Resources for Teaching

MAKING
LITERATURE
MATTER

An Anthology for
Readers and Writers

Resources for Teaching

MAKING
LITERATURE
MATTER

An Anthology for
Readers and Writers

John Schilb
Indiana University

John Clifford
University of North Carolina at Wilmington

Joyce Hollingsworth
University of North Carolina at Wilmington

BEDFORD/ST. MARTIN'S   Boston ◆ New York

For information, write: Bedford/St. Martin's, 75 Arlington St., Boston, MA 02116
(617-426-7440)

ISBN: 0–312–09727–1

Cover Design: Trudi Gershenov Design

Cover Art: Bill Jacklin, *The Park*, 1996 (tapestry detail)

Preface

We designed *Making Literature Matter* to be a flexible pedagogical tool that provides students with help in developing their reading and writing abilities, as well as literature for them to read and write about. But the book is ultimately only a tool, and no text, no matter how carefully constructed, can substitute for a patient and attentive instructor willing to guide individual students through the reading and writing process. For such hard but rewarding work, an instructor's relationship with students is crucial to making the course a success. We hope that *Making Literature Matter* will help you negotiate the challenges of teaching students to read more attentively and write more skillfully, and we hope that the resources in this manual will make your efforts more productive and perhaps easier.

We begin by presenting two sample syllabi, the first for a composition course emphasizing writing about literature and the second for a literature course emphasizing reading skills such as interpretation and evaluation. We then discuss teaching strategies for all of the chapters in Part One, where students learn basic concepts about writing, especially argumentative writing, and about the four genres of literature presented in the book. Supplementing this discussion is an annotated bibliography of sources that you might consult for further ideas about teaching rhetoric, argument, literature, and literary theory.

The rest of this manual — the bulk of it — comprises commentary on the literature in Part Two's anthology, "Literature and Its Issues." We include a discussion of every selection in the anthology, plus commentaries on how every selection works with others in its cluster. Generally we have tried to keep our comments focused on the issues raised by the questions we ask in the anthology, but when appropriate we provide further discussion, which we hope will be useful in raising other issues in the classroom.

Contents

PART TWO
Literature and Its Issues

Contents

9. Loving 116

PART ONE

Ways of Making Literature Matter

Constructing the Course: Sample Syllabi

Both of the sample syllabi that follow are designed for a fifteen-week semester. The first of the two here is for a composition course built around literature. The second is for an introduction to literature course with a writing component.

English 103: College Composition: Writing and Reading

This is a one-semester writing course for students who place out of the two-semester writing requirement. The syllabus should work just as well in a second-semester composition course, where you may choose not to assign any of the genre-specific chapters (3 through 6), instead moving directly from the two opening chapters to the anthology of literature in Part Two.

The course begins with an introduction to Part One, "Ways of Making Literature Matter," before moving on to the six chapters of Part Two, "Literature and Its Issues." In a fifteen-week course, we have found that the two weeks spent preparing students to write using literature is time well spent.

A. The First Two Weeks. During this time, students are introduced to four key ideas:

1. Cogent "meaning-making" is more likely to occur in a literate environment of reading, responding, writing, discussing, and more writing.
2. Arguing about literature is a process of inquiry that entails revision, reason, and reexamination.
3. Finding literary topics to write about involves asking questions.
4. Writing is best thought of as a process involving exploring, planning, composing, and revising.

1

The first idea, about "meaning-making," is the foundational structure for the course. We read, write, discuss, write, make comparisons, and write again. It is in this cycle of literate acts that good writing is most likely to occur. A discussion of Chapter 1 ("Reading and Thinking") is also valuable in introducing students to reading comparatively — the basis for the cluster within the thematic chapters of Part Two. The three poems by Milton, Harper, and Piercy (Chapter 1) can be read in class, perhaps the first day, as can the first writing exercise on page 13.

The second idea, about argument, can also be introduced the first day with an overview of "Thinking Critically: The Value of Argument." The key terms (**issues, claims, persuasion, audience, evidence,** and **warrants**) can be blended into an informal discussion of argument by giving examples from the three poems about work. A fuller discussion will be more useful after students have read this section at home, perhaps also doing the writing exercise on page 30.

The third idea, about the recent concerns of literary studies (p. 32 ff), seems especially likely to benefit students. A class discussion of the writing exercise on page 39 will help students see the multiple topics that are possible in writing about literature.

The fourth idea, about process, is central to any writing course. Chapter 2, "Writing," then, deserves some attention. Although we assign this chapter for home study, at this point it is only necessary for students to understand the general principles of exploring, planning, composing, and revising. Working out the logistics and details is what the course is about. We always need to remind ourselves that many concepts about writing tend to confuse students. We find it best to begin with a reasonable overview. The specifics will come as the class works through the book.

The two-week introduction continues with an examination of the writing process applied to specific literary works. This syllabus uses only one of the four chapters that deal with writing about genres (Chapter 4, "Writing about Poems") as a model for how the writing process can proceed. You can ask the class to read the Frost poems twice and then assign the exploring exercise on page 107; then read the various responses from students. It is especially useful for students to read Sophia's freewrite (p. 117) and to discuss its merits and ways she could revise it. Sophia's final draft is a good example of how to combine rigorous argument and analysis without losing sight of her initial personal response. Obviously each instructor should make individual decisions about how much time to invest in clarifying the key terms (mentioned above) — these ideas are merely the means to an end, and not an end in themselves. The goal is to help students produce strong, serious writing, not obsess about terminology.

B. The Heart of the Course. The syllabus centers on Part Two, "Literature and Its Issues," and devotes nine weeks to four of the six chapters. Students write an essay (four typed pages) for each chapter. They begin with Chapter 7, "Living in Families," and they can work through several clusters in class; it is not possible to work with all the clusters, of course, but students can read other clusters on their own, responding in their journals to questions. Students spend two to three weeks on each essay, from exploring to revising. For Chapter 7 the following clusters are discussed in class: "Memories of Family," "Reconciling with Fathers," "Mothers and Daughters," "Siblings in Conflict," and "Different Children." Depending on the time, you may want the class to read one other cluster.

The syllabus allots time for covering Chapters 8 through 10 ("Teaching and Learning," "Loving," and "Considering Outsiders") in the same way, leaving the last two to three weeks of the semester for work on Chapter 11, "Making Judgments," and a concluding research essay of six pages.

C. The Conclusion of the Course.   Our last chapter is the focus of a research essay. After they have covered about half of Chapter 11, "Making Judgments," students can be asked to choose one of the research-oriented "Writing about Issues" prompts at the end of each cluster to develop into a longer paper. You may want to consider assigning the Appendix, which deals with the longer, more traditional research paper in some detail.

D. Classroom Procedure.   In covering the individual clusters, you may want to begin by assigning the "Before You Read," questions for discussion to raise the students' awareness of the issues involved and help focus their attention. Even if all the reading is assigned for home study, you may want to have students read poems in class and ask them to write after reading. You can have them alternate between specific questions from "Thinking about the Text" and "Making Comparisons" to an open freewriting. Have them record their responses in a journal, which can be checked periodically. In general, you want to begin the class by asking for volunteers to read their responses as a way to open a discussion of possible writing issues.

E. Writing Assignments.   Each cluster ends with four "Writing about Issues" assignments. Naturally students cannot do them all. Our intention was to give instructors a choice, depending on the focus of the course. In a junior-level essay-writing course you may prefer exclusively to emphasize argument, but in the lower-level 103 course it's better to combine elements of argument with personal response, using the literature we read and personal experience as evidence. The assignments are merely prompts; authentic writing comes out of the rich literate texture of reading, writing, discussion, and journal writing. Students tap into that environment for topics that interest them. In the "Living in Families" chapter, for example, the assignment is simply to pick one of the "arguing" assignments in one of the clusters.

F. Semester Outline

| Week 1 | Introduction: Reading Comparatively, Argument, Topics of Literary Criticism (Chapter 1) |
| Week 2 | The Composing Process (Chapter 2), "Writing about Poems" (Chapter 4) |

Week 3-4-5   "Living in Families" (Chapter 7): "Memories of Family," "Reconciling with Fathers," "Mothers and Daughters," "Siblings in Conflict," "Different Children"
- **Essay 1 due**

Week 6-7   "Teaching and Learning" (Chapter 8): "Recalling Lessons of Childhood," "Teaching Children about Society," "Comparing School Culture with the Culture of Home"
- **Essay 2 due**

Week 8-9   "Loving" (Chapter 9): "True Love," "Romantic Dreams," "Completing the Self through Love," "The Appearance of Love"
- **Essay 3 due**

Week 10-11   "Considering Outsiders" (Chapter 10): "Persecuting Outsiders," "Ethnic Outsiders," "Sexual Transgression," "Misfits"
- **Essay 4 due**

Week 13-14-15   Conclusion: "Making Judgments" (Chapter 11): "Moral Law versus Human Law," "Judging Sanity," "Punishments," "Judging Society"
- **Essay 5 due**

English 200: Introduction to Literature

In adapting the preceding syllabus for a course that stresses literature, instructors can simply spend less time on Part One (one week) and work through more of the chapters. It's still a good idea to have students write before they read and ask them to answer selected questions from Thinking about the Text and Making Comparisons. Three short papers (two to three pages) are assigned, spaced over a fifteen-week semester. The topics are flexible; essentially any of the prompts seem appropriate. The two courses are similar, but in the Introduction to Literature course the emphasis is more on reading skills such as evaluation and interpretation rather than on developing topics for essays and direct writing instruction. *Making Literature Matter* was developed to facilitate either emphasis.

Week 1   Introduction: " Reading Comparatively" (Chapter 1), "Thinking Critically: The Value of Argument" (Chapter 1), "Writing" (Chapter 2), "Writing about Stories" (Chapter 3)

Week 2-3-4   "Living in Families" (Chapter 7): "Memories of Family," "Reconciling with Fathers," "Exorcising the Dead," "Mothers and Daughters," "Dysfunctional Families"

Week 5-6-7   "Loving" (Chapter 9): "True Love," "Completing the Self through Love," "Courtship," "The Appearance of Love," "Romantic Illusions," and "Is This Love?"

Week 8-9-10   "Considering Outsiders" (Chapter 10): "Passive Resistance," "The Outsider in a Dreamlike World," "Persecuting Outsiders," "Ethnic Outsiders," "Sexual Transgression"

Week 11-12   "Making Judgments" (Chapter 11): "Judgments about Animals," "Being on a Jury," "Moral Law versus Human Law," "Judging Sanity," "Punishments," "Value Judgments," "Judging a Life"

Week 13-14-15   "Confronting Mortality" (Chapter 12): "The Passage of Time," "Fighting for Survival," "Reflecting on Killing Animals," "Escaping Life," "Returning to Life"

Teaching Writing Along with Literature

We have designed *Making Literature Matter* primarily for courses that integrate literary study with writing instruction. We realize that such courses can be difficult to teach. In particular, the class may get so involved in discussing literary texts that attention to their own writing slides off the agenda. To thwart this possibility, try to make writing part of as many class periods as possible. For example, you might have students freewrite about a particular work before or during a class and then, ask for volunteers to read their efforts aloud. Throughout our book, we present many questions and writing assignments that can serve as the basis for brief composing exercises, as well as for more sustained papers. Needless to say, when students contribute their own writing to class discussion, they are participating more actively than they otherwise might.

Helping Students with Argumentation

In many respects, our book encourages students to engage especially in argumentative writing. We devote much of Part One to it, laying out and demonstrating key elements of argument like issues, claims, audience, evidence, and warrants. Our explanation of argument in Part One acknowledges to students that they may have trouble grasping in particular what *warrants* are. We hope that our discussion of the term does make it clear. But here we suggest that you allow an ample amount of time to help your class understand what *issues* involve. In fact, this concept is often harder for students to grasp than the concept of *claims* is. Remind your class that an issue is a question to which there can be more than one answer. Stress that a worthwhile argument is one that addresses a genuine and interesting issue. Have students review the various kinds of issues we list. At the start of your course, you may have students who write with a sense of grammar and organization but focus on elaborating theses that no one would challenge. They need practice in discovering issues, so that their writing will contribute to real or possible debates rather than merely stating the obvious. To sense the possible issues that a literary work can provoke, students especially have to get in the habit of asking questions. Point out to your class that question-posing is a vital part of discussion. Students who usually feel they can speak only when they have answers may welcome your announcement that questions are valuable, too.

Discussion and Debate

Your students will become more proficient at *writing* arguments if you give them plenty of opportunities to bring up issues and advance claims in *oral* discussion. Consider requiring members of the class to make oral reports on particular authors. You might even call for entire panels on particular issues, authors, and texts. Another possibility is to break the class into small groups and require each to collaborate on a particular task, with the group eventually reporting back to the class as a whole. Bear in mind that small groups are unlikely to be productive if the task you assign them is vague; try to make it precise as well as manageable. Students can also get valuable practice in discussion if you have them undertake various kinds of role playing, even when the text under consideration is not a script. For example, you might have students enact a meeting of characters from various short stories.

Of course, a looming possibility in a class on argumentative writing is the staging of debates. And certainly you can arrange for groups of students to advocate conflicting judgments about a character, for instance. Yet although class debates can be exciting, sometimes they encourage opinions less nuanced than those you want to see in your students' writing. If your class does end up taking simplistic polar positions in a debate, leave some debriefing time in which you encourage more complex views to emerge.

Peer Review

Quite possibly you will also want to integrate writing into your class periods by devoting class time to peer review of students' writing-in-progress. Such review can effectively take place in pairs, but many instructors prefer to set up entire peer review groups. Such groups can remain the same in membership throughout the term; then again, many instructors like to put students in different groups from time to time. A number of students will be comfortable reading drafts aloud to an audience, whereas others prefer to distribute their drafts and have the audience read them silently. Neither procedure is necessarily better, we think. You might even let each group decide which to adopt, or have the class as a whole choose one.

Admittedly, many students need help formulating responses that will be genuinely helpful to the writer. In fact, the typical peer reviewer is afraid to offend. We recommend that reviewers fill out a sheet that contains questions reflecting your criteria for the particular assignment you have given. Moreover, these questions should make clear that the reviewer is responding to the text and not to the writer's personality. We tend to discourage reviewers from directly giving advice; we think they will help the writer more if they focus on rendering their impressions of the text at hand. Occasionally you may want peer review groups to look at work that is considerably less than a full-fledged draft. After all, writers need opportunities simply to test their provisional issues, claims, and evidence, which may take the form of sentences or paragraphs rather than entire papers.

Teaching the Genres

We group most of the literary selections in *Making Literature Matter* by genre as well as by theme. Hence, teachers who prefer to stress elements of genre can easily do so. Even if you prefer a thematic approach, probably you will want to familiarize your students with some of these elements. Therefore, here we offer suggestions for teaching genres. First we discuss short fiction; then we turn to poetry, plays, and the essay. In each case, we refer to examples of the genre found in Part One of the book.

In our experience, students are far more ready to discuss the *content* of literature than they are the structural properties of literature, which much genre analysis emphasizes. We suspect the general public is similarly inclined. Whereas many critics in academe like to ponder a work's symbolism, its plot design, or other technical aspects of it, most readers outside the academy attend more to the text's personalities, events, and ideas. These readers tend to share Kenneth Burke's notion that literature is "equipment for living"; they are not so concerned about its particular nuts and bolts. When you refer to elements of genre in class, your students are likely to be more receptive if you introduce just one or two terms at intervals rather than bringing forth several at once. Students may even lose sight of literature if they have to focus on mastering a whole critical lexicon for it.

We believe that elements of genre are best taught as means to an end, rather than as an end in themselves. Our book envisions a course aimed above all at helping students become more adept as arguers, whether their arguments wind up focusing on literary form or on literary content. Indeed, throughout the book we encourage students to think of their own arguments as a fifth genre, one just as important as the other four. No doubt they will learn characteristics of literary genres more easily if you point out how they can develop claims about these elements in their writing and class discussions. For instance, they will be keener to learn poetic meter if you show them how it can be the subject of the paper you have just assigned on Frost's poems.

How much should you talk in class about the term *genre* itself? That is up to you. Probably most of your students will already have a rough sense of what the term involves. They will know that literature is often divided into fiction, poetry, and drama, although many of them will not immediately assume that it includes essays. To get your class thinking about genres in literature, you might first ask students to identify various film genres, since most Hollywood movies fit into easily recognizable categories. You might even ask how films are classified at local video rental stores, which are conspicuously arranged by genre.

You may want to point out that a genre can be described in various ways. When we discuss genres in Part One of the book, we refer mostly to their technical or formal aspects. In addition, you might note that some writers and literary theorists have associated certain genres with particular kinds of subject matter. For instance, in his book *The Lonely Voice*, short-story writer Frank O'Connor argues that this genre has often dealt with characters on the margins of society. (Try testing his claim by having your class read O'Connor's story "Guests of the Nation," which we include in Chapter 11, "Making Judgments.") In his book *The Situation of Poetry*, Robert Pinsky argues that much Romantic and post-Romantic verse investigates whether the speaker can ever really commune with the physical universe. Similarly, it has often been observed that a great many poems display an individual human being reflecting on the passage of time (the topic of a cluster of poems in Chapter 12, "Confronting Mortality").

You might also have your class situate genres historically, attending to ways genres have reflected or influenced specific societies and eras. To begin this contextualizing, try asking your students to identify genres on screen or in print that have recently changed as a result of changing social conditions. For example, because of exhaustive media coverage of real-life sex scandals like the Clinton/Lewinsky affair, television soap operas can no longer hook viewers simply by presenting fictional hanky-panky. Meanwhile, the growth of Generation X as a consumer force has encouraged an epidemic of youth-oriented TV series like *Dawson's Creek* and *Buffy the Vampire Slayer*. In part because more people surf the Internet and more moviemakers rely on computer technology, Hollywood has produced several science-fiction/fantasy films that examine issues posed by virtual reality (e.g., *eXistenZ*, *The Matrix*, *Pleasantville*, *The Truman Show*). And now that the communist menace has faded, spy novelists like John LeCarre have been forced to invent new villains.

You will have to decide how much to discuss *subgenres* of short fiction, poetry, drama, and the essay. For each of these main genres, certainly you can point out smaller topical categories. In fact, this is what we do with our clusters in Part Two; there, for example, we suggest that certain works of short fiction can be usefully grouped and analyzed as stories about revenge. Obviously you can also refer to subgenres based on form. In the case of poems, for instance, we feature numerous examples of the sonnet and the villanelle, and our drama selections include both Greek and Elizabethan forms of tragedy. Again, though, students need to feel that any generic classification they engage in has some larger purpose, such as helping them write more incisive arguments about particular texts.

Stories

Of all the literary genres featured in the book, probably students will be most familiar and comfortable with this one. Most likely they will have read several works of fiction beforehand, in school if not on their own. In addition, they will have developed some sense of narrative conventions through viewing films and TV shows as well as through listening to songs with story lines. Thus, when you identify elements of short fiction for them, often you will be helping them grow conscious of characteristics they intuitively know. Feel free to bring their tacit knowledge to the surface by encouraging them to compare the fiction they are reading with stories they have already encountered in popular culture. When teaching Rebecca Brown's story "The Gift of Sweat" (p. 78), for example, ask your class to compare it with AIDS narratives they have seen on the screen. You might even invite them to compare Brown's tale with journalistic reports about AIDS, including stories about such HIV-positive celebrities as Magic Johnson.

We find that of all the elements of this genre, students are most eager to discuss plot and character. Try asking your class to analyze at least a few stories using Alice Adams's formula ABDCE (Action, Background, Development, Climax, Ending), which we apply in the book to Brown's story and to Eudora Welty's "A Visit of Charity"(p. 74). Few of your students are apt to know this formula; in fact, we have never come across it in any other introductory literature textbook. Yet Adams's scheme — devised not by a literary critic, but by a veteran short-story writer — illuminates the plot structure followed by many pieces of short fiction. Furthermore, by using it as a benchmark, students can trace how other short stories prove unconventional in design. Of course, your class needs to be familiar in the first place with the plot of any story it discusses. Despite our exhortations to the contrary, we have found that students tend to read an assigned story only once before coming to class, so their memories of plot details must often be refreshed. You might start off your class session on a story by having students write and exchange brief summaries of it. Reviewing their digests, they may discover they do not agree in their identifications of the story's key actors and incidents, including the story's turning points. Such differences in understanding may then spark lively debate.

In Part One of our book, we define short fiction as "the art of the glimpse," a phrase we take from the veteran short-story writer William Trevor. Some stories feature quite dramatic events; for example, Frank O'Connor's "Guests of the Nation"(p. 1257) climaxes with a double execution. Yet other stories mostly present subtle "glimpses" into their characters' lives, and even a dramatic story may have quietly resonant moments. Some of your students may need help seeing the potential significance of a story's lower-key passages. Take the last two words of Rebecca Brown's story: "I ate." These seem ordinary words; furthermore, the narrator's tone seems muted. We would argue, though, that her act of eating is an important signifier in the story. It indicates her ultimate willingness to accept gifts from the man she has tried to help; also, eating is an age-old ritual of communion. To help your class sense implications like these, you might first ask students to list occasions when the declaration "I ate" is an ordinary, commonplace, unremarkable speech act. Then you can explicitly encourage them to consider how the particular context of Brown's story gives this statement more depth.

A good, quick way to discover what your class thinks about a particular story's characters is to have students write down three adjectives for each. You can then go around the room and have each student read aloud the adjectives he or she has devised. Next, you can ask the class to identify and elaborate whatever commonalities and divergences have emerged. You can use this "round robin" method of character analysis to initiate class discussion or revive it. You can even conclude the period by asking whether anyone's adjectives have changed as a result of hearing class members' adjectives. Remember, though, that character analysis is not always the best approach to a story, even if it does come naturally to students. You may find it more productive to have your class address other facets of the story first.

If characters in a story seem to act unpleasantly, irrationally, and/or unproductively, a number of your students may scorn them. Actually, a great deal of modern fiction (and drama, for that matter) centers on characters whose nature and circumstances strike many students as worse than their own. The great literary critic Northrop Frye helps put this situation in perspective. In his 1957 book *The Anatomy of Criticism*, now regarded as a classic account of genres, Frye traces various kinds of heroes that have figured in literature down through the centuries. The first kind was "a divine being," the hero of *myth*. The second was "superior in degree to other men and to the environment of other men"; this was the hero of *romance*. Then appeared the hero who was "superior in degree to other men but not to his environment"; this prototype, Frye argues, was "the hero of the *high mimetic* mode, of most epic and tragedy, and is primarily the kind of hero that Aristotle had in mind." Closer to our own time, there emerged the *low mimetic* mode; this mode features a hero who is "superior neither to other men nor to his environment," so that audiences "respond to a sense of his common humanity." Finally there is the hero of the *ironic* mode, who seems "inferior in power or intelligence to ourselves, so that we have the sense of looking down on a scene of bondage, frustration, or absurdity" (33–34).

Frye seems to refer exclusively to *male* heroes, thus leaving open the question of how much his categories apply to females. Yet many of the short stories we include in this volume fit into his so-called ironic mode. Reading Welty's story, for example, your students may believe that Marian and the adult women she encounters in the rest home are "inferior in power or intelligence to ourselves," caught up in "a scene of bondage, frustration, or absurdity." Even with this perception, a class analyzing Welty's characters may feel compassion rather than contempt. Nevertheless, quite possibly you will encounter animosity toward these characters, as well as toward those in our book's other ironic narratives.

If some of your students do rush to condemn characters, their attitudes may still provoke good discussion, especially if other members of your class are willing to defend or identify with the targets. Often, however, moralistic dismissal is hardly productive at all. At such times, you have various options. To get your students to at least provisionally identify with a character they criticize, you can invite them to report occasions when they have acted similarly or been tempted to. With a little prodding, for instance, many people will recall feeling nervous and uncertain visiting a nursing home, and they may also remember moments during their childhood when they were as self-centered as Marian. Or, you might play devil's advocate, openly proclaiming that you yourself hesitate to indict the characters outright. You also have the option of shifting the discussion from judgment of the characters to analysis of their functions in the story. For example, rather than solicit your class's opinions of the querulous roommates in Welty's story, you might ask how these women serve as obstacles and/or discoveries for Marian. Another conversational tactic is to sketch Frye's history of narrative modes and ask students to supply other examples of the low mimetic mode. You might point out, too, that works of literature enable us as readers to study the complexities of people, whereas we might feel pressured to make snap judgments about them in real life. You can add that works of literature are often *most* worth reading when they complicate an audience's understanding rather than just confirming its righteousness. You might even conduct a "thought experiment" in which all of your students try writing nuanced claims about Marian and her ilk. Bear in mind that many students who offer complex character analyses in class are tempted to be more reductive in their writing. Composing a manageable argument on paper, they suspect, requires claims simpler than those they have put forth in discussion. You may have to remind them that, if anything, a written argument about a work is usually more interesting and credible when it shows that the work is *not* easily decoded and judged.

When discussing the plot of a story in class, usually students need not be concerned with the verb tenses they use. But when they write a paper about the story, you will want them to recount its events with a tense that is consistent. Unfortunately, many students wind up shifting tenses in their papers about short stories. They move back and forth between past and present, as if they cannot make up their minds which to employ. In Part One, we advise students to try sticking with present tense when they write about a fictional character's actions. Whether or not you agree with us, point out to your students what tense you want them to adopt.

Because short stories are short, you may be tempted to have your students read several for a given class period. We find, however, that less is more. That is, we are more likely to engender substantial analysis of a story if we do not make it compete for time with many others. A good limit is one or two per hour. You can, in fact, deal with several if you divide the class into small groups, assign each a different story to analyze, and then conclude the period by having each group report its analysis to the whole class.

Plan to spend at least one class period helping your students understand the role that point of view plays in short fiction. Let them know that a story may or may not feature a character who expresses the author's own thinking. In particular, indicate that a first-person narrator does not necessarily speak for the author; indeed, such a narrator may even be unreliable. You might acknowledge, too, that reliable first-person narrators may still withhold some of their thoughts from the reader. Such is the case with Rebecca Brown's narrator, who waits until near the end of the story before stating what she has found in Rick's kitchen.

Few of your students will be prepared to define or identify free indirect style, although it appears in many stories. Therefore, take time to explain this device. In our Part One discussion of short fiction, we demonstrate free indirect style by citing a passage from Welty's story that exemplifies it. Another way of familiarizing students with this style is to have them write brief passages of their own that use it. Actually, you can have your class practice various modes of narration, including reliable first person, unreliable first person, and direct address to the reader (see the "Narrators Giving Advice" cluster in Chapter 8, "Teaching and Learning").

Poems

Many students suffer what we call "poetry anxiety." Quite simply, they fear this genre. In part, they do so because they find many poems elusive in meaning, hard to figure out. To them, the average poet seems almost willfully difficult. But another reason for their unease with poetry is their feeling that whenever they study this genre they will have to learn many new technical terms. Of course, your class may also include students who love to read poetry, as well as students who have actually written some. You can even invite the poets in your class to bring in samples of their work. Still, when you first turn your class to poetry, it would be a good idea for you to begin by asking your students their general attitude toward it. Let the anxious ones know that you understand their concerns, even as you submit that reading poetry can be pleasurable.

We suggest, too, that you proceed slowly as you introduce your class to the genre's technical features. How many of these features should your students learn? Quite a few instructors believe that the study of poetry should involve extensive practice in technical analysis, so that students develop an ability to identify any poem's particular meter and rhyme scheme. If you are dealing with multiple genres in your course, though, you may not have time for such work. Also worth considering is the level of the course. When our classes consist mostly of first-year students and sophomores pursuing majors other than English, we do not make them regularly engage in scansion. Rather, we draw their attention to various issues raised by particular texts, especially so they can find topics for their own writing. We elaborate on matters of meter and rhyme when we feel they are especially important to a given text's meaning and impact.

We recommend that, whenever possible, you have students read aloud in class the poems to be discussed. Oral delivery helps both reciter and audience sense a poem's sound patterns, while also giving everyone a chance to identify other aspects of it that they may have missed in their first reading. After a poem is read aloud, you can go around the room and ask all of your students to note anything about it they have newly recognized. Needless to say, your reciters will vary in their degree of elocutionary skill, but the practice in speaking is worthwhile for all of them. If they mispronounce a word or substitute another for it, you can patiently correct them.

In our experience, students need help detecting how various words in a poem relate to one another. The task is especially difficult for them when the related words appear in different stanzas. Encourage your students to range back and forth over the entire text, looking for distant connections. Prod them to consider, for example, how the end of the poem is linked to its beginning. We have also found it useful to have students circle what they deem the poem's most important word; usually, interesting discussion ensues as they defend their choices. A worthwhile exercise, too, is having students identify the major stages or phases that the poem moves through, which may or may not coincide with its stanza breaks.

We believe that when students are asked to interpret one of the poem's images, they should be encouraged first to think of all possible associations with it.

In the case of Frost's "Stopping by Woods on a Snowy Evening" (p. 105), for example, you might put the word *snow* on the blackboard and invite students to point out various things it has signified or evoked. To be sure, eventually you can invite them to consider which of their associations fit this specific text. Some of your students may be wary of attaching much figurative meaning to a seemingly simple word like *snow*, whereas you yourself may be inclined to pack it with symbolic import. In fact, poetry tends to be the genre that students most see as in danger of English Teacher Over-Reading. It's in the discussion of poems that our own students are most likely to ask, "But could the author really have had all those meanings in mind?" The best answer to this question, we think, came from the poet Michael Collier when he visited one of our classes. Collier's poetry tends to rely on seemingly plain words like *water*. He said, however, that invariably readers make all sorts of associations with such a common term when it appears in a poem. He acknowledged, too, that several of these meanings may suit the poem well, even if the writer didn't think of them while composing it.

In Part One, our section on poetry as a genre presents three poems by Frost that all feature a first-person speaker. Actually, much of the poetry in our book does so, and contemporary poets seem very much drawn to the "I." Some of your students may automatically identify the "I" of a poem with its author, but we suggest you emphasize that the two may need to be distinguished. Of course, certain poems do seem autobiographical. But, as we point out when we discuss issues of history in Part One, even Milton's poem about his blindness (p. 11) may be presenting just one aspect of Milton rather than his complete, authentic self. You may find, as we have, that unless a first-person poem clearly indicates otherwise, many students refer to its "I" as male. This tendency is not all that disturbing when the poet is male, as is the case with the three poems by Frost. But we are troubled when the poet is female. In one of our classes, for instance, many students used the masculine in referring to the "I" of Maxine Kumin's "Woodchucks" (in the first cluster of "Making Judgments"), even though the poem seems based on Kumin's own experiences as a farmer. When asked why they made such a gender choice, some students revealed a continuing attachment to the generic male as a pronoun, while others assumed that the poem's gun-wielding farmer had to be a man. If this situation arises in your class, take the opportunity to discuss with your students the various criteria they can use in determining a speaker's gender. Our own view is that if the text of an "I" poem leaves the speaker's gender unclear, the critic should write as if the gender of "I" is the same as the author's. But this is only our default strategy, for we realize there may be justifiable departures from it.

Obviously your class will not have time to read all the poems in our book. You will have to be quite selective in the ones you assign. Just as obviously, various principles of selection are possible. We recommend, though, that you try to expose students to all sorts of different forms. In particular, we find many of them unacquainted with blank verse, even though contemporary poets are fond of it. Actually, several of our students have more or less assumed that a poem must rhyme. Your class can learn much when you present examples of poetry that test narrow definitions of the genre. Consider assigning, for example, Carolyn

Forché's dramatic prose poem "The Colonel" (p. 1378). Of course, even poems that rhyme may do so in subtle as well as conspicuous ways. When our students read Frost's "The Road Not Taken" (p. 106), not all of them realize immediately that the poem rhymes, for it closely resembles ordinary speech. Subsequently, a class can get quite interested in the possible relations between a poem's "literary" qualities and everyday discourse.

Plays

When you teach a play, you have to decide how much you will present it to your students as a blueprint for production rather than as simply a text to be read in class. Our own inclination is to make our classes always aware of the play as a script to be performed. There are numerous reasons for stressing its theatrical dimension. For one thing, doing so gives students a better sense of how interpretations can be consequential; after all, performers' understanding of their parts influences their enactment of these characters on stage. Furthermore, referring to actual and/or hypothetical productions of the play helps students see the material conditions that can affect literature. Susan Glaspell created dramatic intensity when she confined the onstage action of *Trifles* (p.127) to the Wrights' kitchen, but no doubt she also relied on a single set because that is what companies like her Provincetown Players could manage in the small theaters where they performed. Also, the emotional dynamics of many plays are hard for readers to trace if they do not have the chance to see an actual staging. For example, this is the case with Strindberg's *The Stronger* (p. 123), in which one of the two characters never even speaks. If students merely read Strindberg's play rather than see any of it staged, they will probably have trouble recognizing how the wordless woman still manages to express herself.

The best reason, however, for treating a play as a script is that you then have a ready means of getting your students up on their feet and actively participating in class. Let students read scenes aloud, or better yet, assign groups to rehearse scenes and then stage them. You can even assign the same scene to different groups; most likely, their different renditions of the scene will get your class talking about how interpretation shapes performance. When students work together on scenes, they will also see how learning can be collaborative.

Do not be afraid of letting a male character be played by a woman, and vice versa. The results may be fascinating. Moreover, such reversal can be good preparation if the class is going to discuss David Henry Hwang's *M. Butterfly* (p. 781) — a play that deals with gender confusion — or a play by Shakespeare, whose female characters were originally played by men. If you teach *Hamlet* (p. 294), you might point out that in modern times the title role has been played by several actresses, including Sarah Bernhardt, Judith Anderson, and Diane Venora. Perhaps you will want your class to consider, too, the current willingness of many professional theater companies to cast a role with someone of another race than the playwright probably had in mind. Sometimes the casting is deliberately provocative, as with the numerous modern productions in which Shakespeare's Caliban is played by a black man. On other occasions, the casting purports to be "color-blind," as when the black actor Paul Winfield played Falstaff in a Washington, D.C., production of *The Merry Wives of Windsor*. (Interestingly, Winfield replaced actress Pat Carroll in the role.) You may know that a few years ago, "color-blind" casting was debated by black playwright August Wilson and white theater critic Robert Brustein in New York City's Town Hall. While Brustein supported the practice, Wilson criticized it, arguing that it diverted America from establishing more black theater companies that perform black dramatists' plays. Your students may be interested in pursuing this debate. If you teach *A Raisin in the Sun* (p. 484), you might ask them what they think about casting whites as the Younger family.

Perhaps some of your students will have acted in high school and/or college. Some of them may currently be theater majors. Try beginning your discussion of drama as a genre by inviting students to report their own acting experiences. You might go further and ask them to report performing experiences of any kind, as a way of beginning to analyze what is involved in making presentations to a live audience. Of course, you can also invite students to recall plays they have seen rather than acted in. Do not be surprised, though, if several students report that they have rarely or never seen live professional theater — all the more reason for having your class actually perform. Of course, you might also encourage your students to see current productions of your college's theater department. Consider arranging a group visit to one.

You may want to augment your class's discussion of a play by showing a video of it. For most of the plays in our book, film versions are readily available on video. For the two Shakespeare plays, *Hamlet* and *The Tempest* (p. 1139), there are various audio recordings in circulation as well. Clearly students can learn much from watching or listening to an actual production. But if forced to be simply an audience for prolonged periods, a class can grow passive. Often a thoughtful discussion can result when students are asked to analyze just a film clip or two. For instance, you might have your class compare Kenneth Branagh's "To be or not to be" soliloquy with Laurence Olivier's or Mel Gibson's. Or, before showing a film clip, you might have some of your students perform the same scene; later the class can compare the two versions. Of course, most film adaptations of plays swerve from the original script, and your students might evaluate changes they spot.

Much of what we have said about teaching short fiction applies to the teaching of plays. In particular, as with short stories, you may find students contemptuous toward a number of the characters they encounter in plays. If this situation occurs, try following some of the strategies we suggested using with short fiction. But with plays, you have an advantage: You can ask someone criticizing a character to perform that character, an exercise that encourages the student to investigate the character's various human dimensions.

In our Part One discussion of plays as a genre, we refer to changes in theatrical conventions. Quite possibly your students will express discomfort with the language and format of *Antigone* (p. 1306), *Hamlet*, *The Tempest*, and Césaire's version of the latter (p. 1206). When you teach any of these plays, there will be times when you have to explain conventions at length. But keep trying to find points of contact between the play and things that your students have experienced, read about, or heard about. In Part One, we stress that even so-called realistic plays like *Trifles*, *A Raisin in the Sun*, and *'night, Mother* (p. 1550) observe certain conventions. Calling attention to these modern theatrical devices may prepare your class for plays that seem less immediately accessible.

Essays

You may be reluctant to teach the essays in our book, suspecting that this genre is not as "literary" as short fiction, poetry, and drama. But as we indicate in the text, quite a few essays show many of the same qualities traditionally associated with the other three genres. Indeed, you may want to emphasize that nonfiction is less a window on the real world than an artful representation of it, exhibiting many of the same techniques of craft that one can find in fiction. Furthermore, reading essays can serve as a bridge between the literature your students encounter in our book and the writing you have them do. Even if you demand that their writing eschew explicitly personal reflections like those of E. B. White, Joan Didion, and Andrea Lee, familiarizing your students with essays expands their rhetorical repertoires. They grow aware of strategies and techniques that can, to some extent, shape their own prose.

Unfortunately, we find that most students have had little previous experience analyzing essays. At best, they have taken an English class that included a brief unit on this genre. Actually, we also have had scant formal training in essay analysis, and the same may be true of you. Moreover, we find that published theories of the essay do not dwell much on specific features of specific texts. Instead, their tendency is to exalt the genre in broad terms. Hence, more than with the other genres in our book, your class's approach to the essay will include evolving a critical lexicon for it. Of course, we try to help by identifying typical elements of essays in Part One.

Many instructors report that their students often refer to essays as "stories." We, too, find this to be so. We have already indicated one reason why students resort to this term: They have not been trained to identify the genre's own particular characteristics. Another reason, we suspect, is that many essays do feature quite a bit of narrative. In a sense, students are not really distorting White's "Once More to the Lake" (p. 155) when they call it a story, for basically it is indeed an extended anecdote. Nevertheless, plenty of essays avoid narrative or include just bits of it, so "story" can turn out to be a misleading term. We recommend that when you move to discussing essays, you spend at least one period reviewing with your class the different amounts and functions of narrative that particular essays entail. Help students distinguish moments of pure storytelling in an essay from moments when the text is more devoted to argument or philosophical reflection. Get them to identify, for example, the claims that White, Didion, and Lee make, in addition to the narrative sequences these essayists spin. Worth noting, too, however, is *where* in the text the claims appear. As Douglas Hesse has pointed out, often an essay achieves its intellectual force precisely by embedding its claims within a compelling and credible narrative.

You and/or your class may very well desire to discuss the extent to which, and the sense in which, a particular essay is "true." Some of your students may simply accept the text's veracity; others may be skeptical, disposed to regard the work as fiction. We encourage our classes to consider how even avowedly objective writing is still a selective, crafted representation of the world. We also suggest that essayists deserve at least some leeway when they attempt to render their past experiences, conversations, and thoughts. At the same time, we acknowledge that readers approach essays and short stories with different expectations. In an important sense, they are willing to accept short stories as fabrication, while being suspicious of essays that seem bent on falsifying the writer's life.

Probably your students will better grasp the craft of essays if you let them try, even briefly, to write a personal account like White's, Didion's, and Lee's. In our experience, one device of essayists that many students enjoy practicing is use of the present tense, even when the experience being described has perhaps already occurred. Didion's essay is an especially good example of how the present tense can give readers a "you are there" feeling. Also worth discussing are the various ways in which an essay can seem relevant to a wide audience even when it dwells on the writer's own life. If and when your students draft their own essays, you can have them consider how successful they have been in making their experience count for others.

Annotated Bibliography of Resources

The following is a list of books and articles that we have found especially useful in teaching literature and composition courses. They have influenced, too, our work on *Making Literature Matter*. The list is necessarily selective; particular items on it may lead you to other good resources for your pedagogy. We have divided the list into three categories: (1) texts on basic principles of rhetoric and argument; (2) texts that engage in rhetorical analysis of literature and/or discuss argumentative moves that literary critics make; and (3) texts that relate literary theory and/or pedagogy to the teaching of writing.

Basic Principles of Rhetoric and Argument

*Aristotle. *On Rhetoric: A Theory of Civic Discourse*. Ed. and trans. George A. Kennedy. New York: Oxford UP, 1991.

Although an ancient treatise (dating from c. 333 B.C.E.), this remains an illuminating guide to basic principles, and most contemporary theorists of rhetoric and argument continue to build on it. Kennedy's edition is accessible as well as sound and up to date in its scholarly apparatus.

*Bitzer, Lloyd F. "The Rhetorical Situation." *Philosophy and Rhetoric* 1 (1968): 1–17.

A key document in contemporary theorizing about rhetorical situations; still worth consulting even though subsequent writers on the subject have pointed out some problems in Bitzer's framework.

*Bizzell, Patricia, and Bruce Herzberg, eds. *The Rhetorical Tradition: Readings from Classical Times to the Present*. Boston: Bedford Books, 1990.

The best compendium we know of primary sources in rhetorical theory through the ages.

*Crosswhite, James. *The Rhetoric of Reason*. Madison: U of Wisconsin P, 1996.

Winner of the Modern Language Association's Shaughnessy Award, this is an extremely lucid and thoughtful defense of written argument as a form of reasoning.

*Ede, Lisa, and Andrea Lunsford. "Audience Addressed/Audience Invoked: The Role of Audience in Composition Theory and Pedagogy." *College Composition and Communication* 35 (1984): 155–71.

Clarifies various possible senses of the term *audience*.

*Emmel, Barbara, Paula Resch, and Deborah Tenney, eds. *Argument Revisited, Argument Redefined: Negotiating Meaning in the Composition Classroom.* Thousand Oaks, CA: Sage, 1996.

> Includes many thoughtful essays that apply current strands in argument theory to the teaching of writing.

*Fulkerson, Richard. *Teaching the Argument in Writing.* Urbana, IL: National Council of Teachers of English, 1996.

> Good introduction to various theories of argument; written expressly for teachers of writing.

*Lamb, Catherine E. "Beyond Argument in Feminist Composition." *College Composition and Communication* 42 (1991): 11–24.

> Despite its title, this article does not go "beyond" argument but rather proposes a collaborative model of it while incisively critiquing "monologic" forms.

*Lynch, Dennis A., Diana George, and Marilyn Cooper. "Moments of Argument: Agonistic Inquiry and Confrontational Cooperation." *College Composition and Communication* 48 (1997): 61–85.

> Detailed presentation of a framework for composition teaching that stresses argument as inquiry.

*Perelman, Chaim, and Lucie Olbrechts-Tyteca. *The New Rhetoric: A Treatise on Argumentation.* Trans. J. Wilkinson and P. Weaver. Notre Dame, IN: U of Notre Dame P, 1969.

> A landmark in contemporary theorizing about rhetoric, especially argument. Details many strategies of informal logic and makes a cogent case for seeing argument as intertwined with considerations of value.

*Toulmin, Stephen. *The Uses of Argument.* New York: Cambridge UP, 1964.

> A significant influence on textbooks about argument, including ours. Foundational especially in its discussion of claims and warrants.

Rhetorical Analysis of Literature and/or Discussion of Argument in Literary Criticism

*Eagleton, Terry. *Literary Theory: An Introduction.* Minneapolis: U of Minnesota P, 1983. 2nd ed. 1996.

> Lucid and witty survey of various schools of literary theory; concludes by recommending they be replaced with a rhetorical approach to literature.

*Fahnestock, Jeanne, and Marie Secor. "The Rhetoric of Literary Criticism." In *Textual Dynamics of the Professions: Historical and Contemporary Studies of Writing in Professional Communities.* Ed. Charles Bazerman and James Paradis. Madison: U of Wisconsin P, 1990. 76–96.

Invaluable survey of the kinds of issues and argumentative moves that literary critics undertake.

*Fish, Stanley. *Doing What Comes Naturally: Change, Rhetoric, and the Practice of Theory in Literary and Legal Studies.* Durham, NC: Duke UP, 1989.

Includes many essays that show the pervasiveness of rhetoric in literary criticism and theory.

*Frey, Olivia. "Beyond Literary Darwinism: Women's Voices and Critical Discourse." *College English* 52 (1990): 507–26.

A forceful call for less agonistic forms of argument in literary studies.

*Graff, Gerald. *Beyond the Culture Wars: How Teaching the Conflicts Can Revitalize American Education.* New York: Norton, 1992.
*———. *Professing Literature: An Institutional History.* Chicago: U of Chicago P, 1987.

Graff's 1987 book is an excellent chronicle of debates among literary critics since the modern founding of the discipline. His later book recommends ways of teaching such conflicts in undergraduate classes.

*Levin, Richard. *New Readings vs. Old Plays: Recent Trends in the Reinterpretation of English Renaissance Drama.* Chicago: U of Chicago P, 1979.

Negative about current practices in literary criticism, but cannily analyzes the field's typical argumentative moves. Especially good on the impulse to "thematize."

*MacDonald, Susan Peck. *Professional Academic Writing in the Humanities and Social Sciences.* Carbondale: Southern Illinois UP, 1994.

Winner of the College Composition and Communication Book Award, this is an incisive empirical comparison of scholarly discourse in literary studies with writing in other fields.

*Mailloux, Steven. *Reception Histories.* Ithaca: Cornell UP, 1998.
*———. *Rhetorical Power.* Ithaca: Cornell UP, 1989.

Two books by a theorist dedicated to showing how both literature and literary criticism function rhetorically.

*Sosnoski, James J. *Modern Skeletons in Postmodern Closets: A Cultural Studies Alternative*. Charlottesville: U of Virginia P, 1995.

Identifies impasses created by current forms of argument in literary criticism; recommends that the field practice a more communal discourse.

*Sullivan, Patricia A. "Writing in the Graduate Curriculum: Literary Criticism and Composition." *Journal of Advanced Composition* 11 (1991): 283–99.

An empirical study of graduate students attempting to practice the rhetoric of literary studies. One of relatively few works on this subject.

*Tompkins, Jane. "Fighting Words: Unlearning to Write the Critical Essay." *Georgia Review* 42 (1988): 585–90. Rpt. in *West of Everything*. New York: Oxford UP, 1992. 227–33.

Drawing on personal experience, Tompkins calls for more civil argument in literary criticism.

*Turner, Mark. *Reading Minds: The Study of English in the Age of Cognitive Science*. Princeton: Princeton UP, 1991.

Advocating "cognitive rhetoric," this book focuses on metaphor as a way of linking literature and other discourse to human beings' everyday acts of perception.

*Veeser, H. Aram, ed. *Confessions of the Critics*. New York: Routledge, 1996.

A collection of essays examining the recent turn to autobiographical criticism in literary studies.

Relating Literary Theory and/or Pedagogy to the Teaching of Writing

*Atkins, G. Douglas, and Michael Johnson, eds. *Writing and Reading Differently: Deconstruction and the Teaching of Composition and Literature*. Lawrence: UP of Kansas, 1985.

A bit dated in its enthusiasm for deconstruction, this anthology still presents many useful suggestions for connecting literary theory to the teaching of writing.

*Berlin, James. *Rhetorics, Poetics, and Cultures*. Urbana, IL: National Council of Teachers of English, 1996.

This posthumously published book is a thoughtful overview of how the three terms in the title have historically been related. Suggests many ways of making composition classes sensitive to the social and historical contexts of literature and other discourse.

*Berlin, James, and Michael A. Vivion, eds. *Cultural Studies in the English Classroom*. Portsmouth, NH: Boynton/Cook, 1992.

Contains several essays that integrate literary study, writing instruction, and cultural studies.

*Bleich, David. *Know and Tell: A Writing Pedagogy of Disclosure, Genre, and Membership*. Portsmouth, NH: Boynton/Cook, 1998.

The latest book by a veteran theorist of writing and literature; offers numerous examples of how to combine the two subjects.

*Booth, Wayne. *The Vocation of a Teacher: Rhetorical Occasions, 1967–1988*. Chicago: U of Chicago P, 1989.

Collection of essays by a highly influential advocate of combining literary study with instruction in writing and rhetoric.

*Cahalan, James M., and David B. Downing, eds. *Practicing Theory in Introductory College Literature Courses*. Urbana, IL: National Council of Teachers of English, 1991.

Many essays in this collection include interesting writing assignments about literature.

*Donahue, Patricia A., and Ellen Quandahl, eds. *Reclaiming Pedagogy: The Rhetoric of the Classroom*. Carbondale: Southern Illinois UP, 1989.

Includes several essays that merge literary theory with composition theory.

*Horner, Winifred Bryan, ed. *Composition and Literature: Bridging the Gap*. Chicago: U of Chicago P, 1983.

Though published in the early 1980s, this is still a useful anthology of essays on ways to overcome the institutional divide between composition and literature. Many of the contributors are leading scholars in both fields.

*McCormick, Kathleen. *The Culture of Reading and the Teaching of English*. Manchester, Eng.: Manchester UP, 1994.

Insightful recommendations for teaching students how to read literature critically and explore its various cultural dimensions through their own writing.

*McQuade, Donald. "Composition and Literary Studies." In *Redrawing the Boundaries: The Transformation of English and American Literary Studies*. Ed. Stephen Greenblatt and Giles Gunn. New York: Modern Language Association, 1992.

Incisive overview of the relations between composition and literary studies in English departments.

*Miller, Susan. "What Does It Mean to Be Able to Write? The Question of Writing in the Discourses of Literature and Composition." *College English* 45 (1983): 219–35.

Provides a model for analyzing both the production and reception of texts, including student writing as well as published literature.

*Pope, Rob. *Textual Intervention: Critical and Creative Strategies for Literary Studies*. New York: Routledge, 1995.

Delightful presentation of assignments that help students learn about literature by encouraging them to write extensions and alternative versions of particular texts.

*Scholes, Robert. *Textual Power: Literary Theory and the Teaching of English*. New Haven, CT: Yale UP, 1985.

Now-classic book on the roles of composition and literary studies in English departments; calls for such departments to affirm writing instruction more and proposes a useful way of analyzing literary texts.

*Young, Art, and Toby Fulwiler, eds. *When Writing Teachers Teach Literature: Bringing Writing to Reading*. Portsmouth, NH: Boynton/Cook, 1995.

A collection that constantly emphasizes the integration of literature and composition.

You may also be interested in four books of our own:

*Clifford, John, ed. *The Experience of Reading*. Portsmouth, NH: Boynton/Cook, 1990.
*Clifford, John, and John Schilb, eds. *Writing Theory and Critical Theory*. New York: Modern Language Association, 1994.
*Harkin, Patricia, and John Schilb, eds. *Contending with Words: Composition and Rhetoric in a Postmodern Age*. New York: Modern Language Association, 1991.
*Schilb, John. *Between the Lines: Relating Composition Theory and Literary Theory*. Portsmouth, NH: Boynton/Cook, 1996.

PART
TWO

Literature and Its Issues

| 7 |

Living in Families

FAMILIES IN FOLKTALES:
A COLLECTION OF WRITINGS
BY THE BROTHERS GRIMM (p. 182)

JACOB AND WILHELM GRIMM
Cinderella (p. 183)

The Cinderella story exists in widely diverse cultures, and many psychological and sociological studies take the Grimms' version as a metaphor for the roles we assume in our families and our family dynamics. For Americans in the twentieth century, the tale resonates on cultural and historical levels, moving beyond issues of how members of blended families work out their lives as individuals. Although students may begin by relating the story to their own lives, discussion and further reading may lead them beyond surface interpretations. Comparisons with the Disney versions of the story — both the cute and conventional animated film and the multiethnic video revision of the Rodgers and Hammerstein musical — invite us to explore the romantic ideal with its bloodless, happily-ever-after resolution and its implications about relationships. The masochistic "good little girl" submissiveness of Cinderella and the cruelty of women directed toward women are issues that have been considered by many contemporary writers, including Nobel Prize winner Toni Morrison, who urges women in the work place to resist the tendency to subvert each other as the stepsisters do. Young men in the classroom are often surprised to hear women eagerly discuss times they have been sabotaged by other women and may be relieved to find themselves briefly off the hook as the designated oppressors. As the class discusses possible historical and cultural reasons why women might feel the need to compete with each other, however, we may find the bases for such behavior in patriarchal attitudes and institutions that relegate women to inferior positions.

The father who absents himself emotionally if not physically, the child in the family who is singled out for the "deformed" and abused role, and the women who mutilate their bodies and souls to be attractive and marriageable are recognizable figures from the literature of psychology, the literary canon, and television talk shows. Students may want to find some of these texts and others that elaborate on the Cinderella story — the Anne Sexton poem that retells the Grimm version, for example, a movie like *Pretty Woman*, or an article about anorexia — and discuss how the stories a society tells to and about its children shape adult roles and expectations.

JACOB AND WILHELM GRIMM
Hansel and Gretel (p. 188)

Children whose parents dare to let them read the uncut tales of the Grimm brothers tend to love this story because the children in the tale are clever enough to outwit the evil or ineffectual adults who seek to abandon or devour them. Rather than being horrified by the situation, children often feel empowered by it. The story can be frightening, of course, and scholars have argued that fear may be a useful emotion for children. Both the dark forests of medieval Europe and the residential streets and information superhighways of contemporary America harbor real dangers for children who wander away from the safety of home or accept candy from strangers. Yet this is a story in which the mother is dangerous as well, and the father lacks the strength of his convictions, choosing not to protect and nurture his children. Certainly the story lends itself to a discussion of child abuse and the complicity of the weak or apathetic parent who enables it. Beyond this, however, students might want to consider its cultural stereotypes — the overbearing wife, the henpecked husband, the witch/woman who seeks to destroy children — and to question their symbolism. For centuries, these have been the stock characters of folktales. Could this be a tale that cautions against the evils of letting women have authority or independence? Does the story imply that this "unnatural" inversion of male/female relationships leads inevitably to the destruction of family values, even the destruction of children themselves? Students may be challenged to recognize the long history of societal assumptions about the roles of men and women by more closely examining the unspoken warrants of the story itself.

Although it would be hard to make a case for taking one's children into the woods to starve, figuratively choosing between one's children and one's own life has been a task that women have long faced, often at the risk of appearing monstrous in the eyes of society. Virginia Woolf writes of the need for "a room of one's own" in order to write, and Tillie Olsen documents the "silences" forced upon both women and working-class men whose labor and weariness have precluded intellectual work through much of history. The father's wavering may be seen as cowardice or as the powerlessness of poverty. The children are the heroes, of course. They find their way out of difficulties with their resourcefulness, their faith in God, and their loyalty to each other. Although they face problems, they pull themselves out of poverty with a little help from a duck. How hard can that be? Why don't all poor people do the same? Why can't all endings be this happy? Many inexperienced readers expect just such simplistic resolutions from all the texts in their literature book and resist texts that are ambiguous or unsentimental. The fairy-tale genre, popular books written for both children and adults, and television dramas that are neatly tied up in thirty minutes all contribute to this expectation from narratives, an expectation that may be carried over unquestioned into our concepts about reality and relationships. An argument could be made that the happy ending may be more detrimental in the long run than the violent images and situations in *Hansel and Gretel.*

The fathers in both *Cinderella* and *Hansel and Gretel* fail to help their children, even though their intentions do not seem as malevolent as those of their wives. It is interesting that the Disney versions of Cinderella have the father die after he has acquired the stepmother and her daughters, whereas in the Grimm version the father is alive and even pronounces his daughter to be "deformed." Gretel and Cinderella are both expected to serve as household help, but Gretel takes matters into her own hands, pushing the witch into the fire and rescuing her brother. Cinderella, however, forgiving to the end, allows her sisters to be bridesmaids, leaving vengeance to the forces of nature or divine retribution. Yet both are magically freed from poverty and the need to handle life on their own. Cinderella becomes a princess, united with her prince in marriage; Hansel and Gretel, with apron and pockets full of money, are reunited with their father. The cultural value of materialism — the fantasy that winning the lottery would solve all our problems — may be obvious. The value of family unity, given the past family experiences of these children, may raise more complex issues, however.

JACOB AND WILHELM GRIMM

Snow White (p. 194)

Like Cinderella, Snow White has entered the American psyche by way of Walt Disney. His earliest full-length animated movie, a product of the early twentieth century, extols the virtues of joyful housekeeping and endorses the dream of marrying a prince. The dwarfs are children, and Snow White mothers them. The values communicated by the Grimm version are startlingly similar, though its images are harsher and its narrative more fully developed. The Grimm story begins with a mother sewing and with the vivid image of blood drops on the snow, followed quickly by Snow White's birth and the mother's death. It ends with the shocking and equally vivid image of the stepmother's dancing herself to death in red-hot shoes at Snow White's wedding. Snow White's "death" occupies the center of the story.

As in many stories in European and American folklore, the heroine goes through three trials, each more severe than the first. Interestingly, since beauty is the supreme value for all the women in the story, her first two trials involve objects that are used to make a woman more beautiful — stays for shaping her figure and a comb for arranging her hair. Beauty is so highly valued, in fact, that the queen will even resort to cannibalism to see that she stays ahead of her competition. The most complex issue to consider here might be whether the narrative critiques the cult of beauty or reveals a particular failing of women not unlike that of Eve, who after all was tempted into eating an apple.

Although women are the enemies of women in this story, we need to discuss the culture in which the pursuit of beauty becomes an obsession that interacts with this antagonism. The fact that women internalize sexist values and act upon them does not mean that the sexist values do not exist. It may be to the advantage of people in power to set less powerful people into conflict with each other, whether this is done intentionally or by following the line of least resistance. In families, mothers and daughters may be in Freudian conflict for the affections of the father, but the conflict may be magnified in American society by advertising's glorification of youthful beauty and by negative attitudes toward aging. Families on television and in movies are often nontraditional ones in which children find shelter with extended family, strangers, or ill-prepared bachelor dads. Critics often argue that such narratives infantilize adults and replace children with spiritual and emotional dwarfs. Others may respond that the traditional nuclear family has not always been the norm, nor should it be.

Rewriting the stories with "bad fathers" and apathetic mothers would be an interesting exercise for examining our assumptions about gender and about the roles of men and women in the family and in positions of leadership or submission. Small groups could work out the details of their revision of the story. In doing so, they would have to come to terms with conflicting and previously unexamined assumptions about roles and power structures that they consider normal within the family. These assumptions, and the romantic assumptions implied in the dreams of being rescued by a prince, can be discussed as the underpinnings for many of our notions about relationships. Like the belief in being rescued by a prince, the belief in magic tends to lead toward inaction and passivity, though often in the stories it seems to be the only solution the character can come up with to solve a problem. There is comfort in seeing bad magic lead to ultimate punishment and good magic to happiness and prosperity, and a case could be made that action does play a part in the lives of the characters, with magic simply being the medium through which the person acts.

MEMORIES OF FAMILY (p. 201)

BELL HOOKS
Inspired Eccentricity (p. 202)

In this piece of autobiographical nonfiction, bell hooks provides an example of the genre at its best. She describes characters, her grandparents Sarah and Gus Oldham, who are three-dimensional and unexpected. And although she interprets their recurring behaviors in the most loving and respectful light, she shows their weaknesses as well. As her title states, they are inspirations to her, but they are not icons. They are, as she tells us, eccentric — different. The author takes pride in their reversal of the conventional roles men and women are expected to take in their community. Her grandfather, seen as passive and henpecked by adult family members and neighbors, is "calm and gentle" in a way that nurtures the child and inspires her to become a writer and a pacifist. Her grandmother seems mannish to those around her, speaks her mind, and carves out her own space. The illiterate older woman's verbal virtuosity feeds the writer as well; her independence makes possible "bell hooks," the bold feminist who chooses to write her name — borrowed from this grandmother's mother — in an eccentric way and to "talk back" to a culture that has long made it difficult for women of color to find voices of power. Hooks emphasizes that it is not one or the other of these grandparents who have shaped her own identity but the two together, a combination that she says burns as hot as the black coals in their fireplace.

While the author traces individual lessons she learned from family members, her interpretations of their influence are seen from the perspective of an adult who teases out the strands of her own personality, based on values that she holds important. Obviously, adults do not always teach what they think they are teaching, even those who consciously consider such things. But bell hooks writes an autobiography here, examining her values and priorities and searching out possible sources, laying out a narrative line — or perhaps the branching narrative lines of a family tree. She knows she seems eccentric to most people, and she likes it that way. She barely touches on her "painful childhood" in this excerpt from her autobiography, but she does mention often being punished. The reader may suspect she was punished for the very traits that she now sees as her strengths, character traits that she may still be trying to justify by writing about them. Like the quilts that her grandmother made, hooks's autobiography is skillfully pieced together in vibrant detail to create something of use and beauty. Students will find many details that contribute to the dominant impression she seeks to project. Perceptive readers will also question the author's views of her grandparents, asking whether the perceptions of the townspeople might have some validity as well. In the writer's attempt to explain her own outspoken individuality, critical readers may discover tensions within the text as well as in the family it describes.

BRENT STAPLES

The Runaway Son (p. 207)

When writing about the life of an individual and the family influences that have shaped that person, the writer must choose what to include and what to leave out. Brent Staples builds his autobiographical narrative around family patterns of loss and separation that continue to haunt him, selecting the family experiences that, taken together, may explain rather complex feelings. The irony implied in the title and opening paragraph of this autobiographical narrative may eventually surface for students who stick with it to the end. Others will wonder when he will finally get to the point and may complain that he seems to veer from his stated thesis. Often Staples does seem to be rambling, and the reader wonders when he will finally reveal the pivotal event that explains his attitude toward innocently wandering children and their distracted mothers. Perhaps he means to contrast this image with the legacy of runaway sons, runaway fathers, and the profound loss of childhood that were a part of his family history. As his narrative ends, the writer has escaped into education and is accused of running away from his family, perhaps from who he is. Many readers will recognize, however, that the true experience of being a son has run away from *him*, as it had from his father before him. Furthermore, since the writer himself is not the only son who runs away in this narrative, issues may be raised about the implications of the title. Who does run away in this story? What causes the narrator's childhood to be lost?

By framing his essay as he does, Staples gives adult perspective and meaning to an appallingly difficult childhood. Without this adult voice, the overwhelming impression would be of a cycle of abandonment and near-neglect in which children are forced into responsibilities that rob them of the security of childhood. Themes might focus on poverty and dysfunctional families. The issues of race and class arise from the beginning images of women and children who are explicitly white and prosperous, who are encountered at beaches and museums and near the doctor's office where the narrator goes for a yearly checkup. Staples implicitly lets us know that he frequents such places, can afford to go to the doctor even when he isn't sick, and is recognized as an equal by the mother whose child he "rescues." His descriptions of childhood come as a shock after this. His scenes are vivid with sensory details that recall long walks to the outhouse alone, mornings building fires, and his sister's burned body. His last paragraph includes another sister's accusation that he has abandoned his own people. Since his fantasies of rescue center on the children of privilege rather than ten-year-olds like himself, questions could be raised about his choice to escape the cycle of loss by shirking the responsibility to rescue those who truly need his help. Must he do this for his own protection? Is he an Uncle Tom?

Because Brent Staples and bell hooks share racial, class, and regional backgrounds and were born a year apart, it would be interesting to look at their differences in terms of gender. Given the complexity of families, the argument could be made that too many variables exist, that their experiences were not the same, and that conclusions made on this basis would not be valid. It may be argued, however, that gender is significant for the writers: Staples identifies his gender in his title, and hooks makes much of being a loud woman seeking the genesis of this character trait. If the child in Staples's essay had been a daughter forced to take over the household in the absence of parents, her story might recall the trials of Cinderella. Would the female Staples, lacking hooks's nurturing grandparents, have hoped for a prince to rescue her rather than turning to education? Would a male bell hooks still feel the need to find the familial source of his independent streak? As students speculate about the changes the writers would make in their childhood experiences, some might argue that difficulties may be what gave these people the strength to become who they are and that they would change little. Both writers acknowledge the importance of grandparents, however, and this may be where we would look for changes if the writers could exchange childhoods. Staples implies that if his father had drawn the education-oriented grandfather as foster father, his character and his family's future might have been much different. And although she celebrates her grandparents' eccentricity, hooks may have allowed her grandmother an education and her grandfather a wider respect. Because the writers acknowledge the complexity of self-image and family influence, students may be able to justify several answers to the question of their attitudes. Overall, hooks seems defiantly proud of who she is but may attribute her character too much to inheritance. Staples seems even more defensive and more ambivalent about his family, even as he acknowledges the power of the past.

N. SCOTT MOMADAY

The Way to Rainy Mountain (p. 215)

This essay has an interesting publishing history, having appeared first as a magazine article, then as the words of a character in a novel, as the introduction to the writer's autobiography, and as a frequently anthologized essay in college writing textbooks. Many students have read it in high school. The essay is highly organized, though students often complain that it lacks focus because it is not a linear, chronological narrative. The narrator begins and ends at Rainy Mountain in the summertime and moves through time and space, interweaving history, myth, and family experience as he goes. Family is central to his story because Momaday journeys into the history of his father's tribe, the Kiowa, and because he uses his grandmother to tie together the diverse strands of the story. The result is coherent, intricate, and uniquely Native American.

By seeing through his grandmother's eyes, Momaday personalizes the historical events, and his vivid sensory images also bring readers into the story, giving a sense of movement down mountainsides and visions of religious ceremonies no one has seen for years. He causes us to feel the heat and to hear his grandmother's voice in prayer. We may recognize that it is an illusion that we can truly see as we think another might see, especially when separated by experience to this extent, but the attempt can open the mind to alternative ways of defining the universe, and Momaday's concrete and specific language keeps us from moving too far away from the senses. Some distances are hard to bridge: Few students have seen a heated anvil, and some need help thinking through the word *deicide*, though the symbolism and cultural ramifications quickly arise as discussion proceeds. Words work as important cohesive devises in this essay, with repetitions and parallel constructions linking ideas together in a way that approaches poetry. In addition, the writer uses his grandmother to bridge gaps that he could not close on his own; he can take her back to childhood to view historical events or have her recount a myth.

By blending genres he makes us see that these ways of seeing overlap and intertwine, especially in families and especially in this specific culture.

Furthermore, he refuses to privilege one sort of text over another: Folklore and history are equally legitimate or indeterminate. He evokes Aho as a person, especially in his observations of her at prayer, and his reverence for her extends to a reverence for the heritage she represents. Yet, although he searches one part of his ancestry, Momaday still observes her as an outsider. Some may argue that he romanticizes Kiowa values or that assimilation has been so intrusive that we have no way of really reading Kiowa values, much less going back to any of them. In his penultimate paragraph, Momaday hints that this may be so. His metaphors speak of death, and he notices how small his grandmother's house now seems.

RECONCILING WITH FATHERS (p. 220)

LUCILLE CLIFTON
forgiving my father (p. 221)

Lucille Clifton's extended analogy between paying one's bills and seeking emotional resolution between father and daughter begins with the language of blunt earnestness. The speaker has been thinking hard. She has come to a conclusion. After many years of delay, it's time for a resolution. Although both her parents are dead, Clifton's speaker focuses on the continuing emotional tug of unresolved pain and disappointment. Both the speaker and her mother had tried to get emotional nurture from the father, but, as she notes, he had never been capable of such commitment. He was too needy himself to give to others, a trait that apparently ran in his family. In the analogy, the father never had emotional reserves to give, but was instead an "empty pocket" to the women who hoped for more. In the last stanza of the poem, the speaker suggests that she is trying to be rid of the exhausting blame game. She realizes that he can give her nothing, then or now. In a kind of neutral reconciliation with herself, she will have nothing more to do with his memory. Neither parent can supply emotional restitution or ultimately satisfy her. Her epiphany that her desires are futile leads to as much "forgiving" as she is capable of giving her father.

The answer to Lucille Clifton's question in line 21 — "what am I doing here collecting?" — seems to be "wasting my time," since the last two lines strongly suggest that no emotional support is forthcoming: no money, no "payday." The speaker seems to suggest that we should face reality, that her father was incapable of giving more than he had, which wasn't much. Her realization that there will be "no accounting" suggests that no matter how she tries to rationalize the situation, it's over. But one could make the case that this poem is a way of settling the emotional tension once and for all. The poet is imaginative in sustaining the analogy from start to finish. Students could be asked to suggest other financial terms she could have used, such as *interest, hoarding,* or *stealing.* They might also be asked to supply connotations for "old dead man" as a way of understanding the poet's attitude. The main contradiction arises as she asks a dead man to pay up, to give what is no longer possible. It is finally resolved by claiming that both parents are "in debtor's boxes," without the resources to pay anyone anything. Some students may see her acceptance of this fact as the way she finally forgives her father, whereas others may argue that forgiving is more problematic, perhaps even closer to forgetting.

ROBERT HAYDEN
Those Winter Sundays (p. 222)

If we assume that the speaker of Robert Hayden's poem "Those Winter Sundays" is the author himself (or a 1920s contemporary), we find ourselves in a Sunday morning atmosphere that may seem alien to students' recent childhood experiences. Students accustomed to central heating may not at first recognize the deprivation and effort implied in making "banked fires blaze" in a wood- or coal-burning stove, furnace, or fireplace to make the day's activities possible in a drafty house in Buffalo, New York. Hayden makes it clear from the first line that it is a *daily* sacrifice that the father makes: "Sundays *too* my father got up early," the speaker says (emphasis added). There is a priestly, almost godlike, quality to the everyday "offices" that the adult speaker, looking back, can view with awe, though the child of the past cannot. The word *offices* here has connotations of religious service, and we are meant to see not only the implications of the title but also other ways in which the father's labors are sacramental. The speaker does not invite us to be overly idealistic or sentimental, however; we are given both the freshly polished shoes and the "chronic angers of that house," both the physical pain of daily labor and the archetypal wonder of creating fire.

The realization that the father is keeping his family alive ("breaking" the cold) through his Sunday fire making, but more importantly through his work throughout the week, is echoed in the last lines of the poem. Repetition of the phrase "what did I know" makes the last sentence more a lament than a question. An answer would consider the difference in perspective that comes with adulthood: an acceptance of ambivalence perhaps, or an awareness that experiences may be interpreted without necessarily assigning blame or assuming guilt. The ambiguities and gaps in the text leave readers room to interpret the poem in the light of their own family dynamics; the working-class nature of the poem's setting provides a context that might add depth to discussion. Images in the poem, such as the repetition of synonyms for *breaking*, gain significance in the context of hard times. The poem's tone suggests personal regret, coupled with the evocation of a specific historical and socioeconomic setting beyond the child's understanding or control.

Although Robert Hayden and Lucille Clifton, both African Americans, describe similar situations in terms of social class, Clifton's tone is less forgiving — some might say more realistic — at least on the surface. Whereas Hayden conveys images of coldness, hints at conflicts he does not reveal, and cloaks the father's labor in heroic significance, Clifton hotly calls names and explodes with anger at her father's "needy" heritage. Clifton addresses her father directly and berates him openly for his failures; Hayden seems to explain his seemingly unloving father to others, placing the shortcomings on himself. Switching to third-person pronouns might have lessened Clifton's accusatory tone, but would have robbed her poem of its power. If Hayden addressed his father directly, the poem might edge into sentimentality, but would certainly lose the subtle sense of love communicated not by words but by inarticulate actions, actions we need to see. In the rhetorical questions asked in the poems, both poets seem to realize the futility of settling accounts completely with their fathers. Each might answer with the resolve to make some sense of it and then let go.

THEODORE ROETHKE

My Papa's Waltz (p. 223)

The images in "My Papa's Waltz" contrast to each other in ways that defy a simplistic reading. Students who would sentimentalize the relationship must deal with the undercurrent of danger implied by the connotations of the words *whiskey, battered, beat,* and even *death.* The household is brought into chaos, and the mother clearly disapproves. Yet those who jump to conclusions of child abuse — a frequent reaction among students — must account for a verb like *romped* and for the child's holding onto his father rather than struggling to get away. In fact, it is the child who holds on "like death" — an ironic simile — and the father whose hands show signs of injury and wear, perhaps a reversal of what might be expected of an abuser. Still, those who argue that the father is an abuser could say that it is the knuckle that is battered. Are these the scars of a man who works hard, or has he been injured by striking something — or someone — with his fist? No, the poem is characterized by playfulness, the sentimentalist could respond. The title refers to the father lovingly as "My Papa," and the regular rhythm and rhyme have a dancelike quality. Father and son participate together in the dance, while the mother — not, we may note, *mama* — stands aside, unwilling to "countenance" such behavior. The formal word used to describe her face invites the connotations of stern disapproval while neatly providing the rhyme. The sense of male solidarity in the rough and dangerous play that excludes the woman may be a subtext worthy of discussion.

With its contrasting imagery of play and danger, the poem expresses both fondness and bitterness, both fear and affection. Such a text invites an issues-based approach. Word choices would strengthen the argument for fond remembrance and affection: If *romped* became *fought,* the meaning would be unambiguously violent; if *waltz* were changed to *dance,* a specific word with romantic and civilized connotations would become a generality allowing less safe, more carnivalistic interpretations — a war dance, perhaps, or the disorder of a whirling dervish. But the poem invites readers to remain open to a more complex reading and may provide an opportunity for teachers to assure students that it's okay to change our views as we write about a text or discuss it with others.

If Roethke had called his poem "forgiving my father," much of the ambiguity and complexity would have been lost. Lucille Clifton can use the word *forgiving* because her tone sounds angry and unforgiving: The use of the word therefore contributes a needed irony to her poem. Both Roethke and Robert Hayden are less open, however; both hint at mixed feelings, intertwining fear and love throughout their poems. Although it may be going too far to say that they miss their fathers, their poems are nostalgic. The three poems express complex feelings about the fathers they describe, but Roethke's speaker reveals the least about what he really thinks, leaving it for the reader to respond to the experience he shows.

SHIRLEY GEOK-LIN LIM
Father from Asia (p. 225)

For most of us, becoming adults involves a movement away from the family and culture of childhood, a questioning of the ideologies and common sense of our parents. We must distance ourselves at some point in order to grow. Yet the feelings involved are complex, a mixture of anger, loss, and guilt, a tangled knot of emotions. Shirley Geok-lin Lim expresses such feelings, which are compounded by the realities of a separation East and West that is equally complex. The first image of the poem, the father's hands as empty bowls, evokes images for an American reader of the empty bowls of the Third World in television commercials for charitable causes. We want to reach out and help. Yet, for the speaker, the need is an emptiness that will eat her up. As the poem proceeds, the rejection of the father by the daughter, of the homeland by the emigrant, is searingly painful. Can she really mean she has learned nothing from him, that such profound distance must be maintained? In succeeding lines, she speaks of her father and/or Asia as a "ghost / who eats his own children" and "who loved his children." Does parental love devour? Imperial China, with a reasoning more like ours than we like to admit, saw itself as the "center of the world," as Lim points out. To move away from our own ethnocentrism may be painful, but the poet implies that going back would be to enter into a cycle that destroys.

The narrator's heritage haunts her, even though she renounces it as one might renounce a false god. Her use of hyperbole, screaming that she will not be held by her heritage, shows its power over her. Her attempts to escape the past lead only to vivid images of pain. Perhaps she writes to shock her audience into deromanticizing Asia, perhaps she writes so that we will protest that she is wrong, or perhaps she writes only to express the intensity of the inevitable loss of culture that comes with change. The repetition of the image of dust in the last line implies a grinding down that repeats itself like some inevitable karma, a renunciation that goes on forever without redemption. This image, like those throughout the poem, expresses the antithesis of life and growth.

If Lucille Clifton's speaker looks at the grave of her father and angrily finds it futile to expect him to give to her, Lim's takes her anger a giant step further and flees across "two oceans" to escape the father whose poverty demands so much of her. Clifton's father is an empty pocket, Hayden's tries without thanks to keep out the cold, and Roethke's spins him dangerously off to bed; Lim's father is emptier, more sacrificial, and more dangerous than any of these. He is a frightening abstraction, and forgiving does not seem to enter into her thinking at all. The easy answer would be that her attitude is the least healthy of the four, but taken figuratively, the impulse to free ourselves from the past — or at least to recognize its power over who we are — is worthy of consideration.

EXORCISING THE DEAD: CRITICAL COMMENTARIES ON SYLVIA PLATH'S "DADDY" (p. 226)

SYLVIA PLATH

Daddy (p. 227)

Often the voice in a poem is quite different from the poet's own, and students need to go beyond the tendency of novice readers to see all poetry as an emotional outpouring of the poet's soul. The poems of Sylvia Plath, however, invite a biographical approach. As a confessional poet, writing as part of a 1950s and early 1960s attempt to bring the life of the poet into the text, Plath incorporated images of her personal psychological struggles into her poetry. For this reason, her poetry might first be approached in the context of the post–World War II society in which she came of age, when the Holocaust and other abuses carried out by fascist movements were within recent memory. Before the cultural changes of the late 1960s, including the resurgence of the women's movement, the expectations placed upon most daughters were rigidly prescribed. Fathers tended to be authoritarian, and husbands to control the lives of their wives and children. Thus contextualizing the poem may help current readers understand the tone and imagery of "Daddy" and allow them to respond thoughtfully to the alternative views of critics.

Like the speaker in Lucille Clifton's poem "forgiving my father," Plath's persona angrily rails at a dead man who has left the business of fatherhood unfinished. His early death has made it impossible for her to challenge her father's power over her self-image through his approval, disapproval, or indifference. She has therefore been unable to function as an adult. Because he is absent, she feels, she has replicated the father/daughter relationship in her marriage. If she is to break out of the victim position, she must kill the inner father who has caused her to be self-destructive.

Because her own father was of German ancestry, Plath metaphorically portrays the father in the poem as a Nazi and the daughter as a Jew, appropriating the imagery of brutality and war for her own personal purposes. This bothers many readers. Other similes seem extreme as well: He is a "black shoe . . . a bag full of God . . . a devil." But images of his replacement, perhaps her husband, seem even more severe, and students may want to discuss the extent to which she is really angry with her father or with someone else. Although Plath claimed that the poem was not her own story, she wrote it on the day her divorce papers arrived. Could blaming her father actually be her way of masochistically blaming herself for the difficulties of her marriage, of remaining a victim who tortures herself with guilt? The poem's assertion that "Every woman adores a Fascist" recalls the I-must-have-asked-for-it thinking of abuse victims.

The childish language of the poem may trivialize it for some; it is interesting that even the bits of German she chooses to interweave are one-syllable words a child would learn. If Plath is describing her inability to escape a role she acquired in childhood, however, the juxtaposition of baby talk and brutality makes sense. The poem seems less about the rebelliousness of young adults and more about the ways in which we may continue to play out the dramas of childhood. Plath seems to refer to her earlier attempt at suicide in the poem, and she would kill herself by sticking her head in a gas oven a few months later, an interestingly symbolic act when considered in terms of her Holocaust imagery here. That she would leave her young children to deal with a loss similar to the one she laments in the poem seems ironic, but may simply reflect a deeply held belief that the loss of a mother could not possibly be as important as the loss of "Daddy."

CRITICAL COMMENTARIES:

MARY LYNN BROE, From *Protean Poetic: The Poetry of Sylvia Plath* (p. 230)

LYNDA K. BUNDTZEN, From *Plath's Incarnations* (p. 232)

STEVEN GOULD AXELROD, From *Sylvia Plath: The Wound and the Cure of Words* (p. 234)

Before reading the critical interpretations of Sylvia Plath's poem, students may need to brainstorm their own ways of seeing it as more than the autobiographical ranting of a middle-class woman unable to come to terms with her neuroses. Because the father's body seems to lie across the American continent, is this young woman living in England protesting that her home country is as fascist as the Third Reich? Does the final scene of villagers dancing remind us of carnival with its implications of overturning authority? What images and words are repeated, and what could this symbolize? Students might look back at the list of issues on pages 19–26 or on the front inside cover for additional questions they could raise about Plath's text.

Mary Lynn Broe sees the speaker of the poem as an actor playing out a scene of exorcism that doesn't quite work. Broe calls the poem "self-parody," implying that Plath is laughing at herself and inviting the reader to see the irony between the intensity and incantation of the speaker's words and the paltry results of her actions. Lynda Bundtzen, on the other hand, while also seeing the speaker as a dramatic persona, uses quotations from Plath to argue that the poem is "a figurative drama about mourning" that describes feelings the poet has already conquered. She is no longer a comic victim, but a victor. Steven Axelrod goes beyond the other critics to say that the poem is about woman as writer, its imagery metaphorically describing the poet's attempts to find her voice in a world of words dominated by men.

Readers will have different ideas about which critic best answers the poem's perplexing questions, though teachers steeped in literary theory may feel that

Axelrod opens up issues of feminism, patriarchy, and the literary canon that give the poem's angry tone a broader context. Axelrod's movement beyond the specifics of the poet's family life differs strikingly from the more limited interpretations of Broe and Bundtzen, but the three critics agree that "Daddy" is a staged representation rather than an autobiographical confession of the emotional turmoil of Sylvia Plath herself.

MOTHERS AND DAUGHTERS (p. 240)

TILLIE OLSEN

I Stand Here Ironing (p. 240)

Readers tend to have strong reactions to texts by Tillie Olsen. Many feel that she challenges class- and gender-based societal barriers, whereas others see her as simply making excuses for failures to overcome them. In her nonfiction book *Silences*, published in 1978, Olsen supports her assertion that both men and women of the working class were long denied political, intellectual, and literary voices by the realities of labor and survival. Olsen was in fact instrumental in bringing texts written by women back into print and into the literary canons of universities during the 1970s and beyond. "I Stand Here Ironing" blends fiction, dramatic monologue, and autobiography. Many of the details of the story echo details of Olsen's early life as a working mother during the 1930s and 1940s.

Today's college students, living with many of the benefits brought about by social movements propelled by Olsen's generation, sometimes have trouble understanding the narrator's situation. In one memorable presentation in an introduction-to-literature class, a student saw Emily as retarded and the narrator as obsessive-compulsive, as evidenced by the fact that she is ironing! A show of hands revealed that several students had never seen their mothers iron. Ironing as a metaphor for oppressive but necessary work may therefore be an elusive concept for young readers. An equally simplistic reading sentimentalizes the characters as victims of poverty, reducing them to cardboard cutouts.

The ambiguity of the ending's optimism or pessimism suggests that the issues are more complex than they appear on the surface. The narrator despairs at ever being able to explain why her daughter needs help, but she holds out hope that the girl will find her own way if she is empowered by self-knowledge. A critique of social conditions is implicit in the text, while the narrator explicitly sorts out her failings as a mother. She may be trying to forgive herself, and this issue — of where personal responsibility ends and societal responsibility begins — may be the major theme of her story. Students could explore other perspectives by acting out an imagined conference among the characters mentioned in the story, perhaps even bringing Emily's father, stepfather, and grandparents into the mix. Reactions to the first-person voice of the narrator vary, with some students sensing an effort to impose a narrative line upon fragmented memories and others dismissing the narrator as a whiner. The narrator may resist a conference with the teacher because she wants to avoid blame, but she seems primarily to resist an intrusive and profitless discussion that would oversimplify complex issues. She also hints that the power for change is not in the mother but in the daughter herself.

AMY TAN
Two Kinds (p. 247)

After Amy Tan discovered that her mother had been forced to leave three living daughters in China, rather than the dead twins that play a climactic part in "Two Kinds," she had fears that her mother would drop her for the "good" China daughters. These fears compounded the already difficult relationship that lends realism to the stories of *The Joy Luck Club*, from which this story is taken. A trip to China with her mother helped Tan place these fears into perspective, however, when she found that her mother was just as critical of her half-sisters, dashing their dreams of the nurturing mother they had fantasized about having. For Tan, writing her mother's stories has become both a way of finding her own voice as a writer and a way of coming to terms with her painful resistance to the older woman's controlling personality. Learning to forgive herself for being the wrong kind of daughter, the disobedient kind, has been a major task for Amy Tan. She says, however, that learning to forgive herself has helped her to forgive her mother as well.

Because the cultural differences between the mother who came of age in China and the daughter born in America are so obvious, the writer admits that the cultural and generational differences are difficult to sort out. These factors and her mother's great personal losses intensify their struggles. Asian American young people maintain that the cultural expectations of their parents still cause similar difficulties in some families, and non-Asian students may recognize their own families in the story as well. Americans who travel to other countries, Tan included, realize that social mobility is more possible here, but we cannot say that race, gender, and other differences do not matter. Perhaps the little Chinese girl can be a prodigy, but she cannot be Shirley Temple. The argument does not settle the matter for either character. The mother is wounded deeply but still cannot accept her daughter as she is; the narrator becomes the wrong kind of daughter but discovers the power of her own will. We know less about the mother's feelings since we see and hear her through the eyes of the daughter, whose thoughts we are allowed to share. Dialogue and descriptions of body language bring the mother to life, as do anecdotes of her failed attempts to create a "prodigy" of her daughter. The characters are dynamic but remain locked in their struggle with each other.

The mothers in the stories by Amy Tan and Tillie Olsen provide a sharp contrast between oppressive control and frantic neglect. Olsen's narrator wishes for her daughter to be empowered and to find her own way. The mother of Tan's narrator seeks to empower her daughter by directing her life and does not see the irony in this attempt. Both mothers unintentionally reject their children but love them and want good things for them. Because the stories are told from different points of view, it's hard to say which daughter has the more difficult life. We know more of the pain of Tan's narrator, but we know that she grows up to be successful and that she wins the battle for selfhood. We are less sure about Olsen's Emily. It may be that living with an overpowering mother is more intense, but less painful, than living without one.

SIBLINGS IN CONFLICT (p. 256)

TOBIAS WOLFF

The Rich Brother (p. 257)

As this story ends, the older brother imagines the voice of his wife calling him to account for his brother. "Where is your brother?" is a question of biblical proportions, and the circumstances here recall at least two similar stories. After killing his brother and thus committing the first murder, the eldest son of Adam and Eve is asked this question by God, and he (Cain) answers, "Am I my brother's keeper?" Much later, Jesus describes two brothers in the parable of the prodigal son. In the parable, the younger son wastes his inheritance in riotous living, and the conforming elder brother is furious when the slacker is welcomed home with ceremony. In Wolff's story, the elder brother seems to accept that he must be his brother's keeper in spite of its injustice. Ironically, the younger brother's prodigality is too Christian for the Christians, and his riotous living is generous and naive to the point of holy idiocy. Still, a bit of doubt remains for Pete that the prodigal may be rewarded with the fatted calf after all. "What a joke if there really was a blessing to be had, and the blessing didn't come to the one who deserved it, the one who did all the work, but to the other." The title begs the question of which brother is the rich one. Pete has all the trappings of prosperity, but Donald is the one who gives everything away, the one who acts with largesse, the one who invests.

The language Wolff uses to describe Pete identifies him as the typical, money-grubbing bourgeois salesman, a literary character we have learned to view with contempt. Donald is the dreamy romantic that we expect to have unexpected wisdom. The hitchhiking Webster seems sinister and even Satanic at first, identifying the darkness as "Stygian," and we expect some terrible thing to happen. Later, when Pete hears a twig snap in the woods as he leaves his brother on the road, we wonder if the terrible thing will now take place. Webster's story of Peru smacks of the formula of romantic adventure, and we agree with Pete that it is not credible. But we view it all from Pete's point of view, and we can't be sure what has happened. Like Pete, we expect the ironic ending, a true climax to the story, but we're left in the middle of the road. Rather than give stock answers based on our past reading of fiction, we might respond by questioning the formulas we have come to expect. Pete and Donald do not fit the stereotypes of fiction when

40

examined closely. Pete, the practical brother, appreciates the mystical experience of skydiving, whereas Donald, the spiritual searcher, questions its cost. There is a mixture of mutual dependency and rivalry between the brothers that surfaces as they sleep or pretend to sleep, as children or adults. The young Pete strikes the young Donald, who turns a blind eye; the adult Pete dreams his brother guides him in his blindness; Pete sleeps while a mysterious contract is made between Donald and Webster. And the reader is left in the dark to fill in the gaps where the issues may really lie.

JAMES BALDWIN
Sonny's Blues (p. 270)

Like the protagonist of Tobias Wolff's "The Rich Brother," the elder brother in "Sonny's Blues" must deal with the question of being his brother's keeper. And although the story stands on its own as a narrative about family relationships, the phrase takes on metaphorical significance in its African American context. Brothers, in James Baldwin's Harlem, must be there for each other but can sometimes only stand and watch. The story begins as the schoolteacher protagonist's younger brother has gone to prison for using heroin. He tells us that his students remind him of his brother, and we walk down a Harlem street with his brother's friend. In a flashback, his mother reveals in their last conversation that his father had seen his own brother maliciously killed by white people in a car that was speeding down a road like an uncontrollable force. We see inside bars and look out the window at gospel meetings where participants call each other brother and sister. Other flashbacks reveal class conflicts within the extended family, and dialogue often carries the story line and the debate between brothers. Baldwin both shows and tells a parable about letting one's brother be who he must be, within both the family and the community.

The story belongs to the elder brother at the beginning, and we continue to see through his eyes. We get to know Sonny better as the brothers' dialogue proceeds, however, and by the end the story belongs to him, as the title has indicated all along. Both brothers are dynamic characters, and we see them struggle — less with each other than with forces beyond their control, the "darkness outside." Their dying mother places the responsibility for Sonny on the older brother, but he is forced by World War II to shift this responsibility to his wife's family, and Sonny must reckon with the judgment of the middle class and deal with his brother's expectations without his presence. In this case, to be one's brother's keeper may be to deny him the freedom to keep himself. At the end of the story, as Sonny plays his music, his brother is finally able to listen to him. Interestingly, this happens as he recognizes that the men playing the blues with Sonny function as a family tuned in to each other, as the real brothers have failed to be. Perhaps our sense of responsibility for our siblings limits our ability to see them as separate from ourselves.

Baldwin's characters come closer to understanding each other in the closing scene. They have talked throughout the story, but music and gesture communicate more in the end. Wolff's brothers are less articulate and less able to find real closure, though perhaps this is because we leave them at a different point in their relationship. Students might want to discuss popular psychology studies about birth order as they look at the conventional older brothers and their passionate siblings. It may be that parents, by making the older child somehow responsible for the younger, subtly suggest the roles that the children will play. Students will choose their own answers to the possible themes of these stories, even going beyond obvious family issues to social, political, or religious ones.

DYSFUNCTIONAL FAMILIES (p. 293)

WILLIAM SHAKESPEARE
Hamlet, Prince of Denmark (p. 294)

Four hundred years after William Shakespeare's tragedy examining the dynamics of a royal household was written, we still find issues that relate to the family and political events. During the impeachment trial of President Bill Clinton, a student from a particularly authoritarian family called the situation disrespectful, arguing that one does not ask impertinent questions of the leader of one's country. This was for her the equivalent of defying the authority of one's father, something that ran counter to the conservative values she had been taught. Although other family values were in conflict with the president's actions, this one seemed paramount to her, especially since her father had recently died. Having been created before the American and French Revolutions and the social and political changes of the twentieth century, the characters of Shakespeare's play wrestle with more severe prohibitions against reversing the order of family or kingdom.

Although we may debate the many reasons for Hamlet's delay in obeying his dead father's urgings to kill the usurper, we can see that his values are in conflict. Any decision he makes will cause him to challenge a person in the position of father, in the personal and the political sense. He is "a little more than kin, and less than kind" (1.2.65) — a position that will require him to go against what he considers to be natural, both as a son and as a subject. Furthermore, Hamlet is also dealing with a supernatural world, and he dares not strike as Claudius prays because he wants to send the false father literally to Hell.

Hamlet's feelings about his mother are more complex, and Freudian issues are often raised to explain them. Does he unconsciously wish to do as Claudius has done, to kill his father and marry his mother, acting out the Oedipus complex? Students may want to examine various productions of the play available on videotape to see how act 3, scene 4, is staged and what tone is used to deliver Hamlet's harsh words to his mother. Some interpretations have a decidedly incestuous slant.

Our argument-based approach to reading the play might best consider how the families deal with their own issues. The royal family in *Hamlet* acts in an emotional frenzy, and all is pathos as they go about making their decisions. The men of Polonius's family are petrified in logos, reasoning out their lives in rhetorical clichés. Questions of ethos arise as values are questioned and characters seek for people who can be trusted. It's all too much for Ophelia, who escapes into incoherence. The play abounds with examples of flawed reasoning and logical fallacies as its families struggle, and for the most part fail, to work out their conflicting issues.

TENNESSEE WILLIAMS
The Glass Menagerie (p. 399)

Tennessee Williams has woven many autobiographical elements into his play *The Glass Menagerie*. The playwright had to interrupt his education to work in a shoe factory; his father, who belittled the son's artistic temperament, was a traveling salesman; his mother was a genteel southern lady; and his sister had a mental illness. Williams sees the question of autobiography in his play as problematic, however, as he shows by the poetic and philosophical comments woven into descriptions of the *dramatis personae* and stage directions as the play begins. He explains to us that we are to pity the mother and see her tenderness even as we laugh at her. He makes explicit the symbolic and metaphorical connection between Laura and her fragile collection of glass animals. He tells us that Tom will have to escape from this trap and that the gentleman caller we are to meet is just "a nice, ordinary young man." He goes on to give the reader the historical and cultural context for the play. But more importantly, Williams reminds us that memory is elusive and tricky, and the line between fiction and nonfiction unclear. He has Tom narrate, calling him "an undisguised convention of the play" and giving him lines that analyze the symbolism of various characters. By showing us the framework of the writing, from the beginning he presents the text as a literary object. As readers we may object, as Tom does when his mother tells him how to eat, and may challenge the playwright's analysis of his own text and his advice to us on how to take it.

By giving us the social context, Williams makes Amanda's desperation to find a husband for Laura seem less neurotic than we might otherwise judge it to be. Yes, she's obsessive, but she also has to worry about how to keep the lights turned on, and women don't have many financial options in this time period. We recognize Laura's emotional fragility and the symbolic nature of the glass menagerie and realize that, like the unicorn, the lightest touch will break her. Her giving of the unicorn to Jim seems more a giving up of hope and love; she has given herself to him in their dance, and there will not be another gentleman caller in her life. Perhaps this is a realistic view of a hyperbolic family. Visitors to the American South are sometimes shocked to find what they thought were the exaggerated eccentrics of fiction having histrionic conversations in the next booth at the breakfast house. Tom truly loves his sister, and she continues to haunt his thoughts after he leaves. That the writer grieves for his broken sister is documented and undoubted. Perhaps the play is for Rose and the final line echoes the words of Tennessee Williams himself. Like Tom, he must say good-bye. It is interesting that Jim at one point says to Laura, "If you were my sister. . . ." Outsiders sometimes can see what to do, while family members continue to spin in circles. Students, at a time when they are finding a place in the world outside of family, may have more to say about the need to break free of destructive, or simply familiar, family cycles.

Both Williams's Amanda and Shakespeare's Gertrude have lost husbands, and both are constrained by the realities of survival. In both cases, their sons tell us how we are supposed to evaluate them. Taking these prescriptions at face value, we may tend to judge Amanda with understanding and to see Gertrude as selfish and weak, but we may want to question why this is so. Hamlet and Tom each live in the shadow of a father whose absence has thrown the family's life out of order. Laertes and Ophelia are obedient children, but we might question when children become adults in their own right. Students may rightly question whether the parents in both plays demand too much of their children's souls. By marrying, Claudius and Gertrude rob Hamlet of the throne, keeping him in the role of son when he should be king. Polonius gives sage and sometimes conflicting advice to his adult children. Tom's mother keeps him in the role of son, waking him in the morning and inquiring into his whereabouts at night. Both he and Hamlet have responsibility and guilt foisted upon them by the previous generation, and both feel trapped. Because both characters are three-dimensional, students will find many traits to draw upon in their comparisons.

DIFFERENT CHILDREN (p. 448)

JOYCE CAROL OATES

Wednesday's Child (p. 448)

In the folk rhyme, Wednesday's child is full of woe. In this story, it is the parents who experience the sorrow while the child apparently feels nothing. Oates's protagonist, the father of a six-year-old autistic child, is an architect concerned with proper forms, a man who appreciates beauty and order. In the story, this concern repeats itself on every page. We first see his house, with its "high handsome roof," described as "firm and wonderfully solid." He hates failure, his wife tells him, because he can't control it. He describes his own speech as consisting of paragraphs — forms — surrounded by silences, and we are told that he hates silence because of its emptiness and formlessness. His daughter's silences are "like terrible monstrous blocks of stone." The child herself is beautiful as a work of art, but it is impossible to discern her inner shape as a person. He wants to teach her the names of things and imagines that it would be terror for her to wake up in the morning without this order imposed on the world. Yet the climax of the story comes as he violently beats a stranger who has collided with his daughter in the park, an act that is the very antithesis of order. Later, the blood on his shoes reassures him that it has really happened, and his daughter's familiar, rigid behavior and silence give him a sense of safety. Her obsessive formalism now brings order into his disorder.

The simple answer to the meaning behind Arthur's act against the stranger in the park would be that such rigidity cannot be maintained, that such tightly reined frustration will eventually explode into fury. It may also occur to the reader that the man in the park is Arthur's disorderly opposite but also represents a part of himself, the part who has fantasized about his daughter's violent death earlier on this Wednesday trip. His daughter Brenda is a flawed work of art for Arthur — a "failure . . . of his chromosomes," as he puts it at one point. He seems to feel little real parental love at first but may have formed a closer bond by the end of the story; they are co-conspirators of a sort, and he can trust her to keep silent. That the daughter almost meets her father's gaze after the incident in the park hints that she knows more than she's telling, and we sense the father's panic that now might be the time that the family fantasy comes true and she chooses to speak. Her silence becomes something solid and trustworthy; a smile from her at this point would plunge them both into chaos. But Arthur's need for order has become more problematic; his touchstone for reality becomes the blood on his shoes and his daughter's crunch of dry pasta, not the street signs that impose order and make it impossible to lose oneself. Against his will, Arthur is the dynamic character of the story, but we are left to speculate about the extent of his change. Caring for a handicapped child requires an intricate balance of hope and realism, as Oates implies when she describes the feelings of the mother and the grandparents. Both parents at some point in the story think about escaping into other relationships. Given a nonjudgmental atmosphere, students will think of a continuum of solutions to the stress of bringing up a handicapped child — ranging from residential schools to group homes to occasional respite care. Some students may have personal experiences that they are willing to share.

KATHERINE ANNE PORTER

He (p. 459)

Until recent times in American society, most developmentally handicapped people were institutionalized or hidden away and often treated as not quite human. Because sexually transmitted diseases sometimes caused birth defects, parents were afraid that the community might think "the sins of the fathers" had been visited on the children and the family's status would be compromised. In addition, such things were feared to "run in the family" and to indicate that the family might have "bad blood." These fears dominate the thinking of the farm family in this Katherine Anne Porter short story. It has been said that the first step toward oppression is to dehumanize the person or group one wishes to abuse or eliminate. And although they may not do it consciously, the Whipples do just that. In the title and throughout this short story, the boy is called by the third-person pronoun rather than by a name. He is given the jobs that other family members do not want, living as a virtual slave despite his docility and his mother's assurances to herself and the neighbors that she loves him and cares for his needs above all others. Like the preacher who assures them that as a holy innocent "He don't get hurt," the parents don't believe he really feels cold, pain, or weariness. His grief at the story's end comes as a surprise; and though his mother continues to rationalize, she finally seems more concerned with her human son than with the judgments of the neighbors.

The family has done little to help Him and have probably done him harm. He loses his extra blanket, must borrow a coat, endures bee stings, and is repeatedly overworked and neglected. The mother wallows in feelings as she butchers the hog, but though the reader catches the obvious symbolism, Mrs. Whipple makes no connection between the creature under her knife and the son she constantly sacrifices for the trivial concerns of other family members, including herself. Adjectives describe the pig as *pink, naked, fat, soft,* and *pitiful-looking.* The connection with the boy seems overdone, but perhaps we are meant to see the irony, the grotesque comedy of her self-deception. Most of us will agree with the doctor that this ten-year-old will be better served away from his family. By allowing us to see this for ourselves as she piles up the mother's silly excuses, Porter makes a powerful argument for communal responsibility and compassion.

In Porter's story and in Joyce Carol Oates's "Wednesday's Child," parents deny the extent of the child's handicap and struggle with what that handicap says about their own worth as human beings. They behave in selfish ways, sometimes in foolish ways that place their children in danger. Although the Whipples may think the problem is about money, Mrs. Whipple's greatest concern seems to be her own status in the community, a status only partly connected with financial standing. Brenda's parents have money, but this seems to give them little control over their embarrassment and frustration. Education and cultural expectations may be the true dividing factors between these families. We may argue, however, that these stories are fiction, after all, and that money matters a great deal in such situations in the real world.

These children stand apart from their families. The result for Him is to be equated with a farm animal. Brenda's silence is a force outside her parents' control, a mystery that disturbs the order of their lives. Her sin is to be mediocre in her insanity, her father says, but her condition seems to dominate her parents' lives in an almost godlike way. Porter and Oates use different strategies to describe the mothers in their stories. We know a great deal about Mrs. Whipple because we are allowed to overhear her thoughts and to judge her actions. Brenda's mother is seen through the limited view of her husband, and we can be less clear about her motives. A comparison of the mothers would therefore require us to speculate more about the architect's wife than the farmwoman. Because most readers of this story will identify more closely with Oates's characters, we may be able to keep more distance from Porter's Mrs. Whipple and to smile ironically at her shortcomings while sympathizing with the more accessible problems of Brenda's mother.

GRANDPARENTS AND LEGACIES (p. 467)

NIKKI GIOVANNI
Legacies (p. 467)

From her first recognition as a poetic and political voice of the Black Arts movement of the 1960s and 1970s to her current involvement with young people as a professor at Virginia Polytechnic Institute, Nikki Giovanni has celebrated and articulated her African American heritage. Rather than following the literary and cultural traditions of white America, Giovanni uses the rhythms and vocabulary of her family and neighborhood in both her message and in the way she delivers it. Like many black people of her generation, she seeks to recover and preserve a distinctive, powerful family and cultural history and to express it to her contemporaries and their children and grandchildren. Her grandmother, Louvenia Watson of Knoxville, Tennessee, is for the poet a tangible link with this heritage, and Nikki Giovanni — now grandmother age herself — serves as such a link to younger people. The poem expresses a strong sense of this continuity, going all the way back to West African customs and ways of being in the world. We therefore need to see beyond the everyday images of the poem to the longer chain of human experience they may symbolize.

In a similar way, the dialogue of the poem has surface meaning, but the granddaughter, at least from the poet's distance, hears instead something unspoken in the dialogue. Although she seems to reject it, the child holds the legacy too dear to spoil it with everyday use, is afraid — superstitiously or otherwise — to touch the gift that her grandmother wants to pass on to her. Folklore can be a way of doing something, such as making rolls. The child seems to be thinking of a more spiritual, mystical link. When the grandmother wipes her hands, she seems to give up on the idea that children will ever be able to grasp the legacy their elders want to give, but we know that the poet has recognized the motives of both generations. What is passed along cannot be articulated by either.

Pride is an important concept in the poem and in the ideology of the poet; being proud of one's heritage is her implicit message. The compressed, idiomatic language and conversational rhythms, although not formally structured, are nevertheless poetic and help prove her point that *this* way of writing poetry — this African American way — is just as legitimate as any other, is in fact part of the legacy. Linguists tell us that the surface meanings of words form only a part of the story of any given discourse. We might encourage students to think of times that they have spoken at cross-purposes with older family members, knowing but not acknowledging that what was said was simply a code for something of deeper significance.

WILLIAM CARLOS WILLIAMS
The Last Words of My English Grandmother (p. 469)

When the most American of poets makes a point of putting his *English* grandmother into the title of a poem, it's fair to question why. Actually, William Carlos Williams did have a paternal English grandmother, his father having been born in England and his mother in Puerto Rico. His parents immigrated to Rutherford, New Jersey, where the poet was born and spent most of his life. Williams takes the language and imagery of his poetry from the sounds and sights of this small town. Much of his poetry has a medical connection, since Williams was a pediatrician who made house calls and cared for people in the hospital. His methods are firmly based in theory, however, though less in literary theory than in that of the visual arts. Like many artists and writers of the early twentieth century, Williams was profoundly affected by the objective approaches to reality he saw in modernist paintings exhibited in the 1913 Armory Show. Like a non-representational artist working with pigments, Williams sought to present words and images without commentary or narrative that would tell the audience how to interpret them. He maintained, furthermore, that rather than search for "poetic" material a poet should take his images from ordinary life and may write about anything that gives him amusement or that is deeply felt. In this poem, we catch a few glimpses of a dying grandmother, and though we are not told of it, an unsentimental but deeply felt compassion seems implicit in the poet's choice of images.

Growing old tends to strip away the need to be tentative and polite about one's needs. Readers will see the grandmother through the eyes of their own experiences, but she says, in what the speaker describes as a moment of clarity, that young people "don't know anything." Perhaps we will not really see what the doctor/poet is able to describe — her renunciation of everything but her own hunger and pain. The last lines of the poem indicate that she is past caring about the objects of the world. There is a profoundly physical nature to the concrete images of the poem — "the rank, disheveled bed"; the old woman snoring and complaining; the fuzziness of her vision — suggesting the reality of the body to one who is dying. Nothing outside of the body really matters. The text invites us to raise issues about a sick person's right to decide about medical care, the desire of the elderly to be cared for at home, and the ramifications of the euthanasia debate.

The grandmothers in this poem and in Nikki Giovanni's "Legacies" both state that young people are unable to understand their elders. Each poet, at least from the distance of adulthood, does understand, however. Each is able to communicate to the reader the crossed communications of an earlier time. It would be difficult to make a case for exchanging the situations or the grandmothers. Each poet makes a point of ethnicity. Yet readers who are not African American can imagine the child who wants to bypass homemaking skills for the memory of the grandmother who magically made rolls as no one else could. And people without English grandmothers can relate to the grandson's problems in Williams's poem. In our comparison of the women themselves and in our speculations about whether they might get along, we are hampered by the vast differences in their situations. At this point, Williams's grandmother is doing the work of death and would be oblivious to the woman of Giovanni's poem, who continues her work as the living center of a household.

GRACE CAVALIERI
Grandmother (p. 470)

In "Legacies" Nikki Giovanni rejects the gift of her grandmother's labor in favor of her spirit. In "The Last Words of My English Grandmother" William Carlos Williams shows the physicality, of death. Grace Cavalieri too speaks of spirit, physicality, and death in "Grandmother." Her dead grandmother visits her as she sleeps, and the poem puzzles out the text of her dreams. She begins and ends the poem with a question, and a question also ends the penultimate stanza. The questions may all be the same question, asking "What is the purpose? . . . What [is the] essential fact? . . . What is the meaning?" The last two questions attempt an answer. She speculates that there is something essential about *motion*, something that has to do with the intersection of body and spirit. Her grandmother is a figure from an earlier Victorian or Edwardian era, but the narrator stresses her nonconformity and independence by picturing her in motion.

The images of the gifts painted in primary colors, especially the last, "a bright clock shaped like a train," reminded us of a painting titled "I Saw the Figure 5 in Gold" painted in oil on cardboard by Charles Demuth in 1928. The painting, abstract and predominantly red and gold, has a similar sense of movement and was inspired by a poem called "The Great Figure."

> Among the rain
> and lights
> I saw the figure 5
> in gold
> on a red
> firetruck
> moving
> tense
> unheeded
> to gong clangs
> siren howls
> and wheels rumbling
> through the dark city.

The poem is by William Carlos Williams! Students need to be assured that personal connections such as this are not irrelevant to their reading of literary texts; idiosyncratic readings often lead to new insights for other creative and critical thinkers.

There seems to be more respect than chiding in Cavalieri's third stanza. The impression is of a grandmother who did a great deal more than the stereotypical grandmotherly tasks of baking, baby-sitting, and cuddling. She is later described as "strong." Ghosts are traditionally compelled by some sense of urgency, and Cavalieri conveys this inarticulate intensity as she describes her grandmother's visits at times when the writer is not strong. Dream analysts tell us that each person in a dream represents an aspect of the dreamer's own personality, and anyone who has ever been in a writer's workshop can testify that hearing one's own texts analyzed is a revealing and not always comfortable experience. Both dreams and poems allow us to work out problems in symbolic form, though the meanings of both types of texts can and perhaps should remain indeterminate. Questions in poems are often rhetorical ones to which the writer knows the answer that she wishes the reader to infer. This is not the case with Cavalieri's questions, however, as is appropriate to the ambiguity of dream interpretation. Students will perhaps find more concrete terms for some of the writer's characterizations of her own lost state, but the argument could be made that the vagueness of the words *foothold*, *direction*, and *way* provides an appropriate contrast with the surety of her grandmother's concrete action.

Nikki Giovanni's "Legacies" and William Carlos Williams's "The Last Words of My English Grandmother" have the feel of everyday life, though we edge into a different state as Williams's dying grandmother's vision begins to blur. Cavalieri, on the other hand, addresses a ghost who appears to her in dreams. Different readers will choose different poems as their favorites in terms of approaches and images, but they might gain personal insights by exploring the reasons behind their preferences. Whether we see the speakers of the three poems as more or less ambivalent about their grandmothers' influence depends upon the details selected by the poets for their varying purposes. Williams keeps his distance, showing us his characters as if we were watching film clips of this particular event, the end of his grandmother's life. The ambivalence may lie more in the reader's interpretation than in the poem itself. Giovanni looks at the grandmother and child from the distance of memory, but we are allowed to know something of the meaning underneath the words. She tells us of her ambivalence, though some mystery remains. Cavalieri speaks directly to her grandmother, still alive in a ghostly way. Her poem is less about a relationship — she confides that there really wasn't one, since her grandmother moved too quickly — than about the narrator herself. Therefore, she selects the strengths that she needs for her dream work, projecting a more positive image than those of the other poems. If these poems are indeed autobiographical, we might expect the writers to worry less about being positive than with presenting a three-dimensional view of complex human beings.

LINDA HOGAN

Heritage (p. 472)

As a Chickasaw, Linda Hogan has a heritage that is a mixed bag, and in this poem she hints at the multiracial history that complicates it. Originally from the Southeast, the Chickasaws were considered one of the "civilized tribes" and were known in the nineteenth century as slaveholders whose cruelty almost matched that of their white neighbors. At the same time, runaway slaves were sometimes welcomed, and both blacks and whites were known to marry into the nation, with children given full recognition. None of this prevented the government seizure of their lands, however, or the forced relocation that took the nation, including Hogan's ancestors, to Oklahoma. Later, when oil was discovered on new Chickasaw lands, white speculators often married Native American women to gain title to mineral rights, further victimizing their families. Hogan traces her blond coloring to such a marriage, explaining why she describes "white breasts that weigh down / my body" and why she calls her "whiteness a shame." Images of deathly white contrast with images of black and brown throughout the poem, with both oil and tobacco — important substances in Chickasaw history — recurring as ambiguous stains. The poem's last stanza recalls a history of dispossession, a heritage of ambiguity and confusion of self, a compass that points in two directions at once.

Homelessness seems to be a negative concept at first, but the first lines of the last stanza raise questions. The grandmother says that "it is wise to eat the flesh of deer / so you will be swift and travel over many miles." This hints at a tradition that predates the "civilized" farming life of the nineteenth century and that sees the return to wandering as an ironic return to Chickasaw roots. Hogan uses her elder relatives to find both a personal heritage and a link to the larger history of Native America, a history that is largely one of loss. The black saliva spilling onto her from her grandmother's snuff can is a startling image, but it becomes "sweet black liquid like the food / she chewed up and spit into my father's mouth / when he was an infant." Anthropologists have speculated that the origin of kissing in human society may stem from mothers and grandmothers chewing up food for recently weaned children, and the concept may be touching if we can get past our knowledge of hygiene. Tobacco in Native American tradition is "medicine" to cleanse the body and "medicine" in a magical and religious sense. The image of being covered by night can be comforting. Still, much bitterness and justifiable anger emerge as Linda Hogan looks at her "heritage." Like Hogan, readers who are brutally honest will at least find ambiguities in their family histories.

Hogan's poem, like her family history, is complex. When oppressor and oppressed exist together in our bloodlines, how do we avoid the self-hate that Hogan seems to battle? Perhaps others deal with the conflict by choosing which ancestors to internalize. Nikki Giovanni, brought up in Ohio, didn't come to know her Tennessee grandmother well until she was a teenager, but she took the older woman as a symbol of strong, black womanhood. Grace Cavalieri's speaker gains strength from her strong grandmother as well and does not mention the weaker family members who may have caused her to carry so much responsibility. William Carlos Williams doesn't bring up his Puerto Rican grandparents in the poem about his English grandmother. Hogan's poem, however, says as much about the ancestors she does not mention as those that she describes. She *becomes* the white ancestor who causes the sufferings of her family.

The last two stanzas of Hogan's poem differ from the earlier stanzas in perspective, and their seeming flatness may reflect the attitude of an observer who has stepped outside of the picture for a moment, much as Williams does in his poem. It may be, however, that Hogan's voice becomes particularly Native American in these stanzas, taking on the tone of orally transmitted wisdom. The tones of Cavalieri and Giovanni are those of adults making sense of the legacies of their grandmothers' spiritual connection to themselves, though there are echoes of the child in both. In each poem, it is the speaker/poet who is dynamic, and the ambiguity allows the reader to be involved in sorting out the heritage the poet describes.

GARY SOTO

Behind Grandma's House (p. 474)

The images of his childhood in Fresno, California, permeate both the poetry and the prose of Gary Soto. Known as a children's writer as well as a poet, he relates stories about streets surrounded by junkyards and tire factories and about being a Hispanic boy playing baseball and attending Catholic school. The Mexican American families of Soto's childhood world are poor but hardworking role models who survive without compromising their values. Because his father died in a factory accident when Gary Soto was five years old, the influence of the extended family of uncles and grandparents — already prominent in traditional families — becomes essential to his upbringing and important in his writing.

Students may not recognize the images from the 1960s. There's Bryl-creem, with its "Kookie, Kookie, lend me your comb" connotations, recalling a television show that featured advertisements for this "greasy kid stuff" hair cream, needed for the Elvis-like ducktail hairstyles of the bad boys in the barrio. The speaker collects glass Coke bottles to return them for refunds, to get money in his pockets. He seeks the trappings of power, and in his imagination he practices being a man who conquers men. The poem ends with a punch line, the punch delivered through the ironic medium of his grandmother. He thus dispatches the macho ideal with self-effacing comedy.

Most readers, male and female, have acted out similar childhood fantasies. We remember both the naiveté and the desperate longing to be grown-up and powerful that lay behind our bravado. Most college students enjoy discussing their grandparents as well and often have just recently gained the distance needed to admit that the older people have both strengths and flaws. In childhood, grandchildren's attitudes range from awe — even fear — to the conviction that grandparents are children like themselves, perhaps co-conspirators. Gary Soto's ten-year-old protagonist has a grandmother who inspires awe, since she is obviously in control of the situation. But there's a sense of equality here, too. After all, she throws the sort of punch we'd expect from another boy. She knocks him and us abruptly into the reality of her commonsense world. The verisimilitude of Soto's concrete detail places us in a particular time and place, and this sense of reality is ironic in the context of his playacting machismo, the minutiae cutting him even more down to size. The profanity lends authenticity but also contributes to the plot of his small narrative. His words, and the noise and vandalism that accompany them, cause the grandmother's action. Although he does not provide an explicit moral, the speaker is able to select events that tell this story, and the poem's existence implies a lesson learned, perhaps that *pride goeth before a fall,* literally.

Some American subcultures, including Hispanic ones, have long traditions involving extended family roles, whereas others privilege the independence and privacy found in nuclear families. However, even in mainstream American culture, many grandparents now play a major part in child rearing, helping with money or time and sometimes actually serving as primary caregivers. Although some older people still move into what have been called *golden-age ghettoes,* the needs of working families, volunteer efforts, and delayed retirement keep some grandparents more involved than ever. Many now communicate with distant grandchildren by way of the Internet. Although the rule of autocratic matriarchs and patriarchs has waned, respect for elders may be reviving in American culture. When the grandfatherly Pope John Paul II made a papal visit in 1999, for example, his most loyal and vocal cheerleaders were young adults. What are the ramifications of children rebelling against the more liberal ideals of their parents' generation to make common cause with conservative grandparents?

In Gary Soto's poem, we see the single exchange between the boy and his grandmother, and whether we see her action as admirable or as child abuse depends as much upon an understanding of irony as on cultural perspective. We can guess that he admires her greatly. Nikki Giovanni's narrator also admires her grandmother, even though she seems disrespectful. We know this because she tells us. Grace Cavalieri respects her grandmother's strengths while describing what society might see as shortcomings. And respect for the gritty old English grandmother comes through in William Carlos Williams's description of her strong-minded battle with those who interfere with her dying. Linda Hogan is brutally honest but accepts her heritage. Whereas inexperienced writers tend to sentimentalize or demonize, these poets give glimpses of complex individuals, and readers can see any of the grandchildren as respectful. None are idealized, though Nikki Giovanni and Grace Cavalieri move in this direction by describing spiritual links. Cavalieri's poem deals most explicitly with women's issues. Although women can relate as well as men to the main idea of Gary Soto's "Behind Grandma's House," the child's male gender is a crucial fact. The poem deconstructs myths of manhood through the action of a strong woman. If a grandfather struck a girl child pretending to be a beauty queen, we would have a very different story.

GAYS AND LESBIANS IN FAMILIES (p. 476)

ESSEX HEMPHILL
Commitments (p. 477)

During the last years of his life, before he died of the complications of AIDS, Essex Hemphill was not reticent about his homosexuality. Above all, perhaps, he was a poet who wanted to be seen and heard. Although "Commitments" speaks explicitly of silences and of the family relationships that depend upon masking his true identity, the longing to be seen and heard sets its tone. He refuses to remove himself from his place in the family, even though he knows that someday some family members will want to literally cut him out of the picture. The opening lines hint at his coming death, and we hear the echo of a cliché about the eternal quality of the soul in his assertion "I will always be there." It sounds like a reassurance, but it is also a declaration of his intention. It says, "I'm here." And it is not his dead body, but his "silence" that will be "exhumed" — dug up from the grave — perhaps when people know him without his mask of practical invisibility, perhaps when he is dead. He names relationships and gives the typical details of a backyard picnic in which the foods identify a family with roots in the American South. But to echo the silence of his earlier stanza, line 16 adds a spatial equivalent of silence; his "arms are empty," childless. And the hopes of his aunts to see his wedding are empty, too. If he could marry the person of his dreams, these aunts might not attend the wedding, and if they did, would not throw rice, the symbol of fertility in marriage. After giving us a vision through the camera lens at holiday celebrations, he repeats his image of empty arms, juxtaposing it with an elaboration upon emptiness: "so empty they would break / around a lover" (lines 26–27). The image is enigmatic, the word *break* making us think of voices breaking in sadness, of vulnerability so fragile it could shatter, or of longing so demanding it would hold on too tightly and break as a result. Although he is part of the family in a pragmatic way, he tells us that he is "the invisible son" (line 32), contrasting emptiness again with the permanent visual record of the photographs and the appearance that all is well. As an African American, Essex Hemphill was familiar with the metaphor of wearing a mask, but his poem subtracts by presenting images of emptiness, rather than adding a protective identity. Like the "invisible man" of Ralph Ellison's novel about the African American struggle to be recognized and made truly visible, Essex Hemphill as a homosexual man in an African American family evokes the tensions of visibility and invisibility, of silence and poetry.

Although questions implicitly give students the impression that they can come up with an answer to explain the conflicting statements in "Commitments," assure them that sometimes a poem may be *about* the conflicting feelings and tensions in a situation. Perhaps we will want to create a different definition of *invisible*, one that takes the possible allusion to Ellison into account or that considers a misreading of who one *really* is as a part of invisibility. A part of the person he is has been buried with his silence, and perhaps will come to light. But things dug out of graves cause fear and disgust, and he is realistic enough to know that his relatives will not welcome the visible breaking of his silence.

In the second stanza, the poet is describing an image in a photograph, not an action, and no verb is needed. The image is so American and so normal we expect to smell the apple pie. Hemphill contrasts this normality with his inability to be completely part of it. His mention of a lover in the middle of this family scene reminds us that his would be a lover, not a husband or a wife. There seems to be a real desire for a place in the family and a concomitant longing for children of his own. Heterosexuals sometimes have problems imagining homosexuals as real people who have desires unrelated to sex. A recognition of the loss he feels as someone who simply does his duty can help readers who do not have gay friends or relatives to see gay men and lesbians as three-dimensional.

The word *commitment* has multiple connotations that the class can discuss. The commitment of marriage is suggested, and we may question whether he feels that this is the commitment that his family implicitly requires of him, as well as the commitment to produce children. He clearly feels that his participation in family life is secondary, even though he is always there for his family in a practical way. In some of the lists that students make to determine what commitments the narrator's family owes to him we can expect to find something like *the insight to see his value as a person* or *the courage to accept him as he is*. Teachers also should remember their responsibility to encourage a safe classroom atmosphere that privileges diversity, allowing legitimate dissent without permitting expressions of prejudice, even when veiled as jokes or platitudes. Perhaps our students' lists will suggest further specific commitments they need from us.

KITTY TSUI

A *Chinese Banquet (p. 478)*

Many Asian American writers speak of conflict when their loyalties to family values and traditions run counter to the separate identity they have developed in the dramatically different world outside of the home environment. Often the family is their only link to the Asian part of their heritage. Amy Tan, David Henry Hwang, Maxine Hong Kingston, and others have taken the stories of grandparents, aunts, and friends of the family as themes for their exploration of what it means to be an American whose roots reach into China. Living as a lesbian or gay man complicates the matter of heritage for an Asian American young person. Even the most Americanized Chinese people of earlier generations tend to look with disapproval upon a gay lifestyle, seeing it as unnatural. Evangelical Christianity has played a large part in forming the value systems of some families, and some condemn homosexuals with communist labels of "decadence and bourgeois false consciousness." Kitty Tsui is Chinese American; she grew up in Hong Kong and England, but has lived in the United States since she was sixteen. In the title of her 1983 poetry collection *The Words of a Woman Who Breathes Fire*, Tsui asserts her complex identity. She is first a poet, a person who uses *words*, usually English words, but sometimes Chinese ones. She is also a *woman* who celebrates the bodies and spirits of women. She is, in fact, a sort of superwoman, a bodybuilder who exudes strength, health, and beauty. And she is a *woman who breathes fire*, a self-proclaimed dragon lady who reappropriates the Western stereotype of the dangerous and exotic Chinese woman and uses its connotations for her own purposes. Rather than serving as the subject of white male fantasy, the dragon lady *breathes fire* and thus becomes the dangerous counter to the romantic knight who lives out his fantasies by rescuing damsels in distress. This dragon gets the girl and dismantles the fantasy.

"A Chinese Banquet" describes the same sort of setting that we encountered in Essex Hemphill's description of a gathering of his African American family.

But Tsui is less accepting of her invisibility in her Chinese family, perhaps because she has not been assigned the role of helpful son but of ungrateful and disappointing daughter. Some of her family's disapproval is culture-specific, as we have seen in Amy Tan's "Two Kinds" (p. 247), and does not have its source specifically in her being lesbian. But Tsui's sense of loss focuses more on the partner who has deliberately been left out than on her loss of family continuity. In spite of her usual skill with words, she is unable to tell her mother how important her lover is to her, how she wishes to bring the woman she loves into all the parts of her life, including her family. In many families, even when a member's homosexuality is open, the seriousness and commitment of relationships tend to be dismissed. One openly lesbian young woman relates that when her first long-term relationship with another woman broke up, her mother minimized the pain she was feeling, acting as if she'd lost a college roommate rather than suffering something akin to divorce. If the son's or daughter's lover can be kept out of sight, even parents who intellectually acknowledge the relationship can emotionally deny the reality of the bond between committed lovers of the same sex, dismissing it as friendship alone. It's likely that Tsui's mother does this, understanding subconsciously but not wanting to admit that her daughter loves another woman.

The conversations at the banquet are aimed at telling the young woman who she should be and what she should do. She imagines telling her mother who she really is, what she really wants. The foods and the manners at the banquet are Chinese. Although boundaries exist in non-Asian families, the traditions of this Chinese American family contrast with the narrator's other reality, showing that the gap she must bridge to get their approval is wider than it might be in other ethnic groups. The phrases that are repeated — "it was not a very formal affair," "she no longer asks when I'm getting married," "not invited" — all have negative structures, are denials of something. Contrasting ironically with the narrator's statement, the details of the banquet indicate what most of us would consider a formal affair, and she presumably has no corsage because she has no escort, not being involved in the formal affair of marriage. Within her mother's silence about marriage lies its opposition. Her mother no longer asks the question, but the question exists beneath its absence. The one "not invited" is conversely the one who is most present to the narrator, the one to whom she addresses her poem. Because she does not use capitalization, the poem also gives a sense of internal monologue.

Like Kitty Tsui, Essex Hemphill would like to bridge the boundaries in his family. His repetition of images of arms indicates this, since arms physically bridge the spaces between people — draped around a shoulder, hugging, holding, reaching out — and are a natural symbol of human connection. In this context, it is interesting that Hemphill uses the verb *break* to speak of arms around a lover, since we might guess that it is his heart that *breaks*. The connotation communicates the same feeling but subverts the cliché. We find visual images in Tsui's poem, as we do in Hemphill's, but other senses are important, too. We hear a great deal of talk, and we feel and taste the foods at Tsui's banquet. The difference in effect is considerable when Tsui directly addresses a specific lover, whereas Hemphill refers to an anonymous and abstract one. Tsui's poem is about relationships and the anger and loss she feels when her love cannot be accepted as legitimate and integrated into her heritage. Hemphill's emotion is a vague sadness that seems more directed toward his place in the family tree and the loss he feels about not being seen for who he is.

MINNIE BRUCE PRATT
Two Small-Sized Girls (p. 481)

Like Kitty Tsui and Essex Hemphill, the poet and activist Minnie Bruce Pratt finds herself in conflict with the values of the culture into which she was born. Hers is the dilemma of a child of the rural American South who loses much by breaking away from traditional mores. In Pratt's case, not only her parents and extended family were lost to her, but her children as well. Her book *Crime Against Nature*, from which this poem is taken, deals with the consequences of the legal term echoed in its title. It was because she was a lesbian that custody of her sons was granted to their father when her marriage was dissolved, and the threat of possible conviction for "crimes against nature" was used as a club to keep her from fighting the court's ruling. Pratt had already been involved in feminist activism when in graduate school at the University of North Carolina at Chapel Hill and had helped to establish women's collectives in the nearby towns of Durham and Fayetteville. She identifies herself as part of a group of "anti-racist, anti-imperialist Southern lesbians."

Along with lesbians and gay men who transform the pejorative *queer* to make it a proclamation of pride, Pratt explores definitions of gender but is also passionate about issues of race and all forms of discrimination. She refuses to accept cultural stereotypes about the body, whether they deal with gender, sex, or ethnic origins. She resists inflexible definitions within the gay and lesbian community, arguing that to criticize some lesbians as being too *butch* and others as not being true lesbians is to fall into the trap of discrimination and oppression. As a Southerner who has taught at traditionally black colleges, Pratt resists biologically determined definitions of human diversity. "I can't be the only one," she writes in a short story, "who grew up trained into the cult of pure white womanhood and heard biological reasons given to explain actions against people of color, everything from segregation of water fountains to lynching." She challenges any attempts to place people into such predetermined categories. Although her poetry has political implications, she explains that she began to write poetry not because she had "become" a lesbian, but because of something more personal: "I had returned to my own body after years of alienation."

Students will differ in their beliefs about "crimes against nature" in terms of sexual behavior. Inevitably, students will speak of ancient laws — even current laws in some states — prohibiting sodomy and making illegal certain heterosexual practices within marriage. In 1999, Minnie Bruce Pratt's home state, Alabama, was debating the legalization of sex toys and aids for medical purposes, with many politicians arguing that since they might be used outside of heterosexual marriage such devices should remain banned. We might want to extend the question outside of the sexual arena. How might a person unfamiliar with the term and its history in America attempt to define "crimes against nature"? As war, perhaps? Or as environmental destruction? Pratt's nature imagery in the poem evokes a hot summer on an Alabama farm, but it also shows the kudzu devouring everything and the wildfire that they set blossoming like some brilliant growth. The garden imposes order on nature, just as the girls turn corncobs into the images of human beings. We can encourage students to explore the symbolic connotations of sensory details that seem at first to be here only for verisimilitude. An issue might be raised about the nature of the kudzu vine, for example, an all-enveloping vine that is not native to the South.

The first numbered section of the poem shows the cousins as little girls on their grandmother's farm. In the second, we see them as adults linked to the earlier scene by certain images — Grandma's bedspread, "rough straw baskets" like the corncobs of their youth, kudzu — and we discover that both have endured custody battles. Pratt compares her "crime against nature," a sexual transgression, to her cousin's desire for a garden, somehow symbolic of her freedom of action. This too has been deemed a crime against nature, an unreasonable demand for a woman to make. The third section of the poem places their different attitudes in political perspective but has a sense of futility; they have traveled different paths but are accused of transgressing, of stepping out of their preordained "natural" roles.

The sections reveal a progression of awareness. Pratt begins with the vague busyness of little girls doing what they have seen others do, moves on to their break with tradition in the present, and ends with the philosophical realization that no matter what path they took, they have been "made wrong." The phrase has a double meaning. They have been made to *seem* wrong, though they have not done anything wrong. But they have also, in the culture's implicit value system, been *made* wrong; with female bodies, they are vulnerable to judgments about how they must behave in the world. A definition of cousins may be made without referring to parents at all; they are people who share a grandparent. The girls are like their mothers at first, shaping their babies from the natural materials at hand. In the second section, we see a shared heritage in their grandmother's crocheted bedspread. But in the final section we see their true heritage, the grandmother who doesn't condemn their fire but instead washes them up after it. Women do this for each other in Pratt's world. Age-mates, the daughters of sisters, provide support; grandmothers give unconditional comfort. Their pain as they think about losing children indicates that family ties are important. But rigid family roles are called into question as arbitrary and unjust.

Both Kitty Tsui's speaker in "A Chinese Banquet" and Minnie Bruce Pratt's in "Two Small-Sized Girls" address women, but their messages are different. Tsui's poem is at times a love song to a person who shares a passionate relationship with the narrator. Her futile desire to find a place for her lover in her family precipitates the poem. Pratt's narrator has a sisterly relationship with the woman addressed in her poem, and they share similar injustices. There is no indication that her cousin is lesbian, and we do not know from this poem how their mothers feel about the behaviors that cause them "guilt from men." Both poems share, however, the sad realization that transgressive female behavior separates family members, sometimes irrevocably. And both resist the culture's belief that such transgressors are worthy of the punishment they receive.

All three narrators in this cluster search for what Pratt's poem calls "kernels of fire deep in the body's shaken husk." Essex Hemphill's narrator is aware of his empty arms and wants integrity as a family member rather than the two-dimensional role of duty. Kitty Tsui's hates the silences behind her mother's words and wants to fill them with truth. And Minnie Bruce Pratt's knows that women must follow the substance of their own bodies and of their desires to walk free and to tend their own gardens without interference.

A FAMILY'S DREAMS: CULTURAL CONTEXTS FOR LORRAINE HANSBERRY'S *A RAISIN IN THE SUN* (p. 483)

LORRAINE HANSBERRY

A Raisin in the Sun (p. 484)

In her autobiographical book, *To Be Young, Gifted and Black*, Lorraine Hansberry describes the struggle of the generation represented by Ruth, Walter Lee, and Beneatha Younger in *A Raisin in the Sun*:

> Out of the depths of pain we have thought to be our sole heritage in this world — oh, we know about love! Perhaps we shall be the teachers when it is done. And that is why I say to you that, though it be a thrilling and marvelous thing to be merely young and gifted in such times, it is doubly so — doubly dynamic, to be young, gifted and black.

In the black-and-white movie version of the play that most of us have seen, the distance from 1959 to the twenty-first century seems vast. It takes an effort to carry students — even those growing up in families where black history is taught at the supper table — back to a time when institutionalized racism was an openly dominant force in American communities. African American students sometimes show contempt for characters who do not openly oppose the system, missing the complexity and the incredible danger their parents and grandparents faced. Many white readers will deny that any sort of racism exists today, insisting that all inequalities have been redressed and that the results of historical policies and actions are not their responsibility.

A close reading of the play makes its action more immediate and focuses our attention on issues of assimilation and heritage. As readers stage the play in their minds and discuss it with classmates, characters become more rounded, and the play deals with the black family and its issues of identity and culture, rather than with whites and integration. Too often, African American characters in literature become the medium through which white characters come to terms with their prejudices, but in Hansberry's play, the white character serves only as one antagonist in a story of dynamic main characters who are black. The conflicts and debates within a specific community, the South Side of Chicago, and the internal conflicts of the individual characters illuminate the historical differences within the wider African American community. The play explicitly raises issues that are still current, especially the question of how — or if — the strengths of a culture can be defined and retained while it gains the benefits of mainstream society.

A *Raisin in the Sun* is largely a play about values, and each character's struggle is an ethical one. Walter Lee is frustrated, desperate, frantically ambitious, and concerned with issues of manhood. He wants to be an entrepreneur. The central metaphor of the title describes him best; he swells with anger and is on the verge of exploding like Langston Hughes's raisin in the sun. His desperation makes him gullible and vulnerable to the trickster, the unseen Willy Harris. When Walter Lee is tempted to take the trickster role, one often taken by slaves as the only way to meet deferred needs, he decides instead to take an ethical stand in keeping with his mother's sense of dignity and honesty. In her eyes, he becomes a true man at this point. Mama has internalized the Christian values she has received; she is devout, sacrificing, resourceful, nurturing, devoted to her family, and forgiving of their faults. Hansberry also describes her bearing as queenly, and though she does not have head knowledge of her African heritage, she epitomizes it. Ruth is even more conventional than Mama. She is in some ways passive and accepting but is desperate for a good life for her family. This makes her choice to have an abortion particularly poignant. Ruth, like Booker T. Washington, pragmatically accommodates to the world she is given. Beneatha, on the other hand, represents W. E. B. Du Bois's "new Negro" point of view. Her aspirations are idealistic, and she sees nothing as impossible. She is intellectual, poetic, and politically and culturally aware — to use Hansberry's words, "young, gifted and black" — but she also has moments of naiveté. Although she strives for independence and individual identity, she ironically does this within the context of dependence upon family.

Beneatha, as the family member in touch with Africa and its history, raises the question of true African American identity. *Which* heritage will be chosen: Nigeria's or Mama's? That of the hardworking father who is held up as an ideal man of his generation? Gender plays a large part in Beneatha's ethical choices, and she stands in a long line of strong black feminists. Gender roles are at least as important as racial ones for all the characters of the play, and students could be encouraged to examine these and consider them in other contexts. Although this play deals with issues that are specific to political realities of 1959, we might also consider its relevance to current debates: choices about abortion; the assimilation of immigrants implied in *English only* legislation; trends toward class-determined, gated communities; and so on. It might also be interesting to consider the values that surface when we speculate on what we might do with a windfall equal in today's dollars to the Younger's insurance settlement.

CULTURAL CONTEXTS:

THE CRISIS, "The Hansberrys of Chicago: They Join Business
Acumen with Social Vision" (p. 553)
LORRAINE HANSBERRY, April 23, 1964, Letter
to the *New York Times* (p. 555)
ALAN EHRENHALT, From *The Lost City: Discovering the Forgotten
Virtues of Community in the Chicago of the 1950s* (p. 556)

The 1941 article that follows the play is taken from the NAACP-sponsored newspaper, *The Crisis.* Its rhetorical purpose is to inspire readers to live up to the ethos personified by the Hansberry family — Lorraine's parents — who had achieved financial and philanthropic goals the newspaper would like others to emulate. Like the Murchison family of the play, represented by Beneatha's suitor, and like Walter Lee in his quest for a business of his own, the Hansberrys were attempting to live out the American dream of the early twentieth century. Quoting from legal documents lends the weight of mainstream authority to the newspaper's assertions about this exemplary Negro family's achievements. Although the move of the Younger family in the play parallels the playwright's childhood memories of her family's integration of a Chicago suburb, the difference in financial means raises issues. Although both families can expect to be alienated from both the rich community life of the segregated neighborhood and the social acceptance of the white middle class, the poorer family has less chance of succeeding. It will have added burdens: the logistics of traveling to work, of maintaining the costs of home ownership once the insurance money is gone, of caring for children when adults must work and the network of nosy neighbors is lost — all the practicalities of everyday existence from which the Hansberrys' wealth cushioned them. Although Walter Lee's stand against selling out to prejudice may be admirable, we are left with the question of what the move will cost his family in both material and nonmaterial terms. Their sense of injustice can be expected to increase and their discontent to fester.

Lorraine Hansberry's 1964 letter to the *New York Times* makes it clear that even a prosperous family like her own suffered a loss of community as they lived out the ideals of the early civil rights movement. *A Raisin in the Sun*, although filled with debates about how to proceed, allows its characters some optimism about the future. They are dynamic, and the insurance money has given them the illusion of choices. But Hansberry questions the wisdom of patiently working within the system as her parents had done. One point of the play is that money, rather than being the answer to the family's problems, exposes other issues with which it must deal. The white defender of "community values" in the Youngers' new neighborhood explicitly warns the Youngers that they will find a welcome similar to the real-life one Hansberry describes in her letter. Differences about how to achieve full equality have characterized the African American community throughout the history of the country, but at the time of Hansberry's letter and of the play itself, the gap between action and accommodation was widening. If she is calling for civil disobedience in the style of her contemporary

Martin Luther King, who would be assassinated just a few years later, many will see her opposition as moderate. Black Power, the Black Arts movement, Black Islam, and the radical political activism to emerge later in the 1960s were stirring. Intellectuals like Lorraine Hansberry and Langston Hughes were early voices expressing a bitterness that would soon explode into vocal and violent responses to inequality.

Although he grants the limitations of lives lived in the class-based and racially segregated enclaves of the 1950s, Alan Ehrenhalt in his book *The Lost City: Discovering the Forgotten Virtues of Community in the Chicago of the 1950s* concentrates instead on the values that were lost when these stable neighborhoods broke up. In sections labeled *Parish*, *Ghetto*, and *Suburb*, he examines three communities in his native Chicago. The parish is the Catholic, multiethnic but thoroughly white, "postimmigrant" bungalow neighborhood of St. Nicholas of Tolentine, ruled with an iron hand by priests, by bosses and union officials at the Nabisco plant, and by the neighborhood network of mostly stay-at-home moms. The suburb is Elmhurst, comfortable but also conventional and limited in ways we recognize from reruns of "Leave It to Beaver." The ghetto is Bronzeville, the closely knit African American neighborhood of *A Raisin in the Sun* that was razed to create the "urban renewal" projects that we now know to be woeful failures. Ehrenhalt maintains that although we have gained opportunities, choice, privacy, and other individual freedoms of a free-market economy, we have lost virtues like family stability, community spirit, and business loyalty. Going back, however, would mean going back to the imposed authority and acceptance of limits against which so many, including Lorraine Hansberry, fought. Integration achieved so much of value that it seems heresy to admit that it required great sacrifice by pioneers leaving ghettoes or cotton fields to make it happen. Yet it is important to recognize that the issues for the characters of the play were not simple, that no way could have been chosen without losing something. As the editor of a magazine directed toward people interested in state and local government, Alan Ehrenhalt plays an influential role in community development issues throughout the country, and he taps into a nostalgia that many decision makers feel for the relative safety of the past. Some city planning re-creates neighborhoods where corner stores and other facilities are within walking distance and street life is encouraged. African Americans are not immune to such nostalgia. A few years ago, school redistricting brought a housing project with a particularly rough reputation into a southern high school. The principal, a man who had grown up in this neighborhood, reassured his faculty that many people who lived there could afford to move out but chose to stay because it was home to them. In the same city, the alumni association of an old segregated Negro high school, now a racially integrated middle school with a math-and-science magnet school next door, meets often to seek out the values it remembers from academic and extracurricular activities. Its members talk about how involved they were and worry that their children feel less free to participate. We need to question such nostalgia, however. If, as Ehrenhalt says, community and deference to authority go hand in hand, students will benefit from thinking critically about the trade-offs implicit both in community planning and in personal choices about social groups and living arrangements.

| 8 |

Teaching and Learning

RECALLING LESSONS OF CHILDHOOD (p. 567)

CATHY SONG
The Grammar of Silk (p. 568)

Both multiethnic and multilingual, Hawaiian culture is sometimes open, sometimes insular. Some residents of the state, when filling out forms, have to add extra lines to proudly include every ethnic group represented in their ancestry. Other families keep to the received traditions of the islands or continents their ancestors left, living and working with people who look and speak much like themselves. Many are personally or vicariously involved in the revival of the Hawaiian language and culture that was submerged beneath nineteenth-century missionary teachings. The groupings are multiple and shifting — Native Hawaiians, Asians with varied histories, American military families of many shades and accents, and tourists. If it is becoming a cliché that America is less a melting pot than a salad bar, Hawaii epitomizes this mix of individual flavors. Or perhaps a better metaphor is the crazy quilt, sewn together from many scraps of life. This would be an appropriate trope, since quilt making has long been an important craft in Hawaii. So when Cathy Song juxtaposes *grammar* and the communal business of fabric shopping in her poem, she does it within a rich linguistic and cultural context.

The learning that Song describes takes place in an informal community institution, the Saturday sewing school for girls. Grammar, too, is learned informally. Linguists tell us that the human brain seems to be wired for the rules of language and that we learn these rules without being able to articulate them consciously. We internalize the speech patterns we hear as children, and these patterns influence how we see ourselves and the world. In much the same way, the girls at Mrs. Umemoto's sewing school learn the rules of what it means to be a woman in a particular society. Sewing, like being a woman in Hawaii, is a language that one learns, and the seamstresses who know it well are "like librarians to be consulted" (line 20). The "mothers and daughters paused in symmetry" are themselves a pattern (line 31). The pattern books are holy texts, like the "stone tablets" of the Bible, a book that provides patterns for lives (line 30). The fabrics have "titles" (line 42), and the remnant the narrator's mother chooses is a "composition" (line 46).

But whereas a composition may be defined in terms of writing, the word takes on added connotations in the final lines of Song's poem, reminding us that patterns can be released into moments of music and freedom. The narrator,

63

looking back, realizes that more was being learned than sewing in Mrs. Umemoto's "pleasant" basement with the "Singer's companionable whirr" (line 8). The sensory images, mostly auditory and tactile, connect the narrator with the women and girls engaged in sewing as a communal activity. They also connect her with history and the traditions of art; the silk inspires awe, "as if it were a piece from the Ming Dynasty" (line 35). The poet is Korean and Chinese, though we might note that the teacher's name is Japanese. It is the continuity that is important, and gender overrides ethnicity. The narrator puzzles out the possible meanings the activity has for the women, now that she can step outside the childhood experience. Beneath images of community, history, and art, she uses words like *sanctuary* and *refuge* to suggest what sewing might represent for these women as individuals.

Song frames her poem by beginning and ending with the experience of sewing itself, but she takes us to the fabric shop in the four middle stanzas. The beginning and end have a meditative quality; sewing, even in a group, is an individual experience, much like the music she compares it with. In the middle section, the rules of sewing are learned in a communal way. Students will have their own interpretations of the mother, but her longing for solitude is explicit in the poem. There may be an implicit desire for individuality and autonomy as well. Though the poem seems mostly positive about the activities of girls and women at the sewing school, the emphasis on grammar, a subliminally learned set of rules, raises the issue of the place of women in a traditional society. The seamstresses in the fabric shop are *like* architects, according to the poem, but they may not think of expressing their art and skill in a less domestic fashion.

Hawaiian culture differs from that of much of the contiguous U.S. Immigration has taken a different pattern, giving Asian and Pacific Rim history and culture a more prominent place than in most states east of California. More important to the poem, however, may be the history of the islands themselves. One of the first changes that English and American Christian missionaries demanded of Hawaiian culture was that the people clothe themselves more thoroughly. Sewing, therefore, became an important activity for women. Many students may come from cultures where textile arts are traditionally female activities that pass down community values. Several texts in this anthology emphasize the importance of quilts or other handmade heirlooms for African Americans or for whites of certain regions. Although Hawaii may be the most ethnically cosmopolitan of states, many strongly held traditions date back to issues of the eighteenth and nineteenth centuries. Many children and adolescents go to schools like Kamehameha, Iolani, and Punahou, private institutions established by church or royal family members to provide formal education for specific groups. Although these schools have broadened their goals in recent years, and although the U.S. government has formally apologized to the indigenous peoples of Hawaii for the forcible seizure of their lands and culture, both formal and informal education teach patterns that owe much to the history of colonial-style conquest. In the midst of this, however, people transform received patterns into strengths, using them both for community and for individuality.

JULIA ALVAREZ

How I Learned to Sweep (p. 570)

Julia Alvarez came to the United States from the Dominican Republic as a ten-year-old girl. She was from a traditional family that expected her to grow up to be a housewife. However, being female in the well-to-do family of her childhood in the Dominican Republic meant living in a compound filled with sisters, aunts, and maids that handled household chores. After moving to America when her father fled political imprisonment or execution in their home country, Alvarez was surprised that she missed the extended family and prosperous circumstances she'd taken for granted. She also encountered prejudice and social isolation, which she had never experienced before coming to America. Alvarez describes the impact of immigration on a child: "The feeling of loss caused a radical change in me. It made me an introverted little girl." Finding her place in the spaces between two languages, she knew as a teenager that she would become a writer, and she speaks eloquently of the power of stories to change us and to help us create meaning. Alvarez weaves her life experiences into stories and poems, often writing about family relationships. Both her knowledge of women in the midst of change within traditional families and her experience with the impact of war and revolution underpin this text, which is from a poetry sequence ostensibly about housekeeping.

Although the speaker of "How I Learned to Sweep" claims that this is a skill her mother never taught her, readers understand that many of the things we have learned were never an explicit part of our education. When she says that she knew what her mother expected, however, the statement is ambiguous. Are we meant to understand that she has picked up the art of sweeping without training? Or are other values being taught? Most students have experienced being kept busy as children so that they are distracted from thinking about serious matters. A child born in 1950 would be a teenager or older when the Vietnam War was being viewed in American living rooms every evening. Is Alvarez expected to do housework rather than dwell on current events because young women need to be distracted from such things? The point may simply be that she should make herself useful, rather than sitting and watching television when the floor is dirty. Whatever the reason, the speaker juxtaposes the act of sweeping and the content of the news program to say something beyond housework.

The poem begins with a regular rhythm and rhyming couplets. The rhythm is much like sweeping, and the rhyme, almost doggerel, gives the action an everyday triviality. This contrasts with the unrhymed descriptions of the televised war scenes in the middle of the poem that are at the same time more realistic and more surreal than household activities. When the poet returns to sweeping, she returns to rhyme for a time. In the closing lines, she has alternate lines rhyme *breath* with *death*. It is ironic that the metaphor of sweeping up the results of war alternates with her mother's innocent praise of her handiwork. In reality, she does not learn to be comfortable with sweeping sacrificed lives aside, as the president may be doing in his television speech. Students will have heard before that

Vietnam was the first televised war. Since the advent of twenty-four-hour-a-day news on cable television, war has become even more immediate, as we know from events in Eastern Europe, the Middle East, and Africa in the 1990s. The usual response of teenagers might be to switch to MTV. Alvarez's Vietnam era girl could have turned on the radio to listen to rock and roll. But her attention has been caught, and the metaphor her mind creates has the sort of power Alvarez attributes to story. The sweeping becomes a frantic obsession, a spell to make death disappear. The mother fails to see the underlying cause of her daughter's success in sweeping. She values cleanliness, orderliness, obedience, and industry.

But the poet may be telling us that reality is messy, that to make reality disappear along with the dust is not as worthy of praise as the mother thinks. The mother easily turns off the news of war but values a tidy house and a daughter who pays more attention to housework than to politics. Studies of Hispanic college women in the 1990s revealed that many still have problems making families understand the importance of focusing on schoolwork. Many parents feel that daughters should be available to help their families first and that college can be dropped to drive a grandparent to a doctor's appointment or to prepare for a family occasion. Students may think of times that they have encountered such conflicts between family attitudes and personal or political priorities, and many will recall being praised by their parents for motives far different from those they really feel. Parents and children may usually sweep away just such differences in worldview, especially when the child knows that the metaphors that bring issues to life can never quite be articulated in a way the parent will understand.

The use of rhythm and rhyme structures a poem, enclosing thought and dictating the readers' pace more directly than the open structure of free verse. The overall effect of Cathy Song's "The Grammar of Silk" is interior monologue. We have a sense of the narrator as an adult musing about the meaning of sewing in the lives of her mother and her friends. Julia Alvarez allows her narrator less distance in "How I Learned to Sweep." Her intermittent use of rhyme pulls us into the action of the moment, as the young woman works out her feelings toward death and war in a physical way. In Song's poem, *sanctuary* and *oblivion* are words connected with peace, a temporary respite from the pace of motherhood and other domestic responsibilities. For Alvarez, oblivion would have less positive connotations. The cleanliness that her narrator achieves as she tries to sweep away the war is a sort of oblivion, an effort to forget reality. But the activity has not been peaceful but frantic, and her mother's happiness with it seems petty and misguided in contrast. Since to receive sanctuary one must flee from the dangers of life, this too would run counter to Alvarez's theme.

The tone that the poets take toward the mothers they describe shapes our interpretation of their actions. Most readers probably sympathize with the busy mother of Song's poem, who must find moments of solitude and creativity in between the activities of life and who teaches her daughter the meditation of work. But we only know what the narrator guesses about her mother's motives, seeing her only from this romantic point of view. The mother of Alvarez's poem may be much like Song's mother, but we see her from a less positive perspective. The daughter learns on her own that work and emotion are interrelated, that sometimes the work we do has symbolic meaning beyond — perhaps opposing — its obvious meanings. But the result is ironic. The mother remains ignorant of her daughter's profound insights about the horror of war, and the reader remains ignorant of the mother's true motives and thoughts. Though some students will protest that the mother is simply practical and the daughter up in the clouds, we can only guess at the mother's thoughts while we overhear the daughter's.

FORREST HAMER
Lesson (p. 572)

Poet and psychologist Forrest Hamer writes that he feels lucky to have been an African American growing up in the South in the 1960s. In fact, when he was an undergraduate at Yale, he felt out of his element, since his rural upbringing set him apart from other black students and he was not yet comfortable with the white establishment. He remembers his childhood as happy and secure. The strength of his parents and grandparents brought him through in a time and place when prejudice could have challenged his confidence and self-esteem. The setting of "Lesson" is a Mississippi highway, a frightening place for a black family to drive through during the specific years of the poem's events. Students may need some orientation, perhaps looking through periodicals from these years or examining pictorial histories and documentaries of the civil rights movement. Freedom rides, bus boycotts, and lunch counter sit-ins had begun a few years earlier, and the South was in the midst of voter registration drives. Some students may have seen movies like *Mississippi Burning* and may realize that "outside agitators" were harassed, even killed. Others might remember reading about violence on the highway at the time of the march on Selma or seeing taped footage of protesters being attacked by police using fire hoses and dogs. It would take only a small misstep for strangers like Hamer's father to become suspect. It may seem odd to current readers that the family sleeps by the side of the road in such dangerous territory, but finding a motel or even a place to eat would have been a problem in the days of "whites only" signs. Forrest Hamer has related that even at home in Goldsboro, North Carolina, the children would fill up on water before going downtown on shopping trips, since it was difficult to find a water fountain that Negroes were allowed to use. Many such childhood experiences make their way into his writing.

His father, too, is an important figure in Hamer's poetic imagery. His father's two tours in Vietnam greatly affected the family, and the changes he saw in the older man after his second return home led Hamer into psychology as a career. If the date of this trip is indeed "1963 or 4," U.S. military involvement in Southeast Asia was just beginning to build up, and Vietnam was indeed "a place no place in the world" to most Americans. To the extent that we know the personal and historical context of the narrator's childhood fears, the poem becomes ironic and powerful. The narrator fears one danger, the very real domestic violence of a 1960s hot summer, but we know that it is the other, unknown danger his father faces in Vietnam that will have the most impact on him. He has said that his father came back a different man, so if — as it seems here — the poet and the voice in the poem are the same person, he really does come to lose the father he needs, and the noises in the dark take on new meaning.

There is an opposition between two lessons in the poem, the one recognizing that his father is not omnipotent against all the dangers of the world and the other realizing that the boy "needs [his] father with him." Perhaps the difference is related to the two major issues of the 1960s, civil rights and Vietnam. The adult narrator knows that his father and other family members have succeeded in bringing him through the wars of prejudice, but he knows that something in his father was lost to him through the war in Vietnam. Could it be the fear of losing a father rather than any concrete danger to himself that requires a boy to keep his father near him? If so, the lesson is singular, as the title indicates. If a father is not all-powerful, the son will have to keep him safely at hand. As a psychologist, Hamer understands that children feel responsible for protecting their parents and that at the root of separation anxiety lies a fear of loss. What is a premonition for the boy is known history to the man who relates the story, and the poet uses this difference in knowledge to create irony for the reader.

By isolating the word *Noises* in line 9, the poet forces us to pause and listen. When he uses the word again, he has just implicitly conjured up for readers the image of soldiers in the jungles of Vietnam sleeping on the ground and listening for danger. He describes the boy as "fixed against noise," and we think of fixed bayonets. From the distance of a new century it may be easy to claim that the father should not have gone to Vietnam, should instead have been there for his son. Students who are quick to judge may be led to consider the consequences for the family if the father had deserted the military. Wouldn't he have been lost to them in another way? During the Gulf War of the 1980s many of the soldiers who were deployed with reserve units were not fathers but mothers, some with very young children. Debates about whether a child needs a father or a mother tend to depend heavily on pathos. We need to steer students toward using psychological studies and other hard evidence to back up their assertions rather than let them depend primarily upon emotion and personal experiences that may or may not be representative.

In each of the poems in this cluster, children learn lessons that involve their parents. But we do not see the parents intentionally teaching these lessons. Cathy Song's speaker in "The Grammar of Silk" speculates that her mother takes her to the sewing school because she wants her to learn how to carve out these times of peaceful concentration when the mind and body work together as one. She believes that the older woman gives her daughter what she would wish for herself. On the other hand, the mother in Julia Alvarez's "How I Learned to Sweep" does not teach her child about housework or about the metaphors of death. She merely sets the learning experience in motion by accident, and the result would be bewildering to her if she realized that her daughter has actually learned the enormity of war along with her sweeping. Like most of the teaching that parents actually do, the lesson that Forrest Hamer's father teaches in the incident described in the poem is unintentional. Most parents don't tell their children that they are invincible, but children make that assumption. Nor do fathers usually tell sons that they are afraid, that they are powerless to protect their children or themselves from war and hatred. Instead, children learn as Hamer describes in his poem, adding up clues from restless sleep, stories they've heard, or the tension in a father's listening body.

As they consider the question of how the poems might be different if written by the parents, students might try writing poems that express the parents' point of view. Song's mother, given time, might speak as her daughter does, but as her life stands, her words might be quicker, with no nonsense. She has been described in terms of music, so perhaps we could expect lyricism in compressed form. Perhaps she would write a haiku in calligraphy. The mother in the Alvarez poem might write greeting-card verse in cliché form. But perhaps this is unfair. She might describe her pride in her daughter, so quick to learn how to make a room spotless with no formal training in the art of sweeping. Or perhaps we will learn that she knew what was going on in her daughter's mind all along, but she knew the child must work it out for herself.

Hamer's father might finally talk about Vietnam; his son said that the father tended to deflect such conversations to the subject of Korea. We might learn what he was thinking that night in Mississippi, what he was feeling about leaving his son. Although Hamer's poem is historically realistic, he only hints at what Vietnam will do to the country and to this family, leaving us to our own associations. In fact, if we assume that the boy in the poem is not identical to the boy who was Forrest Hamer, we can imagine scenarios other than the autobiographical one. The father might run to Canada, for example. Or he might die in the war.

The girl watching television in the poem by Julia Alvarez ironically has more information than the boy who lies near a man who will actually participate. She describes the familiar television image of rescue helicopters, but as she begins to describe the men as dust falling from the sky too quickly to be swept up, the experience becomes surreal, almost a vision. The sheer numbers overwhelm her. Hers is a sudden realization, an epiphany that only begins with the specificity of the television image. His is dread, a presentiment of some lurking, unseen danger to the one soldier who really matters. Although Hamer's poem is more realistic, both poems depend on a grasp of historical events.

TEACHING CHILDREN ABOUT SOCIETY (p. 574)

JAMES AGEE
A Mother's Tale (p. 575)

James Agee graduated from Harvard University the same year that Franklin D. Roosevelt was first elected president of the United States: 1932. As the world entered into the Great Depression and it was becoming apparent that the economy was not going to correct itself, FDR pushed through the programs of the New Deal, transforming the social institutions of the country. Agee, with photographer Walker Evans, used an equally revolutionary approach as a reporter for *Fortune* magazine. The book that grew out of his series of documentary articles was *Let Us Now Praise Famous Men* (1941). The book presents the stories of three families of tenant farmers in the rural South in a way that reveals their battles to survive the literal starvation and appalling deprivation of the Depression. Rather than preaching, however, Evans's black-and-white photographs and Agee's poetic narratives invite readers to come to their own conclusions while allowing their subjects to retain their dignity.

The effectiveness of this style of educating the public seems obvious to readers now, but Agee was the father of this sort of journalism. Students interested in issues raised by Agee's content or style in "A Mother's Tale" will profit from an examination of this ground-breaking text. They might look at other texts of the period, such as John Steinbeck's *Grapes of Wrath* or the movie based on it. Our context for reading the story should also consider Agee's Marxist perspectives and his possible use of the cattle to symbolize workers of the world who should unite against the system that markets their labor and destroys their lives. The foregrounding of death in Agee's thinking is also important. His father died in an accident when he was a child, and this event shaped both his life and his writing, resulting in the novel *A Death in the Family*, published in 1957 after his death. At the time "A Mother's Tale" was published, Agee himself was near death. He had lived as an iconoclast in almost every realm of his life, once saying, "I know I am making the choice most dangerous to an artist in valuing life above art." For Agee, the idea of "pie in the sky by and by" was one way men in power could fool people into accepting oppression, and the true reformer would relieve suffering in the real world by forcing us to look it straight in the eye.

Although "A Mother's Tale" reads like a fable with its talking animals, it uses narrative techniques to suggest that reality must be faced with open eyes rather than with platitudes or self-deceptions. The cattle are dominated by a false consciousness that contributes to their exploitation and destruction. Some students will be offended by the incongruity of cute animals and violent content, and others will not get beyond the surface, perhaps seeing the story as an indictment of eating meat. The class could look back at Philip Levine's "What Work Is" in Chapter 2 (p. 43) and be led to compare the men in line for jobs with the cattle in line at the abattoir. Levine has said of this autobiographical experience that he realized the people in the employment office had deliberately forced them to wait two hours to see who had the desperation or docility to wait it out. Like Agee's cattle, the unemployed workers are at the mercy of a system that sees them only as so much meat. Going further to look at other Levine poems, especially those that feature animals, can illuminate Agee's method. Both writers, to use Levine's words, "give voice to the voiceless," and their twentieth-century working-class parables can be used intertextually. Some students will object to Agee's implication that belief in heaven is for uncomprehending cattle. The One Who Came Back will seem like a Christ figure to them, warning them away from Hell. But we might also think of the trains that took Holocaust victims to their deaths. After all, this story was written soon after World War II, and it could be read as an indictment of Nazism.

Regardless of the historical or religious implications, Agee is pessimistic about the ability of his characters to learn from the experiences of others or from the mistakes of the past. The mother cow passes on the tradition, but her lack of knowledge makes her narrative less convincing to the audience within the story. She is not a true believer, so her tale has the quality of a ghost story or of folklore, used, as she admits, "to frighten children." She moves in and out of belief as she alternately gets caught up in the story and then remembers her audience. There is irony for the reader, since we know that cattle are taken to slaughter in this way and that man is not a kind, paternalistic protector of cows. The mother is unwilling to accept the consequences of true belief, however, because this would mean rebellion for the adults and death for the calves and yearlings. Readers familiar with Toni Morrison's *Beloved* might think of slave women who were willing to kill their babies rather than allow them to live in slavery. As the class discusses the views of The One Who Came Back, we might raise the issue of how far individuals would be willing to go to save themselves or their children from oppression. Those who reject his views should consider how power might be gained when a group finds itself as powerless and bewildered as these cattle.

TONI CADE BAMBARA
The Lesson (p. 590)

Like her young protagonist in "The Lesson," Toni Cade Bambara remembers a childhood in which strong female figures educate younger women and girls. In her most recent book of essays, *Deep Sightings and Rescue Missions,* Bambara quotes one mentor, Miss Dorothy: "Colored gal on planet earth . . . know everything there is to know, anything she/we don't know is by definition the unknown." The older woman teaches the child how to tell stories based on her inner knowledge, and Bambara says that she "taught me critical theory." Later, Bambara would recognize the older woman's advice in her reading. She was taught that stories must be culture specific, that to speak is to assume responsibility. She learned that her stories must be based in the narratives of freedom that make up the oral and literary history of African Americans. Her goal is to "lift up a few useable truths" in a "racist, hardheaded, heedless society." Her voice is thus both political and personal, and she takes seriously the responsibility to pass on what she knows. In "The Lesson" the narrator learns, but the reader is taught as well.

Because the voice of the story moves into present tense in the second paragraph and speaks much as a young girl would speak, the age of the narrator matters little. She has enough distance to choose her details so that we see her begin to realize what Miss Moore wants her to learn from the trip to the toy store, and we see her at the end going off alone to absorb the lesson. Like Paulo Freire, whose pedagogical theory influenced Bambara, Miss Moore knows that one of the purposes of education is to wake up those who are oppressed, to make them see their circumstances so that they can rise up against them. The West African proverb that *it takes a village to raise a child* has become a cliché, but the idea that the education of children is the responsibility of everyone with something to share is central to Bambara's philosophy. In the fragmented culture of slavery, this African precept became even more important than it was before people were forcibly brought to America. Mothers were often strangers who worked from dawn to dark, and elderly women too old to go to the fields cared for the children of many mothers. Furthermore, it was against the law in many states to teach slaves to read and write, so lessons had to be passed on in any way possible.

Traditions that worked for survival and freedom in desperate times continue because children need role models and people who will prod them to think. For many students, Miss Moore's efforts make her seem like a busybody who interferes in family matters. Bambara, whose experience included many such women, would disagree. She and other members of the Black Power and Black Arts movements of the 1970s believed strongly that neighborhood programs must be established to teach children about their heritage and about wrongs that need redressing. Miss Moore has a political agenda, to show the children the inequality that will make them angry. Students may suggest that simply pointing out the problem does not guide the children into finding solutions, does not really empower them. Miss Moore's audience rejects much of what she says because they see no means of acquiring desks for their rooms or microscopes for observing bacteria. Her distance from them, the air of authority that keeps even the adults from addressing her by a first name, makes it difficult for her to build common ground with her audience. They find her boring and have their own agendas. But her Socratic method "contaminates" the youth in her charge into seeing that their lot is unfair, though their reactions vary. Rosie Giraffe's sour-grapes comment — "White folks crazy" — misreads Miss Moore's lesson, accepting the cultural difference without openly admitting the injustice. Mercedes also misreads, thinking the unreachable toys will soon be available to her. Flyboy ignores the issue and doesn't puzzle out the reasons for his weariness. Sugar articulates the philosophy behind Miss Moore's lesson, but there's no sign that she is as distressed by it as the narrator, who internalizes it and makes it her own in the story's final sentence. Race plays a large part in the story, and Bambara would maintain that all stories must be seen in the context of their cultures. But class plays perhaps a more important role in "The Lesson" since it is the economic issue that is most explicitly addressed.

In both stories of this cluster, children are taught lessons about society that are not comfortable ones to learn. In fact, most of the children resist the teachings, misreading or ignoring them because their reality is too hard to face. In James Agee's "A Mother's Tale" the children cannot accept their oppression and looming death, and we realize at the end that they will continue as always to accept and even welcome their fate. There is more hope for Miss Moore's charges, but only one or two will take the hard lesson to heart and find a way to take action. When teachers use such an approach, we sometimes say that their aim is to lead their students into a state of "cognitive dissonance," the awareness that one must work out a way of taking in an uncomfortably new idea. Teachers who challenge us in this way, shaking up our worldviews, make us uncomfortable, but the learning that we acquire becomes our own. The approach of this course is, in fact, a confrontational one. We want students to find their issues in literature and in life and to do the hard work of thinking them through. We want them to examine preconceived assumptions, to explore the reasons for their discomfort with certain ideas, rather than ignoring them or quickly explaining them away. By trusting them with their own intellectual space, we run the risk that only a few will "get" the lesson we think they should. Bambara's teacher succeeds only when she uses this method; her lectures are ignored as educational propaganda. The mother cow is less aware. She passes on the story of her culture, but doesn't quite believe it herself. Both try to make the younger ones aware of oppression, however, and both care deeply about the welfare of their audience.

Writing Agee's story from the perspective of one of the calves would be difficult, since the irony of its last line depends upon the young audience not really understanding the point of the story. The mother cow herself is the dynamic character of her story; she is the one who is moved by the horror she only partly accepts as possible. In Bambara's story we share Sylvia's emotions and know that the lesson has struck her deeply. Because we listen to her resistance, her vow to "not be beaten" is more compelling. We know that she does not simply parrot an answer to please a teacher but that she sincerely owns this knowledge and that this ownership will empower her.

OBSERVING SCHOOLCHILDREN (p. 597)

LOUISE GLÜCK

The School Children (p. 597)

Louise Glück has written that although poems take details from autobiography and the experiences of everyday life, the voice of the poem transcends the specifics of the poet's individual life. For the writer and later for the reader, the connotations of the words in poems change and move away from the incidentals of their original creation. Glück therefore feels free to create her own mythic, surreal world in her poems, moving through time and space. In addition, her attitude frees the reader to create personal meanings and to be an active and flexible interpreter of the poem's imagery. We might explain to our students as we discuss "The School Children" that issues do not always have to be resolved, nor do we need to reach a consensus about the interpretations of literary texts. Sometimes *both/and* is preferable to *either/or*. Readers often find mythological symbols in Glück's poetry. Some students will be familiar with the labor of Hercules in which he seeks the apples of the Hesperides. In contrast to the male hero of the myth, however, Glück's poem tells us in lines 2 and 3 that the "mothers have labored / to gather the late apples" for their children, and we may think of the added connotations of the word *labor* to describe childbirth. The diction of the last stanza carries the biblical tone of edict or prophecy with its parallel clauses beginning with *and* and using the formal verb form *shall*. This poet is often characterized as dreamy, and we find

73

this quality also in "The School Children" as the speaker moves back and forth from schoolroom to orchard.

To be truly universal, a writer must be particular. The poet pictures this group of schoolchildren vividly, though sparely, and we can imagine the rural setting where apples grow and both mothers and children seem to be trapped. But most of us have experienced the rigid demands of conformity regardless of where we grew up, and our first encounter with it often occurred at school. When we are told in line 8 that "they" are orderly, we automatically look back to the last noun phrases for referents, and we may be surprised to find in the next line that the pronoun refers to the nails upon which the children hang their clothes. The speaker could have been referring to the teachers — labeled only by the vague, formal designation "those who wait behind great desks" (line 6). But this leads to another problem with a pronoun. Does *those* mean teachers? But surely the apples are not meant to fulfill the apple-for-the-teacher requirement? Do the women pick apples as workers for a fruit company that has executives who sit behind desks? Alternatively, the pronoun *they* in line 8, a collective pronoun capable of containing any number of referents, could refer back to everyone in the earlier stanzas — children, mothers, and *those* teachers or other authority figures. All are orderly, like the nails; all remain in their designated places. In academic essays, as students support their arguments in an orderly way, we will undoubtedly call them to task for failing to make clear the referents of their pronouns.

Ambiguity can be misleading, even dangerous. (Just recently, a neighbor called to ask if someone could come to the hospital to pick up his child for the night. Speaking of his wife, he said, "Mary was in the hospital visiting her mother and she had a heart attack." It was much later that his neighbors realized with shock that it was his wife and not his mother-in-law who was in the cardiac care unit.)

But poets can break rules concerning ambiguity, and we love them for it. Meanings become multilayered, and we see commonplace events as having a newly discovered intricacy. The indeterminacy of the poem will lead to different interpretations of its theme. It is possible to support the assertion that the poem is about the children or even about the teachers who impose this order upon the young and seem to wield so much power over the lives of the mothers who defer to them. But the mothers seem most active in the poem, and we know the most about how they feel.

Still, we might ask for whom the mothers seek "a way out." If it is for their children, then perhaps the focus changes again. Glück might suggest that the fuzzy focus exists for a reason; that the lives of teachers, children, and mothers are interrelated; that the whole notion of focus is reductive. Though the focus may be unclear, the colors are as sharp and the lines as spare as a Piet Mondrian painting. Aside from the gold of the apples and the gray of the limbs, the colors are primary red, blue, and yellow, colors we associate with the crayon boxes of early childhood. The red and gold of the apples have a magical feel, and the gray limbs signify the bareness of winter and the depression of mothers who have few resources — "so little ammunition" — to use in the battle for their children. The word *ammunition* comes as a surprise in a poem that has not raised issues of war to this point. Is the conflict between the mothers and the teachers who now have charge over their children? Is the conflict the economic one we might expect in the imagery of a more overtly political writer than Glück? We only know that the mothers' efforts are intense, since they "scour" the orchard, a word that recalls the "labor" of the first stanza.

Other phrases are puzzling. The construction "instruct them in silence" seems to be an oxymoron; surely one must communicate in order to teach. The apples of the mothers, on the other hand, are "like words of another language," silent objects that speak but perhaps cannot be deciphered (line 4). Or it may be that the children do understand the labor of their mothers, but now must learn the language of school. The lives of these children have a peculiarly inarticulate quality, and we do not hear them at all. Most of us at some time have encountered teachers who did not understand the community in which they taught or who thought that children should be seen and not heard. In a 1980s movie a teacher known for handing out worksheets and then retreating behind a newspaper dies during class. The punch line is that none of his students notice.

TOI DERRICOTTE
Fears of the Eighth Grade (p. 598)

The reader's first reaction to Toi Derricotte's "Fears of the Eighth Grade" may be skepticism about its basic premise that middle-school children's greatest fear is dying in a war. Students may question the context of the discussion or the relationship between these young adolescents and the adult who raises the issue of fear. In fact, some psychologists say that a major fear of teenagers is talking to adults, and they warn their colleagues that members of this age group are reluctant to reveal their true feelings. One list of the most common fears of adults, teens, and older children puts common fears in order: public speaking, making mistakes, failure, disapproval, rejection, angry people, being alone, darkness, dentists, injections, hospitals, taking tests, open wounds and blood, police, dogs, spiders, deformed people. Fear of dying in a war doesn't even make the top ten. A closer look at the statistics supports Derricotte, however. Although war is not a major fear for children younger than eight or adolescents older than fifteen, it does affect older elementary and middle-school children. Events in the news such as kidnappings, school shootings, and wars cause great distress for children in this age group, and they feel powerless to do anything about such threatening forces. Our images of war take forms learned in childhood. The children of the 1940s and 1950s recall fears of bombs dropping from the sky; boys drew detailed pictures in crayon showing airplanes fighting in the sky. The jungles and helicopters of the Vietnam War preoccupied the next generation. Ironically, children growing up in the 1990s and the early years of the new century may return to the images of air battles and bombings that characterize their parents' wars.

Although "Fears of the Eighth Grade" was published in 1989, it is difficult to place it in time. The "somewhere else" of the second stanza, where women and children gather "at the gates of the bamboo palace," belongs to a generation that sees war in jungle images. Perhaps the default template for war is the poet's own, war being something that happens in an Asian, South American, or African Third World location far from a safe America. Our college students may raise issues about this, arguing that the narrator's assumptions may beg the question of the reality of war for everyone, even those who imagine they are safe in a "little box of consecrated land" (line 9). Some may feel that the last stanza implies that the children are able to see things that adults miss and that when the speaker exclaims "How thin the veneer!" in line 13 she tacitly admits that war can happen anywhere. We can discuss how Americans might deal with war in our own country, how attitudes might be different if our mothers were the ones crying or we were the ones without toilet paper. Those who plan to use this poem in classroom discussion can build the question What things do you fear? into early questionnaires so that they can have the data for this discussion. We have also asked new students, What issues do you think will be most important in the twenty-first century? to get a sense of their values and to orient them to the focus of the course. Most do not mention war, though discussion often raises terrorism issues.

Even in our politically and religiously conservative region, most college students dismiss biblical prophecies of Armageddon or any great conflagration that pits ultimate good against ultimate evil. But Derricotte is speaking symbolically when she uses the word from the Apocalypse, as the writer of the biblical text undoubtedly was doing as well. Her contrasting images in the final stanza support her contention that the trappings of civilization are ephemeral. Our students may be old enough to remember how quickly the Soviet Union shattered into pieces and how they needed to memorize strange new names for political entities. Televised images of the effects of war in Bosnia-Herzegovina or Serbia will be fresh in their minds, and they will recall the swiftness with which events moved. One day in 1999, only dedicated news junkies could find Kosovo on a map, and the next day NATO was dropping bombs and President Clinton was vowing not to send in ground troops.

Derricotte's poem captures the pervasive possibility of war, a potential force that lies beneath everyday life. She implies that children may be sensing something that we are no longer able to see. This may be a romantically Wordsworthian interpretation of childhood, but this does not mean that such fears should be dismissed. Most educators of eighth graders, aware that children see both real and fictionalized violence daily on television, address the issues of war more than they did in the past. Several excellent novels dealing with events of World War II are on reading lists for middle-school students, and teachers may use these as a springboard for discussions of current events. Recently, the journal of a young girl in Sarajevo was published and widely read by American schoolgirls the age of Derricotte's students. Some of our college students may argue that children should be sheltered from such knowledge, and will even object to having to discuss "politics" in a freshman composition or literature class such as ours. Others will recognize that discussing fear — or any other issue — brings it into the realm of critical thinking, where it can be understood and perhaps used to strengthen our ability to solve the actual problems it represents. Students need places where they feel safe to do this. Middle school is the time of preoccupation with horror and the macabre. It may be that children of this age use the imagery of violence to work out fears that are only tangentially related to those they articulate to adults.

The students in Toi Derricotte's "Fears of the Eighth Grade" bring their fears into the light of discussion, and the narrator imagines their visions of Armageddon. The mothers in Louise Glück's "The School Children" work desperately to find the way out of something for themselves or their children, but the narrator leaves the nature of their fears undefined, and her use of the word *ammunition* seems oddly out of place. The emphasis on violence in both poems may be appropriate, but Glück's final lines force us to go back and reinterpret the poem to take the intensity of the image into account. In Derricotte's poem, the structure follows the narrator's thought processes. In the first stanza, we listen in on the discussion in the classroom. The two short middle stanzas move us into the narrator's mind as she reacts to the unexpected response of the eighth graders to her questions. In her final stanza, Derricotte's narrator goes on to imagine what the children see in their minds, moving into the imagery of apocalyptic vision and horror movie. The move is from the realistic to the symbolic. The four stanzas of Glück's poem interweave the realistic and the symbolic, but she also begins the first stanza with a sharply defined image of schoolchildren and moves in the last stanza to biblical syntax and diction that connotes warfare. The emotional impact of both endings leaves the reader unsettled.

Although the persona who narrates Derricotte's poem may be a teacher or a guest in the classroom, the children's voices and the narrator's reaction to them are the focus. This is not a teacher-centered classroom but one in which the children participate. Glück's teachers are like gods who impose order and silence and who must be appeased with offerings. The difference is significant. Our students may think back to their experiences in classrooms where teachers were autocrats and compare these with classrooms where students were encouraged to get involved with their own learning. As college instructors, we may be surprised to find that some students are more comfortable with teachers who supply them with correct answers rather than requiring them to take responsibility for their own critical and creative thinking. We should challenge them to examine their attitude toward authority.

PHILIP LEVINE

Among Children (p. 600)

Philip Levine is a prize-winning poet who has been called the "poet of the factory floor." Having grown up in the gritty industrial city of Detroit, Michigan, during the Great Depression, Levine writes passionately of working-class people. He remembers deciding, while working beside these men and women in various types of factories during the 1950s, that he must "find a voice for the voiceless." Like Tillie Olsen, who writes of the silences of women and working-class men, Levine recognizes that much is lost to literature and intellectual thought by the demands of work in a capitalist society. Like James Agee and Walker Evans, who during the 1930s sought to reveal the plight of tenant farmers, Levine celebrates the dignity and worth of his subjects by presenting them in a concrete and forthright style. His narrative voice speaks with plain words and the rhythms of everyday American speech. Rather than reaching for flowery metaphors or mannered allusions, Levine's poetry is content-oriented, depending upon the authenticity of voice and the clarity of image.

This does not mean that his poems are lacking in allusions or that his voice is devoid of sophistication, however. Like many working Americans, Levine's speaker does not fit a stereotyped blue-collar image. He is a man who thinks, who sees. Students encountering Levine's writing for the first time sometimes miss its complexity because it reads so effortlessly. The poet would appreciate the ease of reading but would want his issues to be considered. In *The Simple Truth* (1994) he tells us in verse:

> Some things
> you know all your life. They are so
> simple and true
> they must be said without elegance,
> meter and rhyme
> they must be laid on the table beside
> the salt shaker. . . .

Though his style is simple, the depth of his philosophy is not. We need to encourage our students to dig deeply into Levine's texts and to look at his poetry in collections and in other sources outside this anthology to see how motifs repeat and enrich each other.

Students will find a variety of adjectives to describe the poem's narrator, but *compassionate, angry,* and *pessimistic* might come to mind. He cares about the children and longs to inspire and strengthen them. But we can sense righteous indignation in his descriptions of their already coarsened bodies and pessimism in his knowledge of "what is ahead." We also sense some distance from the families he describes; he is wise and philosophical in a way that the children and their parents may not yet have discovered. His reference to the Bible might lead students to characterize him as religious, although he claims to be an anarchist in both religion and politics. Nevertheless, the case could be made that he is a profoundly moral and ethical thinker. It might be useful to discuss the difference between being religious and being ethical. The narrator assumes a great deal about what the children think and feel. He characterizes them as victims. The intense image of torn wings in lines 5–6 jerks us to attention after we have seen the ten-year-olds nodding off to sleep in the opening lines.

It seems unlikely that the poet was allowed into the hospital nursery ten years ago, but his description makes us identify with the babies. The imagery of "their breaths delivered that day, / burning with joy . . . / . . . on the hardest day of their lives" (lines 30–38) is too perfectly worded to paraphrase. He imagines the babies to be joyful, filled with wonder, brave, and optimistic. This contrasts dramatically with the pessimism of the poem's beginning and the renunciation of its ending lines as he imagines them as adults. By placing his schoolchildren in the city of Flint, Philip Levine particularizes them and emphasizes the working-class circumstances of the poem. Obviously, they could be schoolchildren in any number of other, similar places, even nearby Detroit; but the name *Flint* lends connotations to the situation, making the setting even more gritty and hard-edged. He also mentions the town of *Paradise*, an ironic name in this context, since the future he foresees for the children is not an idyllic one.

Like Toi Derricotte in "Fears of the Eighth Grade" and Louise Glück in "The School Children," Philip Levine echoes the Bible in "Among Children." Increasingly, college students do not catch biblical or classical allusions. Although we do not need to reopen cultural literacy debates at this point, it is clear that many nuances of literature in the traditional canon are therefore inaccessible to them. But even a poet like Philip Levine, who has the stated agenda of breaking elitist idols, relies upon some shared knowledge. Most scholars would be forced to look up the reference to the horse galloping joyfully into battle, but our students may also miss the connotations of the poet's mention of Job, and they may be frustrated. Searching out the sources of the poet's cultural and personal allusions can add to our enjoyment of reading. When Levine mentions "oranges" in line 25, for example, his fans might think of a later poem, "The Mercy," in which he tells the touching story of his immigrant mother as a little girl being given an orange:

> She learns that mercy is something you can eat
> again and again while the juice spills over
> your chin, you can wipe it away with the back
> of your hands and you can never get enough.

Some readers may argue that the narrator does not take active steps to help these children. But isn't it the duty of a poet to create change through the showing and telling of his words? When he says in the ending lines "I bow to them here and whisper / all I know, all I will ever know," doesn't he take the largest step of all by passing on his knowledge, by educating us as well as them?

Because Louise Glück does not use the pronoun *I* at all, "The School Children" is the most visual and lyrical of the three poems in this cluster. Like Archibald MacLeish, who says that "a poem should not mean but be," Glück presents her poem as an object to be experienced rather than a rhetorical argument to be understood. Toi Derricotte uses the first person in the first two stanzas of "Fears of the Eighth Grade" but drops it as she moves into reverie and imagines what the children see. She seems to be addressing the audience at first, but early in the second stanza we begin to have a sense that we are overhearing her thoughts. In "Among Children" Philip Levine may also be talking to himself, but he tells us of his feelings throughout. He raises issues for us to think about. In fact, he speaks directly to his audience, telling us, ". . . You can see" (line 10). The effect is less of interior monologue than of dialogue with a hint of persuasion. Perhaps Levine's poem depends more on context than Derricotte's or Glück's, but one could argue that all are both specific and universal.

A representative example can say much about a group, can be convincing evidence. The specificity of Levine's poem makes its evidence more compelling, since we could go to Flint and observe the children of factory workers to see if things have changed. And we could extrapolate the results to other children of factory workers if his example is indeed representative. The same can be said of the specifics of Derricotte's poem. A bit of research verified that her assertion about her particular eighth-grade class was consistent with psychological studies. Glück, on the other hand, is less specific, leaves more unanswered questions. We might find through research where the poet has lived, where she might have observed the people and the apple trees of her poem, but we would still be guessing. Ironically, this makes the poem more universal in that the individual may create his or her own reading. But culturally it is less universal, since we are limited to the images of the poem and cannot apply them with confidence to other settings. Levine looks at his fourth-grade children in the context of their whole lives, and this makes his poem significantly different from Derricotte's, which keeps us in the present tense of eighth graders' fears about war. But how can we read about children and war without also looking ahead a few years to a time when the thing they fear could come to pass? Glück's poem could go either way. One reading would have it be a snapshot of the present. But the connotations of the word *labor* when juxtaposed with motherhood hint at a changing relationship between mothers and children as the children file into the school. And the poem also looks ahead, since the mothers seek an escape. Levine's poem has a broader perspective, but the others may not be as time specific as they seem at first reading.

RESPONDING TO TEACHERS (p. 603)

LANGSTON HUGHES

Theme for English B (p. 603)

"Theme for English B" by Langston Hughes raises issues about the writer of a poem — the poet — as opposed to the persona of a poem — the speaker — who may or may not represent the poet at the time of the writing. Students tend to see all poetry as confessional, the outpouring of a soul in the throes of emotion. In fact, those who write poetry often do so to express themselves. But Langston Hughes, especially at the time this poem with its twenty-two-year-old narrator was published in 1949, was deeply involved in experimentation with different voices in both his poetry and his prose. Hughes was then in his late forties and was a well-known and much-celebrated writer who had chosen to live in Harlem. His satirically comic figure Jess B. Semple was articulating the issues within the Negro community of the 1940s and 1950s in a balanced voice that ranged from pain to hilarity, but was never beaten or shrill. He had long been trying out blues voices and was experimenting with female narrators. Of Indian, French, and African ancestry, Hughes grew up with various members of an extended and mostly dysfunctional family in the American Midwest. Unlike his narrator in "Theme for English B," he was born in Joplin, Missouri, and went to high school in Cleveland, Ohio, where he was a gifted student and the only "colored" person in his class. He had traveled to places like Mexico, where his father lived, and to New York, Africa, and France before he and writer Zora Neale Hurston joyfully toured the American South in the summer of 1927. By the time he wrote the poem here, he had also been to Spain during the Spanish Civil War and to Russia as part of the socialist fervor of the early 1930s.

Having pointed out the differences between Hughes and his narrator, however, we may find many similarities between the narrator of "Theme for English B" and the Langston Hughes who arrived by steamer in New York in 1921 to study mining at Columbia University. Columbia is "on the hill above Harlem," as is the college of the poem. The talented, light-skinned Hughes was not the only Negro on campus, but he lived in an otherwise all-white dormitory after initially staying at the Harlem YMCA. He soon was spending all his time with the writers and artists of Harlem, however, meeting W. E. B. Du Bois and other stars of the Harlem Renaissance. He soon became an important participant in this heady intellectual and artistic community. To the fury of his father, who saw education only as a way to make money and who had no respect for poets or for his own African American roots, Hughes left school and became a writer who celebrated his race.

From the distance of adulthood, Hughes has his narrator encounter a typical assignment for a college freshman, the autobiographical narrative. When a similar assignment was given a few years ago in a graduate seminar, at least two students rebelled and wrote essays that resisted the reductive nature of the assignment. Yet their resistance created what may have been the most revealing responses. One woman wrote a poetic piece that touched on the shifting nature of identity, and another wrote an angry explanation of why she could not write an autobiographical essay, in the process writing an essay defining who she was *not*. The assignment as stated in Hughes's poem recalls the "non sequitur" of William Shakespeare's character Polonius in *Hamlet*, that if one is only true to oneself, then it is not possible to be false to any man. But it doesn't follow as the night the day that writing something *true* is that simple. The narrator of the poem critiques the assignment, sounding for a while like Walt Whitman's *Leaves of Grass* as he moves into the street for his self-definition and then pulls even the instructor into the mix.

Even today, to be white in America is probably to be *more free*, especially when the white person is the person in authority, as in the college classroom. In mainstream American culture, white people are the default human beings, with everyone else being defined in contrast to this definition of "normal" humanity. People of color are *different*, are *other*. Of mixed race, Hughes saw himself in the "tragic mulatto" category, not quite accepted as black or white. When a young Langston Hughes traveled to Africa, the black people who lived there would not accept him as being like themselves. They looked at his golden skin and softly curling hair and laughed, "You — white man." America still struggles with the artificial divisions that the history of slavery creates between human beings.

Students who are interested in exploring this topic further might begin with Toni Morrison's brief nonfiction study *Playing in the Dark: Whiteness and the*

Literary Imagination (1992). According to Morrison, much of literature until very recently was directed toward a white audience, even when written by African American authors. This is often true of Langston Hughes, as we hear him constantly speaking to the white person looming just outside the picture, defining and explaining his race to the stranger. But this poem consciously defies the white audience, admitting the impossibility of defining oneself as separate. The rhyme scheme is interesting in this context. The poem imposes the structure of rhyming couplets at the beginning and the end, when the paper is assigned and when it is presented to the professor. This frames the lively rhetoric in the middle that sometimes addresses Harlem, sometimes moves into a jazzy alliteration — as in the "Bessie, bop, or Bach" of line 24 — even occasionally rhymes as if by accident. Hughes often reworked material that was written in earlier years, and he may indeed have turned in a response to an assignment much like this one. We hope that the teacher likes the narrator's impertinence; good writers can get away with challenging the rules. But in 1921 or 1949, and perhaps even today, for college students who are not Langston Hughes, drawing outside the lines entails risk.

LINDA PASTAN
Ethics (p. 605)

Our students come to college with their own ethical codes built from experiences both in and out of schools. But many may be examining these "commonsense" assumptions for the first time. Marshall McLuhan once said that we aren't sure who first discovered water, but it's unlikely to have been a fish. One of the tasks of education is to learn to see the water, to confront the warrants for our beliefs. Ethics can be studied at the college level in introductory and advanced courses in departments of philosophy but may also be a component of other disciplines. Business majors usually must study the ethics of advertising, contracts, and so forth, and scientists look at the issues and principles that affect biology, technology, the environment, and other areas where standards of conduct must be debated and applied. Medicine, law, religion, psychology, political and social sciences: Students of all these disciplines must deal with profound ethical dilemmas. Many of the issues from other discourses find their way into our English classrooms, with argumentative research papers addressing abortion, assisted suicide, animal rights, capital punishment, marijuana legalization, genetic engineering, and a myriad other issues currently being debated in other classrooms and dorms. When we ask our students to define an *issue* as a question about which reasonable people may disagree, we are asking them to make ethical judgments as well as logical ones. The root of the word *ethical* is *ethos*, the same word that we use when discussing the need for writers to appeal to common values or for readers to judge credibility and tone.

Debates rage about the teaching of ethics at the high-school and elementary-school levels. The directive approaches to teaching virtues and morality popularized by William Bennett and other moral conservatives vie with the discursive, decision-making approaches to "values clarification" epitomized by Lawrence Kohlberg and other liberal sociologists and educators. As our college students tackle these opposing viewpoints, they have the opportunity to examine their own reasons for choosing one over the other. Many readers will feel that the teacher's question is inappropriate, that to merely present ethical dilemmas without presenting criteria for making decisions may give teachers insight into the way children think but does nothing for the children. While her theory may have been discursive, designed to force her students to think, the teacher's approach has been ironically prescriptive. She could have seen the narrator as a creative thinker rather than labeling her as a person who refuses to accept responsibility.

Kohlberg maintains that we pass through stages as we develop values over time. In the preconventional stage, children accept what they are told, and are good either because their parents expect it or because they will be rewarded or punished for their behavior. Adolescents may advance to a conventional stage in which they are loyal to groups with which they identify, deferring to the consensus of the family, the gang, the church, and the school. Adults, especially those who consciously think about ethics, may move into a postconventional stage in which they question internalized group loyalties and norms and develop principles that promote universal ideals of justice, human rights, and the greater good for all people. This begs the question of whether values are universal or relative, of course, an issue that lies at the heart of the debates.

The theme of Pastan's poem about ethics also addresses the issue of the stages of life and how our worldviews may change over time. She uses images of fall and winter because she knows they will make us think of the latter stages of life. The children seek the answer that will please the teacher and perhaps earn them the reward of a good grade. The narrator soon learns that divergent thinking will be punished. One year, the narrator thinks of her grandmother, perhaps calling upon the norms of the family group to help her make the decision. Now, as an adult, she sees the whole exercise as reductive, viewing the issue in the light of universality and viewing herself at one with both art and nature. Her description of the Rembrandt painting captures the colors and the use of light but goes beyond surface detail to speak metaphorically and to critique the differentiation between art and life that the teacher's question assumes. The description is subjective, perhaps discarding both logos and ethos in favor of pathos, the emotional component of argument. Her last line resists the whole exercise of teaching children by presenting them with ethical dilemmas. Like many critics of current teaching approaches to ethics, Pastan may object less to the discussion of ethical issues in the classroom than to the inductive method that presents children only with the problems. Philosophers have developed several approaches that could be made available to children and adults to help them solve the problems presented. They might be taught to ask which alternative will lead to the most benefit and the least harm, which most closely respects the rights of all involved, which avoids both favoritism and discrimination, which advances the common good, or which will make us better people. All of these questions are value laden, of course, but we may also admit that bias can never be eliminated and therefore should be conceded. Some people who work with children argue for the power of narrative and poetry in the teaching of ethics, pointing out the long tradition in many cultures of using parables, fables, proverbs, and songs to illustrate principles of conduct or to raise questions about values. Linda Pastan's approach is finally an artistic and literary one that may still avoid confronting difficult choices but that raises new issues for our consideration.

The narrators of both Linda Pastan's "Ethics" and Langston Hughes's "Theme for English B" resist the assignments imposed upon them by their teachers. Both feel that the assignment seeks to reduce a complex issue — a person's true identity, the relative value of life versus art—into simple terms beyond the capability of adults, much less young people, to articulate. Hughes's teacher imparts to his students the truism that most writing teachers have used: Write what you know! But Hughes has his own agenda and wants to say something about the oneness of humanity, the vitality of Harlem, and the inequities implied in the whole situation of white teacher and black student. Pastan also seeks to transform the teacher's question, to make it her own. Writing as an adult looking back, she critiques the warrants underlying the posing moral conundrums to children, continuing to resist what she sees as a false dichotomy. She, too, ends with a celebration of oneness, something that she implies can come only with maturity. Her leap to a later stage in life is significant to a reading of the poems. We must do research to realize that Hughes the poet is speaking from the distance of maturity, and readers therefore may see his narrator as immature and cocky, a slacker just trying to avoid the intellectual work of the real assignment by being flippant and artistic. Pastan explicitly invites us to assume that she now has the maturity and the freedom to object to the teacher's assignment. Students might decide that she cannot get off the hook this easily, that her vague sense of oneness may be beautiful but still "eschews / the burdens of responsibility" (lines 15–16).

Characterizations of Pastan's and Hughes's poems as pessimistic or optimistic will depend upon the readers' interpretations of tone. Pastan undoubtedly has a pessimistic attitude toward the efficacy of placing tough moral responsibilities on the shoulders of children or of reducing life to either/or choices. But she seems optimistic about the interrelationships between the aspects of life that people consider as separate. Hughes also sees life as of one fabric and seems optimistic about Americans being part of each other. But there may be an irony and defiance in his tone that undercuts the seeming optimism. The knowledge that Langston Hughes is not the voice of the poem may lead us to see that the poem's narrator is actually naive, limited, and unreliable. If he is trying to be cheerful and to put the best face on the anger that simmers underneath, then Hughes's poem is profoundly pessimistic.

HENRY REED

Naming of Parts (p. 607)

Known primarily as a writer for BBC radio, Henry Reed wrote only one book of poems, *A Map of Verona*, published just after World War II in 1946. The most famous of the poems in this volume is called "Lessons of the War," and "Naming of Parts" is the first section of this poem. It was reprinted in 1970 with additions, but by then "Naming of Parts" had become the most popular British poem to come out of the war, and many people of Reed's generation can recite it by heart. The poet explains that he wrote it as a joke to amuse his fellow recruits. According to William Scammell's entry on Reed in *The Oxford Companion to Twentieth-Century Poetry* (1994):

> Its good-natured humour, broad sexual innuendo, and lyrical evocations of nature make it instantly memorable. By juxtaposing dry and faintly absurd technical language about the cleaning of guns with the immemorial goings-on of flowers and bees in spring, Reed dramatizes both the ridiculousness and boredom of war . . . and its relationship to the awkward, unbalanced lives of the individuals helplessly caught up in it. (445)

In the context of our poems on teaching and learning, "Naming of Parts" neatly contrasts an instructor's intentions and the student's transformation of them as he learns his own lessons from the teacher's presentation.

If we read Henry Reed's double-voiced poem aloud, it is easy to believe that the author was involved with radio broadcasting, since it is particularly auditory. Students who have grown up in liturgical churches might be reminded of the responsive readings in which the leader reads a line and the congregation responds in unison. Two good readers in the class could be asked to study the poem and to perform it, choosing the places where the voice of the drill instructor ends and the voice of the recruit begins. Or the class might replicate the call-and-response method used in church, with one side of the class reading about the guns and the other about the flowers and bees. Adults seldom get a chance to read aloud to each other, and many students find it a particularly satisfying experience, especially at schools where a strong drama or film studies major is offered.

Students should have little trouble contrasting the voices and finding adjectives for them. Sometimes we hear the military regular characterized as masculine and the responding voice as feminine. We might want to discuss issues raised by this contrast. Much of the enjoyment of the poem is lost if readers do not understand that the voice of the recruit is ironic, even mocking, whereas the voice of authority, the voice of war, is deadly serious. Readers may wonder if the reader means to be making sexual puns. We should assure them that the poet certainly does mean to be talking dirty. What's more, there may be a great deal of significance to the coupling of guns, a phallic symbol, and flowers, the sexual organs of plants, in the same poem, especially since the switch from one to another occurs in midline. In addition, the poem moves from the lyricism of the Japonica blossoms in the first stanza to the violent and clumsy "assaulting and fumbling [of] the flowers" by the bees in line 23. The movements become more violent in each stanza until in the final lines the recruit (or the poet?) repeats lines from earlier stanzas almost incoherently. Readers can decide how far they wish to take the sexual imagery at this point. Although current readers may interpret the poem as antimilitary, Reed may simply intend it as the sort of inside joke that can occur in any group of workers where a particularly self-important person in a position of authority becomes the surreptitious target of a talented and witty mimic. Nevertheless, the poetic voice of the recruit is privileged while those who would worship the weapons of war are ridiculed. The poet uses white space to set off the final line of each stanza. Both the indentation and the space between stanzas emphasize the statement and slow the pace. The effect is a full stop. When the voice of the instructor begins again in the new stanza, he is not responding to the inner voice of the recruit, but beginning a new point in his lecture. By contrast, when the recruit's interior monologue begins each time, it begins in the middle of a line and is enjambed with the first voice. Because the voices are not engaged in dialogue but in separate monologues, this arrangement is particularly telling. The inner voice of the student responds to the spoken words of the instructor, but the instructor is ignorant of what the student really thinks. The repetition also serves as emphasis, but with each repetition the line accumulates connotations. The effect is of an echo, but an echo that is changed, its meaning transformed into an antithesis.

The most obvious difference between Henry Reed's "Naming of Parts" and the previous poems in this cluster, Langston Hughes's "Theme for English B" and Linda Pastan's "Ethics," is the setting of the learning situation. The narrators in Hughes's and Pastan's poems respond to assignments given to them at school, whereas Reed's protagonist reacts to the absurdity of military training in what amounts to a garden. Ironically, Reed's recruit really needs the information he is given, whereas the school assignments come across as sophistry. Some college students have served in the military and recognize the earnest, single-minded instructor as a character who in some respects only exists in this particular setting. But most readers have experienced classrooms or work situations in which the teacher or trainer relayed information according to a boring, detailed script and had no tolerance for questions or deviations. Although the teachers of Hughes's and Pastan's poems ask for a response from their students, they may have fallen into set patterns as well. Hughes's professor makes a perhaps unwarranted assumption that autobiography is possible in a theme for English B, and Pastan's teacher presents the same ethical dilemma every year. Reed is concerned with naming, and Hughes contends with the idea of defining oneself. Both seem to be saying that life is more complex than these teachers assume. Pastan struggles with her teacher's demands that she make distinctions when she prefers to see wholeness. All challenge their teachers and change the rules; Reed plays with the meaning of words, making love not war from the words of his teacher.

WALT WHITMAN

When I Heard the Learn'd Astronomer (p. 608)

Walt Whitman will not be new to most of our college students. He is arguably the most influential poet that America ever produced and is a pivotal figure between the romanticism and decorum of the early nineteenth century and the modernism and experimentation of the twentieth. He created his own rhythms from everyday American speech and Italian opera, from newspaper journalism and the Bible. Although "When I Heard the Learn'd Astronomer" might mislead readers into jumping to the conclusion that he was against science, Whitman was a great believer in science and an early proponent of the theory of evolution. In the preface to his long, unprecedented celebration of human individuality, *Leaves of Grass*, in 1855, Whitman writes, "Exact science and its practical movements are no checks on the greatest poet but always his encouragement and support." In a list that includes astronomers with sailors, travelers, anatomists, chemists, and geologists, but also with phrenologists, spiritualists, and lexicographers, Whitman calls such scientists "the lawgivers of poets" whose ordering of reality forms the infrastructure of poetry. But he goes on to place matters in their proper order: "In the beauty of poems are the tuft and final applause of science." In terms of our cluster on teaching and learning, it seems clear that to Walt Whitman the student is expected to outshine the teacher, to transform science into poetry. Mysticism and science overlap in Whitman's worldview, as they did for many in the nineteenth century. He can see in the Milky Way galaxy the same oneness that he sees linking himself and the universe, and the stars are to him "the visible suggestion of God in space and time." The short poem "When I Heard the Learn'd Astronomer" incorporates in one long, eight-line periodic sentence many of the elements of Walt Whitman's philosophy and prosody.

Whitman's formal schooling ended when he was twelve years old, but he was indeed "learn'd." He sharpened his writing skills as a printer and a newspaper reporter and read widely, referring to the writings of most of the world's religions and to philosophers from Plato to Leibnitz, Hegel, and Kant. He traveled from New York to New Orleans and back. His first publication was praised by Ralph Waldo Emerson and criticized by Henry David Thoreau. He was a force to be reckoned with throughout most of the nineteenth century, and much of the literature of the twentieth century defers to him in some way. Nevertheless, in spite of his own learning and his respect for science, the word *learn'd* has a pejorative tone in this poem; the precision and logic make him suddenly "tired and sick." Whitman must escape from logos into the pathos of mysticism and beauty. The effect of the anaphora, the repeated parallel structures of the first four lines, is often characterized as biblical or sermonic. In this context, however, it seems to emphasize the point-by-point logic of the lecturer as he piles up evidence. When contrasted with the flowing diction and syntax of the last four lines, the repetition of the word *When* projects the poet's sense of frustration, the increasingly longer sentences stretching out the lecture interminably. We might ask students what the poet's reaction suggests about using formulaic approaches to writing arguments or about relying on hard evidence alone to persuade an audience.

Whitman uses a periodic sentence, a form of syntax that does not become grammatically complete until the final line of the poem. The result is inductive, like a mystery story. The reader is kept in suspense, must think ahead throughout the poem to anticipate the revelation at the end. In the first four lines, the narrator hears an empirical argument; at the end, he observes for himself and wraps himself in silence. The easy assumption will be that he proposes another method of education than the scientist's. But we know that Whitman saw science as the father of poetry, at least in 1855. Perhaps, ten years later, he resists the oppressive precision of science that is isolated from beauty. His gazing at the stars is a typically romantic response. He may not learn a great deal about astronomy, but he may learn other things that he values even more. Whitman must use words to convey the "perfect silence" of his last line, and we may argue that this sometimes most talkative of poets contradicts himself. But the word *silence* is placed just before the white space at the bottom of the page where the poem ends, after all the words that precede this last image. The effect on most readers is exactly what Whitman intends, that deep breath of satisfaction at the aptness and beauty of the scene, the unfettered poet out there in communion with the Milky Way. But the poet is wily. Every word has been precise, the structure of the poem as deliberate as any astronomer's chart.

Among the four poems of this cluster, Whitman's narrator is the only student who actually walks out on the teacher. But all the students walk out in one way or another. The young college student of Langston Hughes's "Theme for English B" challenges his teacher by, in a Whitmanesque way, putting the universe, including the professor himself, into his autobiography. Though he does not walk out on the teacher, he walks out on the assignment, choosing, like Whitman before him, poetry over prescribed structure. The older narrator of Linda Pastan's "Ethics" finally walks out on the assignment after many years, echoing Whitman's rejection of cold logic in her revelatory ending. Henry Reed, like a great many students, hides in plain sight; he is present in body but transforms the meticulous details of weaponry into poetry. Whitman, as an adult attending a lecture, has a perfect right to come and go; the others are more or less compelled to remain. Although Whitman does not directly quote the lecturer, he gives us a fairly good idea of the nature of the lecture. Each poem is less about the teacher's words than about the narrator's use of them in his or her own thinking. The narrators find the assignments uncomfortable for more or less "unaccountable" reasons. Whitman's adverb in the line "How soon unaccountable I became tired and sick" is telling. The narrators react against logic, against any *accounting* of reasons and details. They privilege what they obviously consider a higher understanding of reality that is silent and somehow more natural and unified than the compartmentalizing of reality their teachers insist upon. Some readers may agree. Others may question their pathos as vague and baseless, insisting that outside of poetry one must *account* for one's claims.

CHARGING A TEACHER WITH SEXUAL HARASSMENT: CULTURAL CONTEXTS FOR DAVID MAMET'S OLEANNA (p. 610)

DAVID MAMET

Oleanna (p. 611)

David Mamet's postmodern drama *Oleanna* affects audiences much like a Rorschach test. As we try to decipher the inkblots, our readings reveal as much about our own assumptions as they do about Mamet's characters. The play's gaps and contradictions make it less ambiguous than indeterminate, and the text could support directly opposite assertions about many of its issues. Important information is left out, and we are taken by surprise by the dynamics of the characters. What happens to Carol between the first and second scene, for example, to change her character from a seemingly shy and insecure student to a wielder of power? Who are the members of her "Group," and what can we assume about their influence over her? What is she about to reveal to John when the final telephone call of the first scene interrupts, ending their conversation? In many ways, this text deals with critical reading and with rhetoric. The two main characters, the unseen members of Carol's group and the tenure committee, John's family and personal connections, and the readers and viewers of the play all read and misread the situation and the characters' words. Sources of authority are questioned. Carol wants John's book pulled because her group objects to its being used as a "representative example" of the thinking of the university community. Both characters refer to the texts that they have produced, citing them as textual evidence. Each character reads beneath surface meanings and jumps to conclusions about what the other intends by his or her words, projecting personal feelings and experiences into their interpretations. John, in particular, repeatedly assumes that he knows what his student is thinking and feeling, and he constantly silences her by interrupting and anticipating her words. He assumes facts that are not evident. But in a typically professorial manner, he finds her writing imprecise. And both the reader and Carol herself agree that the writing is vague in a way that is typical of student writing, Carol characterizing it as "pathetic." The word has a double meaning, of course, and we are left ironically unsure which one she intends. She may be making a self-evaluation that positions her as an incompetent victim, helpless before the difficulty of the course. But she might be speaking of her rhetoric.

We find examples of all three of Aristotle's types of persuasive appeals in Mamet's play: logos, ethos, and pathos. In later scenes we see Carol using logical, hard evidence to build her case against John, though we have seen with our own eyes that the facts are taken out of context. The play deals with the nature of power and discourse in the university and critiques the theories of education and the philosophical poses that are cynically, carelessly, or manipulatively professed by both teachers and students. To some readers, the professor is the worst sort of chauvinist, the unaware bigot who is self-deceived into thinking that he is tolerant. To others, the female student is an example of political correctness run amok. It is, of course, a junior professor's nightmare, and there is a dark humor and irony to the play for anyone who has spent any time in a university setting. Like the contemporaneous television series *Third Rock from the Sun*, which operates on the premise that the best cover for a creature from an alien planet is as a university professor, *Oleanna* could only take place in this stuffy little office where the dialogue sounds all too normal.

John's philosophy strikes uncomfortably close to home for many of us. He feels that the educators of the past have failed young people, and he is cynical about the assumption that education can be the salvation of the working class. He believes that he wants his students to think for themselves, to put ideas into their own words rather than constantly taking notes and parroting their professors. He is idealistic, identifies with his students, and believes that he wants to help them. He objects to the confrontational approach that seeks to instill cognitive dissonance, to engage in hazing. He enjoys performing in the classroom and trying to solve his students' problems in a personal way. But our student readers will find many ways in which he fails to put his theory into practice and times when his attempts to apply principles backfire. His cynicism devalues what he does, he does not allow his student to finish a thought, and his attempts at establishing common ground go awry. Carol, on the other hand, wants to be told what to think, insists that she has done what he told her to do, has bought and read his book. Eventually, she sees education in terms of groups rather than individuals. She seizes control and forces confrontation.

Ironically, many students identify with John rather than with Carol, missing the ways in which he compromises and undercuts his own ideals. They react against her inversion of the power structure and what they perceive as her irrationality, even paranoia. Actually, she is at times hyperrational, blindly relying upon her evidence and upon written texts. Some readers see Carol as a survivor of child sexual abuse that causes her to seek victimization, citing her bristling at John's contention that he is not her father. The epigraph from Samuel Butler at the beginning and Carol's submissiveness at the end may support this contention, since they hint at self-blame. The class issue is important to other readers, and the second epigraph, from a folk song according to Mamet, mentions slavery. But which character is the slave? And slave to what? Carol's motives are problematic, and although she hints that she has overcome great difficulties to get to college, we are not told what they are. At the end of the first scene, she seems about to reveal something about herself that might have helped both John and the reader to understand, perhaps heading off the events that follow. But John is too self-absorbed to hear her, and this fact may explain a great deal.

Students usually blame the group to which Carol refers for her change in attitude and for the escalating political interpretations of John's words and actions that reverse the dynamics of power as the play proceeds. She instructs him to "consult the report" with its loaded words, characterizing his words and actions as "sexist," "elitist," "classist," "self-aggrandizing," "theatrical," "deviations from the text," and "pornographic." She accuses him of being patriarchal. (She would protest that these are not accusations but proven facts!) By the third scene she is pronouncing sophisticated evaluations of the power relationships in John's classroom and in her conferences with him. Although she may be parroting the rhetoric of the group, a case might also be made for a real change. Perhaps the group has succeeded in making her education meaningful to her by *telling* her what to think. She is no longer an individual but a representative example, has found in the group the sort of indoctrination she desires.

John, on the other hand, personalizes education and fails to realize his place as part of groups and systems or the political implications of his theories. He also fails to realize that he is often a walking cliché. When Carol objects in the final scene that John knows nothing and believes in nothing, we see that she has a legitimate complaint, that his fine theory is a veneer covering vagueness, hypocrisy, and egotism. When he violently finds the strength of his convictions at the play's end, Carol seems to accept his evaluation of her, perhaps finally getting from him the imposition of power that she wants. Many readers will be troubled by the sadomasochistic implications of the closing lines, and may raise issues about the relationships between sex, violence, and power. Mamet's use of fragmented dialogue and the intrusions of personal telephone calls into what should be an academic setting are particularly appropriate to this play. They demonstrate John's inability to listen to Carol or his wife, thus providing insights into his character. Because we know more about his personal aspirations and motivations, readers usually find John more three-dimensional and easier to relate to than Carol, who seems peculiarly flat and symbolic.

Cultural Contexts:

UNIVERSITY OF MARYLAND AT COLLEGE PARK, Pamphlet on Sexual Harassment (p. 641)
HOWARD GADLIN, From "Mediating Sexual Harassment" (p. 645)
ROBERT M. O'NEIL, "Protecting Free Speech When the Issue Is Sexual Harassment" (p. 652)

The University of Maryland's pamphlet on sexual harassment is designed for a specific audience and purpose. Much of the pamphlet is in legal-sounding diction and syntax, stating its message in precise language that uses passive verbs. It outlines information but tries to cover all the possible parties and situations, and it gives its readers a procedure for responding if they are harassed or accused of harassment. Because its purpose is to inform and because there may be legal ramifications to the advice given, the pamphlet's writers try to be as precise and clear as possible. The definition page could perhaps be less formal, but it undoubtedly aims for a balance between the specifics needed for clarity and the comprehensiveness that will include all possible eventualities.

In David Mamet's *Oleanna* Carol uses language similar to that of the Maryland pamphlet when she draws up her case against John. The words *unwanted* and *unwelcome* in the definition of sexual harassment depend upon the state of mind of the victim, placing much of the power in her hands. Her evidence refers to all of the points in the section describing which behavior may constitute sexual harassment, and she uses its jargon, accusing John of "misuse or abuse of power or hierarchal authority" in almost these words. She keeps written records and goes to advisors, her "Group." She bypasses the informal grievance process, however, going straight for the jugular and contacting the tenure committee that has power over his career, reputation, and economic welfare. Ask students to research the process at their college or university and compare the texts the university distributes with the one here. We might consider whether a student would be allowed to take her case directly to the tenure committee and whether John's colleagues would be so quick to accept Carol's version of the events if they were at our school. Does anyone in the class know a person who has been harassed or accused of harassment? What happened as a result?

Howard Gadlin, in his case study of Joanna from "Mediating Sexual Harassment," privileges informal resolutions of sexual harassment issues but maintains that the threat of formal proceedings, even if unspoken, can be used as a tool to make mediation work. Both the student and the professor have their reputations on the line and can be harmed by a formal hearing that becomes public knowledge. When considering mediation, Joanna must deal with her reluctance to meet her harasser face to face; he could have aggressively denied her accusations and possibly talked his way out of them. As Gadlin points out, he could have played the "role . . . of the misunderstood professor," as John's tenure committee undoubtedly believes he does. Since harassment is difficult to prove, Gadlin's contention that formal procedures usually favor the harasser makes mediation sound like a good solution. However, in David Mamet's *Oleanna*, John and Carol engage in behavior that should never occur; they meet alone to discuss the matter without a mediator, allowing the situation to escalate. The best mediation for the characters of Mamet's play might require each to allow the other to speak without interruptions or attempts to *read* or *misread* the words of the other party.

In his article from *The Chronicle of Higher Education*, Robert O'Neil concludes by focusing on the issue of definition. He maintains that tolerating sexual harassment is not an issue but that deciding what constitutes sexual harassment is. This gives us the opportunity to have students recall the definition of an *issue* as "a question about which reasonable people may disagree." Some students might argue with the teaching practices of Dean Cohen as O'Neil describes them in his second paragraph. The complaints that Cohen's student registers could be made about many college teachers, including those using this anthology, which often deals with adult themes. Furthermore, we often make our students uncomfortable as we provoke them to engage in critical thinking. O'Neil's readers do not know from the facts as they are outlined the full context of Cohen's teaching methods.

Sometimes it is not the actual content of a course but the teacher's tone that students find disturbing. And we have seen from Carol's use of the facts in *Oleanna* that facts alone do not always give a true picture of events as another participant or observer would interpret them. Sometimes students, after engaging in many uninhibited discussions of sexual content in past literature classes, will find one class particularly uncomfortable. The problem is not always one we can identify easily; in one case, the elderly male professor seemed more titillated and embarrassed than intellectually stimulated by the content of the course and seemed to think that he was being daring. His students, on the other hand, found his comments quite naive. The issue of sexual harassment never arose in outside discussions of the course and would not have seemed warranted, since no comments were directed at individual students and the atmosphere was not hostile. Like the language of the harassment policy at Cohen's school, the discomfort was vague and imprecise. O'Neil suggests that the classroom environment is hostile when offensive language is directed at one or more students in a way that makes them uncomfortable. Even this might be misinterpreted, however. Who is to decide what is "germane to the subject matter" of a given course? Since we have witnessed both Carol and John misquote or misread each other, students might argue that Carol could have made her case no matter what the guidelines. John, however, might have learned from O'Neil's suggested process what sort of comments would be likely to offend students like Carol and perhaps could have saved his job and his freedom.

COMPARING SCHOOL CULTURE WITH THE CULTURE OF HOME: CRITICAL COMMENTARIES ON RICHARD RODRIGUEZ'S "ARIA" (p. 656)

RICHARD RODRIGUEZ
Aria (p. 657)

Although his essay "Aria" and the commentary that accompanies it in this cluster were written in the 1980s, the issues they raise are still very much alive, and so is Richard Rodriguez — alive and, as usual, kicking against all sorts of conventional definitions. He is a contributing commentator on PBS's *McNeil/Lehrer News Hour,* a much published feature writer for newspapers and magazines, and the author of a second book of essays, *Days of Obligation: An Argument with My Mexican Father* (1992). He continues to be a burr in the saddle of many Mexican Americans, and students often stage protests when he is invited to campuses to speak. He still objects to bilingual education and affirmative action, even turning down university teaching positions because he felt that they were offered to him because of his ethnicity. Richard Rodriguez is in many ways a contradiction. Seen by many non-Hispanics as representative of Mexican Americans, he is actually an iconoclast, constantly at odds with those who advocate for Hispanic causes. He is openly homosexual, yet gay and lesbian issues have only recently played a part in shaping his public persona, and he resists the characterization of homosexuality as a lifestyle, suggesting instead that it is an "emotion." He argues for using the dominant language of cultural literacy, but his doctorate is in the literature of the English Renaissance, an era characterized by the triumph of the vernacular over the cultural literacy of Latin and Greek. His most popular texts speak in eloquent English about topics that surround his non-English ethnicity.

Rodriguez feels that he has been empowered by his command of the English language but claims that he is not an Anglophile. If Spanish suddenly becomes the language of public life in the United States, then he says that he will support the dominance of Spanish in the schools. What he objects to is an education that isolates children from the whole of tradition. He claims that the point of education is not to build self-esteem but to teach children what they need to know, to connect them with people who are unrelated to them but are a part of who they can be. This can and should be uncomfortable for learners. He insists that assimilation is inevitable, that the very act of asserting one's ethnicity is a peculiarly American act. The same is true for individuality in Rodriguez's thinking; to be unconventional is to be conventionally American. In his view, multiculturalism as it is expressed on most college campuses is a political pose, allowing only trendy and politically correct differences rather than true diversity. True to his agenda of paradox, Rodriguez asserts his independence by embracing the mainstream. He says of the book *Hunger of Memory: The Education of Richard Rodriguez*, from which "Aria" is taken, that it was written as a sort of protest. It was "my objection to the popular ideology of that time: my insistence that I am this man, contrary to what you want to make me: my declaration of myself, of my profession — political and personal."

Because he writes beautifully and with confidence, Richard Rodriguez may so skillfully persuade readers with pathos and ethos that they do not hold his logic to the usual standards. Though his title "Aria" may seem at first to refer to the sounds of his early, private Spanish language, necessarily lost, he says, to the public English language, the musical title more likely refers to his speaking out, and to his writing style as well. An aria is a lyrical solo, and Rodriguez insists on singing alone. We need to ask our students if his conclusions follow from the personal experiences that he relates. Even by his own definitions, Rodriguez is not a representative example when it comes to language learning. Why is it not likely that he acquired his skill with language around the dinner table as the family played word games in Spanish? He says that he was a bilingual child, and most linguists would maintain that his language learning occurred long before he finally spoke up in class. Can students imagine other scenarios in which he could have learned the "public individuality" of skill in English without losing the joy of Spanish? Some people might argue that his whole life has been shaped by the attempt to recover what he lost rather than by the voice he gained, since he continues to write about his identity first as Mexican American and lately as Indian. We might also ask if students who would grow up to be math majors would have been as well served by the author's educational experiences, or would this type of schooling have only worked for children who would become English majors? Do students feel comfortable with letting Rodriguez constantly equivocate, making up his own vague definitions? His tone is sad, nostalgic, and filled with paradox as he tries to convince us that his "awkward childhood does not prove the necessity of bilingual education." But why doesn't it? Does it *prove anything*? Many readers understand the sense of loss he conveys when he talks about his parents. No one would contend that children should be denied the language skills that will help them achieve, but many readers take issue with his conclusions that separating them from their home culture is the way to do this.

Although Rodriguez faults "middle-class ethnics" as romantic, some students might assert that Rodriguez uses sentimentality to get us on his side. Many of our students at regional or community colleges are first-generation college students who understand the dilemma of choosing between the person they are at school and the very different person their parents see at home. During the "Ebonics" debates that made the news in the 1990s, many prominent African American writers were eloquent in their appeals to teach children to skillfully use Standard English. On the other hand, it is interesting to hear properly academic English professors who grew up with regional dialects change register in a social or family group from *back home*. Most instructors in college English classes will probably agree that language plays a crucial role in education and that speaking out in class is important. Students may differ, however. The quiet one in the back of the class sometimes surprises us with the depth of her written work. Actually, many may have found that to speak in class is to meet with the sort of "public individuality" that peer pressure sometimes squelches. They have learned to keep their opinions to themselves. The vague generalities and platitudes that we read in student papers may reflect an attempt at consensus, a communal voice. Rodriguez may have a point. To think critically and to speak in one's own voice can be isolating, but profoundly rewarding.

CRITICAL COMMENTARIES:

RAMÓN SALDÍVAR, From *Chicano Narrative* (p. 667)

TOMÁS RIVERA, From "Richard Rodriguez's *Hunger of Memory* as Humanistic Antithesis" (p. 668)

VICTOR VILLANUEVA JR., From "Whose Voice Is It Anyway?" (p. 669)

Ramón Saldívar in *Chicano Narrative* maintains that Richard Rodriguez's narrative serves the interests of political conservatives. Many readers will agree, but others will applaud Rodriguez for challenging political correctness. Underneath his narrative lies the assumption that the only way for a member of an ethnic minority to gain power is to adapt to the dominant culture at any cost. If bilingual education does not empower children who do not speak English, then the government does not have to spend money on such programs. If individual effort, simply learning how to speak up in class, can result in the achievements of a Richard Rodriguez, then why juggle limited opportunities to implement affirmative action? *Those* people just need to speak English at home with their children, so that the children will be able to learn at school, goes the argument. By linking the speaking of English to acquiring a public voice, Rodriguez devalues other languages. Why not study Shakespeare *and* Cervantes, Faulkner *and* García Márquez? The unspoken implication that English is better than other languages plays into the hands of uninformed or racist Americans who use the English Only movement to cover prejudice against brown people. This is especially problematic when Richard Rodriguez is seen as a representative voice of Hispanic peoples or when readers encounter only one text isolated in an anthology. Much of his writing celebrates the strength of Mexican culture, especially its Indian heritage, but most students will only read this essay. His project is to problematize, to complicate, to create metaphors and ironic oppositions that shock his readers, perhaps for his own self-aggrandizement, but perhaps because he really believes what he says. But he is also reductive, sometimes so caught up in creating new oxymorons that a close examination reveals his rhetoric to be meaningless or fallacious. Because he is articulate, vocal, and prolific, many readers are misled into thinking that Rodriguez speaks for a community when in fact he is idiosyncratic in the extreme.

There may come a time with any individual when the choice must be made between home and school. Rodriguez maintains that the break he experienced is true for every child, not just for those whose private and public languages differ. For many readers, however, not just Hispanics, the essay "Aria" dishonors Rodriguez's parents and ethnic heritage in a shameful way. In fact, Richard Rodriguez's mother wrote him a letter asking that he not write about family matters in this way. Some would contend that to destroy the language of a people is to commit cultural genocide, and that when the Irish nuns require the family to speak English at home they engage in a colonial enterprise ironically reminiscent of the sort Ireland itself has endured. Tomás Rivera's critique of the book from which this essay is taken uses Spanish verbs of being to explain that Rodriguez chooses the lesser alternative. In the process, he demonstrates even for English-speaking readers the power of the Spanish language for analysis. Many foreign language instructors are sold on the total immersion technique, however, and some students will insist that only in this way will a child have the incentive to learn the language that will give him a voice in the wider community.

Victor Villanueva, in *Whose Voice Is It Anyway?* responds to the philosophy of Richard Rodriguez by pointing out the institutionalized economic inequalities that historically accompanied the creation of minority ethnic groups as opposed to the free movement of immigrants. He suggests that quite often a racial distinction also exists, with skin color playing a more dominant role than most members of mainstream society are willing to admit. Villanueva recounts the joking of his friends and the stereotypes that they reveal. Rodriguez, along with many others, has pointed out that the image of the lazy Mexican still exists in spite of a work ethic that rivals that of the Puritans. The CEO of Black Entertainment Television recently said in an interview that people in parking lots frequently assume that he is a chauffeur. On the other hand, we know of one blond South African immigrant who, even with a limited education and a working-class British accent, is immediately assumed by most Americans to be highly cultured and finds many doors opened to her in spite of her colossal rudeness. However, Rodriguez, in *Days of Obligation*, points out the power of indigenous peoples to overcome conquest, because cultures have a way of merging. Looking at his own Native American skin and features and those of Mexicans, he asks, "Where is the Conquistador?" The Indians seem to have won the DNA war, even though in many ways Spanish has conquered in the language arena. Ethnicity is complex and constantly in flux, and the direction of assimilation is not fixed. Perhaps the best way to ensure that minorities have an equal opportunity to overcome the barriers of the past is to do exactly what we are engaged in at the moment. Awareness of the issues may be a first step toward attitude changes that accumulate over time. Richard Rodriguez may best serve as a reminder that ethnic groups are not monoliths in which everyone believes the same way. By taking political action of the sort Richard Rodriguez would oppose — multiculturalism in the readings of university students, for example — perhaps we can overcome some stereotypes, making understanding possible and increasing opportunity.

LEARNING IN A COLONIAL CONTEXT: A COLLECTION OF WRITINGS BY JAMAICA KINCAID (p. 672)

JAMAICA KINCAID

Girl (p. 673)

The writings of Jamaica Kincaid immediately raise issues of genre. How are readers meant to interpret these texts? They seem to be short stories or essays or chapters from novels. Yet we can imagine setting them on the page as poetry, choosing line breaks in the quick pauses between breaths, emphasizing the repetitions and collocations. Kincaid's texts also cannot be classed as fiction or as nonfiction. Her stories of mothers and daughters are undoubtedly autobiographical, set in her native Antigua or an island setting much like it, or following the life of a character who, like herself, has left such a place. But she sometimes shifts the details around in time or creates a character from a composite of several real people. Some of her narratives began as stories about her mother's childhood, whereas others are her own. She has said that she does not aim to be factual, but she does aim to be true. We might explore her distinction, perhaps considering it in terms of David Mamet's *Oleanna* (p. 611), in which a character presents the "facts" in a way most will agree is not true. Kincaid writes of intensely close relationships between women and girls, but she cut off communication with her mother for many years after immigrating to the United States, renewing the relationship partly because she wanted her children to know the strong grandmother. The older woman's influence was overwhelming to Kincaid's sense of identity and her ability to grow, and she found it necessary to break free. Many college students can relate to her need to escape the dictates of childhood. Like many Caribbean and African American writers, Jamaica Kincaid chose a new name for herself when she began finding her own voice as a writer. She grew up as Elaine Potter Richardson. Ironically, she gives many of her characters variations of this name. To change one's name is a profound political and personal act, especially for a woman who has struggled for her own identity in the midst of colonialism and sexism. "Girl" is the first story in her first published book, *At the Bottom of the River*, and was the first of many stories to appear in the *New Yorker*, where she also published much nonfiction.

Although "Girl" might aptly be labeled a dramatic monologue, students will find several of the traditional elements of the short story here. The story has a protagonist, though we hear her voice only in the two places highlighted by italics, where she summons up the courage once to defend herself and once to ask a question. And the story certainly has an antagonist, the prevailing voice of the mother. Conflict takes place. The mother gives advice, but she also pronounces evaluations of her daughter in an inexorable stream, like the current at "the bottom of a river," as Kincaid's book title implies. The undertow is so strong that the daughter must eventually leave, but this does not happen until later. At this point, the glow of childhood is being destroyed by the nagging obligations of puberty and adolescence. The fifth item in the catalog instructs the girl in one of the rules of menstruation, and the worries about her future as a slut surface soon after. Women now in middle age, even younger women in traditional cultures, usually are able to pinpoint the year they discovered that to be a woman was to be judged and limited by the culture. A recent study suggests that the self-esteem of American girls tends to take a nosedive somewhere between the ages of nine and fourteen unless concerted efforts are made to see that they find areas of achievement and acceptance. Have our female college students experienced this? What solutions do they suggest for younger girls? Readers will find it interesting that the voice of oppression is female. Our discussions might consider how mothers internalize a culture's evaluations of women as inferior or bad and pass them on to their daughters. Defenders of pornography often cite the women who cooperate with their own exploitation and seem to enjoy it. Do students think this is a related issue? Compare Naomi Wolf's "The Making of a Slut" (p. 1035) in which female teachers and peers take part in similar evaluations of an adolescent girl. Male students are often fascinated as the women in the class relate the experiences of middle school and high school. We should ask men to consider how these hierarchies — from which they benefit — came to be and why they continue to be so powerful. We might also introduce them to some of the literature on colonialism and its metaphors and implications. What do women and conquered peoples have in common? Kincaid's writing style allows the reader to hear the voice of oppression as the girl hears it, as one long harangue that effectively silences her. This may explain why the story is written as one long sentence. The indiscriminate order of the items in the mother's list make us see that her teaching is a recurring event, so pervasive that it washes over the girl every minute of her life. The effect for the reader is shock with a twist of irony when abortion has equal weight with cold cures and fishing. This is a practical matter that a young woman must be told about, especially if her mother fears she will be a slut. It also indicates what we know to be true of many traditional cultures; women can follow certain procedures to subvert the rules that limit choices. Some might argue that this subversion still entails loss, however. Preventing pregnancy depends upon either purity or early abortion. The mother is teaching the girl how to survive in a specific time and place, but most readers will realize that this girl will escape into a culture where her mother's "common sense" must be unlearned. We might have students relate the advice their parents have repeatedly given them and consider what sort of culture this advice assumes. Or might television or music be the current disseminator of cultural lore in the United States?

JAMAICA KINCAID

Columbus in Chains (p. 675)

"Girl" and the other stories of *At the Bottom of the River* describe the education a parent passes on to her child in formal and informal ways; Jamaica Kincaid's novel *Annie John* adds the influence of the school and the structures of colonialism. Annie is a bright, feisty nonconformist. She is competitive and wants to be recognized for her achievements. She is honest, telling us of her evil thoughts and her teasing of classmates without shame. Kincaid writes within a long tradition when she tells her story from the point of view of a naive child, allowing readers to experience irony as they see a reality that still escapes her. Although she is limited as a narrator by her age and by her circumstances as an Afro-Caribbean child under British colonial rule, Annie John's unique view of the world is in some ways more trustworthy because she is open and honest. Annie is taught the worldview of the British Empire. Its goal is to turn her into a loyal, unquestioning subject. There is no question of adapting the superior British view to the needs of the children; these are facts for them to memorize, not issues raised for critical thinking. Rewards and punishments are used to motivate. Most of our students will recognize that such pedagogy is "good" for teaching conformity, though some will argue that the similar education Jamaica Kincaid received makes it possible for her to write as she does. Students might want to compare Kincaid's implicit criticism of her Anglican education with Richard Rodriguez's acceptance of an equally confining Catholic one in "Aria" (p. 657). Whereas Rodriguez believes that he had to devalue the culture of his family to grow, Kincaid's narrator resists the education that positions her as the descendant of slaves. Her caption for Columbus, although innocent, reflects her attitude of resistance. Perhaps the illustration of Columbus in chains is meant to evoke empathy, to show that even great men may be tragically misunderstood. But the humor of her mother's sarcastic comment about Pa Chess sets off intertextual connections in the mind of a divergent thinker. The educators do not see the irony of presenting to the descendents of slaves and oppressed peoples the image of a white man in chains on a ship. The narrator refuses to be reverent about the historical figure who symbolizes the destruction of both Caribbean and African cultures. Like many Caribbean and Native American thinkers, Kincaid does not see Columbus as a hero. To most adults in North America, the European explorers were introduced as achievers, brave men who came to an essentially vacant land and created a great civilization. Even though today's college students may have a less chauvinistic view, they may still feel that education should give us role models at the expense of complexity. History textbooks in elementary and high schools often oversimplify for the sake of time and space on the page, and the desire to uplift and inspire students tends to encourage the perpetuation of myths. Have our college students experienced this, or do they see a trend toward romanticizing indigenous peoples while demonizing figures like Columbus? We do not hear the voice of the teacher Miss Edwards. Kincaid may choose to allow us to see her through Annie John's eyes as more symbol than individual. At the end of the story, Annie's mother lies to her. She is given the native breadfruit but is told that it is some exotic food from Belgium so that she will eat it. In the last image of the story, she sees her mother as a crocodile. At school, also, the child is given a lie rather than something of value, as the educational system pretends that the doctrines of British colonialism will sustain the child of Africans and Caribbean Indians.

The child in "Girl" is given a stream of instructions about how to be a woman. But the implicit message that she is bad underlies the mother's words. In "Columbus in Chains" a girl resists the messages she receives about her value as a person, especially a dark-skinned subject of the British Empire. These messages underlie the rules and formal instructions of the school. The children may be different. If they are, we might expect Annie John to resist the teachings of her mother. But the difference may lie instead in the situations. Annie John is confident at school; because she is so bright, she has a voice, in spite of her teachers. But she seems to be more submissive at home. She seems left out of the joyful interactions of her mother and father, and she does care what they think. The two times we hear the voice of "Girl" she protests or questions, and this behavior is consistent with Annie John's personality. The sassy behavior that makes us like Annie is the sort of behavior that the mother in "Girl" thinks will make her daughter a slut. Kincaid often writes of the loss of paradise that comes when girls go through puberty, when they lose the close symbiotic bond with the mother that characterizes childhood. The foreign colonialism is comparatively easy to resist, but the lore of womanhood that also positions the girl is harder to overcome. The young woman internalizes both, both contribute to her identity, but she will ultimately have to struggle and break with the power of both sorts of education to become her own person.

JAMAICA KINCAID

On Seeing England for the First Time (p. 681)

Following the stories in which we meet a young girl much like Jamaica Kincaid as she learns and resists the lessons of home and school on the island of Antigua, Kincaid's essay "On Seeing England for the First Time" allows us to see some of the results of this education in the woman's thinking. Kincaid takes the reader through her education on England and her changing views of the country so long held up to her as the epitome of civilization, culture, and scenery. A well-known experiment conducted in the early twentieth century in the United States found that young African American girls consistently chose white dolls over dolls that looked more like themselves. They had received the message of the culture that white was prettier and more normal, more human, than their own dark skin. The same sort of message was given to West Indian children of Jamaica Kincaid's generation. England's was the default reality; everything else had to be defined in contrast to it. Kincaid takes us through her education about England, both the formal education and the more powerful informal education. She speaks of first seeing it consciously on a map and then seeing it in historical terms. But it is the privileging of its culture in everyday life, the tone with which it is described, its pervasiveness as the language of reality, that are most powerful. She is affected not only by the way she sees England but also by the way England constructs her view of the world and of herself. However, Jamaica Kincaid, like her fictional protagonists, resists this influence. She speaks of filling up with hatred the gap between the myth and the reality of England. Colonialism and slavery have intended her "erasure" as an individual, and she in turn wants to erase England and its power over her. Her tone asks her audience to feel her outrage and her sense of loss at having been taken over body and soul by England long before she was born.

The narrator of the essay is as open about her negative feelings as is the narrator of *Annie John*. Students might find her too negative, feeling that she is too tough on the current residents of England, people who have done her no harm. After all, she has kept her independent spirit. But the childhood assumptions about the superiority of everything English result in a devaluation of the culture from which she comes, as she points out in paragraph 6. All lessons both in and out of school teach the Afro-Caribbean child to feel ashamed and less worthy because her home and her very self are so different from the English ideal. As Kincaid describes her trip to England, she reminds us of slavery, prejudice, and the ways in which people show contempt for others. After describing in paragraph 14 how her friend changes her behavior and attitude in England as her status is devalued, Kincaid departs from chronological order to show the reader her own reaction to the "slavish, reverential, awed" tones of a salesman as he shows her the prince's crest. Perhaps her organization becomes more topical in this final section of the essay because she wants to drive home her point about oppression for arbitrary reasons. What she finally *sees* in England is the power of colonialism and institutionalized racism over the individual. She subtly points out that personal prejudice, which she admits to feeling along with rage and disappointment, differs from the power "to do evil on [a] grand scale" as England has done by its organized subjugation and colonialism of the hearts and minds of people.

Because it is written as nonfiction, and because the voice of the narrator is that of a bitter adult, readers may feel less compassion for the real Jamaica Kincaid of "On Seeing England for the First Time" than they do for the children who speak in her fiction. Perhaps they take her more seriously. Kincaid's adult voice usually makes white students uncomfortable, since they feel she is directing her anger toward them. In this context, her fantasy in paragraph 12 about enslaving the white people of England and making them more like herself bears examining more closely. She ironically says that this would make them more like the people she loves, and implies that they would be improved and helped, or humanized, by becoming slaves. This may remind some readers that the Christianizing of Africans and other "primitive" peoples was long an excuse for enslaving and indoctrinating them for their own good. "Could I resist it?" she asks. "No one ever has." Similarly, in paragraph 10, she compares her obsession with England and the gap between its myth and reality with Columbus's experience. As she describes him in the essay, he is still the "Columbus in chains" of Annie John's picture, enslaved by the difference between his fantasy about what he'd found and its reality. Although it is not explicitly colonial, we could argue that the short story "Girl" nevertheless reflects customs and traditions of slavery. A conflict is evident between "benna," the music with roots in West Africa and the Caribbean, and "Sunday school," an institution of the Anglican or Methodist church. The mother teaches her daughter how to iron the khaki pants that her father wears, an item of

British colonial culture. She is taught how to set a table properly. The household chores are women's work, but are also the work of the servant.

TEACHING THROUGH LITERATURE (p. 690)

DAVID WAGONER
The Singing Lesson (p. 691)

Whenever our students say a text is *about* life or *about* death, our first reaction may be to scream out the word CLICHÉ. David Wagoner's poem "The Singing Lesson" is obviously an extended metaphor *about* life, however; and it ends with intimations of mortality. He says that life is like singing, and here's a lesson on how to do it properly. Before assigning the poem, we might ask students to come up with their own metaphors for life and to think of others they have encountered in their reading. Many students have read William Shakespeare's *Macbeth*, for example, or discussed the life-and-death symbolism of Robert Frost's poetry. Such activities give us a chance to bring up the concepts of *abstract* and *general* versus *concrete* and *specific*, encouraging students to take abstraction into account in both their critical reading and their own writing. Some may recall a 1999 music video called "Everybody's Free (To Wear Sunscreen)" that humorously parodies the clichés of advice columns and bestsellers filled with warm, fuzzy aphorisms. Set to music by Australian film director Baz Luhrmann, the song's words had circulated on the Internet as a commencement address purportedly by novelist Kurt Vonnegut, who liked it but didn't claim it, before being correctly attributed to *Chicago Tribune* newspaper columnist Mary Schmich. Since nothing ever seems to die on the Internet, students may still be able to find both the column itself, sometimes still credited to Vonnegut, and also parodies of the parody. Each generation probably has its own additions to the wise advice genre. Rudyard Kipling's "If" comes to mind from an earlier century, as do the biblical Proverbs of Solomon from an earlier millenium. Children of the 1960s may remember the poster of *Desiderata* printed in fake calligraphy on yellowed vellum look-alike paper for that natural look. We probably won't share with our students the parody of *Desiderata* posted by Sean Sullivan on the Internet: "Go placidly amid the noise and haste and remember what peace there may be in sleeping through breakfast. Do not speak the truth; it merely upsets the neighbors. Listen to others, even the dull and ignorant; they assign your grade and sign your paycheck."

David Wagoner's "The Singing Lesson" is a dramatic monologue ostensibly spoken by the maestro to his student. When he speaks of *posture, resonance,* or *measures,* he uses the vocabulary of formal voice training. But it soon becomes apparent that he is speaking of more than singing. The first three lines might refer only to singing, but the word *compromise* hints at something more. The words begin to take on added connotations at the end of the third line when Wagoner transforms the expected cliché *best foot forward* into "best face forward" and immediately follows this with the loaded phrase "willful hands." As the poem progresses, we begin to understand that he is referring to an attitude toward art, life, and finally death. The content of the poem deals with the transforming of breath into song, the ironic "inspiring and expiring moments" of line11. The poem's form echoes this by alternating long and short lines. He models the transformation of prose into poetry, reminding us of both poetry and death with the words "final end-stopped movement." We also see the swift movement of the music director's hands as he signals the end of the song. Although the poem does not rhyme, it does follow its own advice to "Keep time." Perhaps he chooses not to rhyme because the singer makes his own song and does not have a script to follow, only instructions about moderation. Most of the sentences are long and complex. This too models the breathing of a singer, but it also emphasizes by contrast the one short sentence of the poem: "Take care to be heard." The effect is like a musical staccato, each one-syllable word separate and clipped. The emphasis on singing with constant vigilance about the audience may be ironic. If the poem is about life, it is about a life lived in public, even in the most private of moments. It is about a life constantly being evaluated. One who is not careful about how he presents himself to others is "asking for it." Do students feel that this is realistic advice about how to live? Or is Wagoner's persona limited by an overly conforming worldview? Is he saying that art requires walking this fine line of moderation, a constant adjustment that finds ease and beauty in order?

THEODORE ROETHKE
The Waking (p. 692)

To attempt an analysis of Theodore Roethke's villanelle "The Waking" is to risk a reduction that goes against its paradoxical message. From its first line, the poem is deliberately indeterminate, resisting the *knowing* that it speaks against. If we read the poem by feeling it, letting it take us where we "have to go," we sense that we understand it in some mystical way. Yet the poem is written in one of the most structured of closed forms, its meter and rhyme scheme precisely determined. What seems free and effortless depends upon great care in construction, revealing knowledge of prosody that stands in opposition to the poem's apparent message. The content is equally mysterious. What does the first phrase actually mean? Does he wake *in order* to sleep? Or rather than waking to the verbal form, the infinitive *to sleep*, does he awaken to some entity that he labels *sleep*, the noun? The first possibility implies that the waking life is a sort of sleepwalking state that he must rise and take part in. Feeling takes precedence, even in the world of daylight, and he goes through life as a joyful zombie. The second possibility implies that he has come to realize something about sleep, maybe about death. He blesses the "Ground" and speaks of the "lowly worm."

For most readers, these images carry connotations of the grave. He is slowly coming to realize the reality of it. He doesn't have a map, doesn't know exactly which way to go, but that's okay. Perhaps the speaker of the poem is on the edge of dying. The first line of the quatrain that ends the villanelle hints that he is ill, recovering from a sickness or a hangover that makes him shake. Roethke was

103

hospitalized several times for alcoholism and mental illness, and he saw such breakdowns as opportunities to gain spiritual insight. He felt a bond with other visionary poets who struggled with the line between reality and mysticism. This poem may reflect the influence of Dylan Thomas, who died in 1953, the same year "The Waking" was published. Thomas's famous villanelle "Do Not Go Gentle into That Good Night" (p. 1533 in the "Confronting Mortality" chapter) addresses his father as the older man is on his deathbed. Perhaps when Roethke says that we must "learn by going where to go" he answers those who speak to the dying. We might question the identity of the person he directly addresses by the pronoun *you* in lines 7 and 14. The word *lovely* in the last line of the fifth tercet makes us think that he may speak to a woman, but the word could refer to the beauty of the experience of being alive — in the "lively air" — before "Great Nature" has her way.

One of the hallmarks of lyric poetry is repetition and echo. Rhyme is most familiar, but assonance, consonance, alliteration, rhythm and meter, even the repetition of whole lines or groups of lines that we find in refrains, play a part in our response to poetry. Often the effect is subliminal. Roethke's repetition of lines, in keeping with the rules for writing a villanelle, are easy to recognize, especially when the form has been explained. They are especially effective in a poem like "The Waking" because they help us find our way in a circling motion that seems to drift in and out of sleep. We replay the action as we do the events of a dream that we try to reenter in the state between sleep and waking. We do not know the way, so the repetitions help us learn as we go. But echoes also occur in other ways. Again according to the conventions of the villanelle, the meter repeats the rhythms of iambic pentameter and the rhyme is limited to the two echoes of the long *o* and the *r* sounds. Roethke departs from this rhyme a bit, with near rhymes allowing slight differences. More subtle is his use of alliteration, the *sl* sounds of the beginning line or the *f*s of the second; his assonance, such as the repetition of the *ee* sounds of *sleep*, *feel*, and *fear*; or the consonance of *lively* and *lovely*. All of the echoes work together with the content to produce a sense of unity between inner and outer realities, sleep and waking, death and life.

The paradoxes of Roethke's poem play into this unity as well. Opposite meanings intertwine in the same line. The poem violates logic by equivocation and vague, undefined terms. We wouldn't stand for such lack of cogency in an argument. But Roethke's poem makes the point that intuition may be a higher sort of learning. Like the devices of the poem, the lessons of life and death may come to us in subliminal ways, through our physical senses. Analysis may discover the patterns underneath, but we respond to them even before logic enters the picture. When Roethke breaks the pattern of the villanelle, the contrast makes us pay attention, especially since he does it to address someone he calls "you" and links with the narrator "me." Although this unseen listener to the dramatic monologue may not be the reader, the effect of this direct address, along with his earlier use of the pronoun *we*, personalizes the poem, lessens the distance. Consequently, when he urges us to learn as we go, most readers will feel that we should at least consider his advice.

Writers who let the content lead them along, writing by enjambment and coming back later to tinker with the finished freewrite, will respond to Roethke's suggestions about learning. Others, perhaps those who like to write from a preplanned outline, will raise issues about the practicality of learning by doing. Some might contend that we can follow the paths blazed by those who have gone before, rather than fumbling in a half-sleep to find our way alone. The answer might be to point out that Roethke does not assume himself to be alone; he even asks his listener which of "those so close beside me" he or she is. This sort of learning can take place in a college course, but it requires a spirit of inquiry and a tolerance for ambiguity. Anyone who gets hooked on the joy of the chase in the course of research or who has found insights in the midst of brainstorming or who has written her way into uncharted territory knows the sort of creative learning that Roethke seems to advocate. For teachers, it requires giving students a great deal of responsibility for their own learning and helping them find the courage to think for themselves, making the assumption that they are willing and able to make. Even then, we may owe them the tools of logic and convention. After all, it is within a highly formal, intellectually ordered structure that Roethke suggests intuitive learning.

When he calls on "Great Nature" in the fifth tercet, Roethke seems to imply that there is a higher power that controls human life and death, especially death. He uses capital letters in two other places aside from the beginnings of lines, in the apostrophe "God bless the Ground!" in line 8 and when he says "Light takes the Tree" in line 10. Both nouns refer to nature but seem to have religious significance. The ground may have multiple meanings, since it could refer to the earth beneath our feet as we walk, the grave we are going toward, or the ground of being that is connected with God. The tree may also be a link to nature. For Roethke, growing things have great spiritual significance. Both the form and the content of "The Waking" imply that there is a natural oneness between life and death at the point when we intuitively let it be.

Although Theodore Roethke's "The Waking" is more formal in structure than David Wagoner's "The Singing Lesson," the tone and content of Roethke's villanelle make it seem freer than Wagoner's less traditionally formal poem. Roethke's narrator accepts the intuitive path toward the process of living and dying. Wagoner's narrator seeks to achieve equilibrium through a carefully maintained set of instructions for performing life and death in an artful way that will be clear and approved. Both are aware of the paradox involved. Both poets instruct. Roethke is less precise but brings his "student" into the awareness of the journey, advising him or her to "take the lively air" and to learn by going. The narrators of the two poems instruct in different ways. Wagoner's stays out of it, at least explicitly, speaking directly to an audience addressed in second person. He may intend to maintain his distance as an instructor, inadvertently slipping into the ironic personal revelations as his monologue takes its course. He may, in fact, be addressing himself. Roethke's narrator, on the other hand, takes the reader by the hand by including both first- and second-person pronouns, sometimes even referring to "we." Our students might consider the rhetorical effects of finding common ground with the reader, as Roethke literally seems to do, as opposed to presenting directives, even symbolically and metaphorically rich ones like Wagoner's.

ELIZABETH BISHOP

One Art (p. 694)

The editors of the selected personal correspondence of Elizabeth Bishop gave their 1994 publication the title *One Art: Letters.* The title is borrowed from the villanelle that she wrote in the 1970s, not long before her death, a text that possibly struck someone as epitomizing her experience of life. Bishop certainly knew about losing. Her father died when she was eight months old, and her mother was lost to her soon after through her institutionalization for mental illness. A lesbian in a time when it was difficult to be open about this in the United States, she lived happily with another woman in Brazil for around fifteen years. But that woman committed suicide, as did another lover. Unlike her contemporaries Robert Lowell or Theodore Roethke, Bishop reveals little of her personal life in her poetry. Although "One Art" is more autobiographical than most of her work, she maintains her distance with wry understatement, choosing not to be openly confessional. A perfectionist, her poems are precisely crafted, but not usually as formal in structure or as dependent upon rhyme as the villanelle. She said at one point early in her career that her aim as a poet was "to say the most difficult things and to be funny as possible." In life she refused to allow anyone to see her take herself too seriously, though she took her work so seriously that her output was smaller than it might have been. She held poems back from publication as she searched for the exact word to express an idea or convey an image. Donald E. Stanford points out in a book review in the Winter 1994 *Sewanee Review* that Bishop does not usually raise political or social issues in her poetry. "She was an artist, not a propagandist," he says. Nevertheless, critical readings will undoubtedly reveal issues for our classes to discuss.

With its five tercets and final quatrain, "One Art" has the structure of a villanelle, and the rhyme scheme follows its traditional conventions. But like much of Elizabeth Bishop's poetry, its tone is conversational and its rhythm departs from the strict iambic pentameter. Bishop also varies the refrain, subtly changing each statement about the existence of "disaster" so that we move gradually and ironically from the denial of the first tercet to the forced admission in the final quatrain that losing "may" affect her after all — "*Write* it!" the voice orders in parentheses. Her tone begins with dismissive bravado, as the narrator proposes to teach her audience the proper way of losing. The tone grows progressively more serious and ironic as the losses become greater, though the sardonic humor remains. By the end of the poem, she is becoming honest about her grief at losing the person addressed, possibly to death, though she still admits only to the appearance rather than the reality of disaster.

We can use autobiography and the motifs that recur in Elizabeth Bishop's poetry to understand some of the losses. The loss of a mother's watch in line 10 reminds us that Bishop may have had only mementos of a mother hospitalized when she was five and separated from her until her death when Bishop was at Vassar. The loss of houses, important in her poetry, also may symbolize the loss of mother or of other loved women. The loss of a continent may recall her loss of Lota de Macedo Soares, the Brazilian woman with whom she shared a home in South America. Part of the practice for losing as detailed in the third stanza seems to require that we give up our dreams for relationships, homes, and "where it was [we] meant / to travel." As a woman who traveled the world and who had lost houses and people, Bishop knows that this renunciation is tougher than she pretends. We might accept her advice if we desperately wish to protect ourselves from the losses that come with living and loving, but the issue can be raised that we would lose even more.

Coming at the end, the rhetorically sound spot for the most important example, we are startled to hear the sudden inclusion of the person addressed — "you" — within the catalog of lost items. The emotion grows stronger. Pain? Anger? Affection, certainly. We try to picture the person who has been lost and wonder if she has simply left or if she has died. Again, we might recall the mother who unintentionally abandoned her daughter as she battled her own demons in the asylum or the lovers who abandoned the poet through their suicides. Her denial that either is a disaster would be ironic. Many readers find the break from the villanelle form dramatic as it allows the voice of the not so gentle muse to intrude. The effect is consistent with Elizabeth Bishop's method. She says the difficult things, but she remains *funny* in her own acerbic way. In recent years, poetry therapy has become a psychological tool. To call what Bishop does therapy would be to oversimplify. Still, the voice of reality that forces her narrator to admit her denial in spite of her inherent tendency to protect herself is the voice of health and honesty.

Elizabeth Bishop in "One Art" and Theodore Roethke in "The Waking" both vary the villanelle form somewhat to fit their twentieth-century agendas. Bishop moves away from the conventions more dramatically than Roethke, for whom the form and content of the villanelle intertwine to enhance each other. Bishop resists the form as she resists the admission of grief. For both, the repetitions have the effect of a mantra or an obsessive chant as the narrators work out their feelings about a serious issue by addressing an unseen party. Although both David Wagoner in "The Singing Lesson" and Elizabeth Bishop in "One Art" assume the pose of teaching a lesson, both seem to be speaking as much to themselves as to the audience. Both show irony, as well, since the speakers reveal their own attempts to carry out the programs they advise to be less than perfect, perhaps achieved at great cost. Both seem in rigid denial as they protect themselves from the revelation of loss or vulnerability, either to others or themselves. Wagoner's narrator speaks to an implied listener in a dramatic monologue, but his own metaphorical revelations are more important to himself and the poem than is any reaction from the student he presumably addresses. Like many teachers, he talks at rather than to the student, beginning with the content of the course but wandering off into his own concerns. Roethke is more intimate, practically throwing back the covers to allow us to wake up with him. The person he addresses may be a particular individual, male or female, living or dead, but

. readers are allowed to feel that it may be they he invites to go with him. Bishop's narrator seems at first to be more like Wagoner's didactic music teacher, beginning with the quotidian and then moving to the poetic. But in Bishop's final stanza, we suddenly realize that the person addressed is not a student but an intimate who has been lost. Logically, we can assume that if she is lost the person is not in the room with the narrator. We know that the poet Elizabeth Bishop was a prolific letter writer, once admitting that given time she'd do nothing else. Perhaps she is writing a letter to her unseen audience, speaking to herself within parentheses as she briefly recalls her love and then orders herself to write.

NARRATORS GIVING ADVICE (p. 696)

JONATHAN SWIFT
A Modest Proposal (p. 696)

From its root meaning of "a dish of mixed fruits," the term *satire* describes a text in which humor and criticism mix in a way that is sometimes gentle, sometimes biting. The satirist walks a fine line. Without the humor and the unexpected twist of irony, satire becomes abusive invective or mournful jeremiad. Rather than persuading its audience to seek solutions, invective tends to make us defensive. When the humorous barbs are intended to hurt someone, to vent bad humor, or to show off, we might characterize them as sarcasm rather than satire. Satire seeks to teach in an indirect manner that causes its readers to reach their own conclusions about the severity of a problem. The satirist uses wit to open our eyes to abuses and to subvert social and political institutions that need changing. Satire is less a genre than a tone that can occur in virtually any mode of human speech or writing: poetry, prose, drama, fiction, or nonfiction. College students have most probably encountered it in comedy routines or in movies and television shows. Because it depends upon the audience's understanding of political and social situations that are specific to a certain time and place, satire can become quickly dated and may require some historical or cultural orientation. British humor is often lost on Americans, for example, and jokes in other languages seldom translate well into English for similar reasons. Some of Jonathan Swift's satire — some of the mock travel tale *Gulliver's Travels*, for example — is inaccessible to most current readers because the individuals and situations that inspired the humor are long dead. "A Modest Proposal" continues to find an audience, however. We get Swift's point that what is done to oppressed peoples is as cruel and unfeeling as the ironic suggestion that those in power eat the children of the poor. That we recognize this so readily may not be a good sign. Enough prejudice still exists against the poor to make Swift's argument meaningful, though most readers will insist that *we* are not oppressors. Although Ireland is no longer wracked by the sort of starvation and deprivation that existed in the eighteenth and nineteenth centuries, large groups of people in the Third World are in great need. Can students imagine this argument applied to people in inner-city slum neighborhoods, to illegal immigrants, or to others who are said to place a burden on the welfare system? Could we as easily substitute homeless people or drug addicts or poor southern rednecks? How different is this proposal, which we recognize as ridiculous, from attempts in modern history to find "final solutions" to deal with minorities through concentration camps, "ethnic cleansing," and other forms of genocide? At the time of Swift's writing in 1729, the institution of African slavery was being developed in the Americas, with its worst abuses still a century away. Native Americans were already being displaced, eventually to end up on lands that would provide little sustenance, leading to the starvation and squalid living conditions that still exist on some reservations. It isn't surprising to find the narrator crediting an American with the idea of consuming the young of an oppressed people.

Swift's narrator in "A Modest Proposal" claims that everyone involved with the problem of poverty in Ireland would benefit from an organized program that paid mothers to suckle their young for a year and then sell them to be used as food. He begins his argument by presenting the problem in a reasonable and compassionate tone, calling upon his readers to consider the pathetic state of the children of the Irish poor. He appeals not only to pity but to the accompanying fear of crime and treason. He says that he wants to provide for the children, to prevent begging, even to prevent abortion. He logically outlines his program for alleviating poverty, giving statistics, citing medical studies, providing specific cost assessments, and suggesting procedures by which his plan may be carried out. In paragraph 29, he catalogs the benefits of his plan and maintains its superiority over other possible solutions to the problem. He lends a sense of balance to his argument by his qualification that the eating of older children would not be practical, since the boys are likely to be tough and the girls would be lost as breeders. What's more, as he points out in paragraph 17, this would not be cost effective and there might be objections that this "a little border[s] upon cruelty; which, I confess, has always been with me the strongest objection against any project, how well soever intended." He further assures the reader of his objectivity in his closing sentence, explaining that he does not stand to gain from his own proposal, since he has no children to sell and does not anticipate having any in the future. His argument is thus a masterful mix of logos, pathos, and ethos. It might be a useful exercise to divide the argument into sections and have students find other such examples of well-developed rhetoric. The warrants underlying his argument assume that his readers will want to find a compassionate solution to poverty, but the point of the satire is that he proposes this solution as a compassionate one. We may have students specifically explore the assumptions he makes about the poor: for example, the assumption that they will welcome the chance to make a few shillings by selling their babies. The implied warrant is that the poor are not really capable of loving their children. But as we look at the argument as satire, we might shift to his warrants about the rich. He explicitly states at one point that since landlords already devour the parents they should have the first chance to eat the children. Underlying the whole text is the warrant that compassion is not being exercised in England's treatment of Ireland's poor, that the current policies essentially devour the lives of these downtrodden people for selfish reasons.

"A Modest Proposal" is highly ironic. Broadly defined, irony refers to the recognition of a reality that differs from the appearance presented; it depends upon opposition and double meaning. Verbal irony is perceived when the actual words used are opposed to the intended meaning. Dramatic irony occurs when an opposition exists between the words of a character and the different reality recognized by the audience. Situational irony is more difficult to define, though we recognize it when we encounter it. Events occur in a way that contrasts with what might usually be expected to happen, but there is an appropriately absurd quality to the divergence that provokes a grim smile. Swift's readers may begin to recognize irony when the narrator refers to human mothers as "dams" and "breeders." Although he seems to care about the plight of the poor, he slips into the terminology of a livestock dealer. The ironic tone becomes obvious, of course, when he relates the claim of his American friend that children are delicious. Even this outrageous proposition is delivered in a reasonable, rhetorically sound tone. It is our recognition of this contrast between the appearance of logic and the reality of cannibalism that produces the ironic response. The verbal irony is sustained throughout the text, since most readers understand that the author, Jonathan Swift, means just the opposite of what his narrator says. His purpose is to make his contemporaries see that political and social policies are figuratively eating up the people of Ireland and that no one seems to have compassion for them. A case can be made for dramatic irony if we look at the narrator as a man who thinks he is making a reasonable argument but does not realize that his underlying warrants are horrifying and obscene. For intelligent readers of good will who recognized Swift's ironic tone, "A Modest Proposal" must have been profoundly moving in its time. Actually, some readers believed that Swift was serious in his proposal and were outraged by the essay. Even readers who understand his purposes may think his images of flaying and otherwise abusing children are unwarranted. History shows that abuses continued in Ireland long after 1729. Still, because they can be extrapolated to other situations in which the problems of society are being mishandled, Jonathan Swift's satires have long outlasted his sermons as an Anglican dean. They provoke readers to think for themselves in opposition to the surface meaning of the text.

DANIEL OROZCO

Orientation (p. 703)

Fans of Scott Adams's comic strip "Dilbert" will recognize the small, weird world of cubicles in Daniel Orozco's short story "Orientation." You might want to take advantage of this intertextuality by introducing Orozco's story with a few representative clippings of Dilbert's difficulties in the workplace, following the lead of the readers of the thousand or so newspapers that carry the comic strip daily. The strip hits close enough to reality to appear on doors and offices all over the country — even the world — and its creator makes a fortune from the use of the characters in corporate training programs. No one believes that he or she is like the pointy-haired boss who fakes any understanding about what the company really does, but readers always feel they have worked for him. Nothing in Dilbert's world is just or fair; in fact, the one thing that he can count on is the arbitrary rule of the absurd. He can't expect his coworkers to work as a team or to provide support. One character warns, "I can please only one person per day. Today is not your day. Tomorrow's not looking good either." Incompetence is to be expected. "I love deadlines," a worker says. "I especially love the swooshing sound they make as they go flying by." One law of work maintains, "Anyone can do any amount of work provided it isn't the work he/she is supposed to be doing." Clichés are transformed to express the irony of the corporate hierarchy: "To err is human, to forgive is not our policy." False religions abound, and a devil dressed in a red suit and carrying a large spoon in lieu of a pitchfork shows up at times when naive workers dare to hope for fairness or recognition. Students who have been operating under the delusion that the completion of their formal education will lead to autonomy and automatic success may miss some of the irony in both Adams and Orozco. But they may recognize the traits of human nature that tend to come out when people feel that they are powerless or that the work they do has little meaning. We might have students look back at Marge Piercy's poem "To be of use" (p. 12 in Chapter 1)and consider the contrast between the total immersion in work that she describes and the arbitrary routines of Orozco's "Orientation" and Adams's "Dilbert." Have they considered the importance of *meaningful* work in their future plans?

Though most students have not been office workers, some may have gone through similar orientations at school or at work. At community colleges and at many regional branches of state university systems, nontraditional students may be coming to college because they do not find their work meaningful and want a more satisfying way to make a living. They may be trying to escape the sort of rigid atmosphere that the story reveals. The language of the narrator in Daniel Orozco's story is as impersonal as the computerized voice mail the worker will be required to use, but he manages to get the office gossip through nevertheless. He advises hypocrisy and noninvolvement rather than the sort of joyful or determined effort Marge Piercy's poem celebrates. But the details of Orozco's story exaggerate absurdly while his narrator delivers the monologue in short sentences in a deadpan tone. This discrepancy and the contrast between the narrator's recitation of the rules of the corporate machine and his matter-of-fact hints at bizarre, idiosyncratic tragedies among the workers produce the same sort of irony we see in "Dilbert." The office gets more unusual as the orientation proceeds. Office crushes are elaborately unrequited, one worker is a serial killer, another has stigmata and the curse of prophecy, one seems to be bulimic and emotionally haggard, another has an autistic child, and a male worker lurks in the ladies' room. But the new employee is admonished not to let on that he/she knows of these things, though the narrator spills it all. Because he does not seem to draw the line between the details of the work situation and the dramatic specifics of his coworkers' lives, and because he coolly passes along the most intimate secrets to a total stranger, the narrator reveals his own character. Readers may detect passive aggression in his seemingly unemotional narrative. But perhaps he simply does not care, has become a cog in the machine. It is interesting that the beautiful view he presents to the new employee is limited, its natural elements hemmed in by other buildings that literally reflect the deadly corporate routine. The order of the narrator's statements matter. The aberrations of the office staff get progressively more bizarre, though his tone does not change. Interwoven with the orientation of the new worker to the rules, revelations of the workers' strange behavior increase the reader's sense of irony.

Both Jonathan Swift's "A Modest Proposal" and Daniel Orozco's "Orient-ation" feature unreliable narrators who pronounce the most horrific facts in a reasonable and logical tone. Swift's proposal of cannibalism comes fairly early in the argument, and he focuses on supporting it, but Orozco's revelations about his coworkers' troubles build gradually, interwoven with what purports to be his true agenda of orienting the new employee to the job itself. Of course, it is altogether possible that the narrator is pulling the leg of the new employee and that the other workers are perfectly normal people. New doctors in a medical clinic familiar to this writer were routinely hazed. They would receive charts for bogus patients with names like "Duck, Donald," whose symptoms became more and more incredible ("webbed phalanges, unusually fluffy epidermal formations") until the intern caught on. Readers may raise issues about whether the size of the audience assumed by each narrator makes a difference. Swift's mock argumentative essay follows the conventions of the genre it imitates, aiming for a balanced tone and seeking to appeal to the intellect and to the emotions of its audience. Orozco's chatty narrator speaks in a more informal setting. We can imagine him ticking off the points he is supposed to make as he goes through the guidelines for orienting a new worker. But the gossip slips in, much as digs against Jews or Americans do as Swift's narrator speaks. The narrators seem much alike, and we can imagine Swift's social reformer as the promoter of office morale. Perhaps he would propose that since their personal emotions lead to so many problems, all office workers should undergo lobotomies and spend their nights in suspended animation in their cubicles in space suits that preclude the need to provide restrooms at all.

PAM HOUSTON
How to Talk to a Hunter (p. 708)

Pam Houston revels in having outdoor adventures and writing about them. After graduating from Denison University in Ohio, she rode across Canada on a bicycle, then wound up in the western United States, where she supported herself with odd jobs and worked on her doctorate at the University of Utah. But she also writes in her nonfiction essays about meandering through water lilies and hippos in Botswana, going whitewater rafting through Cataract Canyon and Satan's Gut on the Colorado River, and galloping horses through wide, open fields. She dismisses her bravery: "You think I spent three summers leading hunters through

Alaska because I like watching guys like David Duke shoot sheep? No. It was because if I didn't go with my boyfriend, somebody else would. I wanted to win." This may be true, but does not explain a continuing way of life. Naive readers may want her to get the man, but more experienced readers may root for the woman herself, wanting her to claim her independence. Her emphasis is interesting in this context. It is less the acceptance of the man than the competition with the other woman that is foregrounded in her disclaimer. She wants to *win*. She also takes the opportunity to make a political statement with her dig at former Ku Klux Klan member–turned–Republican David Duke. A similar subtext turns up early in the story "How to Talk to a Hunter" when she relates the questions her female protagonist, addressed in the second-person "you," avoids asking herself and simultaneously comments on her perplexity about why anyone would like country music or the Republican party. Houston implies that she knows her way of life is not politically correct, and her texts raise their own contradictory issues. We might consider the differences between the environmental movement that many students find appealing and the conservation movement dear to hunters. These discourses can be as different as the rhetoric of Greenpeace and that of the National Rifle Association. If she is a graduate student like the writer, the woman is saturated with the urge toward critical thinking that demands that she eschew the tendency to see in black and white. The hunter lives in a different world, one where the truisms are those of country music, political conservatism, and physical exploits. Do readers feel that Pam Houston's narrator is struggling with the issues raised by these differences and what they mean to her as a woman? Can we be sure that the hunter is not also having mixed feelings?

The narrator is intelligent, educated, and liberal to the extent that she knows she should be asking questions and raising issues. She is sensual, honest with herself, reluctantly romantic. She hears the voices of reason but decides not to heed them. Several voices are heard in the story: the narrator, her female friend, her male friend, words from her education and reading. We hear the "coyote woman" on the answering machine, and we are told of what the narrator's lover, the hunter, does and does not say. The words of her friends and her education enter into dialogue with the narrator and the reader, like a Greek chorus that helps us define and elaborate upon the ambiguous interchanges between herself and her lover. The story, as its title implies, is about communication, about what lies underneath the surface of what is said between these lovers from different discourses. Because we are allowed to overhear her dialogue, readers respect her intelligence, but some may end up feeling that she doesn't make much use of it. We may question whether she is a dynamic character who changes in the course of the story by finally "letting go of fear" or whether she allows herself to be lulled out of language and self-determination by his "humming in [her] ear." Maybe both things happen. Perhaps she accepts the relationship as temporary and understands that this is okay, that she does not need monogamy or commitment. Whether or not the story engages in gender stereotypes begs the question of, Which stereotypes? Certainly the hunter comes across as a typical American *type*, the survivalist mountain man out to prove his masculinity by conquering the wilderness and as many women as he can. And true to the usual assumptions, it is the woman who desires commitment. Other stereotypes tag men as rational and women as irrational, however. A case might be made that the female narrator engages in quite a bit of rationality; she just decides to discard it. We may also want to question the reliability of the narrator. Does she make unwarranted assumptions about her lover's infidelity and reluctance to commit? We have no way of knowing, since we have only her interpretations. Student writers might find a more pertinent issue by exploring the animal imagery in Pam Houston's story. She begins by juxtaposing her own skin (or the skin of the woman she addresses as "you") with the hide of a moose the man has carried "soaking wet and heavier than a dead man, across the tundra." She ends with the howl of the dog accompanying her musings during or just after sex. Her rival has the last name Coyote. Are the women in this story stereotyped as the *hunted*? For women who read the story, the narrator's use of the second-person pronoun is effective, bringing the reader into the story as if she were describing a universal — or at least a culturally common — story about the communication between men and women. Since the struggle between sexual desire and rationality is an experience familiar to many readers, we may find ourselves nodding our heads. Yes, this is what it's like, we think. The word *talk* in the story's title is echoed throughout. The narrator talks to "you," perhaps to herself. But she also talks about talking and not talking. She reads the syntax of his speech for gaps and oppositions. She notes his ambiguity — "I feel exactly the same way" — in response to her declaration of love, and she echoes it later when he admires her body. We might have students note all the instances when the narrator engages in metalanguage, talking about talk or about the disjunction between what is said and what she believes is meant. She tells us what questions she does *not* ask. Overall, she tends to approach love as a text to be subjected to critical analysis. A few romantic readers may approve the final lovemaking as a happy ending. Others will argue that the howl of the dog and the acknowledgment of the shortness of the days project a mournful feeling. Are we meant to see her as winning? Or does she give up the fight?

Although both Daniel Orozco's "Orientation" and Pam Houston's "How to Talk to a Hunter" use humor, Houston's narrator sardonically recognizes the irony of her situation, deliberately creating the humor at her own expense. Orozco's narrator seems oblivious to the humor. The irony lies in the recognition of the audience that his tone and his content do not match. Some readers cannot get past the horror of Jonathan Swift's subject matter in "A Modest Proposal" far enough to perceive any humor in it. But others find it humorous for the same reasons we find "Orientation" grimly funny. Irony — the unknowing discrepancy between the words and the reality or the conventions and their unexpected negation — can be intellectually satisfying in a way that seems so apt that we must smile. The distance of the narrators from their stories constitutes the main difference among the three narratives in this cluster. Houston's narrator focuses upon her own situation, though she does imply that it has some universality by using the pronoun *you*. Orozco's narrator does not directly tell us about himself, focusing instead on his coworkers. Swift maintains the most distance of all, proposing a solution to a sociopolitical issue that ostensibly has little to do with him; he mentions his own situation only to convince us that he is a disinterested party. Each story is highly ironic. Although we have touched on the distinction among types of irony in the teaching suggestions for this cluster, we might have students look up definitions in handbooks of literature or other sources before characterizing the irony of the narratives as verbal, dramatic, or situational.

Loving

TRUE LOVE (p. 715)

WILLIAM SHAKESPEARE

Let me not to the marriage of true minds (p. 716)

Shakespeare's Sonnet 116 seems at first to celebrate the enduring qualities of love between husband and wife. It is, in fact, often recited at wedding ceremonies, an appropriate setting for a poem whose first lines echo the marriage vows in *The Book of Common Prayer*. It is written in one of the most structured of forms, in what has come to be known as the Shakespearean sonnet, though Shakespeare was not the first to use it. Although this poem was published — probably without his permission — as part of a sequence of 154 sonnets in 1609, it may have been written earlier. In 1598, a writer mentioned Shakespeare's "sugared sonnets among his private friends"; imitating and transforming the conventions of the Italian sonnets of Petrarch had become a popular pastime in literary and court circles of the late 1500s. Petrarchan sonnets held strictly to conceits describing unrequited love for an idealized woman leading ultimately to religious transcendence. English writers often toyed with these conventions, however, and Shakespeare inverted conventions and used the poems for wordplay and argumentation about the nature of love and change — and about rhetoric and writing as well.

The form of the Shakespearean sonnet keeps the fourteen lines of the Italian sonnet, but its three quatrains followed by a final couplet allow the poet to form an argument that reaches its conclusion in the last two lines. Predominately iambic pentameter, each line follows the patterns of normal English speech and therefore has a natural ring to its audience, while the *abab cdcd efef gg* rhyme scheme provides a satisfying pattern and sense of closure. However, a closer look at this poem, which seems to proclaim constancy, reveals a series of oppositions that challenge an easy interpretation based on surface sound and sense. Within its closed form, this sonnet rocks back and forth with irregular meter, double meanings, puns, and indeterminate negations. Does the speaker mean to say in the opening lines, "Hold my tongue when the priest asks if anyone knows any impediment that would prevent the marriage," or that he is unwilling to concede that such impediments exist, or that they actually don't exist? Is this a traditional marriage ceremony, a platonic marriage of minds, or — since this sonnet is in the part of the sequence in which most poems are addressed to a man — an argument about a homoerotic relationship? What sort of logic is implied in the second line: . . . *Love is not love?* Even though the enjambment leads to a qualification, a sense of paradox remains. Furthermore, each sentence contains a negative or an absence: *Not, not, remove, no, never, unknown, not, not, never,* and *no* continue to pile up oppositions. Contrasted with this emptiness of *not-love,* the word *impediment* seems unusually solid, and the conventional enemy Time is personified as an inexorable automaton that mows down everything within his *compass,* recalling the circling hands of a clock that signal human aging. Love, on the other hand, receives a negative personification — is defined as a *not-fool* — and seems peculiarly distant and impersonal. The only positive metaphors for love in the poem are linked closely to their opposites: The solitary channel marker, while not shaken, merely *looks on,* and the guiding star cannot really be known.

Having conceded the poem's rhetorical ambiguity, most readers would still undoubtedly be pleased to have such enduring love proclaimed to them. The last lines seem to indicate, however, that the speaker may be defining true love rather than declaring it, since he makes it explicit that he is offering a scientific or rhetorical proof. There's a logical conundrum implied in the words *I never writ.* Obviously, some *I* wrote these lines, but perhaps the speaker is a persona or mask that the poet assumes, and this is the sort of equivocation we often see characters use in his dramas. And the closing line may have either a compound subject or a compound predicate. That is, the poet may mean to say that if his argument is fallacious then *no man* has ever fallen in love; or that he, the poet, never loved a man; or that he never loved *no man* (woman).

Line 12 projects arguably the most powerful image of the poem. Juxtaposed with images of time and of sea voyages, the image of a love that lasts until *the edge of doom* reminds us that we are reading a text written when oceans and continents were being explored and time was being measured in ways never accomplished before. Enduring to the end of the world and going to the ends of the earth may both be implied in such a metaphor, but looking over the edge of either reveals nothingness. Inverting the argument that lovers should seize the day while beauty and youth allow love to flourish, Shakespeare seems to say that love is more lasting than this, and many readers of romance novels and fairy tales will agree without further question. Although we may still agree that this is a beautiful definition of love after reading it more critically, however, we should hold the poet to his challenge in the last lines to examine his evidence. He may be saying that such love does not really exist.

ANNE BRADSTREET

To My Dear and Loving Husband (p. 717)

As the wife of the governor and the mother of eight children in the Puritan Massachusetts Bay Colony of the 1640s, Anne Dudley Bradstreet wrote at a time when few women were literate, much less published poets. Most women in colonial America would have been unable to read what Bradstreet had written, even if her work had been published there. However, she had received a good education in England, as the daughter of a well-connected Puritan family. When a male relative had a number of her poems published in London, in a collection called *The Tenth Muse Lately Sprung Up in America*, she found a wide audience. After her death, her polished versions of these poems, along with several new ones, appeared in *Several Poems Compiled with Great Variety of Wit and Learning, Full of Delight*. The book titles, neither chosen by the poet herself, would be worth analyzing: the first offering a lively identification of gender coupled with classical and poetic allusion, and the second a gender-neutral evaluation or advertisement of the texts themselves.

Bradstreet's poetry hints that some Puritans were not as harsh as law codes and sermons sometimes indicate. Although it would be considered a sin to place physical love and other pleasures of the earth above God, many members of Christian communities saw such things as gifts from God, even as earthly patterns of spiritual truths. The biblical Song of Solomon, for example, with its sensual imagery was considered to be an allegory of Christ the bridegroom and the church, his spiritual bride. In "To My Dear and Loving Husband," the poet uses less explicitly passionate, but similar, imagery. Her poem opens with the image of two being one, alluding to the biblical assertion that marriage causes a man and woman to become *one flesh*. References to gold and riches of the East recall the language of Psalms and Proverbs in praise of God's wisdom, as well as the Song of Solomon's more erotic images. Bradstreet ends her poem with a prayer that her husband be rewarded for his love toward her, and that their earthly love be replicated in some way in the afterlife.

Although the sentiments may seem like naive clichés to current readers, there's no reason to believe they were not deeply felt. As a devout woman, Bradstreet gains permission to be passionate within the bounds of religion and marriage, and the poem has the ring of freely given devotion to her husband, as if he were God. We can be confident that she is not compelled to write by any outside force, since she is doing something unusual by composing poetry as a woman in a woman's voice. In the context of her given situation, she seems to have an independent identity, in spite of her poem's theme of oneness. In fact, Bradstreet was often left alone to manage her household, since her husband's duties took him away for long periods of time, and Massachusetts was a true frontier, filled with physical hardship and danger. The universal danger of two becoming one, of course, is that the submissive partner may become submerged in the more dominant personality, and thus lose autonomy and personhood. Students will probably think of religious institutions and organizations that still encourage women to be subservient to men. They may also discuss why abused partners sometimes remain in destructive relationships, maintaining that they still love their abusers. Bradstreet's poem implies that her conjugal love and her husband's are mutual, though, even within the institutionalized patriarchy implied by its theme.

Like the poet's life, the poem is tightly structured and simple. Most of the poem is written in rhyming couplets of iambic pentameter, with only slight variation from the regular beat of five feet per line — that of one unstressed syllable followed by a stressed one. Interestingly, when the line ends with a stressed syllable, as happens here, we call the line masculine. The last two lines move away from this rhythm, however, giving them a tentative sound, especially coupled with the word *may* rather than *will* or *shall*. With one exception, the rhymes are true, and most of the diction is simple and direct, Bradstreet's plain speech in keeping with her Puritan life. As a Calvinist, she might be expected to speak of predestination and grace rather than *recompense*, but rewards and punishments figure prominently in sermons of the day, and therefore the religious parallels hold true as she tries to think of ways to repay her husband for his love. There seems to be much joy in this marriage; thus her use of the word *persevere* is puzzling. Perhaps Bradstreet means that love is predestined rather than earned, but a couple must also keep working at it, since faith without works is dead, according to the Puritan view of salvation.

Anne Bradstreet's religious vision of love is quite different from William Shakespeare's secular view in Sonnet 116, although both touch on the impossibility of ever doing enough for love. We can imagine Bradstreet agreeing with Shakespeare's contention that love endures "to the edge of doom" and that it is something very solid and sure that nevertheless cannot be fully expressed. Their major differences lie in the responses their speakers have experienced from the objects of their love and in the sources of their imagery. Shakespeare speaks to a changeable lover who doesn't seem to know what love is, and he can only grasp for negative definitions linked to images of science and logic. He works within the conventions of the poetic and philosophical theories of his day and subverts them at the same time. Bradstreet uses hyperbole to describe her husband's value to her, and she uses images of faith to develop themes of earthly and heavenly love. She accepts the social and religious conventions of Puritan culture and writes within that context. Ironically, whereas Bradstreet seems happier and more sincere, Shakespeare's complex imagery of Time's tyranny and Love's elusive persistence is more original and strikes us as more realistic and appropriate, perhaps because it is less sure of itself. Living only a generation or two apart, both poets lived in times when forever was a seldom-questioned reality. Bradstreet undoubtedly took for granted that Protestant theology was correct and that everyone would spend eternity in heaven or hell. Shakespeare and his contemporaries in Elizabethan England were much concerned with the ravages of time, possibly as a result of the queen's concern with aging. That love might not even last a lifetime, much less forever, is a frequent theme. At the same time, Shakespeare can mention doom in a sonnet and expect to be understood, and he can people his plays with ghosts; both concepts presume that life continues after death.

E. E. CUMMINGS

somewhere i have never travelled (p. 718)

An unusually structured and grammatical poem for e. e. cummings, "somewhere i have never travelled" nevertheless uses vocabulary in the poet's idiosyncratic way. As always, reading cummings involves breaking a code, which we can only touch upon in a short introduction. The experiments with syntax and

119

typography that characterize cummings's poems reflect cubism, futurism, and other modern visual art movements. He is also keenly aware of sound, and much of his diction depends upon the musical rhythms of American speech, the punning qualities of the language, and the often highly personal and carefully crafted connotations that he attaches to words. Words for him carry inherent positive or negative qualities, and the connotations of pathos and poetry are opposed to the denotations of logos and common sense. The specific and concrete tends to be privileged, whereas generalities and agreed-upon conclusions are considered deadly. He especially likes words like *alive, Spring, suddenly, young, new, yes, touch, small, frail, guess, dare, open, dream*, and others that symbolize positive movement and energy. He knows the meaning of *is*, contrasting its immediacy with the negative *knows* or *reasons*. "Who" is individual and thus good, but the rhetorical *which, how*, and *because* move into reductive explanations that he abhors. Although cummings was strongly grounded in literary theory and was influenced by Ezra Pound to choose his words carefully, he deliberately traveled the path of extreme individuality. Thematically, his poetry sets the courageous, joyfully spontaneous "anyone," the protagonist of another popular cummings poem, against the oppressive conformity of what he calls "mostpeople." Only this sort of human being is capable of an authentic emotion like love.

So when cummings begins this particular poem with the vague and negative "somewhere i have never travelled," he contrasts it with the positive "any experience," using two words that indicate specificity and spontaneous awareness. To be alive is a hyperbolic experience for which love is necessary. He explicitly compares his lover's touch to that of "Spring," the only capitalized word in the poem, contrasting with the lower-case *i* of the speaker, and his opening up is obviously positive. We should avoid the easy reading that would see the closing-up images of the third and fourth stanzas as negative, however. The word *death* in the lexicons of some poets might denote something negative, but for cummings it may indicate another positive living experience. Addressing his readers, cummings speculates in his introduction to *New Poems*, "if *mostpeople* were to be born twice they'd improbably call it dying . . . you and i wear the dangerous looseness of doom and find it becoming." Other paradoxes in the poem also are consistent with the poet's view of reality. The synesthesia of line 19, "the voice of your eyes is deeper than all roses," mixes several senses together, defeating reason. The whimsical personification of the rain as having hands in line 20 would be laughable if read literally rather than for a beauty that appeals somehow to our senses rather than to our intellects. And although "the power of your intense fragility" in line 14 sounds like an oxymoron, it implies that true power is not to be equated with force or strength. This fragility's "texture / compels me with the colour of its countries," the speaker says, calling upon synesthesia again to pull the reader out of logic and into the immediate world of the senses. The sensory — and sensual — images of the poem hint that love is located at the point of touch where senses intersect and that our understanding of it is essentially physical.

Whereas Shakespeare uses intellectual images in Sonnet 116 and Anne Bradstreet uses religious ones, e. e. cummings borrows the natural symbolism of the flower that stands for physical love but carries it beyond cliché. At times, the speaker is the tightly closed fist of a budding flower opened by the lover, who is compared to Spring, but he later speaks of the woman's "intense fragility" and its color, as if the lover herself were the rose. Cummings is closer in spirit to Bradstreet in the intensity of the two lovers becoming as if they were one person. Inexperienced readers may prefer Bradstreet's simplicity, and some students will relate to her faith. Other readers will delight in the word play of cummings, and some will hate his anti-intellectual ambiguity. Most students will probably find Shakespeare the most difficult of the three because his complexity is complicated by historical distance and differences in language. Although each poet uses the concept of a love that lasts forever, each poem reveals a different perspective on what *forever* might actually mean. Bradstreet's *forever* is in the hands of an omnipotent God who may honor the husband and wife in heaven if they persevere in their love for each other. Shakespeare's *forever* depends upon a lonely, one-sided constancy that endures in the face of loss, uncertainty, and change. Still, his definition of the relationship as a rare but perhaps possible "marriage of true minds" holds out hope. Cummings sees *forever* as part of an eternal *now*, experienced by individuals who are able to be alive and open to each moment. Worldviews and tastes in poetry are both personal and culture-specific, but open-minded readers can step into experiences that are new to them. If Bradstreet and Shakespeare encountered the poetry of cummings, they might be startled at first. The Puritan Bradstreet might be offended by the content, whereas the master of the sonnet and blank verse, Shakespeare, would be offended by the form. But Shakespeare, as a questioner of rhetoric and a lover of wordplay, would undoubtedly understand cummings's motives. And Bradstreet, as the mother of eight, had experience with the physical expressions of love. Because this poem appeals to the senses and is comparatively free of allusions, the poets of the past would seem at least as likely as our students to respond to it as individuals and would need no crash course in modernism.

ROMANTIC DREAMS (p. 720)

LESLIE MARMON SILKO
Yellow Woman (p. 720)

In the montage of texts that make up Leslie Marmon Silko's 1981 book *Storyteller*, from which this story is taken, the writer presents a mixture of autobiographical, fictional, and mythical retellings of the stories of her life as a member of the Laguna Pueblo Tribe of New Mexico. Like many indigenous storytellers, Silko weaves together past with present, dreamlike legend with the mundane verisimilitude of everyday life. She has said that, for her native culture, time is not linear but is like an ocean that surrounds us. The past does not remain past but ebbs and flows into the present. In "Yellow Woman" a young wife and mother, living in a Pueblo household that includes her mother and grandmother, encounters a mysterious stranger. We meet her *in medias res* — in the middle of the story — as she awakens on a riverbank in a sensuous scene with a man who may be a Navajo cattle thief from a neighboring reservation or may be a *ka'tsina*, a mountain spirit. She realizes that she too may be a character in the myth that her dead grandfather used to tell her. She acts out the part of *Yellow Woman*, the heroine of a ritualized captivity story. Depending upon the point of view we decide to take as readers, we may see her as the victim of a seduction, as the embodiment of an ancestral fertility figure, or as a housewife living out a romantic fantasy. The story is disturbing as a rape fantasy, but a sense of freedom surrounds her abduction as well, as she throws off conventions and follows the nature spirit — her own nature, perhaps — to the top of the mountain. Her will seems suspended in a surreal way that follows the logic of myth: "I did not decide to go. I just went. Moonflowers blossom in the sand hills before dawn, just as I followed him." She moves as we do in dreams, forgetting to leave when she intends to go home, and finally going home when she means to go uphill to Silva's place, because going downhill seems safer at the moment. As in her novels, *Ceremony* and *The Almanac of the Dead*, Silko retells a myth in *Yellow Woman* to question the nature of reality and the nature of personal, family, and tribal identity. Though it throbs with danger, the world of Silva, with its intense and sometimes bloody images, puts the narrator in touch with something missing in an inverted world where the younger generation teaches the older how to make Jell-O.

Throughout the story, the woman gives reasons for her actions, but they don't really explain the actions they claim to explain. She stops pulling away from him, she tells us, "because his hand felt cool and the sun was high." She decides that he must be a Navajo because he is tall or because he steals. At one point, she assures us that he has heard her approaching him; she knows this because he speaks to her without turning. She knows that she cannot be Yellow Woman because they have just met the day before. She knows she can escape but stays to eat because she "knew it would be a long walk home." In each case, her attempts at logic reveal that the opposite may be true. She goes because she wishes to go, believes that he really is a *ka'tsina* with supernatural knowledge and that she is Yellow Woman, wishes to stay in this place where senses are heightened and she finds herself "standing in the sky with nothing around . . . but the wind." Linear thinking does not work in this world, which evokes the colors and circular mazes of sand painting. She goes with him because she enters the reality of the myth. Interestingly, her story does not end "happily ever after," as students may expect from their experience with romantic stories in Euro-American culture. Though she stays longer, even the original Yellow Woman of the Pueblo legend returns to her family eventually rather than continuing in an eternal state of romantic adventure. Nor does the story end with her reaping the consequences of sin. The story does not judge the actions of Yellow Woman as a morality tale might, and rather than "learning her lesson" she will simply continue her life as she left it. In mainstream culture, people often try to live out variations on the Cinderella theme that tells every woman she will find her prince if she is beautiful, patient, and good. Equally powerful is the Gothic "beauty and the beast" romance in which the tormented hero is converted into a prince by the insightful heroine who comes to understand him. Advertisements create their own ministries in which romantic fulfillment is achieved by buying the right product or looking the right way. Although college students may gain insight into their assumptions by discussing "Yellow Woman" as romantic fiction, its origins as a myth give it cultural significance for people within the tribe, and its symbols and meanings may elude others. Silko's cousin, Paula Gunn Allen, has complained of Silko's novel *Ceremony* that it appropriates Laguna Pueblo lore that should not have been shared with outsiders, and the issue of whites stealing yet another possession of native peoples is a legitimate one. Myths are tied to origins, to the shared values passed down within a community, to ethos in the classical sense of the term. Perhaps any good story taps into the human need to understand and order the universe. Stories tell us who we are and how we are to behave within a culture. But they also provide us with the enjoyment of reading a well-told tale, and Silko's use of specific details adds to this experience. Students will find many examples, from the tamaracks and willows of the opening sentence to the screen door and Jell-O in the final paragraph. Details contribute to the sense of reality but also serve to reveal characters and to show the state of mind of the narrator. Especially vivid are the piglike description of the white man that Silva apparently kills, the violent and bloody images connected with Silva himself, and the enhanced sensitivity of Yellow Woman's perceptions of the natural setting.

JAMES JOYCE

Araby (p. 728)

The influence of James Joyce on writing in the twentieth century cannot be overemphasized. As lists of the most important books of the century are drawn up, Joyce consistently appears at or near the top. Speaking of the complex and almost indecipherable *Finnegans Wake*, Joyce wryly boasted that his aim was to "keep the critics busy for three hundred years." In *Ulysses*, another novel that continues to keep critics and college students occupied, he allowed his characters internal dialogues that had never before been attempted to such an extent, fragmenting reality into multiple points of view and writing styles. He also dealt with sex and other bodily functions in ways that caught the attention of censors, and the first editions of his books had to be smuggled into the United States. More troubling to many readers, however, especially those in his native Ireland, were his irreverent criticisms of the Catholic Church and of the received morality of nineteenth-century Western tradition. However, in the semiautobiographical novel *A Portrait of the Artist as a Young Man*, Joyce presented himself as a man seeking a higher morality, ending with one of the most memorable lines in literature: "I go forth to encounter for the millionth time the reality of experience and to forge in the smithy of my soul the uncreated conscience of my race." Even though Joyce may have realized the overreaching irony contained within this statement of his hero, Stephen Dedalus, he nevertheless tried to live it out in his writing. Although James Joyce lived most of his life as an exile from Ireland, his fiction evokes Dublin and the countryside and schools of his childhood and adolescence. The

123

short story "Araby" is found in the collection entitled *Dubliners*, a series of portraits intended to reveal the city itself. Each of the stories culminates in its protagonist's experience of what Joyce termed an "epiphany," a sudden spiritual manifestation of insight and understanding. The action of the story takes place within the consciousness of the character and the reader, and is meant to reveal some aspect of reality. In "Araby," the young protagonist seeks a romantic ideal, much as knights of earlier literature sought the Holy Grail, and discovers that his pursuit and its object — his religion — have been trivial and false.

At the end of the story, the boy's "eyes burn . . . with anguish and anger." The reasons for his emotions are revealed earlier in this final sentence. He has been suddenly struck by the realization that he is a "creature driven and derided by vanity." He has seen Mangan's sister as a pure and beautiful goddess. She is a figure of fantasy rather than a real girl, much like the Virgin Mary adored in *The Devout Communicant* or the romantic objects of knightly devotion in *The Abbot* — both books he has found in the room of the dead priest who formerly occupied his house. A third book in the priest's library, *The Memoirs of Vidocq*, a collection of sexually suggestive detective stories, may have contributed a more carnal slant to his thoughts about Mangan's sister, however. Heretofore, he has sublimated his lusts to something he has interpreted as holy, has carried the thought of her through the vulgar streets of Dublin as if it were a chalice, like the most sacred symbol of the Catholic mass, the transformed and transforming blood of Christ. By conflating the two symbols, Joyce suggests that both are equally false idols, thus critiquing both romantic love and the church. At Araby, agreed by many to represent the Vanity Fair of John Bunyan's *Pilgrim's Progress* where Everyman is tempted to buy cheap substitutes for true religion, carnival inverts the ideal of romantic love for Joyce's protagonist. The empty banter of the people at the fair, presumably already initiates into the world of adult sexuality, makes his elevation of love suddenly seem tawdry. Joyce seems to imply that to believe in anything is shameful, and this implication may reflect his philosophy.

Like most of his writings, "Araby" reflects autobiographical events in the author's life; we know that he lived for a time on Richmond Street and that a traveling bazaar named Araby visited Dublin in 1894, when James Joyce was a twelve-year-old boy. Readers may feel that Joyce takes the naiveté acute of his youth too seriously, that his rejection of conventional attitudes toward love and religion is too extreme, especially when based on an event so insignificant on the surface. Most of us have made mistakes like this, however, and still blush to remember obscure humiliations that no one else noticed at the time. Our closest friends would be bewildered by the power these memories still have over us. Joyce's epiphanies are based on just such trivialities, and he might suggest that we examine these experiences for the manifestation of reality contained within them, that we take off the blinders of false consciousness. The beginning of this short story describes Richmond Street as "blind," meaning that it is a dead end, but suggesting an obvious metaphor about the people who live on such streets. At the end of the story, the boy's blindness has been overcome, though he is ironically blinded with tears. He feels anguish, but also anger that he has been fooled by romantic ideas. Beyond the story of a boy who becomes aware of his false illusions, however, "Araby" insists upon an interpretation that connects love and religion equally as types of muddled and confining ideology. An interpretation of Joyce's texts must also consider what is being said about Ireland's collective false consciousness. In James Joyce's thinking, the same institutions and beliefs that diminish individuals also limit cultures.

The boy in James Joyce's "Araby" and the young wife in Leslie Marmon Silko's "Yellow Woman" inarticulately act out the myths of their respective cultures. Joyce's character is the hero of an Arthurian legend, a seeker after a version of the holy grail. He sees the object of his search as something pure, an emblem worthy of his chosen lady, herself an object worshiped from afar. The reader realizes that the protagonist has idealized the Dublin schoolgirl and the sordid carnival to a ridiculous extent, but the boy does not realize this until the end. In a similar way, the female protagonist of "Yellow Woman" moves through a romantic dream, failing to shake herself out of it even as the reader sees the danger and the underlying brutality to which she has exposed herself. It is less clear that she frees herself from the power of the myth than it is with Joyce's character. When she arrives home to the tableau of the older women preparing Jell-O, she is faced with the most prosaic of images, much as Joyce's character is faced with the trivial chatter of the street fair. But the Jell-O, representing the undermining of traditional culture, can be seen as a contrast to the mythological world.

While it is clear to informed readers that Joyce means his character to reject the idealism of myth, Silko leaves the way open for Yellow Woman to return to the romantic, mythological world if the opportunity again presents itself. Perhaps the knowledge that she can return to the world of story is her epiphany. If so, the result is the opposite of the epiphany in which Joyce's character recognizes with shame the unreality of idealism and religion. The door to myth remains open to the Pueblo woman but slams shut for the Irish schoolboy. Whether or not we find one story more realistic than the other may say as much about ourselves as about the narratives.

Readers steeped in the "realism" of Western culture may find "Araby" more realistic, perhaps recalling moments when they came to understand that the idealistic values they had learned in books and religious teachings were not absolute ones accepted by all people. Readers open to alternative views of reality might feel that Joyce's character is too easily robbed of his mythology, agreeing with Silko that the worlds of reality and myth actually do overlap.

JOHN UPDIKE

A & P (p. 733)

If the minutiae of the daily lives of John Updike's characters seem trivial and their preoccupations self-absorbed, this may be the fault of the culture rather than the writer. Updike has been a prolific recorder of the details of American middle-class existence since the publication of his first fiction in 1959, and he continues to tell our stories forty years later. Readers tend to love Updike or hate him. Students who read "A & P" sometimes say it's the best story they ever read. These are usually nineteen-year-old young men who work part time at grocery stores to earn money during their first year at college. Many students, typically young women who spend a lot of time at the beach, are highly offended by the suggestion that Sammy is anything but a sexist pig. Critics are similarly divided on a more sophisticated and ostensibly objective level. John Updike, however, is not a trivial thinker. Interested in philosophy and theology, Updike joins Franz Kafka, Henrik Ibsen, and W. H. Auden as an avid reader of the equally prolific Søren Kierkegaard (1813–1855), the father of existentialism. Seen as the first philosopher of the subjective individual and opponent of "the system," Kierkegaard coined the term "leap of faith" to describe the sort of daring move into a new consciousness that we see Sammy make in Updike's story.

Like many of Updike's characters, Sammy seems more to stumble and fall his way into his future rather than to actually leap. Students often think that Sammy has ruined his chances by a foolish act, using as evidence the final sentence where Sammy realizes "how hard the world was going to be . . . hereafter." We might ask them, however, if coming to such a realization is a bad thing. If Sammy is an incarnation of John Updike, as many of his protagonists are, will he really be better off as a version of the grim supermarket manager Lengel, unable to perceive beauty or to think independently, or as the writer and thinker he will become? Remembering Kierkegaard, we can see Sammy's *angst* as a natural reaction to newly found freedom, and freedom can lead in a positive or a negative direction. That direction is up to Sammy, and falls outside the story, though we should not let that fact stop our speculations about his future.

Although Sammy's reasons for quitting may be based on romantic illusions, the result of his quitting leads to his new, more realistic view of life. Underneath, his quitting may have less to do with the girls than with his reluctance to be one of the trivial name-brands of the A & P, catalogued with great specificity in the story. The customers are characterized as sheep, the workers look like conforming chumps, and the items for sale are as tawdry as the wares of James Joyce's bazaar in "Araby" or John Bunyan's Vanity Fair in *Pilgrim's Progress*. Sammy quits because he pursues, in his crude way, the romantic ideal of individuality. Has he, like the protagonist of "Araby," sought a pure ideal only to realize that the pursuit was vain? Students might want to consider times they have done the right thing for the wrong reasons. Undoubtedly, Sammy is selfish if he quits a job his parents approve of just to gain the attention of girls who hold him in contempt if they notice him at all. But students should be challenged to examine the concept of selfishness as problematic.

Ultimately, the story for both Updike's and Joyce's young knights is not about the ladies — the queens, the false goddesses — they seek to worship and please, but about their own changing perceptions of themselves. Students of the 1960s, who read "A & P" in its first years after publication in *Pigeon Feathers and Other Stories* (1962), may list different priorities than their children do at the turn of the twenty-first century. Breaking free from a conforming society sounded seductively good to Updike's age-mates and the generation directly following him. Current students in our regional branch of a state university often state openly that they are in college solely to prepare for a well-paying career. They have trouble understanding Sammy's dilemma, and most feel that he has his priorities out of order when he quits his job. Sammy, to the extent that he admires the girls for reasons of social class, reveals materialistic values of the same sort, however. This equating of the moneyed class with value may be the false consciousness that corresponds in Updike's American story to the religious dominance in Joyce's Irish one. When Sammy leaves that symbol of homogenized, commercial America — the A & P — he escapes what many of our students actively seek, a job with a secure — if limited — future.

Although we would like to think that the gains obtained by the social movements of the 1960s and 1970s have removed stereotypes about class and gender, students will be quick to tell us that the time frame of the story has less to do with adolescent thought than we would hope. Women are more likely to notice and to challenge sexism in the story, but most students agree that Sammy's attitudes still prevail among the young people that they know. However, we might want to grant him an ironic chivalry that — though misplaced — is preferable in Updike's estimation to the suppression of individuality. The final paragraph takes Sammy outside of the supermarket, and he is able to see the kind of life he has escaped — easy, safe, sheeplike, and paralyzing. Perhaps some students will maintain that, in this case, *hard* is better.

Comparing the three characters at the end of the stories in this cluster takes us back to the cluster's title, "Romantic Dreams." Each character — Yellow Woman in Leslie Marmon Silko's story by the same name, the boy in James Joyce's "Araby," and Sammy in John Updike's "A & P" — acts within a dreamlike world of fantasy, based on the stories and the assumptions of his or her specific culture. Yellow Woman seems to change the least. Her journey into myth has moved her closer to a part of herself as an individual but, more importantly, closer to herself as a strand of a vanishing tribal identity. She is less interested in personal awareness than in continuity with her grandfather and with the people of the stories. It is the Jell-O of the present that is the false thing, not her unexpected and oddly passive interlude into passion and danger. She'll do it again if drawn back into it, but it does not represent a quest.

The young men of the other two stories are active seekers of romance, however, and they both end in a state of disillusionment with the assumptions of their cultures. Individuality and its accompanying alienation are foregrounded in both Updike and Joyce, with the limitations of culture being something to be avoided or changed. The passivity of Silko's heroine, while recovering Laguna myth, is disturbingly similar to that of thirteen-year-old girls of many cultures, and class discussion might address the ramifications of fantasies that portray young women swept up dreamily and helplessly into relationships. Both men and women will recall times that they had unrealistic fantasies about a person or worshipped someone from afar, as the boys in Joyce's and Updike's stories do. The real "anguish and anger" — but also the epiphany — come when we act upon the fantasy. Both Updike and Joyce end their stories on a note of realization that the world will be profoundly different for the protagonists not only because of their actions but, more importantly, because of their changed perceptions of reality.

127

COMPLETING THE SELF THROUGH LOVE (p. 738)

DIANE ACKERMAN

Plato: The Perfect Union (p. 739)

At first, a reading of *Symposium* 5, the section of Plato's dialogues that inspires Diane Ackerman's analysis, invites our laughter. To begin, Plato places the story in the mouth of Aristophanes, a comedian, rather than giving it to a more serious member of the discussion. Then Aristophanes begins by asking his friends to laugh with him, not at him, as he tells his story, a "please don't kick me" sort of request that immediately invites us to disobey. The story, as he tells it, is ridiculous, the original humans described as perfectly round spheres with four legs, four arms, etc., rolling around the earth like so many hamsters in plastic balls. Furthermore, Zeus threatens that if they continue to be impertinent, he'll slice them again, and they'll have to hop around on one leg, a slapstick image. "He spoke and cut the men in two, like a sorb-apple which is halved for pickling," Aristophanes tells us, using a simile that hardly invites respect for the poor things. This reads like the script for an episode of *Monty Python's Flying Circus*. But with the pathos of the divided creatures clinging to their other halves, afraid to unclasp to eat or care for themselves, human beings begin to look a bit tragic, though still ridiculous. And when he begins to discuss "soul mates," we recognize a familiar idea that has its source here in Plato's *Symposium*.

Diane Ackerman, a poet as well as an essayist, who explores the importance of the body and its senses in all aspects of human life, accepts the longing for oneness that Plato's dialogue assumes. But she finds its source instead in the oneness the unborn child experiences with its mother. She frames her discussion of Plato's *Symposium* and its religious, mythological, and literary correlatives with a reference in the opening paragraph to a child waiting for a good-night kiss and a poetic image in the closing paragraph of a child in the womb. Both Plato and Ackerman begin with the assumption that the longing for union with a perfect "other half" is an essential quality of humanity, begging the question of whether this premise is true. Still, Ackerman's science-based reasoning has logic on its side and seems free of the doubleness of Plato's comic narrator, whom we may not be expected to take seriously. She takes many examples from literature, and she is a poet, a fact that Plato's student Aristotle would say also gives her a double voice.

We probably can believe that Aristophanes means it when he speaks of the supermanliness of men whose mates are other men, offering the evidence that "these when they grow up become our statesmen, and these only, which is a great proof of the truth of what I am saying." This requirement for public office might change some things if applied in today's United States! Ackerman asserts, on the other hand, that the human need for complete union finds its genesis in the power of women to carry children and to give birth, undercutting the Platonic assumption that males are superior. Using Plato's logic, the ultimate fulfillment of Ackerman's yearning child would be incest with its mother, whether it is male or female, a variation on Sigmund Freud's Oedipus complex. Students may question whether these ideas about finding wholeness through love explain something innate to human beings or reflect assumptions that are acquired as part of a culture.

The idea that Ackerman is talking about wholeness rather than love is supported by her discussion of religious practices that seek union with God and by her use of the mother and child bond as the underlying reason behind the longing for such wholeness. Yet she fails to develop an equally tenable idea that the union of egg and sperm is part becoming whole in microcosm and that the child who develops from this union carries just as much of the father's biological essence as the mother's. Watching the doubling of cells under the microscope recalls the splitting of Plato's spherical beings, and oneness begins to look quite multiple at this level. Ackerman doesn't try to puzzle out the differences between homosexual love and heterosexual love as Plato does, though she acknowledges a biological heritage in which the sexes coexisted in one body, but she concentrates instead on the "osmotic yearning" precipitated by being torn from one's mother's body at birth.

The question of whether this yearning manifests itself as physical or spiritual begs the question of the nature of spirituality as something apart from the human body. Most students have experienced both sexual longing and religious searching, and most are of an age when they are particularly vulnerable to both. Cults succeed in recruiting members through exploiting this need for ultimate belonging. Romantic ideas about human love can lead to equally destructive situations. Readers might question whether Ackerman's "pinnacle" refers to a long-term relationship with a soul mate, as Plato implies, or a rare achievement that one encounters in rare, brief moments of intense unity with any human being in the right time and place.

GORE VIDAL

The Desire and the Successful Pursuit of the Whole (p. 743)

In his most recent novel, *The Smithsonian Institution* (1998), Gore Vidal takes as his protagonist a thirteen-year-old boy who goes to St. Albans School in Washington, D.C., but has the ability to travel through time. One character in the novel is a twenty-year-old ghost who wanders through the halls of the Smithsonian Museum complex. One task that the young time traveler takes on is to prevent the ghost's death at Iwo Jima. The ghost's name is Jimmie Trimble. The symbolism is — like much about Gore Vidal — brashly obvious. There's no way to know if the real Jimmie Trimble would have grown up to be the satisfying soul mate that Gore Vidal imagines him to be. Readers will question whether they would have encountered each other again or what would have happened if they did, given Trimble's evident desire to marry and remain in the closet. Gore Vidal's willingness to live openly as a homosexual was rare in the generation of men who were born in the 1920s and fought in World War II in their late teens and early twenties. It may be that Trimble, who did die in the battle of Iwo Jima, has been worth much more to Vidal dead than alive, providing him with a fantasy that fuels this chapter of nonfiction and at least two novels. The text that serves in our book as an essay is taken from Gore Vidal's autobiographical book *Palimpsest*, published in 1995. The title is telling. The word *palimpsest* refers to the practice, in times when paper was expensive and scarce, of erasing or writing over earlier texts with new ones on the same piece of parchment. A palimpsest has been written upon, over and over again. Sometimes, as with painted canvases, what's underneath is more interesting and valuable than what is seen on the surface. Furthermore, there's a sense of hodgepodge about a palimpsest, something that distracts the eye from one text to another and perhaps to yet another that jumps out from time to time in fragments. The author may be referring to himself as a palimpsest, but Vidal's memoir also has this erratic quality. He begins telling one story and is reminded of another; he drops a name and feels compelled to relate some gossip. He reminds us that he's part of the political Gore dynasty by birth and that he shared with Jacqueline Bouvier Kennedy Onassis the wealthy and prominent Hugh Auchincloss (the Hughdie mentioned in this chapter) as a stepfather, both their mothers having at different times been married to him. But, though Vidal often strays off his main story, his focus in the chapter titled "The Desire and the Successful Pursuit of the Whole" is his love for Jimmie Trimble, his lost other half.

When Vidal describes his physical union with Jimmie, he contrasts their Arcadia with a "diabolic Eden." Arcadia is Greek, of course, and Eden is Judeo-Christian; and Vidal is describing what is euphemistically called Greek love. But although both are imagined to be paradises, Arcadia represented the ideal, romanticized version of ancient rural Greece, where love had no strings attached. Eden is, of course, the place of original sin, and homosexuality is taboo in much of Jewish and Christian history and culture. Vidal's answer to the question about the origin of guilt would undoubtedly be that it is socially constructed. It's hard for heterosexuals who have never had a physical experience with someone of their own sex to avoid questions of exactly what the partners were doing in the men's room, who was putting what where. And the whole idea of having sex in a bathroom may strike some readers as shocking in a text focused on the Platonic ideal of sexual soul mates. But, as Vidal boasts, he is like Aristophanes in his willingness to be crude and vulgar. There's quite a bit of carnivalistic spirit in Vidal's whole enterprise, as both writer and dramatic human being. He likes to shock his audience and to turn authority on its ear, and telling naughty gossip about famous figures like President Kennedy may be part of this. On the other hand, dropping names may be a way of reminding us that he knows people in authority, lending some importance to Gore Vidal as a result. Vidal's seemingly iconoclastic attitude toward famous people contrasts with his romantic sentimentality where Jimmie Trimble is concerned, but his tone is complex enough for students to support a number of different evaluations of it. Like a palimpsest, his text is scribbled upon by a surface cockiness that covers sincerity, and it's hard to trust much of what we read. His conversation with Jimmie's mother is a gently ironic exchange that works like fiction. It may be that Vidal's fiction is actually more revealing about the man than his attempts to be candid. The most Platonic thing about Gore Vidal may be the fact that he loves the *idea* of finding wholeness in another person more than he loves the actual person. Loving a dead boy he never really knew as a man may be a perfect way to avoid true intimacy.

Whereas Diane Ackerman takes a bit of the fable from *Symposium* to use as a jumping-off place for her own theories about the desire for wholeness, Gore Vidal's retelling captures more of the tale's true spirit. He concedes that it is vulgar and ridiculous, but he has no problems with this, admires it even. And Vidal seems to want the metaphor to be true, seems to need the idea of Jimmie Trimble as a soul mate, as proof that he once really loved somebody. The subject of homosexuality is one of the most difficult to handle in an American college classroom because so many students have been socialized to see it as weak or comical or sinful. Ackerman seems to take a neutral stance, whereas Vidal celebrates his homosexuality while teasing his audience with details we may not want to hear — for example, that Jimmie's hands were too rough for the author's sensitive cock. He undoubtedly thinks the solution to the American public's socialization about homosexuality is to force that public to take a good look.

Many students already believe that there is one person for each of us; Plato's suggestion has had a long life in Western tradition. Both writers seem to focus on the finding rather than the searching. We might question whether the whole enterprise smacks of the rationalization of one's own inadequacies. Students may debate whether time might be better spent developing the qualities we desire within ourselves. Some may feel that a sense of wholeness can be achieved without either seeking or finding a mythical other half.

COURTSHIP (p. 757)

CHRISTOPHER MARLOWE

The Passionate Shepherd to His Love (p. 758)

The subject of popular legend in his lifetime and in the years directly following his violent death in 1593, Christopher "Kit" Marlowe continues to live in the popular culture at the edges of literary studies some four hundred years later. In the 1999 movie *Shakespeare in Love*, playwright Tom Stoppard has a young Shakespeare's competition with Marlowe and his hasty exchange of identity with him lead Shakespeare to believe that he is responsible for Marlowe's being stabbed in a tavern brawl. Stoppard cannot be unaware of the latest wrinkle in the ongoing debate about the authorship of Shakespeare's texts, which maintains that Marlowe's death was a hoax related to his espionage activities in the intrigues between Catholic and Protestant factions. The theory, suggested in 1993 and circulating internationally on the World Wide Web ever since, suggests that a deal was worked out in which the politically compromised Marlowe would seem to be killed, disappear, and then reemerge from some Renaissance version of Superman's telephone booth with a new identity as . . . you guessed it. If true, all of the works of Shakespeare were actually written by Kit Marlowe, the Canterbury shoemaker's son with a Cambridge education and a reputation as a spy and atheistic practitioner of the black arts. Students might enjoy the historicist task of tracking down the myths, legends, and fiercely held beliefs about Marlowe both in his time and in later ones.

We have evidence of the popularity of Marlowe's pastoral lyric, "The Passionate Shepherd to His Love," in the great number of parodies and responses to it that still exist from the early 1600s, when his life and death were still fresh in living memory. In addition to those included in our anthology, John Donne's teasingly sweet variation "The Baite" might intrigue students who are interested in fishing as foreplay, and Shakespeare's comical use of several lines in "The Merry Wives of Windsor" may add fuel to the "Marlowe Lives" controversy. Marlowe's poem reflects his interest in classical themes and is undoubtedly inspired by his translations of Ovid's *Amores* from Latin into English. His setting is Arcadia, with its idealized shepherds and milkmaids living idyllic lives in a trouble-free, natural paradise where love and work are uncomplicated. Such fantasies must have provided a welcome contrast for stressed courtiers during these years surrounding the beheading of Mary, Queen of Scots, threats from political and religious factions at home and abroad, and the anxiety about the future that accompanied the aging of Queen Elizabeth I. The poem's structure may have contributed to its popularity as well, its rhyming couplets in regular iambic tetrameter making it easy to memorize.

"The Passionate Shepherd to His Love" continues to be a much-read poem today, both through its obligatory inclusion in high-school and college anthologies and through its informal and perfectly voluntary circulation on the Internet, a good barometer of current popular culture. The argument is what literary folk would later call a romantic one, projecting an idealized portrait of love. But we know that Marlowe was not himself a simple shepherd, and we can assume that the persona of the poem masks a sophisticated man of the world who realizes that the argument is more charming than logical. The argument will probably succeed to the extent that the lady to whom it is addressed is willing to play the simple milkmaid to Marlowe's simple shepherd.

Even in this idyllic setting, a closer examination raises issues about the world of reality outside of paradise. It is interesting to note that he imagines making her shoes "for the cold" (line 15), hinting that the season may not always be springtime. And although some of his construction materials — like gold, amber, and coral — are lasting, the flowers and leaves will quickly fade, and two types of materials are inextricably intertwined. The whole enterprise, his dressing of her, reflects both his erotic desires and the economic reality that women depended upon men for the clothing they wore. Students might question whether the shepherd's beloved, if she relents, is more seduced by the shepherd or by what he says he will do for her. Seen from an economic perspective, the seduction seems more of an exchange of one commodity for another, the setting and the beautiful trappings traded for sexual favors. Issues may also be raised about the *carpe diem* convention itself. The "eat, drink and make merry" line that we still hear today is from the King James version of the Bible, a translation just around the turn of the coming century from this poem. The biblical context makes it clear that this is a fool's attitude, that the *carpe diem* philosophy is antithetical to the Christian worldview. Students will be familiar with the tension between these philosophical forces in American culture. The same forces also battled in Marlowe's London, with the theaters constantly struggling to stay open in the face of religious and moral arguments against them.

Our discussion of the persuasive techniques of the passionate shepherd could also examine the ways in which advertising and other aspects of popular culture try to sell us on the idea of seizing the day for their own purposes. In an earlier essay in this anthology, Gore Vidal's "The Desire and the Successful Pursuit of the Whole," the writer describes a passionate sexual encounter between himself and another man in a bathroom and says that they were in Arcadia rather than Eden. Considering Vidal's use of the same imagery and symbolism as Marlowe's in a less conventional context could add to the discussion of our assumptions about love, sex, and the settings and circumstances in which they intersect.

SIR WALTER RALEIGH

The Nymph's Reply to the Shepherd (p. 760)

Probably the closest England came to a Renaissance man, Sir Walter Raleigh was deeply involved in the issues of his day. He survived the changing fortunes of a courtier subject to the whims of Queen Elizabeth I to eventually be imprisoned by King James I for high treason in 1603. Before and during his time in the Tower of London, where he wrote a history of the world, Raleigh was a writer and translator of both prose and poetry. Often active in commercial ventures of the sort that planted colonies in the Americas, Raleigh tended to write for self-promotion. The long title of his book about his holdings on the South American continent begins *The Discoverie of the Large, Rich, and Beautiful Empire of Guiana, with a Relation of the Great and Golden City of Manoa (Which the Spanish call El Dorado).* . . . The title's hyperbole strikes symbolically persuasive chords that the author hopes potential investors will hear, but the story is an especially well-written exploration narrative. Other prose reflects a practical interest in war and naval expeditions, not surprising for a man who lived during the age of exploration and the invasion of the Spanish Armada. The arts of persuasive rhetoric are important to Raleigh for pragmatic reasons, since even poetry dedicated to the queen can help him remain in favor at court. Like many poets of his time, Raleigh experimented with the Petrarchan sonnet, an Italian form whose conventions elevated the speaker's lady to a position of worship, a position quite in keeping with that of Elizabeth I. Raleigh's poems reveal his wit and rationality, and he seems to have enjoyed poetry as an intellectual game, played always in the context of his social and political surroundings. This is especially evident in his refutation of Christopher Marlowe's "The Passionate Shepherd to His Love." Raleigh critiques the shepherd's argument, and comes to the conclusion that Marlowe's poem is "in folly ripe, in reason rotten" (line 16). He attacks the ethical and pathetic appeals of Marlowe's poem with the sharp logic proposed by his persona, a woman wise about the effects of time. He implies that a girl would have to be really young and naive to buy Marlowe's argument. Appropriately, these poems are sometimes given the titles "The Milke Maids Songe" and "Milk Maids Mothers Answer."

The key words in Raleigh's refutation are *if, then,* and *but.* The shepherd has offered the milkmaid a deal, and she makes her counteroffer. "Here are my terms," she implies. "See if you can meet them." Since she sets him an impossible task, her counterargument amounts to a refusal of his proposition, for the pragmatic reason that the kind of love he offers will not last. The ambiguity of line 22 raises the issue of how love is to be defined, however. We may agree with the preceding implication that youth does not last, though it is couched as a conditional rather than a declarative statement, but whether or not joys become dated depends upon our understanding of the definition of *joy.* As a true rhetorician, though, Raleigh would probably accuse us of equivocation. The thrust of his argument is that this particular experience of love is fleeting. The tone of Raleigh's poem mocks the impractical idealism of Marlowe's; like a true adman, the speculator who wrote his hopeful account of gold in Guyana knows a con when he hears one. The speaker of Raleigh's poem has a tinge of stereotype about her, though, and this may also be part of the joke. She is a woman as familiar to readers as Chaucer's earlier Wife of Bath, a woman who wishes above all to be empowered by her sexuality, not seduced because of it. Raleigh's poem also stereotypes the young male lover, assuming that his love will only last as long as the flowers he offers his nymph.

Raleigh's poem follows Marlowe's stanza by stanza, refuting each bit of evidence offered by the shepherd to prove love's pleasures. He subverts the *carpe diem* theme by using its basic assumption about the brevity of life to come to a different conclusion, that erotic love will not last any longer than youth will, and a wise woman will not be fooled into thinking otherwise. Raleigh's speaker wants something more lasting. In Marlowe's poem, nature seems pleasant and comfortable, with images of flowers and jewels that sparkle with color and light and birds that sing with the intricate melodies of springtime. The shepherd plucks wool effortlessly to make his love a dress, an especially unrealistic image for anyone who has seen how filthy sheep can become or has thought about the steps involved in getting wool from its raw state to the finished garment. And we wonder, with all this work he cuts out for himself, weaving and embroidering her garments, when he will find time for lovemaking. That Raleigh misses the chance to refute this may betray his gender or his class. Women and men involved in the wool industry wouldn't be expected to let this pass.

The seasons have changed in Raleigh's poem, though, and the floods and cold of winter cause everything to wither and die and the birds to stop singing. He doesn't mention the warm shoes or wool dress of Marlowe's poem, but they didn't seem very practical, anyway. And this is Raleigh's point, of course. Love is not simply a romantic promise. We can assume that Sir Walter Raleigh knew something about love, since he jeopardized his position at Queen Elizabeth's court to marry Elizabeth Throckmorton, and their marriage endured his later long imprisonment. His wife was allowed visits to his apartments in the Tower of London, and a son was conceived in this confined setting, one which — while not uncomfortable — was far from the glow of Arcadia.

ANDREW MARVELL
To His Coy Mistress (p. 761)

As involved in his way with the political issues of the middle years of the seventeenth century as Sir Walter Raleigh was with those around its beginning, Andrew Marvell wrote prose satires and metaphysical verse much admired and ultimately recovered for a twentieth-century audience by T. S. Eliot. Up until this time, Marvell was best known for having served as secretary to the blind poet John Milton. In a poem about Milton's composition of the epic poem *Paradise Lost*, Marvell reacts to Milton's writing process, describing his amazement as he watched the complex structure and lines of the epic take shape before his eyes. Therefore, as a reader in his own time, and later as an influence on early twentieth-century writers, Andrew Marvell is a poet's poet. Some readers of Marvell's lyric poems have speculated that his deceptively light touch, applied to what they see as his profound insight and skilled technique, came as a result of his years as a tutor. Even the most devoted readers of Andrew Marvell therefore concede that to skim the surface of his poetry is to miss an undercurrent that may run counter to the poem as it first appears. Some critics who have examined "To His Coy Mistress" in close detail maintain that the poem sends ambivalent, even confused, messages about love and that its ideas do not bear up under logical scrutiny.

The speaker's purpose in "To His Coy Mistress" is to persuade his reluctant audience to give up her virginity to him without further delay. His logic seems to be that if more time existed, then waiting would be okay; but since there is little time, we should not wait to make love. But the conclusion does not necessarily follow. It would be just as logical — or as illogical — to say, "Since there's so little time, we shouldn't waste it screwing around. I think I'll take that trip to pick up rubies in India before they are all gone." Good authority holds that the poet's argument "affirms the consequent" or commits the "fallacy of the converse." Although some students might know these terms for logical fallacies and enjoy taking a rhetorical analysis further, one could use their interest as a resource rather than expecting all students, or all literature instructors for that matter, to identify examples of faulty reasoning by name. What we might do is ask why so many readers love the poem in spite of our conviction that we would not be swayed by its argument. The answer would undoubtedly lie in its appeal to our emotions and the overwhelming beauty of its style, but even these can be called into question. The issues hidden within "To His Coy Mistress" are best discovered by close reading, something the class can do together. Even the title may confuse students who have never heard the word *coy* or who assume that the word *mistress* implies that she is already his illicit lover, a reading that throws her reluctance to make love into a different light. The woman addressed is assumed by the speaker to be a virgin, and her remaining so until marriage is the expectation of Puritan English society in the 1600s, though birth and marriage records call into question any universal adherence to prohibitions against premarital sex. If Marvell's speaker is meant to be the poet himself, an issue in itself, he is calling for a woman to sin, or at best to marry. He assumes that she will be persuaded to do so by hyperbole, flattery, fear of death and decay, and violently erotic images rather than by logic.

The poem has three major sections, though the rhythm and sense often provide a sense of closure at the end of four lines and the rhyming couplets at the end of two. The first major section elaborates on the first premise of Marvell's argument, what he would do if there were world enough and time, and the final couplet (lines 19–20) sums up his warrant for this action, that she deserves it and he desires it. The second premise, that time prevents such a love, is described in the next section, again ending with a couplet that sums up and gives a warrant for his assertions by citing the finality of the grave (lines 31–32). The final section deals with the third part of the syllogism, with the word *therefore* appropriately used in its first line. He goes on to explain to her, repeating the word *now* at intervals, that he has proven his point, and now is the time to take action. He ends with a couplet that sums up the urgency of these last lines, proposing that though they cannot stop time, they can make it go faster, and this conclusion warrants the rushing violent images of this final part of the poem. The couplet that ends each part of his argument contains an opposition. The poem has a sense of desperation about it, with its images of violent birds of prey devouring time rather than allowing time to devour them, tearing pleasures through iron gates. He proposes that the lovers refuse to be victims, that they turn violently on the enemy, making love a frantic defiance of death. Although some readers may see a threat toward his coy mistress in the last section, others may note that he does not propose that he should direct his violent energy toward her, but that they do these things together, pooling their "strength and . . . sweetness" (lines 41–42). And she seems ready to participate, if we are to believe his description of her body in lines 35–36. Students who have read Plato's *Symposium* may wonder from lines 41–42 if Marvell's reading of classical literature has included Aristophanes' description of divided human beings seeking their other halves, since he saw the original humans as round balls. Despite his fierce images, directed against time and death, the speaker of Marvell's poem seems to desire wholeness rather than rape. Still, readers can legitimately charge him with a rather rough approach to a virgin.

The third of our texts in the section on courtship, Marvell's invitation moves away from the original conventions quite a bit. Christopher Marlowe in "The Passionate Shepherd to His Love" entices the object of his desire by painting a picture of paradise, only hinting at the coldness for which he will devise clothing and shoes to protect her. Sir Walter Raleigh answers in "The Nymph's Reply to the Shepherd" with reminders of changing weather and with indirect references to aging. Marvell speaks of being pursued by an almost demonic time and graphically describes the end result of aging, the grave itself.

T. S. ELIOT

The Love Song of J. Alfred Prufrock (p. 763)

Students may be impressed to know that "The Love Song of J. Alfred Prufrock" is the work of an undergraduate student, published in part in the *Harvard Advocate* when T. S. Eliot worked on the publication in 1910–11. The poem is considered by many literary historians to have invented a new way of writing poetry and to be one of the texts that launched the modernist movement in literature. Building on his education and wide reading, which was filtered through his own sensitivity and eccentricity of thought, Eliot anticipated in this poem his later theoretical ideas in the influential "Tradition and the Individual Talent" and other essays that later solidified into the New Criticism of the mid–twentieth century. His allusions to obscure bits of learning from the classics, French symbolists, Shakespeare, and multiple other sources can confuse even the most erudite of readers. Students need to be reassured that they do not have to understand every phrase. Although critics have maintained that "Prufrock" should not be read as simply a love poem, focusing our reading on this poem's relationship to the *carpe diem* poems in this cluster on courtship can make "Prufrock" accessible to students who are familiar with poems dealing with love and the passage of time. Unlike Andrew Marvell, who speeds up time in "To His Coy Mistress," Eliot slows time down to the pace of a lazy cat slipping like fog into the streets of a city. The speaker of the epigraph is in Dante's hell, where time does go on forever. And since his listener is in the same place, he says, he can tell his story without "fear of infamy," doesn't have to be ashamed. Eliot's narrator wanders through a city whose streets "follow like a tedious argument / Of insidious intent" (lines 8–9), and students who have suffered through dry lectures will agree that few things are more hellish than that. The speaker of Eliot's poem worries about shame, too, constantly asking if he "dares" and finally deciding that he probably doesn't dare, that the romantic adventure is not for him.

Prufrock may be asking himself if he dares to plunge into love as Christopher Marlowe and Andrew Marvell invite their lovers to do, even if there is, as Prufrock claims, plenty of time. Whereas Marvell's persona takes on the sun as an opponent, Eliot's wonders if he has the courage to "disturb the universe" (line 46). In contrast to Marvell's birds of prey devouring time, Prufrock is not sure he has what it takes "to eat a peach" (line 121), an image that evokes sensual pleasures. He worries about growing bald, a peculiar worry for a man so young, implying that he fears the changes that come with passing time. The idea of rejection, of being misunderstood, seems to keep Prufrock wandering through the streets and houses mumbling to himself. Students may conclude that he is afraid of life as well as love. Prufrock has been sounding a great deal like Hamlet, vacillating about whether or not he will take action. But he hints that he is more like Polonius, "an attendant lord" who is characterized by faulty rhetoric, who talks and talks but is laughably unaware of what is really going on. Hamlet kills Polonius by mistake while Polonius is hiding, an unseen observer rather than a participant in the action. A Shakespearean fool, on the other hand, seems to be talking nonsense but sometimes speaks great wisdom. Eliot's tone is filled with irony, transforming the similes of romantic poetry in a startling way. Eliot's contemporaries who were steeped in the usual metaphors for natural phenomena must have been shaken by Eliot's unexpected image of evening as a patient having surgery. There's more than irony here, however, and students could make a case for other characterizations of the tone; certainly the self-mockery that permeates the whole poem begins in the opening lines. Prufrock seems to avoid relationships because he feels that he is not up to the task. His repetition that "the women come and go / Talking of Michelangelo" may imply that the women trivialize art, that superficial social relationships also get in his way. When he says that he "should have been a pair of ragged claws / Scuttling across the floors of silent seas," perhaps his isolation from this society reaches its extremity.

The urgent seductions of both Marvell and Christopher Marlowe would undoubtedly scare the timid and indecisive Prufrock into a corner. T. S. Eliot was a great admirer of Andrew Marvell, however, and brought his poetry into the literary canon. In fact, the repeated "there will be time" of "The Love Song of J. Alfred Prufrock" directly answers Marvell's argument in "To His Coy Mistress" that there is not "world enough and time" for waiting. The contention that line 92 is a direct allusion to "To His Coy Mistress" can be borne out by its juxtaposition with Lazarus returning from the dead, recalling Marvell's reminder that love cannot take place there. It is quite likely that, among other things, Eliot's poem is meant as a modern refutation of romantic love. Not only its ambiguous language but its experiment with form — its varying line length and rhyme in a way that is neither free verse nor closed structure — challenges conventions. This questioning of the sureties of love and poetry reflects the personality of one shy, sensitive, highly educated young man from St. Louis, but it struck a chord with writers on both sides of the Atlantic that sounded through most of the century.

THE APPEARANCE OF LOVE:
A COLLECTION OF WRITINGS
BY KATE CHOPIN (p. 768)

KATE CHOPIN
The Storm (p. 769)

Written late in her career, Kate Chopin's story of passion in the midst of a symbolic tempest, "The Storm," has a close relationship to two other Chopin texts: her novel *The Awakening* (1899) and the short story that first explored the characters of Calixta, Alcée, and Bobinôt, "At the 'Cadian Ball" (1894). In her novel, a sensuous and artistic woman moves toward independence from a stifling marriage into adultery, but more importantly, into seizing her own life. Although the novel's ambiguous ending invites debates about whether its protagonist pays for her sin with suicide or swims into a symbolic freedom, its complex characterization of her sexuality was bold for its time and was shocking to most of the literary community of 1899.

The short story "The Storm," too erotic to be published by a respectable woman during the writer's lifetime, deals with a similar subject but has some important differences. Chopin's female character in "The Storm" is not a member of the upper-class white plantation aristocracy, as is the protagonist of *The Awakening,* but is instead more closely related to the characters in her earlier local-color collections *Bayou Folk* (1894) and *A Night in Acadia* (1897). Although students need not read the earlier "At the 'Cadian Ball" to find issues to discuss, we should consider its perspective, which is often missed when "The Storm" is presented outside its cultural context in literature anthologies. The consideration of any of Chopin's texts must take into account the peculiarly French nature of social institutions in Louisiana in the nineteenth century and must deal with the issues of race, class, and religion that permeated the culture from which these stories arise. All women were bound to their fathers and husbands by the Napoleonic Code, which considered them chattels unable to enter into contracts. Their legal rights were reduced to a greater extent than in any other part of the nation, at a time when women's rights were limited at best. Equally repressive were the dictates of the Catholic Church and of a caste-bound plantation society still greatly influenced by the social abuses and prohibitions of institutionalized slavery.

A reading of the story that first introduced the characters we meet in "The Storm" goes far to explain the actions of its characters, revealing issues that may not arise when the story is considered out of context. The most startling realization, for those accustomed to reading the story in isolation, is that this text deals with love across the color line. Although she is light-skinned with blue eyes and "flaxen" hair, Calixta has African ancestry, and even a "drop of African blood" places her irrevocably outside of Alcée's life as an equal in the eyes of the culture. Yet, as someone who is also known for her fiery Spanish ancestry, she is at first beyond the reach of the adoring, dark-skinned sugarcane worker Bobinôt. However, according to the rules of this ethnically mixed but obsessively hierarchical society, Bobinôt is an appropriate husband, and the passionate storm of her relationship with Alcée can never be anything but an interlude in her life. The earlier story hints at "a breath of scandal . . . when she went to Assumption," a memory that the lovers share in both "At the 'Cadian Ball" and "The Storm," though we learn in the later story that Alcée had refrained from anything beyond kissing at that time, touched by her vulnerability. We discover that Alcée, a white planter, goes to the ball after he has first been rejected by his cousin Clarisse and later has lost a huge crop of rice in a hurricane. Clarisse comes after him, interrupting a flirtation with Calixta, and the story ends with both women proposing marriage to men they do not completely desire. Alcée, surprisingly for readers of "The Storm," is as smitten with the cold and rejecting Clarisse as Bobinôt is with the mocking and distant Calixta.

The events of "The Storm" take place five years later, as hurricane winds blow through the delta yet again. The sudden passion of Calixta and Alcée is inextricably tied to the symbolism of the storm itself; the cyclone is a natural phenomenon outside of the usual expectations of the weather, and the lovers' physical intensity falls outside the constraints of an ordered and constrictive society. Students may raise issues about the sort of love Calixta feels for Bobinôt, but there seems to be a feeling of tenderness in her attitude toward him. She is a solicitous housewife to him, though we might note that they seem to have separate sleeping arrangements. Whether what Calixta and Alcée share is love will also be a matter for debate. We might ask whether love and sex are necessarily linked in this story, or if the story challenges conventions about love within marriage.

Chopin's contemporaries and many of our students may be bothered by the joyful tone of the ending. Unlike the female protagonist of *The Awakening*, Calixta does not suffer for her uninhibited claim to her sexuality; in fact, we are left with the impression that Bibi and Bobinôt have gained from the experience without being aware of it and that Calixta is able to love them more freely. Chopin's story thus runs counter to both the cultural truisms of the day and to the literary conventions she had accepted in the earlier text. Students familiar with soap operas and romantic fiction will recognize that such conventions still apply, since characters who transgress can expect to pay in some way. Chopin further frees Calixta from the *tragic mulatto* motif; rather than pining away for a white lover and dying tragically as a result, she moves effortlessly, without guilt and shame, back into her normal family routine. Although some may see "The Storm" as a celebration of adultery, Chopin seems to be saying much more than this, protesting not against marriage itself but against the legal and social restrictions imposed upon human interactions. In a time when bodies were covered from head to toe, she insists that passion is a natural and joyful part — though only one part — of being a human being. The ironic ending, revealing that Alcée's wife Clarisse is happy to be free of the sexuality that Calixta has welcomed, underscores this point.

KATE CHOPIN

The Story of an Hour (p. 773)

Like "The Storm," the previous story in this cluster of Kate Chopin texts, "The Story of an Hour" was published after the author's death in 1904. Readers today are often as disturbed by Mrs. Mallard's emotions as Chopin's early readers were. Today, we hear students complain that if she felt so confined in her marriage, she should have just left. Readers at its first publication would have understood her unquestioning loyalty to her marriage while she knew her husband was alive but would have chided her for not adapting to her lot as a married woman. They might also point out that to be alone did not mean she would have the power to make her own decisions. Most widows, even if their financial means were considerable, would have found their husbands' estates in the hands of male executors.

It is interesting, however, that Kate Chopin's working title for her novel *The Awakening* was *A Solitary Life*. To Chopin, the very real difficulties — even dangers — of being a woman alone in the nineteenth century were more tolerable than the emotional confinement of most marriages. Divorce was inconceivable to most women around the turn of the twentieth century, although Chopin had less reason to be fearful of women's freedom than most. Her great-great-grandmother had been the first woman in St. Louis to receive a legal separation from her husband and had gone on to raise her five children and run a shipping business alone. Kate Chopin grew up surrounded by such strong women and herself became a widow, with six children, in 1882 after twelve years of marriage. Furthermore, her marriage was characterized by an unusual amount of freedom, with Oscar Chopin apparently not complaining about her smoking, riding streetcars, and walking alone through the streets of New Orleans, actions that scandalized "respectable" people.

"The Story of an Hour" may have its model more in the club women of St. Louis than in the Creole society of Louisiana. Either place, Louise Mallard may have been uncomfortably recognizable, as she would be in some circles today. Married people sometimes fantasize about the death of a spouse, but the thought seems not to have occurred to Mrs. Mallard until the events of the story.

Students sometimes judge the protagonist of this story harshly, seeing her as shallow and selfish, ignorant of the true meaning of love. To do this, however, is to miss Chopin's point that love cannot compensate for lack of freedom. Mrs. Mallard has been unaware of this, but we see her, after her initial grief at her husband's death, beginning to awaken. We see her as if she were a child sobbing in its sleep, her thoughts in suspension, with the joy of being her own person approaching her as if it were an outside force about to possess her. This happens to a great extent because she is a woman bound by cultural restraints, but it is not entirely gender-specific. She feels free, we are told, because she will no longer be oppressed by "that blind persistence with which men and women believe they have a right to impose a private will upon a fellow-creature" (para. 14). Within their cultural milieu, both partners in the marriage are trapped, even if they love each other. Like the stories of Guy de Maupassant and O. Henry, this Kate Chopin story depends upon ironic circumstances for its action. This leads us to assign blame to a twist of fate or to the constraints of nineteenth-century marriage itself rather than to any of the characters.

Although some readers might wish to know something of Mrs. Mallard's life before or to hear the family's reaction to her death, the story's length seems appropriate to its title and its theme. It might, anticipating a Hemingway story about marriage, be called "The Short Happy Life of Louise Mallard," since her time as a free woman is so brief. The brevity of the story nevertheless allows us to see Mrs. Mallard as a dynamic character and to follow her quickly changing reactions first to her loss, then to her freedom, and finally to the loss of freedom that leads to her death. Some students will imagine that Mrs. Mallard is thinking about having a love affair or spending money without having to ask her husband's permission, but we should encourage them to go beyond such easy answers. Many students have experienced unwanted control from boyfriends or girlfriends. Although the status of women and the constraints of marriage have changed, even today, when in relationships, we sometimes intrude into areas our partners would prefer to keep private, feeling that even their thoughts belong to us. We want to control their movements and to tell them how they should feel. It is this intrusion that she is now freed from, and it is her autonomy, her self-determination, that she anticipates. The loss of her newfound self precipitates her death, and the reader understands the irony when the doctor says she has died of joy at her husband's return.

KATE CHOPIN

Désirée's Baby (p. 776)

"Désirée's Baby" is taken from Kate Chopin's first collection of short stories, *Bayou Folk*. Written in the genre termed *local color*, such narratives were a popular type of writing in which setting is an integral part of the theme. Whereas "The Story of an Hour" could have taken place in any number of settings throughout the United States and Europe in the 1890s, "Désirée's Baby" is best interpreted in the light of a specific time and place. Taking her readers back to Louisiana in the days before the Civil War, Chopin describes a society in which everyone knows his or her place. Masters have absolute power over the bodies and souls of their slaves, and men have a similar if more benign power over their women. To have even the hint of African ancestry is to be robbed of all one's claims to humanity. Although Chopin's characters do not question the rules of this hierarchy, living in the certainty of what signifies their place in the order of things, Chopin holds these beliefs up to the light for her readers to examine.

Depending as it does upon foundlings and mistaken identities, Chopin's plot stands in a long line of tradition with William Shakespeare and Charles Dickens, among many others. Around the same time as Kate Chopin used it, Oscar Wilde parodied this plot device in *The Importance of Being Earnest*. African American writers like William Wells Brown and Charles Chestnutt, though, were exploring the complications of mixed identity when applied to questions of race. Issues of passing, assimilation, and the separate cultural identity of people recently freed from slavery occupied the minds of many in the latter half of the nineteenth century. W. E. B. Du Bois was saying at the beginning of the new twentieth century that its major issue would be the troubling question of the "color line," of how the country would overcome the long abuses of slavery and bring Negro people into full equality. Much later, in midcentury, studies would show that a major barrier to the integration of African Americans into full citizenship was the fear of white men that sexual relationships would develop between black men and white women. Sex had long been politicized between the races in the American South, with masters taking advantage of slave women, practicing the equivalent of rape under any of our current definitions of the term.

Throughout her narrative, Chopin subverts the assumption that a person may be defined or classified by race or heredity. As the story begins, we have only the hearsay testimony of Madame Valmondé that her husband has found a baby who calls him "Dada." The enigmatic presence just outside the story's action of La Blanche, the light-skinned slave at whose cabin Armand Aubigny spends so

142

much time, raises unanswered questions about her paternity and that of her children. When Désirée finally realizes that her baby has African characteristics, it is because she compares him with the child of La Blanche, and the reader can infer that the children may look alike in some way. And the story ends, of course, with the ironic twist: Though Armand has driven away his wife and child because of what he thinks is her tainted blood, it is he who carries the inheritance he holds in contempt.

In addition to its challenge to the concept of race, this story, like many other Chopin texts, calls into question the definition of love. We are told that Armand fell in love at first sight, a trait that runs in his family. This statement links Chopin's twin themes, and the ridiculous contention undercuts cultural clichés about both love and heredity. Students will enjoy debating the question of whether love at first sight is possible. Some studies of flirting behavior seem to show that men are subconsciously attracted to women whose body language signals receptiveness and whose symmetry and other physical qualities indicate health and fertility. Moreover, some of these factors seem to be cross-cultural, even universal, with people in widely separated societies choosing the same indicators of desirability. Chopin, like many of her readers, might question whether such attraction constitutes love. Most of us would contend that Armand knows as much about love as he does about how to use his power over his slaves. In fact, Chopin explicitly links Armand's happiness in his marriage to his treatment of the people under his control.

We should beware of using Armand as an example of whether love can overcome racial bias, however, since his father undoubtedly came from the same culture but resisted its constraints, though not openly. Whereas Armand's character seems to show the inability of erotic love to overcome racial barriers, parental love, on the other hand, remains solid, even if, as in Monsieur and Madame Valmondé's case, the child is adopted. Racial prejudice wins in the case of Désirée, however, and we must assume that she allows her child to die with her in the swamps rather than facing life with Armand's rejection. Some readers may be reminded of Toni Morrison's novel *Beloved*, in which a mother kills her child to free her from slavery. For Chopin, too, this may have been a heroic act. Though Désirée has a foster mother with the power to prevent her child's enslavement, she is aware of the realities of plantation life and of her child's limited future. Speculations about Armand's future may range from suicide to freeing the slaves to fleeing to Paris, with most readers hoping that whatever course he takes will be miserable.

It may be more difficult to see how this story relates to breaking cultural taboos in our own time and place. We do not face such rigid role requirements. Still, class barriers based on money and education — and sometimes race and religion as well — are difficult for some to overcome. Many women, especially in certain regions and ethnic groups, are socialized to be subservient, and women often choose to give up their power to men much like Armand. Homosexuals face multiple barriers. Sometimes, babies do not fit the image that their parents have of the perfect child. In 1998, in a case in which babies were switched in a hospital nursery, one mother rejected her birth child as ugly and too black, a commentary on the persistence of internalized racial stereotypes and the self-hate they engender. Although times have changed to a great degree, it is still possible in many homes to bring the wrong type of person home for dinner. We could ask students to imagine what type of person this would be in their own families.

In the three stories in this cluster, the female characters feel quite differently about their husbands. Calixta, in "The Storm," understands the demands of the culture but retains a position of superiority over her husband. She is able to control the household — Bobinôt brings her shrimp and worries that she will be angry about their coming in dirty after the storm. And although she does not actively seek the passion of her lover, Alcée, it is her physical hunger to which he responds. Her husband seems to fit into the same category as her child, Bibi; she loves him, but as someone inferior to herself. Perhaps skin color plays a more prominent role than gender in the power relationships in their story, giving the light-skinned Calixta the upper hand. If so, readers may want to take Chopin to task for this, arguing that her text contains unconscious prejudice. Louise Mallard in "The Story of an Hour," on the other hand, seems to have possessed little power during her marriage. Her love for her husband is colored by this imbalance of power; she muses when she thinks he is dead that she has sometimes loved him, but sometimes has not. She has been the conventional wife of her social class, dependent and childlike, and finds freedom — or death — preferable to the emotional slavery of marriage.

We might ask if love is love when not freely given. In "Désirée's Baby," the young wife worships her husband but is fearful of him. Not only does her own welfare depend upon placating his temper, but the welfare of the slaves — with whom she empathizes and perhaps identifies — depends upon her keeping him happy in the marriage. She is much like the abused wife who thinks that taking the blows will protect her children. Again, we might ask if this is what our students want to define as love, or if Désirée's dependence upon the whims of a tyrant is something closer to masochism. We might question the husbands' love as well. Although we know little of Mr. Mallard in "The Story of an Hour," we may infer that he has been paternalistic and emotionally controlling, and probably loves her as he would love a favorite pet. Bobinôt in "The Storm" is in the opposite position; he adores his wife in a slavish but unequal way. While reading "Désirée's Baby," we question whether Armand's selfish and immature eroticism and pride can be categorized as love at all. The marriage of Bobinôt and Calixta seems the strongest of the three, an ironic fact, since theirs is the marriage that we would expect, according to the usual cultural norms, to find threatened by the wife's act of adultery. The faithful wives of the other two marriages are destroyed.

Kate Chopin's texts consistently question the received wisdom about marriage and its effect upon both men and women. Although her own marriage seems to have been a happy one, her fiction portrays the institution as destructive, especially for women. She does not offer answers, however, arguing against literature that preaches. If she could examine the present state of marriage, including divorce, we could expect her to approve gains in freedom, but perhaps she would focus upon the ways in which power continues to elude women in many cases. She would undoubtedly be proud of the resurgence of interest in her fiction and in the way women of the late twentieth century have received her ideas about their empowerment, ideas in many ways far ahead of her time.

ROMANTIC ILLUSIONS: CULTURAL CONTEXTS FOR DAVID HENRY HWANG'S *M. BUTTERFLY* (p. 780)

DAVID HENRY HWANG
M. Butterfly (p. 781)

Because both the play and the screenplay for the movie *M. Butterfly* were written by David Henry Hwang, the significant differences between the two can lead to fruitful discussions about revision and about adapting a text for a different audience and purpose. Although many of us will not have the available time to show the video recording of the movie in class, watching it together provokes more immediate and open discussion than having students view it on their own time. Substituting a viewing of the film for a reading of the play, however, focuses its interpretation in a different direction, losing many nuances that only the original drama offers. The most dramatic differences come with the linear approach to time and the realistic settings and presentation of action used in the movie, a major departure from the play's flashbacks, surreal atmosphere, and first-person narration by Gallimard himself. The unveiling of Song Liling and the impact of the movie's wonderfully absurd closing scene, kept much as it is in the play, seem to be part of a different reality. Whether the jarring difference in tone at the film's conclusion is appropriate or not is an aesthetic issue that we can debate if we are familiar with both texts. I give students the option of reading the play before we see the movie or waiting to read it later, but set up response assignments to require comparison and contrast. It is also useful to give them some background information about Puccini's opera, *Madama Butterfly*, beforehand and to discuss the preconceived notions that most Westerners have concerning Asian culture. Asian American students in the class can contribute insights about the mixed messages they have received from their families about cultures in China, Japan, Korea, and other countries.

David Henry Hwang, like many children of immigrants, grew up knowing little about Asian culture, since his father was primarily American and fundamentalist Christian. He plays upon the tendency of most Westerners to lump all Asians into one culture, having his French accountant, Rene Gallimard, see his Chinese opera singer as an incarnation of the Japanese geisha in Puccini's opera and himself as the American sailor Pinkerton. Gallimard's notions about "the Orient" are romantic and racially biased, with gender, culture, and geography linked in the drama, as they are in the colonial worldview. The geisha Butterfly in the opera is a male fantasy of dominance. She is fifteen, submissive and obedient, virginal yet eagerly in love, self-abnegating, and possessed of infinite patience. She is an exotic plaything whose adoration is encouraged and abused by the American sailor, who abandons her with empty promises when it is time to move on. At the end of the opera, Butterfly tragically commits suicide, giving up her child to Pinkerton's American wife in the same manner that she has earlier renounced her religion, the respect of her family, and the chance to marry a man of her own culture. Parallels with colonialism and with current Western domination of Third World countries seem obvious but may not at first occur to students. Hwang subverts the representation of Asia as an innocent and exotic plaything by the absurdity of his play, and he ends with the roles having been reversed, Gallimard becoming Butterfly. The Chinese character Song Liling plays the perfect Asian woman, innocent but possessed of esoteric sexual knowledge. Gallimard's self-deception is a factor of his selfishness; had he considered Song Liling to be a real person, rather than an objectified myth, he would not have remained ignorant of her (his) true nature.

Students, like most newspaper readers who first read about it, are shocked that David Henry Hwang's play is based upon the true story of French diplomat Bernard Boursicot's twenty-year love affair with Shi Pei Pu, a singer with the Peking Opera. When Boursicot discovered after his trial for espionage that his lover, who he thought to be the mother of his son, was actually a man and that the whole world was laughing about it, he refused to believe it for a time and then unsuccessfully attempted suicide. The least believable parts of Hwang's plot line actually come from the historical accounts of Boursicot's life, first brought to the attention of Americans — including Hwang — in the *New York Times* on May 11, 1986. Hwang claims that Boursicot's self-deception puzzled him, as it does most of us, until he connected it with the myth that Asian women are like Madame Butterfly and with the principle of Asian theater that only a man can act the part of an idealized woman.

The mystery of Gallimard's ignorance of sex is partially explained by the coldness of his marriage in the play, a marriage of convenience. We are given glimpses of his inadequacy in sexual encounters with Western women. His first experience is shown in flashback, and his affair with an American student named Renee androgynously echoes Gallimard's. Renee, he says, is "too masculine." Only the relationship with Song Liling, which borders on sadomasochism and which gives him the illusion of absolute power, excites and satisfies him. It is hard to imagine how Gallimard can be fooled, and students have trouble getting past their inability to believe that the facts of human anatomy escaped Gallimard or his real-life counterpart Boursicot. The fact that Boursicot was only twenty in 1964 when his affair with Shi began does not convince people of the same age that he could have intercourse with someone and not be aware of his partner's body. His unconscious self-deception, however, is the point of the story, and Hwang provides much evidence for it.

The play's protagonist is fooled because he so deeply desires to be fooled. But the very definition of sexual identity is called into question; perhaps Gallimard desires in Song Liling the qualities he denies within himself. Whereas he thinks of himself as the active male partner in intercourse, Song Liling explains at the trial that Gallimard has been passive, letting Song do all the work. The play's title hints at the ambiguity: To whom does it refer — Monsieur, Madame, Mr., Ms.,

Gallimard, or Song Liling? In addition to raising issues of sexual and cultural identity, the structure of Hwang's play questions the constructions that we impose on reality. As Gallimard explains himself, we enter into his version of reality. The same actors obviously play several roles, further questioning identity. Perhaps this is why the play is more compelling than the more linear and realistic film, where we depend too much upon our own interpretations of what we see rather than relying upon the narrator's point of view. In the courtroom scene in act 3, scene 1, Song Liling makes the play's point explicit when he maintains that men love the fantasy rather than the woman and when he suggests that this is true as well of international relations. Hwang deliberately draws the political analogy between sexual exploitation and imperialism.

CULTURAL CONTEXTS:

PAUL GRAY, "What Is Love?" (p. 831)
ANASTASIA TOUFEXIS, "The Right Chemistry" (p. 834)
NATHANIEL BRANDEN, "Immature Love" (p. 837)

Students tend to be romantics. Many accept the concept of love and are surprised to find that scholars have questioned its universality. While debate rages among social historians about whether or not romantic love is an invention of medieval literature, students see the answer as self-evident: *Of course, it isn't,* they think; *what fool would think it was?* Evolutionary and biochemical "proofs" also strike them as a waste of time, an attempt to quantify the spiritual essence of human relationships. Some eagerly educate us on the matter, using as proof their personal experiences with the difference between infatuation and (their recently or soon to be found) undying love, their sincerity touchingly imprinting the page as they write. While remaining sensitive to their interpretations, we should hold them to more carefully considered evidence. Some may take the view that it's all about sex, with love being a rationalization or a trap. Classroom discussions of multiple definitions of love and of the issues raised by our texts should stress the complexity of love's social construction in cultures and challenge students to examine their first assumptions more closely. These essays lend themselves to assignments in critical analysis, since each presents a thesis about love that is supported by evidence. Students can examine and evaluate three professional writers' handling of a similar theme.

The texts in this cluster that provide contexts for the love of Rene Gallimard for his fantasy of Song Liling deal with playwright David Henry Hwang's native culture: the United States in the last decades of the twentieth century. This is appropriate, since Hwang's play speaks primarily to American attitudes toward love and difference, even though none of its main characters is American. Paul Gray and Anastasia Toufexis produced their articles for a *Time* issue focusing on love for the week of Valentine's Day in 1993. Nathaniel Branden's point of view is more scholarly but more problematic; as a psychologist he has focused on self-esteem, and as a social and political thinker he tends toward the extreme individuality of the objectivist and libertarian movements. Paul Gray in "What Is

Love?" begins with a questioning title, which is followed by a series of questions in an epigraph, as he engages song lyrics in syntactic wordplay. His essay doesn't provide answers. After tracing a bit of cultural history and touching upon some scientific studies, he ends with another series of questions and a final surrender to love's seemingly "preposterous and mysterious" nature. Gray's words recall the tone and theme of *M. Butterfly*, with its paradox that Gallimard is unable to love the real person behind the fantasy of Song Liling. The ironic, black comedy of the play defines the Western male fantasy of love as pathetic (in more than one sense of the word) and absurd. Anastasia Toufexis in "The Right Chemistry" grants, as does Gray, that we do not want our illusions about love explained by science. Like Gallimard, we prefer the fantasy to the reality. Hwang's protagonist and the historical French diplomat upon which he is based practice incredible self-deception to keep love mysterious, illustrating the desire to which Toufexis refers in her closing sentence. Even anatomy is denied to retain the illusion of exotic romance.

Some students may protest that the homoerotic implications of the play's love story make the studies of heterosexual love to which Gray and Toufexis refer seem irrelevant. However, recent researchers of body language state that the same subliminal signals are exchanged by both homosexuals and heterosexuals. The movement of fingers on a drinking straw or the stem of a glass indicates "feminine" receptivity, for example, regardless of whether the person sending or receiving the signal is male or female. Such findings suggest to some scientists that human courtship behavior is learned rather than biochemical and evolutionary, though students may interpret the significance of these findings differently, drawing conclusions about the biological nature of homosexuality instead.

Nathaniel Branden's distinction between mature and immature love, based upon psychological factors having their genesis in childhood, relates most directly to Hwang's characters in the play. Unlike Branden's mature lovers, whose strengths complement each other, Gallimard and Song are both essentially passive, seeking self-esteem from outside sources and from destructive behavior toward each other. Gallimard fantasizes that Song is a Madame Butterfly waiting to be rescued, but he is also an immature lover, seeing her only as a source of gratification and not as a human being. Branden says that one characteristic of immature love is "that the man or woman does not perceive his or her partner realistically; fantasies and projections take the place of clear vision" (para. 15). He goes on to say that the lover subconsciously recognizes reality but chooses not to see it, to play the game. Through most of the 1960s Nathaniel Branden was the lover and anointed successor of philosopher and novelist Ayn Rand, twenty-five years his senior, with the permission of both their spouses. After their break in 1968, precipitated by his adultery with the young woman who became his second wife, Branden went on to become a successful psychotherapist and writer. He departs from Rand's privileging of logos over pathos, arguing instead that emotions should be integrated into reason rather than suppressed. He retains many of her precepts, however, the most relevant here being the assertion that each human being has a right to exist for his or her own sake, neither sacrificing

148

self to others nor others to self. Also important is the prohibition against force, whether exerted by individuals or by groups.

The relationship between the lovers in Hwang's play depends upon illusions of sacrifice and force, and in this sense they are compatible lovers. And at the end, Gallimard, now in his true personality as the masochistic Butterfly, commits the ultimate self-sacrifice, suicide. In the final enigmatic scenes of the play, we see something of Song's needs as well. In analyses of the play, most critics tend to be so taken with Gallimard's self-delusion that we forget that Song also plays the game. He knows that the roles are reversed all along, that he is the one who exploits the innocence of Gallimard. The reversal becomes explicit at the end as he cries out for his Butterfly, his compatible immature lover.

IS THIS LOVE? (p. 841)

ANN PETRY
Like a Winding Sheet (p. 841)

As an African American writing during the 1940s, Ann Petry lends a unique perspective to the cultural changes that occurred as a result of World War II. The short story "Like a Winding Sheet" relates the story of a black man and woman who fill slots in the American work force that might have gone to white men both before and after the war. For instructors using *Making Literature Matter* in courses that introduce persuasive appeals and encourage the analysis of texts for manipulation and bias, the wars of the twentieth century offer unparalleled examples of propaganda.

To provide context for this story, we have students search library and Internet sources for ways in which the war effort was sold to the American public. Several relevant posters can be found currently on the government Web site of the National Archives and Records Administration (http://www.nara.gov). One is the famous workingwoman icon *Rosie the Riveter*, meant to inspire women to take factory jobs while the men were away at war. Although we can point out that this newfound competence advanced women's rights, irrevocably assuring women that they were capable of successfully doing "men's work," Petry shows that her male protagonist has been frustrated by his inferior position as a man under the supervision of a woman. Other propaganda posters of the time ironically encourage the view that Negroes are needed in the war effort, projecting a misleading image of racial harmony in a segregated 1940s America. One poster pictures boxer Joe Louis as an army private; another pictures sailor "Dorie" Miller, who served as a kitchen worker on a ship based at Pearl Harbor but heroically manned the weapon of a white gunman who had been killed. A third shows a black worker and a white worker superimposed in front of an American flag, but interestingly the white worker is placed above the black man.

African American men had been allowed only menial, noncombative positions in the military prior to World War II. They were just beginning to receive limited opportunities to show that they could perform as soldiers, sailors, and airmen. Some students may know the history of the now highly respected Tuskegee Airmen, for example, who were permitted to fly only escort missions because their character and abilities were assumed to be inferior to those of white pilots. Both at home and abroad, black men had the added struggle of maintaining a semblance of dignity in the face of the insulting attitudes of people in power over them. The World War II era was neither the first nor the last time in American history when racial and gender issues came into conflict, with black women often being the greatest losers. Keeping these factors in mind will help students see this narrative as more complex than a question of spousal abuse, though this is certainly an issue that we will discuss.

The tendency readers might have to demonize any man who uses violence is forestalled by Ann Petry early in the story by helping us see the protagonist as a man who loves his wife. When she tells us that he "couldn't bring himself to talk to her roughly or threaten to strike her," Petry raises the possibility that some men might be violent, at the same time foreshadowing the action that follows. We are led into identifying with the protagonist's frustrations; thus it is easier to see ourselves as losing control given similar circumstances. Like the immature lovers discussed by Nathaniel Branden in the preceding cluster, we sometimes demand that our lovers make up for the disappointments and frustrations of our lives. Although the wife in this story seems flirtatious and playful with her husband, some barbs may lie underneath her teasing; she even begins by laughing at his blackness, perhaps a sore subject for a man whose blackness has been a burden to him, through no fault of his own. She is the one who mentions a "winding sheet," an important symbol that students may miss if they are not told that it signifies a shroud. The implication is that he looks to her like a dead man, but the image is repeated to show that he is tangled helplessly in circumstances and emotions from which he has no power to extricate himself. She works as hard as he does but remains cheerful, taking care of him.

Though we should not blame the victim in this story or elsewhere, we might consider how his awareness of her strength contributes to his exhaustion and depression. Some studies of spousal abuse indicate that male abusers often choose seemingly superior women as targets, since dominating strong women increases their perceived power. American culture in midcentury implicitly demanded that men see themselves as stronger and more competent than women. Ironically, the better the women in Petry's story copes with their difficult life, the worse the husband feels. These fictional lives help students see that the working poor are often trapped in situations that call their self-worth into question, causing them to strike out at each other. Statistically, family violence goes up during times of high unemployment and economic difficulties. Petry describes a scenario in which this happens without premeditation, catching the perpetrator of the violence by surprise.

We still hear protests from middle-class students that a way out can be found, no matter how difficult the circumstances. But where is the husband to find a better job, a better home? Where can he turn in a society that offers him no respect and few opportunities? When we stage a mock trial in class, many students will accept no excuses for violence and insist on convicting him of murder. They are sure that nothing could persuade them to do such a thing. A few argue for probation, convinced by Petry's description of his frustration and weariness that he should not be held responsible for losing control, that "to understand all is to forgive all." Most "jurors" opt for manslaughter and find him guilty, maintaining that although they understand his plight, he cannot be allowed to respond to his victimization by victimizing another person, especially one who loves him.

WILLIAM FAULKNER
A Rose for Emily (p. 849)

Just as Ann Petry's "Like a Winding Sheet" gains much from an understanding of its time, William Faulkner's "A Rose for Emily" depends upon a sense of place, of the social world in which the story's events occur. An intricate history of family relationships and social hierarchies structure William Faulkner's imaginary Mississippi town of Jefferson, the county seat of Yoknapatawpha County, where most of his fiction has its roots. Any outsider, anyone breaking the strict rules of conformity, is suspect here. On the other hand, belonging to the right family or having the right connections grants one indulgences, no matter how eccentric one's behavior seems to be. Readers may want to consider issues raised by such a world in which everyone is given a particular role. Love and courtship, like all other parts of life, are the community's business, and the community tells Miss Emily Grierson's story, appropriately using the unusual first-person-plural point of view, *we*. Faulker's story depends upon character and plot, and its impact depends upon its ironic ending.

Accustomed from childhood to stories of the macabre, today's students may be less impressed with the plot and its chilling conclusion than its first readers were in the 1930s, but they are quicker to spot the psychological implications of Miss Emily's strange and oppressive relationship with her father. They also enjoy recent critical speculations about Homer Barron's possible homosexuality, which are based on the narrators' statement that Barron likes the company of men, perhaps simply referring to his preference for barrooms and stereotypically male activities. On the other hand, students who see the recent dramatic presentation of the story on video are led into believing that Emily and Homer consummate their relationship, a reading that assumes facts Faulkner preferred to leave unresolved. Although we often cannot spare the time in class to read the story aloud, a skilled reader can highlight Faulkner's technique, demonstrating how flashbacks, suspense, and narrative pace enhance the story. The long, periodic sentence that closes Faulkner's narrative illustrates his strategy in microcosm, slowing the action for dramatic effect and providing us with an example of inductive organization.

Readers questioning Emily's actions need to consider her earlier denial of her father's death and to think about what might cause such dependency. She is desperate to find a husband in a time and place where women are failures if they do not attract a man, and Emily has been thwarted by her father's possessiveness at

151

the age this might have happened. Emily has inherited or learned a family tendency to hold on past the time of letting go. Because we see their relationship through the limited vision of the town, we do not know what Homer's intentions are, nor do we know how much of the relationship exists in Emily's imagination. Our limited point of view also makes it hard to judge *when* Emily becomes disturbed. When she loses Homer through rejection perhaps? Or much earlier when her father dies? We can imagine cultures that would consider her to be not sick but evil, an aristocrat who is so determined to have her way that she kills out of pride and self-will rather than love. Most cultures would censure her poisoning of her beloved so that she could sleep with his corpse, but we might ask if she simply takes to extremes the dictates of her culture that she must have a man to have self-worth.

The story's perspective adds to the ambiguity of Emily's motives and allows the reader more room for speculation. To give the narration over to Emily might make it an interesting psychological study, but would rob the story of its mystery and irony. It would also remove an important collective character, the town itself. If Southern small-town culture determines who Emily Grierson will be, the influence is mutual. They own her and live through her; the adjectives at the end of paragraph 51 describe their ambivalence and her seeming omnipresence in their lives. The contention that Faulkner is writing less a personal love story than an allegory about the South seems credible in this context. The collective conspiracy to hide and overlook the corruption and the forced ownership of others — body and soul — that characterizes much of the South's history seems aptly symbolized by the events of "A Rose for Emily." And it is interesting that the only character who probably knows the whole story is the black butler who takes care of Emily and thus facilitates her insanity. Some readers might note that the maintenance of Southern society is thus dependent upon the continuance of slavery, even after emancipation. Of course, the story could just as well be a warning about what happens to women who get mixed up with Yankees. Students with roots in the South may provide insights about how the South has changed or remained the same as Faulkner described it in 1930.

The African American male protagonist of Ann Petry's "Like a Winding Sheet" and the aging Southern belle of William Faulkner's "A Rose for Emily" both find themselves prevented from living out the roles that society says they must. Petry's protagonist cannot live up to his presumed role as the strong male provider and achiever because the same society that makes his sense of manhood depend upon this role denies him the chance to assume it. He is unable to deal with it and instead reacts to something in his wife that reminds him of his oppression. Emily, too, finds the ways blocked to filling her expected role in society and in marriage. She takes what she needs to feel like a woman, even though she must kill to keep the illusion. When we vote on possible punishments for Emily, "jurors" are quicker to send her to a mental hospital, and the black man of Petry's story is usually consigned to prison. Because many of our students are old enough to serve on actual jury panels, the issues raised by this difference are worth discussing. Do we forgive Emily more easily because she is a woman? Do race and social standing play a subliminal role in our assignment of responsibility?

Or does she just seem more clearly insane in the legal sense of the term? The stories provide us also with an issue of the definition of *love*. In our evaluations of Petry's and Faulkner's main characters, Petry's protagonist usually wins. Students argue that he loves his wife, and his beating of her is more about his frustration than about their relationship. Others maintain that if he really loved her he would not take out his frustrations on her, no matter what the circumstances. Most readers do not see Emily's feelings as love but rather as the obsession and fantasy of a sick mind.

RAYMOND CARVER

What We Talk About When We Talk About Love (p. 856)

Although earlier characterizations of Raymond Carver as a minimalist have been challenged as a result of his later work in the 1980s, the term still applies to the stories in the collection *What We Talk About When We Talk About Love,* including this one, which gives the book its title. Carver said of these stories that he cut them "to the marrow, not just to the bone." By using a first-person narrator within the story and limiting our knowledge of other characters to what that narrator experiences, Carver allows his readers little information from which to make interpretations, leaving many questions unanswered. Since we have defined an *issue* in this anthology as a question about which reasonable people may disagree, we should therefore expect to encounter many issues in our reading of Carver. When the narrator passes on to us the stories that Mel tells him, for example, we are limited to just what the narrator hears and observes and must further take into account the fact that Mel is probably drunk. Perhaps, because he is drunk, he is weaving fact and fiction or remembering things incorrectly. Or the old saying *in vino veritas* may instead come into play, and we can trust his word *because* he is too drunk to mind his words.

Carver's biography is relevant to "What We Talk About When We Talk About Love" because he lived many years as an alcoholic. His stories sometimes reflect the state of his first marriage as well, one that began too early — making him the father of two children by the time he was twenty — and that ended in divorce in 1982, the year after this story was published. His dialogue captures the realities of everyday life, but the prosaic details of conversations and commonplace actions mask turning points for his characters. Greatly influenced by the Russian writer Anton Chekhov, Carver leads his characters into a "Chekhovian moment," when the soul of the character is revealed in a subtle way. This moment seems to approach for the characters of this story as they come to see the gulf between their attempts at defining love and the glimpse of love Mel gives in his anecdote about an old couple injured in an accident. Perhaps pathos is a more precise answer to this issue of the definition of love than all the logic we can muster.

153

Ironically, we are told immediately that Mel is a cardiologist — a heart doctor — and that this ethos gives him the right to talk about love. He wants to think of love as the Greek *agape*, as something spiritual. His wife Terri, on the other hand, defines love in the context of an abusive relationship that she had in the past with a man named Ed. She can understand the sort of passion that leads one to kill or to die for what she calls love, and her insistence that Ed loved her implies that something is wanting in the sort of love Mel offers. Though Ed is not present and is, in fact, dead, his definition of love is the one with which the characters must contend. The narrator Nick and his wife Laura still bask in the warmth of newlywed bliss; their love is comfortably physical; they touch and kiss from time to time in response to the conversation. And love gets a bit too easy as the neighbors reassure each other that they are loved, cheapening the word *love* in the glow of the gin they are drinking.

The story of the old man who is depressed because they are both swaddled in casts and he cannot see his wife is juxtaposed with Mel's desire to talk to his kids and his fantasies about arranging a painful death for his ex-wife. The result is depressing, and the story ends with the narrator listening to their hearts beating as the gin runs out and the room gets dark. Whatever love is, we can conclude that they don't have it. Although Mel does not drag Terri through the kitchen by her ankles, an undercurrent of hostility and dissatisfaction runs through their conversation, and he sometimes becomes verbally abusive. If, as the cliché goes, love and hate are twins, the intensity of Mel's desire to let bees loose to kill his ex-wife indicates that he has strong feelings for her. His feelings for Terri, on the other hand, seem peculiarly bland. Terri longs for the passion of Ed. Students are likely to conclude that both are fairly sick puppies.

Mel's interest in knights may provide a clue to what Carver is saying about romantic love. Some scholars have maintained that love as we define it comes from the courtly love tradition of medieval Europe. Carver undercuts the idea of a man performing feats of daring for his fair lady through sarcastic humor, profanity, and the increasing inebriation of the conversation's participants. Although the story of the old couple seems to indicate that true love exists, we have to remember that the story comes through Mel. Carver does not articulate a definition of love for us, nor does he come up with one answer for the question implied in his title. Because assigning Carver's story, we can ask students to come up with their own definitions and to relay their anecdotes of love. This will allow a more informed discussion of the subtexts of both their stories and Carver's.

Carver's "What We Talk About When We Talk About Love" allows us to see little of the motivation of its characters, letting us eavesdrop on a conversation. William Faulkner's "A Rose for Emily" also limits our vision, depicting the title character as a statue or idol observed from afar by a close-minded town. On the other hand, Ann Petry in "Like a Winding Sheet" gives us a window on the consciousness of her protagonist; we understand him much better than we do the characters in the other stories. All three characters who hurt others — Ed, Emily, and the husband of Petry's story — are made frantic and desperate by something in their lives, and their strong emotions overflow into their personal relationships. Because we hear of Ed in the context of a discussion of love, we may accept the motive of his violence as connected with the power of his immature love for Terri, but perceptive readers will challenge this assumption as simplistic. Similarly, our views of Terri, Mae, and Homer as victims must take into account the tendency of immature lovers to find partners who play compatible games, as Nathaniel Branden points out in the essay "Immature Love" in the previous cluster. As instructors, we have done best by our students if they leave our discussion with a more complicated view of love than what they had at the beginning.

TROUBLED MARRIAGES (p. 866)

ANNE SEXTON
The Farmer's Wife (p. 867)

Classes that read the fairy tales of the first cluster of the "Living in Families" section of *Making Literature Matter* find themselves in a world Anne Sexton shares. In her 1971 collection *Transformations*, Sexton retells Grimm fairy tales with a feminist slant, reinterpreting characters like Cinderella and Snow White. "The Farmer's Wife" comes from an earlier collection, her 1960 *To Bedlam and Part Way Back*, but it shares with the fairy tales a bitter ambivalence about women's roles in twentieth-century American society. Like Robert Lowell, whose "To Speak of the Woe That Is in Marriage" directly follows "The Farmer's Wife," Anne Sexton is usually thought of as a confessional poet who used the facts of her own life in her poetry. For this reason, much attention tends to be given to both poets for their quite real psychological problems, and students are usually interested in knowing about Sexton's suicide. Nevertheless, each poet often assumes a persona in particular poems, and students who know their biographies should be encouraged to let the poems tell their own stories.

"The Farmer's Wife" is not Anne Sexton, but she is a person whom Anne Sexton understands. The poem is characterized by mixed feelings and unexpected turns of phrase. It begins with phrases that suggest oppressive boredom. The doubled idea of "hodge porridge" describes not married love but their "country lust," and conveys feelings of disorder, dreariness, and the unromantic hungers of the body. It continues in the same vein, referring to the wife as "his habit," and conveying the farmer's only snippet of dialogue, a trivial invitation that good-naturedly takes her for granted. She has flashes of sensual pleasure but no intimacy. The connotations of "sweat" and "the blowzy bag / of his usual sleep" disgust most readers, as Sexton surely intends. This sort of language is mild when compared with the language of Sexton's later poems, however, where she often directs more explicit terms for bodily functions and excretions toward herself.

The ending strikes many as extreme. "Why doesn't she just leave if she's so unhappy?" we hear students ask again, as they so often do of such texts. Surely the answer is that her feelings are complex, that her fantasies are the stuff of romantic fiction and soap opera but represent reasons why a person might *feel* something. Part of our consideration must be the times; the 1960s are beginning to open up options, though maybe not to some farmer's wives. She may not want to be free of him, but to shake him — and herself — into actually experiencing emotion.

The last line is difficult. Why does the speaker suddenly use the first-person pronoun when she has used third person in earlier lines? Some critics have suggested that the poet switches to her own voice, but this seems unlikely. Is the wife addressing her husband? If she is, "my lover" seems a strange way for a farmer's wife to address the husband who calls her "honey bunch," though we might understand her changing a husband into a lover in fantasy, something along the lines of crying out the wrong name during sex. And those who have read the stories of Kate Chopin in an earlier cluster (p. 768) will perhaps understand the motive behind wishing her husband dead, even if she loves him. Even grief is preferable to numbness. Perhaps she imagines that it would be better to dream romantically of a dead lover than to live with an emotionally dead husband.

Readers will say that we are being too tough on the farmer, however, and suggest that they talk it out. We might raise the issue of whether she is actually the one who is unable to get in touch with feelings. She enjoys sex but has no sense of being in love. Students may question whether there is a difference between the two, and how one can tell. The phrase "that old pantomime of love" and other terms she uses to show the habitual nature of the couple's relationship implies that they go through the motions of sex, both deriving pleasure from it, but that this is for her a hollow mockery of love.

Although Sexton's title tells us that this is a farmer's wife, the poem could refer to other relationships. A subtext of the poem is the wife's compliance when the husband yet again assumes his privilege of sex with his ever-available "honey bunch." Perhaps the perennial question does apply: If she is unfulfilled, why does she continue? And why does she keep her discontent to herself? Students might speculate about what his response would be if she did complain of being used. Probably he would be hurt and bewildered. Would she lose more than she gains by telling him? Could she suggest that they have sex less often to increase intimacy? If he agreed, would this help? Of course, one of the joys of poetry is that we can allow the couple to remain forever in the limbo of their farm in Illinois. We don't have to save this marriage. But we can learn from the debate, and it may be comforting for some readers to know that others have questioned whether sex is equivalent to intimacy. Though forty years after this poem's publication women feel freer to express their needs and men more often realize the importance of emotional closeness, it would be naive to think such relationships no longer exist.

ROBERT LOWELL

To Speak of the Woe That Is in Marriage (p. 868)

Speaking of the particular style of poetry that he wrote in *Life Studies* (1959), the collection from which this poem is taken, Robert Lowell denied that all of his "confessional" poems were explicitly autobiographical. "This is not my private lash, or confession, or a puritan's too literal pornographic honesty, glad to share secret embarrassment and triumph," he explains. Well read and well educated, Lowell first followed and then broke with the New Critics of Kenyon College. He wrote poems that are often intertextual, drawing upon his own experiences and upon many other sources as well. The title of "To Speak of the Woe That Is in Marriage" echoes Geoffrey Chaucer's Wife of Bath as she begins her turn in *The Canterbury Tales*. After telling us of her marital adventures, wherein she keeps the upper hand until she marries a younger man who rules her, Chaucer's bawdy narrator goes on to give us the tale of a quest. Her protagonist must discover what every woman most desires. The answer to the riddle is that every woman wants to be in charge, to take the superior position. This raises issues about the relationship of the title to the poem; do they have any connection beyond the common theme "woe . . . in marriage"?

Lowell follows his title with an epigraph from Schopenhauer that links the joys of marriage to the continuance of families and the human race, an important element in Lowell's thinking. His poem seems to undercut both the title and the epigraph. Like the marriage in Anne Sexton's "The Farmer's Wife," this marriage seems peculiarly unsatisfying and lacking in joy. The wife gains temporary mastery by finding a way to keep her husband from driving through the streets looking for sex, but she gains nothing from it. The last lines, comic if read as true rhyme but serious and threatening in the images of clumsiness and impotence they project, make marriage seem like a ridiculous and truly woeful exercise. The poem's forced, imperfect rhymes and slang expressions contrast absurdly with the violent images. The romantic magnolia blossoms of the second line quickly give way to dangerous pictures of a man on the prowl, and the poem ends by comparing him to a beast. He is an elephant, but he is also gored. Women usually experience a "climacteric," the end of their fertility; but Lowell applies the term to "his want," showing us a man without sexual powers. He "stalls." The woman holds the keys to the car, the great American symbol of mobility and power.

The wife says that the man is "unjust." Perhaps the reference is to the Wife of Bath's contention that it is a sin to deny sex to a partner in marriage; he does not give her what she justly deserves, his love. But perhaps what he denies her is mastery. Since we hear what happens through her interpretation alone, we can question the nature of their disputes. Line 5 presents a complex metaphor: the man goes "free-lancing out along the razor's edge." When a person freelances, the implication is that he or she is independent, able to operate without controls. He breaks free of marriage. But if he owes her his love, he also spends it freely — and unjustly — on others less threatening, not on her. There may be sexual connotations to the "lance" as well. What's more, a surgeon might "lance" a boil with something not unlike a razor. The "razor's edge" implies danger and fear. The pledge she thinks he might take may be to no longer have sex with prostitutes. But the wife may fear he pledges to kill her.

Lowell teases us with multiple meanings and with the image of the money and car key tied to the wife's thigh. Students should follow the ramifications of their decisions about the possible meanings of this symbol. If we follow the Wife of Bath scenario, perhaps it is the woman's way of gaining mastery and getting what he owes her, but since he "stalls above" her, she hardly seems in a superior position. And what are we to make of the epigraph? Will they conceive a child as a result of this encounter forced by the wife? In 1958, many marriages did continue in spite of such woe, but two of Robert Lowell's marriages ended in divorce. Some students will still contend that marriage is forever, no matter what.

Both Anne Sexton's "The Farmer's Wife" and Robert Lowell's "To Speak of the Woe That Is in Marriage" present pessimistic views of marriage. Sexton's married couple seems to have the most hope of continuing their relationship, since the husband at least seems content. The husband in Lowell's poem, on the other hand, seems on the verge of exploding. Yet some might argue that at least Lowell's female narrator speaks out, whereas Sexton's protagonist has unhealthy fantasies about her husband's death. It might be more useful to ask if all of the characters in these two poems are asking for fulfillment and self-esteem from their spouses rather than developing these qualities within themselves. If the wives in these poems from the end of the 1950s feel trapped, it may be because the culture told them they would be failures as women if their marriages failed. They feel compelled to stay with the situation, and they love their husbands less because of their inability to choose freely. The husband in Lowell's poem is trapped as well, and he responds to his wife's complaints by escaping in a way that is considered manly to many in the culture. His wife, on the other hand, may be accused of emasculating him symbolically by demanding her due. And most will agree that she is a whiner. Is this the sort of accusation the wife in Sexton's poem fears would fall on her if she spoke out?

Giving these poems to friends about to marry would be cruel. But oversimplifying the difficulties of marriage does no one any favors. We might consider the source of these pessimistic views of marriage. Both poems come from writers who had profound problems with psychological illnesses that perhaps could be treated now with lithium and antidepressant drugs. Personal issues may color their attitudes toward family relationships. Although aspects of marriage have at times been destructive for cultural reasons, the marriages in these poems are — as our title for the cluster indicates — troubled ones, and the institution itself may not be at fault.

A MARRIAGE WORTH SAVING?: CRITICAL COMMENTARIES ON HENRIK IBSEN'S *A DOLL HOUSE* (p. 870)

HENRIK IBSEN
A Doll House (p. 871)

It's been said that when Nora Helmer first slammed the door on her marriage in the final scene of Henrik Ibsen's 1879 play *A Doll House*, the windows shook in houses all over Europe. It was shocking to Ibsen's contemporaries that Nora leaves a loving, indulgent husband for what his first audience would have seen as a difficult and shameful future. The husband's language and behavior, which seem so patronizing and demeaning to current readers, would have been seen as appropriate, even admirable. But it is Nora's desertion of her children that seemed to Ibsen's readers the most unnatural action a woman could take. In some countries, the ending was changed, having her turn back and stay for the sake of the children. This element will probably be the most difficult for our students to understand as well. We need to explain or have them do research on divorce in the nineteenth century so that they will realize that Torvald Helmer has complete power over the lives and welfare of the children, just as he legally has control over Nora herself. Nora will have only the maternal rights he allows her, even if this means she will never see her children again. The first thought of readers, that she should take her children with her to ensure that they will not repeat the mistakes of their parents' faulty relationship, is anachronistic. This is not a possible choice for Nora.

What happens to Nora after the door closes behind her often dominates class discussions. Does she change her mind and return as soon as she realizes how hard life will be for her? Is Torvald capable of changing, as his words at the end of the play seem to indicate? What does happen to those children? The question of what happens after the door slams is so common in literature classes that the British comedy series *Monty Python's Flying Circus* was assured of an audience when it featured recurring scenarios showing Nora's possible fate. The funniest may be the scene that has her walk into the street only to be trampled by a passing parade of Suffragettes. The ironic joke makes sense because we also realize that *A Doll House* invites feminist readings.

Although Ibsen denied that he had a feminist intent in writing the play, Nora's character can only be understood in the context of woman's position in marriage and in the financial world. To our students, Helmer's paternalism toward his wife seems inconceivably controlling, and her manipulation and lying painfully weak — embarrassing to watch. The character traits in Nora that current readers hold in contempt are those reflected in the title; we are disgusted that she behaves as a child, even a plaything. But she sees herself as taking care of her men. She leaves not so much because Helmer has behaved as a petty god, but because he does not carry the "bargain" to its conclusion and rescue her, sacrifice himself for her completely. We cannot emphasize strongly enough that Torvald Helmer lives exactly as his culture told him he should. Students may know men today who live by a rigid code of honor and who control their families like tyrants, and they may in fact recognize their fathers in Helmer. Objections that the childish, manipulative woman stereotype is specific to the Victorian era can be forestalled by juxtaposing almost any 1950s episode of *I Love Lucy* with the scenes of Nora hiding macaroons and elaborately manipulating to hide her financial misdeeds. Lucy Ricardo is cute and dumb, always hiding things and disobeying her husband's rules; Ricky is indulgent and controlling, easily angered, concerned about what others might think. Nor should we assume that the childish role of the wife has disappeared at the year 2000. This writer knows of two young working mothers who have agreed to retrieve mail for each other so that their husbands do not see the credit-card bills until they get their stories straight. Although they deal with financial matters at work competently and honestly and go home to function as good mothers, both tend to slip into roles not unlike Nora's. Ibsen's use of the tarantella is often interpreted as "stage business" that is meant primarily to hold the attention of the audience. But taken symbolically, its frantic, abnormal energy aptly depicts the emotional strain of such relationships. When one partner "dances" as fast as she can to distract the other into allowing her a shred of autonomy, she reenacts the medieval phenomenon that lies behind the tarantella: Bitten by a spider, the victim dances herself to death.

CRITICAL COMMENTARIES:

HENRIETTA FRANCIS LORD, From "The Life of Henrik Ibsen" (p. 923)
CLEMENT SCOTT, "'Ibsen's Unlovely Creed'" (p. 924)
HERMANN J. WEIGAND, From *The Modern Ibsen* (p. 925)
KATHERINE M. ROGERS, From "Feminism and *A Doll House*" (p. 927)
JOAN TEMPLETON, From "The *Doll House* Backlash: Criticism, Feminism, and Ibsen" (p. 931)

 Henrik Ibsen's *A Doll House* inspired controversy in its time and continues to do so. By examining some of the readings that have been applied to the play over time, our students get a sense of how historicist research and interpretation might be done. We are not limited to the immediate social and historical context of a text, nor must we consider it as an object to be evaluated as universal art, but we may also study how it changes over time and in different situations as readers interact with it. Henrietta Francis Lord translated the play and wrote the introduction to the playwright's life in London in 1882; this small excerpt is taken from that introduction. Mrs. Lord — ladies of her generation, no matter how progressive, would expect the title Mrs. — acknowledges that her axiom about freedom is problematic. But she asserts that Nora's husband, and by extension Western culture, has kept reality from Nora. Therefore, she does not have the knowledge to solve problems on her own. This seems reasonable. It also seems reasonable that love is not love if it is based on pretense. We might push our students beyond simple agreement or disagreement with Lord's axiom to suggest how authenticity may be learned, especially in marriages like the Helmers', in which playacting has solidified into habit. Do we always play roles, even when we think we are being forthright?

 In the 1920s, Hermann Weigand could not believe that Ibsen wanted us to take the character of Nora seriously. She is instead a silly, madcap little flapper. We might think ahead to *I Love Lucy*. How cute when Lucy has to admit her foolishness and beg forgiveness of Ricky. The majority of our student readers, especially women, will be insulted by Weigand's patronizing and naive indulgence, which we recognize as unconscious bigotry against women. Katherine Rogers, writing in the 1980s in the context of a women's studies course, would object, of course, to Weigand's talk of the inborn tendencies in women to engage in flirting and playacting to manipulate their husbands. She would maintain that these tendencies and the romantic fantasies about marriage that both Nora and Torvald Helmer hold through most of the play are learned and culturally determined rather than essential to being male or female. Furthermore, Rogers would suggest that our students should question how these and other assumptions still play a role in relationships.

As students search out the most useful and least useful comments in the five critical texts, they should avoid simply summarizing or woodenly comparing and contrasting the writers' opinions. Encourage them instead to create a synthesis that uses the ideas of the critics as a starting point for their own extrapolations, inviting them to enter into the academic dialogue surrounding Ibsen's play.

| 10 |

Considering Outsiders

PASSIVE RESISTANCE:
CULTURAL CONTEXTS FOR
RALPH ELLISON'S "BATTLE ROYAL" (p. 936)

RALPH ELLISON
Battle Royal (p. 937)

In the prologue of the novel *Invisible Man*, Ralph Ellison's unnamed protagonist begins:

> I am an invisible man. . . . I am invisible, understand, simply because people refuse to see me. Like the bodiless heads you see sometimes in circus sideshows, it is as though I have been surrounded by mirrors of hard, distorting glass. When they approach me they see only my surroundings, themselves, or figments of their imagination — indeed, everything and anything except me.

After he thus sets the stage, revealing the protagonist as a trickster who has surrendered to his invisibility, appropriating it to his own uses by hiding in an underground room where he steals electricity from Monopolated Light and Power, Ellison has his hero take us back to his childhood. It is there in his first chapter, "Battle Royal," that we see the protagonist, his idealism intact, beginning his long, futile search for recognition and the fulfillment of the American dream. It was the sense of futility and the ironic and self-mocking tone of the novel that upset many African American readers when the book first appeared in 1952. Nevertheless, Ellison's *Invisible Man* stands as a modernist American masterpiece and offers a surreal and resignedly bitter view of African American experience in the twentieth century. Writing just after World War II and just before the active civil rights and black power movements of the years to immediately follow, Ellison shows the dilemma of a man who is naive and powerless before the political and social forces that seek to define him. Our first step in preparing our students for "Battle Royal" might be to read excerpts from the prologue and to lead them to see that the text is both serious and satirical. It is appropriate for readers to be overwhelmed with empathy for the young boy and to be horrified by the actions of the white bigots. But they can also be led to see the author's anger at the accommodationist ethic that shapes the narrator's response and the satirical tone that critiques it. The background materials following "Battle Royal" in this cluster provide invaluable social, historical, and philosophical background. Jonathan Swift's "A Modest Proposal" (p. 696) might be used to compare satirical methods and T. S. Eliot's "The Love Song of J. Alfred Prufrock" (p. 763) to show an example of the pessimistic, modernist tone used by a writer Ralph Ellison admired and may have emulated.

Although some who lived during the early twentieth century in the South will maintain that the horrors of racial hatred and its perverse manifestations cannot be overestimated, Ellison's story is best seen as symbolic rather than directly representational. The narrator thinks he will be seen and heard as an individual and as a credit to his race, but he instead must go through trials that debase his humanity and both ignore and misuse his voice. He and his peers are set against each other in the battle royal. Students may see the economic ramifications of this, when workers must compete for limited jobs and incentives rather than being able to unite. This becomes especially evident in the electrified rug trial, in which the boys must scramble for money that turns out to be counterfeit. Not only do they compete rather than unite, but the promised reward turns out to be a lie, just as the African American community found themselves divided and their full equality deferred in the century between emancipation in the 1860s and the civil rights gains of the 1960s. The presence of the white stripper easily symbolizes the mixture of fear and pornography implied in miscegenation laws intended to keep stereotypically lustful and bestial black men from presumably overwhelmingly desirable white women: The woman is a temptress, but she is also being used. Students might want to further consider the division between the rights of women and the rights of minorities that was long encouraged to the detriment of both groups, especially women of color. They might also research the cult of Southern womanhood that grew out of race and gender prejudice.

Students may also notice that the boys must wear blindfolds, are denied the information they need to defend themselves. In some states, it had been illegal to teach slaves to read. Later, separate schools, when they existed for blacks, were unequal. In higher education, accommodationist leaders like Booker T. Washington felt that students would be better served by vocational education, and they worked against university education. Students who think the white establishment rewards the hero after his trials by sending him to what is obviously Booker T. Washington's Tuskegee Institute are mistaken, since the school maintains the ideals of segregation.

The bizarre behavior of the white town leaders may be exaggerated for dramatic and satirical effect, but we should not be too quick to assume this. Lynchings were characterized by just such behavior, with castration, burning, and flaying accompanying the hanging. Historical research will provide students with even more horrifying examples than those in Ellison's narrative, with photographs showing not only civic leaders but some women and children, all dressed in their Sunday best for viewing the torture.

The narrator's dream in which his grandfather laughs at him is puzzling unless we consider the irony of his situation. He does not yet realize that he is one of the clowns in this bizarre circus that is twentieth century America. His grandfather has claimed that the only way to fight is to subvert, to be a trickster who hides behind the mask of servility. What is ludicrous is to believe the empty promises, to be willing to wait only to realize that another kind of slavery must be escaped. The narrator has endured the trials because he believes he will eventually be seen and heard. But the only phrase really heard in his speech is the "social equality" slip of the tongue that could potentially get him lynched. Students will propose solutions for dealing with oppression that reflect the debates of passive resistance and violent action, but many need help understanding the complexities of a situation that made direct action so difficult and dangerous.

CULTURAL CONTEXTS:

BOOKER T. WASHINGTON, "Atlanta Exposition Address" (p. 948)
W. E. B. DU BOIS, "Of Mr. Booker T. Washington" (p. 952)
GUNNAR MYRDAL, "Social Equality" (p. 956)
AFRICAN AMERICAN FOLK SONG, "Run, Nigger, Run" (p. 959)

Booker T. Washington's speech at the Atlanta Cotton States and International Exposition in 1895 met with great approval in both the black and white communities. This "Atlanta Compromise" sealed Washington's already considerable reputation as the leader of his race. Ralph Ellison's "Battle Royal" loses much of its irony for readers who do not catch his allusions to Washington's famous metaphors. Ellison's protagonist is steeped in the rhetoric and philosophy of Washington, and the white men at the smoker can be expected to approve his borrowed words. "Cast down your bucket where you are" was a way of telling African Americans to accept the menial jobs they were given to do rather than aspiring toward education and equality. Washington's metaphor of the hand being united in effort while the fingers remain separate in "all things purely social" maintained a myth that encouraged Jim Crow laws and the idea that the races could remain separate but equal. In practice, segregation allowed continued inequality. Because of this, the young man's audience is not threatened by Washington's rhetoric of "social responsibility" that kept Negroes in an economically and politically inferior position. Many students will protest that Booker T. Washington worked tirelessly for his people and that it would have been dangerous to proceed in any other way. He may be compared with the protagonist's grandfather, who considers his submissive demeanor to be subversive warfare. Others might learn from research that some scholars maintain Washington gained a great deal of personal power and influence, while retarding the progress of equal rights for the great majority of African Americans. Although he may have acted as he did for pragmatic reasons, he also harbored doubts about the ability of most black people to ever achieve as the equals of whites.

W. E. B. Du Bois had no doubts about the potential of African Americans, however. As editor of the newspaper of the National Association for the Advancement of Colored People and holder of a Ph.D. from Harvard University granted the same year as Washington's speech in Atlanta, his was a strong voice of opposition to Washington's compromising patience. In this essay from *The Souls of Black Folk*, Du Bois objects to Washington's tacit admission of the inferiority of Negroes at a time when leaders should be seeking full citizenship for members of the race.

Ellison's narrator is still under the influence of Washington, but readers can recognize that he is learning the folly of his subservience to the white establishment. Though he spends most of the story just wanting to give his speech, to show what a good little Negro boy he is, the mask is beginning to slip. At the beginning of the story, we hear the voice of experience as he describes his invisibility. But mostly, doubts surface in his memory of his grandfather's words on his deathbed and later in the protagonist's dream. The grandfather has lived out the letter of Booker T. Washington's law of compromise, but the spirit of his submission is the ironic treachery of the trickster. He implies that only a clown would take seriously the precepts of Washington. "I did what I had to do," he seems to say, "but I kept my sense of self. I was faking it all the time." Perhaps, he would feel that the open declaration of human rights espoused by Du Bois would make him vulnerable to attack. The South is more dangerous for people with dark skins than Du Bois's native Massachusetts, though Du Bois certainly experienced prejudice. Like the protagonist eventually does in Harlem in the novel *Invisible Man*, the grandfather uses his invisibility as a weapon, pessimistically rejecting attempts to be seen and heard as a man. Rather than feeling emasculated, he feels empowered by his ability to fool the white man. What many of Ellison's readers would say about this, however, is that his protagonist therefore chooses the way of the slave in place of Du Bois's stand for human dignity.

Reading Swedish economist Gunnar Myrdal's "Social Equality" provides the most telling information about the significance of the protagonist's accidental substitution for Washington's "social responsibility" catch phrase. Once we understand that "social equality" is a buzz phrase to the men at the smoker, conjuring up images of black men having sexual relations with white women, the protagonist's Freudian slip during his speech and the bristling reaction of his audience take on added meaning. Nothing could be expected to inflame the white citizenry more than the emotions raised by such rhetoric. In 1898, for example, when African American writer Alexander Manley suggested that white women might sometimes *choose* to have sexual relations with black men, his editorial was reprinted over and over by publishers of the local newspaper of Wilmington, North Carolina, to stir up unrest in the white community. As a result, support was found for the armed overthrow of an elected city government that had many black members, reversing the course of racial equality for many years and — to use a term far in the future — ethnically cleansing the city of its most successful citizens of African descent. (Remember that this is the same year as Atlanta's applause for Booker T. Washington's optimistic speech and Harvard's acceptance of Du Bois's doctoral dissertation on the slave trade.) Students may recall examples from early twentieth-century history, like the cases of Emmett Till or the Scottsboro Boys, when black men lost their lives over trivial accusations by white women. Many may have read Harper Lee's novel *To Kill a Mockingbird*, in which a black man is wrongfully accused of rape. We might even go as far back as William Shakespeare's *Othello* for an image connecting racial intermarriage and violence. And, although we might not want to veer into discussions of the O. J. Simpson murder case of the 1990s, a long history of racially charged rhetoric featuring brutal black men and victimized white women may explain much of the extreme emotion exhibited by both admirers and haters of Simpson. Viewing the culture from the outside, Myrdal saw the fears raised by this issue as central to the maintenance of institutionalized racism in the United States in the years immediately preceding World War II.

The folk song "Run, Nigger, Run" rounds out the cultural contexts for "Battle Royal" with its intertextual connection to the final paragraphs of the story. The reward that he finally receives after the efforts of his dream is an engraved document that reads, "Keep This Nigger-Boy Running." The effect is ironic. Readers have known throughout the story that his trust in the power structure is misplaced. Now he begins to see this as well. Like the characters in L. Frank Baum's *The Wonderful Wizard of Oz*, Ralph Ellison's hero has pinned his hopes on illusions. His "scholarship" from the white citizens will not truly educate him but will instead send him to a school where he is expected to learn compliance toward social responsibility and apathy toward social equality. He will run again and again in the novel *Invisible Man* as his attempts to achieve are thwarted. Have students look at the background information that precedes "Run, Nigger, Run" in the anthology for some of the more obscure words in the song. They might also enjoy looking at collections of folk and gospel songs that were created by slaves and fugitives from slavery using a mixture of traditions. In most classes, a number of students have extensive knowledge of music history and theory, and we often use this to advantage in our discussion of outsider issues by considering the role music plays in allowing protest and communication that is otherwise silenced. We might also speculate on what American music would have lost without the African influence.

THE OUTSIDER IN A DREAMLIKE WORLD: A COLLECTION OF WRITINGS BY FRANZ KAFKA (p. 961)

FRANZ KAFKA

The Metamorphosis (p. 962)

The word *Kafkaesque* appears in the lexicons of most modern languages to describe the eerie, dreamlike quality we find in the texts of this cluster, originally written in German by the Czech writer Franz Kafka. An important component of a Kafkaesque experience is the matter-of-fact acceptance of the most unlikely circumstances. Although we know such things could never happen, the sequence of events possesses a weird logic that carries us along, the objective narrator seducing us into suspending our disbelief as we enjoy the irony and psychological aptness of the tale. Kafka's novella "The Metamorphosis" thrusts the reader into its world with the first sentence, one of the most famous first lines in modern literature: "As Gregor Samsa awoke one morning from uneasy dreams he found himself transformed in his bed into a gigantic insect." Some translators insist that the German words might better be translated "monstrous vermin." The comic-book version, adapted by the infamous Robert Crumb, calls him "an enormous bug." Serious critical debates have raged for years over the exact kind of creature that Gregor might have become, though his appearance and behavior indicate something like a cockroach, an appropriately loathsome image for most readers.

Many of our college students have studied "The Metamorphosis" in high school and have discussed some of the possible symbolic meanings. One of the most useful issues to be drawn from the text focuses on the medical implications, reading Gregor as the victim of a deforming disability, either physical or mental. Others see Kafka dealing with his own place in European society as a Jew or as a worker in a particularly bureaucratic occupation. The family relationships invite Freudian readings that explore the challenging of the father's authority, finding evidence both in the text and in Kafka's biography of the son's unsuccessful struggle to deal with the demands of a domineering father. Other interpretations take Gregor's situation as a representation of Kafka's negative views toward humanity itself, a self-hatred projected on a universal scale.

Because a wealth of divergent critical analyses can be found, "The Metamorphosis" makes an interesting text for group projects that ask students to follow particular lines of thought about its possible ramifications. I have students begin by writing obituaries of Gregor Samsa, complete with portraits of the subject during his "final illness." Each group is to assume their information came from a different character: Gregor's father, his mother, his sister, the chief clerk, one of the boarders, the charwoman, or (through some means of communication they invent) Gregor himself. My favorite visual representations include the pasting of Kafka's face on an insect body — a biographical approach — and a drawing inspired by Edvard Münch's painting *The Scream* — a particularly apt intertextual approach. Students who know how to "morph" images on computers can provide creative applications of a group's brainstormed ideas. Agreeing on Gregor's nature so that they can produce a drawing or montage gives students the opportunity to explore their own assumptions as they read the story and discuss it with classmates. If consensus cannot be reached, I ask them to provide a multiple, insect-eye view that includes everyone's input. The obituary requires that they examine the "readings" of Gregor produced by the characters in the story. Reactions to Gregor's nature and disability through the course of the story range from the compassion that his sister first seems to feel to the broadly comic ridicule of the charwoman who finally sweeps him out. Characters respond at various times with disgust, pity, anger, confusion, irritation, shame, fear, horror, callousness, indifference, sentimentality, avoidance, derision, even hate. Gregor's nature and his motives are read and misread, and he is powerless to communicate. He is also cut off from the communications of others, since they isolate him and believe he cannot understand them. Some readers will notice that Gregor too misreads the motives of others and perhaps deliberately misleads the reader as he seeks to justify himself. After exploring their own readings and the readings of characters within the text, groups are asked to go beyond this to the more academic task of writing a synthesis paper that summarizes several texts interpreting *The Metamorphosis* from a particular point of view. Instructors can assign the topics, based on materials we find readily available.

We might also point out that biographies read the facts of Franz Kafka's life differently. Some see him as the suffering, vaguely romantic tuberculosis patient who died of overwork and insomnia, tortured and misunderstood. Biographer Ernst Pawel maintains that though Kafka led people to believe otherwise, his insurance company job was not routine and boring. Kafka carried out major reforms of the insurance industry, implementing safety measures in industry far ahead of their time, forcing changes of unsafe management practices in mines and factories and probably saving thousands of workers' lives. And although he did die of a particularly painful and debilitating form of tuberculosis, Kafka was an admitted hypochondriac who was obsessed with illness long before his diagnosis in 1917. Biographer Sander Gilman links Kafka's absorption with illness with the "racialized" attitude toward illness prevalent just before and after the turn of the century in 1900. Kafka internalized racist stereotypes of Eastern European Jews as prone to illness and went beyond Kosher laws to limit his diet to the point of anorexia. Obviously, readers of "The Metamorphosis" can find parallels in Kafka's life for many different interpretations of Gregor Samsa's strange predicament, but at the same time we must be wary of confusing the two. It may be a wry joke of Kafka's to pose as a person like Gregor, but the real person was far more capable and complex.

Gregor may literally turn into an insect. The text seems to assume this, since the narrator describes Gregor's body and his difficulty in moving in such literal detail. The verisimilitude of insect life, such as scurrying under the furniture, walking with sticky feet on the walls and ceiling, and eating decayed food, are consistent with what most of us have observed insects to do. The reactions of disgust and horror of observers in the story also support this interpretation. Throughout the story it is surprising that no one questions that this is a transformed Gregor rather than something that has come in and eaten Gregor, as logical an explanation as any. But, near the end, Gregor's sister Grete does question whether this is Gregor, supporting the claim that he has really changed into an insect. But others may make a good case for his not being an insect but feeling like one. He may be changed, but in the way someone with a disfiguring illness is changed. Some diseases produce the inability to move, cause the sick person to smell bad, and cause some onlookers to react with disgust or the other emotions we see in the story. Some readers argue that Gregor already feels this way about himself because his family has treated him in an inhumane way, as if he were fit only for the garbage heap. He has been dehumanized, even demonized — used by the family but isolated from it. Like the Jewish people in early twentieth-century Europe, he is the scapegoat upon whom all the burdens of the family fall. Or he is a victim of mental illness; he is not a bug, but he actually thinks that he is, and all of the manifestations described in the story are hallucinations. Readers may find it interesting that a hospital is across the street, and those who have read Charlotte Perkins Gilman's "The Yellow Wallpaper" (p. 1351) may question Gregor's sanity as we question that of Gilman's first-person narrator. Still, the third-person omniscient narrator of Kafka's story lends credibility to a literal interpretation of Gregor's transformation. It may be possible to argue for a physical metamorphosis that manifests the psychological one that already exists. Do we become the thing we think we are?

Most readers will be sympathetic with Gregor, but some may find themselves judging him as weak and self-justifying as the story goes on. Even at the beginning, we find him as rigid in his thinking as he has become in body, so bound by what others will think of him, fearing — albeit justifiably — that he will be fired for one instance of tardiness. He is also as passive in his social behavior as he is semiparalyzed by his physical change. He has simply accepted whatever is thrown at him, as he literally internalizes the apple that his father hurls at him in anger, holding it in until it festers. He is a masochist, a self-proclaimed martyr. As is evidenced by their transformations into self-supporting workers, the family had become dependent upon his labor, taking on the roles of sadistic enablers of his masochism. At work, people do not respect him and are willing to believe the worst. Everyone uses Gregor. His only way out of the trap is to get sick and die. But readers may see this as partly his fault. The story is filled with metamorphoses. Gregor's first change is morphological and seems to have been sudden, happening during his "disturbing dreams" as he sleeps. But his senses change as well. His vision becomes increasingly blurred. His taste has changed from milk to garbage. Perhaps the most profound change is in his inability to communicate. He is silenced and completely isolated. Like someone who has had a stroke, he is unable to get out the words he is thinking in a way that others can understand. And people mistakenly think that he does not understand their speech, he assumes, since no one speaks directly to him. At first the house is hushed, as it might be in a hospital. His sense of himself in space is changed, so that he has to find new ways of moving, leading to mistakes and misunderstandings. Already locked into his room, apparently from the inside, at the story's beginning, his movement is constricted as compared to his former life as a traveling salesman, though some will point out that he has been trapped in the job. Now he is confined to home, usually to his room. Instead of being the provider upon whom everyone depends, he is the problem that everyone must deal with.

Each family member goes through a metamorphosis. We find that his father has been crueler than Gregor thought, since he has hidden away money while Gregor has continued to slave to pay the family's creditors. As in any oppressive relationship, Gregor's oppressors have been debased by their exploitation of him. But the father must transform himself from an inactive old man who reads the newspapers all day to someone who goes out and works, and he is able to do this. The mother, also, finds something to do, in spite of her former position as the sick one of the family. The sister, too, studies and finds gainful employment. Apparently, it takes all three to make up for what Gregor has been able to do alone. Ironically, at the story's end, the parents may have found a way to make use of yet another child, however. They notice that Grete is attractive enough to find a husband, and we can imagine them in another year living off of a son-in-law's money. Whether they have really changed is debatable. Grete, however, changes greatly in the course of the story. She begins seemingly with compassion, though some may argue that she sees her care as a way of helping Gregor recover so that he can go back to work. But by the time the story ends, she wants him gone. The most notable change may be her use of the pronoun *it* to describe Gregor at this point. She has stopped thinking of him as human. Questioning whether the monstrous vermin is really Gregor, she plants the seeds of guilt and despair by contending that the real Gregor would go ahead and free the family of this burden, and Gregor obligingly dies. In the end, his sister's self-sacrifice has resulted in the greatest cruelty of all as she abandons him.

The objective narrator describes the tying up of the "burial arrangements" as the charwoman takes it upon herself to dispose of the body and inform the family, while the family rewards itself with a holiday. Many readers find the effect less convincing than the same voice as it describes Gregor's thoughts and actions. Others see the ending as a continuation of the ironic humor that permeates the whole story. Gregor is sad, but ridiculous in the way any self-pitying martyr might be, perhaps in the way Kafka saw himself. The narration is the epitome of understatement. The most outrageous events are described with the flat tone of a newspaper report. The event is not placed in a specific or unusual time and place, nor is it explained; the situation simply exists "one morning" without any preamble. This causes us to accept the situation more readily as something that could happen anytime or anyplace. The third-person narration achieves some distance between the unreliable Gregor and the voice that tells the story in a reasonable tone. When other changes in Gregor are revealed — for example, the fact that he prefers to eat spoiled food or that he can literally climb the walls — they are related in the same flat tone. His death receives no more emphasis than any other event in the story, and careless readers may even miss it. Realism is achieved not by the believability of the story's events but by the credibility of its omniscient narrator.

Few readers will be cold enough to feel that anyone deserves the fate that falls to Gregor. Whereas some critics may feel that authority is reversed in this family where the father depends upon the labor of the son, we might also see the story as a pessimistic account of the abuse of the father's authority. Surely family loyalty does not require that the son be so subservient to the needs of the father that he gives up his whole life for the family. The role reversal of Gregor's sister and his mother as they contend for authority over the arrangement of his sickroom may reflect a similar conflict between Gregor, the breadwinner, and his father, the dependent. Parents in the story attempt to hang on to authority without the concomitant responsibility. As the story ends, the parents have great optimism, but the reader may ask how the daughter's emerging beauty and maturity will be used. Will they keep their jobs, or will they again rely on a child to provide for them, this time through marriage?

FRANZ KAFKA

A Hunger Artist (p. 995)

Whereas "The Metamorphosis," with its implications of the horrors of illness, was written before Franz Kafka's diagnosis with tuberculosis, "A Hunger Artist" may spring directly from his experiences with the disease. Kafka had a particularly cruel form of tuberculosis that affected his throat and larynx, making eating an excruciating torture for him. Even before the illness, moreover, Kafka had abused his body with extreme diets. He had an aversion to meat and fish, and also refused to eat anything containing sugar or spices. He insisted upon chewing each bite of food a dozen times, a health measure called Fletcherizing. This emphasis upon Spartan diet and unproven health routines was not peculiar to Kafka. In fact, we might look at the cultural contexts for Charlotte Perkins Gilman's "The Yellow Wallpaper" (pp. 1364–75) or view a videotape of the 1994 movie *The Road to Wellville* for a glimpse at the regimen advised by proponents of "rest cures" and related dietary programs in the United States. Some of these theories have proven correct, but others caused more harm than good. Undoubtedly, Kafka's obsession with diet obscured severe anorexia, a psychological and physical disease unknown to medicine at the time. At six feet tall, Kafka probably weighed 135 pounds at his heaviest. He slept very little and tended to work hard at his job during the day and hard at writing, reading, and talking philosophy far into the night. Even before his fatal illness, he suffered from hypochondria and frequented spas and other places where sick people gathered. At times, Kafka seemed to believe that his poor health was predestined as part of his Jewish heritage. He suspected, too, that tuberculosis was more easily contracted by people who used their brains too intensely, a fact he felt to be true about himself. Many romantic figures, especially writers and artists, died from tuberculosis before Kafka did, and the disease had become linked with a certain type of frail beauty and intelligence. Even in Kafka's day, the image of the starving artist was a cliché, so when the writer links the words *hunger* and *artist* in his title, the audience is reminded of the stereotypes associated with artists of great genius who are unappreciated in their time. And along with the starving artist cliché, we may sense under the surface the dying artist coughing in his attic or the insane artist painting underneath the stars with a crown of candles on his head. Or we might look into the piercing eyes of Franz Kafka, burning out at us from a pale, thin face in a black-and-white photograph. When Kafka asked his friend Max Brod to burn his unpublished writings after his death, an act that was not carried out, Kafka made an exception for "A Hunger Artist," a text he was preparing for publication at the time of his death. It may be that, more than any other text, this story presents Franz Kafka as he saw himself and wanted others to see him.

Regardless of who the hunger artist symbolizes, we as readers might first notice that the audience comes in for the greatest condemnation. The hunger artist constantly judges his viewers, critiquing them harshly throughout the story. The hunger artist gives his all, but no one is able to understand his art. The "impresarios" control his performance and keep him within limits. Others insult his sense of integrity by keeping watch to ensure he is not conning them. He especially hates those who try to aid and abet what they assume will be his tendency to cheat. He especially likes the suspicious ones who give him their full attention, then eat in front of him, feeding his sense of competition and superiority. Still, he insists that he alone can judge his work, and this disheartens him because he knows that it is too easy, that he could do more if only allowed. As his story goes on, the hunger artist becomes more misunderstood — more misread — as finally, even the signs on his cage are illegible and he is forgotten, buried under a pile of straw. When he asks for forgiveness, his discoverers think he is crazy. The reader realizes, of course, that the whole idea is crazy. The irony for the artist is that he has done it all along not for art but because of his own needs, because he cannot find food that he likes, so denial is what he prefers. Kafka may mean his parable to symbolize martyrs, like Gregor Samsa of "The Metamorphosis," who renounce their lives for some unworthy cause. He may refer to being Jewish, being misunderstood, having one's strengths seen as weaknesses, never being able to atone, no matter how one sacrifices for an audience who will never understand. More likely, Kafka refers to real artists and writers like himself who place their deepest thoughts and feelings on display for an audience who may not have the capacity to read the text as it is meant. In the long run, they do it for themselves, because they have a desire that cannot be filled.

The hunger artist is ridiculous, of course, and there may be much self-mockery in the story. His art is an absence of something, a refusal rather than a creation. There is a poignancy to the hunger artist's obsession to achieve his goal, but a selfishness in his self-sacrifice. Although readers may feel compassion for the hunger artist, we also recognize that he gets pleasure from his own pain and renunciation. The fact that the impresarios limit his fast to forty days may mean that he represents the suffering servant of the Bible, often interpreted as the Jewish people as a whole. Kafka's Jewish identity was an important part of his understanding of himself, but he had mixed feelings about what this meant. Although we may at first admire the willingness of the artist to suffer for his art or his religion, Kafka undercuts this with the artist's self-evaluation, his contention that sacrifice is actually an act of selfishness, that it is eating, not starving, that causes the real agony. Because he was actually ill with a disease that made eating painful when this story was being written, Kafka may in fact be laughing at his own life in a bitterly ironic way. If this is so, his earlier refusal to eat most foods available to him literally reflects the earlier part of the hunger artist's career. Now, he has no choice in the matter, since he is ill. The hunger artist has no choice since this is the only way he is capable of living. He sees his chance to do his work unfettered by the laws of others, but he gets no satisfaction from it, since it has still been too easy. He has been a fake after all, but not in the way his audience might suspect. If he had quit when he saw that his time was up, he might have been forced to find martyrdom in another way. It's hard to imagine that this character would be happy with a happy ending of any sort. Kafka's character seems to be saying that sainthood or any sort of self-sacrifice is suspect. Perhaps readers will find him admirable for his honesty, but less normal and more pathetic for admitting that his whole life has been a lie.

Still, we may ask, is work or art or sacrifice no longer worthy because its creator does it with ease? Ballet dancers maintain that their art is as athletic as any sport, but more difficult because they cannot reveal the pain it entails. Many models and performers, and ordinary people trying to look like them, starve themselves to be beautiful. And since most art does not pay well, especially in the early stages, and often tends to be misread by the audience, much dedication is required of those who pursue writing, visual arts, or performance. To become successful or to spend a great deal of time at jobs to pay the rent often means being judged by other artists and oneself as selling out. Most artists contend that one must love it or be obsessed by it in order to create anything of value, but criteria for aesthetic judgments constantly change. Sour grapes abound. It is possible to spend one's life avoiding sustenance and calling one's isolation from humanity *art*, wasting energy in critiques of an uncomprehending audience and in the pursuit of impossible goals. Kafka's artist requires not only that his art be perfect, but also that his motives be pure. The panther that replaces the artist, on the other hand, is not concerned with art, but delights the audience with the sheer joy and energy of his existence. Surely, even Kafka meant this as more than an ironic contrast. But, even as we as readers are relieved to be released from the pain of watching the hunger artist, we feel the weight of his judgment. Are we Philistines if we enjoy the panther more?

Both Gregor Samsa of "The Metamorphosis" and the hunger artist of this story live in a world where the unreal seems perfectly logical. Gregor's perceptions change as he adapts to his transformed body, though he tries at one point to hold on to his memories of humanity, as the women of the house lug his furniture out. But his very actions in trying to keep his last possession, the pinup of the lady in the muff surrounded by his artistic fretwork frame, are buglike, as he sticks himself to the wall on top of it. If he is imagining that he is an insect, then his thinking process has become more unreal. If he is indeed an insect, then he is gradually adapting his thought processes to fit his changed reality. He never quite makes the transition, however, but tries throughout the story to make contact with a family we suspect was impossibly distant even before his metamorphosis. The hunger artist lives in a surreal world in which people pay to see others starve. Like Gregor, the hunger artist sacrifices himself for the pleasure of others. The hunger artist, however, is totally self-absorbed. Everything is seen in relation to his art, his starvation. His thinking seems less rational than Gregor's, however, even given a world in which his art is profitable. If he can just fast as long as he wishes, he thinks he will be satisfied, but when he does, he seems to acknowledge that he has been a failure. Just as no food will satisfy him, no achievement will satisfy him. He dies unfilled, unfulfilled, and totally misunderstood. His life has been characterized not by creation but by denial. Few readers will grasp the logic of this. He seems to most resemble the denizens of television talk shows who display their infinite varieties of pain and dysfunction for the pleasure of hooting audiences. Both Gregor and the hunger artist become true outsiders when they are no longer profitable. Both become sick, literally wasted, and people no longer see or hear them. Yet, in both cases, those who surround them are revealed as groups unworthy of the self-sacrifice of the protagonists. Although the hero of each story is alien by his very nature, the insiders are cruel and incapable of understanding.

Readers may differ about which death is more grotesque. Gregor's is ironic. He has been treated like garbage in life, and he becomes garbage in death. The hunger artist's death is equally appropriate. His life has been characterized by emptiness and self-denial. He ends by denying himself credit for surpassing his goals. And he is virtually invisible in death, submerged in the straw into which he disappeared in the cage. Because he keeps his human form throughout, the image of the hunger artist may seem the most haunting to many readers. Kafka leaves us with such images, perhaps to make us question what it means to be human, perhaps to say that death is both final and trivial in the larger scheme of things. He leaves us thinking about the results of all our intense struggling to find a balance between self-sacrifice and selfishness, wondering if they might be the same thing when all is said and done.

FRANZ KAFKA

Before the Law (p. 1002)

Although Franz Kafka was himself a lawyer, his worldview is characterized not by the logic and rationality of law but by a sense of arbitrary and irrational forces that are set up to foil any unwary human creature who dares to hope. His early life may have caused him to feel this way. Kafka's father dominated the family as a total autocrat and was incapable of understanding his sensitive son. At the age of thirty-six, Franz wrote a letter to his father that contained these words: "I kept being haunted by fantasies of this giant of a man, my father, the ultimate judge, coming to get me in the middle of the night, and for almost no reason at all dragging me out of bed. . . . as far as he was concerned, I was an absolute Nothing." His mother was so absorbed in pleasing his father that the young Kafka was unable to turn to her. Further childhood proof that the universe was frightening and arbitrary may have presented itself to him when his two younger brothers died when he was around four years old. Unable to break free from his father's dominance, Kafka continued to endure it into adulthood, living in his childhood home, having affairs with women but never marrying and establishing his own life separate from his parents. Ironically, he is even buried at the same gravesite as his parents, in a Jewish cemetery in Czechoslovakia. It has been pointed out that the cemetery is only half filled, since the generation expected to fill it, including Kafka's three sisters, died in Nazi concentration camps during World War II.

Although Kafka did not witness the rise of Hitler, having died in 1924, the perverse logic of his cruel world seems a premonition of the reasoning that would entrap millions of people into death camps and gas chambers. Certainly, Kafka experienced prejudice because of his Judaism. Racist anti-Semitic stereotypes dominated European and American thought in the early years of the twentieth century. During Kafka's lifetime, beginning in 1895, the Dreyfus Affair in France fascinated and horrified all of Europe; it led to riots and remained fixed in memory for years afterward. The case concerned a French military officer, the only Jew in his unit, who was convicted and sent to Devil's Island based on fabricated evidence of passing secrets to the German enemy. Although the evidence was based on the lie of only one man, prejudice led to its being readily accepted as true. According to French poet Bernard Lazare, also Jewish, Dreyfus was an archetypal Jewish martyr: "Because he was a Jew he was arrested, because he was a Jew he was convicted, because he was a Jew the voices of justice and of truth could not be heard in his favor." Because he was a Jew, but also because he was Franz Kafka, Kafka could write a parable dripping with irony about the injustice of man's structures of justice.

The man who comes from the country naively trusts that he will receive justice if he has patience and determination. Like African Americans who listened to the teachings of Booker T. Washington (p. 948) during the same time period as the Dreyfus Affair, those who believe that the keepers of power will allow them into full citizenship just because they behave well can expect disappointment. Neither assimilation nor accommodation will move an arbitrary and unfeeling system toward change. Kafka's protagonist errs because he expects fairness. But Kafka has learned from his father and from the exploiters of workers and from his experiences with prejudice that judgment is more likely to go against the unprotected seeker of fairness and opportunity. Perhaps the man before the law fails because he comes alone. Each reader will evaluate this tale as cynical, pessimistic, or realistic depending upon their life experiences and philosophies. Students who have had comfortable lives may take issue with the basic premise that there is really nothing the seeker can do to change the results. Kafka seems to be cynically saying that life is unfair, and nothing we can do will change that fact. We'd like to hope that in America at the turn of the twenty-first century the law will treat us fairly, and most of us will find that this is so. But we still need to remember that race still plays a part in decisions made in law courts, and that — like Dreyfus — many people are more likely to be considered guilty because they are outsiders in the eyes of mainstream judges and juries ruled by unexamined assumptions. If the man of Kafka's story forced his way into the sealed system of doors within doors, he would find himself stopped at each one, perhaps eventually being shot. Or perhaps the doors go on forever and he dies before he reaches the end. Or, like Dorothy and her companions in *The Wizard of Oz*, a door finally opens to reveal the law, like the wizard, to be powerless.

The story has much of the folktale about it, and is not meant to be realistic. For example, the invocation of the horror of the third doorkeeper may remind readers of tales in which the hero encounters magical creatures, each one more fierce than the last. But in such tales, the hero emerges from his trials victorious, receiving not only justice but reward. The form leads us to believe, if we aren't aware we are reading Kafka, that the ending might be of the "happily ever after" variety. The situation, like much of Kafka, is surreal. We may be reminded of the dreamlike state the author describes above, in his letter to his father, in which the fearsome judge is quick to bring injustice. Dreams are the kingdom of the arbitrary, and their logic takes strange twists. But if we find parallels with life, we are likely to believe the pattern. We've all been in situations where it seemed nothing we did would have the results we desired. As students think of outsiders who wait for the gatekeepers to open doors, they may think of issues concerning race, gender, immigration, social class, and various other differences that tend to create outsider categories. Sociologists are saying that the gap between those with access to information and those without gets wider all the time. We might consider how colleges and universities act as gatekeepers for people who seek the opportunities they provide. Each time we type in our library password at the computer, opening the door to the thousands of texts available online, we take advantage of an opportunity that has been virtually handed to us because we have been granted a privilege many do not have. Increasingly, students sob to us in conferences that they really must get an A in every class because competition for graduate school is so fierce. Instructors must wrestle with the knowledge that giving the student the C the work warrants might slam that particular door shut. How many revisions can we grade?

Although each of the stories by Franz Kafka that appear in this cluster seems to take place in a world where unfairness reigns, each story has an internal logic that makes it believable. In "Before the Law" the characters behave consistently. The doorkeeper is cold, officious, and cruel, even at times deceptive. The country man is patient to a fault, never giving up. There's a cliché that maintains that God has a plan for each of our lives. In Kafka's story, the plan is devilish, and man is destined to be a victim. Like the man in the "Got Milk?" commercial who thinks he is in heaven as he eats a giant cookie only to realize he is in hell as he opens the refrigerator to find no milk, each person finds that his or her victimization by an absurd fate is tailor made to fit. The hunger artist who critiques his audiences and struggles for the time to create his art to please himself becomes invisible to the audiences that rush by on their way to more exotic attractions, loses all sense of time, and ends by pleasing no one, especially himself. Gregor Samsa undergoes a metamorphosis that clearly illustrates his already disrespected place in the family, and he gradually becomes more and more garbagelike until he eventually is swept out by the cleaning woman. The logical progression makes sense as cause leads to effect, consistent with the characters within the story. Interestingly, in all three stories, the protagonists' vision begins to dim or blur at some point in the story, perhaps reflecting a changing vision as they give up their old sense of reality.

Many students relate strongly to Kafka's characters, especially those who have experienced outsider status because they were considered intellectual or artistic in high school and did not fit into prevailing cliques. They like the exaggerated surrealism of the characters and situations. One student confided in private that she had been treated for anorexia for years, but that a psychologist had recently determined that an obsessive-compulsive fixation on the number four had hampered her life in many areas, including diet. She had known this all along but did not allow herself to tell. She understood the persistence of Kafka's characters in the face of certain failure. Most students, fortunately, do not identify this closely with Kafka, but they recognize caricatures of people they know, especially the long-suffering martyr who is so self-absorbed he thinks his misery is an art form. Perhaps "The Metamorphosis" will strike most readers as particularly dreamlike, especially when we recall our semiparalysis as we try to shake off sleep to get to work or school. A case might be made for either of the other two stories being dreamlike, however, especially in their otherwise illogical settings and in the single-minded determination of their protagonists to accomplish the tasks they have set out to do.

Readers may also see any of the three stories as enigmatic. It is puzzling that Gregor Samsa in "The Metamorphosis" turns into a bug, if indeed this is what happens, and the issue of fact is never settled as to how such a thing took place. "A

Hunger Artist" is quite difficult to grasp, its exact symbolism eluding this reader. And others may find "Before the Law" enigmatic because its details are sketchy, providing little information about characters, setting, or what has led this man to the door. Because it is more fully developed, "The Metamorphosis" is perhaps more understandable to most.

PERSECUTING OUTSIDERS: POETRY OF THE HOLOCAUST (p. 1005)

MARTIN NIEMÖLLER

First They Came for the Jews (p. 1005)

Students and instructors interested in placing the literature of the Holocaust in historical and cultural perspective will find excellent materials in books, in scholarly journals from numerous discourses, and in Web sites on the Internet. Although indiscriminate searches may provide excellent opportunities to evaluate texts of divergent quality, we need to direct students first to legitimate sites such as the U.S. Holocaust Memorial Museum (http://www.ushmm.org). At this writing, the Simon Wiesenthal Center, another excellent source of information, includes at its site (http://motlc.wiesenthal.com) a document refuting thirteen "revisionist arguments" often posted by hate groups. This text can be used both as a source of historical background and as an example of how to effectively respond to opposing views by presenting counterarguments referring to various types of evidence, by clarifying misleading interpretations of statistics, and by pointing out fallacies such as equivocal use of language and false claims of authority.

Experts in the pedagogy of the Holocaust advise that instructors be wary of simple answers to complex questions. We do not want to stereotype either the victims or the "insider" groups involved in this difficult issue. Hitler came to power in 1933, and World War II did not end until 1945. Many complex events and attitudes led up to this twelve-year period. Although it may be convenient to label the German people as bystanders, collaborators, perpetrators, or rescuers, the same person might easily fit one category early on and then be moved by compassion or fear to act differently as the reality of Nazi actions became apparent.

Martin Niemöller is particularly hard to categorize. Students reading his little poem, an expression of guilt written in the first person, tend to think that it describes Pastor Niemöller's own experience. He would not object to this. As early as 1946, German students loudly protested his contention that all of his countrymen shared a collective guilt and needed to beg forgiveness for the crimes done in the name of Germany and Christianity. At this point, the denial of any guilt for the Holocaust had already begun to set in. Despite his willingness to confess his complicity, however, Niemöller and the persona of his poem are quite different, and he is using the dramatic monologue of the poem as a pastor, perhaps to build common ground with his audience.

Far from being a bystander or a collaborator, Martin Niemöller, along with theologian Karl Barth and Christian activist and eventual martyr Dietrich Bonhoeffer, spoke strongly in opposition to Hitler's attempts to use the Protestant churches of Germany to persecute Jews and other outsiders. But he reminds us in the poem that oppression approaches gradually and builds in intensity with each step. For this pastor of a large Lutheran congregation, the realization that Nazi policies were dangerous to freedom came as early as 1933 when the state began to tell the church that Jewish converts and those married to "non-Aryans" should be prohibited from serving as pastors. Gradually, the racist philosophy of the Nazis began to co-opt Martin Luther, the founder of German Protestantism, as an Aryan hero, and some Nazi apologists insisted that Jesus Christ was not a Jew but a godlike Aryan superman. The reading of the Old Testament and the teachings of St. Paul, who boldly declared his Judaism, began to be frowned upon, and SS troops would attend church meetings to see that such policies were carried out. The melding of Aryan racial pride and the trappings of Christianity became very popular as "German Christianity" and the "positive Christianity movement" were preached at rallies and even from many pulpits. The youth programs of the churches began to be supplanted by Hitler youth groups.

Although the early stages of this Nazi appropriation of religion prompted Niemöller's vocal opposition and organized action within the Protestant churches, he did not believe at first that Hitler was responsible for these actions. Niemöller was passionately patriotic, and had worked politically in the years between World War I and Hitler's election to see that Germany found a strong, anti-Communist leader. He had been a supporter of the monarchy and served as a U-boat commander in World War I. He had voted for the National Socialists, Hitler's party, in 1933 and in the previous election, and had even engaged in armed resistance to Communist attempts to gain control of the country. Later, he would come under harsh criticism for unsuccessfully volunteering from a prison cell to command a U-boat for the Axis, even though he was quite aware by this time of Hitler's nature and the evils of Nazism.

Still it is important to understand the strength of Niemöller's patriotism and the complexity of the divided loyalties felt by veterans of World War I and their families. His sons served in the army even while their father was in solitary confinement first in Sachsenhausen, then in Dachau. Hitler's hatred of Niemöller was personal. The pastor discovered Hitler's pettiness and cowardice in 1934 when he attended a supposed meeting of church leaders to find that Hermann Göering had tapped his telephone and used a careless joke to embarrass Hitler and imply that Niemöller considered him easily influenced. When his arrest in 1937 failed to result in a conviction, Hitler told officials that Niemöller was to be considered his "personal prisoner" and was under no circumstances to be released. For a long period of time, Niemöller was literally silenced, allowed no contact with other prisoners and limited in his correspondence, though he was permitted to keep his Bible and hymn book. Never one to hide from inconsistencies, Niemöller's shock in 1945 upon first seeing the crematorium of the concentration camp at Dachau, near his own small cell, was sincere. He was profoundly moved, and took his first steps toward his later pacifism as he preached about the Holocaust again and again. "The guilt has become anonymous and nobody will share the responsibility," he mourned. "Everybody says, 'Go and ask my neighbor. I am innocent.' " But, even in his willingness to shoulder responsibility for German sins against outsiders, Niemöller epitomized the complexity of such issues as he fought as fiercely for humane treatment of German prisoners of war, two of his sons among them, and used his influence to see that postwar Germany received food and other supplies needed for rebuilding. It can happen — will happen — again and again, Niemöller's poem tells us, if people choose to label others as outsiders and to stand by when evil is being done.

Students appreciate the simplicity of "First They Came for the Jews," but they often oversimplify it by assuming the argument to be specific to Niemöller's experience or to a time and place that has nothing to do with us. Most will get the message without explicit explanations, though they may not apply it to themselves. It is important to communicate the complex historical setting, one in which prejudice was accepted throughout Europe and America, with the classes of people mentioned in the poem seen as threats to freedom and cultural values. In composition classes, many instructors use war propaganda along with images from current advertising campaigns to have students analyze persuasive appeals. Reading the literature of the Holocaust in perspective can help students realize how "commonsense" constructions of reality when unexamined leave room for the gradual acceptance of irrational and destructive ideas. Marshall McLuhan once said that we don't know who first discovered water, but it is unlikely to have been a fish. An important goal of education may be to teach the fish how to see the water that surrounds them, to question the assumptions they have internalized as part of a culture. Students might suggest current substitutions for the groups mentioned in Niemöller's poem to make it speak even more clearly to an American audience six or seven decades after the events of the poem.

This poem is didactic rather than lyrical, and its repetitions reflect the author's sermonic style. Many readers find its simplicity moving and find strength in its forthright presentation. As a response to a specific historical event, the poem may be taken literally and its voice added to the list of witnesses whose collective experience educates us about the Holocaust. But it can also serve as a symbolic reminder that apathy can be dangerous and that evil comes on so gradually that we tend to ignore it until it directly affects us. Traditionally, those in power have access to the means of publication, and in many eras and locations these are the people who are heard. But, like the history of the Holocaust, the question of the equal representation of insiders and outsiders in the literary canon raises complex issues. Certainly, many outsiders have found a voice, and the trend in colleges and universities is to open the forum up to representatives of many cultures. Multiculturalism is not without its opponents, however, and even within the academic world, some outsiders may be more warmly welcomed than others. Niemöller himself used his insider voice to good advantage until he was silenced, speaking out for those prohibited from speaking. Like Niemöller, we should hear warning bells whenever anyone in power seeks to silence members of certain groups, even when we do not agree with them.

NELLY SACHS

A Dead Child Speaks (p. 1006)

In *A History of the Jews* (1987), Paul Johnson relates chilling facts about the treatment of children arriving with their mothers at Nazi concentration camps:

> No Jew was too young to die. . . . If a breast-fed baby was a nuisance . . . a guard simply smashed its head against the wall. . . . At Treblinka, most babies were taken from their mothers on arrival, killed, and hurled into a ditch, along with invalids and cripples. Sometimes thin wails could be heard from the ditch, whose guards wore Red Cross armbands and which was known as The Infirmary. (511)

Although it is difficult to determine how many Holocaust victims were children, the U.S. Holocaust Memorial Museum in Washington, D.C., estimates that 1.5 million children — mostly Jewish, Gypsy, and institutionalized mentally handicapped children — were killed in Hitler's state-sponsored genocide and racial purification campaigns. The German public was gradually prepared for the elimination of their "outsider" neighbors. Children were encouraged to persecute non-Aryan classmates. One revealing picture book written for children in the 1930s was called *The Poison Mushroom* and featured caricatures of Jews with warnings about the dangers of being friendly with such inherently evil people, even when they seemed to be harmless. In 1933, the "Law Against Overcrowding in German Schools and Universities" forced most Jewish and Gypsy children out of the schools, and they were prohibited from belonging to the same clubs and social groups as other German children. A eugenics program was implemented that same year, forcibly sterilizing mentally and physically handicapped patients under state control, along with several hundred mixed-race children of German women and African French troops stationed in Germany in the 1920s. Such measures were not unprecedented, even in the United States, but a few years later these same children would be among the first to undergo "euthanasia" in special "children's wards" in hospitals. By 1939, the Nazis would begin the "final solution" to the Jewish problem by disguising gas chambers as bathhouses, sometimes handing those going to their deaths a towel and a bar of soap to deceive them into going quietly.

Great care was taken to use euphemisms when discussing these mass murders, and both German civilians and victims themselves were often deceived, or self-deceived, since few human beings would have been able to bear the conscious admissions of what was truly taking place. Some perpetrators of the violence became hardened to it, however, and some are described as reveling in the brutality of handing a dead child back to its mother. During World War II, many children died from the consequences of war, but children from "outsider" groups were deliberately worked to death or directly murdered in concentration camps; babies born in work camps were often killed shortly after birth; others died as the result of medical experimentation. Although the images of Nelly Sachs's poem "A Dead Child Speaks" are agonizing, they pale before the reality of historical fact.

Sachs gives the story of a child separated from its mother at the concentration camp a universal quality. To be parted from one's mother at an early age constitutes true violence, and the child's subsequent death is painful mostly because it recalls the earlier parting. This is not intended to minimize the child's death, but to place the events in a spiritual and emotional context and to reveal the enormity of this destruction of the most natural of bonds by the most brutal of acts. Sachs and her own mother were able to escape Nazi Germany in 1940, thanks to a Swedish novelist with whom she had begun a correspondence as a young girl. A well-educated child of privilege, Sachs was a mature adult when Hitler came to power, and before the war ended she began writing with empathy about an experience she fortunately did not share. The purpose that runs through all of her poetry, after her escape from what would have undoubtedly been certain death as a German Jew, is the attempt to give voice to those who suffered the anguish of the Holocaust. She seeks to resurrect language after the unspeakable has occurred and to use the sufferings of her people to bring universal reconciliation and healing.

As she speaks in the voice of the dead child in this poem, Sachs focuses on the image that she imagines for the child who has been cut away from her mother. The knife becomes a powerful metaphor for separation. Speaking as the child allows the pathos to emerge in a way that does not seem forced. All of the child's senses are involved in the cutting that continues through the days between her loss and her death. We would expect the mother to understand that losing a child is like losing a part of one's body, but the child's precocious realization is less articulate, perhaps, flashing in sensory images. We know all that we really need to know of the mother's last attempt to shield her child. If we know that this poem refers to the Holocaust and view it in the context of other poems by Sachs and others, we may argue that nothing is lost by limiting the point of view in this way.

Like any Holocaust narrative, true or fictional, the poem gives only one small glimpse that must be added to others to see the larger picture. The experience is much like that of visitors to the Holocaust Museum who are given the name of one concentration camp internee as they proceed through the exhibits, only to discover later whether the person lived or died. Students who have visited the museum can usually give exact details of the person's fate and feel that this view of the issue in microcosm helps them to empathize with all Holocaust victims and survivors.

Sachs is usually praised for her understatement, though some of her poetry comes across as filled with pathos because the event itself evokes powerful emotions. Simply referring to children and atrocity in the same text is horrifying enough, and when we realize that their referents are real there is no need for worked-up emotion. Although students can come up with their own alternative metaphors, the knife recurs as a symbol in other poems by Sachs. For example, in "Peoples of the Earth" she urges all of us to "not destroy the universe of words, / let not the knife of hatred lacerate / the sound born together with the first breath." In

"Landscape of Screams" she broadens the scene of suffering, using the knife metaphor twice, once to describe Abraham's scream when he believes God wishes him to sacrifice his son, and later to describe the catastrophic splitting of the atom: "Oh knife of evening red, flung into the throats / where trees of sleep rear blood-licking from the ground, / where time is shed / from the skeletons in Hiroshima and Maidanek." The knife can kill, but — even more painfully — can tear us apart from each other and from our very humanity.

Both poems so far in this cluster, Martin Niemöller's "First They Came for the Jews" and Nelly Sachs's "A Dead Child Speaks," have universal applications as well as historically specific ones, and readers should be able to readily respond to the avoidance of making waves or the agony of the final parting of a mother and child. Creative writers might try changing the style of the poems, but each seems not only appropriate to the age and circumstances of the narrators but to the voices of the writers themselves. We will forgive Niemöller for preaching, since this is his job, but Sachs, the literary Nobel Prize winner, might be left with her metaphor. It can be argued that Sachs should have provided more context, since someone encountering the poem in isolation might not understand the significance of the event to which it refers. The two poems are causally related, since the apathy of the bystander eventually makes possible the destruction of the family and the murder of the child. Sachs's poem "You Onlookers" seems to speak directly to Niemöller's speaker: "How many dying eyes will look at you / When you pluck a violet from its hiding place?" she demands. "How many hands be raised in supplication / In the twisted martyr-like branches / Of old oaks?"

YEVGENY YEVTUSHENKO
Babii Yar (p. 1008)

"Babii Yar" has been called by some the most famous poem of the twentieth century. It has been translated into over seventy languages and inspired Dmitri Shostakovich's Thirteenth Symphony. One Soviet premier of the 1960s denounced the poem, and another walked out on the symphony, giving the text doubly good credentials as a politically dynamic poem. As Martin Niemöller had reminded his fellow Germans a generation earlier, so Yevgeny Yevtushenko told his Russian compatriots that guilt must not be pushed aside and blamed on one's neighbors or the country next door but accepted and used for redemption and reconciliation. For Yevtushenko, poetry is meant to stir and disturb those in power and to defend and comfort the oppressed. "Politics could humiliate people. Politics could kill people," he insists. And for this reason, poets must care about politics. "Indifference is a kind of crime. I don't think people who are indifferent to the suffering of others can love."

When Yevtushenko visited the ravine of Babii Yar just outside the city of Kiev in the Ukraine, he was shocked to find no monument erected to the people who were killed there when Hitler's troops invaded the then Soviet Union in 1941. Before they abandoned Kiev, Soviet troops had strategically placed bombs in the buildings most likely to be occupied by the Germans. When these explosives killed a great number of German officers and personnel, the SS decided to retaliate by exterminating the entire Jewish population of the city. These people, estimated at over 33,000 in number, were marched to the edge of the cliff, forced to strip naked, and systematically shot and allowed to fall into the ravine. As the German occupation proceeded during the following months, Jews and Gypsies from other parts of the Ukraine were executed at Babii Yar in the same manner, as were Soviet prisoners of war. Eventually, the ravine was estimated to contain 100,000 bodies. Later in the war, fearful that the enormity of the massacre would be revealed, the SS used concentration camp labor to exhume and burn the corpses. When Yevgeny Yevtushenko writes about the need to memorialize the dead at Babii Yar, he remembers the inhumanity of the German atrocities. But he goes further than this to remind his Russian readers of the long, continuing history of anti-Semitism in their own hearts.

Frequently, a poet will assume a voice that differs from his own, taking on a mask or persona. In "Babii Yar" Yevtushenko speaks in multiple voices. In the beginning lines, we seem to stand with the Russian poet as he looks at the cliff and tells us of the fear it evokes in him, but soon the voice takes on echoes from the past of the Jewish people. His journey is biblical, moving into Egypt with Joseph or Moses, then imagining himself crucified, as the Jewish Jesus was. In lines 11–21 he leaps forward to modern history, then quickly back to the book of Judges, speaking in the dual voices of the French military officer Alfred Dreyfus unjustifiably persecuted in Paris in the 1890s and Samson tortured by the Philistines three thousand years earlier. The perpetrators of their torture become mixed as well, since those who are too coarse to understand a high culture are often called Philistines, and the "dainty ladies" trivialize the plight of Captain Dreyfus just as Philistine women like Delilah undermine the biblical hero. What's more, the tables are subtly turned; Samson was one of the "judges" of ancient Israel, but his counterpart in France is now judged. The effect subverts time and space limitations, preparing us for the fact that such persecutions have taken place in Russia, as the speaker quickly moves to tell us in his new persona as a Russian Jew during a pogrom.

For years in Russian provinces, terrorist raids would be made on villages or ghettoes, often using as an excuse the presumed kidnapping by Jews of an innocent child for an unholy, anti-Christian rite Jews were imagined to carry out. Such tales and the concomitant persecutions they encouraged had existed since medieval times, perhaps even earlier. The scene recalls Kristallnacht, the time when Nazi Germany allowed their intentions for the Jews of Germany to be fully revealed, as a pogrom was mounted against Jewish-owned businesses and anyone who got in the way. "Kristallnacht" refers to the sound of shattering glass in the night as shop windows were broken. Russian versions of such anti-Semitic undertakings were no less violent, as Yevtushenko describes in lines 22–42. Not only *could* the atrocities have been carried out by Russians, but such things actually had happened. And what Yevtushenko does not say, speaking in the 1960s during a time of rigid Soviet state control of artistic expression, is that Joseph Stalin had ordered atrocities worthy of Hitler in their brutality. True Russians have seen their homeland appropriated by hatemongers, just as men like

183

Martin Niemöller saw their own beloved fatherland stolen by similar men, Yevtushenko implies.

To further universalize his message, the male poet takes on the persona of the fragile Jewish girl Anne Frank. Yevtushenko's empathy reaches far, as he becomes all of the thousands of dead at Babii Yar; he becomes not only the human being who dies, but the voice of that human being, like "one massive, soundless scream." To be a true Russian is to be at one with the Jews, he concludes. The poet was born in Siberia and is proud of this heritage, but his family found itself there because a grandparent was exiled for political reasons, as were so many.

At the time of the poem's composition it was not unusual for intellectuals to be confined to mental hospitals for their failure to agree with the government's views. The poet's life in the Soviet Union was fraught with danger, and he has more reason to fear than most. As he looks over the edge of the cliff, he cannot know for sure whether he looks at a symbol of history or a premonition of his personal future. Yevtushenko therefore speaks to a Russian audience first, but the poem's wide audience outside of Russia indicates that he has touched more universal emotions. Few nations are without sin in their history or abuses in their present, if people are willing to open their eyes. For Americans to admit the genocide of the indigenous people of the land or the horrors of the African slave system, for example, does not mean that we do not love our country. The Ku Klux Klan raids and lynching of black men in the United States were pogroms of a sort. Imagining what victims must have felt can result in the appropriation of history for cheap emotion, or empathy can be used to call a nation to draw parallels for change.

When Yevtushenko imagines Anne Frank trying to grow into a young woman in the darkness of hiding, he again uses a double metaphor. Anne is herself compared to "a branch in April" just beginning to bud. She is "denied the leaves / . . . denied the sky" because she cannot walk with a lover in the park, but she is also a growing thing that will never reach maturity or her potential as a woman. Later in the poem, the trees that tower over Babii Yar seem "ominous, / like judges" because they represent the people who have died in the ravine. The poem uses metaphor in this subtle way, calling upon each image to communicate layers of meaning. The basic premise of the poem requires that other comparisons be accepted and that readers understand allusions to Jewish figures from history. Because we read it in translation, English speakers may miss some of the poetic quality of the original poem. At schools where there are Russian-speaking students or professors, we might invite them to offer their own interpretations after reading the poem in readily available Russian texts. Perhaps there are connotations and sound repetitions that are lost in translation.

By identifying himself so closely with the Jewish people throughout the poem, then confessing that he is not actually a Jew at the end, Yevtushenko makes it clear that his position is based on a sense of common humanity and spirit rather than a specific ethnicity. True Russians are better than those who would deny these people a place in their heritage, the poet says, and he further implies that they must be better than those who continue to oppress. Even as he compares himself to the Jewish victims, he points out the implicit connection of the Soviets to the Nazis. Americans similarly fall short of the ideals that we think we live by and have been guilty of atrocities we would rather cover up. It is easier to pretend that we are the heroes of the world, to bury our failures, than to accept our mistakes and learn from them. Before reading "Babii Yar" together, we often have students generate definitions of what it means to be a "true American" so that we can compare these ideals.

The first two poets of this cluster, the Lutheran clergyman Martin Niemöller and the Jewish poet Nelly Sachs, were personally affected by the Nazi persecution of Jews in Germany, though neither suffered in the way that many Holocaust survivors did. Niemöller's tiny cell was isolated, but he was not worked to the point of death or tortured physically as many Rabbis were. Nor did he face death in the gas chambers or a volley of bullets at the top of a ravine. Nelly Sachs was able to escape Germany early in the war. Her situation is similar to Yevgeny Yevtushenko's in that she must imagine from a distance the emotions of the Holocaust victims whose voice she makes heard. While Sachs is actually Jewish and Yevtushenko is Jewish in a metaphorical sense, both use the empathy and passion they feel to call for remembrance and mourning for those who were truly victims.

All of the poets call upon universal emotions and behaviors. The mother and child in Nelly Sachs's poem could have suffered a violent separation in Vietnam or Serbia as surely as they do in the concentration camp, though our knowledge of their agony and certain death in this particularly brutal circumstance adds layers of meaning. But Sachs does not have the child speak directly to us for the overt purpose of effecting change, though Sachs has directly addressed the audience in other poems. She leaves us to our own compassion rather than telling us what to do. Niemöller and Yevtushenko have more explicitly didactic motives. As a pastor, Niemöller urges his audience to realize that allowing the persecution of anyone endangers us all. As a political activist, using poetry as a vehicle for change, Yevtushenko sincerely intends that his poem results in a memorial to the victims of Babii Yar, but he also wants his readers to examine themselves for the sort of hate that caused the massacre to take place. When so many voices have been silenced and lost forever, someone needs to speak for them, and this is what the poets try to do. Some readers may complain that this is presumptuous of them, but it is just as valid to argue that such exercises in empathy are the best hope that people will never be so callous or apathetic as to let it happen again. Universalizing the experience of the Holocaust may sometimes exploit and appropriate the pain of the victims, but how else are we to apply its lessons to our own actions, to understand that it really could happen here, in our own hearts?

KAREN GERSHON

Race (p. 1011)

Karen Gershon survived the Holocaust because she was one of the Jewish children evacuated to England in 1939, the year World War II officially began in Europe. Her parents did not survive, however, dying in the concentration camp

185

that would have undoubtedly reserved the same fate for her. When she speaks of her refusal to hate, therefore, her words carry the authority of one who has a great deal to forgive and perhaps even more survivor guilt to carry.

Issues may be raised about the appropriateness of any stance that takes the German people off the hook for their complicity in raising the Nazis to power and accepting the racist views and repressive measures that led to the eventual atrocities. As we have noted in other introductions in this cluster, Nazi attitudes did not develop and continue in a vacuum. People in many countries were willing to let outsider groups be assigned the blame for economic and social problems following World War I and a worldwide monetary depression. Stereotypes that denigrated Jews were the norm in Europe and America. Children like Gershon were denied access to German schools and social services for several years preceding the implementation of the "final solution" of deportation and death to all Jews no matter the age. Some thinkers insist that German civilians must have known what they now deny, must have seen through the euphemisms that thinly veiled the killing of so many. How were they to explain the clothing and other belongings of their Jewish neighbors being passed on for their use during the hard times of war? What fate did they imagine awaited the people on the trains that disturbed their sleep on their way to Poland? Why did the men of Martin Niemöller's family, even Neimöller himself, feel that patriotism required them to serve in the armed forces of a government they knew to be unjust?

Gershon challenges her readers to go beyond the categories that separate and label people. It is interesting that she uses the loaded word *race* as the focus of her poem. Caricatures perpetuating stereotypes of supposedly Jewish features still may be seen in England, Gershon's adopted country, and the same sort of pictures were used in hate literature, as the Nazis consolidated their power, to acclimate the public to racial dehumanization. The concept of race is considered by many scholars to be primarily an invention of the nineteenth century, and the concepts of eugenics and racial purity that proved so destructive under Nazi control grew directly from the idea that race exists and that some races are superior to others. Today, perhaps, we would use the word *ethnicity* to describe the totality of shared values, customs, and history that characterizes a group, and we would not classify Jews or other groups as separate races. We might want to debate in class whether the term should be applied at all. Although access to affirmative action programs and the need for statistical data sometimes necessitate that ethnicity be listed on forms, some individuals choose to leave such spaces blank. At the same time, studies seem to be indicating the importance of genetic inheritance even in the development of personality traits once considered to be learned behavior. Students might consider how such information should be used as the field of genetics develops. How can we resist attempts to classify and limit people? Gershon resists judgments that are based on seeing individuals as symbols of an ethnic group, and by using the word *race* she is able to use its negative and arbitrary connotations to strengthen her argument against such categorization.

When Gershon's speaker returns to her Germany, she finds that her features identify her as part of a group. She indicates that this is not her usual experience, but is something that takes her by surprise. She had expected to blend in. For this reason, we can be fairly certain that she does not imagine her reception, but responds to reality. Writing in the 1960s, Gershon may be voicing the thoughts of most living Jews when her speaker imagines herself as one of the dead. Few families escaped knowing someone who had died, and the sense that one had survived a close call was not limited to Jews on the European continent or those like Gershon who had fled just before or during the war. People who live after being involved in a disaster that kills many of those around them are sometimes said to suffer from survivor guilt, to irrationally believe that they are wrong to have survived when so many have died.

Gershon may also speak for many when she admits her tendency to see all Germans as evil. Even in her rejection of hate, she still assumes that the Germans do harbor thoughts of hate, the assumption still existing, even as she vows not to hate people for their race. In the Bible, Cain is the first murderer, having killed his brother Abel because God loves Abel best. When God asks Cain where his brother is, Cain takes shelter in denial. "Am I my brother's keeper?" he responds. So God exiles him, but places the mark of his crime on his face. Gershon sees the Germans as symbolically bearing this mark of murder and denial. It is this judgment of them that she tries to avoid, afraid that she will become like them. Her title may refer to Jews, Germans, or to the whole human race.

Enjambment makes the poem read smoothly, as if the narrator speaks to us in a conversational tone. But she uses the poetic devices of rhyme, alliteration, and parallel structure to unify the poem in a subtle way. Style does not dominate, however, and the content of the poem seems more important than any self-conscious literary quality. Some readers will contend that wallowing in guilt or anger over the actions of our parents and grandparents serves no purpose, and that such events should be forgiven and forgotten as we move on. Although it is admirable to accept people as individuals rather than as stereotypes, however, there may be value for a culture in examining the structures and attitudes that lead to group actions like slavery, discrimination, and genocide, even though most people now living did not participate in them. Because we live with the results of actions taken in the past, assumptions need constant reevaluation, not so that we will feel guilty or be filled with rage, but so that we see more clearly to make the decisions of today.

Yevgeny Yevtushenko and Karen Gershon both visit Holocaust sites. Yevtushenko, as a non-Jew, must deal with guilt, and he demands that Russia atone for the atrocities. He empathizes with the victims, seeking common ground for understanding them, perhaps moving too far in assuming that he knows what they have felt. Karen Gershon comes to the Holocaust site as a survivor, one who has escaped. Her task is to deal not so much with guilt, but with her own feelings of hate and anger at the perpetrators. Still, because she is not a concentration camp survivor herself, she is perhaps too willing to let go of the anger. In Nelly Sachs's "A Dead Child Speaks" the "knife of parting" has been visible and violent, but we would hardly guess from Karen Gershon's poem that her parents are actually among the bodies in the mass grave. She could have been the dead child, but she isn't, and she keeps a reserved distance from the pain, choosing instead to make this an ethical issue. While Nelly Sachs does not call for hate, she refuses to allow cheap grace to those who forced children from their mothers only to murder both. In "If the Prophets Broke In" she doubts if humanity is capable of the repentance required to hear God's voice and to be forgiven. "If the voice of the prophets / blew / on flutes made of murdered children's bones / and exhaled airs burnt with / martyrs' cries — / if they built a bridge of old men's dying / groans — " Sachs demands, "Ear of mankind / occupied with small sounds, / would you hear?" Many readers prefer Gershon's stand against revenge and prejudice, seeing it as positive, but others find it simplistic, even dishonest, in the face of what happened to her parents and to the children who were unable to escape as she did. As long as the Holocaust is minimized and denied, some contend, healing is delayed, no matter how positive forgiveness sounds.

ANNE SEXTON

After Auschwitz (p. 1012)

Writing in the 1950s, the German Jewish philosopher T. W. Adorno questioned the ethics of creating literature in the wake of the atrocities of the Holocaust. "To write poetry after Auschwitz is barbaric," he insists. No one could possibly capture the horror of what took place, some Holocaust scholars maintain. To attempt to express in art what can only be expressed by a scream is to trivialize and take aesthetic pleasure in the agony of victims who are no longer alive to speak for themselves. And it is particularly offensive, according to these thinkers, when a non-Jew like Yevgeny Yevtushenko in "Babii Yar," Sylvia Plath in "Daddy" (p. 227 in the "Living in Families" chapter), or Anne Sexton in "After Auschwitz" appropriates the specific agonies of the Holocaust for imagery and symbolism directed toward more universal concerns. Others, however, feel that because the voices of Holocaust victims have been silenced forever by their deaths, someone must express the experience with them in mind, speaking as survivors or as artists possessed of imagination and empathy. There is no doubt that Anne Sexton's title "After Auschwitz" refers to Adorno's well-known quotation. Does she challenge his assertion by deliberately writing poetry about the Holocaust to prove that producing art is not barbaric? Does she choose to act without sensitivity because she does not care what anyone thinks or because she doesn't like being told what to do? Or does she accept Adorno's thesis and support it by producing a barbaric poem? Her use of hyperbole is also puzzling. Although she communicates the horror of the Holocaust, most readers are accustomed to interpreting exaggeration as irony, suspecting that the writer means the opposite of what is said. But to read Sexton's poem as satire would be appalling, since this would mean that she is ridiculing Adorno and others who grieve over the atrocities of the Nazi concentration camps. Her image of the Nazi consuming the baby in the first stanza seems to mock the precise documentation and statistical proofs of Holocaust historians; the image is ridiculous, and perhaps describes one of the few things Nazis have *not* been accused of doing. But her short second stanza that introduces the personified death may explain the hyperbole of the first stanza. Here she retreats into understatement, and the contrast is chilling. An immense but trivialized horror has taken place, and death does not care. The bitter anger of the third stanza condemns all of humanity, and although we find ourselves nodding as we recall the Nazi atrocities, we may suddenly remember that *man* — humankind — includes the mother and child of Nelly Sachs's "A Dead Child Speaks" and the willowy Anne Frank of Yevgeny Yevtushenko's "Babii Yar." Are they included in the creature unworthy of living? If so, doesn't the voice of this poem speak not for the victims of the Holocaust but in the spirit of their murderers? But the counterpoint is repeated in the fourth stanza, as death is vulgarly unconcerned about the ranting of the speaker. In the fifth stanza, Sexton's speaker takes Adorno's admonition several steps further, again calling upon what seems to be hyperbole, though we suspect by now that she means it seriously. Adorno argues that art after Auschwitz is barbaric, and Sexton's poem seems to ask, "Well, what isn't barbaric after Auschwitz?" How can we possibly live — do the simple, everyday things or the profound, beautiful ones — if we think about what humankind has been capable of doing? God should wipe us off the face of the earth, she implies. And as if she suddenly realizes the unspoken implication, the narrator of the poem takes back her curse, turning it into a prayer. Seen as a response to Adorno, perhaps the poem means to say to the philosopher, "Yes, you are right. Art is barbaric after Auschwitz. But so is everything else. Do we really want to give it all up?"

If she doesn't mean the curse she speaks "aloud," repeating parallel words and phrases like an incantation, her purpose may be to express the horror and guilt all human beings must feel when confronted with our capacity for brutality. Maybe the destruction of humanity should take place, but the speaker may be, like most of her readers, reluctant to let go of life. Although Sexton eventually committed suicide, she fought against the compulsion to do so for many years, even beginning her career as a poet as therapy to literally keep herself alive. The poem has a quality of attempted suicide about it. She has taken the sleeping pills one by one, then panicked and called the hotline at the sight of the empty bottle. When asked if certain images in the poem should be changed because they are offensive, students usually agree that the situation to which she responds merits strong and blunt language. Her inclusion of words that parents use to admire a newborn baby — the "small pink toes" and "miraculous fingers" — make it clear that it is all of humanity that she sees as evil. Some readers find this disturbing. Most would gladly see the Nazis condemned, but not the babies. Sexton's speaker does not let us off the "black . . . hook" of her anger. We are all covered in excrement, as she sees it. Her shrill tone, which may offend some readers, is mitigated by the alternating of the three long harangues with three understated, one-sentence stanzas that we can imagine spoken through the teeth. In two of these, death puts things into perspective, as he "looks on with a casual eye," while in the third, the narrator calls upon "the Lord not to hear." The personified death is arbitrary, unfeeling, and nasty; but so is man.

Karen Gershon in "Race" refuses to allow hate to turn her into a person like the ones who have killed her parents and would have killed her as a child, given the chance. Although she has valid, personal reasons to be filled with rage, she is unwilling to lump all Germans into the category of people worthy of hate. Anne Sexton, by contrast, has spent the war safely in middle-class America and has no grounds for personally hating the perpetrators of the Holocaust. It is not her issue; yet she screams invective against the whole human race. Her ambivalence in the last line does not ask for forgiveness or even for undeserved redemption — nothing in the poem indicates that she sees humanity as anything but evil and worthy of total destruction. What she actually seems to ask of God is that he be a bystander, even a collaborator, in the face of atrocity.

Student readers often prefer straightforward expressions of anger like that in "After Auschwitz" to subtle evocations of grief like Nelly Sachs's "A Dead Child Speaks." But in this chapter on outsiders, we need to ask why Sexton's narrator, as an outside observer of Auschwitz, depends upon hyperbole and explicit images of evil, whereas Sachs's dead child, speaking with the authority of an insider, communicates her *pathos* with quiet understatement and metaphor. Perhaps it is best not to change any of the multiple voices that poets have used to speak out against the Holocaust in the texts of this cluster. Readers will differ as they choose the one that comes closest to expressing their feelings about the Holocaust. Students often like Martin Niemöller, Anne Sexton, and Karen Gershon because their language and straightforward approaches are accessible without a great deal of literary interpretation. Mature readers may find Yevtushenko powerful, but students often feel bogged down in cultural, historical, and biblical allusions for which they lack the context. Nelly Sachs is a Nobel Prize–winning writer, and we would invite readers to explore her poetry in depth. She makes every word and image count, metaphorically and symbolically, as she compresses imagined experience and emotion into a few short lines. But the emotions she evokes are both historically specific and universal at the same time, and any reader willing to give her the time will be rewarded. Rather than being barbaric, the poetry of Nelly Sachs, after Auschwitz, speaks in the voices of many human beings who need to be heard.

ETHNIC OUTSIDERS (p. 1014)

CHRYSTOS

Today Was a Bad Day Like TB (p. 1015)

Even before Europeans arrived on the shores of mainland North America, their diseases preceded them, spread by travelers from the islands where contact first took place. Measles was especially deadly. Some historians maintain that explorers and settlers from Europe found little resistance because so many of the indigenous nations of the eastern seaboard of the Americas had been decimated by epidemics, leaving large areas seemingly uninhabited and ready for the taking. Native Americans have been particularly susceptible to tuberculosis, and as the disease reappeared with new force in the 1990s, statistics reveal that new cases numbered 16.5 per 100,000 people among Native Americans in 1995. The rate means that this ethnic group has more than twice the risk of contracting TB than the general population in the United States and five times the risk for non-Hispanic whites. So when Menominee poet and activist Chrystos says in her title "Today Was a Bad Day Like TB," the metaphor has added meaning. Tuberculosis was given to Chrystos's people unintentionally by whites who intruded into a land already occupied, spreading their diseases before them. And as she sees it, whites continue to intrude. Moreover, they continue to take what does not belong to them and fail to see the cultural significance of the customs and artifacts they appropriate.

European attitudes toward the first people of the Americas have been characterized by misreadings based upon arrogance and self-interest. The earliest stereotypes portrayed Indians as primitive, uncivilized, and simple, having no real language with which to communicate complex ideas, and thus incapable of philosophy or metaphysical thought. They were ignorant heathens in need of salvation, teaching, and paternalistic protection. This myth soon gave way to the stereotype of the bloodthirsty savage, as competition for land and alliances of native groups with rival European powers made demonization a more useful construct. At the same time, romantic ideas of philosophers like Rousseau led many to regard non-Europeans as noble savages living in perfect harmony with nature, a stereotype that continues to oversimplify Native American culture in the minds of many enthusiastic onlookers. More recently, all Native Americans are characterized in popular thought as victims who have been robbed of culture and dignity, unable to cope with the modern world but cut off from tradition. Perhaps each of these stereotypes began with a grain of truth — clichés usually do. But the stereotypes are also fallacious oversimplifications or overgeneralizations about a group that is heterogeneous and complex in history, culture, and degree of involvement in mainstream society.

Some people of this diverse ethnic group prefer the term *Native American*, for example, whereas others insist on being called *American Indians* or on using their specific ethnicity: *Choctow*, *Laguna Pueblo*, and so forth. Richard Rodriguez insists that, far from vanishing as a racial and ethnic group, Indians live on in the faces and many of the customs of Hispanic Americans. But Chrystos, who did not grow up on a reservation and calls herself an Urban Indian, has chosen as a political act to discard all of the European ancestry of her mother's family and to fully identify herself as a Menominee like her father. Growing up feeling like an outsider, she moves to the inside of the Native American group and fights to retain the distinctiveness of the traditions that remain. She angrily battles against the theft of items of culture for economic gain in "Today Was a Bad Day Like TB" and in other texts. In "Vision: Bundle" she rages, "They have our bundles split open in museums / our dresses & shirts at auctions / our languages on tape / our stories in locked rare book libraries / our dances on film / The only part of us they can't steal / is what we know." A "bundle" is a sacred religious object. To tear it apart is comparable to desecrating an altar or any other holy object. This sort of ignorance and insensitivity makes Chrystos sick, and she compares her rage to tuberculosis.

191

Some academics who are members of Native American groups argue that there can be no written Native American literature because tradition requires that stories and chants remain oral and within the clans to which they belong. They insist that such precious and sacred things should not be shared with outsiders. To Chrystos, those who buy or sell the trappings of Native American culture and history, which often have profound religious or ancestral significance, merit contempt, even if their motives are based on admiration. Many middle-class whites feel as if they do not have a culture of their own and romantically seek to become linked in some way to the traditions of indigenous peoples. But Chrystos is angry that such people take the symbols without doing the work of learning what they mean. If someone has an "Indian grandma back in time," this does not mean that he or she has a right to "own" and desecrate his or her heritage. In fact, it means that someone has discarded the memories of the ancestors and failed to pass them on, has opted out of the group by passing into the mainstream through assimilation. Furthermore, the targets of Chrystos's anger do nothing concrete to help Indian people in need, continuing instead the European tradition of taking unthinkingly. The poet's assumptions imply that underneath ignorance lie arrogance and selfishness. Those who clap during a Lakota dance see the act as a performance done for their pleasure rather than the celebration of something spiritual. This assumption recalls the initial European images of Native Americans as incapable of understanding metaphysical concepts. It also assumes that the white onlookers are the reason for the dance, and that others exist only in relation to them. When the speaker retches, trying to "get it out," she compares her rage to tuberculosis. But the disease does not go away as she painfully coughs up her own body fluids. Like a bacillus, the harm done by the destroyers of native culture cannot be expelled. Both are the result of the same sort of invasive callousness. Students should not deceive themselves that Chrystos is speaking metaphorically when she expresses rage toward all whites. Yes, she is angry with us. Even the punctuation and the structure of the poem deliberately subvert the rules of traditional English verse.

The crude language of the poem's final lines is appropriate to the theme. Subtlety does not work with those who are unable to see the enormity of their intrusion, as she shows us in earlier lines. Many students believe that the anger of Chrystos, or Native Americans who protest the appropriation of cultural symbols for sports team names, is extreme and unjustified. They see such complaints as whining about inconsequential matters. Many will defend prejudiced characters in stories by maintaining that "this is the way they were raised," so their actions are excusable. Since "the chop" at Atlanta Braves games is not intended to insult anyone, just to have a good time, they say, why should anyone be insulted? The only counter to their defensiveness may be to present scenarios in which their own cultural or religious icons are desecrated. A few years ago, for example, much controversy raged over an NEA grant that went to an artist who submerged a crucifix in urine. Perhaps we could think of other such images to present to our students before we read the poem and discuss the views of Native American activists.

LOUISE ERDRICH

Dear John Wayne (p. 1016)

Although college students usually recognize photographs of John Wayne and perhaps have seen his old movies on television or videotape, we no longer can assume that everyone will understand the cultural connotations evoked by his name. Children of the 1950s and 1960s, even in the effete East, came home from school to serialized Westerns on newly acquired black-and-white television sets. They went en masse on Saturdays to matinees at movie theaters with names like "The Bijou" to throw popcorn and whoop as ancestors circled their wagons against the brutal savages that swept down from the mountaintops, making hearts thump with terror. The cavalry would arrive just in time, raising long guns to bloodlessly pick off the feathered demons as they raced by on their horses, shooting their flaming arrows at the Conestoga wagons and the innocent blonde women and children cowering below. Little boys would ask for cowboy hats and cap pistols for Christmas, and Christmas morning smelled like brimstone as they joyfully shot at Indians skulking behind the decorated tree. On television, *Wagon Train* continued the story of the trek west, where Indians were a constant menace. In an earlier American time and place, Walt Disney's version of Davy Crockett and television's manly Daniel Boone — both played by actor Fess Parker, thus confusing American history for a generation — fought scowling, painted, and shaven Mohawks, though occasionally there were friendly Indians willing to help the innocent settlers. Tonto offered solemn assistance to the heroic Lone Ranger, and everyone read about Squanto and Sacajawea at school.

Some movies categorized Indians as wise and friendly or wild and hotheaded, depending upon their willingness to accommodate white expansion. Sometimes the white hero would raise issues with misguided government officials, standing up for Native Americans who were apparently unable to speak for themselves. But mostly — everyone could repeat the proverb — "the only good Indian was a dead Indian." John Wayne, shown in Technicolor in the theaters at night or on the huge outdoor screen at the drive-in movie, was the hero for teenagers, grown-ups, and the few lucky kids whose parents took them out in the evenings. But his name is linked inextricably with all the other images, a 1950s version of the heroic, manly struggle to conquer the West for the good guys. It was no coincidence that the same face represented the American victory in World War II or the heroic figure standing against the Communist threat to everything wholesome and fine. It was so romantic when he turned the sassy Maureen O'Hara over his knee and spanked her to show who was boss! America was tall, blue-eyed, unquestionably male, and unconquerable. This is what everyone knew without a doubt, and few doubted whose side God was on.

As the speaker of Louise Erdrich's poem watches the larger-than-life images of John Wayne fighting the stereotypical enemies, impossible to identify as belonging to a specific Indian nation, she realizes as a Native American that she is not the intended audience for this picture. Until recently, when they went to the movies, African Americans saw no representations of Buffalo soldiers riding to the rescue of their fellow U.S. Cavalrymen, and Native Americans saw only misleading and demeaning images of people who looked like them. As the culture presented heroes for emulation and self-identification, and for the economic benefit of producers and advertisers, the message to minorities was clear: You are inferior. When Thurgood Marshall presented his case to the U.S. Supreme Court against the "separate but equal" doctrine that justified the segregation of African Americans, he used as evidence of its destructiveness an experiment in which little girls were asked to choose the prettiest doll. Presented with white dolls and dolls that were black like themselves, children almost always chose the white doll as the best representation of human beauty. A culture that privileged whiteness as the ideal had told these children that they could not measure up unless they could become whiter. The same principle is at work as children decide what qualities determine manliness, or even define humanity itself. The visual images of television and motion pictures are especially effective in communicating the values of a culture, even unintentionally, since the audience tends to simply absorb them rather than thinking consciously about the assumptions viewers are internalizing. Native American children watching a John Wayne movie are as likely as anyone else to identify with the hero. But how are they to deal with the message that the only good Indian is a dead Indian? Do they accept the evaluation of inferiority or brutality, even behave in ways that lead to self-destruction? Do they deny their heritage and try to be as white as possible? Or do they protect themselves by treating it all as a big joke, at least on the outside, rolling on the hood of the car and "slipping in the hot spilled butter," as in lines 24–25?

Born in 1954 in Minnesota, Chippewa writer Louise Erdrich was a young child during the cold war, when such movies were at the peak of their influence. Americans had already taken such assumptions about the inherent inferiority of people of color into battle in Korea and soon would find their confidence in such beliefs challenged by the Vietnam War. Erdrich becomes no longer part of the intended audience for the movie when she begins to read the images closely and to enter into dialogue with the text she sees on the screen and surrounding her at the drive-in theater. Critical thinking is antithetical to stereotyping. As America was forced to reevaluate its warrants during the late 1960s and the following decades, and many Native Americans became active in seeking political change and redress of grievances, movies attempted to challenge stereotypes. Often, however, high-budget films exchanged one stereotype for another. In *Dances with Wolves*, for example, the Native Americans are noble savages rather than bloodthirsty ones, but the blue-eyed Kevin Costner is still the star. As Native Americans take the opportunity to speak for themselves, as Spokane/Coeur d'Alene poet Sherman Alexie does in the 1998 film *Smoke Signals*, the human complexity of their lives will perhaps become clear to more people, and Native American children may find more realistic role models.

Louise Erdrich uses multilayered language to question stereotypes. The teenagers sit on the hood of a Pontiac, a model of automobile that evokes the 1950s and creates some verisimilitude. We might not notice at first reading that the car is named for an Ottawa chief who fought the British at Detroit in the

1700s, then went on to make an alliance with them. How many of our students ever heard of Pontiac's War? A name that might have been well known if Native Americans were deciding the content of history books is trivialized into a gimmick for selling cars. The "slow-burning spirals" that create smoke to deter insects also capture the drive-in experience for older adults who were part of it as children or adolescents, but college students may need explanations. Even so, this image too carries a double meaning, since smoke signals used by Indians were a movie cliché.

Furthermore, Erdrich echoes the image of smoke and fire throughout the poem. The spirals are "slow-burning," as anger and resentment may be. The "smoke-screen" literally fails to repel the mosquitoes. But we are aware of many smoke screens that were set up to deceive Native Americans as their lands were stolen. Her juxtaposition of statements about mosquitoes and statements about Indians create a metaphorical connection between the two as pesky creatures that get in the way. The hordes of Indians are not individuals in the movie but are an indiscriminate "bunch"; they seem more like inanimate objects superimposed on the landscape or weapons of mass destruction than people. She ironically describes them as "barring progress."

The poem implies that ownership of land is a European American concept and distinguishes between the selfish lust for land and real understanding of it. Seeing with one's eyes is not the same as seeing with one's heart. The forces of western expansion, as represented by John Wayne on the screen, selfishly assume their right to anything they see, but under the surface they are willing to destroy the souls of people to get what they want. Erdrich's speaker hears John Wayne say *"we've got them / where we want them, drunk, running."* Alcoholism is a complex medical and social issue among Native Americans. Though not entirely stemming from low self-esteem, the disease thrives on internalized self-hatred and contempt, and prejudiced images of drunk Indians in popular culture do not make it an easy addiction to battle. The use of the word *running* might remind some readers of the ending of Ralph Ellison's "Battle Royal" (p. 937), in which the note in the protagonist's dream says, "Keep This Nigger-Boy Running." The point of both texts is the same, that those in power have a stake in keeping minorities in a position of inferiority. What John Wayne actually thought, consciously, is beside the point. People can justify actions to get what they desire, whether they want to settle on "unoccupied" land, and thus must kill or weaken the pesky Indians who protest, or to create a box-office success by promoting images that implicitly label groups as outsiders and promote destructive stereotypes.

All people learn subconsciously what the insider groups expect of them and either accept these dictates unquestioningly or find ways to resist through critical thinking. Many people sleep through history class, and their only sense of their identity as Americans comes through visual media. Students may debate the extent to which film studios have a responsibility to provide positive portrayals of ethnic diversity in America. Perhaps we do not want filmmakers to teach us who we are. Most people do not realize, however, the degree to which this already happens. Deliberate propaganda hardly seems the answer. Encouraging and funding outsider groups to write their own history on film to provide multiple alternate views may be the most effective approach.

Whereas Chrystos in "Today Was a Bad Day Like TB" projects a bitter and angry attitude, Louise Erdrich's tone in "Dear John Wayne" is more objective and ironic. She is angry, as well, but focuses on reading the implications of the text of oppression rather than centering on her own response to it. Both poets challenge white readers to look underneath the surface of their careless actions and stereotypes to see the harm that they do through ignorance and the selfish assumption that everything is theirs for the taking. Both think that whites see Indians as cardboard cutouts or symbols rather than as real individuals with a particular heritage that is of value in its own context. In Erdrich's poem, the John Wayne type sees land as his right, while the white characters in Chrystos's poem buy sacred things and unthinkingly desecrate them. Readers may excuse the whites because they do not understand what they are doing, but the Indian speakers imply that their ignorance stems from the refusal to learn. As Erdrich's speaker says, "the heart is so blind." There is something basically evil about refusing to see, as Erdrich goes on to show in her final lines. Erdrich watches and studies the dynamics as a Native American audience responds to a text created by whites. Chrystos describes whites as they assume they are the audience for Native American religious and cultural ceremonies and works of art. If their roles were reversed, Chrystos might choose images from the movie and show how specific cultures are appropriated and misread by the filmmakers. Erdrich might be more likely to engage in dialogue with the "young blond hippie boy" in Chrystos's poem and to read the subtext of what he says. In each poem, the audience is caught up in the text being presented, but harm is done to the outsider culture in each. The disjunction between presentation and audience leads to misreading at the dance and the possible internalizing of negative stereotypes at the movie. In both cases, however, the perceptive reader — the poet — uses the text to raise issues that others ignore.

DWIGHT OKITA

In Response to Executive Order 9066 (p. 1019)

Quickly scanning through Executive Order 9066, issued by President Franklin D. Roosevelt on February 19, 1942, the reader might believe that a benevolent government wished to do a favor for Americans of Japanese descent. Internment in concentration camps is not mentioned. Instead, military officials are instructed to "prescribe military areas . . . from which any or all persons may be excluded," with no specific indication of what people are intended. Anyone the military considers a threat may be kept out of "military areas" as defined by "the appropriate Military Commanders." This is to be done to prevent "espionage and . . . sabotage to national defense material, national defense premises, and national defense utilities." There is no indication in the order that such categories include the prosperous farms and businesses of Japanese Americans who had spent years carving out lives for their families in California, Oregon, Washington, and Hawaii. It is not surprising that it came as a shock to some families when they found themselves first in makeshift stalls or shacks thrown up on racetracks, fairgrounds, and livestock enclosures, and later in deserted areas that amounted to prison camps. Executive Order 9066 states in two separate places that the people excluded from sensitive areas must be provided for with "medical aid, hospitalization, food, clothing, transportation, use of land, shelter, and other supplies, equipment, utilities, facilities, and services." But food was often spoiled and inedible. When internees of one camp protested the theft of food by guards, many were injured and two killed. Barbed wire and guard towers surrounded the camps, and those trying to escape could be shot. In his 1995 novel *Snow Falling on Cedars*, David Guterson imagines how it might have been: "He remembered Manzanar, the dust in the barracks, in the tar-papered shacks and cafeteria; even the bread tasted gritty. They'd worked tending eggplants and lettuces in the camp garden. They'd been paid little, the hours were long, they'd been told it was their duty to work hard" (162). Many sons and husbands also felt it was their duty to serve their country, the United States, in the war. They fought, even while their families were imprisoned as potential saboteurs. The school writings of children who were interned in the camps reveal physical discomfort, mixed with cheerful trust in the goodness of life. They complain about the cold or the heat, the sandstorms, the fence, and the cramped conditions requiring whole families to share one room. But they enjoy the outdoors as children might on a camping vacation and wax eloquent about "the good drinking water, the free food, the free electricity and free water." Unlike their parents, they did not have to be concerned about what would happen when it was time to resume their lives. Even before the war, laws prohibited free and clear ownership of property by Asian immigrants, and many were cheated out of years of hard work when their internment made their homes, lands, and businesses available to looters and opportunists. In 1980, the U.S. government officially apologized to the internees still living, about half of those who had endured the camps. A commission reported that "the promulgation of Executive Order 9066 was not justified by military necessity, and the decisions which followed from it . . . were not driven by analysis of military conditions. The broad historical causes which shaped these decisions were race prejudice, war hysteria, and a failure of political leadership."

In the first stanza of "In Response to Executive Order 9066," Dwight Okita's young female speaker tells the relocation officials that she has packed "three packets of tomato seeds" in preparation for her journey. She introduces her friend Denise, who calls tomatoes "love apples." When the speaker's father says "they won't grow" in the internment camps, the obvious connection is that love probably can't survive there either. Although the next three stanzas continue to describe the speaker's relationship with her white friend, a friend who abandons her as a result of prejudice, the tomatoes are not mentioned again until the final stanza, thus framing the poem with a metaphoric image. Once the seeds of friendship have been planted, young Miss Ozawa claims, they will come to fruition, given time. The assumption seems optimistic about the ability of love to overcome hate, given time. Perhaps this is based on naiveté. After all, her letter begins with a polite acceptance of the government's "invitation," as if it were a

197

vacation. She is being a good girl when she packs her galoshes, since this is the sort of thing a mother might remind her to pack. This is ironic if she is going to Manzanar or another desert camp, however, and again implies that she doesn't grasp the situation. But Denise is naive as well, accepting the assumptions of her elders that Japanese Americans will be more loyal to Japan than America. Furthermore, no Japanese American was convicted of espionage against the United States through the whole course of World War II, a fact that cannot be wholly attributed to concentration camps, since none in Hawaii were interned and many Japanese Americans served heroically in the U.S. military. It is an especially effective device to have a young girl speak about such prejudice, since the audience can empathize with someone who is obviously no danger to her country. Both the content and style — concrete words like *hot dogs* or *messy room*, for example — indicate that she is American rather than Japanese. Her friend's rejection seems doubly hurtful because the injustice is so clear. Because the bombing of Pearl Harbor came as such a shock, many Americans could not believe that the Japanese had been able to carry it out without help from collaborators in Hawaii. There was great fear that such an attack would be mounted against the West Coast of the United States. Nevertheless, as government studies maintain, the main reason for internment seems to be the visibility of people who looked like the enemy. "Japs" became demonized as a racial group, while animosity toward the enemy in Europe, so like mainstream Americans in appearance and culture, tended to be focused upon the figures of Adolph Hitler, Benito Mussolini, and their followers, rather than all ethnic Germans or Italians.

Chrystos in "Today Was a Bad Day Like TB" is furious at the betrayal of her culture by those who sell Native American possessions to whites who reveal their unconscious biases by misusing the artifacts. Her tone is bitter as she takes the insider stance as a member of a group that has been wronged, condemning the outsiders — the whites — who fail to understand. The speaker of Dwight Okita's "In Response to Executive Order 9066" does not condemn. Her tone is innocent and hopeful in the face of betrayal. Her friend's prejudice bewilders her. Okita's use of a naive narrator allows the reader to know more about the reality of the situation than she does. He may be speaking in the voice of his mother as a young girl; she and other family members were interned during World War II, then moved to make a new life in Chicago after losing all their possessions as a result. The voice seems authentic, but we can only guess at Dwight Okita's emotions. Louise Erdrich in "Dear John Wayne" seems to be recalling an experience from her youth, and we assume that the speaker's views are similar to the poet's own. Even though she speaks in the present tense, we sense the distance of mature reflection in her reading of the movie and its immediate audience. A less direct approach might have had one of the "laughing Indians" explain why he laughs. Chrystos gets in the reader's face with her direct expression of rage, and we hear the speaker and the political activist/poet as one voice. An exercise in irony might have Chrystos go further in reading the minds of the people who clap, the hippie, and the people with Indian grandmas who forget their heritage, giving them each a chance to reveal themselves in narration. The alienation in Okita's poem is based on true alienation, since his narrator will be totally isolated from her insider life, segregated behind a fence under armed guard. This is painful and unjust. But some readers may feel that the psychological isolation of the speakers of Erdrich's and Chrystos's poems is equally profound, perhaps more so because they are so angry and their betrayers hide their prejudice, even from themselves.

JANICE MIRIKITANI
Doreen (p. 1020)

Like many students in the late 1960s, Janice Mirikitani worked as a political activist, demonstrating for minority admissions and for implementation of a multicultural curriculum at San Francisco State University. As an Asian American woman, her participation as a writer and speaker broke with tradition. Ironically, her cause called for recognition of the very traditions that her radical stance undercut. Third-generation Japanese American women like Mirikitani struggle with which elements of American culture — their own culture — they will embrace and which ethnic customs they will maintain in recognition of family and individual identity. Ideals of beauty are problematic. Does one attempt to adapt to the "American feminine" image, internalizing racism and self-hate, even surgically changing one's body to look more European? If not, does this mean it is necessary to accept equally stereotyped Asian ideals that set one apart as an outsider? In her 1989 poem "Yea, She Knows," Mirikitani has her speaker wonder if current college students like her daughter understand the issues their parents fought over in the 1960s. She decides that they do, because racism continues:

> She tells me that she was called ugly
> cause she's a chink.
> She laughs . . . we all look alike.
> Yea. She knows.
> Some whites visiting her roommate say
> to her about the Japanese
>   ". . . they were right to put the japs
>   into concentration camps."
> She tells them to shut-up. Her family was in the camps.
> They say:
>   ". . . they deserved it. The japs are so crazy —
>   you know, those kamikazis — they shouldn't be
>   allowed to run around free in this country."
> Yea. She knows. (qtd. in http://www.oxy.edu/—kareem/Janice.htm)

Janice Mirikitani deals with the ways racism causes problems for girls from Asian ethnic groups as they construct identities and find their place in American culture. Students might want to compare "Doreen" with a later text in this chapter, Naomi Wolf's "The Making of a Slut" (p. 1035). The teenaged "Dinah" of Wolf's essay finds herself in a similar adolescent situation to Mirikitani's Doreen, but the sorting process works against her because of social class rather than ethnicity. In "The Making of a Slut" Dinah is unfairly categorized because she defiantly carries herself with pride and has artistic aspirations that break stereotypes for lower-class girls. To the high-school culture, economically disadvantaged girls with large breasts are sluts, so this is what Dinah must become. The anger of the other high-school girls toward Doreen seems more justified. She rejects her own culture to the point of abasement, and though the speaker claims that her classmates are "sad" when she is injured, most readers can't help feeling that her disfigurement is ironically just, though certainly sad. Doreen's story begins with ridicule about her Asian features and ends with their total erasure. This seems a rather high price to pay for self-hate and internalized racism.

Like a kidnap victim or a hostage, Doreen comes to identify with the people who take advantage of her. She may not realize that she is obvious and ridiculous as she tries desperately to change her very identity. Rather than not caring what people think, she seems to care desperately what the insider culture thinks of her, rejecting the evaluations of other Japanese girls. She rebels against being categorized as Asian, but she fails to become a true rebel. Doreen's rebellion is turned against her own body and soul rather than against the structures of discrimination. She seeks to break out of racism on her own, thus losing the support and guidance of others in the same situation. Her position is essentially one of denial, and this leads to her exploitation and eventual erasure. Young adolescents are brutal to each other, and college students discussing this issue can give numerous examples from their experiences. As a result of school shootings in the 1990s, scholarly discussions of how the prevalence of cliques and the outsider status of some students may lead to violence are taking place in many discourses. Typically, boys tend to express their distress about social status through violence, whereas girls act out sexually. Having said this, however, we recognize that sexism plays a role in categorizing students and that sexual transgressions still label girls, whereas boys may be forgiven or even admired for similar behavior. In her attempt to fit in with the insider group, Doreen accepts violence and name-calling against Asians like herself, laughing about it when confronted. Since Doreen could only relate her own story if she had engaged in self-examination and realized that she had been ridiculed all her life for her misguided efforts to acquire status, the effect of a first-person account would be pathetic and tragic, and we would miss the irony of the ending lines. Creative writers in the class might like to experiment with a poem in her voice, however. Perhaps Doreen laughs about the stories about Korean War atrocities because she is nervous and embarrassed, but the narration gives no evidence that this is so. She chooses to relate these stories to her classmates. She may have identified so closely with her warped view of mainstream America that she takes pleasure in the destruction of anything Asian. In taking such gruesome pleasure in violence, Doreen seems also to reject the typical female role, becoming as hardened as her veteran boyfriend. Doreen's assimilation is as extreme as her makeup. Like African Americans accused of acting like "Uncle Toms" or "oreo cookies" — dark on the outside and white on the inside — Doreen believes that she has successfully overcome racism when she has actually betrayed herself and others within the excluded group. Often, individuals in outsider groups will "pass" for members of the dominant group if their appearance allows it. Although this denial of one's ancestry is usually viewed with contempt by insiders and outsiders alike, the impulse may be natural. Children, especially, want to be on what they perceive as the winning team. We can't do this by changing sides, however, but by making sure that everyone has an equal chance to win. The numerous civil rights movements of modern history are filled with examples of people who rebelled against cultural norms in ways that had positive consequences for humanity as a whole.

Mirikitani seems to put the blame on Doreen rather than focusing on the societal abuses that lead to her desperate need for acceptance. Chrystos might spread the blame around more, expressing anger toward the boys and men who take advantage of her distress and toward the culture that tells her that her Asian features are not pretty. But Chrystos would not ignore Doreen's complicity; she rails against those who have forgotten their Indian grandmas and sold their heritage. Whites in Mirikitani's poem are represented primarily by men who sexually use the Asian girl and commit atrocities against Asian men. They seem less positively presented because their motives are not considered. This is not a poem about white oppression, but about internalized racism. In the other poems of this cluster, we might find ways to make excuses for characters who do not realize the depth of their disrespect for outsiders. Doreen evokes our pity because we realize that she is damaged even before the automobile wreck. Her youthful desire for inclusion in the mainstream is touching in spite of — perhaps because of — its exaggeration. Dwight Okita's young female speaker in "In Response to Executive Order 9066" seems closest to Doreen. She is culturally American, and the prejudice of her classmate takes her by surprise. Although the sadness is less intense, it is evident. Other readers might see Doreen as similar to the Native Americans who laugh at the John Wayne movie, sad characters in that they are exposed to denigrating images that tell them they are inferior.

DAVID HERNANDEZ

Pigeons (p. 1023)

Many people in the Chicago area credit David Hernandez as the inspiration behind a revival of interest in poetry, especially its oral performance. Born in Puerto Rico, Hernandez moved to the continental United States as a child, and is strongly concerned with multicultural issues. He writes in both English and Spanish. He believes in taking poetry to the people; he first recited his poetry on playgrounds and street corners as a community activist in the 1960s. He performs with a group called "Street Sounds" that integrates his spoken poetry with Afro-Cuban, pop, folk, classical, and jazz rhythms and motifs. He frequently reads his poetry and conducts writing workshops for students ranging from elementary school to college age, and he often performs at public events. In 1987, he was commissioned to write a poem celebrating Chicago's one-hundred-and-fiftieth anniversary. His poem "Pigeons" communicates some of this appreciation for the people of the city and his pride in his Hispanic ethnicity. The structure of the poem is puzzling, but if you turn it sideways and squint your eyes, it takes the shape of a city skyline with a hodgepodge of square and slanting rooftops. Raising carrier pigeons is a hobby popular with a number of ethnic groups, especially city dwellers who keep conglomerations of cages on the roofs of apartment buildings. Pigeons are hardy and gregarious birds, and some live to be over thirty years old. Still, they do have a bad reputation. We think of them as nasty, since their droppings fall in inconvenient places. They sometimes visit bird feeders in abutting residential neighborhoods and voraciously devour the seed intended for the more colorful cardinals and blue jays and the cuter chickadees.

Ostensibly, in Hernandez's metaphor, the word *pigeons* is the tenor and *spiks*, the vehicle. This would mean that we are discussing pigeons here, that *pigeons* is the abstract and general concept to be illuminated by the more concrete and specific *spiks*. Actually, Hernandez does just the opposite. As he pretends to use stereotypes of Hispanics to help us understand pigeons, he obliquely forces us to examine our preconceived notions about the people rather than the birds. He characterizes them as survivors in the face of poverty. They are lively — move to the beat of the music — but also seem a bit threatening, are flashy "young street thugs." They seem ethnically in between and are therefore discriminated against by everyone. Even those who find them worthy of help often do more harm than good. His larger argument may be that Puerto Ricans slip through the cracks of society, as things now stand. By saying that our attitude toward Hispanics resembles the bird lover's attitude toward pigeons, the poet accuses mainstream America, especially liberals, of pushing this group to the side for more colorful minorities. He speaks of assimilation, as some "try to pass," but points out that language is also a factor. His accusation seems valid, especially when we consider political resistance to immigration and bilingual education, reflected in laws and propositions directed against the menace. In any argument, analogy may be the most vulnerable type of evidence. Both writer and reader may find that metaphor can be taken too far. Some may object, for example, to the application of the housing project example specifically to Hispanics. Does he mean to say that such environments are more destructive to Puerto Ricans than to African Americans or other minorities? Others may feel that the word *spik* should not be used in a poem, since it is degrading even when used by someone within the ethnic group to which it refers. There is an ongoing debate about the use of the word *nigger* by African American comedians. Some prominent African American thinkers disagree with its use by anyone, leading to circumlocutions like attorney Chris Darden's euphemistic lecture on the N-word during the O. J. Simpson trial. Others insist that it is important to transform the enemy's language by appropriating the symbols as one's own. Thus, we may read *Queer Theory* in an English course, though it would still be inappropriate for a heterosexual to hurl the word *queer* as a homophobic slur. Similarly, readers may enjoy the word *spik* as an ironic statement by a Hispanic writer, while realizing that his usage does not give non-Hispanics permission to do the same. Hernandez has said earlier that "pigeons" — read Hispanics — are perceived to "move funny," and his play on the word *pigeon-toed* may refer back to this. But he implies that the misguided efforts of liberals have injured the pigeons' feet, so he may also refer to the results of malnutrition and other diseases that result from poor living conditions. Hernandez does not treat kindly those who try to help, referring to them as "pigeon ladies, renegades, / or bleeding-heart Liberals." He does not say they should turn aside, but he implies that their methods ignore the specificity of Hispanic culture. Rather than treating Puerto Ricans and others of Spanish ancestry as if their needs were the same as other ethnic groups or forcing them to change in order to assimilate, the poet implies that other Americans should recognize them as unique. Foreign language departments at many universities cannot accommodate the increasing demand for Spanish language classes as more English-speaking college students aim for fluency in this important American second language. Perhaps expanding such programs into the community would be most useful and in keeping with Hernandez's project of taking language to the people where they are.

Hernandez in "Pigeons" communicates a message similar to Chrystos in "Today Was a Bad Day Like TB." Both call for whites to think before they act, respecting the differences of other ethnic groups. The preceding poems of this cluster center primarily on the experiences of specific narrators or characters, whereas Hernandez considers a whole group of people. He may be trying to paint a fuller experience of discrimination. We should not forget, however, that specific, representative examples may be as effective as broader views in getting a point across. Some readers may be more convinced by the pathos of one schoolgirl than by a metaphorical argument about a whole group. Readers will vary in their responses to the poetic techniques in this cluster. Some will prefer the extended metaphor of Hernandez's "Pigeons" whereas others will respond to the straightforward presentations and dialogue of other poems. Some may be offended by the accusatory tone of Chrystos, Hernandez, or Erdrich, feeling more comfortable with the innocence of the speaker in Dwight Okita's "In Response to Executive Order 9066." Whatever their choice, encourage students to explain specifically why they find one poem effective and another less so, asking them to examine their own hidden assumptions.

SEXUAL TRANSGRESSION (p. 1025)

MAXINE HONG KINGSTON
No Name Woman (p. 1026)

In 1976, Maxine Hong Kingston's *The Woman Warrior: Memoirs of a Girlhood Among Ghosts* jumped straight off the presses into the multicultural literary canon in university classrooms. The book is interesting for a great many reasons. Its style is filled with metaphor and concrete imagery, often reading like poetry. Characters are as three-dimensional and dynamic as those of any short story, and they evoke a specific situation in a way that both insiders and outsiders to its culture can grasp. But perhaps most interesting is Kingston's interweaving of the nonfiction of autobiography with fictional leaps into imagination and myth. Just as the author lives in the borderland between her Chinese ancestral heritage and her American individuality, her narrative exists in the intersection where genres overlap.

In her adaptation of the stories of her childhood, Kingston critiques both American and Chinese cultural limitations, especially the racist assumptions of white America and the patriarchal structures of China that reduce women to shameful beings who are less than human. To be a girl is to be worthless and bad. Girls grew up to move into other families, so every mouthful of food given to a girl was stolen from the true children, the boys. In China, where infanticide has long been accepted, female children were often disposed of, especially in times of starvation. So when the young Maxine Hong begins to menstruate, her mother tells her the story of her aunt, the No Name Woman of this narrative, an excerpt from *A Woman Warrior*. The assumption is that the warning is needed so that the young woman will not commit the sexual transgressions that will embarrass the family. But the author comes to see that the true punishment dealt to her aunt has been her erasure. Her fate has been a sort of "reverse ancestor worship" in which she continues to pay for her sin against the family. She has no name, and all memory of her has been wiped out, except as a bad example.

Kingston imagines scenarios that explain her aunt's shameful pregnancy, imagining at first that she was forced, then briefly that she had been promiscuous, and finally that she had sought out a lover, deliberately attracting and winning his love. She even realizes the possibility of incest. Kingston's aunt is one of the ghosts who haunt her girlhood, and continues to haunt the woman twenty years later. Her affinity for this particular spirit is not altogether safe and wholesome, she admits at the end of her narrative. By filling in the gaps of her mother's cautionary tale to find the personality behind it, Kingston imagines her aunt's motives and explores her own assumptions about gender and society. The reader is invited to do the same because Kingston acknowledges the open quality of this mystery story.

The argument behind the narrative that Kingston's mother tells is that a woman is always being watched, and though she is prone to be bad, her punishment will be certain. Women students who read the story may be able to recall such exemplary warnings by their mothers against forming relationships too early or having unprotected sex. Often, parents see such warnings backfire, as children say, "Well, I guess I take after that aunt you told me about." Like Kingston, most young people find that such anecdotes make them curious to know the reasons behind the behavior the parent disapproves. Most contemporary parents might ask daughters to consider how focusing on a sexual relationship will interfere with education and the chance to establish a career. "Don't give up your power," we tell them, pointing to women who are abused or otherwise dominated by men. Most American students will not have comparable punishments to share with the class and will think of the aunt's treatment by the villagers and her family as unforgivable abuse. Some American parents shun adult children for choosing the "wrong" partner or lifestyle, cutting off communication entirely, but this is rare among our students. Some girls in any given class may have ended unplanned pregnancies with abortions, either by their own choice or because of their parents' insistence. Sometimes they mention this privately to the instructor, but usually they keep silent. We might want to keep this in mind as the class enters into the discussion of sensitive matters, maintaining a noncondemning atmosphere. Young men might be asked to consider what they would do if they realized they had impregnated someone; can they imagine covering this up by being among the villagers who invade the woman's household? Although discussing their punishments for minor infractions may seem trivial in the light of what happens to No Name Woman, this is an illuminating way to discover the values of our families and to think about the warrants we bring into adulthood. Students also might want to share the stories their parents tell, usually to laughter, about their childhood or adolescent infractions. Have fathers shared with sons their college drinking escapades? Or times they got arrested for a political demonstration? Sometimes, Kingston tells her readers explicitly that "No Name Woman" is a tale of gender inequality. For example, she tells us in paragraph 15, "To be a woman, to have a daughter in starvation time was a waste enough." But the whole story is implicitly about the greater burden that sex places upon a woman. It is she who is punished by the family and the village, must bear the child and give birth alone, and is driven finally to commit murder/suicide because she cannot provide a respectable life for the baby. We can believe the part of the story told by Kingston's mother, though she leaves many gaps. We can also trust the information the author provides about herself and her own childhood experiences. Her facts about Chinese customs can be verified. But she only guesses about her aunt's experiences and motives, often signaling this with the word *perhaps*. When she speaks of her aunt haunting her, she speaks metaphorically, but in an emotional and psychological sense this may be equally as true as the numerical fact that there are only one hundred surnames in all of China.

As we have seen in many of the texts of this anthology, writers often distinguish between things that are true in a human or spiritual sense and things that are merely factual. Kingston's imagined events give flesh to the sparse facts of her mother's cautionary tale and her knowledge of her Chinese family and history. Kingston reiterates the assertion that the crime of No Name Woman was severe because it happened in the context of famine. "Adultery is extravagance," Kingston says of the Chinese view. Thirty or forty years ago in America, a daughter's pregnancy would have brought shame to her family in most regions and subcultures. Girls were sent away to "homes for unwed mothers" and their babies disappeared into the adoption market. Neighbors often guessed the reason for the young woman's absence, but secrecy reigned. Sometimes, family members found ways to quietly claim the child as their own, and there are tales of people discovering in adulthood that the woman they thought was an older sister or aunt was their biological mother. Those with cooperative family doctors often had a "D&C" to discover why their periods were "irregular," effectively removing any fetal tissue that happened to be there without anyone outside the family knowing for sure. And, of course, we have all heard stories of illegal abortions. For contemporary women, pregnancy does not usually carry a stigma as a sign of sexual activity, though peers may judge harshly the failure to use birth control or safe-sex measures. Church members who once might have been condemning of unmarried pregnant women find themselves in the incongruous position of praising them for not choosing abortion, though premarital sex and adultery are still considered sins. An American woman in the position of Kingston's aunt would probably be able to get help with the support of her child, but keeping the name of the father a secret would not be encouraged, since he would be expected to contribute financially. While sexual transgression is shrouded in moral and religious prohibitions, economic factors may be the most important underlying reasons for cultural taboos against sexual activity outside of marriage.

NAOMI WOLF
The Making of a Slut (p. 1035)

Of all the texts in this anthology, Naomi Wolf's "The Making of a Slut" tends to raise the most familiar and accessible issues. Young women talk eagerly of the sorting that begins in elementary school and continues into high school. One wrote in her response of being called "Tits" all through high school because she had developed early, as Naomi Wolf's young protagonist does. This young woman did not have Dinah's social-class problems and did make the cheerleading team. However, she related the time that a male classmate seemed to compliment her by saying how much he enjoyed watching her cheer, only to follow up with the detail that he loved the way her breasts bounced up and down. Before coming to college, this young woman had breast reduction surgery so that she could be judged in this new situation for the person she was — a fine student and a lively drama major — rather than for a physical quality that singled her out as a sexual phenomenon. Though she did not discuss this in class, she agreed to allow her example to be presented anonymously. Other young women recall the cliques that freeze out girls whose clothing, social skills, appearance, and so forth do not fit the narrow, arbitrary, constantly shifting standards of the insider groups. One girl spoke of being accepted completely at a school in one state, moving one year to a more affluent area and experiencing slut status, then moving back to her home state to again be a nice girl. She could think of nothing about her behavior or appearance that had changed, other than her relative economic status.

Coupled with texts that describe Cinderella stories pitting stepsisters against each other, these narratives leave young men open-mouthed and feeling temporarily off the hook as sexists. We have to remind them, however, that though women are complicit in perpetuating the structures of patriarchy, the devaluing of women is a societal issue that has taken centuries to develop. In Wolf's examples, as in Janice Mirikitani's poem "Doreen" earlier in this chapter, men benefit sexually from the distress experienced by young women seeking social status in self-destructive ways.

As an introduction to this cluster, one can have students bring in pictures of sluts and then discuss the warrants underlying their selections. The first year we did this, the Monica Lewinsky scandal broke, and several students chose her photograph. We discussed the reasons why a Jewish psychiatrist's chubby daughter in an upscale school might find herself the person placed in the slut niche, as seems to have happened to Lewinsky. Did the behavior come first, or did the behavior develop in response to the arbitrary evaluation of her peers? Why were people so willing to accept James Carville's characterization of Paula Jones as "trailer trash"? And what specifically about living in a trailer makes one trash? The class question seems important. One person brought in a picture of Bill Clinton as a representative slut, and we talked about why this is usually a gender-specific word, why we are willing to separate a man's sexual activity from his leadership ability when we might not allow a woman the same leeway. Even if students bring in sexually explicit pictures for shock value, this opens up discussion of the issues surrounding the necessity of objectifying human beings before we can harm or exploit them. This gives us a chance to turn to Naomi Wolf's words about "sex workers" being forced into more and more degrading acts, ironically due, she says, to progress in the sexual freedom of ordinary women.

Wolf asserts that, even with the increase of sexual freedom for women, some girls and women continue to be assigned roles that scapegoat them. She gives examples to show that sexual rules are unequally applied, beginning with an extended narrative about her school friend Dinah, who seems to be forced into the "bad girl" role while still "technically a virgin" simply because she looks the part. Wolf concludes that middle-class girls who engage in secretive sexual behavior are assumed to be innocent, whereas lower-class girls who dare to be visible are labeled as sluts, even if they are not sexually active. But readers may argue that Dinah is not required to accept this evaluation. They feel that some of the behavior Wolf describes may lead to Dinah's lowered status rather than the factors Wolf focuses on. Dinah could persevere in her ambitions, they say, in spite of the cultural barriers. Most importantly, women should claim their own sexuality, or choose to wait, rather than seeing sex as a "performance" for the benefit of men. Wolf proposes that women refuse to allow individuals to be singled out for blame. Although the expressions of censure against women's sexuality are culture specific and change over time, Wolf's last example — the young woman strangled and submerged in a German bog — shows that the history of the condemnation of women for sexual expression is long. Readers can turn to Seamus Heaney's poem "Punishment" (p. 1380 in the "Making Judgments" chapter) for another reference to the same woman, and can see pictures of her preserved body in the archeological account *The Bog People* (1969) by P. V. Glob.

Whereas male students often complain that Wolf's evidence is anecdotal and that her examples may not be representative, female students usually find that her narrative squares with their own experiences, even when they disagree with her conclusions. The overt participation of adults in this categorizing, as in the cheerleading episode, is not as readily apparent, since it usually occurs in more subtle ways. However, many girls relate that responses of principals and teachers to their complaints of sexual harassment — usually inappropriate touching by male classmates — are perceived as tattling. Some even recall being told not to flaunt themselves in front of the boys. The sexuality of young men is accepted and tacitly condoned, at least when it is heterosexual. Whereas girls become outsiders because of their perceived sexual availability, boys may be singled out for ridicule or contempt for other reasons, quite often because they do not fit stereotypes of masculinity. Although Wolf does not deal with the issue here, we might bring up the fact that the suicide rate for gay and lesbian teenagers is much higher than for heterosexuals in this age group, a statistic directly related to societal pressures toward conformity. Many experts contend that when boys use violence they do so in an attempt to overcome outsider status and to seem manly in the eyes of their peers. At some point, both boys and girls seem to be looking to the evaluations of male peers to bolster their self-esteem.

Wolf may use her discussion of fellatio for shock value, and these examples seem less convincing than her description of the stereotyping process. However, they do bring home the point that the "sluts" of this story wind up thinking sex is to please men, not themselves. It's unclear what Wolf wants women to do about the problems of "sex workers" becoming objectified and debased. Perhaps she touches on a solution when she says, "We are all bad girls." By *bad girls*, she seems to mean women who are aware of their bodies and refuse to apologize for being sexual beings. If women stop condemning each other for being sexual and begin to realize that sex is not simply a performance done for men, she says, we will no longer see certain girls and women singled out for arbitrary punishment. Wolf asserts that society imposes such judgments on "bad girls" so that other young women will find incentives for controlling their own sexuality, thus keeping themselves "safe" from a similar fate. If a bad example does not exist, the group will have to invent one so that the insiders know how to define themselves.

Economic factors play a large part in constructing sexual rules in both Maxine Hong Kingston's "No Name Woman" and Naomi Wolf's "The Making of a Slut." Because keeping the family fed is a pressing concern in a China intermittently plagued with famine, girls who will grow up to provide no income for their family are extra mouths to feed. If they become pregnant, especially if they give birth to girls, they have brought the family closer to starvation. The young wife in Kingston's narrative is separated from her husband for economic reasons, so that he can go to America to work and send money home to his family. In Wolf's narrative, the child from the lower socioeconomic class is denied a position she merits because cheerleaders "represent the school" and teachers depend on stereotype and prejudice in their decisions. Wolf feels that Dinah's self-respect and high aspirations are misjudged as improper because of economic factors. Social class sets the agenda for sexual behavior in Wolf's world, and behavior has little to do with it, though modern Americans like to think of our society as classless and tolerant. In Kingston's world of Chinese villagers, in China or in America, a woman's sexual behavior can affect the social class of her family. The villagers destroy the belongings of the family, even the crops that will feed them, because a daughter has committed adultery.

References to the stories of mothers begin both narratives in this cluster, but both move on to show the inadequacy of the mothers' views for daughters living in another social context. Wolf contends that the sexual narratives of her mother's generation need to be revised because they describe the experiences of virgins finding sexuality, whereas contemporary women are "sluts" who must explore sexual issues in a different light. Kingston goes beyond the warnings of her mother's story to imagine the emotions and motives of the woman presented as a bad example. Both say they are "haunted" by the transgressors whose stories they hear; both identify more with these women than with their mothers.

Boys and men in the two narratives are somewhat peripheral to the concerns of the writers, although male actions have important consequences for the characters within the stories. These stories — like female sexuality — are about girls, not boys. Kingston is aware of male power that leaves women little choice about whether or not to have sexual intercourse but punishes women for the results. She imagines at one point that No Name Woman has been raped and that her abuser organizes the retribution of the villagers. Wolf describes the dehumanizing effects of male demands on prostitutes and shows boys as the eager recipients of the sexual favors of girls, oblivious to the emotional cost to the young women. Peer groups are central to both the problem and the solution in Wolf's view. In Kingston's narrative, the peer group is made up of all the neighbors, and their judgment is violent and unforgiving.

Thinking about what Dinah might say to No Name Woman across time and culture is difficult. Dinah's reaction to her own rejection by society when she fails to make the cheerleading squad is that one does not really know what to say in the face of such injustice. At this point, Dinah keeps her identity and pride intact, but she does not seem to realize that her rejection as a cheerleader will be a watershed event for her. "Keep standing tall," she might tell No Name Woman. "Don't let them get to you."

THE MYSTERIOUS EXILE: CRITICAL COMMENTARIES ON HERMAN MELVILLE'S "BARTLEBY, THE SCRIVENER" (p. 1042)

HERMAN MELVILLE
Bartleby, the Scrivener (p. 1042)

The mysterious Bartleby of Herman Melville's story is himself an indeterminate text that the narrator tries to decipher as he relates his escalating problems with the employee who "prefers not" to do what is requested of him. Critics too have tried to explicate the character of Bartleby, coming up with wildly differing conclusions. Some raise issues of Herman Melville's personal biography, identifying Bartleby and the narrator/lawyer as specific Melville family members. Some contend that Bartleby is Melville himself, frustrated by financial pressures to write popular novels and misunderstood when he writes with literary depth. *Moby-Dick*, for example, mystified Melville's contemporary audience, as did this story. Scholar Robert Gale makes a convincing case for the narrator's representing Melville's father-in-law, Judge Lemuel Shaw, who often supported Melville financially, tried to secure diplomatic posts and other paying jobs for him, and worried obtrusively about Melville's health and depression. Such hovering by Melville's wife and her family hampered his creativity and interfered with his writing and may have been seen by Melville as similar to the narrator's uncomprehending and perhaps misguided benevolence. Another approach considers the philosophical issues current in the 1850s, especially the influence of Henry David Thoreau's writings on civil disobedience and passive resistance. Melville sets out to show that Thoreau is misguided, perhaps, since the end result of such nonaction is psychological paralysis and eventually death. To carry it to its logical conclusion is silly. It may be that Melville demonstrates similar drawbacks of Christianity, with its emphasis on charity and forgiveness at all costs. Thus Bartleby is sent by God to test the narrator's patience, a reading with which the narrator agrees at one point, thinking that he may have found his God-given mission in life in providing for Bartleby. On the other hand, the narrator refers to Bartleby as an "incubus," a demon sent from Satan to suck out his life and to damn his soul. The narrator's reading of his esoteric text wavers from one extreme to another, anticipating future audience responses.

For some readers, Bartleby is a hero, critiquing the dulling effects of the industrial revolution that reduces human beings to machines in the service of economic forces, and the lawyer/narrator is the capitalist villain consumed with self-interest. The mysterious clerk is the ultimate hippie dropout, staging a sit-in to protest the abuses of the system. The problem with this interpretation is that Bartleby does not articulate a social or political agenda and is totally alienated from all other human beings. The most popular student analysis agrees with the youngest employee of the firm, Ginger Nut, maintaining that Bartleby is "luny" and arguing that his symptoms indicate autism, schizophrenia, or an obsessive-compulsive disorder. In this context, it is interesting to compare Melville's character with the insane characters of Edgar Allan Poe, especially in stories like "The Black Cat" or "The Cask of Amontillado" (p. 1388), in which the narrator coolly relates walling his victim in. Melville's narrator even thinks of this solution, and recalls a famous murder case in which a murderer crates up the dead body and attempts to ship it out of town. There is evidence for the story's Poe-ish quality, as critics have noted.

Instructors may be more likely to see the narrator's dilemma as a failure of leadership and authority. Even before Bartleby enters the picture, the narrator is ruled by the moods of his employees, and we are told that the nature of his law practice allows him to avoid ambition and conflict. Power is reversed in the office when he procrastinates each time he is faced with Bartleby's escalating resistance. This reading interprets Bartleby's refusal as passive aggression. He becomes the center of the work environment, and even the other employees unconsciously use the word *prefer*, as Melville shows in one especially comedic exchange between the narrator and Turkey. The cataleptic figure becomes the focus of conversations among the workers and even the clients. The striking employee has become, in effect, the boss. He becomes the de facto landlord, forcing his employer to walk around the block until he is ready to let him enter his own offices. The lawyer's decision to vacate his offices, leaving Bartleby there, is hilariously ironic, and startling in its cowardice and abdication of authority. The narrator is as passive as his employee, and though he tells us about his spiritual agonizing over Bartleby, he continually ducks his responsibility as the person in authority. Like the stray messages that make their way to the dead letter office, Bartleby as a person is a text that is lost to its immediate audience, the narrator, and remains ambiguous to those who finally try to read him as a character. The narrator may misread because he is a man characterized by "assumptions," as he tells the reader. He jumps to conclusions: For example, he assumes that Bartleby's first refusal to copy is made because his eyes are bothering him. He uses the common sense and philosophy that seem reasonable to him — his accumulated constructions of reality — but his warrants do not work in the context of Bartleby's mysterious, walled-off world. Like the narrator, readers reveal their own concerns as they fill in the empty spaces of the Bartleby template. As Maurice Friedman notes in his critical commentary on "Bartleby, the Scrivener," this indeterminacy that demands so much of the reader anticipates existentialist writers like Franz Kafka, whose characters are similarly isolated, single-minded, and mysterious.

Like Herman Melville and other serious writers, Bartleby fills blank pages with words. He works furiously at first and is obsessed with writing day and night. He works in isolation, and it is when he is asked to submit his work for others to read and to engage in the proofreading of their work that he begins his refusals. Perhaps he experiences an "anxiety of influence" when he becomes part of a community of writers or cannot face the thought of rejection or criticism of his work. He may have writer's block. If he represents Melville or other creative writers, he has been captured at a low point. Like Melville, he may feel that the work he does for money is in conflict with the work he wants to do, ambitious and mighty work like *Moby-Dick* that will not pay the bills because the reading public fails to understand it. If we think of Bartleby as an artist, then his refusal to do meaningless work is a positive statement. He stands by his principles rather than mindlessly bowing to the expectations of others. But nothing in the story indicates that Bartleby is an innovative creator or a romantic rebel. His refusal seems just as obsessive and rigid as his earlier attentiveness to the task of copying the words of others. Like the walls that surround him, creating a "hermitage" where he sits like some early Christian martyr, Bartleby is static; he seems the antithesis of the rebel.

Most of us have been tempted to rebel by refusing to do tasks we have not chosen for ourselves. Every semester, students leave college because they have procrastinated until assignments are late or because they have missed too many class meetings to pass the course. We usually interpret this as immaturity and poor time management rather than direct refusal, but many may be unconsciously rebelling because they lack a focus of their own and are merely coming to college because their parents assume that they should. Bartleby achieves autonomy, even a sort of power, but his hardly seems a pattern that we should emulate. We see Bartleby through the descriptions of the bewildered narrator, who rationalizes his own passive abdication of authority. We see Bartleby as a mysterious, immovable object that interferes with the peaceful completion of business tasks. His deviation from expectations disturbs the narrator and leaves him baffled. The narrator's limited assumptions and his desire to keep his reputation as a "safe" lawyer lead him to extreme measures to avoid conflict. His narration seeks to explain to the reader why he is blameless for what happens. But we recognize him to be a poor manager, failing to even check the references of the new employee, then shifting the responsibility to the new occupants of the office.

If Bartleby himself told the tale, we might learn the reasons behind his behavior, as happens with Kafka's "A Hunger Artist" (p. 995). The reasons might operate with a different sort of logic, but we would no longer share the narrator's bewilderment. Perhaps Bartleby would be baffled that the lawyer doesn't bring him ginger cookies in prison, since he knows what he likes. We might find out what mysterious activity is going on when he prefers not to open the door to his employer. Third-person point of view would be less ironic and subtle, causing our judgments of the lawyer to be more severe. We might be just as mystified by his behavior as by Bartleby's. Ginger Nut would go with the interpretation that Bartleby is mentally ill, and Nippers, at least in the morning, might characterize him as lazy and good for nothing. Both would probably give some views of the lawyer that would surprise him. However the story is told, it is a tale of two men who avoid stressful work situations, rather than just one striking employee.

The penultimate line may mean that if the narrator had been able to properly read Bartleby — if Bartleby the text had found its perceptive ideal reader — whatever message he was trying to communicate would have been understood. The final line implies that all human beings may be in the same position as Bartleby, destined to be a mystery to others. In this epilogue, Bartleby's story seems closest to that of Melville, whose most profound and complex literary messages seemingly go astray without finding the audience he desires. Reading "Bartleby, the Scrivener" from the other side of victories accomplished through civil disobedience by twentieth-century figures like Gandhi and Martin Luther King, we understand the effectiveness of passive resistance in achieving social change. We would admire him if he were passively resisting participation in horrors like the Holocaust. But we do not know why Bartleby resists, and resistance is only meaningful within a context. His silence makes it impossible to judge the ethics behind his act of refusal. To apathetically refuse to act can actually be an act of evil in itself. We might think of bystanders during the Holocaust who refused to speak out against the Nazis or preferred not to take the risk of helping Jewish neighbors to hide or escape. Oppressive governments make civil disobedience a crime or institute laws that make strikes illegal, seeking to prevent mass refusals. Most readers will agree that this should not be done. Still, the arbitrary refusal to work, without a clear articulation of the reasons behind the resistance, only serves to make life more difficult for others, and we can hardly blame Turkey when he wants to take charge and blacken Bartleby's eyes.

CRITICAL COMMENTARIES:

MICHAEL PAUL ROGIN, From "Class Struggles in America" (p. 1069)
LEO MARX, From "Melville's Parable of the Walls" (p. 1075)
MAURICE FRIEDMAN, From "Bartleby and the Modern Exile" (p. 1079)
ALFRED KAZIN, From "Ishmael in His Academic Heaven" (p. 1084)

When Alfred Kazin sums up in our excerpt his longer argument refuting both the reasoning and the scholarship of various esoteric interpretations of Herman Melville's "Bartleby, the Scrivener" he calls for a straightforward, commonsense approach to its reading. But, as we have seen, Bartleby invites multiple, contradictory interpretations, and his readers, beginning with the narrator, tend to make first one assumption and then quickly discard it for another. When one first looks at the comparative question in the anthology about one of the commentaries being "commonsensical," one misreads and scans the selection by Michael Paul Rogin to see if one agrees that it was fairly easy to understand. Not far into it one begins to realize that something was wrong with one's reading of the question, since one could imagine students raising many objections to the essay's level of difficulty. As consumers of literary theory from deconstruction to phenomenology to new and old historicism to the latest flavor of the year at the MLA convention, college instructors become accustomed to ways of thinking that may bewilder our non-English-major undergraduates. If one reads an entire article that analyzes all of the characters in terms of the "predominant oral imagery" and the resulting "symbiotic relationships" in the story, one might be tempted to mention this as we tackle Rogin's first paragraph. But we would probably resist and make sure students understand words like *protagonist*, *modernist*, *existentially*, and *abstraction* as they are likely to be used in critical discourse. To stay on the same page with this commentator we don't have to be clear about who Georg Lukács and Tocqueville are, but students tend to give up when so many names are dropped. Since most have read some Henry David Thoreau, they may perk up again when he comes into the conversation, but students will undoubtedly agree that this is not a straightforward, "commonsensical" essay. If we are using this book in a class that includes the teaching of academic writing, we might have students practice summary and paraphrase techniques with the Rogin text, asking them to make its meaning understandable to a high-school audience. Although students may feel that Leo Marx's "Melville's Parable of the Walls" is a bit "far out" in its examination of the various walls in the office, they will probably find it more focused and easier to understand than the essay by Rogin. They may be surprised to find that critics look at specifics in such minute detail. Many students prefer the sort of broad, overgeneralized views that we are likely to slap a C on when they turn in their papers, and they may not realize that academic writing expends so many words on such microscopic details.

The excerpt from Maurice Friedman's "Bartleby and the Modern Exile" is perhaps the most interesting of the commentaries because it links Melville's story to Franz Kafka, whose work appears earlier in this chapter. The intertextual parallels are striking, especially with "A Hunger Artist." Perhaps students who read these writers together will also notice the similarities of spirit between the two and respond to Friedman's commentary. Nevertheless, many students will feel lost in Friedman's discourse, as they did when reading Rogin. For example, some instructors are old enough to remember when the "death of God" debate was a hot topic in the 1960s, and others might remember it from philosophy courses. But students may be puzzled, even with the help of Friedman's definition, and we may also need to explain some of the connotations of the term *modern exile* in the title. We can't emphasize strongly enough to our students that, when they first begin reading in an unfamiliar discourse, they will not understand everything they read, but more connections will become clear as they stick with it. Students who avoid scholarly materials will end up with a *Reader's Digest* worldview, but we know that many choose that route because they feel overwhelmed by academic style and content. College-level reading takes perseverance and tolerance for ambiguity that some students "prefer not" to apply.

All of the commentators hint at reasons why Bartleby haunts critics and other readers. Friedman feels that modern readers find a common human connection with Bartleby, since we all struggle with our "unique tension of compulsion and responsibility" as we try to become authentic human beings. Rogin states that "the power of Melville's short story comes from its abstractness." He goes on to place Bartleby in historical context, but he ends by insisting that it is because Bartleby exists outside of history that he haunts the reader. Although Marx does not directly explain why Bartleby haunts the reader, he argues that Bartleby is Melville himself at a time of particular hopelessness as a writer. Readers are often fascinated by autobiographical elements in fiction, and this may explain why some readers find the character haunting. Finally, Kazin's view agrees with Friedman's, that we see ourselves in Bartleby. He calls the story "a fable of how we detach ourselves from others to gain a deeper liberty and then find ourselves so walled up by our own pride that we can no longer accept the love that is offered us." Kazin also agrees with Marx that the story is about Melville himself in the sense that "he drew . . . on his own situation and his bitter understanding of himself." In his analysis, Rogin refers to specifics of Melville's biography, such as his loss of a father and a brother, to explain Melville's connection to Thoreau and thus to Bartleby's passive resistance. Friedman's only mention of Melville in his passage, on the other hand, is in the connection between Bartleby and Melville's Ishmael character in *Moby-Dick*. Both, he says, are modern exiles. Interested students might want to go to the book from which this excerpt is taken to see if Friedman discusses Melville himself as a modern exile in other chapters.

MISFITS (p. 1085)

NATHANIEL HAWTHORNE
Young Goodman Brown (p. 1085)

Nathaniel Hawthorne's "Young Goodman Brown" invariably raises issues of historical and biographical context and intertextual relationships with other treatments of the Puritan struggle against perceived manifestations of sin and evil. Students may have read Hawthorne's frequently anthologized story in high school, and perhaps have read his novel *The Scarlet Letter*, itself a famous text dealing with the issue of outsiders. Arthur Miller's drama *The Crucible*, a retelling of the Salem witch trials, also appears on high-school reading lists. Less familiar, but recommended to students interested in an alternate fictional view, is *I, Tituba, Black Witch of Salem* by Caribbean writer Maryse Condé. This novel tells the story of the Salem witch trials from the perspective of the Barbadian cook whose stories and Afro-Caribbean lore may have interacted with Puritan credulity about evil to fascinate a group of young girls into hysteria. Colorful and imaginative in the midst of the mostly humorless and somber members of the Salem congregation, Tituba, a black servant, was the first person blamed for the strange behavior of the bewitched girls. Sarah Good, a woman whose behavior and appearance may sound to current readers like a description of a "street person" — annoying respectable people with her smelly pipe, her pleas for food, and her neglect of her children — was accused soon after Tituba. Those claiming to be tormented also pointed out Sarah Osburne, a woman who was known to have lived with her husband for several months before their marriage. Each of these women was an easy target, since each was in some way an outsider, a transgressor against the accepted views of proper demeanor and behavior for a woman. Most readers will know the story of how the hysteria spread and how, to use the words of the seventeenth-century Boston preacher Cotton Mather, "some of the Witch Gang . . . [were] . . . Fairly Executed." Ironically, Mather's study of the matter may have stopped the hysteria, since he argued against the use of "spectral evidence" in which victims claimed to see various members of the community behaving like witches. Since he maintained that evil spirits can take any shape, claims to have seen a neighbor in a manifestation of evil were not proof.

Hawthorne uses these ideas and others about witches in "Young Goodman Brown." Nathaniel Hawthorne, writing in the 1830s, long after the 1690 trials, knew the history well, since his family had been intimately involved with the prosecutions. In the generation preceding the witch trials, Hawthorne's ancestor had become known for fighting heresy, forcing a Quaker woman to be whipped out of town. Students can read about this in Hawthorne's autobiographical preface to *The Scarlet Letter* called "The Custom-House" or in various biographies and critical studies of the author's life and work. Like James Joyce would later do with Dublin, Hawthorne found himself inextricably bound to writing about Salem, even though he was happiest elsewhere. Hawthorne takes his witch lore from both oral and written sources, including official Puritan doctrine like Mather's. Mather mentions the "multitude and quality" of the accused, and speaks of a woman "who had received the devil's promise to be queen of hell," words Hawthorne uses in his story. Names of his characters come from actual people who were brought to trial; for example, Goody Cloyse and Goody Cory both appear in the historical record. Hawthorne's ancestor John Hathorne interrogated Goody Cory. The recipe for witch ointment was published — one hopes as a joke — in a popular magazine Hawthorne was connected with, but it is interesting that brave souls who have tested a mixture of smallage (hemlock) and wolfsbane (aconite) say that it produces a sensation of flying. The inclusion of the "fat of a new-born babe" perpetuates a common belief about witches as baby killers, a story still heard today. There are also hints that Young Goodman Brown has made an agreement with the devil before the story begins, another motif that we recognize from multiple adaptations of the Faust legend and other sources.

In allegory, abstract ideas are represented as people, objects, places, and so forth that play symbolic roles. Hawthorne read John Bunyan's early Puritan allegory *Pilgrim's Progress* many times, and he also enjoyed the long allegorical poem *The Faerie Queen* by Edmund Spenser. He employs the genre in a less ambitious way than the writers of these classics of English literature, but Hawthorne's narrative does have many qualities of allegory. Names are most obviously symbolic. The narrator refers to the protagonist always as "Goodman" and the implication is that he represents the quality of goodness, as Bunyan's "Everyman" stands for the ordinary human being. We may need to point out to students that "Goodman" is the character's title, similar to *Mr.*, rather than his name. "Goody" is short for *Goodwife*. But, ironically, the people who seem to be good are revealed in Young Goodman Brown's nightmare — or his actual experience — to be evil. The good man of the story is actually a hypocrite who goes out for a night of adventure or in response to a bargain made earlier. He goes on an evil quest, unlike Bunyan's hero, who perseveres toward salvation. The Puritan husband expects that he may leave his good wife alone long enough to indulge in evil this one night, and then return to the "arms of Faith." His wife's name is equally symbolic. In fact, readers may find that the double meaning as he cries, "My Faith is gone," lays it on a bit too thickly. He ultimately finds a vision of evil that causes his alienation from all goodness and joy, and the report of his funeral indicates that he goes on to eternal damnation. Our interpretation of his discovery depends upon our answer to the narrator's question: "Had Goodman Brown fallen asleep in the forest and only dreamed a wild dream of a witch meeting?" The reaction of his wife and neighbors as he returns to town after his night out gives no indication that they have seen him or have been engaged in secret ceremonies. If we recall Cotton Mather's warning about accepting "spectral evidence," we have further evidence for believing that Young Goodman Brown has not actually seen his neighbors. He may have dreamed it, but it is equally possible that evil spirits have fooled him, disguised as his wife and fellow church members. Whatever has happened, the protagonist makes a case against the townspeople, holding them to a higher standard than he demands of himself. He feels betrayed, but he had been willing to sin, in spite of all his wavering.

Later, Hawthorne would write about Herman Melville's unresolved crisis of faith, that Melville had "pretty much made up his mind to be annihilated; but . . . will never rest until he gets hold of a definite belief. . . . He can neither believe, nor be comfortable in his unbelief; and he is too honest and courageous not to try to do one or the other." Puritans agonized over whether or not they were truly of the elect. One record tells of a woman who threw her baby into a well, explaining that now she knew without a doubt that she would go to hell, and the misery of doubt about her salvation was over. However, Goodman Brown wants it both ways: to have Faith, both the wife and the abstract quality of character, but also to have the adventure of sin. The anticipation of those traveling to the meeting in the woods hints that they may expect experiences of a sexual nature, since women are excited about the new young man they have heard will be inducted, while men look forward to a new young woman. We may remember that Faith has begged him not to leave her alone, but he rejects her for his errand. Even if she has been at the devil's meeting, she is at least as reluctant as her husband. But he does not grant her this virtue. As a result of his experience, the earnest young man cuts himself off from faith and fellowship and lives as a bitter misanthrope, unable to trust. We might suggest to him that he think of alternate readings of his experience, that he consider evidence that the neighbors and his wife have not attended the Witches' Sabbath. But he sees the text as fixed, much as Puritans see their interpretations of the Bible and the predestined salvation of a selected few as not to be questioned. The devil in Hawthorne's story doesn't allow the shifting of blame. *Evil has a human face* is a cliché because our experience says this is true. When the devil relates the sins of Brown's neighbors, he lists secret sins that happen within the family: incest, wives poisoning husbands, sons killing fathers, infanticide. When he describes his knowledge of Brown's family, he claims to have helped his grandfather as he "lashed the Quaker woman so smartly through the streets of Salem" or his father as he burned an Indian village. The religious and racial bigotry of Hawthorne's Puritan ancestors are thus characterized as evil, ironically so since they believed they were taking a godly stand against evil. Young Goodman Brown's naiveté hides an arrogance that is based on either/or reasoning: People are either saints or sinners, rather than having elements of both good and evil. Students may recall President Clinton's impeachment trial as they consider the standards we require of leaders. Although the scandals involving television evangelists are old news by now, we may want to recall them. The public judges such figures harshly perhaps because we hold them to a higher standard of conduct than we do ourselves, much as Young Goodman Brown does church leaders. But we may also be angry with such role models when they tell us how to behave but fail to follow the rules they set for us or to be honest about their own shortcomings.

FLANNERY O'CONNOR

A Good Man Is Hard to Find (p. 1095)

Flannery O'Connor's texts mix comedy and tragedy in a manner usually termed Southern grotesque. "Why don't you ever write about any *nice* people?" a relative not unlike the grandmother in "A Good Man Is Hard to Find" once asked her. Like the ghoulish and ridiculous figures perched on medieval cathedrals, O'Connor's characters lurk on the crumbling rooftops of the Christian religion and in the shifting shadows of the American South of the mid–twentieth century, both repelling and fascinating us with their odd humanity. Readers who have grown up in the South laugh, cry, and blush with shame at the perfection of her characters' obsessions and their dialogue. We know these people. They are our mothers, grandmothers, aunts, and cousins we don't talk about in company. To say this is not to sentimentalize or forgive them. Students will find many critical studies of Flannery O'Connor's work, and the author herself has commented on her stories, often confusing readers more than clarifying the ambiguities of the text. Critics who disagree with O'Connor's interpretation of a character or event often remind us of D. H. Lawrence's advice to trust the art rather than the artist. After the writer is finished, the story has a life of its own, and the author's opinion is no more authoritative than any other, according to this view. When Flannery O'Connor comments about the meaning of her work, she speaks as a Roman Catholic theologian rather than a writer, some contend. And often, she perversely compounds the mystery, purposely deflating people who analyze and dissect her stories.

Each reader will have his or her own opinion of "A Good Man Is Hard to Find" and its ambiguous protagonist. In fact, students sometimes differ over whom they identify as the protagonist. Usually, we think of the grandmother as the main character. We see most of the story from her point of view, and she is the only character whose thoughts we overhear. But a few readers argue that The Misfit is the protagonist, since the whole story belongs to him, beginning with the foreshadowing of the opening paragraph and ending with his existential pronouncement about life in the final sentence. Even minor characters ring true in a Flannery O'Connor narrative. Students will enjoy the connotations of names. Bailey, for example, may get his name from "Bill Bailey Won't You Please Come Home?" — a song in the same blues/jazz genre as the one that gives the story its title. (One can begin discussion with a recording of Billie Holliday singing "A Good Man Is Hard to Find" and point out its second line: "You always get the other kind.") The rude son who supplants the authority of the father has the name of the founder of the Methodist Church, John Wesley, certainly a dig at the Protestant usurpation of Catholic authority. The Misfit explicates the meaning of his name; rather than describing his outsider status as we expect, his name is a philosophical statement on the misfit between sin and punishment.

The Misfit engages in rationalization about his violence, but he seems to do this for his own purposes rather than as an excuse for his actions. He attempts to construct a logical argument with evidence that convinces him that his punishment is warranted. He is frustrated because, although written documentation exists — "They had the papers on me" — it does not clarify matters for him and he has no memory of his original sin. Therefore, his punishment seems out of proportion to him, does not fit. Because of this, he makes sure that he signs his work, leaving clear evidence of his crimes, so that he will know when the claims made about him are valid. When the psychiatrist tells him that he was really killing his father when he committed his crime, The Misfit interprets this literally instead of symbolically, refuting the doctor's assertion with evidence. He provides specific facts as proof, offering the date, the diagnosis of his father's final illness, and the precise location of his grave. This is hard evidence, he maintains, because "you can go there and see for yourself." Jesus is a logical conundrum for The Misfit. He attempts a theological decision based on his own brand of logic: If Jesus raised the dead, then we must give up everything and follow him; but if Jesus did not raise the dead, then any "meanness" that gives pleasure is permitted. But The Misfit is frustrated again by the lack of concrete evidence to guide his decision about Jesus. An essential step in the chain of logic is missing. Since he has not observed with his own eyes whether Jesus raised the dead or not, he finds no pleasure in anything. By raising the issue, if not the dead, Jesus "thown everything off balance" and makes reasoning impossible.

The grandmother, too, encounters problems as she attempts to create persuasive arguments. When we first meet her, she is trying to convince her family to go to Tennessee instead of Florida, using appeals to fear. She further attempts to manipulate, unsuccessfully employing the non sequitur that going to East Tennessee will broaden the minds of the children. Later she will persuade the family to seek out the old mansion by appealing to the self-interest of the children and winning them over to her side, but ironically bases her argument on an assertion that is false. At the trip's beginning, she convinces herself that the cat might turn on the gas in the house and die, an improbable hypothesis, so she ignores opposition and sneaks the cat into the car, including it on the trip, along with her other hidden agendas. As they leave town, she collects statistical data — the mileage and how long it takes to get out of Atlanta. She passes on information to an unheeding audience, makes aesthetic observations, and reveals her racist and class-driven assumptions. The ethos of Red Sammy Butts's credentials along the roadside may lead her to draw the hasty conclusion that he is a good man, though her evaluation of him may simply be an ingrained tendency to use the fallacious false-flattery appeal. The conversation in Red Sammy's "filling station and dance hall" is sentimental and filled with cliché. These people and the grandmother understand the discourse of small talk. The Misfit, on the other hand, finds such conversation difficult, fumbling around for comments about the weather, and he uses the grandmother's attempts at sentimental flattery and manipulation to discuss theology and philosophy.

The end of the story raises issues for critics. Some think that the grandmother mistakes The Misfit for Bailey because he now wears the shirt that she has last seen him wear. Her disorientation and her obvious distress about Bailey — she keeps calling his name — lend credence to this interpretation. Others insist that she feels compassion for The Misfit, recognizing him as vulnerable, and reaches out to him as a mother. She has noticed his thin shoulder blades and she hears the crack in his voice. He seems to her to be on the verge of crying. Some readers take her statement that he is her child as a cowardly, desperate attempt to persuade him not to kill her, the strongest argument saved for the crucial point just before the conclusion. O'Connor has increased the ambiguity by insisting that this final scene between The Misfit and the grandmother is a "moment of grace" that has religious significance. In Flannery O'Connor's stories, as in James Joyce's, characters move toward epiphanies, moments of clarity. Just before she calls him her child, the text says that "the grandmother's head cleared for an instant." How we interpret the ending depends upon our interpretation of the grandmother. Students often feel that her sins do not warrant the punishment she receives, but The Misfit would say that this squares with his experience as well.

Religious orientation, or the absence of it, will also enter into the reading. It has been seriously argued that the grandmother confuses The Misfit with Jesus at one point or that she speaks with the authority of God when she claims her killer as her child. O'Connor abhorred hypocrisy and arrogance. Just before the grandmother dies, the falseness and self-centered pride that have characterized her throughout the journey have, by some interpretations, been stripped away. If this is true, The Misfit is correct when he implies that it has taken this crisis to make her a "good woman." The grandmother goes through her whole repertoire of persuasive appeals and finds them wanting as she tries to save her life, but we don't see her using any of them to save her family, not even the baby. Her obsessive drive to get her way leads her family to death, and her impulsive identification of The Misfit seals their fate. As the epigraph to the story suggests, The Misfit has been the dragon by the side of the road that this sinful pilgrim must pass on her way to God. How does one deal with a dragon?

In Nathaniel Hawthorne's "Young Goodman Brown" the protagonist loses faith in the goodness of his wife and neighbors. In fact, he rejects Faith — both his wife and his naive trust in the church people of Salem — when he returns from his encounter with evil, and his empty life is the result. The Misfit of Flannery O'Connor's "A Good Man Is Hard to Find" either loses faith in justice and the power of God or he has never developed it. The grandmother, perhaps the true misfit of O'Connor's story, loses faith in her own rightness and goodness, a loss she sorely needs. Goodman Brown operates under the assumption that some human beings are good while others are evil. He is unable to go beyond this polarized view and becomes bitter and mistrustful of all humankind. The Misfit tries to make sense of theological issues, insisting on reasons and evidence in an area where only a leap of faith is appropriate. He sets up an unsolvable dilemma and alienates himself from the laws and emotions of the human community because proofs cannot be found to satisfy him. "Young Goodman Brown" has a dreamlike, supernatural quality. This sets up ambiguity, so that the reader is not sure if the events have really occurred. In its own way, the sequence of cause and effect in "A Good Man Is Hard to Find" is just as improbable. But the characters seem so real, even if exaggerated, and the setting so down to earth, that we go along for the ride. The importance of realism depends upon the genre. Willing readers enter worlds that are internally consistent, even if they are very different from the "realistic" world of our daily lives.

ENCOUNTERS WITH FOREIGNERS (p. 1108)

GISH JEN

What Means Switch (p. 1109)

Gish Jen's first novel, published in 1991, bears the title *Typical American*. The choice of words is revealing. According to Jen, immigrant families, from Chinese to Irish, tend to refer to native-born Americans whose ethnicity is not apparent as "typical Americans." The title has a double meaning. Members of the Chang family, who appear in the novel and in many of Jen's short stories, are typical Americans in more ways than they realize. Even the problem of agonizing over one's ethnic and personal identity is typically American. This is Jen's point. As one of the Chang daughters, Mona, negotiates her way through what it means to be Chinese American in a predominantly Jewish American junior high school in "What Means Switch," she must get past the "Oriental" stereotypes that even she accepts. Mona feels that she must either be exotic or be invisible to her classmates. She fails to recognize the dual and constantly changing quality of her identity. Jen says that people often ask her if she's really Mona and if the Changs are her family. They aren't, but she suggests that Mona is a more outgoing version of herself. Like many junior-high-school students, Gish Jen picked up a nickname from the teasing of classmates and made it her own. Her first name is actually Lillian, and someone was reminded of the film star Lillian Gish. Choosing one's own name, Jen says, is empowering in a similar way to writing. Like many American girls, Jen was influenced by Louisa May Alcott's *Little Women* and by the novels of Jane Austen. Her favorite play is William Shakespeare's *King Lear*. Interestingly, all these texts involve young women and family dynamics, as Jen's fiction does.

Jen began writing poetry in college and switched her major from premed to English; she now writes fiction because of her love of dialogue and plot structure. She is also interested in complexity of tone, mixing the comic with the tragic. She claims that this is part of her Chinese heritage — sweet and sour, *yin* and *yang* — where opposites exist within the same context. When considered in these terms, it is not necessary to switch from one culture to another, since both are contained within her. Jen resists the idea that her fiction seeks to reclaim her Chinese heritage at the expense of her American environment, or vice versa. "What Means Switch" raises issues about the categories we use to sort out identity. Characters sort Mona by appearance and racial criteria rather than culture, throwing her together with a Japanese boy because they "look alike" and because the boy's mother has asked that her son be placed with other "Oriental" children that attend the school. Mona shares in this racial classifying at first, claiming to know karate — a Japanese technique, not a Chinese one — to impress her friends. But gender categories are also important to the narrator and her peers, along with the status of being desirable and discovering sexuality. Sherman gains points with the boys for actually knowing the martial art of judo, not so much as a sign of exotic difference but as proof of masculine ability. The girls see him as a sex object, a status he resists — along with Americanization — as he throws Mona to the ground, switching from the romantic scenario to a combative one.

Numerous instances of switching occur in the story. The narrator's parents begin by switching neighborhoods from Yonkers to Scarsdale because they privilege education as the road to success in America. The real estate agent tries to warn them that ethnic and financial criteria may play a part in their adjustment to the neighborhood. The narrator tells us, "This is my first understanding of class," and she learns to switch her ways of behavior to find her place in the school. The move requires that Mona switch her status from a "laugh-along type" to the purveyor of sexual information. She also finds her ethnicity gaining positive attention for her rather than prejudice, so she invents exotic details about herself and her heritage. At the same time, she is becoming more like her classmates, just as her mother "fudges" her calligraphy and insists that tomatoes are an ancient Chinese food. Gradually, they "switch" without fully realizing the extent of their adaptation. Sherman Matsumoto, on the other hand, is in the United States temporarily and has no intentions of switching his allegiance from his native Japan. Mona maintains that he could become American, just as she could become Jewish. "You only have to learn some rules and speeches," she argues. His classification system is nationalistic and assumes the superiority of being Japanese. When Mona's mother reacts so strongly to Sherman's flag drawing on her refrigerator, it becomes clear that the distance between the Chinese and Japanese cultures is much wider than that between an Americanized Chang family and their Jewish neighbors. His portrait of their nationalities implies that Japanese people are capable of independent thought and action, whereas the Chinese — as represented by his one example, thirteen-year-old Mona Chang — slavishly look to others, are too willing to switch. Later, when he suggests that she could become Japanese and she retorts that he should be the one to switch, he flips her. But there's more going on here than differences of nationality. Mona and Sherman are also dealing with gender issues. His story of his father bowing to his mother is a description of a shocking switch, the man submitting to the woman, considering her feelings. When Mona has the temerity to ask Sherman to be the one to adapt, he switches from treating her as an American girl to putting her in her place. At the story's end, as Mona hears her parents discuss the specific, idiosyncratic problem that only this family in this particular living situation would have to discuss — something as concrete and down-to-earth, literally, as a wall — she accepts the individuality of herself and her family. She can't switch, she decides. Identity has to do with specificity.

Mona's school situation doesn't allow for much individuality. The school shares in the stereotyping that assumes the two Asian students will have something in common. Teachers could have chosen another student to show Sherman around, but they choose Mona, revealing unconscious assumptions about race and ignorance of culture and history. Peers immediately assume that they will become a romantic couple. Few readers who recall their own middle-school years will fault Mona for embroidering the truth to find status in her peer group. But Jen's point seems to be that part of growing up involves finding an authentic self based on unique personal experience rather than playing into the stereotypes we are given. She shows us this in a comic way, but it takes being knocked off her feet for Mona to come to this understanding. Some readers may see this as a switch to a serious tone, but we might recall that Jen deliberately mixes sweet and sour throughout the story. Sherman resists change that runs counter to his received values. Mona has been too willing to "switch" her identity. At the story's end, however, she seems to have gained wisdom.

Part of the story's comic charm comes from its presentation by the naive narrator. Although the story is told in the present tense, we move with Mona through the year and accompany her through her changes as a dynamic character. Students may want to acquire a copy of Jen's novel *Mona in the Promised Land* to compare the differences that third-person narration make. A logical prediction would be that the reader would feel more distance from the protagonist if we watched her change as outsiders to her motivations.

MARGARET ATWOOD

The Man from Mars (p. 1722)

Travelers to North America are sometimes surprised that when we say, "How are you?" we do not necessarily want a detailed description of the respondent's health. Nor do we always expect acquaintances from that foreign vacation to show up on our doorstep with bags packed for an extended visit in response to our invitation to stop by if you're ever in the neighborhood. Cultural differences in body language may lead to misreadings that are embarrassing, if not dangerous. While it is important to be aware of such differences on a personal level, governments can also assume that they are understanding matters in the same way when grave cross-communications are taking place. Though Margaret Atwood would not want us to carry the analogy too far, it is interesting that she tells us implicitly that the clinging foreigner of "The Man from Mars" is Vietnam. When the story was first published in 1977, the Vietnam War had recently drawn to an ignominious close. The United States still reeled from years of bewildering contention over how to end a situation created by unwise decisions based on cultural ignorance and arrogant assumptions. The issue had haunted all of North America, though Atwood's Canada had taken the moral high ground. By identifying her alien character as Vietnamese, Atwood may intend for us to recall the strange relationship between Southeast Asia and North America, but the parallels are indirect.

Atwood is known for her outspoken stance against political oppression, but she trusts her art to take its own circuitous route rather than forcing it to teach a lesson. She warns writers against the impulse to begin with politics and then try to make the literary text fit, comparing such efforts to the bed of Procrustes. Procrustes is a mythical Greek figure who welcomed guests but required that they fit the bed in his special guest room. If they were too short, he stretched them to fit. If they were too tall, he cut off their feet. Atwood says that she refuses to take such measures with her characters, and she resists simplistic answers to serious issues. So while we will find a number of social and political issues arising from her story, their unraveling will be complex, and the aptness of the narrative will come first.

As the protagonist of "The Man from Mars" looks through newspaper accounts of the war, she realizes that she cannot differentiate one of the foreign faces from another. She does not even know whether he is from the North or the South. He has been for her, to use her mother's euphemism, "a person from another culture" rather than an individual. Outsiders to a dominant culture often point out that they exist in the thought and literature of the mainstream only in terms of how they help insiders define themselves. The strange man's pursuit of Christine raises her status with her friends, transforming her from a tolerated outsider to someone worthy of attention. Her fantasies begin to reflect her new vision of herself. But, ironically, she discovers her successor to be a far from romantic figure, a nun in late middle age. The man's intentions remain a mystery. She reverts to her nondescript alienation, but she becomes obsessed with her stalker, now that he is out of reach.

From the beginning, the third-person narrator of the story gives the reader details that lead us to see Christine as boring and unattractive. Her face is described as "chunky, . . . reddish, . . . like a Russian peasant's," and we are told that even the old men in the park don't find her appearance worth a second look. Although she is from a family of privilege, she is an outsider even there. She gets no respect from the help. She is sexless, intellectually mediocre, completely without imagination. We know this both because the narrator tells us and because we are shown her actions, even when she is in private. Her body language and tone of voice should indicate to the stranger that she is not the sort of person who is accessible. She is courteous and helpful when she first meets him, but dismisses him with "a terminal smile" after being imposed on to make a map. But he does not pick up on her signals. The details we are given about the man lead to mixed feelings. His pursuit of such a rigid and uninteresting person may strike readers as funny. The story can be seen as an ironic exaggeration of failed cross-cultural communication, with the poor little guy just trying to make friends and fit into his new homeland. We may feel compassion for him. He seems emotionally needy and naive. His pathetic physical appearance, chewed fingers, and frayed clothing make us feel sorry for him. Then again, we wonder, can he be playing a con game? When he takes a picture of the two of them in what could be construed as a compromising pose, we wonder if she will be blackmailed in some fashion. Since in recent years stalking has come to be understood as a serious crime, the story may strike many readers as horrifying rather than ironic and comedic. This will be especially true of people who have themselves been victims of stalkers.

Like Margaret Atwood's frequently anthologized story "Rape Fantasies," this narrative raises issues about the nature of the victim position, especially when confused with romance. Suggestions that women may sometimes be complicit in their victimization may anger some readers. But Christine benefits from the stalker's attentions and indirectly encourages his maladaptive behavior to continue. It is the housekeeper, not Christine, who puts a stop to his actions. Usually, both male and female readers would be more likely to fear a male stalker than a female one, since men are more physically powerful and because rape is a real threat. Atwood's story defuses this somewhat by making it clear that the woman being stalked is large and athletic, while her pursuer is small and weak. But a psychologically disturbed female stalker can also wreak havoc on a man's personal life. There have been accounts of women thinking they are the wives of famous men and consequently breaking in to take their rightful places.

The news that the strange man is Vietnamese and may be in danger because he was deported to what has become a war zone haunts Christine, and may also cause the reader to see the story as more tragic than comic. The political connotations of that particular war cause us to think of the tragic results that come from failing to understand the nature of another culture, and these resonate with the details of the story. Do we blame Christine for exploiting the foreigner for her own aggrandizement rather than finding a way to let him know that his behavior was inappropriate? This perspective turns her victimization around, making her the oppressor who has been responsible for his rejection, perhaps even his death. Because he is so mysterious, there are gaps that allow alternate interpretations of the man.

It's ironic that Christine imagines him as an interpreter, since he seems to have failed so amazingly to interpret the rules of behavior during his stay in Canada. She too has been unable to interpret him, and she has not even given him the attention needed to determine the basic facts about his life. Rather than concentrating on reading him for comprehension, she has been absorbed in her own reader response. One student reader of "The Man from Mars" was so led astray by the title of the story that he missed the whole Vietnamese reference and interpreted the man as being an alien from outer space. To overemphasize the Vietnam connection may also be a faulty interpretation, however. Often, students read literary texts in the same way they read academic textbooks and wonder why the writers do not present information in a straightforward way. Such readers react much as Christine does, unable to get beyond the narrow confines of their own Procrustean beds to open up to new perspectives.

Gish Jen in "What Means Switch" tells us Sherman Matsumoto's name and his country of origin because the differences between his culture and the Chinese American culture of Mona Chang are important to the cause and effect of the story's plot. "Typical" Americans are often unaware of the history of Asia and the pronounced differences between nations and cultures there. This leads to situations like the one in which Jen's young adolescents must decide to what extent they will switch cultures. On the other hand, Margaret Atwood's "The Man from Mars" presents a character who lacks the vision even to ask the foreign person any personal questions. Like many in a dominant culture, she doesn't really think of the outsider as a real person. He is a mystery and a problem. Because there are gaps left in the readers' knowledge, our view of him is blurred for most of the story, and reader responses to Christine's pursuer may vary more widely than their thoughts about Sherman. The reasons behind Sherman's unexpected judo move against Mona remain a mystery to the reader, however, and we may get some interesting variance in interpretations of its significance.

The first-person narration of Mona's story brings the reader into her immediate thinking as a thirteen-year-old in a specific situation. With the limited third-person narration of Christine's experience, we watch as observers. Though we are allowed access to some of Christine's thoughts, we are told about them rather than experiencing them directly as we do with Mona. Margaret Atwood uses a frame technique for "The Man from Mars," beginning the story in an unspecified present that we return to in the end. In the middle lies the story that we are told happened "a long time ago." Most readers identify more closely with Mona because of the narration, but also because she is a more congenial character. Most readers do not like to think of themselves as being like the lumpy Christine, but do remember being middle-school students longing for acceptance like Mona. Mona's misreadings of cultural matters are more understandable because of her youth. But Christine is a college student — even one who has been involved with international students — and readers may feel that her passivity and naiveté are destructive of both herself and the man who follows her. While Mona's lack of understanding will change — has begun to change even before the story ends — Christine's ability to function as an active adult in the world shows no sign of developing further.

COLONIAL INSIDERS AND OUTSIDERS (p. 1138)

WILLIAM SHAKESPEARE
The Tempest (p. 1139)

Students and instructors approaching William Shakespeare's last play, *The Tempest*, have a multitude of background materials from which to choose. First performed for King James I in 1611, then again for the royal wedding of the king's daughter in 1613, the drama was designed for an audience of privileged insiders, providing colorful masques of exotic settings for their entertainment. But the play raises many issues about outsiders as well. *The Tempest* questions the nature of authority and social class. The pubescent Miranda in her exaggerated innocence and her joyful awakening to the discovery of the "brave new world" of sexual attraction offers modern readers an interesting contrast to characters in other coming-of-age stories. In the person of Prospero, the play explores the problematic role of literacy, a skill that can separate or empower. Some scholars link Prospero with Shakespeare himself, a word master whose dramas magically recreate nature. But *The Tempest* is at its most powerful as a text about the European voyages of exploration and their political, social, and intellectual ramifications. The seeds of colonialism and empire were being planted during Shakespeare's time, and attitudes and methods for dealing with indigenous peoples of newly discovered islands and continents were taking shape.

Although the play's setting is magical and fantastic, reminding readers of Shakespeare's earlier A *Midsummer Night's Dream*, many historical and literary connections can be found as students explore the background of *The Tempest*. Readers interested in the issue of how language plays a part in empire should begin with Stephen Greenblatt's discussions of "linguistic colonialism," looking at attitudes revealed in the relationship between the original inhabitants of the island, Caliban and Ariel, and the various types of newcomers represented by the other characters. As many Europeans believed of the people they encountered, Prospero contends that Caliban must be taught to speak before he can approach any definition as human. But Caliban complains that he has only learned to curse. Even speech and exposure to the Bible do not make him human, it seems, since he attempts to rape Miranda after she and her father have taught him language. He assumes an equality that merely being human does not allow him in the European view. The play presents him as demonic at core, and therefore, in the perspective of the early 1600s, Prospero is justified in abusing and enslaving him.

At times, Europeans condemned the people they encountered as beasts or thralls of the devil because they did not understand Spanish, English, or another "human" language immediately. Indigenous languages were not considered human speech. The Spanish, however, sometimes behaved as if their language should be grasped without any tutoring. In 1513, the Spanish drew up a legal document called the *Requerimiento* that explorers were required to read each time they encountered new people, explaining their rights and duties as newly conquered subjects of the king and queen of Spain and as expected converts to Catholicism. This was read in much the way criminals are read their Miranda rights by police officers in twentieth-century America, but with no real attempt to explain it in a language that could be understood. The consequences of noncompliance were severe: "We shall take you and your wives and your children, and shall make slaves of them, and as such shall sell and dispose of them as their Highnesses may command; and we shall take away your goods, and shall do you all the mischief and damage that we can, as to vassals who do not obey," the disclaimer reads. What's more, this will be your fault, the document tells the uncomprehending people, so don't say you haven't been warned.

Opposition to this trampling of human rights arose early. Bartolomé de Las Casas, a Dominican friar who was a contemporary of Christopher Columbus, objected to the enslavement and maltreatment of the indigenous people of the Americas. He paints a picture of them as gentle, peaceful, and vulnerable to the cruelties of the Spanish *conquistadores*. In 1583, Las Casas's writings were translated into English and disseminated as propaganda against the Spanish, beginning a legend many of us learned as children, that the Spanish treated the first Americans much more cruelly than the more civilized English did. Shakespeare may have been acquainted with this text. There is evidence that he knew the essays of French thinker Michel de Montaigne, who saw Native Americans as noble savages but nevertheless popularized the image of them as cannibals who ate human flesh. The name Caliban comes from the word *cannibal*, as does the name of the Caribbean Sea, from the name of a tribe

227

encountered by the first Europeans in the area. This view of newly encountered people as so depraved as to break the most sacred taboos of Christianity made their subjugation more acceptable to Europeans. Like Caliban, the natives also excited and scandalized the Europeans in their sexual behaviors, a fact sometimes used to condemn and at other times used to take advantage of native women. Rather than native men raping white women, the reverse was true, as accounts from as early as the voyages of Columbus show. The relative nakedness and sexual openness of the Caribbean and South American natives had shock value when reported to Christian Europe. But, if people can be dehumanized or demonized in this way they can be exploited without guilt. Obviously, no real human beings lived in these new lands. The stage directions for Shakespeare's play identify his setting as "an uninhabited island" even though people already live there. Prospero enslaves Caliban without any apparent qualms and frees Ariel only to force him into indentured servitude.

Readers interested in placing *The Tempest* in an English colonial context might look at arguments that Shakespeare was inspired by a shipwreck that occurred off Bermuda in 1609. Although he literally places his characters in the Mediterranean, many critics have noted that the connection of magical phenomena with the Bermuda Triangle is by this theory at least four hundred years old. Students may also be interested in some of Richard Hakluyt's *Voyages*, sea stories that are roughly contemporaneous with Shakespeare. Connections exist, for example, with Sir Walter Raleigh's account of his journey to Trinidad and Guiana in 1595. Promoters like Raleigh who wanted to exploit the riches of the Americas are echoed in some of the attitudes of the play. When Gonzalo proposes his ideas for a new "commonwealth" on the island in act 2, scene 1, for example, Shakespeare may be satirizing both the glowing advertisements of men like Raleigh and the utopian ideas of Montaigne, Sir Thomas More, and others. Many literary texts — the poems of John Donne are only one example — directly relate to the shifting perspectives that medieval assumptions and the contact with new lands and people forced Europeans to take. Instructors who use visual texts as introductions to critical analysis techniques could use the drawings of Theodore De Bry, which combine accurate depiction of cultural artifacts with biased portrayals of Spanish rivals and American "savages." Students might also go beyond this in their research to find texts that reflect a Native American point of view. We should also keep in mind that African slavery began almost immediately after Europeans began seizing lands in the Americas. People were voluntarily or forcibly being moved across oceans in both directions. When Stephano and Trinculo, representing lower-class whites out to make a buck, propose to place Caliban on display, they too have historical parallels. Explorers took individuals back to Europe to exhibit as exotic oddities, but also as proof of the journey and as tools to be taught "human" language and taken back to the Americas as interpreters.

By setting *The Tempest* on an island, Shakespeare creates a world of cultural contact in microcosm. He limits the movements of the characters both by the insularity of the setting and by having Ariel use magic to separate them into groups. He also emphasizes their vulnerability to the environment. These most powerful of men, kings and nobles, for example, are at the mercy of the elements of nature and would starve if others did not provide food for them. Because the island is so sparsely inhabited, however, the playwright must resort to magic, calling on classical deities for the feast. While later readers and directors may find such scenes distracting, especially if we are drawing colonial parallels, Shakespeare's audience at the court of King James enjoyed the colorful displays. The shipwreck in the opening scene begins the play with chaotic noise and movement that tests the imagination of set designers but that immediately pits different groups of characters against each other. The rules of society that work in one situation do not work in others, as the noblemen get in the way of the seamen.

Language and class distinctions are raised as explicit issues from the beginning. The shipwreck and calculated magic separate the men into social groups. The ship's crew find safety and disappear from the action. The noble characters, both legitimate and usurping, are cast together so that intrigues and discussions of proper government can continue and character can be revealed. Through these characters and their social equal Prospero, the play raises issues concerning the qualities that make a person fit to rule, refusing to accept simplistic answers. Prospero has Ariel isolate Ferdinand, the young heir apparent, so that he can encounter Miranda and so that he can learn to work. Through the barriers Prospero places in his way, Ferdinand's character is tested. The comic characters Stephano and Trinculo represent the bottom of the social ladder among the shipwrecked passengers. In status, they correspond to Caliban, and their comic encounter with him reveals a great deal when interpreted in a colonial context. They misread his nature, thinking he is some sort of monstrous, alien creature; then they introduce him to alcohol and seditious ideas. They mean to exploit Caliban, but they make him conscious of his plight. For these characters there is no middle ground between abject servitude and the complete freedom to do anything one desires. Whereas Caliban is bestial by nature, Stephano and Trinculo are depraved and evil. Their attempts to overthrow the social order leave them appropriately covered with filth and pursued by the hounds of hell, ending up with cramps for their efforts. The play assumes that there is a proper social order and that each person has an essential character and place in society that can be revealed through difficulties.

Characters are capable of change, however; and Prospero is especially dynamic. Prospero has been a scholar who loves learning above political power. He recalls of his approach to exerting authority that his "library / Was dukedom large enough" (1.2.109–10). But his retreat to the ivory tower of learning results in his loss of political power and his exile. His books give him access to a different sort of power, however. Like the playwright, Prospero can create illusions. He seems most like William Shakespeare, ready to retire to the country, in the speech addressed to Ferdinand that begins "Our revels now are ended" (4.1.148–62). Prospero speaks of the visions on his magical island, but Shakespeare speaks also of drama and life in the words " We are such stuff / As dreams are made on, and our little life / Is rounded with a sleep" (4.1.156–58). And later, Prospero/Shakespeare imagines that upon his return to Milan/Stratford "Every third thought shall be my grave" (5.1.312). Like a theater artist, Prospero manipulates and shapes his characters to his own purposes. Although he seems to love his daughter Miranda, he withholds information from her and demands her total obedience, keeping her the ingenue. He develops tests for the castaways that create subplots consistent with their characters. His relationship with Ariel and Caliban is one of master and slave, though he treats Caliban more harshly. We must remember, however, that Caliban poses a real threat to Miranda and demonstrates through the course of the play that he is subject to manipulation by false authority. Though current readers have the historical perspective to see slavery as inherently evil, Shakespeare and his audience would have felt that Prospero treats Caliban as he must be treated for the protection of the social order and Caliban's own welfare.

Ariel is obligated more by a legal contract than by a slave mentality. Like an apprentice actor contracted to the company, Ariel is essential to the execution of the magic. In the colonial situation, he may be more like the indentured labor provided by poor English settlers, exploited for a set time and then freed, whereas Caliban corresponds at first to the American Indian and later to the African slave, whose human rights are ultimately denied. Although we will illuminate class discussions by raising historical issues of slavery and colonialism, we must warn against anachronism. The greatest abuses of labor in the Americas were to come in later centuries as practices current in 1611 escalated. We may sympathize with Caliban more readily than Shakespeare's contemporaries did. We don't like the way Prospero addresses him and understand when he responds in kind. But, although he can be played as pathetic and comical, Caliban is also crude and dangerous. Students might be asked to compare him with other sinister outsiders like The Misfit in Flannery O'Connor's "A Good Man Is Hard to Find" (p. 1095) or the Frankenstein monster from old movies. Whereas Ariel is intelligent and Miranda innocently naive, Caliban seems steeped in ignorance. He possesses his own type of knowledge, offering to show Stephano and Trinculo how to find delicacies on the island, but this skill is not highly valued. When Prospero acknowledges Caliban as his own, perhaps he admits that he has tampered with nature in his enslavement of Caliban and in his efforts to convert him. Caliban as he has become is the creation of his master. Or he may mean that since he has laid claim to Caliban's labor, he is responsible for him, must bear what later generations would term the "white man's burden."

When students seek to classify the genre of *The Tempest*, they will need definitions of the literary terms *romance, comedy,* and *tragedy*. Instructors may choose to give these to the class or to suggest the types of sources where students can find definitions for themselves. Some students might be asked to look at introductions to Shakespeare, others at definitions that relate to dramatic works in general, others in dictionaries of literary terms. Students who have read Shakespeare's *Hamlet, Prince of Denmark* (p. 294) will readily identify it as a tragedy, since essential qualities of its royal characters lead inexorably to their downfall. *The Tempest* ends happily, and few would see it as unrelieved tragedy. But it is not strictly comedy either. Many students will have seen the 1999 movie version of *A Midsummer Night's Dream* or have read it in high school, and recognize it as a comedy, ending happily after revealing human frailties in a way that makes us smile or laugh. They may also recognize elements of romance in *A Midsummer Night's Dream* because its world is filled with unreality and magic. *The Tempest* — sharing elements of tragedy, comedy, and romance — is more difficult to classify. Although *The Tempest* fits most definitions of a tragicomedy in its improbable plot and unnatural situations, it doesn't focus primarily on love, as examples of the genre usually do. Instead, it questions relationships involving power and authority, with even its love story dominated by the machinations of a loving but controlling puppeteer.

AIMÉ CÉSAIRE
A Tempest (p. 1206)

In 1939 in Paris three black scholars from widely separated locations of the French colonial empire — Léopold Senghor from Senegal, Léon Damas from French Guiana, and Aimé Césaire from Martinique — initiated the négritude movement as a call for ethnic solidarity among all people of African origin around the world. In the 1950s and subsequent decades, as the old colonial regimes began breaking up, the writers of the movement became major voices in literature and thought among readers of the French language, and they were influential among politically active young people of many cultures. Senghor became the first president of the nation of Senegal after it gained independence from France in 1960, serving until his retirement in 1980. For many African Americans, the cultural values of négritude inspired separatist movements and political action that rejected the patience of passive resistance and assimilation. They found common cause with people of color in Third World countries. Young writers of the Black Arts movement — like Amiri Baraka, Nikki Giovanni, Etheridge Knight, and Sonia Sanchez — began to produce revolutionary texts that shocked audiences with their explicit diction and their outspoken anger. Malcolm X became an important rhetorician for black separatism and direct action. People of African descent all over the world — in what has come to be called the African diaspora, a scattering like the Jewish diaspora — became interested in recovering their African history and culture.

Readers can find glimpses of the impulse to find one's roots in several of the texts in this anthology; Lorraine Hansberry's *A Raisin in the Sun* (p. 484) and Alice Walker's "Everyday Use" (p. 1420) provide two examples of educated characters who look to Africa and the distant past for their identities. Walker's text is critical of pretentious African Americans who deny the living heritage of their parents and siblings while reaching back for an earlier history they fail to understand. Some African thinkers agree. Yoruba Nigerian poet and dramatist Wole Soyinka, for example, scorns négritude as a Westernized movement that is interested in external symbols while it fails to understand the essence of a culture that still lives. Like the elements of any culture, the indigenous religions of West Africa are continually changing while in many ways remaining the same. Therefore, the Yoruba god of metals and creativity, Ogun, expands to become the god of roads and workers in a developing Nigeria. And Sango — the Shango of

Caliban's songs — remains the god of thunder, but takes on a new role as the god of modern electrical power. The West African deities are further transformed as they move to Caribbean islands like Haiti and Césaire's native Martinique or become submerged in folk practices in New Orleans and other areas of the American South where African influences were not completely stamped out by slaveholders.

Some students may know facts about voodoo or about the African religious roots of reggae and other Caribbean music. Interested readers might look into the literary theory of Henry Louis Gates's *The Signifying Monkey* for further studies of African influences in African American art and culture. In his reading and rewriting of William Shakespeare's *The Tempest*, Césaire begins by making two changes in the *dramatis personae* of the play. First, he adds Eshu, the Yoruban god of fate, who is also a trickster and likes to subvert the order imposed by gods and men. And he specifies that Caliban and Ariel have African ancestry. In a Caribbean culture that tends to assign social class according to skin color, Césaire challenges traditional values. Second, he makes Ariel, the mulatto, an accommodationist who counsels patience and submission in the face of promises that are long delayed in coming to fruition. Caliban becomes the symbol of négritude and Black Power. And in Césaire's retelling of Shakespeare's story, Caliban wins. This runs counter to the usual state of affairs in postcolonial or plantation societies where mulattos traditionally take positions of social and political superiority after the whites let go of power. Prospero, on the other hand, is one of the diehard colonials who is unable to let go. Decadent and crumbling with age, he clings to the delusion that he retains power while Caliban sings his freedom. For Césaire, the negation of European exploitation requires a claiming of nonwhite pride and history and a reconquest of one's own identity. He sees this not as reverse racism, which he considers limiting, but as an embracing of universality, of a culture that is worldwide rather than nationalistic. He calls for a global diversity in which all peoples are allowed a voice. Césaire has written that "nobody can colonize with impunity, there is no innocent colonization. There will be a heavy price to pay for reducing humanity to a monologue."

Césaire's version of the play is less elaborately staged and more open about its workings than Shakespeare's original. The love story and all the speeches are pared to a minimum, and Eshu interrupts the fanciful masque by offending the matronly goddesses. The play begins with the assigning of roles, with editorial comments by the master of ceremonies. Each actor chooses a mask. This reminds us of Greek tragedy, in which all players wore masks. It also recalls the origins of the literary term *persona*, in which the speaker of a poem or monologue assumes an identity different from the voice of the writer. Moreover masks have significance in African rituals and play a part in Carnival festivals in the Caribbean. The speech of the master of ceremonies also reminds readers that we are interacting with a text. Like the actors, we choose the characters with whom we most closely identify, and this choice reveals something about who we are. Later, as Miranda worries about the ship's sinking, Prospero reassures her that this is only a play. Like Shakespeare, Césaire keeps his reader aware of the metaphorical connections between magic and drama and life. The result of

Césaire's postmodern technique of denying us the illusion of reality lets the reader into the creation process, privileging the ironic voice of the author. But at the same time, it keeps us distant from the characters of the play by subverting the verisimilitude that involves us in the action. If a production of *A Tempest* has the characters keep on their masks throughout, the audience is likely to feel even more separate from their emotions.

As readers consider the differences between Ariel and Caliban in act 2, scene 1, they might also look back at the writings of Booker T. Washington and W. E. B. Du Bois in the first cluster of this chapter. Ariel, like Washington, believes that African Americans can eventually acquire freedom and equality through patience and cooperation with the white establishment. And, like Martin Luther King and others who seek to obtain rights through nonviolent means, Ariel has dreams of the brotherhood of all humanity. Caliban — like Du Bois, who died a citizen of the West African nation of Ghana — knows that compromise will fail to gain equality. And, like Malcolm X, Caliban wants to resist injustice in a concrete way, to achieve freedom *now*. Both desire freedom, but they disagree about the means through which it will be achieved.

Césaire's addition of Eshu and his calling upon Shango through Caliban shift the balance of power on the island. In Shakespeare's play, all of the spirits and cosmic forces are subservient to Prospero and his agent Ariel. In Césaire's version, the African gods sabotage this power. Though Shakespeare's 1611 drama draws on some elements of colonialism that were already appearing as cultures came into conflict, Césaire's 1969 retelling explicitly makes Prospero a failed colonial entrepreneur and his island a Caribbean one. It is interesting that the crime he is accused of by the Inquisition involves knowledge of geography and of "demonic tongues" like Arabic and Hebrew. Ironically, the church oppresses Prospero for being a scholar, but his scholarship is of the sort that would actually make him useful to the church in the age of exploration. As a legal document, the notice read by the friar in the flashback of act 1 is reminiscent of the Spanish *Requerimiento* informing the natives of the newly discovered lands that they must submit to king and church or be enslaved or killed. Recent studies of Columbus see his initial motives as primarily religious. He was trying to fulfill prophecies concerning the second coming of Christ and saw no problem with forcibly requiring heathens to convert to the true religion both for Christianity and for their own good. Césaire's Prospero chooses to remain on the island and convinces himself that he does so for the good of Caliban. He remains because of the arrogance that can claim "from a brutish monster I have made man!" and "This isle is mute without me" and (to Caliban) "I've tried to save you, / above all from yourself." Césaire has him stay to prove the falsity of this interpretation. The island becomes overrun with what Prospero sees as "unclean nature" as he shoots wildly in his attempts to "save civilization" even while he loses the distinction between himself and the slave about whom he now obsesses. This is an obvious metaphor for the problems of dismantling empires after long mutual dependence between oppressors and oppressed. Most informed audiences are capable of grasping Césaire's point, regardless of race, and it is unlikely that any audience members will identify with Prospero. The differences between black and white readers may have been more pronounced in 1969, however, when issues of separatism versus integration were more intense. The debate continues, and we might expect to find more differences between African Americans who vote Republican versus those of a more liberal bent than between racial groups.

Readers will find many differences between the two plays, though they keep the same characters, except for Eshu, and the same basic plot lines. Some may feel that the most pronounced difference is one of tone. Césaire is postmodern, confrontational, and openly political. His play boils Shakespeare's drama down to its essentials as an analogy of empire, and his characters are emblematic rather than three-dimensional, with the possible exception of Caliban. Shakespeare creates a Renaissance romance filled with fantasy and magic, and his characters are complex and multilayered. It is difficult to imagine how a reader unfamiliar with Shakespeare's *The Tempest* would make sense of Césaire's play. Césaire can be confident that readers will catch the allusions, however, and he counts on our reading the two as a palimpsest, one text interweaving with and peeking out from behind the other.

There is not a video recording of Shakespeare's *The Tempest* that captures the magic of the play for American college students and there is not one that exists of Césaire's *A Tempest. Prospero's Books*, a 1991 film based on Shakespeare's play, uses a black actor effectively as Caliban, but unwary instructors should be warned to preview it and consider the sophistication of their students before showing or recommending it. Even readers who have studied *The Tempest* in depth can get lost in the surreal and sexually explicit images of the Peter Greenaway film. It makes sense to cast the original inhabitants of the island as African or as colonized minorities, even in Shakespeare's play, especially if the purpose is to present it as a statement about empire. For today's audiences, this casting moves us closer to Césaire's message but perhaps further from Shakespeare's more complex themes. Because most current readers are socialized to view the oppressor as the villain, casting the servants as people of color almost guarantees that we will not identify with Prospero's struggle to come to terms with conflicts between knowledge and power. As with any presentation of a text to an audience, purpose and focus determine choices about style. Because Césaire depends upon Shakespeare for elaboration, it is difficult to see his as the better play. Students may find him more accessible, however, because his central idea is more focused on the issue of colonialism, whereas Shakespeare may be approached from many different angles. If the class has students who are bilingual in French and English, it would be interesting to get reactions about the quality of translation of Césaire. Shakespeare, too, requires some "translation" for American students, especially those who tend to give up at the first ambiguity.

| 11 |

Making Judgments

JUDGMENTS ABOUT ANIMALS (p. 1240)

MAXINE KUMIN
Woodchucks (p. 1241)

Interestingly, though the poem "Woodchucks" predates 1999 "ethnic cleansing" in the Balkans by more than a quarter century, Maxine Kumin's daughter knows about this particular current event firsthand, since she directed a United Nations refugee program in Belgrade, in the former republic of Yugoslavia. Perhaps a mother who finds ironic parallels with the Holocaust in attempts to exterminate a clan of rodents from her garden marks a daughter for rescue missions. We can't be sure, however, that the poem is directly autobiographical. Maxine Kumin does live in New Hampshire, on her PoBiz Farm, where she raises horses, sheep, and a variety of other animals. Now that her children are adults, she jokes that animals have become her family and that she writes more and more about them. But though she raises sheep and writes poems about butchers and "lambs for slaughter," she is virtually a vegetarian, and her poems ironically question the concept of nurturing animals only to destroy them. When she sells horses, she only does so after carefully screening new owners to make sure the animals will be treated well. Many of the animals on her farm have been rescued from inhumane conditions before arriving there. And she has protected the wildlife on her property — bears, foxes, and presumably woodchucks — by designating undeveloped land as a conservation area.

Perhaps this poem describes an actual experience from the family's early days on the farm. But we should remind students that poets often assume a persona and should not be confused with the poem's speaker. While the poem's narrator seems to approve the "quiet Nazi way," the poet ironically questions both the killing of woodchucks and, by implication, the Nazi atrocities. We may even go beyond the literal situation of the poem and its explicit Nazi parallels to see Kumin as raising issues about the taking of life under any circumstances. If the poet were not an animal lover, we could conjecture that "Woodchucks" is a mock epic that makes a trivial subject ridiculous through hyperbole and a more serious tone than is warranted. But she seems to be serious about both the humane treatment of animals and the lessons of the Holocaust. If anything, it is the speaker's self-righteousness that is satirized.

Maxine Kumin has close connections with a number of poets of her generation who use the imagery of the Holocaust for their own purposes. Unlike Sylvia Plath, who compares her father to a Nazi in "Daddy" (p. 227), and Anne

Sexton, who rails against the Nazis as representative examples of human evil in "After Auschwitz" (p. 1012), Maxine Kumin is Jewish. This perhaps gives her a more legitimate right to the "property" of the Holocaust as a poetic device. Still, some readers may criticize her for trivializing such horrors by juxtaposing them with the exterminating of garden pests. A close friend and collaborator with Anne Sexton on children's books, Kumin may be suspected by some readers of participating in a faddish appropriation of the historical pain and death of millions of people for a cheap effect. Others may argue that by including such references in their poetry, Kumin and her contemporaries keep Holocaust memories alive and show us how we may apply their lessons to our lives. We can read "Woodchucks" as a text that reverses the apparent tenor and vehicle of Kumin's metaphor. Rather than using Nazi atrocities to make us see the horror of killing woodchucks, she personifies woodchucks to remind us of the enormity of killing human beings. Just as the speaker of the poem is haunted by the baby faces of the woodchuck family, the reader sees that we cannot guiltlessly destroy people unless we dehumanize them and turn our faces away from our deeds.

The poet gives words a double meaning, raising additional issues. When she uses the word *case* in line 4 we can read this word to mean both a physical trap and a rhetorical or legal argument. If we stay with the specifics of the poem, most gardeners will understand the need for driving out the current inhabitants of the land so that the vegetables can grow and human beings benefit from the produce. We may know from Kumin's biography that the farm at the time of the poem's composition was simply a summer hobby rather than a source of sustenance for a subsistence farmer. But we can imagine a speaker with a more pressing need and thus justify the extermination of the woodchucks. Few readers would be opposed to hiring an exterminator to get rid of rats in an apartment building. But we may also recall that the Third Reich justified aggression against neighboring countries and implementation of the "final solution" to eliminate minorities by citing the need for living space for the German people. Many of the reasons given in the "case" against Jewish and Gypsy minorities were economic. The poem's speaker begins by seeking a "merciful" method for eliminating the woodchucks, but when this does not work, she "righteously" finds excuses for exerting direct power using survival-of-the-fittest arguments. Her language hints at both the excitement of killing — "thrilling / to the feel of the .22" — and the equivocation involved in going against one's ethics — "a lapsed pacifist fallen from grace / puffed with Darwinian pieties for killing." But as the narrator kills the animals, they become more human and she becomes "the murderer . . . the hawkeye killer." She ends the poem as a stalker obsessed with killing the old woodchuck that refuses to die. The speaker's transformation has proceeded gradually, as such things do, and is now complete. If the poet had not used first person, the voice of the poem would seem accusing, and the audience would be less aware of the changes that have taken place in the speaker's attitude. Third-person perspective would allow us to be outside observers with the distance to be horrified at the killer's actions, just as we can be safely appalled by Nazi atrocities, sure of our inability to agree to such programs. As the poem stands, readers find it difficult to avoid the implication that we too are capable of the gradual metamorphosis that the poet describes.

Kumin's poem rhymes, but she does not use a conventional pattern, and the result echoes sounds rather than obtrusively imposing structure. Readers will find alliteration in several lines; the s and sh sounds of lines 5 and 6 are one example. In this example the sound interacts with the content, since we can imagine the speaker making shooing noises and hissing to drive the pesky critters away. Kumin draws deliberate parallels between the evolving attitude of the poem's speaker and the human propensity for becoming gradually tolerant of violence. She also raises issues about our willingness to accept killing we do not see as opposed to looking at the faces of those that we destroy. Some readers are more moved by descriptions of the killing of animals than they are of similar actions toward human beings. It would be reductive, however, to discuss this poem as simply about whether or not we should kill animals.

D. H. LAWRENCE
Snake (p. 1242)

Students interested in exploring the deeper meanings of D. H. Lawrence's "Snake" will find many critical studies. Since the snake is a phallic symbol in many cultures — even to some ways of thinking an archetypal symbol connected universally with male sexuality — the poem invites Freudian readings, and undergraduates are often surprised to find analyses of Lawrence's Oedipus complex as they look for interpretations of the poem. A reading of his novel *Sons and Lovers* may convince them that this is a reasonable assumption, though some Lawrence scholars contend that he'd written his way through the worst of his feelings about his father by the time he wrote "Snake" on a trip to Sicily in 1913. In a personal letter, Lawrence himself once wrote that human beings are freed by "phallic consciousness . . . [which is] the root of poetry, lived or sung." For Lawrence, sex was at the core of everything human, and such interpretations can usually be supported with ample evidence.

Critics who focus on Lawrence's ideas about women see in the poem's approach to nature a similar impulse to his desire for relationships in which the woman does not become submerged in the man but finds her own passion and integrity. This is a nature poem, but Lawrence tries his best to fight the cultural demands to subdue nature, to kill the symbol of evil. Lawrence privileges nature over received conventions in his work. He admires poets like William Blake and John Keats, whose work is characterized by structure, but Lawrence wanted to catch a sense of experience in the present, rather than "recollected in tranquillity" as William Wordsworth taught. Readers will find this sense of immediacy in "Snake" as the speaker argues with himself throughout the poem, then acts impulsively, and ends with his spiritual task unfinished.

Critic Ross Murfin maintains that it is impossible for D. H. Lawrence or any other writer after John Milton's *Paradise Lost* to view a snake without making a conscious or subconscious intertextual connection with the biblical serpent and

Satan. Murfin sees Lawrence as unsuccessfully trying to break free of this and other cultural connotations to interact with the snake in a natural way. Before reading the poem, we might have students brainstorm or free-associate their own connotations for words like *snake, serpent*, and *python*, and invite them to relate stories of encounters with snakes on camping trips or growing up in rural areas. Some may think of expressions like *snake in the grass* to describe someone who turns on us unexpectedly. We may recall the folktale of the "bosom serpent" in which a man befriends a snake only to have his kindness repaid with a poisonous bite. The moral is that we must be careful who we "pick up" and take to our hearts. But some may connect Lawrence's presence on a Mediterranean island with Greek stories that link the python with Apollo and his oracle at Delphi, endowing the place where the god killed the snake with supernatural wisdom and power. The python is usually taken to represent an earlier religion connected with Mother Earth and supplanted by the male god Apollo. Lawrence would have known this.

Those of us who were fascinated with snakes as children recall a mixture of fear and attraction that attaches to no other animal with the same intensity. Lawrence reflects this ambivalence in his poem. He tells us that "the voice of [his] education" says to kill the snake. He feels "afraid" of the snake, but "honoured" to be sought out by it. He hints at mythical allusions, the snake disappearing into the underworld to be crowned as king. The nearness of the volcano and the snake's withdrawal into the darkness of the earth remind us of Hell and the biblical (or Miltonic) connections of Satan and the serpent. Lawrence hears the voice of logic and science first, telling him that "black snakes are innocent, the gold are venomous." Then he hears the cultural voices that try to shame him into proving his manhood by killing the snake. Since the Bible speaks of the "enmity" between man and the snake, perhaps this is the voice of Judeo-Christian religion that Lawrence so strongly resists in his work and his life. It is the snake's "Deliberately going into the blackness" that impels him to throw something at it. The horror that the speaker of the poem feels has something to do with the blackness rather than with the snake, which he has continued to admire. Perhaps for Lawrence this withdrawal is a rejection of relationship and of life, but he blames his reaction to it on the "voices of [his] accursed human education." He feels that he has momentarily done something unworthy. He uses words like *paltry, vulgar, mean*, and *pettiness* to describe his action, comparing his throwing a log at the snake to the shooting of the albatross in Samuel Taylor Coleridge's *The Rime of the Ancient Mariner*.

It would make sense to read portions of Coleridge's poem in class to help students unfamiliar with it to understand the allusion. The ancient mariner must wear the dead seabird around his neck until he has learned to appreciate the wonders of nature; he is finally released from his penance when near the point of death from thirst he takes joy in the beauty of the luminescent sea snakes. Some readers see Lawrence's judgment of his action as exaggerated and quite different from the action of Coleridge's ancient mariner. The narrator of "Snake" is thoughtful about nature and does not seem unthinking or unfeeling at all. But he denies the snake his natural behavior, sees the darkness of the earth as a horror, and recoils from the union of the snake and the earth with its sexual connotations. Perhaps this is his sin that must be expiated. He has lapsed from faith in nature because of the temptations whispered in his ear by the "voices of education." The biblical story wherein the serpent is the tempter is thus reversed. Lawrence's use of the word *and* to begin many of his sentences recalls the syntax of the King James Bible. This usage also gives the poem a sense of ongoing thought and spontaneity that contributes to Lawrence's purpose of communicating the present moment as it is happening.

If we compare the pettiness of the narrators of Maxine Kumin's "Woodchucks" and D. H. Lawrence's "Snake," the shooter of woodchucks gets the award as most petty. Both wrestle with conflicting impulses, but Kumin's protagonist wages an escalating war whereas Lawrence's acts on impulse, almost as an afterthought. And for most audiences, Lawrence's speaker could make a legitimate case for killing a solitary venomous reptile more easily than Kumin's can for killing mammals that seem like a human family. On the other hand, the snake does not really bother anyone, so attacking him is an arbitrary act of cruelty. The woodchucks interfere with a human activity, giving the narrator a warrant for getting rid of them; the cruelty is a side effect of the failure of the would-be killer's methods.

Although both speakers seem equally self-divided, the different tones of the poems make the internal dialogue of "Snake" seem sincere whereas the conflict of the speaker of "Woodchucks" seems more like rationalizing. Both poets use a conversational style and allow the reader to share the thoughts of their narrators. Students may see Kumin's poem as more traditionally "poetic" than Lawrence's since it has rhyme and a more visible structure. Lawrence's poem is in free verse, but we should urge students to look for alliteration and other repetitions. His use of parallel structures is especially effective and may remind some readers of Walt Whitman.

ELIZABETH BISHOP
The Fish (p. 1245)

Elizabeth Bishop is known for her precise observations and evocations of objects in the world. She begins with something concrete and specific, as she does in "The Fish," and lets the imagery carry the meaning. She doesn't tell us what to think about it but simply paints the picture for her readers to interpret. For instructors using this anthology in a writing class, Bishop's poem provides an opportunity to discuss diction, syntax, and descriptive techniques. Students may notice that "The Fish" is really a sort of fish story, a narrative about the one that got away, or rather the one that the narrator allowed to get away. It has unity, beginning with a straightforward statement of what happened and describing a series of observations that culminate in the narrator's letting the fish go. The details of the story build until she notices the evidence that this fish has already been caught five other times. This leads to what most critics have agreed is an epiphany, a sudden insight into reality spurred by some ordinary object or incident. There is a flash of joyful recognition as the concrete details converge for the speaker as "rainbow, rainbow, rainbow!"

We can ask students to look at the poem's diction, plotting words along a ladder of abstraction. For example, the word *tremendous* is fairly abstract and general, since readers' images of the fish may range from a foot long to something like the great white shark of the movie *Jaws*. When the poet says that the fish's "brown skin hung in strips / like ancient wall-paper," the image is more concrete, and the images that different readers have will come closer to being the same. Students can also be asked to find similes and metaphors like the wallpaper one and to look for other ways that the writer provides precise descriptions. When she says that the fish "hung a grunting weight," several senses come into play, since we see the fish, but also feel the tug of holding it and hear the sound of grunting — whether from the fish or the fisher is unclear. Color plays an important role, too, coming together in the penultimate line with the rainbow. The phonetic qualities of words are important to poetic diction. We can read closely to find alliteration — "tarnished tinfoil," for example; or assonance — "full-blown roses" or "green weed" or "frayed and wavering"; or unexpected rhymes and vocal echoes like "shallower, and yellowed" or "backed and packed"; or the unexpected couplet of lines 46 and 47, ending with "jaw" and "saw." Students should also consider the syntax of the poem. The poet uses straight-forward, declarative sentences at first. There's a breathless quality to the series of short parallel sentences of lines 5 through 9. But the sentences get longer and more complex as the poem proceeds and the speaker becomes absorbed in her minute descriptions. She seems almost to look through a magnifying glass.

As the speaker observes the fish more closely in the course of the poem, her attitude changes. At first, the fish is a fairly abstract and undifferentiated weight, though the word *venerable* hints that the fish is elderly and worthy of respect, foreshadowing the insight that is to come. Gradually, the fish becomes even more real as the speaker mentally dissects it. Finally, the fish becomes personified, the old fishing lines in his jaw becoming "a five-haired beard of wisdom." Although her description is precise and seemingly unemotional before the outburst of passion at the end, the details she chooses to give reflect her values. The evidence of hard-won survival that the fish exhibits moves her. From her early description of him as "battered" to his "frightening gills, / fresh and crisp with blood" through many other images of his age and endurance, we finally come to the old fishing lines that prove his struggle to survive. She also values the precision of nature's machinery. For example, she is fascinated with "the mechanism of his jaw." She values the aesthetic, even when seen in the imagined internal organs of a fish; she sees beauty with an artist's eye. (We might note that Bishop was a painter as well as a writer.) When the poem's speaker uses the word *victory*, she refers to the fish, but may also refer to herself. But rather than the victory of catching the grand old fish that myths are built on, hers is the victory of epiphany, of being struck by beauty and the will to live epitomized by the brave old fish. One critic has ironically termed Bishop's fish an "old man of the sea," alluding to Ernest Hemingway's character who tenaciously holds on to his catch, another symbol of endurance.

In a sense, the whole poem is about seeing. But the writer begins to make this explicit when she looks into the eyes of the fish in line 34. His eyes are like "tarnished tinfoil / seen through the lenses / of old scratched isinglass." Isinglass was used as a cheap substitute for window glass before the invention of plastics and is translucent rather than transparent. One sees through such a glass darkly. Like the other images of the poem, this one emphasizes age and endurance. The fish does not return her gaze. But later the speaker says that she "stared and stared." The rainbow itself has to do with visual perception, the breaking up of light into the colors of the spectrum. The speaker refers to the fish as *he*. Perhaps the only reason for the fish being male is the convenience of his having a beard made up of fishing lines. We have to admit, however, that if the fish were female, we might find her pathetic rather than enduring. The warrants for this reaction are worth discussing.

All of the speakers of the poems of this cluster use the animals they encounter for self-examination. Elizabeth Bishop's narrator seems more admirable than those of Maxine Kumin's "Woodchucks" and D. H. Lawrence's "Snake," since she releases the fish. But she has been just as willing at the beginning to take a fish as a trophy; she merely changes her mind as she gets to know him as a character in a narrative she imagines. Lawrence's narrator respects the snake as well, and seems no worse than Bishop's impulsive fisherman who opts for allowing the fish his life. The speakers of Lawrence's and Kumin's poems are more self-reflective than Bishop's, so they leave themselves open to our judgments. Lawrence lets us hear the internal dialogue as he examines his warrants for not killing the snake. Cultural assumptions tell him that he should kill it, and he eventually gives in to them half-heartedly, then feels guilty for caving in to the conventional pettiness that he has been socialized to exhibit toward snakes. Kumin's speaker also reveals her thoughts, but we feel that she has been caught up in actions she cannot stop. Some readers may feel that she reveals more than Lawrence, since she allows us into her dreams. Bishop is least explicit about her thoughts. She shares her observations, even the flash of joy, but she allows the reader to determine what these experiences mean.

Bishop's poem is a descriptive narrative that describes a single event. It makes sense to focus it into a structure that looks like one continuous block. Lawrence also describes a single event, but he describes his thinking process as the event takes place. This calls for the separation of thoughts into separate stanzas as he moves from one mind state to another. Kumin uses a closed structure of uniform stanzas with a fairly regular rhyme scheme. Each stanza tells of a different stage in her war on the woodchucks. D. H. Lawrence would be especially pleased if we recognized that content often suggests its own form. Good poets keep this in mind.

WILLIAM STAFFORD
Traveling through the Dark (p. 1248)

William Stafford's narrative, in which a speaker finds a pregnant deer dead beside the road, reads more like an objective newspaper account than a poem. This provides us with the opportunity to discuss his style and tone and the distance he maintains from his emotionally charged topic. When students write the obligatory autobiographical narrative in our first-year composition classes, they often have trouble separating themselves from the powerful feelings evoked by the events they want to write about. Our first instinct may be to tell them to postpone the telling of their loss of a high-school classmate or another traumatic experience until they have more distance. Their deeply felt emotions often come across to us as sentimental clichés.

The difference between emotion and sentimentality is difficult to communicate, especially to young people, for whom the experience and the expression of it are fresh and original from their perspective. The key to distinguishing the two has to do with focus. Sentimentality focuses on the feeling itself — something along the lines of being *in love with love*. There is a falsity to it, though it may be sincerely intended. A few years ago, when a young woman drowned her two young children by pushing her car into a lake, her acquaintances kept bringing up evidence of how much she had seemed to love the children. Her writings about them were revealing, however, showing a self-absorbed preoccupation with her own emotions about the role of mother rather than a sense of the children as separate human beings. Her voice when she spoke of them had a similar tone, and her comments were filled with clichés.

While some poets successfully focus on their own feelings, most twentieth-century readers resist a solipsistic outpouring focusing on the speaker's emotions. A writer like William Stafford can offer a useful counteracting example. Though some readers find him cold and unfeeling, he succeeds in making *the reader* feel something through his understated recital of this waste of life. He doesn't weep over the deer or preach at us, Look what happens when we carve roads through the wilderness! He lets his audience come to its own conclusions through the evidence he presents, and he trusts us to be perceptive enough to feel the emotions that are submerged beneath the details of the story. As a leader of creative writing workshops, Stafford emphasizes the need to communicate emotion without falling into the trap of sentiment. This is done, he teaches, by writing not about one's feelings but about the scene, the time of day, the sensory images that accompanied the emotion. If these concrete details are connected with emotion for the writer, they can evoke a similar reaction for the reader. The effect created is one of immediate, shared experience. Having said this, we should concede that many readers feel that Stafford goes too far in the other direction when he seeks to avoid sentimentality and to show rather than tell. When we assign the autobiographical essay, we urge students to go beyond narrative and description to ponder the significance of the event. But don't tag on a moral! we warn. The line is a fine one. But though he does it in a subtle way, William Stafford places his narrative in a philosophical context by letting us see his momentary "swerving" from the necessary deed.

When Stafford uses the pronoun *us* in the final stanza of "Traveling through the Dark," he invites multiple interpretations of the word. He has just mentioned "our group" in line 16, seemingly referring to himself, the pregnant doe, the still-living fawn in her womb, and possibly the personified automobile with its purring engine and aimed lights. He also introduces the character of the wilderness, imagined as a silently listening audience. And then there is the reader, a sharer with the writer in a common humanity. All of these entities may be implied as he ponders the situation for "us." The poet frames the narrative with references to "swerving." Although it's possible that a hunter has seen the deer and shot for the joy of killing, the context of the poem seems to imply that the deer has been hit by a car. Most of us have swerved to avoid hitting animals when we travel roads through habitats and ranges, and we have all seen the mangled bodies of raccoons or opossums who did not successfully avoid their collision with civilization. Although some states have laws against taking road kill home to eat, presumably discouraging the deliberate use of an automobile as a weapon, few drivers would deliberately swerve to hit a large animal like a deer. If so, they would not leave the carcass. This is an accidental, arbitrary death — the result of the narrow mountain road and the deer occupying the same space in the wilderness. It's unclear when the speaker says that "to swerve might make more dead" if he means that people would be killed as their automobiles swerved off the road or if more animals might be killed as the cars swerved to avoid this dead one. The ambiguity of the poet's diction implies equality between the two. But the swerving that he mentions in the final stanza is a figurative one. He knows what he must do — sacrifice this individual life within the dead doe to prevent further accidents — but he cannot do it without pause. The empathy implied in his swerving touches the reader most, though we may understand that the kindest act is to proceed as he does.

We might wonder if animals seeing automobiles hurtling down the road interpret them to be fierce beasts of prey. Stafford personifies the car in "Traveling through the Dark" by making it seem like a large cat at rest after taking its prey, the verb *purred* describing the sound of its engine. The verbs in this fourth stanza give the automobile credit for its "aimed" and "lowered" parking lights, conveying the impression of the eyes of a sentient being guiltily avoiding the sight of what one of its kind has done. The last sentence of the fourth stanza also personifies the wilderness. The absence of sound becomes the wilderness "listening" as the human being, the only one with the power to take action, to accept responsibility for this clash of realities, hesitates. Those who object to the image might be asked if it is possible to hear silence or to see darkness. The listening presence of the wilderness may be a key to the significance of the poem. It is as if humanity is on trial for this death. The judgment of the wilderness is implied in the stopped motion and the silence that surrounds the tableau on the mountain road. The action of the speaker is the most merciful course of action. The fawn will die slowly if he chooses any other alternative. But in the stillness, readers briefly mourn this collision between the natural world and the machine-driven world of human beings. Like silence, the word *dark* indicates an absence of something. Although the protagonist of the poem's narrative has stopped in his travels, the title may imply a figurative journey in which we always find ourselves with insufficient light, making decisions we'd rather not make to redeem sins we have not ourselves committed.

For each of the writers in this cluster, a barrier exists between the human speaker and the animal he or she encounters. To varying degrees, the human

243

protagonists of these poetic narratives respond to qualities that hint at a bond with nature that is almost, but not quite, possible. Maxine Kumin's woodchuck killer sees their faces and allows them other human attributes, even as she tries to exterminate them, and explicitly draws parallels between this attitude toward nature and our ability to justify the killing of our own kind. D. H. Lawrence resists the learned impulse to do harm to the representative of nature almost to the end, but instead demonstrates the power of the received ideas that would judge nature as evil. Elizabeth Bishop's narrator at first sees the fish as an object, but enters into a bond through her close observation and through this oneness is able to let the creature of nature go back into its own world. William Stafford's speaker is forced to let go in a different way, but he too hints at a disjunction between the world of nature and the artificial environment of the human world that leads to the death of the natural creature. Had Stafford's speaker left the deer by the side of the road or made fumbling attempts to deliver the fawn, his act would have been unnatural. Except for Bishop's speaker, who comes to a moment of revelation, the human characters in these poems must deal with the guilt of knowing the cruelty of which human beings are capable. And even with Bishop's fish, it is the creature's many struggles with its human antagonists that reaches the speaker.

All of the texts in this cluster have an air of sadness and regret that we are so separated from the natural world in which we live. All of these speakers think hard for all of us. Readers who admit that they also struggle with human cruelty and alienation from nature will get the most from these poems. The exercise of comparing the clarity of the poems with our aesthetic and reader-response evaluations of them will provide interesting insights into our own warrants as we read poetry. As instructors we should do this before we ask our students to try it, thoughtfully examining our own criteria, but not imposing them on other readers in the classroom. If students do not like the texts that challenge them to look at unflattering facts about humanity or that demand close reading, we have the opportunity to discuss the purposes of literature. Do we want to read sentimental clichés that cover up the unpleasant issues of life or to face the conflicts involved in being aware human beings?

JUDGMENTS ABOUT ABORTION (p. 1250)

ANNE SEXTON

The Abortion (p. 1250)

Of all the controversial topics used in argumentative writing classes, abortion is the most problematic for many students and instructors. Because the issue is so emotionally charged, writers find it difficult to maintain a reasonable tone, regardless of their position as pro-life, pro-choice, or wavering someplace between the polar opposites. The abortion debate provides many examples of logical fallacies and arguments that seem to take place on parallel planes that never touch. Often debaters on both sides of the issue build straw-man arguments, attacking enemies that do not exist. For example, antiabortion speakers prefer to describe horror stories of late term abortions, though statistics show that these procedures are not the norm. They like to discuss abortion as if it were chosen lightly as an easy means of birth control, *abortion on demand*, although few women would purposely seek either the difficult decision or the procedure. Pro-choice debaters, on the other hand, find easy straw-man targets in fanatical or disturbed people who bomb clinics or shoot abortion doctors, although the majority of abortion opponents are as horrified by such acts as anyone else. It is easier to build an argument against an extreme stereotype of the opposition than to counterargue substantive points. Non sequiturs abound when spokespersons for the two camps meet. In a recent debate on the question of whether antiabortion rhetoric leads to violence, one speaker threw in the comment, "Well, the clinics don't provide adequate counseling." This had nothing to do with the debate at hand, and certainly did not follow from the previous comments about the effects of hate speech on the actions of violent individuals. We could even classify it as a red herring in this context, designed to take the argument off track, though perhaps the speaker meant to connect it with pro-life attempts to provide information, a free-speech issue. Others construct slippery-slope scenarios in which abortion rights are eroded to the point where back-street abortions are again the norm, and wire coat hangers are waved as symbols of something that can never again be tolerated.

With the support systems that women have developed, some may question whether history would repeat itself in this particular way, even if access to abortion became limited. But the issue is complex, and those most concerned are often very young women who have little information and less power and whose voices are seldom heard. Manipulation of emotions occurs on both sides. When we juxtapose the image of a twelve-year-old victim of incestuous rape being forced to give birth with descriptions of saline solutions and infant brains being sucked out of cracked skulls, how is the reasonable reader to choose between two such worst-case scenarios? How can we forget historical situations in which women routinely were forced to continue pregnancies or to end them against their wills? Even the preferred labels of each faction indicate the cross-purposes of the debate. Most people are pro-*life* if the term is taken literally, especially those who live life to the fullest, feeling free to express their sexuality. And anyone who values freedom and American values must be pro-*choice*, since we prize the rights and responsibilities of the individual to make informed decisions. But opponents prefer terms like *pro-abortionists* or *baby-killers*, *antichoicers* or *hatemongers*. Both sides have been compared to Nazis, one for imposing their values on others, the other for taking the lives of innocent victims. The basic problem with rhetoric on the issue of abortion may be that each side is often guilty of begging the question.

Students write eloquent arguments against abortion that fail to convince because they begin with the assumption that abortion is murder or that biblical quotations provide authoritative evidence for a secular audience. Still others make the equally facile assumption that the embryo is simply a mass of tissue, a sort of benign tumor. Ethical issues of when human life can be defined as beginning are complex and constantly shifting. The discussion of abortion overlaps with ethical debates about *in vitro* fertilization and multiple births, cloning, the harvesting of fetal tissue for medical research, surgery performed on fetuses in *utero*, legal issues involving unborn victims, and ownership of frozen embryos. Although the abortion issue is not a comfortable one to discuss, we can use its rhetorical aspects to promote critical thinking. Sometimes the issue is not simply an academic exercise for our students but a decision they really face, and approaching it through literature can provide a safe forum in which to weigh the pros and cons.

Anne Sexton's poem "The Abortion" is painful to read. Its overall tone is sad, regretful, approaching depression. There are images of budding life, but these are soon followed by images of emptiness. The speaker drives south through Pennsylvania, through coalmining country that we associate with poverty and a particularly brutal digging out of the earth. She describes the features of the terrain as "sunken . . . / a dark socket from which the coal has poured." The image anticipates the final line of the poem in which the blood pours from the woman's body after the abortion. The emptiness contrasts with the "fullness that love began" of line 19. The voice is realistic rather than sentimentally emotional or guiltridden. The refrain, repeated three times and emphasized in italics, expresses an emotion that the speaker must confront. To feel this remorse is natural.

Abortion is not an act that is undertaken lightly, especially in the time period of the poem, when its illegality placed women at the mercy of unsanitary, unprofessional, often life-threatening conditions. The repetition of the two-line stanza, "*Somebody who should have been born / is gone*" gives it the haunting quality of a lament. The pause before the last two words emphasizes the cutting off of what "*should have been born,*" echoing the imagery of emptiness and loss that permeates the poem.

If the last three lines of the poem had been left out, we might see this refrain as the theme, and interpret the poem as an agonizing description of grief and guilt, an indictment of abortion and a self-condemnation of the speaker. But another voice undercuts this reading. She allows herself this mourning, but gives herself the warning that "such logic will lead / to loss without death." She forces herself to make the experience concrete, ending with the raw truth of the last phrase — "this baby that I bleed" — surely one of the more powerful lines in modern poetry. The voice of realism rejects the sentimental sinking into depression that will compound the loss.

Anne Sexton wrote a series of poems that represent her readings and retellings of the European tales collected in the 1800s by German folklorists Jacob and Wilhelm Grimm, and her allusion to Rumpelstiltskin refers to the same source. The story only runs two or three pages in most volumes of the Grimm brothers' tales, so reading it in class would not take much time. The class might discuss the extent to which her father, the king, and the manipulative Rumpelstiltskin control the life of the young woman and her rights to her child. The "little man" of the story gets the woman out of the situation set up by the patriarchal structures of family and state, but he requires a high price, her first-born child. She is able to escape this bargain because she guesses his name, the most magical part of the story for children lucky to first hear it told by a dramatic narrator who stretches out her teasing of the little man with name after name. In Sexton's poem, the German imp sounds a bit like a leprechaun as she concedes that he is "not Rumpelstiltskin, at all, at all." This woman loses her child through the little man's services, after all.

We do not know the circumstances under which the poem's narrator decides on an abortion. Often women let the men in their lives influence the decision in one direction or the other, surrendering their choice to concerns that run counter to their own feelings in the matter. Even if the decision is hers alone, she still grieves her loss in these moments immediately following the abortion. Some biographers maintain that Sexton's poem describes an autobiographical experience. This knowledge adds to Sexton's credibility in the view of some readers, and they respect her courage in writing about it at a time when the subject was taboo in most circles. Others object to Sexton's confessional mode, preferring poetry that is less subjective. Interested students might enjoy other Sexton poems that speak to issues of concern to women. For example, "Unknown Girl in the Maternity Ward" makes an interesting companion poem to "The Abortion," since its speaker is a young woman who addresses the six-day-old baby that she will give up for adoption.

GWENDOLYN BROOKS
The Mother (p. 1252)

Students who have read Lorraine Hansberry's play *A Raisin in the Sun* (p. 484 in the "Living in Families" chapter) will recall that one of its characters, a married woman, decides on an abortion for economic reasons. The Younger family of Hansberry's play lives in the Bronzeville neighborhood of Chicago, a real community of African American families at the time that both Hansberry and her contemporary Gwendolyn Brooks were living and writing in the Chicago area. In the 1940s, when "The Mother" was written, Brooks was perfecting her art in the poetry workshop in Chicago's South Side Community Arts Center and was describing ordinary people with honesty and compassion. In her 1944 collection *A Street in Bronzeville*, she painted a portrait of her neighborhood. Her purpose was to show "that Negroes are just like other people; they have the same hates and loves and fears, the same tragedies and triumphs and deaths, as people of any race or religion or nationality." The quotation strikes us as sadly revealing. Why should this articulate poet have to justify the common humanity between her subjects and her readers?

Later, after meeting Amiri Baraka and other black literary thinkers at a conference in 1967, Brooks would worry less about explaining African Americans to an establishment audience and would express more forceful anger at racism and sexism. Her style would change as well. In "The Mother" Brooks uses rhyme, but is already experimenting with varied rhythm and line length, motivated in part by her admiration for Langston Hughes. The speaker of the poem addresses the children that she has lost to abortions. Like Ruth Younger in *A Raisin in the Sun*, the narrator does not abort because she is selfish or because the timing of her

247

pregnancies is inconvenient. She chooses not to complain or shift blame, only hinting that she has not willingly chosen their fate. She tells them, "Believe that even in my deliberateness I was not deliberate. / Though why should I whine, / Whine that the crime was other than mine?" (lines 21–23). She grieves but rejects self-pity. To understand the speaker of this poem, we must take social and historical issues into account. Some students, often African Americans, do not grasp the vast differences between the opportunities available in the ghettos of a rigidly segregated America of the 1940s and those open to college students sixty years later. It is true that the people who live in the high-rise urban-renewal projects that replaced the neighborhood of Bronzeville face problems even more debilitating than those of earlier generations and that racial prejudice and injustice still exist. But if we imagine a situation in which reliable birth control and access to medical care were not available at the same time that social services for families were virtually nonexistent, perhaps we will judge less harshly.

Readers may find the speaker of "The Mother" brave, enduring, sad, grieving, longing. These ghostly children haunt her, much as the ghost of her child haunts Toni Morrison's Sethe in the novel *Beloved*. In Morrison's story, a woman kills her living child rather than have her returned to slavery. Brooks's speaker imagines nurturing these babies and apologizes for taking away their identities and their lives from birth on through to natural death. The speaker must sacrifice her desire to mother all of the children she conceives presumably because she does not have the resources to raise them. The poem does not make abortion seem like a good thing. But it doesn't argue against it, either. Abortion must be available to her because she has no other choice. The implied argument is implicitly directed toward a culture in which she is forced to deny herself children.

In the poem's first stanza, the speaker uses the second person to imply that the experience she describes is common to many people. The focus is on the mother's experience. She describes the loss in negative terms: Here's what you don't get. She lists some of the everyday joys of motherhood, ending in line 10 with a delicious sensory image that captures a feeling most parents know, the desire to "Return for a snack of them, with gobbling mother-eye."

The second stanza shifts to first person, as the speaker makes the loss concrete as she speaks to her aborted children. She seeks a definition of what she has denied to them in a series of parallel clauses beginning with *if* followed in turn by the verbs *sinned*, *seized*, *stole*, and *poisoned*. But she does not claim that abortion is the equivalent of sinning, seizing, stealing, or poisoning; she only says that *if* this is the case, then she did not intend these deeds. She goes on to seek her definition of abortion in what has happened to them, rather than what she has actively done. She says at first that they are "dead," tacitly accepting the equation of abortion and murder. Then she revises her judgment to suggest that perhaps they were "never made," going with the definition of the embryo as not equivalent to a baby. Finally, she decides that they "were born, . . . had body, . . . [and] died." The "damp small pulps" of the first stanza are redefined as children who had a life, albeit an abbreviated one. Like the speaker of Anne Sexton's "The Abortion," this mother insists that she must come around to the "truth," to speak plainly rather than trying to duck the responsibility for her decision.

In the third stanza, Brooks's speaker begs her aborted children to understand that she loved them. The repetitions intensify the force of the feeling, and the rhythms remind us of the rocking movements of a mother comforting an infant. The isolation of the one word *All* in the poem's final line is powerful. Perhaps this mother, like many, has living children that she is able to bring up but has chosen to give up others as her responsibility to them. If this is the case, the final word is more touching, since mothers usually do love all of their children and would not want to choose between them. When the speaker pleads for the children to believe her, repeating the word three times in the course of the poem, she reveals the fear that they or some other judge will not believe her when she says that she did not mean to take anything from them, that she does love them. It is unlikely that she reiterates her love for them three times for any reason beyond emphasis and the symmetry of poetry, though we might guess at deeper reasons. Perhaps she has aborted three children. We know that there are at least three, since she uses the word *all* to refer to them. Perhaps each declaration of love is for one of the poem's stanzas, since she says between the first and second statement of love that she "knew" them, and it is in the second stanza that she works out the logic of their nature.

The feelings that the speaker expresses are those of a loving mother, and most readers will grant her the title. A few may judge her as insincere or engaged in an unhealthy obsession. If we knew this woman, we would try to find counseling for her so that she could work these feelings through. But if the abortions have not been her choice, as seems to be the case, then we understand her grief. It would be difficult to adapt this poem enough for it to make sense as a father's mourning for his unborn children, though certainly men experience a sense of loss if they have wanted a child that the mother chooses to abort. Though he wouldn't be able to communicate the physical sensations of longing to bear a child or to nurse one at the breast, he might ache to hold the child in his arms, to carry her on his shoulders, or to peek in for that second look at him asleep. If the father has shared in the decision for similar economic reasons as those implied in the context of the poem, we might expect his distress to be profound. But if he has usurped the decision and is similarly explaining it to the aborted children, we are likely to judge him harshly. The imposition of abortion on a woman's body is as oppressive as forcing her to carry the child to term.

Because she speaks directly to the children, the speaker of Gwendolyn Brooks's "The Mother" seems to be dealing with more guilt than the speaker of Anne Sexton's poem about abortion. Brooks's narrator carries the additional burden of having made the decision several times, whereas Sexton's seems to refer to a single incident. On the other hand, the speaker of Brooks's poem, living in difficult economic circumstances, may have more pressing reasons, and this would be expected to mitigate guilt. In Sexton's poem the focus remains on the woman's feelings of emptiness, and the aborted fetus is a distant "*Somebody*" until it is called a baby in the final line. Brooks imagines the fetuses as children throughout the poem, hears their voices, talks to them, and may even end with a lullaby. Both speakers feel compelled to define abortion in raw, blunt language and to allow themselves no excuses, no shelter in abstractions. "The Abortion" by

Anne Sexton is structured as a journey to have an illegal abortion. The voice of the refrain mourning "*Somebody*" interweaves with the stages of the trip and the return. The three stanzas of "The Mother" by Gwendolyn Brooks are structured more as a rhetorical argument with a beginning, a middle, and an end. Whereas with Sexton we have a sense of immediacy, the aftermath of an event that is occurring even as we overhear the speaker's thoughts, with Brooks the mourning is a recurring experience, something that "will not let you forget."

MARGE PIERCY
Right to Life (p. 1254)

When we present the poems of Marge Piercy to our undergraduate classes, some of the young men will groan and say — directly or by a roll of the eyes and a shifting in the chair — "Oh, God. Not another damned feminist." Whereas the earlier poets of this cluster show women struggling with the ethics of abortion, Piercy is unabashedly pro-choice. And she places blame squarely on patriarchal traditions that make women into chattel, the equivalent of livestock. Just as it is difficult to take both black and white students back in their imaginations to times of slavery or Jim Crow laws and to show them that vestiges of racial prejudice still live in language, unexamined behaviors, and unquestioned assumptions, it is difficult to open the eyes of both men and women to the pervasiveness of sexist warrants underlying the "common sense" of male/female relationships. Students can look at other poems by Marge Piercy for a fuller vision of her message. In "The Moon Is Always Female" she communicates the pain of a clitoridectomy, sometimes called "female circumcision," though male circumcision seems like clipping one's toenails by comparison. She brings home its horror by graphically applying the details of the mutilation to the male anatomy. She goes on to generalize about historical appropriations of women's bodies: "For uses of men we have been butchered / and crippled and shut up and carved open." Both our male and female students will protest that these are extreme examples. In "A Work of Artifice" Piercy brings the issue closer: "With living creatures / one must begin very early / to dwarf their growth: / the bound feet, / the crippled brain, / the hair in curlers, / the hands you / love to touch." We come into a world that has already been constructed for us, and we absorb a culture that seems as natural as the invisible air around us. Feminists question "common sense" about what it means to be a man or a woman. As we have encouraged them to do throughout this course, our students must learn to examine the warrants for their own beliefs about this issue, as they do about others. Defensiveness and denial of blame are reactions that are beside the point. A man or a white person or a member of another privileged class coming of age in the twenty-first century is not responsible for the sins of the ancestors, but he is responsible for coming to grips with their residual power in his thought and behavior. Similarly, women need to think through their internalization of cultural assumptions that are self-destructive. Does this mean that we will agree with Marge Piercy on every point that she makes? Possibly not — but we can allow her voice into the conversation without raising the palisades.

In earlier centuries, European women often died young as a result of giving birth to a new child almost every year, attempting to ensure for husbands the survival of one male heir or the replenishment of the family work force. Piercy begins her argument for abortion in "Right to Life" with the point that even in nature such annual abundance is not the norm. She provides negative definitions that describe the nature of a woman by stating what a woman is not, but hidden within the denials are the cultural assumptions that the poet resists: She "is not a pear tree / . . . not a basket you place / your buns in . . . . Not a brood / hen . . . . / Not a purse . . . . / Not a bank." The cliché of the pregnant woman having a bun in the oven makes the reader smile, breaking down a bit of the resistance to its negation. She continues her argument in the third stanza, directly accusing her male readers of using the products of nature for self-serving purposes. We may have already noticed her use of the phrase "mutations in the tainted / rain" in stanza 2. Now we notice that she inserts a fish kill into the last two lines of stanza 3. Could she be drawing an analogy between the misuse of the fecundity of women and the raping and poisoning of the earth? In the fourth stanza, she makes the connection between woman and land explicit. We wonder if she is being ironic, even sarcastic, about the negatives of this part of the argument. Is she repeating what the audiences she accuses would like to believe about themselves?

Stanza 5 undercuts the claims of the previous part of the argument. If claims of prosperity and family values are true, then the events of stanza 5 would not take place. Here we get to the specifics of abortion. Tragically, the woman dies because of lack of funding and unsanitary conditions. Piercy raises the issue of child abuse and juxtaposes it with the image of a botched abortion. Here are two things that can happen when safe abortion is not made available to everyone, she implies.

In the sixth stanza, the speaker of the poem gets to the crux of her argument and ties in the expectations set up by the title "Right to Life." Everyone has a right to come into the world as a person who is valued; if this does not happen, all of society pays in the long run. Piercy ends the poem with a stanza that sums up the argument for choice. She moves back to the negative definitions of womanhood but personalizes them with the first-person pronoun. Her poem ends with a proclamation, a declaration of independence from colonization by the male audience and by the representatives of capital, religion, and law. By appropriating the slogan of her opposition for her own argument, Piercy takes back the meaning of the words themselves. The speaker declares that she has a right to her own life, and she claims it.

Piercy's imagery has an ecofeminist slant. She links the female human being of her poem to the land and describes her child as a growing thing that "has a right to love / like a seedling to sun." Just as she reclaims the words of the title, the speaker transforms the destructive notion that sees the land as analogous to the female body: Yes, I am like the land, but I will not let you do to me what you have done to the land. Near the end of her poem, Piercy leaves open the possibility for

251

voluntary union between the female speaker and her male audience for a time: "This is my body. If I give it to you / I want it back. My life / is a non-negotiable demand." No longer does this mean that the man owns the woman. She has a right to life. In our class discussion, students may raise issues of what this really means in practice. How does it impact marriage? Could we say the same thing to an employer? To those around us who wish to harm the environment?

Many of our students do not believe in abortion. But the declaration with which the speaker ends does not require that the woman involved choose abortion to achieve autonomy. Nor do we have to believe in abortion to promote medical care, family counseling, proper education, and all the freedoms ironically claimed in stanza 4. The links connecting unplanned pregnancy with child abuse are not unbreakable; other means of birth control and perceptive intervention could make it less likely. Perhaps we do, however, have to trust women to make their own choices.

In Marge Piercy's "Right to Life" the pronoun *you* addresses an audience that seems to be male. Like the persona in a dramatic monologue, the speaker in Piercy's poem seems to be engaged in developing her side of a debate already in progress. When she lists things that a woman is not, she refers to metaphors that have been posited by someone — perhaps the voice of the culture. This is the "You" addressed by the "I" who declares her independence. Anne Sexton's "The Abortion" presents an internal dialogue that the speaker engages in with herself. She is at the same time the "I" who narrates the story of the trip, the voice that haunts her in the refrain, and the "you" she addresses as she jerks herself into a realistic acknowledgement of this concrete situation. Gwendolyn Brooks in "The Mother" has her speaker refer to herself and possibly a communal "You" — one that may include the reader — as she describes the power the act of abortion has over a person. When she moves on to address her aborted children, however, she becomes "I" and the children become "You." Piercy's tone in "Right to Life" is strong and confident. She has her mind made up and is prepared to make her points. She has a social and political agenda. Sexton is ambivalent, hard-edged, raw, shocking the senses with her imagery. She allows us to view her conflicts with herself over the emotional meaning of abortion. She is a woman of an earlier time period than Piercy, and she is less prepared to tackle the philosophy of abortion. She does share with Piercy, however, the parallels between the woman of the narrative and the land through which she travels.

Brooks allows her speaker to express more emotion that the other poets give to theirs. Her tone is emotional, but she grapples with definitions as Piercy does. Ethnic attitudes, generation, gender, and life experiences play a part in the tone used by the writers and will undoubtedly affect student readings. Piercy's poem is explicitly political. She discusses problems with capitalism and the exploitation of nature along with her discourse on abortion and women's rights. Political and class issues are implied in the context surrounding Brooks's text. Socioeconomic issues having to do with racial inequality make abortion a reluctant decision that takes away her autonomy rather than serving as a declaration of independence. Sexton's speaker seems absorbed in her own experience; but the reader will notice that she has the means to drive a long distance and to pay for an illegal abortion.

Some thinkers maintain that all texts are ideological. Even the choice to keep silent about political matters is a political decision.

JUDGMENTS ABOUT DUTY (p. 1257)

FRANK O'CONNOR
Guests of the Nation (p. 1257)

Students and instructors will find many ways to discuss Frank O'Connor's short story "Guests of the Nation." We first provide — or have students research — the historical and cultural context of Ireland's relations with the English and the ongoing political and religious issues that motivate O'Connor's characters. We sometimes use intertextual connections with other Irish writers, perhaps bringing in William Butler Yeats's poem "Easter 1916" for another perspective on the same conflict that is taking place in O'Connor's narrative. Students may be confused by references to "the German War" in the dialogue of O'Connor's story, and they need to know that the war in the story is a different one that takes place concurrently with and continues after World War I. The British are involved in both, and the British soldiers here have been sent to curb what Great Britain sees as civil unrest in territory under their control.

The story takes place during the time usually referred to by the Irish as "The Troubles" — troublesome both because the British sought to stamp out Irish rebellion and because Irish factions engaged in armed combat about the way to proceed politically. The nation of Ireland had not yet gained independence, and independence was one of the issues involved. The partition of Ireland kept several northern counties as part of the United Kingdom; this partition continues to be a source of conflict even now, and students may remember President Clinton's and the First Lady's 1990s involvement with drawing up peace accords. Writing at the beginning of the 1930s, between World War I and the ideological upheavals in Europe that would culminate in World War II within a decade, Frank O'Connor describes events and has his characters discuss debates that his contemporaries would have understood immediately. The British soldier Hawkins and the Irish Republican Noble echo in microcosm the major debates of the day. Many thinkers of the 1920s and 1930s, for example, saw communism or anarchy as the answer to economic and social problems. When Hawkins accuses the Roman Catholic clergy of collaborating with political forces to keep workers from complaining, he echoes Marxist rhetoric that labels religion the "opiate of the people." But for these characters the debates are merely theoretical arguments, not qualitatively different from the card games that fill their time, and they are surprised when patriotism and "duty" force them to play out the ideology of war in solid reality.

O'Connor wrote his story out of his own personal participation in this conflict as a young man. He had been held prisoner at one point because he disagreed with the treatment his fellow Irish Republicans dealt out to women who transgressed. "Guests of the Nation" grew out of his chance hearing of the experiences of other participants (quoted in volume 162 of the *Dictionary of Literary Biography*):

> One day, when I was sitting on my bed in an Irish internment camp. . . . I overheard a group of country boys talking about two English soldiers whom they had held as hostages and who soon got to know the countryside better than their guards. It was obvious from the conversation that the two English boys had won the affection and understanding of our own fellows, though it wasn't the understanding of soldiers who find that they have so much in common, but the understanding of two conflicting ways of life which must either fight or be friends. (255)

In addition to considering issues of historical, cultural, and biographical context, readers often evaluate "Guests of the Nation" in terms of aesthetic, philosophical, and ethical issues. Some critics consider this Frank O'Connor story a flawless example of literary art. They praise the lyricism of his language, especially in the descriptive imagery of the final paragraph. The plot of the story lends itself to analysis, with the forces of cause and effect leading inexorably toward the climax and the final event being foreshadowed in earlier dialogue. Since the sections of the story are numbered, questions about narrative structure enter into our analysis as well.

Students might enjoy discussing the names of characters and comparing these with the traits that they reveal. In this context, it is interesting that O'Connor gives the rigid, duty-bound Donovan his own family name. (O'Connor was born Michael O'Donovan and invented a pseudonym from names in his mother's family to allow himself the freedom to express independent ideas as a writer and still retain his Irish civil service job as a library administrator.) "Hawkins" is a Kiplingesque name for a low-ranking British infantryman, and "Belcher" has similarly "common" connotations, while the Irish rebels carry mock heroic names like "Noble" and "Bonaparte."

Students can debate the extent to which these names and other aspects of the story are ironic. They might look at external and internal conflicts confronted by the characters. Issues of philosophical and ethical evaluation may arise as they discuss the conflicting codes of honor that drive the characters. Hawkins cannot believe that his "chums" would break the code of friendship by taking his life, and Donovan judges the situation by rules of patriotism and duty to God and country. Hawkins is even willing to change sides, since treason does not go against his ethics. Bonaparte and Noble, however, struggle with ethical dilemmas as these codes come into conflict. If they had known they would be called to execute their hostages, they would never have turned them into friends.

Donovan, Noble, and Bonaparte have been assigned the duty of watching the hostages Hawkins and Belcher. Noble and Bonaparte fail to realize, however, that their duty may eventually include executing their "guests." Donovan, on the other hand, seems prepared, even eager, to carry out this ultimate duty. Bonaparte responds to Donovan's comments about duty with the thought, "I never noticed that people who talk a lot about duty find it much of a trouble to them." And just before his execution, the English soldier Belcher says, "I never could make out what duty was myself." One point of the story is that the ethical concept of duty is problematic. Much depends upon whether the warrants for interpreting a certain action as one's duty are based on loyalty to friends, religion, one political entity versus another, or some other nebulous concept of right and wrong action. Belcher takes on the duty of helping the landlady, whereas neither Hawkins nor the Irish soldiers feel an obligation to do so. Belcher may also demonstrate the duty a soldier owes to himself to die bravely. Perhaps soldierly ethics also explain why the hostages do not run, despite Bonaparte's desperate wishes that they would. The story makes no explicit judgments about which duties override others but implicitly critiques the blind duty that accepts without questioning. Anticipating by two decades the Nuremberg Trials that condemned Nazi war criminals for simply "following orders" regardless of the atrocity of the orders, O'Connor's story asks whether in some cases individual human judgment should supercede political ideology.

Bonaparte and Noble are most upset because the killing of the prisoners has been for them an "unforeseen" occurrence. The word *unforeseen* becomes a refrain in Bonaparte's commentary on the events. The English soldiers have become like household pets, he implies at one point, and if the guards had realized they would have to kill their hostages they wouldn't have become so attached to them. As we have seen elsewhere in this anthology, a recurring theme in many literary texts is the need to dehumanize before we can justify doing harm. Of O'Connor's Irish soldiers, only Donovan is able to shut himself off from acknowledging the humanity of the prisoners. When he is faced with Belcher's dignity in the face of death and can no longer ignore him, Donovan explains that he is only doing his duty, shielding himself from the emotion that the other characters cannot escape. Although the ending completes the narrative in a wonderfully satisfying way, and readers familiar with the short story will not be surprised, O'Connor allows us the full impact by keeping us in suspense. There's always the chance that they will run; after all, we have been told that Hawkins knows the countryside better than the Irish soldiers, and we could expect the landlady to hide Belcher if asked. Or perhaps a reprieve will come. But, as it turns out, this story belongs to the narrator and is about the impact of deliberately killing men one has considered to be friends.

While Hawkins argues against religion and capitalism throughout the story, at the end he also argues against the betrayal of friendship. Readers will vary in their judgments about his sincerity and his depth of understanding of Marxist theory. His arguments fail both to convince his religion-bound listeners and to prevent his execution. Some may see his willingness to change sides as cowardly, whereas others will read it as an appropriate action for an anarchist to take. His only duty is to himself and his friends as individuals, not to the institutions he sees as oppressive. Most readers see Belcher as more admirable, especially as we finally hear his voice at the story's end. Hawkins has been the talker, but we know little of him as a person. Belcher reveals a great deal about himself in his few words at the story's end. The two English soldiers are revealed most by their actions and their attitudes toward their executions. Most revealing may be Belcher's kindness to the old woman and his placing of his own blindfold over his eyes. He is helpful to the end. Hawkins, on the other hand, does not go gentle into the good night of the bog. The English hostages are alike primarily in their lack of true commitment to the cause that has sent them to their deaths. Hawkins serves in one of the most controlled and conservative institutions in his world, the British army, yet he strikes the pose of a radical and turns out to be apolitical at best. Belcher admits that he has no real comprehension of the duty that sends him to Ireland, but he stoically accepts his death without really questioning its necessity. While Hawkins argues that the Irish are pawns of capitalism and religion, the two British soldiers epitomize such victimization. Though we are struck by their differences, they are equally dead.

Undoubtedly, O'Connor's original audience of the 1930s needed less exposition to understand the context of the story. Although historical information is helpful, the story can stand on its own as an exploration of the competing claims of friendship and patriotism. Each generation of readers will think of its own parallels. At this writing, three American prisoners of war were just released from Serbian control through the efforts of Jesse Jackson. Expressions of gratitude toward the guards who treated them humanely headed their lists when they spoke to reporters and when they returned home. Though we often hear of hostages coming to identify with their captors, "Guests of the Nation" shows that the bond can be powerful from the other side.

HARUKI MURAKAMI
Another Way to Die (p. 1266)

As we read Haruki Murakami's narrative of an incident that he imagines took place during the Japanese occupation of Manchuria in northern China, we might look at other war stories, like the preceding "Guests of the Nation" by Frank O'Connor and "The Things They Carried" by Tim O'Brien (p. 1480). We can illuminate cultural and historical issues through texts like Gish Jen's "What Means Switch" (p. 1109), in which a Chinese American mother educates her daughter about Japanese atrocities against the Chinese, or through David Henry Hwang's *M. Butterfly* (p. 781), in which stereotypes about Asians are skewered. The novel from which "Another Way to Die" is excerpted is called *The Wind-Up Bird Chronicle*. It takes a surreal journey through several generations of Japanese history, including elements of fantasy and science fiction that strike some readers as Kafkaesque. Murakami has been compared to Gabriel García Márquez in his attitude toward history, a subversion of chronology that compresses or elongates time and brings about impossible meetings and recurrences. Although "Another Way to Die" has a realistic tone through much of its action, the final scenes pick up a postmodern surrealism and a warping of time. Interested readers might compare Murakami's style to the texts by García Márquez (p. 1522) and Franz Kafka (pp. 962, 995, and 1002) in our anthology.

Readers of "Another Way to Die" may note the musical quality of its carefully paced action and its interweaving of visual imagery and narration. Some see

Murakami as jazzlike, citing his occupation as the proprietor of a jazz club in the 1970s and 1980s. Other critics take issue with his subversion of genre, finding his inconsistencies confusing. Murakami likes to imagine alternate lives, and his texts are multilayered. For example, in *The Wind-Up Bird Chronicle* the protagonist moves in and out of dreams — sometimes dreams within dreams — in which other characters tell stories, act as mediums, or leave messages on the computer. But it is difficult to know which alternate reality is which, or whether one character is actually living out another's experiences in a transformed way. At one point in the novel, the main character, Toru Okada, uses a baseball bat to beat his politically manipulative brother-in-law to death in a dream. In the part of the novel retold in "Another Way to Die" the baseball bat becomes a weapon in the hands of another character's father years earlier. The wind-up bird that is heard as this story ends is also a recurring motif. The bird screeches every morning — is a sort of "wake-up call" — that signals a day has begun, but could as easily not begin. It symbolizes the tightly wound tension and the "inescapable ruin" that permeate life for human beings. In Murakami's story, the killing seems without real purpose. This is made clear by the instructions to kill the zoo animals, the most innocent and vulnerable victims one could imagine. War, like history, is as arbitrary and logical as a nightmare.

Although some readers may argue that "Another Way to Die" is too violent, we wonder if it is possible to communicate the effects of war on human beings without picturing the violence. Most readers would expect, as do the characters, that a killing with a baseball bat would be more physically brutal than an efficient bayonet thrust. The details of the story convince us otherwise. The second paragraph thrusts the reader immediately into the arbitrary nature of war with the pathos of the animals' silenced "voices" and the information that specific animals — tigers, leopards, wolves, and bears — have been "liquidated — eliminated." Alert readers will associate the month and year given a few lines down with the date near the end of World War II when the United States dropped atomic bombs on Hiroshima and Nagasaki, literally liquidating and eliminating innocent women, children, and other noncombatants. In the English translation, presumably a fair rendering of the original Japanese, the words have euphemistic connotations that remind us of Nazi doublespeak or current language that uses terms like "collateral damage" to refer to the injury and death of human beings not actively involved in fighting. Later, the narrator mentions Hiroshima in passing. The violence resonates.

The veterinarian sees himself in the hands of fate, and though the narrator characterizes him as "not passive," he becomes a literal bystander as atrocities are carried out. Later, he is called upon to perform a duty because of his medical training, to pronounce the last Chinese victim dead. But he is literally "pulled into" the war against his will by the death grip of the soldier. We are told in the flashforward of the ending paragraphs that he will eventually die as a Siberian prisoner for his collaboration. But we also see that no action of his would change any of the events that take place, and honest readers may wonder if they would behave any differently. He is a Japanese national and would be guilty of treason by one code of ethics if he acted to prevent the deaths of either the zoo animals or the Chinese men.

We associate zoos and baseball with the innocent play of childhood. By interjecting these images into a war story, the author makes the events more nightmarish and horror-filled. The effect is heightened by the concrete details, a technique Murakami's narrator makes explicit: "This was reality — as real as the sink and toothbrush he saw in front of him." And we have the further juxtaposition of haikulike sensory imagery describing the natural setting. Readers might be reminded of Henry Reed's "Naming of Parts" (p. 607), in which the blunt instructions of a drill sergeant are juxtaposed with the sensual imagery of flowers and bees in the surrounding garden. A similar voice of education is heard when the lieutenant explains to the veterinarian how a bayonet is used and when he instructs the young soldier in how to use a baseball bat. The coaching results in a perfect hit, but the suspense is agonizing as we wonder whether he will botch the job in some horrible way.

The visual incongruity of the Chinese men "disguised" by the numbered baseball uniforms reverberates with connotations. We think of the enhanced identification the uniforms have provided both the group and the numbered individuals, the "friendship" games these men have played, and the similarities and differences between sport and war. The zoo, also, where dangerous beasts have been imprisoned and then executed, echoes with implicit metaphors and analogies. It would be interesting to have students draw up free-associated lists of their own connotations for zoos and baseball games in relation to war.

Readers of the novel may have a different understanding of the symbolism of the wind-up bird than those who read the story in isolation. This sudden switch to an alternate reality is interesting but puzzling. The ending of Murakami's short story may remind readers of the ending of Frank O'Connor's "Guests of the Nation"; both suggest the impact of an event on the future of the characters. Murakami takes the postmodern approach of magical realists like Gabriel García Márquez and allows his narrator, now taking the young soldier's point of view, to see or to imagine the future. But Murakami's text questions the very concept of reality, and we cannot be certain if the young man knows what will happen or if he is engaged in a dream or a vision of one of many possible futures. The symbol of the wind-up bird signals a change of reality, an enhanced awareness that is similar to the epiphany we see in writers like James Joyce and Flannery O'Connor. We have thought to this point that the story belonged to the veterinarian, but it turns out to belong to the young man who wields the baseball bat. Like Frank O'Connor's narrator Bonaparte, it is the naive young farmboy who is profoundly changed by his participation in an execution in the midst of war. Both stories end with what amounts to a prose poem, with the language lyrical and dreamlike. Students proficient in Japanese may find it interesting to read the story in both languages. Haruki Murakami's books are best-sellers in Japan, selling millions of copies. Since most of his fiction crosses cultural boundaries — *The Wind-Up Bird Chronicle* being his most Japanese text — he is also developing a following among readers of Jay Rubin's English translations of his work. Like American readers of the Vietnam War narratives of Tim O'Brien,

Robert Olen Butler, and others, Japanese readers may be uncomfortable with the brutally honest depiction of the behavior of Japanese soldiers during World War II. But the history of atrocity in war is documented by historical evidence, and all nations have been complicit in such activities at one time or another. Some readers may claim that cultural differences made Japanese soldiers more brutal than Americans. They fall into the prejudicial stereotypes of earlier generations who found it necessary to demonize "Japs" and "Gooks" to distance them as the enemy. "Another Way to Die" counters this image; the characters are human beings engaged in the ethical dilemmas and rationalizations of war, just as American readers can imagine themselves doing under the same circumstances. Furthermore, Western readers are reminded again that Asian cultures are highly diverse and differentiated, with histories that still influence attitudes.

Although Frank O'Connor uses a first-person narrator in "Guests of the Nation" and Haruki Murakami uses a third-person narrator in "Another Way to Die," the differences in distance and degree of knowledge revealed are slight. Murakami limits the reader for much of the story to the perspective of one character, the veterinarian, and we know only what he knows. Later, he shifts the point of view very briefly to the lieutenant, and then finishes the story with the young soldier whose knowledge seems to approach the omniscient. We stand at a greater distance through most of Murakami's story than we do in O'Connor's, since we — like the veterinarian — are primarily bystanders, whereas Bonaparte brings us intimately into his own thoughts and action.

We might also expect to feel differently about O'Connor's characters than we do about Murakami's, since their names give them individual identities. This individualization is undercut somewhat by the emblematic connotations of the names, however. It is more important that we hear the victims speak in a language we can understand, whereas Murakami's victims are silent for the most part and we never hear their words. We look in on the card games and the political debates of O'Connor's characters but are only told of the baseball games of Murakami's. We also notice that, as Hawkins has been willing to do, the Chinese soldiers change sides when the opportunity arises. Until they know the Soviets are on their way, the Chinese men have been training in a facility of the puppet government controlled by Japan. Perhaps their donning of the baseball uniforms is more symbolic than the action at first appears, since this seems to be where their true allegiance lies. They are a tiny army of their own.

The veterinarian uses the numbers on the uniform in an attempt to humanize them, making them separate individuals. But the killers are more distinctive, even though they are named by their function in the army rather than by their names. We know about the veterinarian's family and about the young farmboy's chasing dragonflies and playing sword games. We know that the lieutenant is inexperienced at killing. Perhaps more readers empathize with the narrator of "Guests of the Nation" since we see him struggling with his emotions. The theme of O'Connor's narrative has to do with his conflict between the duties of friendship and the duties of war. Murakami's characters do not make friends with their enemies, but underneath their attempts to distance and control their emotions, their struggle seems equally real. None of the characters really seem to want to kill. Donovan in "Guests of the Nation" and the lieutenant in "Another Way to Die" are the most rigid and most willing to follow the orders given them from authorities far from the immediate events. But even they attempt to shield themselves from the act. Their seeming coldness may be self-protection. There are distinct similarities between the reactions of Bonaparte and the veterinarian as they are gripped — one of them literally — by their experiences. There are major differences, however. Bonaparte is young and inexperienced. The animal doctor is older, reflective, and philosophical. Murakami's shift in perspective at the story's end provides a more likely candidate for comparison with Bonaparte: the young soldier who grew up on a farm. They are similar in their innocence and in their transformations. Both end with insights about the future, engage in a reverie filled with sensory imagery, and ponder the changes in perception that can occur as a result of participation in such an event.

BEING ON A JURY (p. 1279)

SCOTT RUSSELL SANDERS

Doing Time in the Thirteenth Chair (p. 1280)

Courtrooms provide excellent examples of the sort of rhetorical issues we deal with in our first-year college English classes. Since the advent of courtroom television, instructors can mine the presentations of lawyers and the responses of witnesses for both positive and negative illustrations of persuasion. With their opening and closing arguments, their critical questioning of opposing sides, and their hodgepodge of logical, emotional, and ethical appeals, the professional rhetoricians of the courtroom often surprise us by the means they use to achieve their purposes. Each witness imposes his or her own narrative line upon events and sees the chain of cause and effect in a particular way. In the college classroom, as we teach our students to critique the arguments of other writers, we urge them to be on the watch for logical fallacies. Use the ABC rule, we advise: Examine evidence for its appropriateness, its believability, its consistency and completeness. Make sure one idea follows logically from another. Be alert for emotional manipulation. Don't be fooled by false appeals to authority; judge the ethos of the writer for knowledge and trustworthiness. Question warrants and underlying assumptions. But, time after time, we find lawyers convincing juries through appeals we would never accept in academic discourse. The use of pathos, no matter how obvious and manipulative, often carries the day. Experts list their degrees, building a case for their ethical credibility, and bore everyone to tears with impressively detailed hard evidence; but showmanship, humor, and folksy anecdotes get everyone on the side of the expert with the most style. Jurors see the defendant and his or her community as foreign and terrifying; as a result, they distance themselves and make judgments that the evidence may not warrant. Although we want students to recognize and write cogent arguments in which the chain of reasoning is flawlessly connected, we need to point out that logic alone may not be as persuasive as we would like to believe. People are not computers, and most audiences are moved by subtle factors like tone and style. And sad to say, many are moved by prejudice, loaded and slanted language, or appeals to class, race, sexual orientation, gender, or religion. As writers, we face ethical decisions about how to present a fair and reasonable argument that effectively persuades without resorting to trickery or demagoguery. The stars, the really great lawyers, know the audience their particular brand of rhetoric can reach most effectively. They choose accordingly.

Scott Russell Sanders titles his essay "Doing Time in the Thirteenth Chair" and uses the time motif to unify the narrative. We hear the ticking clock in the first sentence, and the narrator imagines that there may be "bombs or mechanical hearts" inside the walls. The Poe-like image comes close to personification but leaves the impression of inhuman machinery instead. The bombs reappear later in the essay as some of the jurors relate a frightening incident in front of the courthouse, as we imagine the defendant's Vietnam experiences, and as the jurors come out of the room after finding Bennie guilty, looking like survivors of a mine explosion. We notice that the narrator's backpack reads "NO NUKES."

Time is important throughout the essay, along with the metaphorical expression "doing time." Sanders is losing his Christmas vacation, the other jurors lose time at work, and the defendant loses fifty-four years, presumably the rest of his life. "Time, time," Sanders intones, "it always comes down to time: in jail, job, and jury box we are spending and hoarding our only wealth, the currency of days." He brings up the image of a ticking heart again, recalling the sound of his unborn daughter's heart as heard through the stethoscope. Time is like a force of nature, "raining its ticktocks down on us." After he has been selected as the alternate juror, Sanders throws in the one-word sentence, "Ticktock." We notice that he is number thirteen, and recall that both clocks and juries only go up to twelve. This allows Sanders to occupy the perfect position for a writer, that of observer. But it keeps him out of what he sees as the final act of the play. Like anyone who has just escaped deliberating on a jury, the writer has mixed feelings.

Sanders portrays the jury in a positive way and imagines that their conflicts about convicting the defendant resemble his own. We wonder, however, how they reach the conclusion that the evidence overcomes reasonable doubt, since it seems unconvincing as Sanders presents it. The social distance between the jurors and the defendant may strike readers as minimal, since several jurors are unemployed. The writer's keen observations individuate them, but they still remain somewhat anonymous, known mainly by their occupations. One he characterizes as "a boisterous old lady" and another as "a meek college student with the demeanor of a groundhog." Both comments seem slightly derogatory. We wonder if they resent not knowing that the law would require them to take away the rest of Bennie's life because of the habitual offender statute. Since we, like the narrator, are locked out of deliberations, we miss the most important details of the jury's interactions. This is a disadvantage for an observer, and readers may notice that the old men hanging around the courthouse and the young men doing "penance" seem more vivid than the jurors. The narrator sees them as akin to Bennie, at some point along the continuum from misdemeanors to long prison sentence to electric chair or lonely old age.

Sanders never truly becomes part of the "community" of the jury. He paints himself as an outsider from the beginning and is sure that this will keep him from being chosen to serve. He views Bennie and his "community" with a mixture of compassion and guilt, as almost but not quite an insider of this unsavory group. He has a great deal of insight about Bennie's situation; he identifies with him as an age-mate, as a person whose appearance defies the conservative norm, and as a reminder of his own working-class roots. Sanders's father comes from a similarly large working class family; Bennie's little girls remind him of his childhood playmates; an uncle died on the railroad tracks and Bennie was arrested on the railroad tracks; Sanders has escaped the Vietnam experience that Bennie claims has damaged him. The writer/professor feels a there-but-for-the-grace-of-God-go-I bond with the part-time garbage collector on trial for selling drugs. At least twice, he doesn't want to look at Bennie, doesn't want to see his pain and common humanity. But his portrayal is not wholly positive. Bennie's supporters are "a parade of mangled souls." The defendant's "mate" is described with animal imagery: She is "tigerish," is as capable of retaliation as Sanders once believed of "snakes, bears, wolves," and "mountain lions." The jurors reveal their view of Bennie's community when they fear at first that "Bennie's mean looking friends" have thrown a bomb at the courthouse. Bennie seems to know an uncommon number of betrayers and "snitches," and his testimony is filled with shifted blame and excuses. Yet the representatives of the community called by the prosecution seem no better, and Bennie's arrest borders on entrapment.

The writer himself steps back from time to time and provides a contrast from his own real-life community. He presents a short dialogue with his son, who seems to have a romantic cops-and-robbers view of his father's jury duty. He reveals tacitly that he has been keeping up with the news: juxtaposing an item about the government's passive acceptance of the drug trade and elaborating upon a prison suicide. He does not have to tell us that the relative weight of the damage and punishment in both cases, when compared with Bennie's case, seems ironic and hypocritical.

It would be interesting to have your students vote on whether or not they agree with the jury's verdict against Bennie and to discuss the quality of the evidence pro and con. The judge claims to know additional information that leads him to believe that Bennie's conviction is justified. But readers may recall the facts of the case — characterized by the narrator as "a mess." According to the state's evidence, Bennie's gross income from the sale of drugs to I90 amounts to thirty-three dollars — even if we believe an informant's self-serving testimony and the garbled tapes and notes of a police officer. The jury learns even before they are surprised with the habitual offender issue that Bennie understands he can get over thirty years in prison. Few readers believe that the punishment fits the crime, even with his earlier convictions factored in. Others raise issues about the damage Bennie has done if he actually is a drug dealer, citing above all the effect on Rebecca's daughters of living in a house where drug deals occur. The jury is supposed to consider the law of the matter, however, and perhaps these are ethical issues. Has the prosecution proven its case through the evidence of I90 and his handler? The jury decides that it has. Although Sanders emphasizes the uncertainty of the matter, many readers could make a good argument for reasonable doubt.

JOYCE CAROL OATES
I, the Juror (p. 1294)

The title of Joyce Carol Oates's essay "I, the Juror" plays on the words of the Mickey Spillane title *I, the Jury*, the novel in which his famous fictional detective Mike Hammer tracks down and wields his own brand of justice upon the murderer of a friend. Spillane's character, in the first of several 1950s best-sellers, becomes the judge and jury as he pronounces sentence and exacts revenge. Oates links herself with Mike Hammer through the allusion. Her attitude toward the African American male defendant is not vindictive, however. She goes along with the decision to find him guilty of a lesser charge, despite her feeling that his female victim is being blamed. But Oates ends her essay with a statement that indicates the real targets of her judgment, the jury system itself — and this jury in particular — as representative of a bigoted, classbound, "not serious" citizenry. Perhaps the essay itself is her revenge.

We ask students to examine the diction and syntax of Oates's narrative as they determine her attitude and tone. She begins by musing about the "abstract principle of Justice," using a capital letter J to emphasize the symbolic nature of the word. Abstractions and generalizations are problematic, since they invite divergent interpretations, and Oates foregrounds this fact. She begins with her own abstract notions and her conflicting emotions about jury duty, preparing us for the specific, concrete working out of the trial-by-jury concept in practice. She shares her thoughts leading up to this particular jury duty as a way of giving background and providing context for the crushing of her "romantic illusions" at the trial's end. As we assign the reading, we brainstorm our own definitions and metaphors for justice — writing on the board *Justice is . . .* and having students call out completing phrases. We find political and philosophical differences and discuss the possible reasons underlying responses. Oates tells us her connotations for the word in her first two paragraphs, developing them further as the essay proceeds. Her syntax in the opening is poetic in its balance; she begins with a fragment and follows with a series of parallel repetitions of words and sentence structures. We find alliteration and assonance. This seems an especially appropriate way to begin a piece of nonfiction about the nature of justice, since we would hope for balance and satisfying order in the jury process. But even here Oates points out the conflicts. Her word choices in the essay critique the absence of the human touch in the system itself. She receives a "smudgily computer-printed summons," at first appreciating its "impersonality"; doesn't explain her professional name because it might generate "a punitive misfiring in the unimaginative computer brain"; and tells us the jury list is "stored in the computer" and thus names cannot be removed. She refers to the system as a "gigantic grinding machine," and later repeats the image: "an antique machine clanking and grinding and laboring." The system is "archaic, cumbersome, inefficient, outmoded, punitive," characterized by "an air of menace and threat." The courthouse is "generic." The jury as first seen is "a rambling herd," and her view of them grows even more negative. Even without her overtly negative evaluations of her fellow jurors, the procedures, and the court workers — her "overseers" — Oates's loaded words alone make judgments.

One worker tells Oates, when she challenges the routine as "punitive" and "inefficient," that the process has been streamlined, that it used to be worse, and that people had to accept it. The worker, perhaps correctly in view of the writer's judgmental attitude, takes a defensive stance, feeling personally criticized. Some readers feel that through much of the essay Oates comes across as arrogant, negative, and inconsistent in her criticism of everything around her in the courthouse. Isn't it fair to speculate that juries, too, have changed as the culture has changed, that people are no longer as willing to shoulder the responsibilities of jury duty or to accept any discomfort outside their own self-interest? Like reluctant schoolchildren, potential jurors come unwillingly, and perhaps they must be pursued and punished when they play truant. Nevertheless, as Oates points out, the great majority of those called have been excused before these few are forced to show up. It has been ironically asked if anyone would want to be tried by a juror who was too stupid to avoid jury duty. Does the oppressive atmosphere of the courthouse make people reluctant, or does the resistance of citizens to participate and cooperate make such rules necessary? Oates criticizes both the informal dress of fellow jurors and the churchy trappings of the court. Isn't this inconsistent? She carps about both impersonality and bias.

Interestingly, juries may have been even more biased in the distant past, before the two-week imprisonment the court worker describes or the systematic randomness of computerized selections. In some areas of the country in the past, the issue of bumping black jurors from the panel would not have existed, because African Americans would not have been called for jury duty at all, most having been barred from voter registration by Jim Crow laws. The original "grandfather clause," instituted in many localities in the 1890s, a generation after slavery was declared illegal, prevented men from voting — and consequently serving on juries — if their grandfathers had not been qualified to vote. Oates herself would not have served in the past, since women were not called either. In the 1930s unemployed young men hung around the courthouse, hoping to be called for jury duty. It worked a bit like plasma donation. Local white men over the age of twenty-one could be pulled in off the street to serve, earning a dollar or so and — if sequestered — free room and board for as long as they could keep the hot debates going, taking whichever side was necessary. Would this sort of volunteer jury pool be preferable? Oates implies that African American jurors might have been able to try this case more fairly. Although few readers would condone racial loading of juries in either direction, we feel intuitively that cultural experiences play a part in judgments. However, it is just as likely that African American jurors — even women — would blame the female victim. Trying to decide who in the jury pool is truly a "peer" of the victim or the defendant would be a risky and even more prejudiced approach than the current one. Readers who find Oates's complaints about the jury system persuasive should consider the ramifications of changes. Placing the justice system in the hands of a few judges or professional jurors, as some have suggested, seems especially conducive to elitism, a charge that could be leveled at Oates herself.

Some readers respond positively to Joyce Carol Oates because she is a keen observer and an articulate, highly respected writer. She gets us on her side with balanced considerations of the pros and cons of jury duty and with self-revelations about her idealism and her fears. She seems to have compassion for the woman who has been beaten, for which most of us judge Oates positively. Her criticism of the jury centers primarily around their willingness to condemn this woman and the others of her community because the jurors are unable to place themselves in the situations described. This is a major problem. Recently, in a televised trial in Texas, both the prosecution and the defense made shockingly open attempts to play on the jury's distance from the people of "that neighborhood" of Mexican Mafia members, glue-sniffing boys, "breeding" women, and careless girls. "Send a message to *those* people," the prosecutor actually said. "How could you expect this young boy to know how to behave given these role models?" the defense attorney countered, pleading for life in prison rather than death. The eighteen-year-old was sentenced to death row. Readers may find it frightening to contemplate that most jurors are more swayed by overt or unconscious race, class, and gender bias than by a careful consideration of the facts. Because it is a story that involves a black man beating his wife, Ann Petry's "Like a Winding Sheet" (p. 841) makes a useful companion piece to "I, the Juror." Students can compare their possible votes on a jury panel that is trying Petry's character with the verdict in this case.

Readers sometimes feel that Oates judges the jury too harshly, especially when she characterizes them as not taking the process seriously. Who is she to condemn their clothing and their offhand remarks? Others will agree with Oates that justice for the victim should be uppermost in jurors' minds. Since Oates also participated in the deliberations, however, we wonder why she did not stand her ground if she wanted a harsher verdict. Her generalizations are questionable both because her experience may not stand as a representative example, and because the writer herself may be biased in terms of class and education. Throughout her narrative, Oates seeks to separate herself from the other people in the courthouse. Only the judge — an articulate, educated woman who tells Oates later that she recognizes her — seems to be accepted by Oates as her moral and ethical equal. Some readers question the identification of the Princeton professor and award-winning writer with the black woman who is beaten, seeing Oates as taking merely an ideological stance. Those who know Oates's biography and work will perhaps see her position as consistent and sincere. Still, it hardly seems fair for one who stands aloof in her judgments of her peers to fault the jury for being equally distant from the world of the defendant and his victim.

Although Sanders is less critical of his jury than Oates is of hers, the behavior of the Indiana and New Jersey panels does not seem qualitatively different. Both panels feel that the people they are judging are not their peers. Both juries engage in small talk. Sanders relishes the revelations of personality and common humanity in such exchanges as relieving the boredom, whereas Oates feels that this is time wasted and would like to contemplate the evidence. The ordinary, presumably respectable, people on the juries see a different world from their own in the drug- and violence-ridden world of the underclass. Oates's jury lashes out in judgment against the victim, while Sanders's jury — seen only from the outside view of an alternate juror — nervously jokes about bombs. Both narrators are professional writers and English professors and feel the intellectual's estrangement from the middle class and imaginative empathy with the underclass — Sanders with the scruffy defendant and Oates with the battered victim. Both writers have working-class roots that give this perspective some legitimacy, though no reader would believe either could have truly exchanged fates with the individuals with whom they identify. Although he does not criticize as harshly as Oates, Sanders supplies ample details for the reader to judge that what happens to the defendant in the Indiana trial is terribly unfair, and he makes it clear that it is the system and not the jury that causes this injustice. Because Sanders dedicates more space to the defendant, his wife, and the witnesses from the lower-class community in the Indiana trial, they are more three-dimensional than Oates's emblematic abusive man and victimized woman in New Jersey. We have only Oates's judgment and the few glimpses that she gives us to decide whether the victim and the defendant in the New Jersey trial receive true justice.

By relating her story in the past tense, Oates gives a sense of having thought through the meaning of the events, but she also takes the chance that we will step back and observe her, as she does others. Sanders's use of the present tense allows the reader to share his observations and frustrations first-hand. He shows more than he tells. The use of the present tense seems especially effective when Sanders uses the time motif to unify his narrative. We hear the clock ticking along with him. Both writers use images that emphasize the inhuman, mechanical nature of legal institutions. Both feel limited by the waste of time and by their confinement in space. Oates speaks of the tedious nature of the testimony and the dead time when the jury is kept from hearing information. The trial "traced and retraced the same narrow terrain, like a snail with a motor imbalance," Oates says, linking the frustrations of time and space in the same simile. "The facts are a mess," Sanders generalizes, leading into his concrete metaphor. "They are full of gaps, chuckholes, switchbacks, and dead ends — just like life." Unlike the witnesses, each writer finds a way to focus the jury experience for the audience. Scott Russell Sanders uses the repetition of time images to impose a narrative line on the jumbled observations of an alternate juror. Joyce Carol Oates structures her essay through a chronological arrangement. She first considers her thoughts about justice and jury duty before the trial, then shows her change and frustration as she finds that her ideals are far from reality, and ends with an "Afterword" that ponders the meaning of the experience and her changed views. She ends with a question rather than closure, projecting the issue into the future for the reader to consider.

MORAL LAW VERSUS HUMAN LAW: CRITICAL COMMENTARIES ON SOPHOCLES' *ANTIGONE* (p. 1305)

SOPHOCLES

Antigone (p. 1306)

In other places in our anthology, students have been exposed to the concept of persona in poetry, used to describe the speaker of a poem who is obviously not the poet. The term originally referred to the masks worn by the exclusively male actors in Greek drama to indicate to the audience who they were supposed to be. When a man acted the part of Antigone, Ismene, or Eurydice, therefore, gesture and voice were all that were available to him as he sought to suspend the disbelief of his audience. The audience was called upon to imagine it, to be an active participant in reading the human emotion portrayed. The more we allow ourselves to become involved emotionally in the drama, the more likely we are to experience catharsis, the "cleansing" that comes as we work out feelings of pity and fear as we share in the conflicts of the characters in the play. In *Antigone* the moral family obligation to bury the dead and to cry out in mourning is one of the few public roles allowed to women, one the Athenian establishment in the home city of Sophocles historically sought to control and limit. The tension of the play exists between the human laws of government — an arena of exclusive male dominance — and the emotional imperative of honoring the death of a loved family member, thus preserving traditions of family and religion — an activity important to women. This reality of Greek life underlies the conflict between Antigone and her uncle, Creon, who has become king of Thebes on the death of her brothers.

Instructors will want to provide more background about Antigone's father Oedipus and the reasons behind the situation his children experience. Some students will have heard Oedipus referred to in psychology classes as the archetype for the desire every little boy presumably feels to get rid of his father and be united with his mother. Instructors who are unfamiliar with the story can find it in any number of reference books about classical Greek mythology. The actuality of Oedipus inadvertently committing this primal sin brings a curse upon his family; in addition, during his old age and blindness, Oedipus has cursed his sons explicitly for their perceived failure to help and honor him properly. One tragedy leads to another in this family.

To Antigone, the daughter of Oedipus and his mother Jocasta, another monstrous event seems about to take place. Her brothers have killed each other contending for control over their dead father's city Thebes. Their uncle in his role as the new king will not allow proper burial of Polynices, who had allied with a competing city in his attack. Both Antigone and Creon have warrants for their actions. The king feels that it is proper to deny glory to Polynices by leaving his body unburied because he has committed treason against the city, even though such handling of a body is not the tradition in their city. Antigone, however, operates under an ethic that sees this as a horror, going against religion and tradition.

There may be personal grounds for her obsession as well. It is a woman's duty to care for family members in death as in infancy. Creon's action further denies to her the only public voice and participation in ritual a woman is allowed in ancient Greece. Women are not citizens, but Creon devalues women even beyond this, telling his son that "there are other furrows to plow." Women are interchangeable, he implies, and Antigone is less than nothing, even though she is a king's daughter. Creon accuses her of hubris, the overreaching pride that brings the anger of the gods, because she challenges male authority. He sees her as irrational and insane. But he too is arrogant and habitually acts in rash anger rather than taking the time to reason out his actions.

Scholars debate how *Antigone* fits the traditional elements of tragedy. How can Antigone be a tragic hero, since she is a woman? Would the audience have been moved to pity by her desire to bury her brother, or would they have seen her as a hateful feminist dangerously out of control? Interested students can look up descriptions of Greek tragedy and debate the issue of tragic flaws and other qualities of the hero to determine if Creon fits the role. Some argue for Haemon, who plays a small but important role, dying for the love of a woman and the shame of his father's actions. Students will be reminded of Romeo and Juliet on a grander, more intense scale.

Haemon's conflict with his father is warranted by his belief in reason as opposed to rigidity and unbridled emotion, respect for the gods, and the importance of considering the will of the people. He therefore stands between the obsessions of Antigone and Creon. But like Antigone he disobeys the ruling authority. He comes close to committing patricide like Oedipus. If Haemon is the hero of the drama, perhaps this willingness to overturn the order of society and family is his fatal flaw in the eyes of Sophocles and his immediate audience. He ends as a suicide, and his death leads to catharsis as his mother commits suicide and his father cries out in mourning and guilt. The chorus drives home the point that suffering can lead to wisdom.

Modern readers tend to see Antigone as tragically heroic and as an early feminist who stands up for what she believes is right. Students may see her as determined, idealistic, passionate, and loyal. Others may feel that she is obsessed, shrill, and hysterical (a word with pejorative connotations toward women). We sympathize with her and see her as morally superior to Creon, though cultural differences may stand in the way of our understanding of her intensity about this particular subject. Some readers may feel that at some point she loses moral authority as the issue becomes more a matter of defying Creon than burying her brother. We have more difficulty sympathizing with Creon. He seems especially irritating when he is accusing people of being money hungry. He constantly shifts blame. He flies off the handle easily and allows matters to escalate as he rigidly holds his ground. Perhaps, at the end, when he has lost his whole family, we feel pity for him and hope he will gain the wisdom the chorus speaks about.

Ismene comes across to modern audiences as lacking in courage, though she tries to stand with Antigone by sharing the blame for something she didn't do. She comes in for some harsh judgment from her sister, but she is following the rules and tradition set out for women to follow. She is also aware of the tragedies the family has already endured and shies away from yet another public shame. Ismene is a good girl. The first audience for this play might have seen her as more normal than the manic Antigone.

The chorus is the unified voice of the elder statesmen of the city, and its wisdom varies. When Creon announces that he will not allow Polynices to be buried, the chorus agrees, going against its better judgment in the face of his power and determination. This shows the chorus's imperfection, as does its handling of Eurydice at the play's end. The chorus hopes that she will retire to her quarters to work out her feelings in private, and it watches her go, even though it partially suspects that she will harm herself. Often, however, it interprets events for the audience, mixing its reading of the current situation with philosophy. It tells us about the nature of mankind, the gods, and fate. It recalls historical events and genealogy. Students who have read William Faulkner's "A Rose for Emily" (p. 849) may see in the first-person-plural perspective echoes of the Greek chorus, interpreting events surrounding Miss Emily as normal citizens would have explained those surrounding the royal personages of Greek tragedy. We might also remember that Faulkner's story involved an unburied body, with the heroine taking a stand quite different from Antigone's.

Most viewers of Sophocles' tragedy prefer the Greek tradition of keeping the actual violence offstage. Creon entering with his son in his arms is a moving scene, evoking our pity more strongly because we only hear the telling of the events that lead up to it. We do not need to see the struggle between father and son to feel the agony of a man whose father has killed the woman he loves, nor do we need to see Eurydice slashing herself in grief to recognize the suffering of a mother who has lost a son. Students may disagree, having observed realistic violence in films, on television, and in video games. The Greek audience had probably seen more actual death than we have in our protected, modern-technology-enriched lifestyles. But we have become emotionally hardened through experiencing violence and death vicariously, and catharsis becomes more elusive. Although students will think of many examples of violence in slasher movies and films in similar genres, the most vivid recent evocation of realistic violence may be the movie *Saving Private Ryan*. Students could argue for the importance of showing such violence in historical reenactments so that we understand the enormity of war. Others say that the opposite will happen, and we will yawn at seeing yet another televised image of an actual war, perhaps even complaining that the angle is not quite right, undercutting the realism.

CRITICAL COMMENTARIES:

BERNARD KNOX, From *The Heroic Temper* (p. 1346)
MARTHA NUSSBAUM, From *The Fragility of Goodness* (p. 1347)
CHARLES SEGAL, From *Interpreting Greek Tragedy* (p. 1349)

Both Bernard Knox and Martha Nussbaum compare Antigone with Creon. For Knox, both characters are caught up in their own personal battles, but they use higher causes as justification for their stands against each other. Creon places the good of the *polis*, the state, above everything whereas Antigone privileges the family over the state. Knox points out that in the end it is Antigone's love that differentiates her from Creon. He loses not only the family he rejected, but the state and the favor of the gods. Antigone's stand turns out to be best not only for the family and gods, whom she honors, but for the state that she has opposed.

Nussbaum sees Antigone and Creon as similar in their oversimplification of complexity that reduces life to death. Creon sees people as bodies to be used, even those that he loves. Antigone is in love with death, seeks to serve the dead, and welcomes death. This relieves her of the complexity of living. Nussbaum too sees Antigone as superior to Creon, since she at least believes that there are higher claims than the pragmatic exploitation of owned bodies.

Most students will see Nussbaum's discussion as a bit strange, but we are talking about two people who spend a whole play in conflict over a corpse. Some readers argue that Nussbaum is correct in seeing Antigone as cold. We have only to consider her attitude toward her sister or to recall that her only real concern for her lost marriage and barrenness comes as she enters the underworld, where love leading to children is no longer possible. Other readers will agree with Knox that her actions have been motivated by love, since she does not abandon her brother even though he is dead. She sees love as eternal.

Although Segal sees Antigone as totally embracing her womanhood, some scholars argue that she is manly in taking on a public rather than a private role. This is what Creon means when he accuses her of *hubris*, and he sees their conflict as her defiance of his right to rule. Stereotypically, she has female qualities that are concerned with family, blood ties, care and mourning for the dead, and the willingness to sacrifice herself for others. But she takes on male prerogatives when she takes public action rather than remaining passive, speaks boldly to the king rather than keeping silent, and becomes concerned with the glory of winning her argument and compelling political change.

Creon, on the other hand, is not always rational. He sticks to his plan, even when it becomes obvious to everyone else that it is not proper in any way. Like a writer who has committed to an outline, he will not adapt his thought to new information or insight. Rather than being characterized by rationality, he is absorbed in emotion, and the play ends with his taking on the role of the female in the care and mourning of the dead, since his wife has killed herself over the results of his rash actions. Of course, this has been made necessary by his denial of the importance of family roles that have emotional — as opposed to rational — content.

Gender is conceded to be an essential theme in *Antigone*, but Segal's characterizations, taken in isolation, oversimplify the ethical dilemmas Creon and Antigone face as they weigh the competing values of religion, state, and family. Rules for which activities and what sort of speech are appropriate for men and women are not as rigid in the United States at the turn of the twenty-first century as they were in 441 B.C.E. In our politically correct environment, students may think of more examples of "obsessive masculine rationality" than of "full acceptance of . . . womanly nature."

Perhaps the theme of the drama, even in Sophocles' day, would be the inadvisability of single-minded obsessions about anything. Each person, male or female, needs balance. Having students divide a page in half and list "masculine" traits on one side and "feminine" traits on the other might lead to interesting discussions, but some students resist any such examination of warrants, preferring to deny any possibility of gender bias in their psyches. Others loudly defend cultural dictates about what is proper behavior and speech for men and women.

JUDGING SANITY: CULTURAL CONTEXTS FOR CHARLOTTE PERKINS GILMAN'S "THE YELLOW WALLPAPER" (p. 1351)

CHARLOTTE PERKINS GILMAN
The Yellow Wallpaper (p. 1351)

The narrator of Charlotte Perkins Gilman's 1892 short story "The Yellow Wallpaper" — a married woman who has a young baby she is not required to care for — writes a series of surreptitious journal entries while undergoing treatment that prescribes complete rest from physical, social, and mental activity. The context of the entries, separated by spaces, suggests that there are eleven of them, written over the course of the summer. As the narrator records her thoughts, they become increasingly disordered and her tone becomes gradually more manic. The change is particularly evident when the story is read aloud by a skilled actor. Our class listens to an especially good audiotape, allowing the voice of the narrator to sweep the audience inexorably into her delusion. Gilman's narrator is unreliable, and readers question her interpretations of the situation. Is the narrator in a country house with her husband, or is she actually in an insane asylum? Is she delusional, or does her early comment that the house may be haunted indicate that this is a ghost story in which the figure of a woman really does come out of the wallpaper? Would she be crazy anyway, as students sometimes contend, or does her condition become worse because she is treated as a foolish child and forbidden intellectual activity?

Gilman's sensory imagery creates an impression of gradually altered perception. The wallpaper has unattractive and ominous connotations from the beginning. The narrator's first description of its color uses words like *repellant, revolting, smouldering, unclean, lurid orange,* and *sickly sulphur.* Her reaction to the pattern is even more revealing. Curves "suddenly commit suicide" and "destroy themselves in unheard of contradictions." Two weeks into the summer stay, in the second journal entry, the narrator has begun to personify the wallpaper, suspecting that it has knowledge of its effect and a will of its own. She begins to see horrible faces in it; "the pattern lolls like a broken neck and two bulbous eyes stare at you upside down." As her solitary confinement and forced idleness continue, the narrator comes to believe that a woman is imprisoned in the wallpaper, and she takes action to help the woman get out.

At a point late in the narrator's illness, the images become synesthestic — melding two senses into one as sometimes occurs with schizophrenia. The wallpaper now has a "yellow smell." By this time, the narrator claims off-handedly to have been the woman in the wallpaper, who has finally been released, in spite of Jane and the husband. This is the first time we have heard this name; Mary is credited with caring for the baby, and Jennie does everything else. The logical conclusion is that Jane is the name of the narrator, whose derangement we have followed through most of the story. Now, the narrator implies, the woman behind the wallpaper has escaped. Where then is Jane?

The narrator moves from a cheerful though frustrated attempt to submit to the authority of her husband/physician and other male authority figures to a determined, single-minded "creeping" that takes her right over the husband's prostrate body, which has collapsed in shock. Read strictly in a psychological way, her story is one of a slide into madness, brought on by society's denial to her of any real fulfillment of her intellectual and emotional needs as an adult. But some readers feel that she achieves a victory of sorts, is finally freed from oppression and has become her own person. No longer can her feelings be waved aside and dismissed with baby talk. Students usually enjoy diagnosing her psychological illness. Postpartum depression is certainly indicated, though bipolar disorder and schizophrenia are sometimes suggested. Research on neurasthenia, a faddish diagnosis for women with vague symptoms around the turn of the twentieth century, will turn up interesting facts for students with medical and psychological interests. Similar symptoms in recent years have resulted in increased labeling of patients with hypoglycemia, chronic fatigue syndrome, fibromyalgia, and so on. By the end of the story, the narrator has the symptoms of an obsessive-compulsive disorder; she focuses on the need to tear down wallpaper, chew up the furniture, and creep along the edge of the wall.

Although critics like to emphasize the cultural and historical issues of patriarchy and women's societal position in the 1890s and beyond — a focus consistent with the author's concerns — it is possible to read Gilman's story as a psychological thriller like those of Edgar Allan Poe. Readers find ample evidence that the narrator reveals the truth of her illness to us in bits and pieces, sometimes misleading us because she herself does not realize the truth. From her earliest musings about the house, we wonder whether it has been used as a madhouse before or if she has been here longer than she indicates. There is a locked gate at the top of the stairs, bars on the windows, and "rings and things in the walls." Although she assumes that the room has been a nursery and a gymnasium, we do not have to accept this evaluation. Even at the beginning of the story, the wallpaper "is stripped off . . . in great patches all around the head of my bed, about as far as I can reach." We see that the bed is damaged long before we see her take a bite out of it. Some readers question whether she has already begun to damage the furnishings or if the room has housed a previous resident who rips wallpaper, perhaps a woman who is now trapped in the wallpaper. To read the story in this way is to enter into her madness, but it provides a valid perspective.

The wallpaper becomes a symbol of the circumstances of the narrator. Forbidden the order of work and adult activity, the narrator's mind is as confused and disordered as the lines of the paper, and she feels as sick as its colors and as full of poison as its nasty fungi. She is trapped within the constraints of dependency and societal rules and frantically grasps for the action that will allow her to be free and whole. She feels suicidal — thinks at one point of jumping out the barred window — and the wallpaper writhes with images of choked people and women behind bars.

The joy of reading "The Yellow Wallpaper" with a new class each semester is the opportunity to read the story from multiple perspectives. Students who choose to write papers about Gilman's story could experiment with playing a believing-and-doubting game with the text, first completely trusting the narrator's words that these supernatural events are taking place, and then questioning everything. Though some readers see Jane as a freakish madwoman who is merely displayed for our horror, much like Kafka's hunger artist, many others find her persistence in the face of patriarchy admirable. We empathize with her resistance to forced isolation and insulting condescension and are able to imagine our own reactions to such abuse. Students who dismiss her as simply crazy might be asked to consider if this is proper treatment for her even if she arrives at the house mentally ill. Isn't Gilman correct in her contention that being forbidden to work, exercise, read, or see friends makes a depressed person feel worse?

Through her use of the present tense, Gilman allows us to observe the progression of the narrator's reading of the wallpaper and to be startled by the sudden inconsistency and disjunction of certain remarks. At the end of the fourth entry, she sees the shape of a woman, or many replications of the same woman, and she says, "I wonder — I begin to think — I wish John would take me away from here." We are not told what it is she wonders about, but we know that at this point it frightens her. By the ninth entry, the present tense allows her to nonchalantly drop her own method of "creeping" into her musings about the woman she now believes she sees creeping outside every window. We do not know what happens after her husband awakens from his fainting spell. If the story were told from the past tense, we would sense a narrative line being drawn to explain either her recovery or her continuing illness. As it stands, the reader must decide what happens next and ultimately must decide the meaning of the story.

"The Yellow Wallpaper" lends itself to a discussion of symbolism, cause and effect, theme, and social and historical context. Most critics take the story to be a condemnation of the cultural barriers that work against equal treatment of women. By creating a composite character in the narrator's husband John, making him both her husband and a physician, Gilman broadens her critique to include not only the medical profession but also marriage and, by implication, the other institutions of a patriarchal society. John's paternalistic control over his wife is complete. She has no power and no voice, since she is virtually imprisoned and all of her thoughts are dismissed as foolish. Readers doubt whether John could really understand what love between equals entails. He is his wife's keeper, and she is his pet. Yet, in her time, many of Gilman's contemporaries would wonder what the woman has to complain about. She lives like a princess, they would think. She is even robbed of the conflict that women of past generations felt between the need to do meaningful, creative work and the need to nurture and love husbands and children. She is allowed neither, and instead must occupy the position of a fragile doll. She is expected to be cheerful and docile, denying any of the feelings that she needs to work out.

CULTURAL CONTEXTS:

CHARLOTTE PERKINS GILMAN, "Why I Wrote
'The Yellow Wallpaper' " (p. 1364)
S. WEIR MITCHELL, From "The Evolution of the Rest
Treatment" (p. 1366)
JOHN HARVEY KELLOGG, From *The Ladies' Guide in Health
and Disease* (p. 1370)

From a perspective of more than a century, it may be difficult for young men and women in college to imagine the inferior position to which women were relegated in the 1890s, when Charlotte Perkins Gilman was facing gender discrimination as a writer and as a person. Students tend to blame the victim in "The Yellow Wallpaper" for the distress she feels as a result of her limited options for self-expression and meaningful work, dismissing her as her husband does as foolish and weak. Because Gilman was subjected to S. Weir Mitchell's "rest cure" in the wake of her own postpartum depression, many readers have assumed that the events of the short story are autobiographical. In her response to such hasty conclusions in her own time, Gilman states unequivocally that although she and the narrator of "The Yellow Wallpaper" share some experiences, they are not the same person. "I never had hallucinations or objections to my mural decorations," she quips.

Gilman mentions S. Weir Mitchell by name in the short story, keeping him in the distance as a threat to the narrator but not a person directly involved in her treatment. In the nonfiction piece "Why I Wrote 'The Yellow Wallpaper' " she does not give his name; however, she does cite "friends" of the "specialist" who say that he "admitted" to changing his treatment methods after reading Gilman's story. He may have done this privately, but the public speech that is excerpted here gives no indication that he has abandoned his methods.

Health professionals today would agree with some of Mitchell's techniques — the use of massage, perhaps — but would be horrified by the lack of exercise and the insistence upon "overfeeding" in his regimen. This alone tends to make Gilman's objections to his advice seem reasonable to modern readers, despite what Mitchell says. Gilman's evidence for her statement that Mitchell has been influenced by her story is weak, however, since it is based on hearsay and not attributed to a specific, reliable source. This possibly erroneous statement of the doctor's views, undoubtedly without his permission, comes across to some readers as a false use of authority in her defense of her story.

The physicians she answers in this piece raise two issues. One praises her description of insanity as believable and asks if it is autobiographical. She responds to this by a frank admission that it is true to her life to an extent, but then counters Mitchell's methods by maintaining that going directly against his advice saved her. In response to the doctor who says that her story could drive people crazy, she insists that "The Yellow Wallpaper" has achieved its purpose of saving people from mental illness. She gives a single example of a woman whose family was influenced to stop such treatment, but presumably her final statement refers to the alteration in Mitchell's program, a fact in question. The core of Gilman's explanation, like the main idea of her story, remains convincing, however: She speaks from experience. Mitchell's advice to avoid intellectual stimulation and to give up her creative activity almost sends her over the edge, and she emerges from the experience convinced that work empowers women.

In Gilman's day, a woman of her social class was often denied work and education and was then seen as inferior — perhaps underneath it all as "a pauper and a parasite" — as a result of her dependence. Some readers may raise the issue that Gilman's experience is not necessarily representative and that the failure of Mitchell's cure in her case keeps her from fairly evaluating its efficacy for others. If a person is mentally ill, such readers insist, it is difficult to know whether poor treatment causes decline or whether the disorder would have taken the same course in any event. Nevertheless, for most readers, Gilman's first-hand knowledge of depression and of the "rest cure" lends weight to her story. Her clarification about the extent of her illness is especially useful, her "escape" from the fate of her narrator giving her a survivor's credibility and distance. Biography is most helpful when the reader is able to see the world of the story as informed by the facts of the writer's life but as not identical to them.

Although he does not acknowledge feminist and fiction writer Charlotte Perkins Gilman, it is obvious that by the time S. Weir Mitchell discussed his methods in "The Evolution of the Rest Treatment" in 1904, he had come under a great deal of attack from other quarters. His tone in the essay is defensive. He has been labeled a charlatan. He says in his closing paragraphs that he has "suffered keenly" from accusations that his methods are unscientific. In this passage, he emphasizes his discovery of massage as an adjunct to the rest cure, and defends his method as pragmatic but also "defensible in the end by scientific explanatory research." He separates himself from "quacks" like osteopaths and Swedish massage practitioners, whom he judges as too rough. He describes several cases in which his cure has been successful, but does not provide the evidence of controlled studies that we would expect today. Students find it ironic that one proof of success is weight gain, an effect that many people today would see as a sign of an unhealthy lack of exercise. Mitchell takes his patient's illness seriously, and we may approve his defense of her against the label of hysterical woman. He recognizes the pejorative quality of the word *hysteria*, maintaining that "calling names" and labeling don't really lead to recovery.

Mrs. G. is like Charlotte Perkins Gilman and the narrator of "The Yellow Wallpaper" in that she is essentially placed in solitary confinement and forbidden to work, but Mitchell emphasizes massage and "electric passive exercise" in which the muscles are stimulated by mild electric shocks. She gets better, he claims, and he is able to "overfeed" her and to sneak iron supplements into her food. Everything about her treatment is decided for Mrs. G., but readers do not sense the level of condescension that Gilman's narrator receives from her husband. Perhaps this is because we hear Mitchell's tone as he addresses other doctors, and not as he speaks to Mrs. G. Unlike Gilman, she stays with the program; and unlike the narrator of Gilman's story, she does not slip into madness. Mitchell takes full credit: The woman remains at the time of his speech "what I made her." Implied in the description of Mrs. G., however, is the notion that she suffers from exhaustion because she seeks to go beyond her strength. There is no way to know from this distance what Mrs. G.'s problem was or why Mitchell's treatment worked in her case and not in Gilman's.

Mrs. G. is offered as evidence of success, not as a case study that gives detailed observations from which his audience can draw their own conclusions. The gaps make comparison difficult, and readers are usually too influenced by our reading of Gilman and our knowledge that isolation and lack of exercise are debilitating. Still, we may appreciate the need of busy people to have some respite from the duties of life and the recognition that it is not a good idea for a woman to have babies too often. Mrs. G. may recover in spite of Mitchell's treatment.

Modern readers cannot miss the signs of anorexia and bulimia that would indicate a need for more calories and mineral supplements and would cause weakness that might require bedrest. It may strike young working mothers as appropriate that this woman's case comes up in the same speech as descriptions of what we would now call post–traumatic stress syndrome in American Civil War soldiers. Today's women often feel embattled. When stress is the cause of illness, rest alone may bring relief. Mitchell's description of the male patient with "locomotor ataxia" is more puzzling, since some physiological condition seems to be involved. The gaps in his description are too great to draw any real parallels with Mrs. G. or Gilman's character. From the details we are given, the woman's care is managed more closely. Students may find it significant that Mitchell distinguishes between his male and female patients. In speaking of men with battle fatigue, which he sees as a variety of "Neurasthenia," Mitchell says that such cases are "more certainly curable than are most of the graver male cases which now we are called on to treat." Does this imply that female cases are less grave or that male cases are taken more seriously? One wonders too if Mrs. G. would have received such solicitous, albeit intrusive, attention from the famous doctor if she had been of a lower social class.

In the passage from John Harvey Kellogg's 1882 *The Ladies' Guide to Health and Disease*, women are advised about their responsibilities as childbearers. Like today's nutritionists, who encourage women of childbearing age to eat a diet high in folic acid and other nutrients that prevent birth defects, Kellogg encourages a healthy diet and exercise, arguing that these should begin even before conception occurs. But his tone reveals warrants close to those of the eugenics movement of the nineteenth and early twentieth centuries as he uses words like *stock-breeder* and *propagate*. Prenatal care for mothers focuses on the breeding of superior children. He assumes as fact some notions about prenatal responsibilities of mothers and fathers that modern readers find laughable. The mother's "mental condition" at the time of conception is important, Kellogg says, though he states with no apparent fear of contradiction that the father's condition as the couple is having sexual intercourse is naturally more important in forming the child's character. One is reminded of medieval descriptions of homunculi, tiny beings implanted in the mother's womb wholly through the father's influence, though women were blamed, of course, if the child was the wrong sex. With no real understanding of genetics and prenatal development, Kellogg reveals his warrants as he suggests reasons for symptoms of fetal alcohol syndrome and perhaps other birth defects in the opening paragraph. If the child is retarded, both parents must have been "in a state of beastly intoxication" when the child was conceived. Because the child can be further marked during gestation, the mother "should not yield to the depressing influences" of pregnancy. The assumption is that she should be happy to find herself pregnant, her opportunity of "molding a human character" being a "God-given" one.

Although Kellogg differs from S. Weir Mitchell in his emphasis on a vegetarian diet, exercise, and "interesting conversation, reading, and various harmless and pleasant diversions," he agrees with the avoidance of excitement and the need for the woman to think happy and calm thoughts. If she wants her child to acquire high culture, the pregnant mother must concentrate totally on the art in which she wishes her child to excel. One presumes that if the child is born without talent, she didn't think hard enough. If she does not want her child to crave stimulants, she should avoid spices, coffee, tea, and so forth. But throughout his list of suggestions, Kellogg gives the impression that women must be saved from their emotional tendencies and that husbands should gently control the lives of these flighty bearers of their children if they want healthy progeny. When he goes on to discuss "puerperal mania" — or postpartum depression — the connection of this text with Charlotte Perkins Gilman's "The Yellow Wallpaper" is evident. They seem to be describing the same woman. We might ask students considering majors in medical or social science fields to research current knowledge about this condition. Some readers will recall the biography of poet Anne Sexton, whose psychosis following postpartum depression led both to a career as a writer and to her ultimate suicide. As late as the middle of the twentieth century, Sexton insisted that her work as a poet kept her alive rather than contributing to her psychosis. It was in spite of her intellectual activity that her mental illness finally won out. Even though the condition is taken seriously in Kellogg's 1882 quotation from a medical expert, the wording borders on the pejorative; there is a "sullen obstinacy," for example, and a shocking "immorality and obscenity" sometimes occurs in patients' speech. This "insanity of childbirth" is characterized by "active mania" much like that of Gilman's narrator. Kellogg's text implies paranoia in the frequent suspicion that one's food is being poisoned, whereas Gilman's protagonist centers her paranoia on the wallpaper and the house.

In both texts, however, postpartum symptoms may trigger underlying tendencies. Gilman's narrator tells of childhood experiences in which she saw her surroundings in an imaginative way that may either reflect the fantasies or presage mental illness. Whereas Gilman's narrator is freed from the responsibility of caring for her child and doesn't seem to think much about the baby, Kellogg describes the rejection of the child and even its attempted murder that we sometimes read about in court cases today. One of the ironies of Gilman's story is the husband's unwillingness to accept his wife's condition as real. Many mental illnesses are now being recognized as having a physiological basis in brain chemistry and function. Although Gilman blames the treatment of her narrator for driving her over the edge, Gilman did not try to raise her own child. Given the climate of divorce at the time, perhaps she had no choice. It is more likely, however, that she feared the recurrence of her illness or her inability to function as both mother and writer. Like Mitchell, Kellogg advises isolation during the manic phase of the disorder and counsels against excitement. He prescribes a change of scene, as the husband of Gilman's narrator has provided for her. But Kellogg ends with the suggestion that a "dear friend" could be called upon to visit. Readers wonder if her obsession might have been avoided if John had allowed his wife to have her cousins visit, as she so greatly desired.

If Kellogg's text were published today, readers would find a great many of his assumptions faulty. We know that genetic and congenital factors play a large part in the development of a child, but not in the naive ways assumed by Kellogg. Still, many pregnant women cultivate a peaceful atmosphere for the unborn child, playing classical music to influence developing neural pathways. Many of Kellogg's insights about eating whole foods and vegetables rather than meat are more accepted today than they were in his time. We are horrified when Gilman's character is forced to eat meat and to avoid exercise and when Mitchell fattens up his patients as they lie idle. We find Kellogg's ideas about sex a bit odd, however, and would not prohibit sex during pregnancy for fear that this might make the children more prone to sexual activity. We usually allow diet and exercise to naturally take care of constipation and do not fear poisoning by the "effete products" of digestion. While his warrants may be outdated, many of Kellogg's ideas about diet, exercise, and the avoidance of stimulants during pregnancy would be accepted today. Most modern readers find his assumptions about the treatment of mental illness in women to be more problematic, however.

PUNISHMENTS (p. 1376)

ROBERT BROWNING
My Last Duchess (p. 1376)

One of the most anthologized poems in the literary canon, Robert Browning's "My Last Duchess" epitomizes the dramatic monologue form and opens up our class discussion to issues of persona. As an audience of drama, a genre Browning tried with little success, we easily accept the notion that the actor who delivers the lines may differ a great deal from the character being portrayed. And in fiction, readers understand that the *narrator* and the author are not one and the same. In poetry, however, students tend to have more difficulty separating the voice we hear in the poem, usually called the "speaker," from the poet. This may be because we are accustomed to reading confessional poetry or texts inspired by William Wordsworth's romantic dictum that poetry should relate intense emotional experience "recollected in tranquillity." When students say that they do not like poetry, this is often the sort of poetry they mean. Dramatic monologues, with their links to the soliloquies and dialogues of drama, help students to recognize that poetry too may have a fictional element. The Greek word *persona* originally referred to the masks worn by actors in classical dramas like Sophocles' *Antigone* (p. 1306). When the speaker of the poem is obviously not the poet, we usually refer to the character we hear speaking in the poem as a persona. Usually, the speaker of a poem is not called a "narrator" unless the poem tells a story.

Although Robert Browning's biography does not play a direct part in the interpretation of this poem, since it presents a persona quite distant from his own personality, students may find it interesting that the dramatic monologue was an experimental form in his time. Robert Browning was a bit out of step with other Victorian poets like Alfred, Lord Tennyson, and Browning's wife Elizabeth Barrett Browning was more popular than her husband for her lyric poetry.

Students usually enjoy researching the romance between the Brownings. When he was thirty-four, Robert rescued Elizabeth, six years older, from a life as an invalid, hovered over by a domineering father. Students who have read Charlotte Perkins Gilman's "The Yellow Wallpaper" will recognize the sort of inactivity that was imposed upon Elizabeth Barrett before her marriage to Robert Browning, which was followed by a fifteen-year residence in Italy and the birth of their son. All evidence indicates that they were an extremely happy couple from the early days of their courtship until her death. Because "My Last Duchess" is about a bad husband, to put it mildly, Browning's biography thus provides an interesting contrast to the poem. Though the 1842 poem predates his romantic marriage to Elizabeth and their time in Italy by several years, it shows Robert Browning's ability to imagine the subtleties of power and sex in an Italian Renaissance setting where a rich man could do whatever he pleased.

Some scholars have pointed out that the dramatic monologue affords Browning the safety of speaking indirectly, forcing us to read the implicit meaning hidden beneath the actual words of the poem's persona. Because we want our college students to do just this, to go beyond the literal or reductive interpretations of textbook reading to explore less obvious issues in literature, "My Last Duchess" serves as a good starting point. Browning's complexity of characterization and his colloquial and experimental style have been linked to his literary ancestors William Shakespeare and John Donne; his contemporary Victorians, novelists Charles Dickens and George Eliot; and future modernist poets like T. S. Eliot and Ezra Pound, who both admired and parodied him. Because Browning's speaker suggests to his unseen auditor, the marriage broker about to get another young woman into a fine mess, that he "read" the portrait of his first wife, we may further use this poem to discuss the concept of reading a text. We like to bring in prints of paintings and have students read them from different

279

perspectives. They can then write descriptions or narratives, think of personal and intertextual connotations, make aesthetic evaluations, and/or discuss historical, sociological, or psychological issues. In class, we look for gaps and oppositions, consider audience and purpose, and talk about any other interpretive aspects of reading particular paintings. We define a "text" at this point as anything that can be read and interpreted, ranging from the anthropologist's reading of a cultural group to a jury's reading of the evidence in a court case to our various interpretations of literary works in a college literature class. We also explain that although it may be possible to misread a text, there is seldom only one valid reading of a given text and our interpretations often tell us as much about the readers — ourselves — as the text. Browning's poem connects well with this exercise, since the Duke of Ferrara, as the poet imagines him, seems to have had his young wife killed because of his reading of her demeanor with other men. As we listen to his reading, we judge him more critically than we do the young woman he describes.

The speaker of Browning's poem is based on the historical Alfonso II, Duke of Ferrara, who lived in Renaissance Italy in the 1500s, at the height of the flowering of art taking place in that country's city-states. The duke's very young first wife, Lucrezia, died mysteriously in 1561 after just three years of marriage. Soon after her death, the duke began negotiations with representatives of the Count of Tyrol, whose capital was in Innsbruck, to marry the count's niece. Here, the duke is expecting to replace the dead beauty with a count's daughter. In the dramatic monologue, we are to imagine the shocked wedding negotiator as he listens to a cool description of the preceding wife's shortcomings and the duke's response to them. Her sin has been what may be a pretty woman's tendency to flirt or simply a sweetness and kindness that reaches out to everyone. Her husband feels that such attention should be saved only for him, and seems to be especially bothered by her pleasure when the portrait artist compliments her beauty. She is not discriminating enough, he feels. He insists that it would be beneath his dignity to complain about her lack of decorum or to give her a chance to explain. There seems to be no suggestion that she has committed adultery or betrayed him in any way, though some readers can't resist blaming the victim, suspecting her of hidden sins. He tells the marriage broker that it is because she smiled at people more and more that he "gave commands; / Then all smiles stopped together." The reader is left to conclude that the speaker has ordered his wife killed because she is cheerful and friendly to people other than her aristocratic husband. Readers familiar with studies on spousal abuse see symptoms of a typical abuser in the duke. But unlike many abusers, this man possesses the power to get away with the ultimate abuse of murder. Some readers may be reminded of court cases in which wealthy defendants with skilled lawyers evade punishment. This is not even a question for the Renaissance nobleman in Browning's poem, since no one will dare call him to account. His complaints seem petty and arrogant to most readers, and his discussion of this topic with the agent of a potential bride's family has ominous implications. He's a scary, menacing man.

Although it is difficult to think of any positive qualities about the duke, some readers may admire his power and decisiveness. The duke is an art lover, obviously. But one wonders what happened to the fictitious Frà Pandolf, the artist Browning imagines creating the portrait of Lucrezia. Titian painted the duke, but there is no known painting of his young wife. Ironically, the duke now controls who gazes at her beauty; only he pulls the curtain aside. The duke may be warning the family of his new bride that he will be in complete control this time. Perhaps the first instinct of the count's agent is to bolt from the horror of what he has learned; the duke at one point feels the need to verbally pull him back and tell him that they should leave together. But another motive for revealing the painting may be to show off this object of art to the representative of an equally cultured household; the duke seems just as interested in pointing out the statue of Neptune by an artist from the count's own city. This is the duke's own private stash of art for his eyes only, and he thinks of wives in the same terms. The count's daughter will simply be an addition to his private collection of aesthetically pleasing objects. The duke speaks of these things matter-of-factly, almost off-handedly.

The monologue may be read in a conversational tone as one long speech, as Browning's choice of keeping it as one undivided stanza invites. Syntax and meter fight against each other in "My Last Duchess" in a way that submerges rhyme. If we follow the sense, we do not pause for a full stop at the end of lines, but let enjambment take us to the end of a sentence, often in the middle of a line. The poem is written in heroic couplets; that is, two successive lines in iambic pentameter rhyme with each other. Instructors might want to introduce definitions of poetic terms as we listen for the effects of Browning's stylistic choices. Because a dramatic monologue works best if it sounds as if a real person were speaking to an unseen listener, the poet may sacrifice some of the lyrical effects of poetry when he chooses this genre. Many of Browning's Victorian contemporaries frowned upon what they judged to be his clumsiness. Reading poetry in the wake of modernists who take their lead from Browning and others who were willing to be colloquial, and with a post-Whitman appreciation for free verse, today's readers usually are not as bothered by the conflict between syntactical rhythms and counted meter. The dramatic monologue allows Browning to develop a character who reveals himself through his own words. The poet trusts his readers to work through the difference between the message of the poem and the words of the villainous character, just as we deal with the disjunction between traditional meter and conversational sentence rhythms. As twentieth-century readers of a nineteenth-century poem about a sixteenth-century character, we might expect barriers to understanding.

Students inexperienced with reading poetry sometimes do feel at a loss when they first read the poem. It helps to provide the sort of context we've touched upon here. We could show students a few examples of Renaissance portraiture to set the mood. Reading the poem aloud may give the best grounding and allow the instructor to choose an emphasis; for example, the word *last* in the title and the first line needs to be read in a way that lets us know another duchess is waiting in the wings. Once they catch the character of the speaker, today's readers recognize the sort of snobbish, self-absorbed person that still exists and certainly existed in the 1800s. Although few men in Browning's time had the power of a Renaissance nobleman, we read of many autocrats who terrorized their wives and children. Later, when Browning would defy Elizabeth Barrett's father, he would be dealing with a similar sort of authoritarian man who felt he owned the women in his family body and soul. The laws in most countries in the nineteenth century, including the United States, would have allowed or even encouraged a man to beat his wife. We often read of women today who are in abusive relationships, "punished" by husbands or boyfriends for actions no less innocent than Lucrezia's seem to be. Browning's duke is more psychologically interesting than the ordinary bully, however. Rather than lashing out in anger, he acts in secret, never really approaching his wife with his dissatisfaction with her. Misplaced pride often keeps a person from revealing true feelings to a partner, and we often insist that the other person guess what is upsetting us, to anticipate our needs without our having to "stoop" to express them. Our students may have stories to share about when this has happened in their relationships, though it will be easier to recall when others have done it to us than when we have been guilty of it. Both men and women sometimes build scenarios in their minds that interpret innocent behavior according to a suspicious narrative they have imposed on a partner. Students might enjoy comparing the duke with the protagonist of Robert Olen Butler's "Jealous Husband Returns in Form of Parrot" (p. 1594), in which a husband makes similar judgments about his wife's behavior with more humorous results.

CAROLYN FORCHÉ
The Colonel (p. 1378)

Poet and peace activist Carolyn Forché calls her prose poem "The Colonel" a "documentary poem" and considers her work a "poetry of witness." We ask students to consider the possible reasons for Forché's use of these terms, exploring the ways in which "The Colonel" fits this description. Like a reporter with a video camera, the political poet records injustices for her audience to view. Although she provides some commentary, she primarily presents the details of what she sees, challenging the reader to make judgments about the subject. As a witness, she passes on the facts and holds them up to the light. She makes no apologies for having a political purpose, however, and does not pretend — as some writers might — that she is an objective observer. Like a photographer who aims the camera, the writer directs our gaze by the details she selects.

But the topics chosen by Carolyn Forché and other poets who write about social and political issues strike some American readers as inappropriate to poetry. Perhaps this is a reaction against moralistic and didactic literature that relegates art to an inferior position as the means to a political end. But most readers do not believe Forché's poetry sacrifices the subtleties of imagery and metaphor for the sake of her message. They feel that the poetry is more vivid because of its strong purpose. Forché reminds us that literary artists in many countries occupy a place of influence and respect, often holding positions of leadership in government or resistance movements. The way she usually tells her story, Carolyn Forché stumbled into international affairs, naively landing in El Salvador in 1978 just as war was breaking out and later finding herself in Beirut, Lebanon, as strife was heating up there. The fact is, however, that she has consistently taken stands for human rights, and as a commentator for public radio and an investigator for Amnesty International, she often finds herself in hot spots, since these are the places where human rights are likely to be abused.

As a teacher in the creative writing program at George Mason University and in workshops for writers in various parts of the country, Forché sees her job as equally proactive. She says that such programs play a subversive role in the academic world, "democratizing" education by privileging the voices of students. For her, teaching means involving students in creative and critical thinking. She advises students to learn to write by reading, suggesting to potential poets that they keep books of poetry in the bathroom and use their time there to read at least one poem a day. She conducts programs in which writers in graduate school creatively document in words and photographs the particular issues of an economically depressed region or move outside the university to research the experiences of Holocaust survivors. In 1998, Forché received the Edita and Ira Morris Hiroshima Foundation for Peace and Culture Award, an international prize recognizing her work for human rights and the "preservation of memory and culture."

In "The Colonel" Forché describes an arrogant man who would undoubtedly judge her work for human rights as without value. He mocks the power of the poet to accomplish any change that will stop men like himself: "Something for your poetry, no?" he says as he shows off his trophies, a batch of severed human ears. His action seems crude and sophomoric, reminding instructors of students who think they will shock us with lurid descriptions of adventures with drugs, alcohol, and explicit sex. He is "mean," both in the word's connotation of willingness to cause pain and in its sense of pettiness and poverty of spirit. The poet uses the natural symbolism of the ears, however, to catch our attention, to shake us into awareness of present tyranny — "this scrap of his voice" — and to be alert for approaching tyranny, with our ears "to the ground." The ending calls us back to the opening line of the poem, which suggests that we have "heard" something about the colonel's brutality and perhaps have dismissed it as folklore. The poem makes him seem ordinary at first, simply a family man having dinner. But we soon learn that he is cruel to the extent of turning even his house into a weapon. The colonel controls and dominates language. He is even compelled to silence the parrot, and the narrator's friend warns her to keep quiet as well, knowing that the colonel is getting ready to show off his trick with the ears.

Although the narrator's — and therefore the reader's — awareness of the colonel's barbarity escalates as the poem goes on, we feel his menace from the beginning lines. For example, the presence of a pistol is juxtaposed with details of everyday family life and with a poetic metaphor that compares the moon to a light bulb in the interrogation room of a prison. As we argue about whether or not Forché's text is really a poem, we should consider its use of metaphor, symbol, and imagery. The vivid visual image of the ears looking like peach halves and then coming to life in the water is not lyrical, but it is a simile that has symbolism and sensory power. Its conversational tone does not preclude its definition as poetry; compare, for instance, Robert Browning's "My Last Duchess," which directly precedes Forché's poem.

One aspect of poetry is compressed language that distills experience into a few carefully chosen words. This is therefore a poetic text, and the prose quality is more a factor of typography than genre. The short sentences could have been lines. Small groups of students might work together at a computer station to make "The Colonel" look more like a traditional poem, explaining to the class their decisions about where lines should end. Part of Forché's method is to make this poem of witness a documentation of the egotism and terrible small-mindedness of a military dictator. Not only does she make it look like prose, but she justifies margins so that they are perfectly straight, as a legal document would be. By turning his attempt to shock into a poem that reveals his character, the poet takes back the power of speech that the colonel seeks to undermine and control. He has meant the *text* of the ears to symbolize his power, but the poet uses it to ask her audience to listen attentively. Her decision to bury his words in her poem without quotation marks further emphasizes her linguistic coup. His words are no more important than the television commercial or the parrot's meaningless *hello*. We give him our attention only because we know he must be stopped and that others like him must be listened for. Although the story of the colonel has the ring of folklore, Carolyn Forché claims that this incident really happened, that the man was notorious for entertaining dinner guests in this way. Like narratives about war atrocities, the details seem too outlandish to be true, and we don't know whether to believe the author or not. Although it is fair to assume the colonel is based on someone the writer met in El Salvador, it is a good strategy to keep his exact identity generic. Tyrants exist in many times and places, and the colonel's universality helps us remember to be alert for them wherever they crop up.

The twentieth-century Central American dictator of Carolyn Forché's poem and the sixteenth-century Italian nobleman of Robert Browning's "My Last Duchess" could be the same man. Each seeks to subtly bully a guest, to send a warning that he has the power to command violence and will not hesitate to do so on the smallest pretext. Although we do not know who the victims of the colonel are, our knowledge of the arbitrary nature of political murder in El Salvador, especially the brutal killings of priests and other noncombatants, causes us to see their deaths and mutilations as unwarranted. A man who would coldly have a wife killed for smiling too much would have no trouble carrying out political executions or bragging about them at the dinner table.

The listeners in both poems are forced by caution to be passive. Nothing would be gained by challenging the dangerous tyrants of these poems. Forché's listener is the speaker of the poem, a persona who may be very close to the poet herself. Although she has the sense to remain silent in the presence of the colonel, she goes on to write a poem, a political action of potential consequence. We know less about the listener of Browning's poem, since it is the menacing duke whose voice we hear. There is a hint that the listener makes a move to leave, perhaps involuntarily; but he does not possess the power. Perhaps, he will advise the count to keep his daughter in Innsbruck, but we will never know.

Our students find Forché's diction easier to understand, since its simple, declarative sentences have an American directness that we are accustomed to hearing every day. Browning takes more work, both because his nineteenth-century British poetic style is more formal and because he is portraying a Renaissance character. Even though Browning's poem rhymes and has an underlying meter, both poems have the effect of conversational prose. Both writers deliberately choose this style to suit their content and the dramatic situation they have imagined. With their block form, the two poems even have a similar visual appearance.

SEAMUS HEANEY
Punishment (p. 1380)

In Northern Ireland where poet Seamus Heaney grew up, large areas are covered with peat bogs. Heaney tells of being fascinated even as a child with the amazing variety of objects that fall or are thrown into the bogs only to be found years later, preserved by the unique chemical properties of the watery, vegetation-rich soil. He recalls that people would store butter under the peat in the days before refrigeration, keeping it fresh for long periods of time. In his earlier poem "Bogland" Heaney mentions butter being discovered after hundreds of years still "salty and white," and he describes the quality of the bogland as "itself . . . kind, black butter." He remembers as a child the recovery of a prehistoric skeleton of a "Great Irish Elk" from a local bog and the newspaper pictures of his neighbors posing with the huge antlers.

This land had a habit of remembering, and Heaney himself came to see history as something that still exists in the present, each object reverberating with it and each human being echoing a heritage and mythology that does not die. As a Roman Catholic in Northern Ireland, Seamus Heaney would have been hard put to avoid a sense of history and politics. Students may be aware of religious and political issues that have plagued Ireland for centuries. They may have read poetry by the late-nineteenth-/early-twentieth-century writer William Butler Yeats, like Heaney a Nobel Prize laureate who wrote about Ireland's unique culture and history. Some may know about Irish culture from background reading on James Joyce. Instructors may need to remind many students of the social and historical context of Heaney's texts, however. Classes that have read Frank O'Connor's short story "Guests of the Nation" (p. 1257) in which Irish Republican soldiers are called upon to execute their English prisoners will find intertextual connections. We may recall from O'Connor's biography his imprisonment by an Irish political faction because he spoke against the brutal punishments dealt out to women who were judged too friendly to men of opposing political or religious groups. Heaney's poem "Punishment" refers to similar treatment in modern Belfast. Irish Republican Army sympathizers have been known to humiliate women who date British soldiers by shaving their heads, stripping them, coating them with tar, and then handcuffing them to railings for public ridicule.

With his knowledge of such politically motivated actions, his contact with history and mythology, and his personal experience of growing up near the peat bogs of Ireland, Seamus Heaney's reading in 1969 of *The Bog People* by Danish archaeologist P. V. Glob led to a powerful convergence of interests that energized Heaney's writing. The book contains photographs of preserved bodies from bogs in various locations in northern Europe. The details that remain of faces, bodies, and artifacts are stunning. Glob's book was published by Cornell University Press in 1969. If the book is available to you, take it to class; nothing can replace seeing the photographs themselves, and students will understand why Heaney was impressed by them. Readers of our anthology should also turn to the final paragraphs of Naomi Wolf's essay "The Making of a Slut" (p. 1035) in which the writer — perhaps inspired by Heaney — describes the same young girl. Glob sees some of the bog people as human sacrifices, offered to a pre-Christian earth mother deity, and Heaney makes that connection in some poems in his sequence inspired by Glob's book: for example, "Bog Queen" and "The Tolland Man." The poet sees "an archetypal pattern" in these deaths and explains in his nonfiction "Feelings into Words" that the photographs of these ancient victims converge for him with similar images of "atrocities, past and present, in the long rites of Irish political and religious struggles" (58). Glob goes to first-century Roman historian Tacitus for a hint about the girl who inspires Heaney's poem "Punishment." His account describes a situation chillingly like that of her Irish counterparts. "Tacitus names a special punishment for adultery by women," Glob writes, "but says nothing about male adultery. The adulterous woman had her hair cut off in the presence of her relatives and was then scourged out of the village. This calls to mind one of the bog people in particular, the young girl from Windeby, in Domland Fen. She lay naked in her grave in the peat, her hair shaved off, with nothing but a collar of ox-hide round her neck and with bandaged eyes" (153). Elsewhere in the book, Glob describes her burial in minute detail, telling us that she was around fourteen, that her hair was originally light blonde and had been chopped off and shaven unevenly, that her hands and facial features were "delicate," that she hadn't been getting enough to eat. Pollen samples show that she was roughly contemporary with Tacitus. Her woven blindfold would have been bright red and yellow at the time she died. She wore only this and an ox-hide collar. She had been drowned and covered with birch branches and a large stone. Glob includes with his description three photographs: one of her body, one of her face, and one of her remarkably preserved brain (112–14).

Heaney weaves many of the details from the archaeologist's written and visual texts into his poem. The scientist's account is written for a popular audience rather than for experts; he even includes in his introduction letters from a group of English schoolgirls interested in his discoveries and dedicates his book to them and his own daughter, Elsebeth. It is not surprising, therefore, that we detect empathy in his descriptions. These are real people for him, and we cannot look at the photographs without feeling their individuality. Seamus Heaney uses sensory imagery that empathizes even further, evoking the physical sensations she must have felt, especially the cold. He shows us her fragility; her rib cage is "frail," she is "Little" and "undernourished," and she is like a "sapling" — a slender young tree.

He shows her as vulnerable, using the word *naked* and referring to parts of the body we think of as tender, her "nipples" and the "nape / of her neck." She is passive, since we feel and see what is done to her, but not what she does. We feel compassion for her and perhaps a touch of sexual or aesthetic attraction. The poet does not address her directly until the sixth stanza. This shifts the perspective somewhat, now focusing on the feelings of the speaker while the reader has previously envisioned the girl herself. This allows a movement in time. He first projects us into the past and brings the individual victim to life. After we have felt something for the first-century woman, we are more prepared to hear the comparison with the political present and the speaker's status as a "voyeur," a silent witness to modern "tribal" vengeance. For Heaney, the bog woman drowned for sexual transgressions, the Belfast girls tarred for similar crimes, the speaker of the poem, and the reader who joins him as a bystander are all part of the same story.

A key to one possible theme for the poem is Heaney's use of the word *scapegoat* in the seventh stanza and his allusion to "stones of silence" in the eighth stanza. Both are biblical referents that symbolize the shifting of the sins of a culture to a selected victim. The scapegoat in ancient Israel was driven into the wilderness, carrying the evils of the community, as a way of acting out repentance and absolution. We have come to use the word to refer to a person or group unfairly punished for the misdeeds of others, often the person or persons exacting the punishment. The "stones of silence" may refer to an incident in which Jesus defends a woman accused of adultery, a crime punishable by stoning. He implies that no one really has the right to judge and punish the personal behavior of another since no human being can claim moral perfection. The allusion may also relate to another biblical stoning in Acts 7:58 in which Saul, not yet transformed into St. Paul by a dramatic conversion experience, stands by and holds coats as a mob murders the first Christian martyr Stephen. The poem's speaker feels that he engages in a similar complicity in which he does not fully participate in political violence but understands the emotions that underpin it. Heaney has lost friends to terrorism, and, as a Roman Catholic raised just thirty miles northwest of Belfast, he understands the reasoning behind the rage against British occupation and those who go along with it. But he shows the victim in the bog and her future sisters in Ireland to be incongruously fragile and pathetic targets.

The speaker calls himself "an artful voyeur." A voyeur is usually defined as a person who obtains sexual gratification from observing the sexual activities or the bodies of other people. The reader joins the speaker in looking at the naked body of the victim. (Who wouldn't find the image of her nipples as "amber beads" irresistible?) But we go even further to invade the "darkened combs" — the valleys — of her "exposed" brain and to inspect her skeleton. In a sense, to read is to be a voyeur, and to write is to be an artful one. The poet uses her for his art, and we find pleasure in the images he creates. But whereas the speaker may do nothing about the violence that he witnesses, this cannot be said of the poet, since he does not stand idly by. He takes the action of writing the poem. By exposing our own voyeurism to us, he may challenge us to act.

In the speech Seamus Heaney gave when accepting his Nobel Prize for Literature in 1995, he relates the story of a busload of men stopped by a masked band of gunmen in Northern Ireland. When the men, presumed to be Protestant terrorists, shouted for the Catholics to step forward, the lone Catholic in the group felt the passenger next to him squeeze his hand to pull him back with the silent promise that his Protestant friends would keep his religion a secret. The Catholic decided to stand up for his faith and stepped forward anyway. He was the only survivor. The terrorists pushed him to the side and opened fire on the Protestants, and the Catholic lived to tell of this small gesture of peace. It is this squeeze of the hand that Heaney calls for, the small sign of friendship and solidarity that refuses to hand over the scapegoat for condemnation.

In the last stanza of "Punishment" Heaney admits that the issues that divide are complex. The poem's speaker faults himself for being willing to "connive / in civilized outrage." The word *connive* implies an action that disregards or tacitly consents to a wrongdoing. The word has pejorative connotations. If we called someone conniving, we would be hurling an insult. But his usage is ironic. He leaves some question about the act he takes himself to be silently condoning. Is it the "revenge" that he sees as the wrongdoing? Or is it his own sense of "outrage" that he sees as a betrayal? Does he connive when he shares the outrage directed at the woman who has sinned against the community or the world's outrage against his fellow Catholics who punish her? The tarring of the woman who has committed treason by sleeping with the enemy is an act against one's own: A "tribal, intimate revenge" that the speaker claims to understand. Though readers tend to romanticize such relationships as Romeo-and-Juliet situations, we might have students imagine scenarios in which we saw our nation occupied by an oppressive enemy. Would we easily forgive someone who willingly formed relationships with the men who abused our fathers and brothers?

As a writer, Heaney is sometimes criticized for being disloyal to his own Northern Irish Catholics, failing to take a strong stand against oppression. Others fault him for raising such political issues in poetry at all. Still, by linking the treason of the Irish women with the presumably less political adultery of the bog woman, and by painting her with such compassion, Heaney makes the brutality toward these women seem to be directed primarily toward their sexual transgression. Seen in this way, the revenge of the "tribe" reminds readers of the Chinese villagers who punish the whole family of an adulteress in Maxine Hong Kingston's "No Name Woman" (p. 1026) or of the men of some Muslim cultures who execute daughters and sisters who go against their sexual mores. Rarely are men punished for having sex that does not involve violence, but women often are.

Seamus Heaney uses down-to-earth language — no pun intended — to describe the woman in the bog. Many words are one syllable. He ends the fourth stanza with the hyphenated "oak-bone, brain-firkin," reminiscent of the Anglo-Saxon rhythms of *Beowulf* or the inventions of Gerard Manley Hopkins, a favorite poet of Heaney's. A firkin is a small cask. She is therefore a container for the brain whose complexity he admires with voyeuristic interest in a later stanza. Because his diction consists mostly of strong, terse nouns and verbs, the adjectives he does use stand out vividly: *naked, amber, frail, drowned,* and so forth. Rather than depending on meter and rhyme, Heaney's rhythm emerges as a natural consequence of word choice and content. Much of the sound depends on subtle assonance and alliteration. Notice in stanza 9, for example, the repetition of the consonant *b* and the vowel *o*, with the deliciously mouth-filling vocalic echo of *combs* and *bones* filling in for formal rhyme. If the poet had substituted the synonym *valleys* for the more localized English word *combs*, much would have been lost. The single-syllable words of the poem's first line literally pull us into the poem, communicating a feeling of forced movement that exactly fits the sense.

In the three poems we have read in this cluster, punishments seem far more brutal than the crime would warrant, and all are even more disturbing because they continue after the victim's death. Robert Browning's "My Last Duchess" describes a murder that seems to have been prompted by nothing more than a young girl's pleasure in social interactions. Her blush may as easily have been interpreted as modesty that honored her husband. But her husband degrades her memory by describing her supposed sins to a stranger who will provide her replacement. Carolyn Forché's bully in "The Colonel" goes beyond merely killing his opponents to mutilating them and desecrating their memories with a tasteless show. The women of Seamus Heaney's "Punishment" are stripped naked before the community, subjected to attacks on their beauty, and held up to public humiliation. The bog woman is drowned and weighted down, perhaps being sacrificed in a religious rite meant to return the community to proper order.

In each poem, control is maintained through the extreme exercise of power, and the language is controlled as well. The subject of silence is implied in Browning's poem, since we hear only the voice of the duke. He has ownership of language in his world, and the listener in the poem cannot escape it. He has silenced even the nonverbal expressions of his wife. The listener will have to decide, however, if he will share the information he is given with the father of the duke's new bride. The theme of listening is foregrounded in Forché's poem from beginning to end. The colonel seeks to control language, the severing of ears being a symbolic image of this attempt. But the final image of ears pressed to the ground subverts his power, as does the poem itself. Again, the reluctant audience must make a decision to listen alertly and to act upon what is learned. The speaker of Seamus Heaney's "Punishment" gives us the metaphor "stones of silence" and the image of himself standing "dumb" as he watches the humiliated women. To keep silent is sometimes to take an action, he implies. To stand aside may be to assist in wielding a weapon.

It is difficult to imagine such extreme punishments taking place in the contemporary United States with the approval of the community. However, students may suggest examples of subtle ways that we punish individuals, symbolically overreacting to transgressions or opposition. Do they know people who have been punished by their families for forming relationships outside of their religion or ethnic group? Do American subcultures enforce silence on some, seek to control language, or hold transgressors up to humiliation? Perhaps class members can offer examples from their own experience of the double standard that punishes women for sexual behavior accepted as the norm for men.

SHERMAN ALEXIE
Capital Punishment (p. 1382)

Spokane/Coeur d'Alene Sherman Alexie likes to shake people up. If there is a stereotype to be broken or a genre to be challenged, he is the man to do it. He is first a poet, but his poetry edges into narrative and prose poetry, whereas his short stories — some of the "sudden fiction," short-short-story genre — have the feel of poetry. He has been called "a storyteller with a poetic streak." Alexie says that his poems are essentially stories and acknowledges a "strong, narrative drive" in all of his work. In the introduction to his screenplay for the movie *Smoke Signals*, published in paperback by Hyperion in 1998, Alexie talks about genre:

> When people ask me, and they do ask me, how I feel about making the difficult transition from writing novels to writing screenplays, I am not always sure what to say.
>
> I mean, screenplays are more like poetry than like fiction. Screenplays rely on imagery to carry the narrative, rather than the other way around. And screenplays have form. Like sonnets, actually. Just as there are expectations of form, meter, and rhyme in a sonnet, there are the same kinds of expectations for screenplays.
>
> Of course, free verse poetry subverts all expectations of formalist poetry.
>
> So, I wonder aloud, who is writing free verse screenplays? (x)

Though his movie is not free verse, it begins and ends with poetry and includes songs, some of them written by Sherman Alexie and his cowriter Jim Boyd. For Alexie, songs are people's poetry. One of the songs in *Smoke Signals* bears the memorable title "John Wayne's Teeth." Students might enjoy viewing the movie and comparing Louise Erdrichs poem "Dear John Wayne" (p. 1016). *Smoke Signals*, loosely based on Alexie's 1993 book of interconnected short stories *The Lone Ranger and Tonto Fistfight in Heaven*, breaks new ground as a movie written, directed, coproduced, and performed by Native Americans.

Like his poetry, Alexie's movie challenges stereotypes of American Indians as necessarily shamans or warriors, and his texts exist in the present rather than a romantic *Dances with Wolves* past. His characters are not magical holy men and women who turn into deer or possess supernatural spirituality. Alcohol and poverty play a part in their lives because these are realities of reservation life, but his characters are not pathetic victims who say, as Dustin Hoffman's character does in *Little Big Man*, "Today is a good day to die." Alexie says that there is no such thing as a good day to die, and he parodies the line: "Today is a good day to play basketball" or "Today is a good day to have breakfast," his characters quip. Humor and irony energize all of Alexie's work.

It has also been pointed out that his work also takes an argumentative rhetorical stance. This is an angry young poet, and he has a right to be. The first peoples of the Americas have endured a Holocaust, and Sherman Alexie and other Native American writers represented in this anthology do not intend to let anyone forget this fact. Consider the texts, biographical headnotes, and instructor's manual discussions (in the order in which they appear) for N. Scott Momaday, Linda Hogan, Richard Rodriguez, Leslie Marmon Silko, Chrystos, Louise Erdrich, and Gabriel García Márquez, and the representation of Caliban and Ariel as indigenous peoples in William Shakespeare's *The Tempest.* In addition to the "should be simple" equation in line 98 of "Capital Punishment" — "1 death + 1 death = 2 deaths" — Alexie has suggested a more complex equation: "Survival = Anger × Imagination" or sometimes "Poetry = Anger × Imagination." Ironically and appropriately, we may interpret his variation to mean that no one simple answer exists to any problem, or we may notice that the equations suggest another truth for Sherman Alexie and other forthright voices in current Native American literature: Poetry = Survival.

Alexie argues against the death penalty in his poem "Capital Punishment" first by raising the issue of racial inequities in the system. He goes on to bring up the implicit point that the electric chair constitutes cruel and unusual punishment by relating the story of "a black man" — reiterating the inequality — who was executed twice because the chair malfunctioned. Readers may recall true horror stories of the flames, smoke, and other physical atrocities Alexie describes in the lines following line 74. The speaker eats from the plate of the man to be executed and hopes to be with him in his death. He develops this idea further in the last three stanzas of the poem to imply that "any of us" — the speaker and the reader united in the first-person plural pronoun but alone in the unique *any* — could be connected with the executed man, that we have all "sinned" and all are equally vulnerable to death. The arbitrary connotations of being struck by lightning add to his argument against the unjust selection of those to be executed.

Since any of us in a college classroom are likely to be called for jury duty during the next few years, it makes sense to think about our attitudes toward the death penalty. We might have students look back at this point to Joyce Carol Oates's observations of jury bias in "I, the Juror" (p. 1294). Ironically, people who admit to being against capital punishment are not allowed to serve on "death-qualified" juries when such a verdict is legally possible, a fact that may skew judgment more surely against mercy for the defendant. Students may recall the furor from usually vocal advocates of the death penalty like Jerry Falwell who were protesting the execution of a pretty, white, born-again Christian woman on death row in Texas for a brutal murder. Gov. George W. Bush refused to pardon the woman, opting for consistency. Alexie questions why we feel that one person's death is more acceptable than another's. Some readers may not change their minds about the death penalty no matter how rhetorically effective they concede the opposing argument to be.

One of Alexie's most compelling points revolves around the definition of the word *kill*. Proponents of the death penalty when challenged with the biblical commandment *Thou shalt not kill* contend that the Hebrew word should have been translated *murder*, referring to guidelines in the Bible for carrying out capital punishments. The term *capital punishment* is itself a euphemism, as is *execution*. Alexie describes the procedures linguists use to edit dictionaries, a process students may not realize is based on studies of how words are actually being spoken in social and written contexts rather than on prescriptions for proper speech. In line 82, the poet repeats the word *kill*, refusing to gloss over the reality of what is taking place. We may try to sugar-coat it, but killing is killing.

Alexie refers to the divisiveness of the issues surrounding victimization and punishment with the observation that we "throw the killers in one grave / and victims in another. We form sides / and have two separate feasts." In most traditions, funerals are accompanied by eating. Readers may recall Hamlet's ironic observation that it was thrifty of his uncle to make the funeral feast do double duty as a wedding reception. Alexie is equally ironic in making his speaker a cook who prepares the last meal for the execution victim. He imagines a vestige of his own being reaching the body of the man as he is dying, a sort of communion.

Just as he demands an honest definition of the word *kill*, the speaker questions the meaning of the word *witness*. We recall that Carolyn Forché calls hers a "poetry of witness." Sherman Alexie has a political agenda as surely as she does; he may in fact have more legitimacy because he is a person of color who realizes the part prejudice plays in deciding who goes to the electric chair. The speaker's first claim that he is not a witness simply seems to differentiate the role of official witness to an execution from the role of cook. But he moves soon after this first denial into an assertion about the racial inequality of execution, and tells us that this can be proven by the facts — hard rhetorical evidence that we can verify. We remember that a witness may be someone called upon to testify, to offer proof. In line 22, the denial that he is a witness becomes a refrain, a line that will echo throughout the poem. This time, the context indicates that he will not stand as a witness against a man who loves another man, that he does not pass judgment. The next negation of his witness status comes after he has told "a story" about a failure of the electric chair and the subsequent double execution of a man. This is hearsay evidence and is anecdotal, so we would not be expected to give it as much rhetorical weight. He does not have the authority of a true witness. The irony, of course, is that such evidence tends to be extremely persuasive, though we like to think we are more swayed by logic and facts. The next repetition comes when the speaker is trying desperately to block out the reality of what is happening by sitting in the dark and chanting to himself "not to look at the clock." At this point, the claim that he is not a witness has the panicky tone of a prayer or a mantra — *Please God don't make me be a witness*, he seems to say underneath the words. After powerful imagery describing the body's reaction to the jolt of electricity, he again claims not to be a witness, though he sounds like someone who knows what he is talking about, and we now trust the ethos he projects. Finally, in line 102, he admits to being a witness to the culture's denials, curiosities, and divisions, if not to the execution itself. He witnesses with his anger and imagination from the pit of the stomach of the executed man.

It cannot be denied that race is a factor in the dealing out of punishments in the United States. Some readers will find that Alexie's ethnicity lends authority to his argument, whereas others may feel he has an ax (a tomahawk?) to grind and his ethos is therefore undermined by his lack of objectivity. Some readers see Alexie's argument against inconsistency as more persuasive than his argument against capital punishment per se. Whereas the movie *Dead Man Walking* juxtaposes the faces of the victims with that of the executed man as he dies, Alexie's speaker imagines himself as present through the sharing of food. This is not a story about the victim or the crime but about the execution and the nature of witnessing. The victim in Alexie's poem is mentioned matter-of-factly, in spite of the violence of the image describing his death, and the speaker follows quickly with a joke about the stereotype of Indians gambling. The humor works on multiple levels, since casinos are one of the few sources of economic power that tribal governments have, but gambling can be a seductive addiction like alcohol.

Games and sports took the place of war in the history of several tribes, and the "Indian killer" in the poem stands ironically in a tradition, even as we laugh at Alexie's subversion of the stereotype. This particular use of humor is typical of Alexie's style, deflecting pathos, bitterness, and prejudice with irony. In the notes to his screenplay for *Smoke Signals* Alexie praises actor Irene Bedard for ad-libbing a "very Indian moment" as Suzy Song. As she hands over the can of ashes containing the cremated remains of Victor Joseph's father, she jokes deadpan, "This is Arnold. He ain't looking so good." Alexie's conclusion is that filmmakers should learn from this: "Cast Indians as Indians, because they'll give better performances" (162). At the end of the poem "Capital Punishment" Alexie offers another image that readers could interpret as ironic. Electricity is electricity, whether in a chair or in lightning, just as killing is killing whether it is done by an Indian or a government. We — the speaker, the poet, and the reader — are not qualitatively different in our humanity from the man who is brought by just one of his sins through a system as arbitrary as lightning to "headlines and ash." Although readers may vary in their guesses about their possible epitaphs after standing on a hill in a thunderstorm, an appropriate one might be, "We knew she didn't have enough common sense to come in out of the rain."

Both Sherman Alexie in "Capital Punishment" and Carolyn Forché in "The Colonel" assume readers who critically question what they are told. We want convincing evidence, so they offer it. But they also trust their readers to think for themselves as they consider the images the poets project, to come to as reasonable conclusions from the implicit messages as we would from more overt polemics. Like the word *witness*, the word *tribal* has divergent connotations. For the first peoples of the American continent, identification with a tribe is both legally and culturally important. Different tribes require different degrees of genetic inheritance for full tribal membership and the benefits that now accrue from belonging to a separate nation within the nation of the United States.

Such identification has had its drawbacks in the past, to say the least. Writers wishing to describe ethnicity constantly rephrase to keep from saying *Native American* yet again, knowing that editors will probably cut out references to *American Indians*. But some people within these ethnic groups object to the pretentiousness of the term *Native American*; one Internet Web site of the Choctaw Nation, for example, proclaims "No Native Americans here, just Indians!" Using tribal names seems more precise, but this doesn't help when a person is qualified by ancestry to register as a member of more than one tribe. Nevertheless, the word *tribal* in this sense has an objective connotation, serving simply as a descriptor.

As a person becomes involved in the characteristics that make his or her particular group unique, *tribal* can take on positive cultural undertones, can be a source of self-esteem. When Seamus Heaney uses the word to describe the actions of his own Irish "tribe" of Roman Catholics, however, the word takes on pejorative connotations. Just as non-European or non-Christian societies were long considered "primitive" and without culture, Heaney's characterization of the extreme revenge carried out against women as *tribal* implies negatively critical connotations. The division he describes by the word is similar to the one Alexie evokes by his image of separate funeral feasts. In Carolyn Forché's poem, too, the colonel acts tribally, in Heaney's sense of the word, as the leader of a faction who feels justified in any action taken against the opposing tribe. The taking of ears may remind us of scalping, of accounts of ancient Assyrians piling up body parts as trophies, of heads of Catholics or leaders of peasant revolts impaled on the railings of London Bridge.

Whereas the first two poems of this cluster confine their documentation of a character's speech or action to a one-stanza block, Seamus Heaney and Sherman Alexie allow more white space to separate the phrases in their speakers' stories. When white space is used, whether at the line or stanza breaks of a poem or at the beginning of a paragraph of prose, the pace slows down and the words nearest the white space are emphasized. Like the spaces within the geometric solid shapes of a sculpture or the rests in a piece of music, the pauses of a literary text count. Students might be asked to note the words that come just before a break in Alexie's two-line stanzas to determine if they tend to convey important images. One result of the slowing of pace is an increased sense of spontaneity and intimacy. Rather than demonstrating a character's control of language, the poet gives space for our entry into the issue, allowing a dialogue between reader and speaker as we think about what is said. This does not mean that the poems of Heaney and Alexie are more or less effective in communicating their message than those of Browning and Forché, but simply that their method and purpose are different.

REVENGE (p. 1388)

EDGAR ALLAN POE

The Cask of Amontillado (p. 1388)

Most students have read Edgar Allan Poe in high school, perhaps the spooky novella *The Fall of the House of Usher*, short stories like "The Telltale Heart" and "The Black Cat," or the much-anthologized poems "The Raven" and "Annabel Lee." They may even be familiar with "The Cask of Amontillado." Rather than covering territory with which they may already be familiar, we invite students to address issues they may not have considered before. If they have studied the story in high school, they may have considered its suspense and other narrative elements. In a college class, they may explore instead how the story illustrates the issue of carnival, in which the rules of society are turned upside down. Or they may consider the implications of class in nineteenth-century America and speculate about the writer's decision to set his story in an anonymous European setting.

Students enjoy researching and debating details of Poe's various and conflicting biographies. Since the writer even sensationalized himself, and readers often have difficulty separating the creator of his texts from their narrators, issues remain open about his addictions, his romances, his family relationships, and the extent of his genius and his madness. Many college students will relate to the problems that arose between Edgar Allan Poe and his foster father John Allan when the poet was their own age. His heredity must have presented cause for concern to both men as Poe came of age and his artistic temperament and eccentricity began to manifest. The carnival quality to his life before his mother died when he was two years old and he came into the aristocratic Allan household would surely have been seen as a foreshadowing. His parents were itinerant actors, just a step up from vagrant gypsies in the eyes of polite society in 1809, and his natural father had been an alcoholic unwilling or unable to take responsibility for his family. To understand nineteenth-century views about parental influence on character and the implications for Poe's self-image, we might turn to the theories of John Harvey Kellogg (p. 1370) in the cluster of background materials for Charlotte Perkins Gilman's "The Yellow Wallpaper."

Some critics believe that "The Cask of Amontillado" reflects Poe's relationship with his foster father. Conflicts with John Allan had begun even before Poe flunked out of West Point because he felt his allowance was inadequate and the military atmosphere was oppressive, and therefore stopped attending classes. Poe had already seen some literary work published by this time and turned to writing as a profession after it became apparent that he would be disinherited. Perhaps the flighty, alcohol-soaked Fortunato, with his carnival trappings of a fool, represents the ungrateful son in a bit of ironic self-parody, and the bitter and revengeful Montresor represents the rigid, unforgiving father tormented by a "thousand injuries." The hyperbole of the narrator marks him as unreliable, and the reader is left to wonder if Fortunato has truly insulted Montresor or if the narrator is simply paranoid. Interested students might compare this narrator with other insane protagonists in Poe's fiction. The symbolic walling up of a victim is a recurring motif, appearing in both "The Telltale Heart" and "The Black Cat" — stories in which the narrator imagines himself to be clever but gives himself away.

Montresor seems to be successful, however, and much more in control of himself than the usually manic and hallucinating madmen of the other stories. He is actually quite funny to some readers; we laugh at his ironic assurances that Fortunato will not die of the cold and niter, his toasting of Fortunato's "long life," and his revelation of the trowel underneath his cloak as proof that he is a mason. He ridicules the secretive Masonic brotherhood, itself an elitist organization, reversing the ceremony in which the initiate moves from darkness into light. The narrator's echoing screams and laughter can be imagined as hilarious if the reader decides to agree with Montresor that Fortunato deserves his fate. They are nightmarish otherwise. Readers may decide to read the story first in total agreement with Montresor and a second time with doubts.

Dramatic irony is added to Montresor's verbal irony because the audience understands that Fortunato's unknowing descent into the bowels of the earth is a descent toward death. The niter reminds us of hellish brimstone, and the flambeaux — the torches — are described by a word that reminds us of flames. Montresor's coat of arms makes a visual allusion to a verse in the Bible directed toward the serpent who tempts Eve to disobey God in the Garden of Eden. When God expels humanity from the garden in response to this original sin, he also curses the serpent, saying that Eve's offspring "shalt bruise thy head and thou shalt bruise his heel" (Genesis 3:15). This gives Montresor a Satanic aura. His family motto — *Nemo me impune lacessit* — means *No one wounds me with impunity*, a sinister threat, but also the motto of Scotland and the Stuart kings. Some scholars see in this yet another connection to John Allan, a man of Scottish descent and a Scottish Rite Mason. By this interpretation Poe would be the hapless Fortunato.

The name is symbolic, indicating that Fortunato has been blessed. Perhaps, like Poe, he has been fortunately rescued into privilege. Whether we believe that he has really harmed the narrator or not, we recognize Fortunato as an elitist. His pride in his ability to judge fine wine marks him as an aristocrat who needs to be taken down a notch. Seen in this way, it may be Fortunato who symbolizes John Allan and other moneyed representatives of the upper class and Montresor who fulfills Poe's fantasies of revenge. When Poe ends the tale with the epitaph *"In pace requiescat!"* he continues the irony. The words traditionally mean, "Rest in peace," but experts have pointed out that *In pace* can also describe solitary confinement in a monastic prison.

As students think about who the narrator may be addressing, they may recall the dramatic monologue of another nobleman, Robert Browning's Renaissance duke in "My Last Duchess." Although they are writing in different countries, Browning and Poe offered the two texts to a public audience at roughly the same time. Perhaps Poe's narrator has a similar motive to Browning's; he may be giving the listener a sinister warning that he is a person to be feared. If he is speaking fifty years later, however, he may be justifying his actions to a confessor or another person attending his deathbed. Montresor accuses Fortunato of adding insult to injury, but he keeps to these abstract, general descriptions, so the audience does not know what Fortunato has done. No matter what the crime, we cannot envision its being severe enough to warrant being buried alive. Therefore, it is best left unexplained.

Like Browning's Duke of Ferrara, Poe's nobleman does not stoop to discuss the matter with the person he sees as challenging his pride. This would give him away. But, unlike Browning's character, Montresor feels that revenge must be carried out personally with the full understanding of the offending victim. The carnival setting makes possible the image of the ridiculous victim, drunk and dressed like a clown going foolishly to his death. He is amazed by the luck of finding such fine wine during carnival and is drunk enough from his Mardi Gras revels to accept as sincere the false flattery praising his expertise. Montresor uses reverse psychology to entrap Fortunato into volunteering. Poe establishes early that Fortunato is a con man, but that he knows his wine. Montresor's victory is sweeter for his success in conning a con. Perhaps he uses the word *amontillado* so much to parody the name dropping of rare vintages engaged in by pretentious foreign charlatans who make a living from "imposture upon the British and Austrian *millionnaires*," as the narrator describes this Italian *quack*, Fortunato.

When Fortunato pleads with Montresor at the end of the story, saying "For the love of God," Montresor mocks him by throwing the words back. Students may feel that this blasphemy indicates that Montresor is completely evil. Others may argue that he feels so justified in his revenge that he believes God is on his side against the sinful and frivolous Fortunato. Readers may recall that in the second paragraph of the story the narrator anticipates the "immolation" of his enemy. The word *immolation* refers to a human sacrifice. Fortunato does not answer Montresor's final mockery, and Montresor throws a torch into the wall with the imprisoned man. At this point the bells jingle in reply, perhaps as Fortunato moves involuntarily to avoid the flames. When this sound sickens the narrator's heart, he attributes his reaction to the atmosphere of the catacombs and leaves. With the jingling of the bells, Fortunato has the last word, since the narrator cannot echo him in ridicule.

Many readers will identify with Fortunato because he seems merely foolish whereas the narrator commits premeditated murder in a heartless manner. Hardier souls may temporarily abandon their morality and identify with the ironically single-minded Montresor. A case can be made for Montresor as satanic. Others may see him as the wildly insane epitome of an Edgar Allan Poe unreliable first-person narrator.

LOUISE ERDRICH

Fleur (p. 1394)

Most readers of Louise Erdrich's short story "Fleur" in our college classes will approach it as a self-contained text. Instructors who have read Louise Erdrich's complex series of interwoven novels, composed of interrelated short stories about several interconnected families, may be tempted to explain more about the characters than students are ready to hear. Instead, we can invite interested readers to explore the longer fiction on their own, noting how the author makes changes to fit her new purposes. "Fleur" becomes a chapter of the novel *Tracks*, for example, and another short story that deals with the narrator of "Fleur" as an adult — "St. Marie" — makes its way into the novel *Love Medicine*.

The narrator of "Fleur" is Pauline Puyat, who grows up to be the cruel nun, Sister Leopolda. Perhaps in the story here we glimpse the source of the child's bitterness and rage as an adult. Interestingly, the narrator speculates that Fleur might have been compelled to stop in this particular town because of the spire of the Catholic church. But although this may be a symbol of power for Pauline, there is no indication that Fleur is attracted by this particular brand of the supernatural. Fleur, at least in the reading of the people around her, is connected with forces in nature that are fatal to men. The author, Louise Erdrich, is affected by both the Roman Catholicism and Black Forest witchiness of her European ancestry and the windigos, water monsters, and transformed animals of her Chippewa side. It's intriguing in this context that Erdrich's contribution to a feminist book about rape issues includes a photograph of herself in her white confirmation dress and veil. "The veil is the mist before the woman's face that limits her vision to the here, the now, the inch beyond her nose," Erdrich writes. "It is an illusion of safety, a flimsy skin of privacy that encourages violation. The message behind the veil is touch me, I'm yours. The purity is fictional, coy. The veil is the invitation to tear it away" (in Emilie Buchwald et al., *Transforming a Rape Culture* [Minneapolis, MN: Milkweed, 1993], 335–39).

The issue has been raised that this story might better be titled "Pauline" since she is the narrator who exacts revenge for the brutal rape of Fleur by Pauline's stepfather and the other men at the butcher shop. But Fleur Pillager is the central figure of the story. In Pauline, we have the sort of child narrator often used in fiction to give a fresh perspective to the activities of adults. Pauline is less naive than is usually the case with such narrators, and we may notice that the date of the story indicates that she is recalling this from the distance of old age. One element of the story is Pauline's pathetic understanding of her own invisibility to the men. She, like the title character, is a female who is shunned by her community.

But it is Fleur who affects everyone around her so strongly that they die from her influence or avoid her in fear or rape her to take revenge on her for exerting power and independence. The supernatural elements of the story keep the power in Fleur's hands; otherwise, she'd be a pathetic victim. We do feel compassion for her, since from her childhood she seems to have been blamed for things that are not her fault. The "results" of the curse of saving her life on the hapless Chippewa men are laughable to the reader just plunging into the story. But most readers come to accept her special relationship with nature and may notice that the animal imagery connected with Fleur begins in the first paragraph, where she shivers like a dog.

The narrator frames the story of Fleur's sojourn off the reservation in the mean little town of Argus with scenes of Fleur at Lake Turcot. The story recalls recorded legends of monsters in lakes. In one story, a girl strikes off the tail of a "lion" in Leech Lake and it turns out to be pure copper, which her father sells, making the family's fortune. Some folklorists speculate that the use of the word *lion* to describe a creature already in Native American mythology comes from contact with the British coat of arms. Its stylized lion may have reminded the Chippewa and others with this legend of the copper-scaled lake spirit. Erdrich's description is vivid, and we're willing to believe that Fleur's children bear a family resemblance to Misshepeshu.

Fleur herself is changed by her drownings, or perhaps by the reactions to them, and she becomes a woman who breaks the rules of female decorum and tribal tradition. This repels the Chippewa and attracts and eventually enrages the lecherous white men of Argus. As Pauline describes her, Fleur seems like a lake creature herself, "her hips fishlike, slippery, narrow." She wears a green dress that clings to her body, and she is variously described as like a bear or a wolf. Her teeth curve and her braids look like animal tails.

The narrator prepares us for the violence that erupts when the men will no longer tolerate Fleur's strength and supernatural luck. We follow the plot as Lily gets angrier about Fleur's teasingly winning only a dollar each night. The setting, in a place where animals are butchered and boiled, smoked and hung in an ice-lined compartment, seems overwhelmingly brutal and disrespectful of nature, and readers may question Fleur's willingness to throw herself into such work. It may remind us of historical accounts of buffalo hunters piling up stripped carcasses to rot. Readers of Native American mythology will be reminded of windigos, men turned into mad, voracious, cannibalistic giants. But whereas the men seem to be brutalized by this atmosphere, Fleur shows that she can gently give the young girl respectful bits of attention.

Erdrich foreshadows Pauline's betrayal of Fleur by having the child describe herself as "the shadow that could have saved her." While racial differences are foregrounded by Lily's exaggerated whiteness, the inability to see Fleur's supernatural power is where the white men exhibit their difference from Native Americans. Although the Chippewa do not treat Fleur well, they recognize her power. When the white men finally see that she has tricked and beaten them at a man's activity, they want to destroy her. But this reaction may be less about race than about gender.

Ironically, the narrator describes the rape in one sentence. She concentrates instead on the forces of nature unleashed by the attack. Erdrich thus makes use of a cultural stereotype that links nature with both women and the indigenous people of a land. She can always blame this on the narrator. Pauline believes that Fleur is magic. She describes Lily's violent encounter with the sow as a sort of dance, wrestling match, and knife fight combined. Later, when the tornado approaches, it has a similarly bestial aspect. "The odd cloud became a fat snout that nosed along the earth," Pauline says, "and sniffled, jabbed, picked at things, sucked them up, blew them apart, rooted around as if it was following a certain scent, then stopped behind me at the butcher shop and bored down like a drill." She watches a surreal movement of weird objects, reminding the audience of a scene from *Alice in Wonderland* or *The Wizard of Oz*.

Pauline has landed in a nightmare, and she judges herself more harshly than most readers do at this point. We question how she could have stopped the men. Perhaps, by calling attention to herself, she too would have been raped. Most of us even applaud when she takes the revenge of locking the men in their death chamber, ensuring that they will remain after the tornado buries them alive. We may notice that the child has remained out of sight and mind as the men have selfishly taken shelter without concern for her safety. We recall that the stepfather has forced the girl to leave school to do the tasks her dead mother would have done. And these men are rapists, a fact that for many readers fully justifies Pauline's act. The cold selfishness of the whole town is revealed when we discover that they have not even noticed that the men are missing. They are even less concerned about Fleur, presumably because she is an Indian.

Pauline blames herself for Fleur's rape, and revenge is her way of making amends. It also brings her into solidarity with Fleur and the natural elements that conspire to see that her rape is avenged. Their continued connection when both return to the reservation indicates that Fleur does not condemn Pauline, though one of the scanty details the narrator gives of the rape has Fleur calling out her name. The events bring them together.

Although the narrators of both Edgar Allan Poe's "The Cask of Amontillado" and Louise Erdrich's "Fleur" entomb their enemies, we understand Pauline's motives more clearly than we do Montresor's. This is partly because we observe the "injuries" the men at the butcher shop inflict, whereas Fortunato's sins against Poe's narrator remain vague. Also, Pauline's act, although premeditated and unrepented, is less deliberate and planned than Montresor's. Finally, she is a child, numbed by several traumatic experiences in a row, and by what modern readers see as ongoing abuse and neglect. Most readers are therefore more horrified by Poe's narrator. Others, however, dislike the explicit violence and images of death at the butcher shop in Erdrich's more realistic horror story. It is harder for some readers to distance themselves from the animal heads boiling in Fleur's pot than from the human figure in motley jingling his bells in the wall of the catacombs.

Both stories use a framing technique in which the first-person narrator looks back on an event from the distance of old age. When we leap forward at the end of Erdrich's story, we do not advance to the present but to the same location that we saw in the beginning. The time period is later than the major action of the story but still takes place in the past, when Fleur's children are young. Pauline is reflective and does not seek to justify herself or to impress the reader with her own cleverness as Montresor does. Poe's narrator ends with the ironic "Rest in Peace" whereas Erdrich's ends with an aura of the supernatural. Erdrich has her narrator offer an assertion at the beginning of her closing section, placing her characters in a continuum of family or tribal inheritance. Poe's narrator is concerned with family pride, too, but the effect is negative. Obviously, Montresor has not been able to rest in peace about his murder of Fortunato, since it still preys on his mind fifty years later, but there is a sense of closure in his remark. Erdrich's story projects us into a possible future, however, with the knowing smile of Fleur's little girl, an omen of things to come, we suspect.

Throughout her story, Erdrich has shown people reading the text of Fleur's life and coming up with various interpretations. But she remains a mystery with no one solution. We enjoy this for the same reasons we enjoy *The X-Files*: The eerie mystery provides the delicious thrill of wondering if we are surrounded by an invisible world with different rules. When the men speak of "not knowing," we recall the blindness of the men at the butcher shop to the women in their world. As we read both Erdrich and Poe, readers need to cultivate a tolerance for ambiguity. Students often prefer texts that give all the answers. We can help them appreciate that writers show respect for their readers when they allow us to imagine some of the answers for ourselves, even if this means we find different interpretations each time we read the same text.

ANDRE DUBUS

Killings (p. 1404)

By giving his short story about revenge the one-word plural title "Killings," Andre Dubus subtly avoids the definite or indefinite article that would particularize one of the specific killings that occur in the story. This universalizes the situation he describes. Any parent or spouse can imagine taking action to avenge a child or to save a partner from agony. Young people can imagine their own fathers desperately taking such matters into their own hands. But the title, like the story at its end, does not allow the interpretation that revenge murder is without cost. The two murders of the story share equal billing. He implies, as Sherman Alexie does in "Capital Punishment" (p. 1382) with his equation "1 death + 1 death = 2 deaths," that killing is killing, no matter what the warrant.

This does not mean that Matt Fowler does not face an ethical dilemma or that he would act differently given another chance. This is the true conflict of the story. He is left knowing that his action has cut him off from his family. His wife has not participated in the act of revenge physically, and she wants to use their lovemaking as a celebration and communion in vengeance. But for Matt, everything is now literally anticlimactic. He has also robbed himself of a full relationship with his living children, since he cannot make them accessories and he knows that they will think, as he has arranged for outsiders to conclude, that his son's murderer has run away. The reader is complicit in the killing, since we go along for the ride and agree with him that this boy does not seem as worthy of living as Matt's son, especially since we are sure he will not be punished severely. Revenge is not sweet, but empty, Dubus tells us with his narrative.

Dubus introduces a collection of short stories with a quotation from Flannery O'Connor. "The man in the violent situation reveals those qualities least dispensable in his personality," O'Connor said, "those qualities which are all he will have to take into eternity with him." Ironically, Dubus once told an interviewer that he doesn't read Flannery O'Connor because she *frightens* him. Like O'Connor, Dubus is a Roman Catholic — it is her religious symbolism that scares him rather than the violence in her stories — and he has been characterized as a profoundly moral writer. He realistically portrays ordinary Americans who struggle with definitions of moral behavior and sometimes lose their spirituality in the process. Andre Dubus maintains that the foregrounding of violence in his fiction has to do with being American, that "violence is a reflection of American consciousness." But the acceptance and action of killing goes against nature, Dubus believes; Matt Fowler at the story's end is therefore "forever removed" from nature, and he will never recover the life destroyed by his son's death and his own surrender to anger and revenge.

In his justification of the premeditated murder of Richard Strout, Matt Fowler uses the warrant of protecting his wife. This is what a man must do, take charge of the evil that has been directed toward his family. Everywhere she goes in their town, Ruth sees the killer of her son, and Matt takes action as a good husband. But he is also angered by the young man's apparent flaunting of his freedom to enter a new relationship with a woman, to go out drinking, and to otherwise boldly continue his life. Richard Strout may not be capable of feeling the remorse that Matt Fowler will endure for killing him, and this is part of the story's irony and perhaps part of Fowler's motive for murder. We read the story from Matt Fowler's point of view and tend to agree that he has reason to take revenge. We sympathize with the grieving father and admire the cleverness of the plan to make it look as though the murderer has fled.

Strout is humanized for us, however, by the details of his room, his obedient packing, and his respectful attitude as he addresses the older man as "Mr. Fowler" like one of his son's high-school friends might have done. The audience has been led to think of Strout as defiant, but here — in the situation of violence described in the Flannery O'Connor reference — he is touchingly vulnerable. His own killing of Matt Fowler's son has been more impulsive, and he has been wronged. Though this does not excuse his actions, we see a qualitative difference between the murder that American society would once have condoned as a "crime of passion" and the calculated execution that the wronged father carries out.

Readers may point out that Strout epitomizes another American attitude of the past that sees women as chattels legally owned by men. In both murders, men use the feelings or actions of women as the warrant for their own violent actions. We are back to the Garden of Eden, with Adam making the excuse that Eve handed him the apple. The younger man tries to reason with the avenging father as he pleads for his life: "I'll do twenty years, Mr. Fowler; at least. I'll be forty-six years old." He assumes that his life will essentially be over by then, but the older man sees this from the perspective of fifty-five. Twenty years in prison does not seem just punishment for the loss of his son and the family's way of life. Earlier, Strout argues that he had reason to kill Matt's son Frank, because he had violated Strout's marriage and was keeping him from pulling his family back together. Neither man takes the step of seeing how the other's family has been sinned against.

Willis Trottier's motives are even more questionable, since he makes revenge possible and participates fully, though he does not have the excuse of family as a warrant. Perhaps he represents an outraged community with law-and-order values, the type of vigilante who takes action when the courts are seen as weak. He may even have baser, more criminal assumptions about the validity of personal revenge. We do not imagine him wrestling with guilt. Ruth, too, is not troubled by the act of murder, has encouraged it and has known what her husband would do in response to her expression of her needs. She does not realize yet the impact that this second killing will have on her marriage and family.

Interested students can trace the attitudes toward women that the men demonstrate in Dubus's story. Matt is less judgmental of Mary Ann than his wife is. He defends her marital unfaithfulness and the fact that she is older than Frank. He too finds Mary Ann attractive, but he also feels compassion for her. The Fowler family is gradually accepting the young woman and her boys when their son is killed in front of Mary Ann's children. Dubus keeps this fact from his readers at first, delaying our judgment of Strout on this account. It makes less credible his claim that he was trying to reestablish his family, and it reflects upon his character.

It would be interesting to explore whether the theme in "Killings" relates as much to what it means to be a good husband and father as to judgment and revenge. Strout is neither a good husband nor a good father. Matt Fowler, on the other hand, mourns the loss of "the quietly harried and quietly pleasurable days of fatherhood" even while he recognizes that he has "wandered through" most of these days. As he carries out his obsessive act of revenge, his life becomes focused. Dubus focuses his story at this point as well, slowing the narrative pace and taking us step by step through the deliberate murder, thus matching style to content.

Focus obtained through obsession dehumanizes a person. Edgar Allan Poe's narrator in "The Cask of Amontillado" is chillingly focused on his revenge, and we see him as evil to the point of the demonic. Dubus's avenging father in "Killings" does not know that he is robbing himself of the human connections he has so highly valued, and he earns our compassion, even as we realize he has taken the wrong action. The narrator of Louise Erdrich's "Fleur" acts more impulsively, but if we go beyond the context of the short story to look at her future as Sister Leopolda, we realize that she too will pay with a loss of humanity. On the other hand, readers may say that the treatment of women to which Pauline responds with revenge is actually what dehumanizes her. Because she realizes that she is burying the men alive, terrorizing as well as killing them, her alliance with the avenging forces of nature comes across as equally cold and brutal to the murders committed by the men in the other stories in this cluster on revenge. In law, we are told that premeditation does not have to take very long; it just requires a deliberate action taken with the knowledge of the consequences to the victim. Pauline is young and acts quickly, but she is not innocent. Whether we agree that the men at the butcher shop are worthy of death is another issue.

Of the three narrators in this cluster, only Matt Fowler in Andre Dubus's "Killings" seems to truly approach remorse. Poe's Montresor feels a momentary twinge as he immolates Fortunato, but brushes it aside as attributable to the atmosphere of the catacombs. Pauline is able to keep quiet for days about her entrapment of the men in the debris of the tornado and coolly enters the meat locker to observe the dead bodies. Andre Dubus is the most realistic of the three writers in the attention to verisimilitude that convinces the reader this could have really happened. He shows everything from the socks and underwear neatly in Richard Strout's drawer to the meticulous details of the location and organization of the gravesite where Matt Fowler and Willis Trottier shoot the young man. We feel the gun kick and watch the victim die. Erdrich's settings, on the other hand, seem dreamlike and selective in the details they give. We learn in more detail than we would wish the inner workings of the sweat-and-tallow-filled butcher operation. But we know little of the neighbors who shrug at Fleur's disappearance, don't think to look for several missing men, and are not even considered as possible avenues of help as Pauline blames herself for Fleur's rape. It seems reasonable that a young girl would block out the details of the rape itself, but Pauline's concise description conveys what is symbolic to her — Fleur's crying out in her Chippewa language and the incantation of the narrator's own name. The fight between the swinelike Lily and the sow stands in for other details of the rape. The details are nightmarish. Other scenes are similarly surreal as Pauline watches cows and other objects flying past her in the tornado or weaves folklore into Fleur's experiences at Lake Turcot.

We are aware in Erdrich's story that the narrator communicates events in the light of her own interpretations and that her vision of Fleur is permeated by the supernatural. We cannot trust her reliability. Edgar Allan Poe, of course, is the modern inventor of the unreliable narrator along with the American short story, and his self-satisfied murderer is the least trustworthy of all. We know that such catacombs exist under Italian estates, but the journey he describes feels like a descent into hell, and the temporal setting of carnival adds to the unreality. With Poe's story, the reader is entitled to have grave doubts about the existence of the setting outside of the narrator's nightmares. We willingly suspend disbelief, however, because we recognize the genre of the Edgar Allan Poe tale of horror.

VALUE JUDGMENTS:
A COLLECTION OF WRITINGS
BY ALICE WALKER (p. 1419)

ALICE WALKER
Everyday Use (p. 1420)

One of the major themes of Alice Walker's short story "Everyday Use" is the indeterminacy of history and identity, especially for African Americans. Walker's characters raise issues about what constitutes a family's heritage. As autobiographers must, we all identify the major events in our lives and the characters representing our ancestry by choosing those that fit into the narrative line we have chosen for our story. We look back at the poem we wrote in third grade and interpret this as a signpost along the road to the career in English studies, foreshadowing the budding literary giant we hope to become. Since we didn't become Michael Jordan, we omit the hours perfecting the free throw on the basketball court or we reinterpret them as evidence of perseverance. We choose our ancestors as well, literary or otherwise. Alex Haley finds the West African *griot* and the courageous Kunta Kinte as he explores his *Roots* and writes the text that becomes a culture-changing miniseries on television. Never mind that some of the details are borrowed; this narrative explains Alex Haley to Alex Haley.

As we approach Alice Walker's story, we might ask students to tell about ancestors — genetic or chosen — that they claim as their own. Alice Walker picks fiction writer and folklorist Zora Neale Hurston, a Harlem Renaissance literary figure who gave voice to the African American storytellers of the rural South. But she also searches out the strengths of her mother and other remarkable, everyday women of Minnie Tallulah Grant Walker's generation —

and earlier generations — who paved the way for the independent African American woman who strides through today's world. These are the women who worked in the homes and took care of the children of white families or broke their backs on farms to battle for the education and equality — and survival — of their own children. Most of the students coming into our college classrooms today know these women, if they see them at all, as elderly neighbors and grandmothers, and their struggle seems far away.

Like the mother in "Everyday Use," many women of Alice Walker's mother's generation found ways to send one or two promising children away to college. As often happens in working-class families, regardless of race, the hard-bought education sometimes separates the young person from people back home, and what was intended to uplift may lead to conflict and isolation. In her poem "For My Sister Molly Who in the Fifties" (in *Revolutionary Petunias* [New York: Harcourt Brace Jovanovich, 1973]) Walker describes the gradual move of a college student away from her roots. From reading stories to her family and trying to make changes in the household, the sister moved on to:

> Another life   With gentlefolk
> Far less trusting
> And moved and moved and changed
> Her name
> And sounded precise
> When she spoke   And frowned away
> Our sloppishness (18)

Now, African American students born in the 1980s find the afros, the daishikis, and the earnest quest for black pride of their parents' 1960s and 1970s youth distant, glimpsed perhaps in the stereotypes of television reruns. Ironically, though "Everyday Use" could be taught until recently as a contemporary view of conflicting values about history, today's students need a historical context to understand the characters in Walker's story and the issues of concern to them, including the trendy Dee/Wangero, who now seems dated to many readers.

Although we are meant to see Dee and her male companion as pretentious and ironically humorous, Alice Walker's treatment of them in 1973 was not applauded by all African Americans. She was questioning blind political correctness before the term was invented, and there was a risk involved in holding black pseudo-intellectuals up for ridicule. What was to stop white Americans from interpreting her text to mean that a person of color is ridiculous unless he or she remains in poverty and ignorance? In this context, we should raise the issue of audience and purpose. This is not a text written to explain black folks to the white reading public, but a text about cultural issues within the African American community. Readers who are not African American can also be cruel to family members, however, and thus miss much of value in their own heritage. The story thus has universal applications. We may also benefit from the reminder that there is no one monolithic "African American community."

Most readers will agree that Walker visualizes an audience that needs to be reminded that family and community values are not to be discarded simply because one acquires an education. There is history that we read in books, and this is good. As a writer and speaker, Walker has shown that she knows this sort of history. She has lived in Africa, and the topics of her writing are international. In her imaginative fiction she has traveled as far back in African history as one can go, which means she has traveled as far back in human history as one can go. But there is a history that is not found in books or formal archaeological and anthropological studies, and this sort of history is good, too. This is oral history, the true if not always factual history of folklore, the material history that can be touched in a handmade quilt or churn or bench, and the living history of parents and grandparents.

Dee seeks her roots because this activity is in style, and she is more concerned with style than substance. She thus misses her chance to see the more immediate history that her mother could pass on to her, because hypocrisy and arrogance blind her to its value. Most college readers can understand Dee and would probably feel more comfortable having coffee with her than with the formidable narrator and her pathetic daughter Maggie. We'd be more likely to hang the quilt on the wall than to put it to everyday use. Looking at a portrait of Alice Walker, we *know* she would not join them in a dip of snuff. But we can imagine her sitting in a nearby rocking chair, really listening and learning.

The problem with Dee is that she comes to take, not to share in her true heritage. She gives the distant kiss on the brow instead of the full embrace. She grasps and insists and belittles. Her self-esteem depends upon pretense, and she must protect herself from her true history and identity. Like many African Americans and others who acquired names reminiscent of slavery or colonial domination, Dee has chosen a new name. This can be a positive act, an assertion of independence from a constant reminder of oppression and stolen identity. But Walker seems critical of Dee's choice to do this. Perhaps she opposes the superficial, imitative, faddish quality behind the decision for some people.

For Dee, the impulse differs on the surface from slavish assimilation into white society, but underneath lies a similar falseness and fear. Dee and her friend *pass* for political thinkers who celebrate their African roots, but they *bypass* the living family heritage. Walker has the narrator remind us how much is owed to the hard-working people who lived and created in between the romanticized African ancestor and the beautiful, educated woman of the late twentieth century. Their names deserve to be continued and put to everyday use. But the newly christened Wangero denies this honor to the Dees in her ancestry. Students interested in exploring the social and historical issues raised by the discussion of Alice Walker's texts might turn to other texts in our anthology that deal with similar issues. They might compare Dee with Beneatha Younger in Lorraine Hansberry's *A Raisin in the Sun* (p. 483); compare the place of the quilt in bell hooks's "Inspired Eccentricity" (p. 202); or compare generational conflicts in texts by Nikki Giovanni (p. 467), June Jordan (p. 1633), and writers in the "Living in Families" chapter. We can have them research contemporary African American and Caribbean writers to determine how many have chosen new names and what reasons they give for the change.

The conflict in values between Maggie's and Dee's joint desire for the quilts raises the definition of culture. Dee represents "high culture" and art. To people who see culture in this way, Maggie and the narrator are uncultured. The work of family members is not art, but craft, and is desirable because it is quaint and currently in vogue among sophisticated people. Maggie, however, knows how to make quilts. She values them because they are links to people she has known and valued, her grandmother and her aunt. She uses the education they have given her to create new ones. She is willing to give them up because she has the memory without needing a material reminder. She knows the stories behind each object because she has paid attention. The creators are not anonymous to her. Her mother remembers the hands that have worn the marks on the churn.

The narrator does not share the story of the blue piece of cloth from the Civil War uniform or the knowledge that Dee's name goes "back through the branches" much farther than the younger woman realizes. Dee has cut herself off from the family tree and chosen other ancestors. She devalues Maggie's keen memory, saying that her "brain is like an elephant's." Their difference highlights the difference between recorded history — fixed in writing or displayed on museum walls — and oral history and folklore — worn and constantly changing with everyday use. It is easy at this point to see these views of history as being in conflict, and it is true that the narrator must choose between their competing values. But the question is complex.

We may look forward to "In Search of Our Mothers' Gardens" in which Walker describes being inspired by an exhibit in the Smithsonian Museum, a quilt created by an anonymous black woman. Obviously, if the quilt had not been hung on a wall, Walker would not have experienced it. In "Everyday Use" Walker has her narrator choose the way of human love and compassion, choose to value the one who needs uplifting rather than the one who unwittingly takes on the role of spoiler and oppressor. To Dee the quilt is an object, just as the man who accompanies Dee looks at the narrator as an object, "like somebody inspecting a Model A car" — and just as their ancestors were objects to slave traders and slave holders.

At one point in the story, the educated daughter proclaims of her former identity as Dee, "She is dead." For her, culture and family history are reduced to lifeless commodities, things that can *belong* to her but are no longer filled with the memory of life that gives them value to Maggie and the narrator. Dee has been influenced by her education and by the political movements of the time, as represented by the farming collective that operates in the neighborhood, one of many efforts to organize people and to better economic conditions in the South. Her friend makes it clear that he is not involved in this sort of active labor. The implication is that he wears the trappings of black pride but doesn't allow the philosophy to sink in to the extent of helping others or breaking a sweat. Dee seems to be influenced by him. But she has always been concerned with whether or not something was in style, had even refused the quilts as "old-fashioned" when she left for college.

Few readers would suggest that Dee should be like her mother and sister; what she needs most is to learn to respect them and to find out who they are and what they know and value. This is not easy. Walker has given them qualities that have figured in racist stereotypes and have been used in some African American groups to sort by social class. The narrator and Maggie are dark-skinned. Numerous people of color have spoken of the "paper bag rule" or the "blue vein society" that kept women out of debutante balls and social clubs if their skin was a shade darker than the bag or too dark to see the vein on the inside of the wrist. The beauty criteria of white society thus continued to oppress and influence class even in social arenas where no whites were involved. Dee, on the other hand, is a golden girl — light-skinned, intelligent, strong-willed. The mother anticipates her visit as if she were a famous movie star, even fantasizing about a television meeting in which she herself becomes miraculously lighter-skinned and less heavy.

Her weight also contrasts with Dee's trimness, which reaches even to her "neat" ankles and feet. The narrator is so heavy she has difficulty moving. This makes her look like the stereotype of "Mammy" in *Gone with the Wind*, a Bertha-type housemaid and cook, or an Aunt Jemima. We learn that she works like a man. She is the image of the black woman as the "mule of the world" who shoulders all the burdens and takes all the abuse. We can admire and respect her strength while we understand that Dee would not want such a difficult life for herself, nor would we, nor — we can assume — would Alice Walker.

We feel compassion for Maggie. She may remind readers of Celie in Walker's novel *The Color Purple* in her shyness and the extent of her pain. Her life is limited not only by her burns but by her future with the husband with "mossy teeth in an earnest face." Students sometimes ask if Dee has set the fire that burns down the hated house and damages her sister. The story does not reveal this, and there is no sign that the narrator suspects such a thing, but we notice that Dee is absorbed in her own thoughts rather than the injury to her sister even then. She seems more self-absorbed than evil, and this seems to be the message that Walker sends to those who have escaped unscathed, perhaps including herself. Open your eyes and ears. Respect those who have endured labor and pain. By making Maggie a burn victim, Walker insists that we feel compassion for her rather than seeing her as backward or stupid. Some readers see the story as an allegory of the conflict in values between intellectuals and the working class that makes their success possible. Others argue that it is about shaping an identity for oneself as changes take place in society and fooling oneself by donning trendy masks rather than dealing with real issues. It has been interpreted as a reversal of the parable of the Prodigal Son. Other critics interpret the narrator's attitude toward Dee as idolatry that she comes to see as false. We can focus our reading on the character of Maggie and the empowerment her mother achieves by supporting her.

Most readers will take the story seriously, though they recognize the humor and irony. Certainly there is nothing funny about the image of Maggie's arms sticking to her mother or about the rejection the other women feel from Dee. But we laugh when the narrator humorously refuses to understand the name of the man who comes with Dee. She first pretends that she confuses his name with the greeting — meaning *Peace be with you* — that she has heard used by people at the collective farm; then she mispronounces his Muslim name to sound like he's a barber. This makes him look ridiculous, as does Dee's African greeting, which we know she does simply to show off. The characters are exaggerated, and the hyperbole makes us smile. On the other hand, hints of a real political situation are understated. The narrator has gone out of her way to see the farmers guarding the collective with rifles after whites poison their cattle. This contrasts with Dee and her companion, who play-act at fighting oppression while others do the work. The narrator seems justified in her evaluation of Dee's world as characterized by lies and make-believe. She speaks of Dee's reading to everyone as if it were a punishment. It is as if she reads *at* them rather than *to* them, using reading as a weapon. But don't we value reading and make-believe? Do we agree with the definition of fiction as *lies*? We may be left with the question of how far Alice Walker may have reeled us in with an unreliable narrator and convinced us to accept her value judgments as correct.

ALICE WALKER
Nineteen Fifty-Five (p. 1427)

Most instructors are quick to admit that many students know more about the history of rock and roll than we do. Some of us can remember, however, when Elvis Presley first came on the scene. No one needs to be told that Elvis had roots in both country and rhythm and blues. Actually, country music owes much to the blues tradition. Listen to the original Jimmie Rodgers — the one from Meridian, Mississippi, who sang railroad songs, not the ersatz folksinger of the 1950s and 1960s. Rodgers is in the Rock and Roll Hall of Fame and is also called the father of country music, but his sound comes straight out of the Mississippi Delta. Whenever we get the chance, we like to interweave musical texts with lessons on reading. Students will enjoy doing their own research on American popular music, perhaps looking at some of the origins of rap music and their connections to the literary theories of scholars like Henry Louis Gates. We shouldn't pass up the opportunity to incorporate the texts that may have inspired Alice Walker's story — the 1950s versions of "You Ain't Nothin' but a Hound Dog" first by Willie Mae "Big Mama" Thornton and then by Elvis Presley. Since Walker mentions Bessie Smith as a rival to her character Gracie Mae Still, we could listen to her, too, and to Ma Rainey, who recorded a hound dog song in the 1920s or 1930s.

The earliest blues recordings are by women, and some students of African American history and culture would say that though there are great blues men, it takes women who "fool around with a lot of no count mens," as Gracie Mae says, to have really lived the blues. And Alice Walker might say it takes black women with the weight of history and culture on their backs enduring *still* (to echo Gracie Mae's last name). On the other hand, some experts make a case for Otis Blackwell as the true model for Elvis Presley. Blackwell wrote "Don't Be Cruel" — the flip side of "Hound Dog" — and other Elvis hits, "All Shook Up" and "Return to Sender." He also wrote for other singers: "Great Balls of Fire" for Jerry Lee Lewis and "Handy Man" for James Taylor, for example. In 1955, Goldy Goldmark of Shalimar Music Company, where Blackwell went to promote the song, persuaded the African American artist to sell half his copyright of "Don't Be Cruel" to Elvis Presley. Elvis was already beginning to fulfill the dreams of record entrepreneur Sam Phillips, who knew that if he could find a white singer with a black sound he could revolutionize the music industry and sell "race music" to a white America steeped in prejudice. Elvis parroted all the nuances of Blackwell's demo, and little white girls found someone they could lust after without breaking the particular taboos our students should read about in Gunnar Myrdal's "Social Equality" (p. 956).

Recently, a history scholar tried to imagine what the American character would be like if African slavery had never existed. As we begin to draw up possible scenarios of America without the African influence, we realize how profoundly race defines our culture and how impossible it is to imagine an America without the pain and guilt of slavery and its aftermath. Some say the American colonies would not have broken with England in 1776 at all, that economic factors would have required that we maintain British ties, lacking the exploited and renewable labor force. But what is most difficult to imagine is what the culture would have been like without the vibrant African soul. And what would the music have been like without that and the profound blues of being a slave, a Negro, an Afro-American, a black, an African American, a person of color in a United States that pretended everyone was equal, but only took and never freely gave?

Yet, like Traynor's uncomprehending and shallow audience — and like the grasping and false African American pseudo-intellectuals of "Everyday Use" — Americans may never understand the depth of feeling, experience, and spiritual power in what we so willingly take as our own. This hollow, grasping ignorance is what Gracie Mae fears at the story's end: "One day this is going to be a pitiful country," she thinks. Alice Walker's "Nineteen Fifty-Five" personalizes in the composite character Gracie Mae Still the appropriation by white entrepreneurs and imitators of the music invented by African Americans. And in the story a white boy named Traynor does a pretty good Elvis impersonation. But, as we have seen, perhaps Elvis was himself an impersonator.

Traynor — the Elvis character — does not understand Gracie Mae's song because he does not understand the experience out of which it grows. Trying to figure out the music's power becomes an obsession for him. We hear first through the "deacon" — whom we recognize as a not too exaggerated caricature of Elvis's manager Colonel Tom Parker — that Traynor has "cut his teeth" on the music of "you people." In one masterful sentence, Alice Walker raises two issues. She recalls the debt and emotional dependence of thousands of white children raised literally at the breasts of African American women, the milk for their own babies appropriated, as Toni Morrison shows so compellingly in her novels. In addition, she puts in the mouth of the man in power the words *you people*. During his campaign for president, Texan business tycoon Ross Perot was bewildered by the reaction of an African American audience as he attempted to build common ground by referring to his listeners ingratiatingly as *you people*. The words separate and sting, are reminders of hate and oppression. They reveal a prejudice so blind it does not even recognize its own existence. Gracie Mae and J. T. share the irony of the deacon's unknowing double insult, laughing at it. The deacon is unambiguously out to make a sharp bargain.

Traynor, on the other hand, senses the ethos of the music he parrots. He becomes a slave and a prisoner to his own success, but he is unable to wake up and pull the power out of his blues that would enable him to be healed by the music. He continues through the twenty-two years of the story to puzzle through the meaning of Gracie Mae's song. Two years after his manager buys all the rights to her song for one thousand dollars, Traynor doesn't even catch the injustice as he remarks in passing that the song earns forty times that in a day. He wants to know what the song means, and she relates it to being a woman mistreated by "no count mens" — ironic in this context, since he is a man who has exploited her talent.

A few years later, he is writing her about his lack of success in writing his own songs, and we realize the irony again as he pinpoints the problem; his songs are dead because he has not lived them. Thirteen years after they first meet he has given her a farm, which she sold, wondering if the meaning of the song has something to do with the rural setting. He's researched her life and learned about some of her men, but he reveals more about his own poverty of spirit. His failure to recognize that Horace is not J. T. — *they all look alike* being the implied cliché — further reveals his inability to really see the people whose lives inform the art he seeks to understand. If he fishes for her to teach him or to create another song for him, she doesn't take the bait.

By this time, the song begins to take on mythic and historic proportions, and we realize that trying to identify it as a particular song and Gracie Mae as a particular blues singer may be a mistake. She has been in a fight over it with the legendary Bessie Smith, and she herself admits to not understanding it when she wrote it as fully as she does now after living longer. Perhaps age or generation is as much a factor as gender and race. Traynor comes close to getting it as he realizes that the "feeling" of the song has something to do with the alienation he feels in the midst of a world of strangers. The remainder of their dialogue suggests that the meaning of the text relates somehow to audience. His audience does not read deeply enough to realize the mystery of the text. It prefers the imitation, and he has enough insight to be contemptuous of its misreading.

The key to the story's theme may lie in his struggle with the superficiality of his audience: "They want what you got but they don't want you. They want what I got only it ain't mine. . . . They getting the flavor of something but they ain't getting the thing itself." In a neatly ironic simile, considering the song that may have inspired the story, he compares his audience to "a pack of hound dogs." Gracie Mae answers by trying to explain the communion between an authentic creator and an "honest" audience. Traynor is fake, dead, half-asleep. He knows he is the shell and she is the kernel of nourishing substance, but he does not know how to get from his emptiness to her fullness.

Some readers feel that Traynor tries to bribe and manipulate Gracie Mae with his gifts. It seems more likely, however, that he seeks to establish a connection in a search for understanding. He knows she has something he needs, but he can't figure out what it is; its mystery is locked in the song. She comes to address him as a son, feeling perhaps the sort of affection that women have felt nursing the slaveholder's child. At one point, she says that "one way or another you talk to rich white folks and you end up reassuring *them*." Perhaps the gifts are meant to make Traynor feel better, too, to assuage his guilt. But we notice that he does not allow her to share in the profits and decide for herself how to spend the money but bestows paternalistic gifts, laughing that he is *spoiling* her, a word one would use with a child — or an inferior. As students write epitaphs for Traynor, they will have to decide on his essential qualities, perhaps centering on his emptiness.

Gracie Mae and Traynor both get fat, and Gracie Mae is concerned with this throughout the story. Both have health concerns. At times, the narrator downplays these, seeing the waddling, plump Traynor in his successful years as too rich to have to worry about such things and herself as looking "distinguished" and formidable. But later he looks like a "fat Dracula" — an ironic simile for an appropriator of culture — and fat is mentioned as one of the possible causes of his death. Gracie Mae realizes at last that "my fat is the hurt I don't admit," and we suspect that Traynor's fat comes from a similarly emotional cause, from his aching hollowness and lack of truly satisfying human relationships.

Both Gracie Mae and Traynor depart from Standard English, and Alice Walker captures their two varieties of Southern speech. The letters, with their formal phrases mixed with Southern diction, are especially realistic. Both are aware of performing an act of literacy, and they take this seriously. We could fault Walker for one or two inconsistencies: For example, when Gracie Mae speaks of Traynor's "awareness of the transaction," we sense a break in the natural rhythm. And although the narrator is certainly intelligent enough to speculate about Traynor's estate looking like England or Wales, this isn't the sort of comparison we expect her to make, and the effect is jarring. She effectively communicates the foreign nature of the way Traynor lives, especially in the symbolic image of the magnolias dying as the atmosphere gets too high and cold. We hear the voice of Alice Walker momentarily slipping in, though.

We may need to explain to some students that Walker does not mean for us to see her narrator as ignorant because she does not speak Standard English. Black English has its own rules of grammar and is as logical as Standard English, more so at times. For example, when she says, "I had done unlocked the screen," there is a sense of completed action. This is similar to the often misunderstood *be*. A speaker of Black English might say, "She sick," to communicate the information that someone has a cold from which she will soon recover, but say, "She *be* sick," to describe a condition that is ongoing or more permanent. The usage conveys meaning similar to the Spanish *ser* and *estar*, making distinctions that take more words to communicate in Standard English. Interested students should be directed toward linguistic studies of dialects, and all students should be introduced to the basic linguistic assumption that language is arbitrary and pragmatic. Experts on language are more interested in descriptions of how people actually speak than in prescriptions for a proper, socially elite language. At this point, we share with students the comment of one South African that American English — as opposed to British pronunciation — is a "bastardized" language. After they cool down, we discuss the warrants underlying this assertion and consider how this relates to the condemnation of Black English as somehow inferior.

Despite linguistic theory, however, African American students tell us that the use of Ebonics is a subject of debate around dinner tables, with most parents arguing hotly for the use of Standard English. Many African American leaders infer from rationales for Ebonics programs that educators assume African American children are not capable of learning the kind of English that will be needed in respectable, good-paying jobs. Others maintain that the bias that forces the same dialect on everyone needs to change, not the children. Children in some neighborhoods face ridicule from both parents and peers for trying to "talk white" when they use Standard English. Gracie Mae's manner of speaking is as alive as her blues song, and most readers respect it, but we should be aware that this is a complex social and historical issue.

White students often have trouble understanding why members of ethnic minority groups object to the compliment given when others enjoy their culture enough to imitate it. They fail to consider the economic injustice done when the white performer's records get promoted and played on the radio and the black artist behind their creation gets a pittance. They also believe that some people are oversensitive, inferring insults where none are intended, whining about things that don't matter — being addressed as "you people," for example. Others argue that crossracial borrowing is a fact of life in a country where more contact and more exposure to various American cultures take place through film, television, and even multicultural reading anthologies like ours. Students can be asked to generate a list of current examples. At the time of this writing, most adolescent boys wear the baggy clothing popularized by rap artists whose music crosses racial boundaries, in spite of content that is often specific to a small subculture.

The narrators of "Everyday Use" and "Nineteen Fifty-Five" both talk about appearing on television, a major catalyst for crosscultural borrowing since the mid-twentieth century. In "Everyday Use" Mama fantasizes about a "This Is Your Life" sort of television show in which a celebrity is reunited with those who have shaped his or her success. She imagines herself slimmer, lighter-complexioned, witty, and sophisticated. Alice Walker tells of her own mother's absorption in the lives of the all-white characters in television soap operas, recalling that her mother asked at one point if her daughter didn't agree that these beautiful people were somehow *better*. It is hard for current college students to picture television and movies with virtually no African Americans. Although many people in minority groups watched television faithfully, audiences were simply assumed to be white. When Gracie Mae appears on the Johnny Carson show, she too worries about weight, but she is too grounded to let the audience judge her value. Dee's mother, too, comes back to earth fairly quickly. Both have a sense of who they are. The television scene in "Everyday Use" comes at the story's beginning and serves as a contrast to the narrator's actual meeting with the undeservedly adored daughter and the mother's decision at the end to embrace the values of home and true identity over pretense and make-believe. Gracie Mae's appearance on Johnny Carson's show comes near the end of the story and brings us to Traynor's climactic realization that his audience will never see the power in the authentic music of Gracie Mae.

The narrators of the two Alice Walker stories lead different lives, but they both understand about the value of creating art that is grounded in human experience. Mama's perspective is more limited than Gracie Mae's; her experience has involved mostly family and hard physical labor. Gracie Mae quickly gets out of the kitchen to the front porch when Traynor unconsciously acts on the limited stereotype, and she has sung in juke joints, fought with Bessie Smith, and had several husbands and lovers. If we are looking at Alice Walker's spiritual ancestors, perhaps the narrator of "Everyday Use" is closer to her mother, whereas Gracie Mae has a great deal of Zora Neale Hurston in her, vibrant and artistic but knowing suffering and knowing the value of her heritage.

Traynor and Dee both partly see the value of the creations they try to make their own, but they fail to grasp the spirit of the creation. Both come into the home of the older woman and take over. Traynor turns up the television, and Dee rifles her mother's personal belongings. Both mimic African American culture. Dee has a more legitimate right to do this, but she sees her culture as something to be put on when it is in style and rejected when it is inconvenient. Traynor senses the value, but can't understand it. Dee assumes she understands, but fails to see the authentic value. Neither is able to achieve the true contact with other people that would give meaning to the art they desire to make their own.

Because "Everyday Use" focuses on a single day, whereas "Nineteen Fifty-Five" spans many years, we see more change in the characters of the latter story. Although the mother in "Everyday Use" is a dynamic character who moves from worshiping a distant daughter to valuing herself and her other daughter, we don't have time to see the effect of this experience on Dee or the changes that she experiences. We tend to judge her harshly because we do not see beneath the surface. In "Nineteen Fifty-Five" the greater space of time allows us to watch the dynamic of the relationship between Gracie Mae and Traynor. Most readers feel compassion for him, even though he continues throughout the story to misread Gracie Mae and the song that obsesses him. We see his gradual decline from a "womanish" sixteen-year-old to his pathetic death. The implied allusions to the life of Elvis Presley in dates, descriptions, and circumstances make this more vivid. But overall the two stories have similar themes — the value of the art of African American women of a certain generation and the difficulty of perceiving its value in the absence of respect and shared experience.

ALICE WALKER

In Search of Our Mothers' Gardens (p. 1438)

The title of Alice Walker's much anthologized essay "In Search of Our Mothers' Gardens" recalls for some readers the opening scene of Steven Spielberg's movie version of her novel *The Color Purple*. The screen is filled with brightly colored flowers, contrasting sharply with the later suffering of Celie. But in Walker's vision the flower gardens, songs, stories, and hand- or machine-sewn creations of women artists serve as an outlet that maintains sanity — even provides salvation. Although students may have read "In Search of Our Mothers' Gardens" in high school, our college classes can reread it as theoretical background for the fiction we read earlier in this cluster.

Walker explains here her attitude toward the art of the African American women of past generations, helping us to understand characters like Mama in "Everyday Use" and Gracie Mae Still in "Nineteen Fifty-Five." She makes it clear with her discussion of Phillis Wheatley, for example, that we can respect the hunger to create that impelled women of the past to find an outlet in whatever way this was allowed. And women of today can be inspired by the heritage they sometimes invisibly passed on. This does not mean that the gifted and fortunate Dee must become like her mother or sister. But she needs to respect them, to appreciate their spiritual worth, and to listen and learn from them. Alice Walker's philosophy invites, in the wrong hands, the sentimentality we warn our students to avoid in their writing, and she has been facetiously compared to artist Norman Rockwell who painted glowing, idealistic portraits of a New England that didn't quite exist.

Students can judge for themselves whether or not she succeeds in tempering her loving celebration of these matriarchal artists with realism and rationality in her essay. Certainly, those who know she has tackled such difficult subjects as rape and the mutilation of female circumcision realize that Alice Walker does not oversimplify issues of patriarchal or racial oppression of black women. The questions in our anthology direct readers toward a rhetorical analysis of this text. Because so many college students have come to us with formulaic notions of how an argument should be constructed, they may object to what they see as lack of structure in Alice Walker's essay. Many have been taught that personal experience should not be included in persuasive writing. Analyzing Walker's rhetorical strategies will help them see the movement of her argument and to note the effectiveness of Walker's use of both literary and personal examples to call for a specific change in attitude in her readers and listeners. Classes that have read the stories in this cluster might imagine an audience in which Dee/Wangero is a member whose eyes are opened and a reading public that includes Traynor, seeking to understand the power of Gracie Mae's art.

We can approach a text for summary and analysis by reading it through first for general understanding, perhaps freewriting a response or jotting down questions and reactions as we read. Some instructors teach students to use a double-entry page in which they write paraphrases, quotations, and summaries of textual materials on the left and their own thoughts on the right. Others encourage annotations in the margins and within the text itself. If we need to write a summary of the whole essay, we can parcel it into discourse blocks and determine the main ideas within each block. Unlike methods in which the paragraph is considered a unit, this approach concedes that a point may be made in a short space or developed in a longer block.

The title, for example, is the first unit of discourse, shaping our reading of what follows. Walker presents beneath her title a long quotation from Jean Toomer's *Cane* describing women of the 1920s, and then goes on to elaborate on

Toomer's ideas. She echoes this later in the essay when she introduces another section by referring to her own mother in the 1920s. In her first paragraph, Walker reveals some of her underlying assumptions — that black women were not consciously aware of their capabilities, were "abused and mutilated," and were misread as "selfless abstractions." She signals a turning point with rhetorical questions, then goes on to answer them with an important idea in her essay — that these women are the mothers and grandmothers of the speaker and her audience of highly educated African American women like herself. This establishes common ground, reflecting the original rhetorical situation of this text.

She goes on to develop her description of black women of the early twentieth century, slipping in allusions for the alert reader to Toomer's quotation and to Zora Neale Hurston, Martin Luther King, and the Bible. Students may identify her thesis statement as the first sentence of paragraph 9, in which she asserts that these women were "not Saints, but Artists." In this emendation to Toomer's views she gives us another turning point as she moves on to talk about the barriers that thwarted creativity, referring through her examples to both slavery and patriarchy. She moves to a new discourse block with yet another rhetorical question: "How was the creativity of the black woman kept alive . . . ?" She answers by acknowledging the expression allowed to them in song and mostly lost to them in literary form, then gives her "paraphrase" of an African poem that laments their loss.

The word *But* at the beginning of the following paragraph signals a change in direction. It brings us to the extension of her main idea: African American women of her mother's generation found a way to keep an artistic heritage alive in spite of the barriers they faced. The remainder of the essay develops this main idea. We may note another transition as she begins a paragraph with the phrase *One example*, signaling a move from general to specific. First, she explains how 1700s American colonial poet Phillis Wheatley illustrates the sublimation of creative genius. As part of her discussion, Walker introduces the important feminist text *A Room of One's Own*, using brackets to focus Woolf's text on black women in particular. We might remind students of this use of punctuation to distinguish between quoted material and our own additions, so they can use it in their own writing.

In the middle of her essay, between the example of writer Phillis Wheatley and the example of her mother that follows, Walker places her call for action. Being a black woman and an artist is difficult, she says, so black women today must take hold of their creativity. Students may notice that she begins this paragraph with the transition word *Therefore*, signaling cause and effect. She goes on to explain how the title relates to art. Her own mother is also an artist. Walker defines art in various places in her essay as singing in church, singing blues songs, sewing clothing and quilts, telling stories, and making gardens, as well as the convention-bound literary efforts of Phillis Wheatley. Unlike the formula that begins with an explicit thesis statement and then takes the reader point by point through an argument, Alice Walker's text leads us into her main idea gradually, interweaves examples, letting one idea lead to another, then comes back to ideas mentioned earlier and develops them further. Students should note that she achieves coherence partly through the use of words that signal the course of her thinking: *but* or *yet* to signal shifts, *and* to signal more of the same. Although they may have been taught to avoid beginning sentences with conjunctions, they'll notice that literary nonfiction writers use these simple connecting words effectively to help readers follow their arguments. Walker's essay is quiltlike, a mix of genres, sewn together with smooth transitions. Walker's mother's artistry with sewing leads us to a vivid description of a quilt in the Smithsonian Institution whose attribution to "an anonymous Black woman" leads us back to Virginia Woolf and her suggestion that *Anon* — the unknown creator of literary works — was a woman. From here Walker moves to descriptions of her mother's storytelling, but most importantly, her gardens. She vividly explains how her mother made growing flowers an artistic endeavor. Then she includes a poem about the "Headragged Generals" of her mother's generation who acquired the literary knowledge for their children that they did not have themselves. We may recall that Walker has earlier given us the detail that her mother only loses her temper when fighting for her children's education.

Alice Walker's speech ends with one sentence following the poem, summing up the influence of her mother's generation. She lists three values in this sentence that may give us a key to the themes of her stories: "heritage . . . love of beauty and a respect for strength." In the essay, however, she adds three more paragraphs. The ending of the speech is pretty, but it has a pat sense of closure, reminding the reader of a moral tacked onto the end of a fable or a parable. We almost see her pause and lower her head for the applause that comes after the performance. But the essay needs the echo of Phillis Wheatley and her connection to the deep past. As she does in so many of her texts, Alice Walker imagines an ancestor — a mother — for the African child bought by the Wheatley family the year she lost her front baby teeth and came across the ocean in a slave ship. Alice Walker and Phillis Wheatley are thus linked in a long line of artistic women, and the essay's unity is enhanced.

Both "Everyday Use" and "In Search of Our Mothers' Gardens" refer to quilts. Both texts describe these as part of the artistic heritage of African American women. They are of value not as objects to be collected, but as material creations of the hands and artistic spirits of ancestors. They are reminders of the past and are imbued with power beyond simple artifacts. We might think of the crayon art of Minnie Evans or the quilt created by the last queen of Hawaii as she sat confined in her palace by Americans out to steal her kingdom. Walker says of her mother's gardening that it was "a daily part of her life," reminding us of the everyday use Maggie will make of the quilts, remembering her grandmother and Aunt Dee all the while. Walker similarly sees song as an artistic creation that has been permitted to black women. In "Nineteen Fifty-Five" song is the expression of Gracie Mae's life and heritage. Reading this essay gives us a clearer idea of what this might mean. If a person is allowed only one way of creating, then all of her energy and spirit go into it. So do the oppression, the abuse, and the failures of men to understand. Interestingly, Bessie Smith is mentioned in both texts, this time as a singer of Ma Rainey's creations.

317

The narrators of the short stories in this cluster and Alice Walker's mother as described in the essay have much in common. The heritage of slavery and its consequent alienation from Africa play a part in the lives of these enduring women. Slavery and its soul-scarring ramifications are barriers to creation for artists denied education, time, materials, health, respect, and understanding; and Alice Walker sees that the frustration of their creativity has driven some of these women insane or led them into self-destruction, as Jean Toomer described in the 1920s. But gender plays as large a role as race in this waste of artistic energy. For centuries, movements for women's rights and the rights of African Americans have been in conflict. This places black women in a double bind. Students might like to look up the famous anecdote of Sojourner Truth demanding bare-breasted of an audience of female activists, "Ain't I a woman?" Even the men who should support them or at least recognize their contributions and desires see them as "the mules of the world," as Walker points out. Mama in "Everyday Use" does hard physical labor. Gracie Mae has often provided financial support for her men. Walker's mother works in the fields as the equal of her husband, does domestic work, and still creates her gardens, quilts, and stories. Limited both by the poverty and inequality that followed in the wake of slavery and by the patriarchy that subjugates women to men, the women Walker writes about manage to create and grow strong in spite of these barriers. Walker has called her philosophy *womanist* rather than feminist, and all of her texts celebrate in some way the value of women.

JUDGING WRITING (p. 1447)

ROSEMARY CATACALOS

David Talamántez on the Last Day of Second Grade (p. 1447)

Students in teacher education programs need to post a copy of Rosemary Catacalos's evocation of "David Talamántez on the Last Day of Second Grade" beside their bathroom mirrors to read every morning. It wouldn't hurt for college instructors to read it from time to time either. It has been more than two decades since Mina Shaughnessy's 1977 *Errors and Expectations* gave instructors of basic writing at the college level the practical insights we needed to help our students improve their own writing. They make mistakes, she says, "not because they are slow or non-verbal, indifferent to or incapable of academic excellence, but because they are beginners" (5). They see writing as a *trap* — as Shaughnessy terms it — or a test for which we refuse to provide clear-cut questions, rather than a means of communicating real ideas to real people. If we look together at patterns of errors, we can help them find these for themselves as they edit and proofread late drafts. Like David Talamántez's spelling, errors in college essays tend to have a logical basis that students can learn to spot with attention.

Before this, however, we have to get past the fear of judgment that has become connected with writing for so many students. Some have overcome this and made good grades by writing according to the set patterns laid out for them, giving the teacher exactly what the directions require. "But what did I do wrong?" they demand, when their mechanically perfect but lifeless essays earn them a B– in their first semester of college. We try to work through issues of form and content in conferences and emphasize that writing is a process, that our nebulous ideas and fragmented logic seldom fall into beautifully organized prose in the first draft. Discovering their own content and form through writing is a new experience for many students, who assume we are unorganized and unable to articulate exactly what we want them to write, as previous teachers have done.

Accountability issues have placed high-school and elementary-school teachers in a difficult position. Standardized testing of writing works against all that we have learned about critical thinking and the need for form to follow content. To make their school's percentages look good on the test, students must reduce a complex issue quickly to an oversimplified thesis statement, then follow specific guidelines about how many points to make. In recent formulas that middle-school teachers must follow in one state, even paragraphs have a predetermined form, beginning with the obligatory topic sentence, but also dictating the degree of specificity of the following set number of sentences. This practice ignores studies showing that professional writers seldom follow such rigid order and that a large percentage of paragraphs in published prose do not have topic sentences. Unfortunately, some college instructors carry this prescriptive pedagogy into higher education. One teacher at a community college measures margins, counting points off for misalignment. Another has students place the main ideas in the paragraphs of a published essay into a formal outline with Roman numerals, letters, and so forth in the same way she breaks them down, with a topic sentence and exactly three points in each paragraph.

Grammar, punctuation, and spelling also count heavily with these instructors. Students quickly learn to keep their essays short and safe, avoiding any risk that will cut into the grade. This makes grading simpler, but the focus at college thus becomes similar to what we see happening already to David Talamántez in elementary school. Creativity and originality are squelched. Rather than being allowed to enter the academic dialogue with a fresh perspective on the issues being discussed, they must concentrate instead on semicolons. In the 1970s when composition theorist Lil Brannon taught in Wilmington, North Carolina, the local newspaper quoted her in an interview as saying something like "Grammar and punctuation are the last thing we worry about in a college writing class." Angry letters to the editor followed. The writers thought she expressed contempt for proper English and that contempt epitomized all that was wrong with liberal education. They saw a defiance of standards bordering on a Socratic contamination of the morals of the young.

What she meant, of course, was that we first get the ideas down on paper somehow, not letting issues of correctness make us tense or limit our thinking. We don't censor ourselves, understanding that we may learn something interesting from that wild thought about why birds are warm-blooded, even if we are

319

technically wrong. Then we organize and rethink, perhaps get some more ideas and throw away a few others or save them for other essays. We test the quality of our evidence or examples and then make connections and clarifications to help the reader follow the argument or narrative. Then we tinker with sentences, and finally — as the last thing we worry about — read to make sure we have used the conventions that will make it easiest for our audience to understand our ideas without distractions.

It isn't that linear, of course, and computers make the process a bit different, inviting even more backtracking and shifting of materials. They also allow spell-checker howlers like *cereal killer*. Of course we get some lazy or overextended students who throw something together at the last minute and expect to get the A their work received in high school. And some have both talent and solid grounding in critical thinking before they come to college; they construct cogent essays with admirable style. But most students dread having their writing judged as much as we dread judging it. And too many college students can relate experiences at school that battered their spirits. If this is true of those who succeed, imagine the struggles of those like the little boy in Rosemary Catacalos's poem who experience such negative evaluations consistently.

Catacalos creates in David Talamántez a character who seems real. Even after being told that he is a composite, we still see him vividly and feel that we know him, because she gives details of his personality. We watch him in action and hear his voice. We have seen his artwork and know how he thinks: His warrants for knowing that birds are warm-blooded have to do with their lively movement and the complexity of their expression. We are hurt that the teacher is unable to see the beauty and creativity of his mind, its liveliness and complexity, which is so like his warm birds. We are conscious of his ethnicity because he has an Hispanic surname, because we see a few details of the neighborhood, and because he has difficulty with written English, spelling it just as he hears it. But most second graders have some difficulty with the spelling of English, a notoriously inconsistent language. The "whole language" approach to reading and writing takes this into account, allowing students to invent spellings so that they are not slowed down as they first begin to write. But David's teacher doesn't cut him any slack, nor does she seem to take his probable bilingual learning situation into account.

Although in some ways it is important that English is probably not David's first language, the experience is not confined to his being Chicano. He could as easily be limited by an English dialect or by cultural or class differences that separate him from mainstream American speech and concepts. He could simply be a child whose learning style differs from the one privileged by an obviously unperceptive teacher. Studies have shown that evaluations of a student's work can be influenced by misinformation planted by researchers. If the teacher is prejudiced, even unknowingly, against Mexican Americans, her bias clouds her expectations of David's abilities. Other forms of bias might affect expectations of other students.

This teacher assumes that everything belongs in its proper place and should be done in the proper way. Neatness counts. Creativity and originality are punished. Rules are important. So are correct spelling and "nice details." Readers readily conclude that the teacher values conformity. In her classroom, students learn rules rather than critical and creative thinking skills.

David, when we first meet him, may be angry, but he is most of all determined to make "his mark," to shout out his name to the world. There is something triumphant about his contribution of language to the world. He "publishes" his literary and artistic creations like broadsides or flyers thrown from an airplane. If David were a part of speech, he would be an active verb, and readers might count the verbs and other references to movement in the poem. By inscribing his name in place of the teacher's evaluation of him, he reclaims his identity, replacing the negative minuses of his grades with the positive "yes" of his worth. His voice rings out confidently and his affirmation is large, unlike the small letters he uses for schoolwork. He has not been beaten down yet. But readers usually characterize this poem as sad. Perhaps this is because we hurt for children who suffer judgments from teachers who fail to recognize their strengths. "But we should have standards," teachers object. We might answer that students do need to learn language skills that will help them in life, but it is not necessary to ignore the value of a child's identity while teaching him. Interested students might review "Aria" by Richard Rodriguez (p. 657) for another view on the role of teachers in giving a Mexican American child a voice of his own. Some readers of Catacalos's text maintain that bilingual education would help David to express himself in a more familiar language while learning skills in English.

But the issue seems more universal. It involves a difference in philosophies about education. School boards and principals can influence the type of teacher who is hired, screening for attitudes that fail to take difference into account. Teacher training programs have a great influence, as do English departments at universities. Many teachers try to find something positive to say before raising a negative issue with a child or her parents, a policy that tends to build self-esteem and good will. Some activists call for the elimination of grades altogether. We might ask our college students how they think such an action would affect their current learning experiences. If they think they would expend little effort, we might ask them if the result would be the same for young children, eager to learn and create. Most of us recall thinking of grades as somehow involved with good or bad luck or the teacher's personal dislike or affection for us. This is especially true of evaluations of writing or art, since our identity is so closely bound up with such efforts. Some teachers think like the computer, sticking to the rules and disregarding the differing purposes of poetry and prose, along with any other difference.

The enjambment of the poem gives syntax importance, since we keep reading to the end of the sentence for the sake of meaning. Nevertheless, punctuation and line breaks allow smaller units of discourse. In the middle of the first line, for example, we have the phrase "whose mother is at work" set off by commas. This gives us an indication of David's family life, since he is going home on his own and his mother will probably not be home until later. The commas emphasize this fact, but the poet just mentions it in passing, not explaining anything but instead leaving it for us to simply note, perhaps to think of it later as we see the drawing of the crowded dinner table with "To mush noys!" We see that perhaps David could be valued more as an individual even in his family, though this is just a fact of his life, not something that is singled out for judgment. Enjambment allows the smallest of pauses to occur at the end of each line, thus emphasizing by the white space the words that occur in these spots. For example, the first line could have come to a full stop at the end of the word *mark*, and we do pause there, left for a fraction of a second with the idiom "leaves his mark," meaning to make a difference in the world. But the indented phrase that comprises the second line modifies the meaning. Therefore, we see that the syntax and the punctuation and line breaks maintain a tension between the headlong action of the text's narrative and the more measured and intermittent pace of the poetry.

BILLY COLLINS

Workshop (p. 1449)

This poem could be characterized as a *meta*text, a piece of writing that is about itself. Those of us who have written for an audience of peers in a creative writing workshop recognize the tentative tone of the reader who is trying to find a gentle way to critique the poem of a classmate. Or as instructors, we may recognize our voices as we attempt the positive expression that cushions the blow of the mediocre grade. The poet may be talking to himself, evaluating his poem as he writes it. We who have been there — including most of our students — may suspect that an assignment is due and the student in the poetry class has written something — anything — to meet the workshop deadline. Although for most of us it is a mistake to edit too strenuously in the middle of the creative process, as the speaker of "Workshop" seems to do, a key to effective writing is learning to be one's own editor.

New college instructors are often shocked by the first batch of papers from first-year undergraduates. Many obviously have not been read through by the writer or anyone else before coming across our desks. If the students sit down with us in conference or if they consult with someone at the college writing center, they quickly catch convoluted sentences or failures to connect ideas in their own work. One can tell them that invention and other early steps of the writing process are right-brain activities whereas organizing and proofreading are left-brain activities. The activities feel different. Too much rationality tends to stifle the free flow of ideas, often leading to writer's block. Yet the organizing and revising of later stages depends upon stepping back and reading critically. When peer editing groups function as they should, students learn to clarify their ideas for an audience and for themselves. But often readers in a group are at a loss about what to say and how to say it, like the apologetic speaker of Billy Collins's poem. Their comments offer little real sense of the text's effect on an audience.

Some professional writers object to the workshop format so prevalent in graduate M.F.A. departments and other creative writing programs, feeling that literary texts lose spontaneity and individuality when they are adapted by and for a small "incestuous" audience. It sounds like a cliché to suggest that the success of a workshop or a peer editing group depends upon the mix of personalities and the instructor's clear guidance in creating a community of readers and writers, but we all know that this is true. Most of us have been in groups that were worse than useless in helping us judge our own writing and in other groups that gave insightful readings that were invaluable to our development as writers. In the best of academic and literary worlds, students carry the critical reading skills they learn from analyzing the texts of others into their own writing and editing process.

Billy Collins's "Workshop" hints that the poem refers to itself in the first line, as it gives a reader response to the title. The second stanza mentions "the first couple of stanzas" and the poem's "mode of self-pointing" — giving more evidence that this poem is the one being judged in the workshop. The inconsistent voice brought up in the third stanza communicates a reality about workshops and takes a sideswipe at the pomposity of academic judgments. One of the criticisms of workshops — and the whole notion of teaching creative writing in the university — is that the writer's unique voice may become submerged beneath the other voices in the class. The fourth stanza refers to "the middle stanzas, / especially the fourth one," and this self-reference to both the poem and the workshop experience continues throughout the poem. But there's also the feeling that some of the lines are out of context: The speaker refers to lines we are seeing for the first time that seem to be from a different poem. This may be one of the poem's points, however; the poem is made up of snippets from the metaphor collection in the desk drawer or the daily journal, and is so far a jumble that doesn't connect for a reader, perhaps because the writer does not yet have a focus. The speaker's judgment shifts, beginning on the obligatory positive note, but tiptoeing into criticism with the "But" of the third stanza. He wavers back and forth throughout the poem, unwilling to give a definitive reading, aware that ambiguity is supposed to be okay, seeming to wonder if the problem he's feeling with the poem is how it's written or if his perception as a reader is in question. The speaker's tone and vocabulary parody feedback in a creative writing workshop. We recognize the allusion to Samuel Taylor Coleridge's "Rime of the Ancient Mariner" in the fourth line, but wonder if the speaker uses it ironically or has slipped into cliché. The metaphors in the second line reach too hard for a fresh way to say something, and they may hint that the text being judged is garbage or that the poet is casting pearls before swine — the readers in the workshop. The tentative "if you know what I mean" and "maybe that's just what it wants to do" and the repeated apology that perhaps "it's just me" ironically echo the discourse of peer review and instructor feedback. They also reflect the lack of confidence we tend to have in ourselves as readers. As we analyze this poem, we hear ourselves lapsing into the jargon it parodies. We wonder if we would have been among the philistines unable to recognize the genius of T. S. Eliot and James Joyce. In the workshop of Collins's poem, the reader refers to specific aspects of the text, groping for reasons behind their effect upon him as a reader. This may be the best a reviewer can expect to do. Sometimes students who have met in peer groups in their first year as undergraduates continue to give each other feedback on papers they write for other classes, a fact that counts as a measure of success. Creative writing seminars produce ongoing relationships, sometimes literary movements or "schools" of interrelated poets, but more often informal arrangements between writers who trust each other's judgment. The members of Robert Lowell's group demonstrate the empowering effect of such relationships for poets with their own strong voices. For example, Maxine Kumin tells of keeping a telephone line open to Anne Sexton as they worked independently, each poet reading drafts to the other as the poems developed. Billy Collins's poem is clearly satirical, striking at the pomposity of professors, the clichés and contrived metaphors of texts written to be judged, the indeterminacy of such judgments, and the questionable value of teaching writing by consensus. We might ask students to decide if the poem parodies the response of a reader who is too obtuse to recognize a good poem or a reader who is trying to be polite about a mediocre one.

If Rosemary Catacalos submitted her poem to the workshop of this poem, Collins's speaker would have something to say about tropes, perhaps finding significance in the way that the thrown pages "catch on the teachers' car bumpers" in the second stanza. He wouldn't be sure, but might think this signified a *catch* that snags the boy up like a *Catch-22* or a *catch in the voice*, or perhaps it is meant to *catch* the readers' attention like an ancient mariner. Students should have fun writing a parody, and there should be a variety of responses that *catch* the polite, unsure tone of the speaker. The rules of Collins's workshop include courtesy and specificity. The creations of writers in "Workshop" are treated with respect — to a fault, some would say. The teachers at the elementary school in "David Talamántez on the Last Day of Second Grade" could give their students a similar sort of understanding. The pattern in writing workshops is to have each reader respond to the text in detail, giving it focused attention. Ironically, children in school seldom receive this sort of attention. The teacher focuses on telling David what is wrong and is concerned mostly with rules. In the workshop, we hear nothing about spelling or the placement of the writer's name on the page, and its readers would certainly have something positive to say about the creativity that the second-grade teacher frowns upon. On the other hand, perhaps the adult writers in "Workshop" could handle a more critical reading than they are given.

PHILIP LARKIN

Fiction and the Reading Public (p. 1452)

As we move into reading Philip Larkin's "Fiction and the Reading Public," which purports to give advice to the writer, students will enjoy hearing other poems by Larkin. Most relevant may be "A Study of Reading Habits," a much-anthologized poem that takes its rowdy speaker through a life of living vicariously through books and ends with the memorable line, "Books are a load of crap." Ironically, Larkin was a librarian. He never married, and he cultivated the personal image of a man who had no adventures, romantic or otherwise, though recent biographers dispute his reputation as a recluse. But his brash poetic persona earned him one biography with the apt title *An Uncle Shouting Smut,* echoing a line from another poem, "The Whitsun Weddings."

Larkin's tone is ironic — both humorous and sharp — and his agenda since his days as an undergraduate at Oxford University in the early 1940s was to skewer pompous and mannered style in poetry. He liked to side with a popular audience against the obscurities of modernism, feeling that "this myth-kitty business" of allusion to classical or biblical themes pretentiously sacrificed originality in order to show off one's education. He uses slang — British, and thus sometimes obscure to American readers — and obscenities that shocked more readily in the 1950s and 1960s than they do now. He's good at bitter one-liners that raise cultural and psychological issues: "Sexual intercourse began / in nineteen sixty three" or "They fuck you up, your mum and dad" or "Life is first boredom, then fear." But his seemingly democratic verses are steeped in irony, and when we take tone into account, members of the popular audience may feel less complimented.

He can also write gentle, somber lines like the first stanza of "Cut Grass" (1974): "Cut grass lies frail: / Brief is the breath / Mown stalks exhale. / Long, long the death. . . ." Or he can juxtapose his blunt diction with a poetic echo of Sir Philip Sidney's Sonnet 31 from *Astrophil and Stella* (1591) in "Sad Steps" (1974): "Groping back to bed after a piss / I part thick curtains, and am startled by / The rapid clouds, the moon's cleanliness. . . . / The way the moon dashes through clouds that blow / Loosely as cannon-smoke to stand apart / (Stone-coloured light sharpening the roofs below) / High and preposterous and separate. . . ." Considered a minor poet for a time, turning down the office of poet laureate on principle, Philip Larkin has come to be considered the major voice in British poetry in the late twentieth century. That he has also reached "the reading public" is evidenced by numerous postings on the Internet.

The reader Larkin depicts in "Fiction and the Reading Public" wants sensation. He wants verisimilitude, giving the writer the tried-and-true advice that he should write what he knows. We might use the adjectives *superficial* and *intrusive* to describe him. The reader is also moralistic, wanting sunshine and happy endings. He's really not interested in art or the writer's happiness or self-expression. He's a practical capitalist, his warrants reminding the writer where his bread is buttered. The speaker's tone is arrogant and demanding. The poet's tone, on the other hand, may be sarcastic, revealing the crassness of the "reading public" through his own imagined words.

Many readers in their first year of college don't have a taste for subtlety and prefer the upbeat and straightforward popular fiction Larkin describes, if they read for pleasure at all. Others, on the other hand, like science fiction and horror or psychological thrillers that present a darker view than that of Larkin's 1950s popular audience. We might recall that Mickey Spillane's Mike Hammer detective stories topped the best-seller lists in the United States when Larkin's poem was written. The average woman preferred romantic fiction. But the 1950s in the United States also brought writers like Eudora Welty, Flannery O'Connor, Saul Bellow, Norman Mailer, Ralph Ellison, John Updike, Bernard Malamud, and others who raised issues even as they surprised readers with their style and shocked readers with their frankness. Many of our current students are beginning

325

to find the authors that make them think even as they share in the "thrill" and the "kick" of realistic or imaginative worlds of fiction. Books that Oprah Winfrey chooses for her televised "book club" achieve instant success, even when they are difficult texts that have been around for years, like Toni Morrison's *Song of Solomon*. Despite predictions that electronic media would kill reading, bookstores in the mall and online sell millions of books.

It's usually a mistake to identify a writer too closely with the speaker of a poem. Larkin enjoyed the role of misanthrope and did not seek out honors, perhaps saw bad reviews as a challenge. And he kept his need to make a living separate from his writing; therefore, he did not depend on reviewers and promoters for his income, as is implied in the third stanza. He knew that his work was respected, but may not have known it would become as highly valued as it has, especially since some of the colloquial language should have dated it sooner. This and the fact that he wrote little poetry during the last decade of his life argue for an ironic bitterness in the last two lines.

Larkin's "reading public" goes for the type of fiction that usually doesn't make it into the literature books or get much space in the Literary Supplement of the *New York Times*. But when Larkin doesn't differentiate between this sort of "pulp fiction" or Harlequin romance genre and the fiction that gets reviewed, today's readers may feel that he lumps together many different audiences. Perhaps we could determine who is part of the current "reading public" that fits Larkin's description by looking at who buys books from the supermarket and drugstore rather than the bookstore. The lines between art and trash are difficult to draw, and we are increasingly less willing to draw them.

The simple rhyme scheme of Larkin's poem is part of its theme that popular audiences want writers to stick to conventions they understand, to make things easy and pretty. He mocks the criticisms of readers who prefer uplift to artistic or serious fiction by putting quotation marks around words they are likely to overuse to the point of cliché. By doing this so many times in the space of one stanza, he calls attention to the usage and engages in a humorous hyperbole of punctuation that makes complainers seem ridiculous.

The readers Larkin describes would look at Rosemary Catacalos's "David Talamántez on the Last Day of Second Grade" and say first of all, "I don't get it because it doesn't say what it means," and secondly, "I don't like it because it's sad." They might fault Billy Collins's "Workshop" as too artsy, too separated from real life. The teacher of Catacalos's poem has a great deal in common with Larkin's reader; neither wants the writers to go outside the lines to get too creative or try to *express* themselves. It's puzzling that the teacher seems to like the picture that David draws of his family with the line implying that life at home is too noisy. One might think at first that she might like it because it plays into her prejudice about overcrowded Hispanic homes, but there is no evidence for this. What she praises him for are the "nice details." This seems to be what Larkin's reader wants: verisimilitude "that'll sound like real life." Collins's workshop member too might go for this advice and repeat some of the jargon of Larkin's second stanza as he talks about reader response.

Rosemary Catacalos's poem achieves most of its effectiveness by sounding like "real life." We know this kid exists, even if he is a composite, and we want to do something to rescue him from a school experience that threatens to kill his spirit for no good reason. For a limited audience, Billy Collins also writes a poem that rings true in our experience. Although poems do not always have to be realistic, we expect a sort of internal consistency that works in the world of the poem itself. The poem that Billy Collins's reader works with in "Workshop" puzzles him because its metaphors do not seem to work together. They are consistent if this is a poem about the difficulty of reading and writing for a workshop, but if we imagine another poem in which the images occur, they don't really hang together as we are given them. Larkin's poem reads the mind of a reader who probably would not consciously realize that he wants these particular things of a book, and wouldn't say them in this way. Here, we are conscious throughout of the voice of the contemptuous writer making fun of his readers. Ironically, the poem that imagines a call for realism is the most contrived.

JUDGING SOCIETY (p. 1454)

WILLIAM BLAKE
London (p. 1455)

It's always a good idea with William Blake to read one poem in the context of other poems that share the same symbolic motifs. This is especially important with the companion volumes *Songs of Innocence*, written in 1789, and *Songs of Experience*, written in 1794. Blake set up these poems and illustrations — Blake was first an artist and engraver — as "contraries" that relate to each other. The poems in *Songs of Innocence* reveal a dark, fallen world as seen through the eyes of naive narrators who are unable to envision the horrors that the reader understands are suggested. The companion poems of *Songs of Experience* picture the same world through the perspective of someone older and thus able to confront the oppression and evil all around him. To use examples that will be familiar to most readers, contrast "The Lamb" in Songs of Innocence with its companion piece "The Tyger" in *Songs of Experience*.

The world of *Songs of Experience* is frightening and ugly, peopled by human creatures chained by poverty, disease, war, and the exploitation that uses women as prostitutes and children as chimney sweeps. Repressive morality and a loveless church add to the pain. In Blake's view of history, human sacrifice was the charter of civilization, and the images of the poem "London" epitomize the continuation of this atrocity. While people around him had good reason to believe that Blake was crazy — he had hallucinations and showed signs of paranoia — Blake pointed out the madness of London and industrialized England. For Blake the salvation from this institutionalized, mechanized horror lay in the human imagination. Imagination can take us beyond the naiveté acute of our first innocence and the pessimism of experience to a state of "organized innocence" that includes the earlier states but spiritually transcends them. Blake believed that unmasking evil through art and literature could break the passivity that allowed abuses to continue. As an observer from afar of both the American and French Revolutions, he had a keen awareness of the political and social issues of his time, and conversed with radical political theorists like William Godwin and Tom Paine.

Blake is not an easy poet to interpret, since he created an idiosyncratic mythology. His symbols condense personal connotations into recurring images and key words filled with meanings beyond their commonsense denotations. To better understand "London" students should first be acquainted with other poems that refer to chimney sweepers, who symbolized for Blake the exploitation of the most vulnerable members of society. Because they were small, these young boys spent their days engaged in the filthy, dangerous job of going into the chimneys of London, breathing soot and risking falls. All who should have protected children from such abuse — their parents, the church, members of the poem's first audience — actively or passively conspired in this child abuse because it was economically expedient.

In the first version of the poem "The Chimney Sweeper" in *Songs of Innocence*, the child escapes the "coffins of black" in his dream, and the poem ends with his innocent and ironic moral that "if all do their duty they need not fear harm." We hear his lisping pronunciation of *sweep* as " 'weep," since he is too young to speak plainly. His word sounds like the synonym for *cry*. This image is repeated, along with others that implicate parents and church, in the later poem titled "The Chimney Sweeper" in *Songs of Experience*. These intertextual connotations should already be in the minds of readers as they look at lines 9 and 10 of "London," where Blake explicitly links the *cry* of the chimney sweeper with the "black'ning Church." Another poem — "A Divine Image," which begins with the line "Cruelty has a Human Heart" and includes the image "The Human Dress is forged Iron" — seems particularly relevant to a discussion of "London." Although most of us lack the time to become experts on this complex poet, to a certain extent we can allow him to explain himself to our students in his own words.

Repetitions of words are particularly important in the first two stanzas of "London," where Blake begins by repeating the words *chartered* and *mark/marks*, moving on to repeat the words *every* and *cry*, almost as a speaker might pound his fist on the lectern for emphasis. The context invites the interpretation that the repetitions echo the sound of a prisoner clanking rhythmically as he shuffles in his chains. The repeated word *chartered* traditionally refers to the legitimacy of London's existence as a chartered institution, literally meaning that the city is "at liberty" to govern itself. The connotation of democratic government is thus here, and this sounds like a good thing. But we must remember that Blake equates the origins of organized human society with human sacrifice. The word *chartered* also refers to land parceled off, owned as private property, and rented out. Thus the river that should be a part of nature has been appropriated to artificial uses.

The speaker uses the word *mark* as a verb for seeing and noting, but what he sees are *marks*. The perspective of experience does not allow the blemish that the city smudges on its inhabitants to be ignored. The repetitions, therefore, build meanings as they accumulate connotations, and they hold our attention. The word *every* is repeated five times in the stanza that ends with the image of "mind-forged manacles." The perverted imagination of civilized humanity thinks up ways to enslave everyone from the oldest to the youngest; it is like the hellish furnace of an iron foundry, a negative symbol for Blake. The word *ban* relates to the repression suggested by the word *manacles.* A ban confines socially in the same sort of way manacles limit physically. A ban can be a prohibition, a taboo, or a public condemnation. Furthermore, its plural sounds like the word *banns,* the public announcement that a marriage is about to take place, thus limiting love to the confines of church and state.

Although the specific abuses Blake describes are not accepted by society with the same apathy they received in the eighteenth and nineteenth centuries, students will think of modern equivalents. When women are forced by drug addiction into prostitution and their children live in cockroach-infested squalor, for example, we might consider them to be wearing "mind-forged manacles," especially when no concrete action is taken to help them find better solutions to end their "weakness" and "woe." The final stanza of Blake's poem suggests that the problems of London will not be confined to the present. His reference to the "infant's tear" is usually taken to have the double meaning of sorrow and the "curse" of venereal disease that causes the infants of infected mothers to become blind. By ending with the juxtaposition of marriage and death, Blake may refer to the carrying over of disease into marriage.

Blake's poem ranges from the universal abstract implied by the word *every* to less general images like the chimney sweeper, the soldier, and the harlot. These are representative characters, however, and do not refer to specific people like "Tom Dacre" or "Dick, Joe, Ned, and Jack," who are mentioned in one of the chimney sweeper poems. We don't know much about the appearance of the "marks" Blake's speaker notices. Are they scars from disease or violence? Or smudges from the gritty surroundings? The poem describes an ongoing situation, happening too often to too many people, and the level of abstraction appropriately allows for this feeling. But some images are concrete enough to give us a vivid picture; for example, the "Soldier's sigh / Runs in blood down Palace walls." This poem is thoroughly negative because Blake sees the situation of humanity as desperate. But he counts on the reader's imagination to transform society once its horrors are revealed. Recognizing that apathy leads to cruelty, Blake is hopeful that readers will identify with these symbolic characters and thus seek out the "Mercy, Pity, Peace, and Love" that he writes of in his poem "The Divine Image."

WILLIAM WORDSWORTH
The World Is Too Much with Us (p. 1456)

Like his contemporary William Blake, William Wordsworth developed his poetic vision with an awareness of the social, political, and intellectual revolutions in the world of his time. As a young man, he traveled to France to

329

place himself in the midst of the French Revolution, falling in love and fathering a child while there. Earlier, Wordsworth had traveled to Switzerland, a trip that also represented a kind of revolution. From our distance on the other side of the Romantic Movement that Wordsworth to a great extent fathered, it is difficult for us to realize that communion with nature has not always evoked positive emotions for human beings. For earlier generations, nature represented the fearful forces of a realm outside the control of God and civilization, and mountain and ocean views would have been viewed with horror and distaste.

In Wordsworth's time this attitude toward the natural world began to change. For the poet, gazing at the ocean or climbing an alp to be thrilled by the rugged landscape below led to an experience with what he called "the sublime," a rush of awe and heightened emotion. Like Blake, Wordsworth contrasted this depth and beauty of the countryside with the ugliness and oppression of an urban England entering the Industrial Revolution. Wordsworth, his friend and fellow poet Samuel Taylor Coleridge, and others of what came to be called the Romantic Movement spent time walking in the Lake Country of England, energizing their writing with "emotion recollected in tranquility" — to use Wordsworth's definition of poetry.

Wordsworth set out to revolutionize poetry in the same way the political revolutions of the day were changing society and views of humanity. He resisted the neoclassical detachment and formalism in vogue in the generation preceding him, choosing to use diction that was closer to everyday speech and to seek out down-to-earth subjects like leech gatherers and old soldiers. He saw peasants and children, who are capable of spontaneous joy and oneness with nature, as wiser than the people who were running the world. Though he would become more conservative and receptive to orthodox religion in later years, the early Wordsworth of "The World Is Too Much with Us" might be termed a pantheist who sees all nature as charged with spiritual depth and energy.

Not only did he resist the received wisdom about class and decorum in poetry, but he deliberately rejected the new ideas of Sir Isaac Newton that permeated Cambridge University at the time the young poet was studying there. He saw the warrants of Newtonian physics as reducing the universe to a dead clockwork mechanism of cogs and wheels, in opposition to the organic, mystical whole shimmering with joy and life. Like Blake's "dark, Satanic mills," the worldview that reduced nature and humanity to objects to serve the ambition and selfishness of others was the antithesis of Wordsworth's Romanticism.

With Wordsworth and Coleridge's 1798 *Lyrical Ballads*, poetry began its transformation into an expression of individual emotion and imagination. All poets since Wordsworth must contend with the assumptions that he articulated, deciding how far they will walk alongside him and where they will diverge. Ironically, although Wordsworth privileged colloquial diction and innovation rather than externally imposed forms, his language often sounds self-consciously "poetic" and his forms are rigid to current readers, who are accustomed to the free verse and hard-edged irony of modern and postmodern writers. It's hard to believe that Wordsworth became a virtual rock star of his time, besieged by fans that trampled his lawn and listened to him intone his poetry and philosophy extemporaneously. By then, the old revolutionary was poet laureate of England, solidly ensconced as a figure of the establishment.

"The World Is Too Much with Us" is an Italian, or Petrarchan, sonnet that consists of an octave — eight lines — whose rhyme pattern is *abbaabba* and a sestet — six lines — with an alternating *cdcdcd*. Rhetorically, this divides the poem into three parts, the first four lines stating a proposition, the second unit of four lines elaborating on it, and the final six taking a logical turn. Wordsworth varies the rhetoric a bit by delaying the change a half-line, but he keeps the traditional rhyme. We could restate his argument in three points: We have traded our ability to experience nature for economic gain; we are therefore "out of tune" and numb to nature's beauties; it would have been better to experience the joys of nature in a pre-Christian world that peopled nature with deities than not to feel it at all.

Students may be confused by Wordsworth's rejection of the "world" in the first line and his praise of nature in later ones, since in some definitions of the word, nature would be part of the *world*, a concept used interchangeably with the *earth*. We should discuss this issue of definition early, inferring from the context that Wordsworth means the world of economic concerns, perhaps with the biblical connotations of conforming to the evil nature of a fallen humanity rather than being spiritually renewed. The "powers" that we have lost in trading away our hearts are powers of perception and awe in the face of natural wonders. The "sordid boon" refers to the results of the barter, not the human heart.

In Wordsworth's view, humanity has become separated from nature and can no longer relate to the natural world because this other world gets in the way. Certainly, many people of Wordsworth's time would have seen nature as something to be conquered, tamed, and fenced off into a proper English garden. Few people would admit to this politically incorrect attitude today, even as they vote in plans to pave wilderness so that people can park their RVs and be close to nature. Most students today are environmentally aware and may have a stronger grasp of what Wordsworth fears than his immediate audience did. We might raise the issue, however, of the convenient excuses we make to justify just one more high-rise resort on a shifting beach or one more stand of old growth lost to development. Environmentalists are in fact often criticized as being romantics, a characterization meant to pejoratively imply that they are impractical and out of touch with "the world." Perhaps such critics also refer to the outpourings of emotion about nature that seem exaggerated to modern ears. But the sensory imagery so valued in both poetry and prose today may owe a great deal to Wordsworth and his peers.

In "The World Is Too Much with Us" Wordsworth appeals first to the visual senses, even using the word *see* to describe our perceptions of nature, now dulled by trade. He goes on to give us the startling personification of the Sea in an attitude of unselfconscious nakedness, exposing herself to the moon. This is definitely visual. But the next line invites us to imagine the howling of the wind, an auditory image. We visualize the flowers in line 7, recalling ones that open up in the morning and close at night. But in the next line, we are listening for the note when we are told we are "out of tune." In the sestet, we similarly alternate between the eye and the ear, ending with "the sight of Proteus" and the sound of Triton blowing on a conch shell. And there is a bit of the kinesthetic as we feel ourselves standing on the beach with the poet and envision the sense of movement as the sea "bares her bosom" or imagine "Proteus rising from the sea."

Although William Blake and William Wordsworth differed greatly in personality and in the mythology and symbolism they used, they opposed the same social and political forces. Both speak against the selfish objectification of humanity and nature for purposes of monetary gain. Wordsworth wrote several poems about London that students might want to compare with Blake's. Whereas Wordsworth's famous "Composed upon Westminster Bridge, September 3, 1802" describes the city's beauty at dawn in tones of admiration that he usually reserves for natural settings, the attitude of "London, 1802" is closer to Blake's darker view. In the latter poem, Wordsworth cries out to the seventeenth-century poet John Milton, telling his poetic ancestor that England has become "a fen / Of stagnant waters."

Although "The World Is Too Much with Us" is only one stanza, readers aware of the conventions of the sonnet do divide the poem into parts, as described above. Blake's "London" consists of four stanzas of quatrains, rhyming verses made up of four lines each. If they were jammed together, lacking the pattern of the sonnet, some of the nuances would likely be lost. Two eight-line stanzas might work, however, since the first two stanzas look in a general way at all the denizens of the city, while the final two stanzas are more specific. The word *But* at the beginning of the final stanza signals a connection to the last line of the previous stanza. (We might note that it also breaks the pedantic English teacher's rule never to begin a sentence with a conjunction.)

Whereas Wordsworth explicitly includes the reader and himself with those who have dulled their perception of nature, Blake in no way lets us off the hook because he does not use first-person-plural pronouns. He hits us in the face with the reality of the suffering and evil in which we are complicit if we do nothing. Neither poet points a finger directly at the reader; both seek instead to open our eyes to what has happened to humanity.

MATTHEW ARNOLD

Dover Beach (p. 1457)

William Wordsworth's long life spanned the era of Romanticism that he to a great extent initiated. But his life overlaps with a major voice of the succeeding Victorian age, Matthew Arnold. The two knew each other, the young Matthew Arnold sharing long walks with the elderly Wordsworth, who was a family friend. As the son of a famed headmaster of the English preparatory school Rugby, Arnold found himself in the midst of debates about social, political, and intellectual issues from the beginning of his life. In his prose, he tackled educational and literary issues directly. He felt that education would change society by changing the middle and lower classes, bringing culture to "the little ploughboy" who would eventually hold the reins of political power. In his thirty-five-year tenure as an inspector of schools, Arnold was in a position to put his philosophies into action.

As a literary theorist, Arnold privileged the accessible diction and "high seriousness" that would uplift the reader. Religion was losing its power to transform, and he believed literature should possess qualities that would allow it to fill the gap. He wanted to bring "culture" to the class he called the "Philistines," people like those described by Wordsworth as dulled by "getting and spending." For Arnold, culture could be defined as an awareness of the art, literature, philosophy, and so forth of Western civilization coupled with a mind unwilling to blindly defer to authority. These issues are reflected in his most lasting poem, "Dover Beach," in which a speaker proposes that human beings hold on to each other in lieu of a retreating faith in God.

The last half of the nineteenth century, and perhaps all of the twentieth, witnessed the ramifications of Charles Darwin's *Origin of Species*. Darwin's book appeared in 1859 to a storm of controversy, eight years before "Dover Beach" was published. We might ask students to consider how Arnold's poem addresses issues related to debates about Darwinism. Because students usually get a kick out of it, we like to use Anthony Hecht's irreverent parody "The Dover Bitch" to compare the earnest "high seriousness" of Arnold's text with the irony of a twentieth-century reinterpretation of the same scene.

In "Dover Beach" the sea serves as an extended metaphor for faith, as the poem explicitly states. Arnold saves this statement of his theme for the third stanza, however, using an inductive method to prepare the readers for his point. The opening stanza describes the sea itself — specifically the English Channel separating England from the continent of Europe. As the speaker calls his companion to the window to look at the sea, he asks her to listen to the effects of the waves on the shore. He ends by saying that a "note of sadness" is evoked by the ceaseless sound.

In the second stanza, the poet takes us back to ancient Greek drama for an allusion to Sophocles' same reaction to the sound of the sea. He refers to lines 657–778 of *Antigone*. Since the play appears on page 1306, students should turn back to it and read the passage for themselves. Sophocles specifically refers to tragedy's reverberating consequences through the generations of a family like that of Oedipus. In Christian theology, the equivalent is the proverb that the sins of the fathers are visited on the children. The sea in *Antigone* is "a great mounting tide / driven on by savage northern gales, / surging over the dead black depths / roiling up from the bottom dark heaves of sand." The sea's "moaning / echoes" bring to mind human grief. All this stuff keeps getting dredged up, Sophocles says. The sea does not keep still about family secrets. Arnold universalizes the allusion.

Though he has gone from sadness to misery, the third stanza makes the story literally worldwide. Faith once rolled up on every shore like the sea at high tide, hugging the hips of the land like a sash wrapped around the earth's body. But just as the sea rolls out at low tide — or as a woman might slowly unfurl her clothing for the night — faith is going away, leaving our souls as bare as the rocks on the shore or the unprotected body of the woman. This brings the speaker of the poem to his final point. Since we are now vulnerable without the authority of religion to make us feel safe, we have only our human love.

We discover at this late point that the speaker addresses someone he loves, probably a woman. The sounds of the ocean echo like the sounds of warfare as the speaker thinks of vulnerable humans alone "on a darkling plain" without the sure expectations faith once provided. Although the speaker calls someone to the window in the first stanza, revealing that the poem is a dramatic monologue overheard by us as he addresses another character whose voice we do not hear, we know little about the relationship. Anthony Hecht's parody assumes that this is a good way to get someone into bed, especially if the speaker is a soldier going off to war. Knowing something of Arnold's philosophy, we assume that he has higher motives. He is suggesting obliquely to his readers that we need to rely on our own critical thinking and good will to our fellow human beings rather than on authority. His vision of the world intensifies the value of love. The speaker wants to be in a relationship in which lovers are *true* to each other. Issues of definition may come up in class discussion about exactly what Arnold means by this. Students might enjoy writing their own scenarios for a soap opera about this couple.

The poem begins in the present tense, and the imperative sentences that invite his companion to the window and urge her to listen increase the sense of immediacy. But by the end of the first stanza, he raises the issue of eternity. At this point, he moves into the literary past "long ago" for a few lines before leaping back to the present again before the second short stanza is over. In the third stanza his movement back and forth in time is like the tide he describes. Finally, in the last stanza, he proposes a plan for the future, in view of the present condition of the human world, which he elaborates upon more fully. Misery is eternal; faith sufficed for a time as a counter to it; now faith is gone and we must counter it with love.

We might look back to William Wordsworth's implicit definition of "the world" to interpret the retreat of Arnold's speaker at the poem's end. We can't look to the world — or the sea of faith — for any of the positive values he lists in the final stanza. We therefore must look to each other as human beings. Perhaps the speaker places too great a burden on love, which most people today would say can't solve the problems of an individual. Some readers will feel that the speaker — and the poet — will be as disappointed in seeking comfort from love as he was from religion. Others will contend that he is on the right track as he seeks human solutions to human problems.

Wordsworth sees the answer to the evils of commercialism and industrialization in a renewed vision of nature as a living entity. Arnold sees the solution to the decline of faith in a commitment to human love. Both recognize that values they cherish are being lost in society, and they use poetry to inspire people to truly see what is happening to humanity. The sea for Wordsworth is filled with personified life; first it is like a woman, then like the sea god Proteus who could change his shape at will, and finally like Neptune, the god-king of the sea. Arnold's sea changes like Proteus; first it is a symbol of sadness and misery, then a symbol of faith, and finally a reminder of the contentious and dangerous nature of the human world of the mid–nineteenth century. Although Blake in the poem "London" remains in the city and does not use the sea as a symbol, he too is dealing with the eternal problem of human misery and also feels, as do Wordsworth and the later Arnold, that the world has become unnatural. The repetition in the second stanza of Blake's poem has the ebb and flow of the sea, even though he is far from it. He does refer to the river Thames, but he points out that it has come under the negative control of man.

Blake and Wordsworth might have called for a sense of spirituality rather than a retreat into human love alone, as expressed in Arnold's poem. In a poem like Arnold's, where rhyme is irregular, readers tend to notice content before they notice form. The balance of Arnold's lines, however, gives the text a poetic cadence and rhythm reminiscent of the ebb and flow of the waves. Even though Arnold particularizes the changing perceptions of humanity by having his speaker address a lover, he still deals with the universal themes the other poets address. Both Blake and Arnold use the first-person pronoun, whereas Wordsworth includes the listener in the *we* of his poem. Because the speaker of Arnold's poem is a character in a drama, he keeps his reader more distant. However, his focus on two specific people does not diminish the relevance of the issue or make him seem self-centered. Just as the examples mentioned in Blake's poem do not eliminate the mill worker, who is not mentioned, Arnold's use of only two people does not mean that the poem is *about* these two people. Most readers will recognize that the poem is also about us.

ZBIGNIEW HERBERT
Report from the Besieged City (p. 1459)

As our instructor's manual is being written, Pope John Paul II has returned to his home country of Poland for what is expected by everyone to be his final visit. Huge crowds wait and pray as he struggles to recover from a fall and the flu. It seems as if Catholicism has always been there, as indeed it has, though in a quieter, more submerged form for a time. As a Polish citizen, the pope had helped to inspire the solidarity movement that many believe first revealed the fallibility of communist power in Eastern Europe. A few years later, the world woke up to newspapers telling of the breakup of the Soviet Union. We watched on television as the Berlin Wall was dismantled. But as we also watch as the Balkans continue to function as "the sick man of Europe" whose sufferings affect us all, we are reminded again that things both change and remain the same.

This quality of history is one theme of Polish poet Zbigniew Herbert's "Report from the Besieged City." In this poem time, space, and history are not static and linear. Earlier times interweave with the present, and geography encompasses a specific space with the understanding that the places of the world are interconnected and that the refugee takes the homeland with him as part of himself. References to time begin in the opening lines as the speaker tells us he has been assigned the job of "chronicler" because of his age. The old-fashioned word, in English at least, carries the idea of time within it. A chronicler records history as it happens. But history won't let itself be pinned down. All of the events of the past converge. In lines 4 through 6, as the biographical headnote points out, the invasions of the past and the present merge together in what the speaker explicitly tells us is a "loss of the sense of time." We move from the partition of Poland in the 1700s to a 1981 December defeat of democratic reform, then to the 1939 Nazi invasion and the 1944 Soviet takeover, both symbolically present in the reference to the month of September. The human attempt to order calendar time does not succeed. Weeks are "interminable," and days hold one unthinkable disorder after another. References to "spice merchants" and the plague have a medieval connotation, further linking modern events with the events of the distant past that keep recurring, that have never really stopped. The compression of the facts of war in stanza 5 evokes a sense of panic and the numbness that comes when too much happens in a short time.

With irony, the poet describes the change in the children, who symbolize the future. Because these children have become dehumanized, the dream for the future that comes in the last line seems less likely to come to pass. In the eighth stanza, the speaker states that the situation has been going on for "a long time" and lists the various invasions of history; in the ninth stanza, it becomes "a siege as long as eternity." Peace accords are just a temporary pause in the inexorable increase of the dead. Though he leaves us with the persistence of dreams, we wonder, with the weight of history behind us, if his implication is true. Perhaps this is where we might go outside of the poem to look at the spirit of the Polish people, who kept the dignity of their dreams throughout their long oppression.

Less obvious than the theme of time, but also present, is a sense of space, an attempt to define the homeland. In the fourth stanza, the speaker talks about holding on to a particular place. In 1999 we might be reminded of the conflict between Serbians and ethnic Albanians in the province of Kosovo in the former Republic of Yugoslavia. Diplomats speak of partition yet again, but each faction has an emotional attachment to the same place, the Kosovars wanting to hold on to the homeland of family and community and the Serbs singing folk songs that celebrate the ethos of their tragic defeat at the Field of Blackbirds. Looking back at the failure of partitions of the past, readers may recall Solomon offering to cut a baby in half. A picture sometimes appears in history books depicting the rulers of the great military powers of Europe in the 1700s dividing up a map of Poland. It reminds us that the warrants for drawing boundaries seldom have anything to do with the actual land and the people who preserve it. For the speaker of Herbert's poem, the borders are not marks on a map but "the frontier of our uncertain freedom." But stanza 11 makes a major point: The city may have no boundaries; it may exist within the individual and go with him into exile.

The speaker's comments about the world outside of his "besieged city" are laced with irony. Although he identifies with oppressed people of the modern era, listing other peoples under fire from major communist powers in stanza 9, all of them are isolated and unable to band together in a common cause. He is ambivalent toward the people of the West, recalling the betrayals of World War II — "the second Apocalypse" — when Hitler's German forces were allowed to invade Poland unopposed by the United States or other Western powers. People who could help don't want to hear the pathos that might move them to compassion; they only want "the facts." The speaker ironically calls these betrayals "distant ancient matters" and decries the ignorance of Americans that come along with "good advice" and relief packages. His moralizing about how the city's people should be grateful mocks the arrogant attitude with which the United States often assumes a stance of moral superiority, forgetting its abandonment of nations in need and the inconsistency of its helpful gestures.

The city is caught in a cycle of despair and inhumanity. It too becomes a target of the speaker's ironic tone, when, in stanza 7, he claims to speak "with a certain pride" of the "new species of children" that have developed from the violence and deprivation. The speaker hints that "foreign markets" are his audience. He fears that the listing of events will not "move anyone," indicating that his purpose is at odds with the intolerance of his audience for anything beyond facts. Readers recognize the poet's irony here, since the bare listing of the realities of war coming one after another — beginning with the ultimate symbol of the hunger that reduces besieged people to eating rats — *does* move us to see the horror. We see that people are turning on each other and that even the enemy betrays the rules of war. But the facts are not enough for the chronicler. He is supposed to "avoid any commentary" but slips more and more into the imagery of poetry.

The title indicates that the text is a factual report. The speaker is a war correspondent of sorts, keeping track of events as an eyewitness. He attempts to be "exact" as the conventions of genre demand and tries to avoid pathos, to retain the objective voice. But, as most of us are aware, objectivity is at best a pose, and the chronicler shares his feelings. In stanza 8, the conventions of poetry take over as he lapses into sensory sight and sound images and vivid metaphor, the colors of the enemies' flags evoking comparisons with "delicate bird's yellow" and the changing seasons.

The declaration that the city lives within the citizen, no matter where he goes, would seem a good place to end the poem. We know the statement to be true, even if we simply consider voluntary literary exiles like James Joyce, who never really left Dublin even though he never returned to it physically. But this city has been painted with a gloomy past and present that seem to foreshadow a gloomy future. Will the exile carry the horrors of the siege as do the ruins of the beloved homeland? Perhaps Herbert gives us the remaining lines to counter this impression and to hold on to the dignity of dreams, ending with hope.

Besieged cities are surrounded by forces that will not allow them to escape. When we read of historical sieges — of St. Petersburg, Russia, for example, during both World War II and the earlier Napoleonic Wars — we think of hunger, thirst, cold, fear, and the atrocities to which such deprivations can lead some desperate people. The people of William Blake's "London" are besieged in much the same way as the people of Herbert's symbolic city. Forces they cannot control cause children to be robbed of the normal joys of childhood, soldiers to suffer bloody deaths, and mothers to pass on a heritage of disease and misery.

337

William Wordsworth in "The World Is Too Much with Us" speaks to human beings spiritually besieged by their choice to embrace the dark, commercial world of Blake's poem, blinding themselves to nature. Matthew Arnold describes a civilization besieged by doubts about religion, deprived of the values that it sorely needs. The connection of Herbert with Wordsworth and Arnold stretches the definition a bit, but Blake makes an apt comparison. Although Wordsworth and Arnold are less overtly political in that they do not show vivid pictures of abuses as do Herbert and Blake, all four poets have political agendas. Both Wordsworth and Arnold articulated their intentions to use poetry to effect changes in society. Blake's message is passionately political; he is exposing evil incarnate in industrial England and seeks to impel his audience to rescue innocent victims.

Of the four poets in this cluster, Blake seems the most concrete. He simply shows us the dark city, lets us listen to its sounds with him, and gives no real commentary to sum up his message, though his words are filled with double meanings that speak volumes. Students may differ in how they rank others, depending on their warrants and their definitions of abstraction. Perhaps Herbert follows next, since he refers specifically to events in the current situation in Poland under Soviet-dominated communism. Arnold and his listener in the dramatic monologue observe a specific sea, the English Channel at the white cliffs of Dover, looking across to France. His poem is situated in the poet's present day, when the issues of religious faith and the new idea of evolution were hot topics. Wordsworth's world seems the most abstract.

Readers will differ in their evaluations of the poems. Most current readers prefer the concrete, and though the diction and syntax of Wordsworth and Arnold reflect the everyday speech of their time, they still come across as too "poetic" to please many students. Herbert is more accessible because he addresses current themes, though some readers resist texts that confuse them with allusions they must refer to in explanatory notes. We like the slight hint of the science-fiction or fantasy genre in Zbigniew Herbert's medieval references and his movement back and forth in time. Students will probably prefer the down-to-earth, deceptively simple, concrete imagery of William Blake.

JUDGING A LIFE (p. 1462)

PERCY BYSSHE SHELLEY

Ozymandias (p. 1463)

A few years ago the Rameses exhibit from Egypt toured the United States. The museum had reassembled the huge statue of the monarch that had been shipped in pieces, and it stood like a redwood tree for one's admiration. One young woman at the exhibit was suffering through the agony of a disintegrating marriage, caused perhaps by a dominating tyrant of a husband. This may not be as irrelevant as it sounds. Although one point of the poem "Ozymandias" is undoubtedly the irony of *how the mighty have fallen,* exhibited in the person of a boasting Egyptian monarch of the thirteenth century B.C.E., the poem may also apply to common folk. Another cliché has it that *what goes around comes around,* and the meanest small-time tyrants may find themselves in positions that contrast ironically with the ones they planned for themselves. The oppressive husband becomes the ex-husband who is subject to the dictates of a divorce court. The proud military and political bully winds up with his face in the dust. Even the good readers of Shelley's poem are subject to the eroding changes of time, and we will all die and risk having our words read differently in new contexts. The judgment of a life is complicated by the perspectives of those who interpret it.

Students are usually interested to learn that Shelley was expelled from Oxford University for writing a pamphlet praising atheism and distributing it to his professors. The eighteen-year-old expected to stir a logical debate in which the issue would be hammered out. He was surprised when his academic audience judged him rather than the idea he had presented for discussion. Interested students might delve more deeply into Shelley's biography for judgments leveled against the poet's radical lifestyle. They will be interested in his complicated relationships with women, in his radical political activities, and in his death in a boating accident at age twenty-nine. If we believe Reynolds Price's quotation in the "Before You Read" prompt that precedes "Ozymandias" on page 1463, Shelley was a little over ten years shy of being able to understand that we owe much of who we are to those who have gone before us. Shelley lived as if he truly thought he'd invented both life and poetry. Although the Romantic poet is still studied extensively, it is ironic in the context of this poem that many undergraduate students may not recognize his name but can immediately identify his second wife, Mary Shelley, as the author of the Gothic novel *Frankenstein.* Shelley, a man with supreme confidence in his own genius, has become for popular readers merely a footnote. In this respect, he resembles his Ozymandias. Perhaps this is because he finds himself in a barren desert in terms of readers.

"Ozymandias" is less emotionally charged and has less of the dizzying sequence of poetic images and hyperbole than do most of Shelley's lyrical poems. Because it speaks more directly to emotions we can understand — pride and folly — "Ozymandias" is frequently included in anthologies, and students may have read the poem in high school. If so, we might ask them to challenge any definitive readings they came to then by looking for oppositions that complicate their judgment of the Egyptian monarch's life. Or they may decide instead that the poem is really about the artist who created the statue. Some readers interpret the ambiguous line 8 to refer to the creator of the monument instead of its subject.

Although "Ozymandias" follows some of the conventions of a sonnet, meaning is not sacrificed to rhyme or to meter and traditional divisions. Rather than taking a sharp turn after the eight lines of the octave, the sestet continues to elaborate on the scene, seemingly without pause. But by reading closely we find that subtle divisions do exist. The early lines tell what the traveler saw, describing the statue but also making the observation that the artist who did the work was a perceptive reader of the "passions" he represented. The sestet moves outside of the original text of the statue and its subject and creator to quote the words of Ozymandias. There is a cause-and-effect relationship between this "caption" to the work of art and the ending lines of the poem. We obey the king's command and see only an empty desert. We might therefore read his quotation with irony, interpreting it to mean that he thought rival rulers would continue to be cowed by his kingdom after his death. We can see that a discrepancy exists between his expectations and the reality of the wasteland in which he stands. But a less orthodox reading might argue that he predicted rightly. The mighty should look and see that it all comes to nothing in the end, and for this reason they should "despair."

Ozymandias might be seen as scornful or supercilious, judged by his "wrinkled lip, and sneer." His "frown" would indicate that he is disapproving or judgmental. The word *cold* shows him to be insensitive to those to whom he issues his orders. Words like *warlike, arrogant, proud*, and *boastful* come to mind to describe the man who issues the words of lines 10 and 11, though some might choose to see him as a confident, bold, in-your-face leader. We may describe his present state as powerless, impotent, or broken.

Shelley begins the poem as if he is already engaged in a conversation with the reader and uses this anecdotal evidence to elaborate upon a point he is making. Perhaps the discussion is about art, and the speaker who is the *I* of the poem wants to say something universal about the creative process, that the artist has to be acquainted with the emotions he conveys in his art. Or he may want to talk about the fact that art does not remain intact, either, but lasts only somewhat longer than life. Line 8 gives the artist power over the monarch, since his hands are able to mock — both to imitate and to ridicule — the passions of a king. As the English proverb says of a cat, an artist too may look at a king.

Shelley and the ancient Egyptian sculptor both understand the passions of others because they are acquainted with passion. There is no doubt that this is true of the intense Shelley, and he imagines it for the sculptor. Often, in our literature or writing classes we emphasize to students that a text can be anything one reads, from anthropologist Clifford Geertz's Balinese cockfights to a work of art to the books we read at school. We also read each other. In order to create a work of art, the sculptor or painter or writer must first interpret what he or she sees. The audience, in turn, reads the reading. In "Ozymandias" Shelley reads the tale by a narrator who reads the statue that represents the artist's reading of the king. And it may be that his frowns indicate a reading of a situation in his world that we no longer have the context to understand. Little survives in the poem but the sands of the desert, but the poet is able to read the shattered ruins, and it could be argued that he makes the memory of the Egyptian king and his sculptor last a few centuries longer. Recently, the footprint of what seems to be a boy of about twelve years old was found in a cave believed to have been sealed for 20,000 years. The art nearby has lasted that long, as has the sign of his living presence. Art seems to last pretty long, after all.

STEVIE SMITH

Not Waving but Drowning (p. 1464)

Biographies of Stevie Smith, whose real first name was Florence, always contrast her limited personal life with the energy and turmoil of her mind. From a family reduced to lower-middle-class circumstances, she worked for many years as a secretary, lived in a London suburb with an elderly aunt, and didn't marry. But as a writer she was a woman gifted with multiple personalities, using many different personas. Most of her poetry mixes tragedy with satirical wit in a style that has been characterized as what you'd get if you crossed William Blake with Ogden Nash. Perhaps the paradox behind "Not Waving but Drowning" is the knowledge that more is usually going on beneath the surface of an ordinary life than one might think.

Some readers have had the experience of being caught in a rip current, trying simultaneously to remember to swim parallel to the shore while desperately trying to get the attention of swimmers who had the good sense to stay in the shallows. We speak metaphorically of "getting in too deep" before we realize we are "out of our depth" in a given endeavor. We don't know what the drowned man was attempting that proved to be more than he was capable of handling, but apparently he'd been faking nonchalance for a long time.

There are three parts to the situation that leads to his drowning. First, there's the cold, suspected of causing a heart attack by its suddenness. But the drowned man says that "it was too cold always." We can only guess, but perhaps the coldness represents a lack of real love in his life. This could affect one's heart, in a symbolic sense. People can be "alone in a crowd" — getting no real warmth from human relationships even though from the outside they seem to be doing okay, with plenty of friends and lovers. The second difficulty involves being out too far, a situation the man declares has been a lifelong habit. Maybe the drowned man is one of those people who to this point has been unable to say no and winds up overextended. In his moaning, he now reiterates the word *no* as he seeks to explain his death. Or perhaps he is one of those people recognized for his talent and ability, inexplicably to him, and he feels the need always to prove himself or to fake his way through, pretending wisdom he knows he lacks. Since he has a reputation for "larking," he may plunge into play too enthusiastically, getting into things that are risky, and this is what he means by going too far. Or finally, the risk may be an emotional one; perhaps he has been drowning in his intense feelings, even while pretending to be a light-hearted clown. Whatever the details, he tends to excess. Finally, he drowns because he is "not waving but drowning."

This image is funny in an ironic sort of way, and the words have surely been spoken many times at beaches every summer, though not by dead men. Bystanders at the scene of the tragedy say, "We thought he was waving!" Stevie Smith's protagonist was drowning and now is dead, but he's still "moaning" to let his companions know that he has been terribly misread. But if we fake it all our lives, how does anyone know — how do we even know ourselves — when we are being real? We all know the class clown who covers his insecurities with laughter, and many comedians claim to be shy people at heart. This is a version perhaps of waving *while* drowning.

Although the basic scenario is presented in the first stanza, the second stanza lets us hear how the people around the drowned man view him. We understand why they didn't take him seriously and hear their guess about the cold. This invites his elaboration in response. In the third stanza we get the important information that the drowning is the result of a lifetime pattern, not something ironic that just happened one day at the beach. The dead man attempts to explain himself, and his moaning implies hidden misery. Now that he's dead, he wants everyone to know. It's ironic to have a dead man speak, but somehow it doesn't feel unrealistic in the poem. It's like a dream of attending one's own funeral or like writing an epitaph or a sealed letter to be opened *in the event of my death*. Writing one's own epitaph is an interesting exercise in trying to define who you are in a few words, and we might suggest that students voluntarily give it a try.

Comparing the words of Stevie Smith's drowned man to Shelley's "Ozymandias" shows the modern character admitting his shortcomings, perhaps realizing the irony of his crossed communication, whereas the Egyptian monarch tries to ensure that the pose continues after his death. Most readers feel closer to the drowned man, and feel that this is the sort of stupid thing that would happen to us. He seems honest enough after death to admit that he has made mistakes. We have more trouble relating to the bravado of Ozymandias, partly because such boasting is chillingly dangerous in a man with the power to carry out his threats. On the other hand, Ozymandias may arouse our pity because he is so blind to the fact that death will end his power. It isn't likely that the man in Stevie Smith's poem has the same power as the Egyptian king, though a member of British royalty might have this combination of overreaching and insecurity. He seems more of an ordinary fellow, though — perhaps like a lower-middle-class poet who fakes her way using wit in the circles of the literary elite. In Shelley's poem, the equivalent of the people who speak of the drowned man is the glimpse we get of the artist who "mocks" the king's arrogant features. By creating a portrait, he makes judgments, giving the man's personality his own particular reading. We can realize, by the way, that the Egyptian artist of the thirteenth century B.C.E. was working within strict conventions at the dictates of the government, whereas Shelley read the artist and his art through the eyes of a nineteenth-century Romantic. Unlike the drowned man, the sculptor doesn't get to tell us that Shelley misread his intentions.

JAMES WRIGHT

Lying in a Hammock at William Duffy's Farm in Pine Island, Minnesota (p. 1465)

Like many writers, James Wright comes out of a working-class family and carries his work ethic with him into his poetry. It's been said that Wright worked as hard at his poetry as his father worked at making glass. Wright felt some guilt about not becoming like his father. This is an inevitable burden shouldered by the children of the working class; it's a variety of survivor's guilt. He had the talent to study his craft at Kenyon College under John Crowe Ransom. Theodore Roethke also became a literary mentor, and Wright co-wrote with Robert Bly. His life experiences included a tour of duty during the American military occupation of Japan, a Fulbright scholarship to study in Austria, and time spent in Italy, where he wrote some of his later poems. By choosing the intellectual and literary life, Wright at times felt personally isolated from community, homeless, and rootless; but his poetry is rooted in the Midwest, and his early life shaped his subjects and concerns.

Poetry saved his life, he believed, from the hard labor and forced layoffs his father endured as a factory worker. Like William Wordsworth or Matthew Arnold, he approached poetry as if it could save others, too. Wright said that he "wanted to make the poems say something humanly important instead of just showing off with language." He identified with outcasts and derelicts, and put them in his poetry. But he is criticized for his tendency toward sentimentality and, in the early stages of his career, the self-absorption characteristic of the chronic alcoholic. Although he later pulled himself out of alcoholism and gained some personal happiness, his poems often deal with the guilt and self-hatred of a man who feels that he has failed.

The last line of "Lying in a Hammock . . ." is one of the most famous last lines in twentieth-century poetry. It comes to the reader as a shock, since nothing in the poem seems to prepare us for it, and we backtrack quickly to read the poem again for clues. Wright confessed that the line might not be as autobiographically profound as some have surmised. It was "a statement of mood, not an Augustinian confession," he said. Nevertheless, it seems fair to question whether he means that he has wasted his life heretofore by not attending to the details of nature that he now relaxes enough to see or if he refers to his present idleness. Earnest students often interpret the poem to mean the latter, whereas people long stressed by the activities they impose upon themselves — such as instructors — lean toward a reading that privileges the hammock. Critics sometimes take it to mean that the poet's former concerns with structure were a waste and are now giving way to free verse. Others consider in their reading details of Wright's life, like the breakup of his first marriage and his alcoholism. They note that he was homeless at this time, like the chicken hawk that looks for a home. Certainly, the poet is connecting with nature.

Although it does not have the form of a Japanese haiku, the poem's observations feel like condensed snapshots of natural details in the environment. The image of "the bronze butterfly, / Asleep on the black trunk" seems static and artistic in a particularly Asian way, reminding the reader of a lacquered design on a chest or a painted screen. Some might see Wright's observations as objective, but they have a Zen-like sense of peace and oneness with nature; even the unlikely image of horse manure is transformed in a way characteristic of Eastern religious thought. All of the images are odd ones that don't lend themselves to rational analysis. This seems appropriate for that unique state of mind between sleeping and waking that a person might have drifting off in a hammock on a summer afternoon.

Considered rhetorically, the poem has an inductive arrangement. Details are given first and add up to the point that is made at the end. This allows the surprising ending that forces the reader to reevaluate the preceding images. If the poet had begun with the line "I have wasted my life" and proceeded to list natural observations as evidence of this assertion, we probably wouldn't be reading his text in a college anthology. We'd want him to do more explaining. At the time the poem was written, Wright was experimenting with long titles and short poems. The title of any written text is always its own discourse block, passing along the first bit of information or otherwise catching the reader's attention. This one serves as the first line of the poem, functioning a bit like the stage directions of a play. We don't hear of the hammock in any of the lines in the body of the poem, so it's important to our understanding that we read the title. By naming the owner of the farm, the poet produces verisimilitude.

Wright was open about his admiration for the poetry of Robert Frost, and we recall that in the familiar "Stopping by Woods on a Snowy Evening" (p. 105) the speaker does not know who owns the woods. Wright does know, and his knowledge lends realism and credibility to what his speaker will say. Wright's observer of nature in a rural setting has much in common with Frost's, however, coming in the end to what may be a similar conclusion. Both are suspended for a moment but find fresh resolve or insight in the end. The setting in a place called "Pine Island" makes us imagine woods nearby, and the agrarian setting may remind readers of critical theory that Wright was after all a disciple of John Crowe Ransom. And although the name "Pine Island" might refer to a geographical place, the word *Island* hints at isolation or solitude. Since Minnesota is north as well as midwest, we picture a certain quality of light. Therefore, we find that Wright has compressed a great deal of semantic and semiotic meaning into the twelve words of the title. The ending, by contrast, is tantalizingly vague. By not telling us how the speaker "wasted his life," Wright invites readers to imagine their own concepts of exactly what a "wasted life" would entail. Sharing our differing definitions in class discussion provides a chance to examine some of our warrants for the ongoing decisions we make about careers and lifestyles.

Stevie Smith's drowned speaker has wasted his life as surely as Wright's meditator in the hammock has wasted his, as far as we can judge. He has not lived in a way that others take seriously and has failed to be an authentic person, so has literally wasted his life. We only have the speaker's own evaluation in Wright's poem, but he tells us he has wasted his life. What Wright actually seems to mean is that his speaker has been wasting his *time*, doing things other than lying in hammocks and observing nature. He has cheated himself out of a life in which one really *sees*. Waste in Shelley's "Ozymandias" is symbolized by images of ruins and crumbling monuments and prefigures the sort of wasteland that later poets would visualize. Much of the effort expended to create the colossus has been wasted, because the work of art has begun its gradual erosion back into the sand of the desert. Nature in James Wright's "Lying in a Hammock at William Duffy's Farm in Pine Island, Minnesota" leads to the conclusion at the end that may change the direction of the poet's life or art. In Stevie Smith's "Not Waving but Drowning" the ocean provides the only reference to nature, and it seems to symbolize an unknown endeavor that overwhelms an unwary participant. Therefore, we might say that the only nature reference in Smith's poem is symbolic. However, if this is a true drowning, the sea — representing nature — is a terrifying environment in which one may die from unknowingly taking dangerous risks. In Shelley's poem, too, nature, in the form of the desert, overcomes the efforts of a man to immortalize himself, and the scene at the end is not an uplifting one.

SHARON OLDS

I Go Back to May 1937 (p. 1466)

The speaker in "I Go Back to May 1937" by Sharon Olds traces her own identity to the spring her parents graduated from college and married. Although Olds insists that the poem should not be considered her autobiography, it is certainly part of the speaker's autobiography. And like all who seek to sort out the threads that have led to the person one has become, Olds's poetic persona interprets all of the events of the past in the light of her interpretation of the present. She imposes a narrative line on her life, and she sees the path that leads inexorably to the future divorce and abuse that dominates her view of her parents. Like the child looking through the family album, she asks only, "But, where am I? What about me?" The first-person pronoun is in fact the first word of both the title and the poem. It occurs only ten times in thirty lines, but at the heart of the poem is the line "you are going to do bad things to children." When one looks at the block of the poem on the page, the accusatory predictions in the parallel lines that leap out from the center seem somehow much longer than just four lines. We get the impression that the emotions expressed in this part of the poem are also at the core of the speaker's being, coloring all of her self-definitions.

We are inclined to accept the speaker's judgments and predictions at first, since she has the benefit of hindsight and knows that her parents will make each other and their children incredibly unhappy. But her assumptions imply that this path was inevitable, and readers may disagree that this is so. The predictions of the speaker, if she really had been able to go back, would have had the degree of certainty, perhaps, of an astrological chart. One warrant for believing that these two people are fated to fail in their marriage and parenthood assumes that something fixed about their characters and personalities cannot change or adapt in any way that will change the future. The only choice is for them not to marry at all. There is no possible divergence in the road in Sharon Olds's yellow wood. The child decides before it even takes place that the answer to the question, Can this marriage be saved?, is a resounding *No*. She decides therefore that because they produced her, and she wants to come into being, that the inevitable misery must develop as it does. She can imagine no other future.

Olds often writes bitter poems about an abusive father, and "I Go Back to May 1937" hints at the menacing nature of the young man who is the potential tyrant. Our first indication that the parents in this poem will not be viewed in a sentimental way occurs when her simile in lines 4 and 5 introduces the startling image of blood. The "bent / plates of blood" sound scientific, like platelets under a microscope, but the connotations of blood relationships are also contained in the word. And we may remember the proverb *How the twig is bent, so grows the tree*. What's more, the red image glints "behind his head" like a sinister halo. The gate behind her mother has "sword-tips black in the May air," almost as if she is being held prisoner by primitive warriors. When she states in line 12 that "they would never hurt anybody," the seeds have been planted for us to understand that this assumption her parents make about themselves is not true, that just the opposite will be the case. Her mother's face is "hungry, pretty, [and] blank," and her father's face is "arrogant, handsome, [and] blind." The two descriptions predict that the woman — emotionally needy and vulnerable — will be crushed by the man, who is unable to perceive her needs because of his egotism. The elements of sadism and masochism are present. But Olds links them in the plural *you* as she chants out their fate. Both will cause pain; both will suffer. The repeated "you, you, you, you" at the beginning of succeeding lines is like a finger jabbing at their faces, though the speaker's tone toward her subjects has a note of compassion and implied forgiveness — though not a willingness to forget.

At the beginning, the poem implies this open attitude in the first two lines and later in the fifth and sixth with the words *I see*, a phrase used to express understanding. Of course, it also indicates perception. The speaker is able to see what the young couple cannot. She is also like the fortune teller sitting before her crystal ball intoning "I see . . . I see . . ." as she looks into the future of the lovers. In the parallel constructions and repeated words of lines 21 through 24 she describes their innocence and the personality traits that will destroy the marriage. She has both of them "turning to me," the speaker. And the repeated *I* of line 25 drives home the point that this poem is about the speaker herself and her parents, not really about the two young people who graduated and got married in May 1937.

Some psychologists argue that family secrets are dangerous to keep, that they need to be let out before health can come. However, readers may argue that it is not necessary to let everyone in the reading public have access to such information. The banging together of the paper dolls is a childlike motion, thoroughly realistic to anyone who has watched little girls having Prince Charming and Cinderella kiss. But this speaker, a grown-up but still a child where her parents are concerned, has them bang together at the hips, reminding us more of the play therapy used to ferret out indications of child sexual abuse. English majors may be interested to know that such a profession as play therapy exists, functioning much like music or art therapy. It uses both the reading and writing of poetry as a means of discovering and working through complex, often hidden emotions and ideas that are causing distress. We might offer this as a possible avenue for students who are wavering about studying literature because it seems impractical and isolated from the "real world."

Readers of literary works need to be vigilant about separating the speaker of a written text from what we imagine is some essential quality of the poet. Perhaps, like the figures in dreams, every character in a piece of fiction or every voice in a poem is actually an aspect of the living person who envisions it. But we can dream about — and imagine — persons quite different from our waking selves at any given point. What's more, we constantly reinvent our images of ourselves. Although biography can place a poem in context and help us understand the worldview out of which it came, we should not try to fix the poet on a pin and require that she forever be the person she has presented to us on the printed page. Some readers think the interviewer who insists that Olds admit that these are her parents is intrusive. Others feel that by choosing to discuss such issues in her poetry for all the world to read, Sharon Olds invites the sort of questions that interviewer Terry Gross raised.

The poems in this cluster deal with past, present, and future as they judge individual lives or relationships. The speaker of Olds's poem looks back at the people her parents were and wishes they had not endured the pain caused by their marriage, though she is glad she herself exists. She ends with the prediction "I will tell about it," which is not simply the resolve of the child who threatens to hang out the family's dirty linen but the voice of the speaker who intends to continue talking about the difficulties of her family history, perhaps because she must. James Wright's speaker lying in his hammock lives very much in the present throughout most of his poem, but he realizes at the end that he has wasted his life in the past. The future is only implied, but epiphanies such as this cannot be ignored once one gets out of the hammock and goes on with life. The waste, once recognized, has to stop. Stevie Smith's drowned man listens as the people around him misread his past, one in which he was always out of his depth, desperately trying to get the attention of people who misunderstood. His plan, one assumes, can only be to continue being dead, but what he seems to want is a proper epitaph to take his defined memory into the future. Shelley in "Ozymandias" has his narrator look to the past and give evidence of humanity's impotence in the face of passing time. The implications for the present and the future may be that the desert will continue to erase the monuments we build out of our pride. The setting of Shelley's poem in ancient Egypt has the advantage of the desert's unique ability to both preserve the past and to wear it down and bury it. Stevie Smith uses the familiar seashore setting and the "not waving but drowning" experience that fortunately results more often in eventual rescue than in death. Since it's an easy situation to imagine and picks up on the familiar idiom of *getting in too deep*, the poem makes us smile because it overturns cliché, even while we recognize its tragic elements. James Wright's setting on William Duffy's farm gives his speaker the environment of solitude and clarity needed to open his eyes to an important fact about himself.

Sharon Olds, by placing her speaker's parents at their respective colleges just before graduation, sharpens the details we might see in old photographs and catches them at the moment of innocence and fresh hope, at the threshold between single life and marriage. Olds judges her parents rather than herself, and may invite the accusation of shifting the blame for her implied unhappiness to something essentially bad about these people as a couple. The judgments made in Stevie Smith's "Not Waving but Drowning" are more problematic; the onlookers judge the drowned man as trivial and caught by surprise in the surf, whereas he judges himself to have had a pretty hard time all his life. He may judge the others for being too obtuse to recognize his distress. Wright's man in the hammock, usually assumed to represent the poet himself, judges himself as having wasted his life, though he does not give us the information we need to evaluate this judgment. Shelley's Ozymandias has judged himself to be the king of the world, but is proven wrong, and the artist who created the statue must judge his passions in order to represent them. We need to take the judgments of others, whether they are self-evaluations or accusations, with a grain of salt until we understand the warrants and hidden assumptions that underlie them. Our own judgments can benefit from such examination as well.

| 12 |

Confronting Mortality

THE PASSAGE OF TIME (p. 1471)

JOHN KEATS
Ode on a Grecian Urn (p. 1471)

John Keats knew a great deal about confronting mortality. When he was a child, his father died in a riding accident. His mother died of tuberculosis when he was fourteen, and he would later nurse his brother through the same illness. Keats himself would die of tuberculosis in 1821 when he was barely twenty-five years old. Perhaps it is with the pale, delicate young poet with so much unfulfilled life and promise that the disease itself begins to take on romantic connotations. The myth would develop that people with tuberculosis were too gifted, too intense, too intelligent, too sensitive and fine for this world. Keats perhaps served as a model for this stereotype of the consumptive artist. During a five-month period in 1819, he produced an amazing amount of original, creative work, including the poem we include here. Like his critical writings proposing the idea of "negative capability," "Ode on a Grecian Urn" reflects Keats's belief that we should leave ourselves open to uncertainty, rather than reducing all of life to logic and reason. We might encourage our students to follow his lead, especially in the early stages of examining an issue, encouraging a tolerance for antithetical beliefs, a willingness to speculate, and a skepticism that does not make up its mind too quickly. Keats was the youngest and last great writer of the Romantic movement. Romantic poetry sounds old-fashioned to most of today's readers, and its passionate, lyrical outpourings about nature and art may strike our students as mannered, even silly. Much of the poetry of the Modernists of the twentieth century reacts against the style and attitudes of the Romantic poets and those who followed them in the nineteenth century. But we need to remind our students that the revolutions of one generation quickly become solidified into the idols that the next generation must topple. The Romantic poets, responding to the American and French revolutions and to newly discovered knowledge about Greek and Roman "antiquities," were doing something fresh and exciting. John Keats was insisting upon ideas that we now take for granted: that we can process personal experiences, emotions, and realizations about life into poetry; that images should be concrete and sensory; that poetry may be suggestive and ambiguous; and that intensity and control can interact to "surprize by a fine excess."

After having students try to visualize or draw the vase described in the poem, we might look at examples of this genre of Greek ceramics. Scholars theorize that the "Grecian urn" of the poem is a composite of several that Keats might have seen in a London museum. Some details may come from the poet's imagination.

The surface of the vase would be rather crowded if it depicted all that the poet sees. His words catch the essence of the original but go beyond the details to imagine the scene as a moment frozen in time. This idea is familiar to current readers, since we can pause time on a videotape or freeze the frame of a film, but even photography did not yet exist for Keats and his contemporaries. Most readers will see his description as imaginative and subjective rather than objective.

Both the first and the fourth stanzas of the ode ask questions about the people in the scene. The poem's speaker seeks to place the myth or the ceremony in context, to historicize it. In fact, he addresses the vase as a "historian" in line 3, asking the personified object to explain itself. Like the scenes described by Christopher Marlowe and others in the "Loving" chapter, Keats's images of love recall the conventions of pastoral poetry where lovers live in rural bliss in the rural fields of ancient Greece. But some readers might question whether this sort of love is blissful for everyone described. The "maidens" of the first stanza seem to be fleeing rape. Even the designation "unravished bride" may have violent connotations. But all of this is forestalled, stopped in the moment of desire for the male lover and in the moment of flight and intact beauty for the female. Ironically, Keats became engaged to Fanny Brawne later in the year these words were written, but he may not yet have realized that he had contracted the tuberculosis that would keep the physical expression of their love in a similar suspended animation.

Though the poem sounds passionate, even seeming to prefer the urn's suspended love to "breathing human passion" in the third stanza, he calls the image a "Cold Pastoral" in the final stanza. Perhaps his mention of the empty town prepares us for this antithesis. It comes just after a description of human passion in the third stanza that sounds more like tuberculosis than love. In the long run, the object is empty, cold, and even reminds us of eternity and old age, though he still seems to value it as "a friend to man." Many conflicting explications exist for this ambiguous poem, reams of paper being expended to discuss just the last two lines. In the course of discussing the inconsistencies in the poem students may raise many of the issues that literary scholars have brought up in the past, and we should resist imposing our own interpretations. The poem resists definitive answers. We cannot even be sure who is speaking in the final line, the poet or the urn. We may guess that the concrete images of the poem define what the speaker means by "beauty," but we may raise an issue of definition about the meaning of "truth." We may raise issues of theme: Is the poem about beauty, truth, love, art, mortality, immortality, or some combination of all of these? It seems useful to consider the ode in terms of Keats's own literary criticism of William Shakespeare in which he privileges the open mind that allows opposite meanings to coexist.

GERARD MANLEY HOPKINS
Spring and Fall (p.1474)

Writing in the nineteenth century, but virtually unpublished until the twentieth, Gerard Manley Hopkins consciously wrote as a poetic innovator ahead of his time. Hopkins chose to keep his poems out of print partly because he was a

Catholic priest whose superiors in the church were unlikely to have approved of his writing, but he also may have realized that the literary world would not have fully appreciated his poetry either. Later generations, however, have embraced his experimentation with rhythm and language, seeing them as an antidote to the mannered lyricism of the Romantic poets and the structured forms of the Victorians. Readers of "Spring and Fall" will notice the accent marks Hopkins supplies to make clear what he called the "sprung rhythm" that characterizes his poetry. Rather than counting the regular beats of meter in a line as the conventions of English poetry dictated, he aimed for rising and falling patterns of speech that borrowed from the time and tempo of music, as well as those of the Welsh language. His language is experimental, too. He coins new words, like "wanwood leafmeal" (line 8). Or he uses words in unexpected ways, like "unleaving" (line 2); the reader's mind searches for definition; at first, *unleaving* seems to connote permanence — something that doesn't leave — but we then realize that it refers to the trees divesting themselves of leaves. The opposing definitions interact as we read the poem. We often find such puns in Hopkins's poems. The meanings become complex as all of a word's possible connotations intertwine. Alliteration, internal rhyme, and other devices that depend upon sounds further elaborate the connotations. Odd syntax forces the reader to see meanings in new perspectives, to follow a tortuous path to interpretation. Hopkins believed strongly in the power of words, attributing to them an essential, spiritual quality. He aimed in his poetry for something he called "inscape," an inward pattern of language that exactly expresses a specific reality.

The subtitle, perhaps the dedication, to the poem "Spring and Fall" is "To a Young Child." The seasons of the year provide a source of natural symbolism for people who live in the parts of the world where they occur. Fall stands for passing time, old age, and approaching death. Spring is associated with youth, fresh beginnings, and life. We easily associate Margaret with springtime, though the scene and most of the poem's images reflect autumn. Aside from her "fresh thoughts" (line 4), there is little of spring. The words for both seasons have double meanings, however. Adam and Eve lost their innocence in another garden, and forever after we have called the results of their actions the "Fall." Some, perhaps including the poet, believe that every human being lives out that particular fall as he or she goes through the seasons of life. Margaret will come to the knowledge of good and evil and eventually recognize that she is grieving over her own mortality. And there are other meanings for "spring," one of which Hopkins juxtaposes with sorrow in line 11. The springs of her sorrow are in her spirit, and are an inevitable consequence of being human. Although the speaker seems to address a young child, the issues may be raised that most adults would not actually say these words to a child and that most children would not understand them. Overhearing the speaker as he seems to speak to Margaret herself has more impact on the actual audience for the poem, however. Imagining how we might explain the sorrows of life to a child, or defending our reasons for distracting or lying to her instead, leads Hopkins's readers to contemplate our own humanity from the perspective of adulthood. Telling us about the passage of time and the accompanying sorrows using Margaret as an example might seem too preachy, might even reduce the poem to trite cliché. When Hopkins compares the "things of man" to dead leaves, he may be revealing his religious philosophy about what endures and what does not. The view of human life is pessimistic, seeing sorrow, perhaps even death, as "the blight man was born for."

As a Jesuit priest in working-class sections of large industrial English cities in the late 1800s, Gerard Manley Hopkins saw more than his share of human suffering. In other poems, Hopkins celebrates the power of God — as revealed in simple, natural objects — to overcome man's blight. Some readers may feel, however, that the implied separation between the child and nature that will come with adulthood reflects a stance in this poem that removes humanity from nature and is thus against what they consider to be truly religious. Students will differ in their definitions of the word *religious*. Do they see it as having similar meanings to the words *spiritual* or *mystical,* or do they define it in terms of established systems of ethics, worship, or belief? In looking at alliteration, rhyming, and unusual words, students have much to choose from. We might ask them what they think "wanwood leafmeal" means or if "Goldengrove" is likely another coinage rather than a real place. Have them dig for how the words sound, other words they are reminded of, connotations, and even how the words feel in the mouth as they are spoken aloud. In addition to the alliteration of the *g* and *v* consonants in line 2, for example, the assonance of the repeated *o* vowel sounds makes reading the line a physical experience beyond hearing and seeing the words, perhaps bringing the reader close to the "inscape" the poet seeks.

Though readers differ, most will probably respond more easily to Gerard Manley Hopkins's "Spring and Fall" than John Keats's "Ode on a Grecian Urn," for a number of reasons. Even though the narrator of the Keats poem allows us to experience his emotions and thoughts as he addresses an object of art, he is separated from us in time, and the object itself is even more distant. The scene he describes, furthermore, is static; time stands still. The speaker's excited utterances and animation may seem exaggerated to many student readers. They may be disturbed by his ambiguity and seeming inconsistency, feeling that the whole exercise is artificial and worked up. Hopkins speaks to a child in a garden and contemplates the passage of time in an understated, gentle tone. The scene is dynamic, since he imagines Margaret's growing up into real sorrows that will replace this vague feeling of grief she does not yet understand. His tone, though sad and pessimistic, is consistent. The scene depends less upon context than experiences common to many readers. Most readers will relate more easily to a child than to an artifact, even though people are represented on the vase.

Others may think it morbid to speak to a child as Hopkins's narrator does and will be more comfortable with Keats. The scene in Keats's poem is an eternally fixed Spring in which leaves will never fall as they do in Hopkins's autumn *Goldengrove.* In "Spring and Fall" even the springtime of childhood foreshadows the inevitable changes of season. A case could be made, however, that the two poets reveal similar attitudes toward the passage of time and the mortality it symbolizes. Keats sees the figures in the painting as blessed because they are spared the changes of time, even the sexual consummation of the lover's chase.

Hopkins sees Margaret as grieving because, though she does not realize her reasons, she senses the changes of time. The implication is that she will gain knowledge (truth?) but lose her connection with the beauty of nature. As a child, however, she senses a truth in the beauty of the falling leaves. Whether we believe that Keats really equates truth with beauty in his ode depends upon which of many possible readings we decide upon. Readers can successfully argue that both poems are about mourning, although Hopkins is more clearly so. Keats mourns the things of life that do not remain by praising an object that contrasts with the world of the living in its unchanging permanence.

ROBIN BECKER
The Star Show (p. 1475)

The title of contemporary writer Robin Becker's third collection of poetry, *All-American Girl*, has ironic undertones. Growing up in Philadelphia in the 1950s, Becker is American, certainly, though she has traveled widely. But writing about being middle-aged and the accompanying task of confronting mortality, she is hardly a "girl" in the traditionally youthful definition of the word. Writing as a lesbian, she sometimes crosses gender, giving the word *girl* a double irony. In one poem, she shares her desire as a young girl for the freedom of "the boy across the street / who hung upside down from a tree / and didn't care / that his shirt fluttered over his bare / chest." Or after making love with another girl in a Philadelphia hotel room as a teenager, she is "happy as the young / Tom Jefferson." Her poems deal with the totality of life, however, not about issues of gender and sexuality alone. Becker looks back on a lifetime of experiences honestly and reflectively, exploring her losses and gains, her winding journey toward self-definition and insight. She writes about her Jewish grandmother who wants to have her granddaughter's nose fixed (she declines) and about her sister who commits suicide. In "The Star Show" she recalls a childhood experience in Philadelphia, the transformed reality of a visit to the planetarium, but the poem may be *about* much more.

The poem begins with the writer's present situation. Becker has spent a good deal of time in the American West, where it is possible to look up at "the enormous sky." In years when meteor showers are active, groups of people often get together at night to watch shooting stars, and her poem may describe such an experience in the first stanza. She establishes here that she is no longer a child, but an adult having an experience with a real star show. Unlike the narrated, scripted excitement of the planetarium that she will remember, a star show is something you glimpse, something words cannot really keep up with or explain in the present tense. If the beginning had been omitted, the most recent scene of the poem would be the ending, where the children jarringly leave the other world of the planetarium and the spell is broken. With the opening scene, the sense of wonder is recovered before we know it is lost, and the poem is significantly different in tone. The night sky and the planetarium are of one substance; it is the "autumn afternoon" into which the children are thrust after the planetarium show which seems out of place. The planetarium lecture takes the children through the seasons of the year, though interestingly begins with winter night and ends with autumn day. This seems more to reflect the way such lectures are conventionally done in planetariums rather than a cheap use of symbols of time by the poet. The adult voice that begins the poem pinpoints the time at midnight, perhaps a logical place for an adult narrator at the end of life. But midnight can as easily be the beginning of something as the end of something. And autumn, usually associated with middle age, is still with the children as they leave the planetarium, far too early to fit the usual metaphor.

The seasons and other signs of the passage of time do not seem to be used in a conventional or trite way. The interlude of night is religious and mythic in quality. The speaker refers to it as the "miracle spreading overhead" and the "sky's mysteries." She compares the lecturer with a rabbi discussing Moses, then brings up Galileo and the Inquisition. But we soon move away from established religion into the wonder of the Native Americans, the climax of the story that causes the child to weep "for what I'd lost." The lecturer turns out to be a sort of Wizard of Oz, a false god who gets the students caught up and then rewards them with the mockery of "a grown-up laugh" as he takes the heavens away from them. We suspect at this point that the narrator knows something about feeling betrayed by grown-up laughter, has felt let down by religion. That she compares him to a rabbi makes us wonder if she has lost her faith. But the wonder of the sky remains.

Memory is always selective; we impose a narrative line upon the elements of our experiences, making them match up with the story we have taken for our own. The story of the planetarium star show belongs to the woman lying at midnight out west watching a meteor shower, and she interprets the child's experience through the filter of the years since third grade. But the details may be the ones the child stores up; maybe the woman who would travel out west is shaped by the child who hears stories of the Hopis in a planetarium in Philadelphia. Maybe the woman adds stories that she heard much later, traveling out west. Many writers maintain that a story may be true without being factual, and vice versa. The poem does not have to be realistic. A case may be made that the theme of the poem is not the stars but the language used to discuss them. Words are inadequate, the narrator tells us at the outset. Words are seductive, she tells us during the planetarium star show; they can bring us into wonder, but toss us as quickly out again. And words are inadequate, she tells us again at the poem's end; they are meaningless, ordinary, derisive, destructive.

Both Gerard Manley Hopkins and Robin Becker attribute more wisdom and religious sense to a child than may seem warranted. Hopkins assumes in Margaret the foreknowledge of a fact of life that surfaces in the child as vague emotion. He sees the child as an innocent but intuitive being who will grow into the knowledge of sorrow. Becker gives her narrator — perhaps herself as a child — a spiritual and intellectual experience in which she recalls connections to major religions, Hopi myth, changing seasons, and loss of faith. But she is able to return as an adult to the wonder of the sky. The child of Becker's poem seems more aware, but this may be because we see Hopkins's Margaret from the outside. These two poems and John Keats's "Ode on a Grecian Urn" may end on a note of despair. It would be hard to make a case that the Hopkins poem does not end with despair, though there is a sense of appropriateness about the grief that the protagonist, like all humankind, will come to know. The narrator may feel acceptance rather than despair. On the other hand, "Ode on a Grecian Urn" is ambiguous. Some readers might see it as transcending despair by maintaining the immortality of beauty. Others interpret the ending as filled with despair, especially if the writer's close acquaintance with sickness and mortality is taken into account. Becker's ending startles the reader with its brusque quality after we have experienced the wonders of the sky with her. Yet we may read it as only temporary, citing the beginning as closer in time to the adult narrator, who seems less despairing than matter-of-fact as she watches the meteor shower and admits that it cannot be narrated.

Becker's commentator is like Hopkins's at the beginning: He is calm as he speaks to the children, sad as he describes Galileo's trial for heresy, cold as he moves them into winter. But he is like Keats's narrator in his changes and in the way he woos them with beauty that we think for a while might be truth. The sky in the planetarium, although it is a great teaching tool, is not the real thing. Without her words telling us that she felt "bereft," we would see Becker's lecturer at the planetarium as a wonderful teacher and storyteller. In fact, her complaint may be that he is too good. Keats's narrator might talk about the timeless circling of the sky, and he might ask questions and make exclamations about the figures he saw in the constellations. He might point out that Polaris stands still and shines steadily, unlike the flickering candles of our daily lives. Hopkins's narrator might notice the young girl who is so moved by the trip through the seasons and remind her that she will feel this again looking at the stars as a middle-aged woman. With either Keats or Hopkins, style is important to content. Students who attempt to write a commentary for Keats should use a lyrical style, whereas those imitating Hopkins might create new words or combinations of words to describe the night sky.

VIRGINIA HAMILTON ADAIR
A Last Marriage (p. 1478)

Although she did not publish her first collection of poetry *Ants on the Melon* until she was eighty-three years old, Virginia Hamilton Adair has written thousands of poems. Many of them appeared in literary journals during the years she taught literature at California Polytechnic University, but she writes primarily to please herself. Like the less prolific Californian Tillie Olsen, Adair explains that she was too involved with life to consciously write for publication in her younger years. "I got tremendously interested in teaching and scholarship and getting married and then the three children," she says. The poet lives in a retirement community and continues to write, even though she is now blind from glaucoma. Her touch typing sometimes goes awry, resulting in gibberish, but she laughs about it. It is the joy of creating poetry, the process itself, that counts for her, and she has no problem letting the poem go once it is finished. It was only at the urging of a friend, another professor, that she went through years of typed texts to choose the poems for the collection.

She claims T. S. Eliot and Robert Frost as influences, but unlike most poets first being published in the 1990s, she has actually met both of them. Her compressed style has been compared to the poetry of Wallace Stevens, and one critic rates her as the best poet to come on the scene since Stevens. Adair's texts tend to be autobiographical, sometimes intensely personal. She writes in the poem "One Ordinary Evening" of her husband, a history professor who took his own life in 1968: "Later that year / you were dead / By your own hand / Blood your blood / I have never understood / I will never understand." Our knowledge of the poet's intense encounter with death — Douglass Adair killed himself in their bedroom — gives added depth to Virginia Adair's description of a widow in "A Last Marriage."

"A Last Marriage" begins with a recitation of losses: children forming their own relationships, husband dying, mother's death being remembered, friends dying. Like many older people, the woman of the poem has lost all of her intimates. She does the work of grief, working out emotions until "day by day . . . she recovered stillness." Since so many have "gone underground," the woman enters into communion with the earth, taking greenery and wood into her home and using it to nurture her through the winter. She makes peace with life and death, is able to accept and appreciate the space of time in which she lives. Whether the garden is real or not is an issue that may be argued from either side. The poem says that "her flesh was jabbed by thorns" (line 13) and speaks of death being "tangible" in the garden (line 9). This deliberate reference to physical reality may indicate to readers that she actually goes through the physical labor of clearing an overgrown garden. This sort of activity makes good grief therapy. But whether the garden is real or not, the extended metaphor is plain: Grieving is hard work, but there is great compensation in digging out the "deadwood," all the complex emotions, especially the negative ones. This may be particularly important when at least one of the losses is from "a bullet in the head." The survivor of a partner's suicide must have a great deal of anger and other difficult emotions to work through. For Adair, perhaps the poetry itself has been a sort of garden that she toils in and ultimately finds strength from. But this poem is written in the third-person "she" rather than the autobiographical "I." This gives the poem a greater universality, making its theme more about the process of grief than about the individual woman herself.

Statistically, women outlive men in North America, and widows outnumber widowers. It also may be a societal norm that women tend to be more oriented toward relationships than men and are more consciously affected by such losses. It may be easier for men to find new, often younger, companions and lovers. Yet it is arguable that grief is not gender specific, that the protagonist of the poem might as aptly be a man as a woman. Perhaps we would expect a man to be more stoic than a woman, to either plunge into a new marriage, or into work, or to die soon from a stress-related disease. The protagonist of Adair's poem does not short-circuit the grief process by avoiding emotion, and she is able to work her way through to peace. It may be that women have permission to do this in our culture, whereas many men do not.

Rhyming couplets by virtue of their form provide a sense of closure. Perhaps this is why she uses one to end an otherwise unrhymed poem. The couplet also provides a sense of balance that is consistent with the sense of acceptance at the poem's end. There is quiet after the passionate labor of the earlier lines. The final image of the poem, "a fine crystal of snow," which is the vehicle for her metaphor for "each breath," may at first seem to symbolize winter, the end of life, and perhaps it does. But other meanings are contained within it. She has also come to the peace that lies at the end of grief, and winter is a quiet season when the work is done. But it is not simply snow that she makes us see, but a snowflake. The unstated truism that each snowflake is different lies behind our understanding of the metaphor. Each breath has now become unique. Although the poem does not rhyme, many sound patterns are used. Both consonant and vowel sounds echo; in the opening line, for example, *gone* and *grown* alliterate and are also near rhymes, sharing similar vowel sounds. This alliteration and consonance continues in the second line, as *gone* is repeated and *underground* added. The words *ash* and *shamefast* share phonemes in the third line, with the neat reversal providing a vocalic echo. We hear another echo in the fifth line as *crash* unexpectedly rhymes with the earlier *ash*. An internal rhyme pops up in the seventh line with *alone* and *overgrown*. Throughout the poem, sound patterns make the poem cohesive in an unobtrusive way, and close examination will provide numerous examples.

Three of the poems in this cluster refer to weeping. Virginia Adair's protagonist ironically does not let us see her cry directly in response to the losses the narrator describes, but in the course of the hard labor in the garden, her "eyes stung by mould and tears" (line 14). Crying may also be implied when we are told, "Sweat, anger, pity / Poured from her" in lines 12 and 13. Her crying is linked to frustration and strong effort, and both the tears and the sweat seem equally cathartic. The child in Robin Becker's "The Star Show" cries as she feels herself losing a beautiful, almost-religious experience that she is helpless to retain. Whereas the protagonist of Adair's poem cries in the midst of taking control, Becker's speaker recognizes something that cannot be taken in by language, something outside of her control. The young girl in "Spring and Fall" by Gerard Manley Hopkins is even less aware and in control of her emotions, though the narrator implies that she will come to know what causes her crying.

All four poems in this cluster refer to the seasons and to some extent use them as a metaphor for the passage of time in an individual life. John Keats in "Ode on a Grecian Urn" compares the eternally green and flowering season in which his characters are fixed with the inevitable old age and woe of living human beings (lines 46–47). Unlike the realities of human life in which fall and winter, sickness and death inevitably come, the only truth that the urn needs to know is a beauty that does not change. Gerard Manley Hopkins in "Spring and Fall" takes the romantic emotion a young girl seems to be experiencing at seeing the falling leaves and extrapolates the sorrows that she will encounter as she reaches a later season of her life. Robin Becker in "The Star Show" reaches a height of emotion and oneness as the lecturer at the planetarium takes his audience into the coldness of December, as her adult narrator similarly experiences at midnight. She does not want to return to the reality of the warmer seasons, or the "autumn afternoon" that represents everyday life. She contrasts the harshness of its "jeers / and curses with the wonder of the stars in winter or at midnight. Virginia Hamilton Adair also finds peace in winter, after the work of earlier seasons has been completed. A case might be made that the attitudes and associations these writers make with the seasons of the year differ dramatically, with the twentieth-century writers calling the conventional symbolism into question.

All four writers use the seasons as a means of confronting mortality or their own humanity. The gardens of Adair and Hopkins seem very different, though the difference may lie less in the gardens than in the narrators' involvement with them. Adair's grieving woman, presumably an aged woman, deals consciously with grief by working in a tangled, overgrown garden — a garden we can expect to symbolize her own soul. She takes something that is hurtful and full of effort and appropriates it for her own healing and peace. Adair's poem is filled with verbs of action, with both the woman and the garden as actors: She hacks and drags, but is "jabbed by thorns" and "jerked by twigs." Adjectives refer to her garden as she begins her work as "overgrown / shapeless and forlorn." Its roots are "Self-strangling." But later she refers to its "green tenderness" and "reviving ground." With the falling leaves, she — perhaps Margaret grown up and proving the poet wrong — does notice their passing. But, in the penultimate line, we are told that this is the "season to sit still with time to know." The sorrow seems to have passed with the leaves. We see the "Goldengrove" of the Hopkins poem in a few glimpses and must decipher its nature from four words: *Goldengrove, wanwood, leafmeal,* and (perhaps) *blight.* The connotations of *golden* are rich, warm, pure; and *grove* makes us think of life and pleasantly rural but tamed surroundings. Perhaps it represents the innocence and beauty of youth, though some readers will maintain that the word *golden* refers to turning leaves. The other words imply lifelessness, decay, and disease. The progression of the images is the opposite of Adair's. The ground of Goldengrove does not revive, at least not in Hopkins's poem. In Keats's poem, the garden remains green; we will never see this grove "unleaving." This is the poem's point. The actual coming of autumn, symbol of old age and approaching death, is held at bay by art. In Robin Becker's poem, the "meadow drenched with light" may be an equivalent of the garden, but it has negative connotations, since it awakens the children from their encounter with eternity.

FIGHTING FOR SURVIVAL (p. 1480)

TIM O'BRIEN

The Things They Carried (p. 1480)

In a sense, the stories in Tim O'Brien's collection of interrelated narratives about the Vietnam War are stories *about* stories. One piece has the title "How to Tell a True War Story" and begins by swearing to the reader that the story is true.

But the narrator will later explain that "a true war story cannot be believed. If you believe it, be skeptical." At times, O'Brien will tell the same story with differing endings, confiding to the reader at one point that the first ending is true and later insisting that another one is what *really* happened. In his mystery novel *In the Lake of the Woods*, he leaves the reader with no resolution of the plot, maintaining that the point of the story is the impossibility of ever knowing the secrets that people keep within themselves. Imagination and memory interweave in autobiography or fiction, and the fact that they do is part of the story for O'Brien.

Like many writers we have encountered in our anthology, he distinguishes between facts and truth and insists that we must sometimes lie in order to tell the truth. "Stories save us," he believes. This may especially be true about Vietnam War experiences, since conflicting political narratives about that war have been part of our culture since the 1960s. People like Tim O'Brien, who were eyewitnesses and (often reluctant) participants, find their actual experiences so bizarre and surreal that they foreground the incredibility of the account. And like Kiowa in "The Things They Carried," they find that the incredibility compels repetition. The story must be told again and again to be confirmed as true.

It would be futile to attempt a sorting of the fact and fiction in a Tim O'Brien narrative. Much of it is certainly autobiographical, and there can be no doubt that the war still haunts him. He says it was an image of himself, still loaded down with the physical and spiritual burdens he carries from Vietnam, that prompted his writing of this story, though he has written about the war both before and since. Ironically, given his teasing of readers with the fuzziness of the line between truth and fiction, Tim O'Brien says that he does not write for catharsis but for *communication*. He is a perfectionist about his writing, working long hours and editing out much more than he keeps in a story. Students sometimes complain of the long catalogs in O'Brien's story, missing the subtle shifts of emphasis and the connotations and wry puns that layer meanings. Assure them that every line of "The Things They Carried" is crafted in minute detail. Much will be missed if they rush through it.

The lists of things carried have a cumulative effect that builds as the story humps on, interweaving physical, mental, emotional, spiritual, cultural, and political burdens. The story presents itself as a sort of factual account of items carried. From time to time, there is white space as the narrator takes a breath and renews the rhetorical tone of nonfiction. At times, the tone is of the formulaic classification paper that students too often use for every possible occasion. You can almost see the numbered outline: things carried out of necessity, things carried as a function of rank, weapons, variations by mission, things carried out of superstition, and so on. By the time we get to the last bit of separating white space, the narrator can be obvious about the complex meanings underlying the concept of carrying things and tells us how the soldiers carried themselves. The last sentence ironically includes the military jargon "Carry on," which we now recognize as full of meaning. But soon into the story, the coolly objective narrative voice unexpectedly varies the pattern; for example, in the midst of describing "odds and ends" like New Testaments and vitamins, the narrator throws in, "They all carried ghosts."

His delivery continues to be deadpan, even when he slips in bit by bit the central event of the story, the death of Ted Lavender. Buried in the middle of a list of things they carried from necessity, we first hear of this in past tense, as if it were just another trivial detail. Yet it is the event that effects the change in the dynamic character First Lieutenant Jimmy Cross. It seems unlikely that Cross's daydreaming about Martha is the cause of Lavender's death. Scared, high, concentrating on urinating and zipping his fly, Lavender is as much to blame as anyone. In the long run, none of the soldiers is at fault: The war is beyond their control, and death for some is a given. But Cross must exorcise his consciousness of the things of the other world in order to carry on as the leader of these men. We may question whether his change will be for the better.

In the mid-1990s O'Brien returned to My Lai, where his platoon had been stationed a year after the much-publicized burning and killing of civilians by American soldiers. Writing about the trip and the implications of the massacre, he suggests that lost love and the insanity of war interact to produce such atrocities. In the light of this, it is interesting that the platoon in "The Things They Carried" carries out just such an atrocity after Lavender is killed.

The story is set up in a way that encourages the reader's identification with Cross as the main character of this story. We are allowed to know what he is thinking. Perhaps he is preoccupied with Martha's virginity because he needs her as an ideal, a fantasy to contrast with the reality of war. He may reflect the mores of the times: Contrary to stereotype, many young people of the 1960s had conservative ideas about premarital sex. We have no reason to believe that she does not love him, since he is an unreliable judge of her feelings. Some students might use the word *paranoid* to describe his obsession. Others might point out that he is in an insane situation and that his seeming paranoia is understandable. We might also keep in mind Tim O'Brien's preoccupation with the shifting nature of any narrative, even fantasy. His point may be that the story Cross tells himself about Martha is destructive. Or he may instead be saying that fantasizing about Martha is the thing that keeps Cross human. Or he may be saying that both readings are true, that for Cross and his men to survive under the insane conditions of war, he must give up the story that makes him vulnerable, and thus human.

Other members of the company become more rounded in other stories of O'Brien's intertextual group of narratives. Kiowa, for example, will later die in a shit field, smothered in excrement. In the realistic details of "The Things They Carried" readers will find a cross section of young American manhood. Characters are clearly distinguishable from each other. As a group, they are protective of their pride, filled with bravado, irreverent and mocking in the face of death. The best word to describe them might be *burdened.*

The best comparisons to make between Tim O'Brien's story and the stories of earlier wars might be found in Ernest Hemingway. In his nonfictional *If I Die in a Combat Zone,* O'Brien says that he is greatly influenced by a Hemingway character who has the courage to walk away from war in *A Farewell to Arms.* "Henry was able to leave war being good and brave enough at it, for real love," O'Brien writes, "and although he missed the men of war, he did not miss the fear and killing. . . . Henry, like all my heroes, was not obsessed with courage; he knew it was only one part of virtue, that love and justice were other parts." But the Vietnam War challenges such abstractions, and "The Things They Carried" is the epitome of the concrete. The brutality and lack of idealism in O'Brien's characters bring home the ugliness of war. This is an antiwar story because it shows the dehumanization of the men involved and the meaninglessness of the activities in which they are engaged.

JAMESON CURRIER
What They Carried (p. 1494)

The fight for survival described by Jameson Currier in "What They Carried" and in his 1998 novel *Where the Rainbow Ends* has much in common with the dogged effort of men to stay alive in Tim O'Brien's war stories. Lost love, fear, the indignities of death and dying, and — perhaps above all — the loss of autonomy and control over the simplest things of life are common to both war and the catastrophic illness AIDS. Currier points out, however, that medical advances of recent years have somewhat lessened the grim death sentence the diagnosis of HIV signified at the time this story was published in 1993. Nevertheless, the story reflects the early days of the AIDS epidemic of the 1980s, times that shaped the lives of many people who were coming of age, especially in the homosexual communities of large cities. Currier, a southerner transplanted to Manhattan, remembers the first time he heard about the disease that would take many of his friends, business associates, and lovers. "I clearly remember the day in Central Park," he writes in the *Lambda Book Report* (February 1999), "a summer morning in 1981, waiting to meet my friend Kevin and reading an item in the *New York Times* about a rare cancer being found in gay men. That morning is ingrained in my consciousness. My immediate reaction was one of confusion and skepticism, but I was also aware of being caught up in an historical moment, yet uncertain how the future would play itself out." He goes on to speak of being haunted by his first few friends who contracted the disease and by the fear that he remembers as he visited them. Like O'Brien in his concentration on themes of war, Currier finds himself writing about AIDS not only because its existence has been a central conflict to be dealt with in his life but because its stories are the stuff of literature.

Some readers, including this one, may miss the fact that a flashback is framed by the activities of Adam's funeral. We are not explicitly told at the beginning that Adam is dead, and the reader might assume that the flowers are for someone who is still in the hospital after a long time. Rereading explains John's confusion and Danny's help. Still, the flashback does take us back to an earlier time, when Adam checks himself into a hospital as his disease moves into a more severe stage. Flowers are carried at the story's beginning, and we are told of Adam's carrying only his briefcase to the hospital. All of Adam's friends wind up carrying food to him, and the story ends with Danny carrying plates to the table as they get together after the funeral. They bring him things to read and changes of clothing to replace those he keeps throwing away. Danny carries lists of things to carry, mostly medicines and other items to help Adam feel better. He carries the most, eventually including items for his own needs as he stays by Adam's bed, even though John is Adam's partner. This seems to be because Danny has done this before. When Adam goes home, medical equipment is carried into the apartment, and paperwork and insurance forms are soon carried there as well. But some things that are carried are not physical. At first, everyone carries hope. Later, when a doctor speaks of people carrying the virus, Danny responds angrily that they know this: "It's the fear every gay man carries today." Finally, Danny carries the ashes of Adam's body, surprised at how heavy they seem.

Although Adam's disease brings about the major conflicts of the story, Danny seems to be the main character. Most readers will probably identify most closely with Danny, since we experience the story through his perspective. He is a hero of sorts, giving a great deal of time and energy with no apparent hope of reward. We tend to feel pity for Adam, who seems to bravely fight the disease. John is more problematic. We understand that he is grieving, but he seems to distance himself from Adam; it is Danny who is available. And Danny is there for John when Adam dies. Much is left out of the story. We wonder why Danny is so dedicated and why he has so much time to give. Why does John keep his distance? Where is Adam's mother during the illness? We know little of the other members of the circle of friends, but they seem supportive, and this may be what counts. The narrator is objective, telling the story in third person, but the point of view seems to be limited to Danny's perspective. We know his thoughts and feelings, but not those of other characters. This, and the lack of direct quotations, allows a distance that keeps the emotions of the story in check. We do not get bogged down in pathos, though it permeates the situation. Perhaps the writer intends for us to observe the impact of AIDS on a circle of friends and specifically on the caregiver. A first-person account or a narration that focused on Adam or John might cause us to see the disease as something affecting an individual or a couple rather than an interconnected community of people who care and try to help.

If Currier borrows Tim O'Brien's idea about the physical and spiritual burdens of war, applying it to the battle against AIDS, he tempers it a bit. For example, he doesn't constantly repeat the phrase *They carried*, as O'Brien so effectively does. To do so would border upon plagiarism, no matter how sincere the motive. Surely, Currier would have been aware of a book that was a finalist for the Pulitzer Prize and other major awards in 1990, only a few years before this story's publication. If he borrows the concept deliberately, the metaphor adds to Currier's story. Fighting AIDS is like fighting a nasty war, he implies, and the friends of the victim are the troops. And someone, like Lieutenant Cross or Danny, must be there to take the lead, to give up something to carry others.

Readers will accept or resist the characters of O'Brien's "The Things They Carried" and Currier's "What They Carried" based on their own biases, though some may protest that they are not prejudiced, *but*. . . . Listening to others in a discussion group may allow unconscious assumptions to surface. Cross's romantic vulnerability and his weeping with guilt may surprise readers who see soldiers as grim fighting machines, while the brutal aspects of war portrayed by

O'Brien undercut sentimental views of "our boys overseas." People who see homosexuals as predatory and promiscuous exploiters may be surprised by the solidarity of the friendships and the altruistic actions of the caregiver described by Currier. Unexamined warrants may come to light as students discuss their emotional reactions to the two stories. The violent images and harsh language of O'Brien's narrative might offend some readers, preventing their involvement with the characters. They may, in fact, be repelled by the characters themselves, and feel angry at O'Brien for portraying the soldiers of the Vietnam War in this way. Many of our current college students are the children of O'Brien's contemporaries and do not like to think of their fathers in this way. Others may recognize some of the realities of war for the first time, feeling compassion for soldiers who are about their age. Currier's characters are human beings surviving the death of a friend. Many readers have known people with catastrophic illnesses and can relate to the universal experience of losing someone to death. We can usually head off homophobic reactions by matter-of-factly introducing the story and tacitly setting the tone for a tolerant atmosphere. Although ignoring the issue of AIDS as a "gay disease" may go against the stance of Currier's narrative, each instructor has a sense of a particular class's dynamics and how much confrontation falls within his or her own comfort zone.

IMAGINING THE END:
A COLLECTION OF WRITINGS
BY EMILY DICKINSON (p. 1504)

EMILY DICKINSON
I like a look of Agony, (p. 1505)

As instructors using *Making Literature Matter* in composition classes we encourage students to discover analysis techniques that work for them. Students often have no idea how to begin. Some feel that only one correct way to approach a text must exist; and since they do not trust their own ideas, they lean too heavily on research or safe but superficial interpretation. To help young writers realize that analysis involves creativity and intellectual risk-taking, we often share our real-life writing tasks at different stages, assuring students by example that invention and organization involve personal choices. We want them to catch the excitement of becoming actively involved in reading, researching, and writing about literary and academic texts. One of the writers of this instructor's manual shared her writing process for the entry on Emily Dickinson with a group of first-year composition students to help them understand how such decisions may take place with a real audience and purpose in mind. She emphasized to them that another writer would undoubtedly read Dickinson's poem from an entirely different point of view, but that we all have an opportunity at college to enter into the academic dialogue already in progress and to make our voice heard. We cannot do this by simply repeating the received wisdom of experts. The surprising response of many students was that they simply did not realize they were "allowed" to explore their own original thoughts about a literary work. Written in an informal "I-Search" style, in the present tense, the remainder of this entry is one teacher's idiosyncratic approach.

In the midst of finding my way into Emily Dickinson, another part of my mind chews on how best to guide my freshman composition students in their current task of writing an argumentative research paper on another topic. They are having trouble choosing an issue to write about, narrowing it down, and finding their way into the research. I wonder how my process might inform theirs as I fish for my angle. So much has been written about Dickinson. How do I best serve the needs of my audience of college professors and adjunct lecturers and graduate teaching assistants, et al., without covering ground they may know more intimately than I do?

So, as I nag my students to do, I begin by writing, starting with sentences that sound a bit like turning over the engine of a car on a cold winter morning. I've underlined the second line of each stanza of Dickinson's "I like a look of Agony," because these phrases seem to express a main idea or theme. The speaker of the poem — perhaps Dickinson, but perhaps another persona — does not like hypocrisy. I have done some background reading on Dickinson, as I have instructed my students to do on their topics, and I know that the poet valued intellectual honesty, especially in religion. I know that she resisted the sort of Christian conversion that demands a total renunciation of self in return for the promise of victory over death, even though most of her friends and family publicly made this religious commitment and urged her to do the same.

As I think about how to present this text to students, I realize that many have been brought up in fundamentalist religions much like Dickinson's, though 1990s culture is not permeated with religion in the way that Amherst, Massachusetts, was in the poet's time. I know that Emily Dickinson lived from 1830 to 1886, an era when many people died young of diseases like tuberculosis and women were expected to maintain a watch over the dying. And I know that she often wrote about death, though she wrote about many other issues as well. I've also read about her love of metaphor, what she called telling things "slant." From reading other Dickinson poems I know that the poet herself is not always identical to the speaker in the poem. So, I go back to the poem again, with this in mind.

This time, I notice the word *Convulsion* in the third line. It strikes me as odd that the speaker says people "do not sham Convulsion." I'd just been looking through the index of a biography of the poet, searching for the word *conversion*, along with other words that might help me find pages that discuss her attitude toward religion and death. The words are so similar that they raise an issue for me. People cannot pretend *convulsion*, but under circumstances like the fervent revival meetings that took place regularly in Dickinson's church, family, and schools when she was in her teens, a person could be mightily tempted to fake a *conversion*, if for no other reason than to get everyone off her back. Could the poet be playing with the configuration and phonetic echoes of the two words, punning or otherwise counting on the connotations of one working with the other, with most readers subliminally absorbing the "slant" vibrations between the two? If I were writing an argumentative research paper, I would now have an issue about which I could make an assertion.

As I think about the issue of Emily Dickinson and her deliberate decision to resist the surrender of autonomy that comes with conversion, it strikes me that the voice of the poem might be an ironic persona, expressing her idea of a perverse and unloving God's attitude toward death and suffering. From what I have read, I believe that I could make a case for this interpretation. At this point, if I were going on to write an argumentative research paper on this poem, I would direct my reading toward its being Dickinson's ironic protest against a God who demands suffering and death. One critic has described the voice in this poem as "almost a hysterical shriek." Reasonable people may disagree! I think it is an ironically defiant mockery of either God or the Angel of Death. Given this, how might I refute the characterization of Dickinson's poem as *hysterical* — a word full of pejorative, sexist connotations?

First, I would point out that the word is loaded and that the critic's assertion is inconsistent with what we know of the poet's wry humor and defiance of death. I would try to find evidence of other times that Dickinson takes an ironic tone in relation to death and times when her content is boldly heretical. I would keep in mind my first reaction, that Dickinson does not like hypocrisy any more than God does, but would argue that she often hides behind the protective coloration of metaphor. I'd have to work out the seeming inconsistencies of this statement, perhaps arguing that Dickinson knows she cannot fool God and simply throws his absurdity back in his face. She is totally honest with God, herself, and any reader who cares to discover the joke. One Dickinson biographer makes the point that Dickinson believed in the existence of God because she was convinced by evidence of design in the physical universe, but that for equally logical reasons she had difficulty believing God has humankind's best interests at heart. To Emily Dickinson, the evidence of suffering and death supports the thesis that the designs of God, as interpreted by Protestant theology, are less than loving.

Whether the poem is a "hysterical shriek," a satire describing a harsh god's view of suffering and death, or the sincere though brutal imagery of an honest woman who has seen many people die, the speaker's attitude toward hypocrisy is clear. Taken at face value, the poem seems monstrous, but there is something to be said for reaching the point where pretense is shed. If the tone is ironic, the agonizing deaths of the Civil War are simply historically specific examples of exactly what the poet is talking about. Is agony the price of authenticity for this speaker?

The poet capitalizes most of the nouns. By doing this, she implies personification in some cases: "Agony," "Convulsion," "Throe," "Death," and "Anguish" become entities. They also become emphasized as emblems or symbols, as do "Eyes" and "Beads upon the Forehead." They seem to shout or stand out on the page. The first stanza describes pain and critical sickness or injury; the second stanza takes one step further and describes death itself. Anguish is described in the second stanza " homely." This word, and others in the poem, may have both denotations and connotations that are unfamiliar to students, and we might look them up in small groups in different dictionaries. In the first definition in most dictionaries, *homely* denotes unattractiveness. However, since the speaker claims to "like a look of Agony" and other forthright manifestations of suffering and death, the secondary definitions may be more apt: "simple; plain; or unpretentious" — even "comfortable in the manner of home; cozy."

We might be reminded of the women of Emily Dickinson's day, sitting up with dying relatives in the home and then preparing the body for burial. We may picture Anguish as a grieving aunt or sister, keeping her hands busy in the death watch, placing beads one by one on a string as she patiently waits, and finally placing them on the dead face. The image may refer to the beads of perspiration that might linger after a sick person has finished a death struggle. If Dickinson were Catholic, we might think of a rosary, since this would be an appropriate emblem to place with the dead. Upon first reading, we might expect the image of death to end the poem, and readers may fault the last two lines as anticlimactic. On closer reading, however, we may see the honest sweat that clings to the body after death — put there by authentic, down-to-earth anguish — as an appropriate concluding image.

EMILY DICKINSON
I've seen a Dying Eye (p. 1506)

Emily Dickinson observed death from multiple perspectives in her poetry. In the well-known poem that begins "My Life had stood — a Loaded Gun — " the speaker may be the Angel of Death himself, according to some critics. In many of her poems, including the two that follow "I've seen a Dying Eye," the speaker is the person who has died. In "I've seen a Dying Eye" the narrator observes as a person looks frantically around the room as he or she dies. It has been pointed out that the phonetic coincidence between the word *eye* and the first-person pronoun *I* is sometimes used by Dickinson to evoke a double meaning when speaking of death. When the eyes close for the final time, this also signals the end of the "I," the human individual that Dickinson values so highly.

In an era when people usually died at home under the watch of the women of the house, Emily Dickinson had seen many close friends and relatives die. Her letters to family members often include lists of the sick and dying or accounts of the deaths of friends, including the young woman who had been her college roommate at Mount Holyoke Seminary. Of an age-mate who died when they were thirteen, Dickinson wrote a friend two years later,

> There she lay mild & beautiful as in health & her pale features lit up with an unearthly — smile. I looked as long as friends would permit & when they told I must weep no longer, I let them lead me away. I shed no tear, for my heart was too full to weep, but after she was laid in her coffin & I felt I could not call her back again I gave way to a fixed melancholy.

Poetry may have been Emily Dickinson's way of dealing with this close acquaintance with death and dying.

"I've seen a Dying Eye" tells as much about the speaker as it does about the person who dies. We do not know what the dying person searches for as he or she looks intently around the room. The effect as the speaker describes it is desperate, purposeful, but helpless. The dying eye does not seem to find what it seeks. The speaker does not flinch. Like the thirteen-year-old Emily Dickinson, who must be led from the room by the adults as her friend lies on her deathbed, the narrator of the poem observes the stages, not looking away until the eyes are "soldered down" — welded shut forever. Some might find this attitude morbid, ghoulish, or sick. Others might find it brave, honest, and realistic. Perhaps the speaker simply reveals a probing, curious mind that wants to know the whole business of death. She observes with an almost scientific detachment. The active verb *Run* describes the eye, not the dying person. The contrast creates a tension between dying and searching for something or someone just before death. This seems to be something important to the dying person in the speaker's view. Her language makes it seem as if this search is something the narrator may have seen more than once.

Part of the mystery of death is that we do not know, and the dead person can never tell. This seems to be the point of the poem. The poet does not make clear whether the blessing comes to the dying eye. There is no smile, which perhaps means both the speaker and the dying person are left unfulfilled. The *m* sounds are clustered in the middle of the poem as the search comes to an end and the vision is obscured. This is the moment of dying, and perhaps the hum describes the last breath, like the sound of a fly buzzing that we will hear in the next poem of this cluster. "I've seen a Dying Eye" focuses upon vision throughout, however. The word *seen* of the first line is repeated in the last, but the perspective is quite different. At the poem's outset, the verb describes the keen observation of the speaker, whereas its use in the final line occurs within a verbal structure that leaves unclear whether the dying person has *seen* anything or not. The movement of vision in the poem follows the same progression as death, from clarity to obscurity.

The eye darting around the room in "I've seen a Dying Eye" seems to be more conscious and purposeful than the look of agony described in the previous poem in this cluster. This eye searches for "Something," whereas the person in "I like a look of Agony," seems absorbed in his or her dying rather than looking around. The word *look* is ambiguous. The narrator of "I like a look of Agony," seems to like the way the dying person appears, the sincerity of the look of death, not the way the person looks around the room. A case might be made for either interpretation. The moment of death itself seems the same, however. One poem describes the way the eyes "glaze," and the other says that the eyes "obscure with Fog," both implying the end of the ability to see. Both death scenes are vivid, and the people who are dying have business to do. The differences are subtle, but the death scene in "I like a look of Agony," seems more violent, and its dying protagonist seems to be busy with the illness itself. The dying person in "I've seen a Dying Eye" looks outside of herself, and we do not know why — perhaps for help, perhaps to search out the Angel of Death, perhaps to find a familiar face or to take care of unfinished business with the living.

EMILY DICKINSON

I heard a Fly buzz — when I died — (p. 1506)

Like the two poems that precede it in this cluster, "I heard a Fly buzz — when I died — " catches its subject at the moment of death. But whereas the other poems show the dying person from the perspective of an observer, this one lets us into the mind of the person who dies. The image of the fly subverts any romanticizing of death. Rather than flights of angels or something else as elegant and high-minded, the poet gives us an image that conjures up absurd and down-to-earth connotations. We do not see the painful death throes of "I like a look of Agony," or hear the serious tone of "I've seen a Dying Eye." For people of the nineteenth century, the fly could be a homey, everyday image. A children's song of the time was "Baby-bye, Here's a Fly" in which a mother playfully invites her child to watch a fly with her. A fly is a trivial irritation that one might brush away. It has no sting. But the fly can have other connotations as well. We associate it with decay and physical death, and a biblical demon is named Beelzebub, the Lord of the Flies. The humming sound of the fly in this poem may remind readers of the *m* sounds that we noted in "I've seen a Dying Eye" just at the moment of death. "I heard a Fly buzz — when I died — " could be a companion piece to the preceding poem, providing a view from the deathbed to explain the observations of the watcher. The progression is similar, and the buzz of the fly may be the source of a noise that the dying eye seeks before the vision is finally obscured and she cannot "see to see."

Because the poem minimizes both the horror and the romanticism of dying, some readers will find a grim humor in it, almost a ridiculing of death as something insignificant that we might brush away from our face. The under-statement implied in the calm voice that speaks of death as a failure of vision lends an ironic tone that some will read as amusing. Rather than giving us an inside view of the look of agony described in an earlier poem, the speaker relates the business of making a will, though this may be meant symbolically. Death seems rather prosaic here. Others will find the poem horrifying and oppressive. The juxtaposition of the fly with death may call up images of rotting bodies. They will note the deadly stillness in the room and the onlookers steeling themselves for the end. Part of the poem's irony is the use of the dead person as a speaker. Literal-minded people may find this too improbable. Others will argue, however, that we do not know at what point death actually comes or what it is like. It may be that Emily Dickinson, with her intimate acquaintance and keen introspection about death, makes as good a guess as any.

The repetition of the word *Stillness* in the first stanza explicitly communicates the sort of feeling some of us have experienced in the eye of a hurricane. We can feel the weight of the air, and perhaps are reminded of the stillness that awaits in the heavy airlessness of the coffin. The word denotes an absence of both movement and of noise, and is a uniquely appropriate word to use in connection with death. The word *see* also has a double meaning, referring to both vision and understanding or logical thinking. For Dickinson, loss of the "eye" and loss of the "I" — the self — are related. When the speaker says she "could not see to see," she may mean that she no longer has the vision to engage in rational thought. This loss of conscious self is death.

The poet frames the business of death that relates to the others in the room, the living, with the actual dying of the first and last stanza where she hears the fly. The middle stanzas convey a different sort of reality, the part that concerns the living. This provides a sort of flashback to earlier observations and even earlier activities. It provides suspense of the sort that we saw in earlier poems before the eyes glaze over, but it allows the actual dying to be a personal experience. Death here is not *about* the survivors, and it is a profoundly different experience for this speaker than for the witnesses of the preceding poems.

To refer to the eyes as the windows of the soul may have been a cliché even in the 1860s, and to argue that the final image of the poem is such a metaphor may be an oversimplification, though it is often read in just this way. Dickinson may use the obscured view implied when the "Windows failed" to be consistent with the image of the fly. Most readers have seen a fly beating itself against a window to get out. Perhaps the windows give way to the fly, allowing the dying person to break past the barrier between life and death. In a similar poem "I felt a Funeral, in my Brain" the speaker experiences her own funeral, with the final stanza implying a similar crash, this time through "a Plank in Reason." The poem ends as does "I heard a Fly buzz — when I died — ," with one of Emily Dickinson's enigmatic dashes. Because the poems are so closely related in persona and theme, some readers might find it interesting to compare and contrast the two. In both, the loss of vision may be important, but it is the loss of reason that seems to concern the poet most.

The difference in point of view between this poem and the two preceding ones produces an ironic effect. "I like a look of Agony," is horrible to read, its speaker perhaps an evil God who glories in the authenticity of the death struggle. "I've seen a Dying Eye" is more compassionate but still evokes pathos for the dying person. It is difficult to feel sorry for the matter-of-fact narrator of her own death in "I heard a Fly buzz — when I died — " because we hear her tell her own story. The last line is poignant, but not horrifying. Like a place we have read about for years and finally visited, death has an everyday quality when seen from this more familiar perspective.

Most Christian readers will assume that the King is Jesus Christ, since he is sometimes called the King of Kings in the Bible. If the poem had been published in the Amherst, Massachusetts, of her time, Emily Dickinson might have kept her silence and allowed this safe interpretation. But most Dickinson scholars think that the title probably refers to a personified Angel of Death or death itself. Some might read this as the "Something" that the dying person searches for in the room in "I like a look of Agony."

The poet's use of "eyes" in all three poems of this cluster is consistent with her connections between vision and the ability to think. Emily Dickinson insisted upon her own vision, her own independent worldview. When a person dies, he or she loses vision in this symbolic sense. If this poem was written in the early 1860s, as it is usually dated, Dickinson was experiencing some frightening vision problems, almost going blind. The thought of not being able to read was horrifying to her. Perhaps this threat to her access to texts and the critical thinking they provoked explains her linking of literal and figurative vision in her poetry. Her focus in these death poems on vision and on stilled breath peels away the things of the body, focusing our gaze on the essentials of death — the loss of voice and the power to see, to understand.

EMILY DICKINSON

Because I could not stop for Death — (p. 1508)

In 1847, when Emily Dickinson was sixteen years old, a friend just a few years older, Olivia Coleman, died of the complications of tuberculosis. This happened as Olivia was taking a carriage ride. Perhaps the memory of this death, one of many among Dickinson's friends and relatives, underlies the imagery of "Because I could not stop for Death — ." It is perhaps her most anthologized poem, and many students will have read it in high school.

The poem describes a courtship or, more likely, a marriage. It has been popular in recent years in our town for the bride and groom to ride from their wedding to the reception in a horse-drawn carriage. Royal weddings in England may also come to mind. Readers may also recall images from state funerals in which a carriage carries the body to a place of burial. Although readers a century and a half distant from Dickinson have no everyday associations with carriage rides as the poet would have had, perhaps our images are even more appropriate to the poem. Weddings and funerals are ceremonial occasions, and we understand the sort of "Civility" that ironically accompanies these most dramatic of events. When a death in the family takes place, we tend to be surprised for a while that life goes on, that children still play and the sun is still in the sky. The allegory of the believer as the bride of Christ may also be implied in the poem. Some readers see Death as merely the driver of the carriage, with the bride going to wait for the bridegroom who will come to receive his bride at a later time. By this interpretation, she is still waiting at the poem's end. The speaker does not reveal any strong feelings about this. Though the poem implies no horror, the speaker's eerie passiveness equally denies ecstasy.

The active life implied in the first line sharply contrasts with the timelessness and stillness of the final stanza. As early as the fifth line, we find the elongating of time. And we are given to understand the change in the speaker from busy movement to total stillness when she reverses her perception of the sun's movement between the third and fourth stanzas. At first she speaks of the sun's standing still as she passes it, then corrects herself to describe the transformed reality: It is she who is stopped in place. Like an observer who watches a moving train and feels as if she herself is moving, though actually standing still, the poem's speaker realizes that the world is literally passing her by.

Immortality is personified in the poem, but seems a strangely static character. If the speaker is immortal, it may be because time no longer has the same meaning. Centuries of death do not contain as much time as one day of life. Some may read the final stanza as an expression of contentment of a time-flies-when-we're-having-fun quality. Others may argue that this person who so filled her time that she could not stop for death is now cheated of both time and activity, a reading that rejects the implied optimism of a romantic view of death as a contented marriage. The adjectives that readers choose to describe their images of death in the poem will depend upon their interpretation of the poem as optimistic, perhaps even Christian, or as an ironic challenge to this traditional view. The speaker has "passed" away, and the poem describes the things she has passed in her passing: the school, the fields, and the sun. But each is described oddly. Rather than seeing the children at the school as they played, the speaker remembers that they "strove," a word implying struggle. Rather than gazing at the grain in the field, she sees the grain as gazing at the carriage as the passing takes place. And she realizes that it is the sun that moves rather than the carriage. All that she passes contrasts with her new position as one who can no longer strive, see, or move. This is not a marriage she has chosen, but she has lost the vital powers she needs for resistance.

The grave is a house in the last two stanzas, continuing the extended metaphor of death as a wedding procession. At thirty-three, Emily Dickinson would have been considered in her day to be a spinster, an old maid too old for marriage. She had seen many deaths of people younger than herself. Current college readers may consider her to be about the right age for marriage, certainly too young to die. There is no warmth to this macabre marriage. Some might find it comforting. Others will question as overly sentimental the assumptions that find a happy ending here.

The death described here, unlike those of the earlier three poems in this cluster, is sudden. The dying protagonists of "I like a look of Agony," "I've seen a Dying Eye," and "I heard a Fly buzz — when I died — " die in the presence of witnesses who observe the stages of death. They have business to deal with — going through the agonies of sickness, searching the room with frantic eyes, making wills — so perhaps the difference is one of perspective. Here, death is a journey that takes place outside of the sickroom. Perhaps the protagonist actually dies on a carriage ride, as Olivia Coleman had many years before at the young age of twenty. Perhaps, like the speaker of "I heard a Fly buzz — when I died — ," her experience of dying has a different focus from that assumed by her observers.

Unlike the other deaths, this one involves the whole body, and we have a change in perspective rather than a blurring of vision. Some readers will find this incompatible with the descriptions of death in the earlier poems. Others might argue that the first two lines of "Because I could not stop for Death — " summarize the experience described in the earlier poems. Now we are beyond the actual dying, journeying to the place death takes us to. Perhaps the journey described here takes place at the time vision blurs in the earlier poems. The images of this poem are sunnier, but we also feel the chill of death. A case could be made for this poem's metaphor being even more horrible than the honest imagery of the earlier poems. It is difficult to see the Emily Dickinson of the earlier poems really meaning us to take it at face value.

Students are entitled to their favorites, but they should examine their reasons for ranking certain poems higher than the others. "Because I could not stop for Death — " will be the favorite of many, because they find it more optimistic. Experienced readers often like it the least, finding it a true horror story, much like William Faulkner's "A Rose for Emily" (p. 849 in the "Loving" chapter) or other stories that reek of necrophilia.

CONFRONTING THE DEATH OF A STRANGER (p. 1510)

KATHERINE MANSFIELD
The Garden-Party (p. 1510)

Like most young people, the main character of Katherine Mansfield's short story "The Garden-Party" is in the midst of constructing her view of reality and finding her place in the social structure of her society. The music, the clothing, the activities, and the attitudes that surround her all contribute to Laura's developing worldview, deliberately and subliminally telling her who to be and what to believe. In the world in which the garden party takes place, reality has a predetermined order that remains unquestioned by most of the characters. They accept the social constructs as givens and do not examine the reasons underlying class-determined behavior. This world is not unlike the colonial hierarchies of the New Zealand of Mansfield's childhood. The British Empire imposed its own structure upon the lives of its colonized peoples, and the lines between social classes continue to rule manners among the children and grandchildren of settlers. A garden, with its courteously blooming roses, its potted lilies, and its manmade constructions obscuring the karaka trees, symbolizes the taming of nature by the hand of "civilization."

Katherine Mansfield, in her life if not her fiction, resisted this imposition of societal rules. An early marriage lasted only twenty-four hours, and two affairs resulted in miscarriage or abortion. She lived with John Middleton Murry for several years before their marriage in 1918. By this time, she had manifested the tuberculosis and heart disease from which she died in 1923 at the age of thirty-four. Although she spent her adult life in England and other European locations, she recalled her South Pacific childhood with pleasure. Like the protagonist of "The Garden-Party," she grew up with sisters and shared a special bond with her brother, Leslie Beauchamp, whose early death she felt as a great loss.

Although she read and wrote about her contemporaries in the early Modernist movement, enjoying T. S. Eliot but finding James Joyce vulgar, Katherine Mansfield — like the later student of middle-class manners, Raymond Carver — was most influenced by the Russian master of characterization, Anton Chekhov. Writing to her husband just weeks before her death, Mansfield may have been referring as much to herself as to Chekhov: "We know he felt his stories were not half what they might be. It doesn't take much imagination to picture him on his deathbed thinking, 'I have never had a real chance. Something has been all wrong.' "

Students, like critics, will interpret Laura's reaction to death differently, since her newly found definition of "life" is left unfinished. Many readers find her shallow, seeing Laura as fixed in the unreality of romanticism. The woman at the dead man's house has perhaps expected to shock the young aristocrat by forcing her to look at the body; Mansfield describes the woman's movement as "sly." Instead, Laura sees him through the same glowing filter through which she has earlier seen the workers in the garden. Her reaction recalls the sentimental Victorian song her sister sings earlier with no thought to the meaning of its words, and our discussions will gain much from a consideration of the lyrics. The prosperous family members have no understanding of how "weary" life might be for those who do the actual labor of their household and seem able to interpret life only in relation to their own concerns. This superficiality also includes Laura.

At the story's beginning, Laura indulges in poses and generalizes romantic views of the workers as they go about their work and she plays at directing them. In the grieving household, she must appear as incongruously decorative as the trappings of the party. But there are hints that she recognizes this, as she asks the corpse to "forgive" her hat, and she makes assumptions throughout the story that reveal her view of the workers as people with feelings similar to her own. Although she sees her family as "heartless" in having the party despite the man's death, she too may seem to some readers to have very little substance at her core. She is easily distracted from her empathy by her own appearance in the new hat. The implication of the word *heartless* may be that the upper-class family live on the surface because they are hollow, lacking in real emotions. Some readers will maintain that it would be unrealistic for the family to change their plans because a worker has died, arguing that it is Laura who is romantic and impractical. Warrants may reveal attitudes about social class but may also be related to experiences with death and varying ways in which subcultures and families deal with it.

Laura clumsily tries to ignore class distinctions, but her efforts are naive, since the workers and their families have their own concerns. She exaggerates her own importance to them. They look at her "queerly," and a woman speaks to her with an "oily" voice. Although she fantasizes that they are more natural, making much of one worker's sniffing a sprig of lavender, it is a worker who suggests placing the marquee in front of the karaka trees, hiding their natural beauty. Some students might point out that if the family had called the party to a halt, it would be at best a hollow gesture, and the band, at least, would be out of a job. Despite its title, the story shows little of the party itself, since the events that affect its protagonist occur in the encounters with workers that take place before and after the party.

We see the family's attitudes toward the people they consider inferiors, there for their own comfort and amusement; for example, a household servant is referred to fondly as "good little Hans" and the band is laughingly compared to frogs. We are told that Laura's sister Jose "loved giving orders to the servants, and they loved obeying her. She always made them feel they were taking part in some drama." This contrasts sharply with Laura's naive, democratic fantasies, which make everyone uncomfortable. Although readers may applaud her intentions, it is unclear whether Laura will grow beyond her immature attempts at finding common values with the people across the road to a philosophy based on true respect. In the long run, the story is *about* the impact of the working class on the consciousness of an aristocratic character. She tells her brother that her confrontation with mortality has been "simply marvelous," a comment that seems to trivialize the death of a human being, turning it into a learning experience for a silly girl. However, it is at the point when language fails her that Laura may reveal the dynamism of her character: No longer able to reduce life to romantic cliché, she is silenced by its complexity.

GABRIEL GARCÍA MÁRQUEZ
The Handsomest Drowned Man in the World (p. 1522)

In 1955, a small Colombian destroyer ran into heavy seas on its return to Cartagena. Several sailors were swept overboard and lost, and all died except one, who survived for ten days at sea, clinging to a life raft. When he eventually washed ashore, the castaway became a national hero. The government of dictator Gustavo Rojas Pinella immediately claimed him for propaganda purposes. The man traveled the country making speeches and starred in advertisements for watches and shoes. Eventually, however, a guilty conscience led the sailor to confess that the cargo of his ship had been contraband and the sailors had fallen overboard through their own incompetence. There had been no storm. When the story was offered to *El Spectador*, a newspaper in Bogotá, the assignment fell to Gabriel García Márquez to act as the ghostwriter of a serialized narrative. The dictator was furious, and García Márquez's editor felt that it was time for his reporter to serve for a time as a European correspondent. Soon after this, the government shut down his newspaper, but by this time García Márquez was beginning to see his fiction published.

Considering the surreal nature of most of his work, it is interesting to read that this master of magical realism says that his starting point for any story must be a *real fact*. Although he includes texts that he has read as real facts — for example, the flying carpets and genies of *The Thousand and One Nights* — he insists that such adventures correspond somehow to real-life experiences. His grandfather's experiences in the Banana Wars and his grandmother's superstitious tales equally serve as material for his fictional worlds. Readers could make a case for "The Handsomest Drowned Man in the World" as prompted by the real facts of the sailor's tale first written as nonfiction in *El Spectador*. Beyond the bare fact of a man's being washed up on shore, however, the fictional tale may owe more to the reception the sailor received. Like the drowned man of the story, whose character and narrative are imagined by the villagers, the surviving sailor became a text to be read and rewritten by the government, the adoring populace, and finally the newspaper reporter.

Like its companion story "A Very Old Man with Enormous Wings," in which a winged man appears after a storm, "The Handsomest Drowned Man in the World" is subtitled "A Tale for Children." Both stories may have elements inspired by the lurid, superstitious tales the writer heard from the grandmother with whom he spent his first eight years in the coastal Colombian town of Aracataca. He confesses that her stories so frightened him that he was afraid for a time to venture outside the house. These were the folktales of *mestizos* and *costeños*, racially and culturally mixed descendents of Spanish pirates, African slaves, and indigenous peoples of the Caribbean coast of northern South America — an ethnic heritage García Márquez wears with pride.

His subtitle is certainly ironic. These are stories that question the warrants of adults as they seek to read the strange, new text of a godlike drowned man or a winged ancient, and children would perhaps have nightmares or, at best, would be unlikely to understand them. Yet the real irony may be that, because he was not protected from such tales, the frightened little boy grew up to become a Nobel Laureate. He has related the breakthrough that led to his mature style when he realized on a trip out of town that the key to the narrative he wanted to write should be the perfectly deadpan style of his grandmother as she told the most incredible of tales. He turned around, went home, and began to write like a madman. This matter-of-fact acceptance of the most unlikely of circumstances is the essence of magical realism.

In "The Handsomest Drowned Man in the World" the appearance of the dead man is presented as a fact. The story is about the unfolding reactions of the villagers to him. All are in awe of his size and manliness, and we are told that after they see his face, their imaginations cannot contain him. As the women lovingly clean and clothe him for burial, he becomes an object of desire as they compare their husbands unfavorably with him. They give him the name *Esteban* — Stephen — the name of the first Christian martyr, who in Acts 6:15 is portrayed as having the face of an angel as he preaches the new religion in the temple just before the mob stones him for blasphemy. Interestingly, however, the first African man named as a traveler to the Caribbean, perhaps a symbolic ancestor for the writer, is also *Esteban*.

Whatever the name's significance, the women have given him further definition by giving him a name. They come to love him for his vulnerability, now seeing him as like their husbands. The men are equally awed, but as the women delay, they become jealous and call him names that degrade and dehumanize him. However, even the men come to love him. At the beginning and later at the end, he is compared to a whale, and they come to pity him, seeing him as ashamed and sincere. Readers may be reminded of Herman Melville's *Moby-Dick*, a text quite familiar to García Márquez, in which the whale becomes a symbol for characters and readers alike. The drowned man becomes a kinsman to the villagers, forever identified with the town. Like a god — or a text — he becomes a mirror reflecting the people who interpret him. This is not unlike the funerals of friends and relatives; sometimes we hardly recognize the person we knew as we listen to the various glosses upon his or her life.

There is a great deal of ironic humor, almost slapstick comedy, in the story. The godlike creature is an object of awe, but the children play at burying and reburying him in the sand, the women imagine householders fearing that he will break their chairs, and the doting women almost make the men trip over him as they delay the parting with their big toy. At first, the children even think he is a ship! The manner of telling is realistic, and the villagers seem naive but believable; but the drowned man is fantastic. Long sentences give a breathless quality to the prose. For example, after the one-sentence paragraph in which the women praise the Lord that the drowned man has not been claimed by another village and thus belongs to them, much of paragraph 8 is made up of one long sentence in which the women delay and the men get irritated. We are told at the paragraph's end that "the men were left breathless too," and the style models this breathlessness.

At a recent funeral, the minister made the statement that the woman being buried had died peacefully because no mortician could have artificially placed such an expression on her face. Some of his listeners knew, however, the distress that her husband had felt when he saw the distortions of her face in the hospital after the medical team's strenuous efforts to resuscitate her. The clergyman's interpretation revealed more about his own views, or perhaps his purpose in comforting mourners, than they revealed about the manner of the woman's death. Much the same thing happens as the characters of Katherine Mansfield's "The Garden-Party" and Gabriel García Márquez's "The Handsomest Drowned Man in the World" view the dead.

In both stories, the observers of the dead engage in idealistic fantasies. Readers whose warrants involve the view of death as a rest from one's labors may find Laura's view sensible. Others may see her reaction as similar to her earlier submerged attraction to the worker who smells the lavender. To find the reactions of the villagers sensible requires that the reader enter the fantastic world of the story. We assume that there must be some good reason behind all of the villagers seeing Esteban as desirable in some way, but we also realize that the story may be about the projection of desire onto the blank page of the dead man's face. The villagers are forever affected by their encounter with the drowned man, since they are now identified with him; their village is now Esteban's village. We are not as certain about Laura, since the story ends ambiguously. Perhaps her new understanding of the complexity of life will keep her from conforming to the social distinctions and shallow selfishness that characterize her mother and sisters.

At the garden party of Mansfield's story, even the flowers defer to the upper-class family. Roses bloom on cue. Lavender can be plucked from the lawn. There is a "lily lawn" and the mother has even more lilies brought in. Even Laura's hat is flowered. She realizes instinctively that taking the flowers to the house of mourners will be pretentious on top of the "scraps" from the party. As Laura looks at the body, she knows that he has no need of flowers. By contrast, the seacoast village is barren of flowers, is like a desert. But neighbors bring flowers for Esteban's funeral, and later the villagers paint their houses bright colors and plant so many flowers on the cliffs that people far out to sea can smell their aroma and see the sunflowers. The whole village has come to life.

DON DELILLO
Videotape (p. 1526)

When John F. Kennedy was killed in 1963, Americans felt for the first time the full impact of television in creating the shared experiences that define a culture. A generation now middle-aged and older can recall exactly where we were when the news came. Although we did not see Kennedy's death at that time — the Zapruder film was released later — many of us saw Jack Ruby's killing of Lee Harvey Oswald as it happened. Later, after viewing the videotape of the parade made from the film — women wearing head scarves milling about, the blow to the head, the wife in her pink suit reacting in panic — many of us think we have a memory of the scene itself. Not only is the videotape real to us, it seems somehow more real than living memory, has the official stamp of reality upon it. It is hard evidence that we can go back and verify, unlike our own experiences, by comparison vague impressions with the quality of dream about them. A few years before Kennedy's assassination, Walker Percy wrote about the phenomenon in his novel *The Moviegoer*. Describing a scene in which a young man lights movie star William Holden's cigarette, Percy tells us, "The boy has done it! He has won the title to his own existence, as plenary an existence now as Holden's. . . . An aura of heightened reality moves with him and all who fall within it feel it."

In the forty years or so since Percy's novel and Zapruder's grainy film, the power of the visual image has continued to increase exponentially. As we pull this book together in April 1999, the twenty-four-hour news channels on cable television compete for images in the wake of a school shooting at Columbine High School and the NATO bombings in the former Yugoslavian province of Kosovo. A year ago, most Americans had never heard of either place, but we now recognize their televised faces better than we do those of our own relatives. We weep at the funeral services of children we have never met, ache for homeless refugees. At the same time, a television talk show is being sued for allegedly embarrassing a man into killing a gay admirer who expressed a fantasy on a videotaped episode. The young killer is said to have feared that his grandparents would see the tape and think that he was gay. It is unclear why he might have thought that killing his admirer would prevent this. Court TV shows the talk-show episode over and over again as they announce with no apparent sense of irony that the tape was never aired. A few years ago we watched Rodney King beaten by police officers, and we have argued about the guilt or innocence of O. J. Simpson, whose dead ex-wife we know on a first-name basis. A few weeks ago, Dr. Jack Kevorkian was convicted of second-degree murder for the assisted suicide of a man on a weekly television newsmagazine. Those with the heart to do so watched the man die. The seventeen-year-old boys who carried out the Columbine school shooting, then killed themselves, are said to have acquired inspiration and information from the images of video games, German techno-rock, and the Internet.

News analysts discuss issues of censorship and other measures to protect kids. A few years down the line, we and our students will add fresh examples of the impact of television and other information sources on our definitions of reality. Electronic images have become the materials from which we construct our reality, determine common sense, and explain our judgments of the world. Don DeLillo writes most of his fiction about the power of the image to dominate reality. His novel *Libra* retells the Lee Harvey Oswald story, the first major example of the bizarre, unreal reality of the televised news event. The short story "Videotape" examines the effects of this easily accessible technology of the image on its audience.

As digital technology advances, students will probably see videotape as only a step along the way, as dated as cassette tapes have become in the days of compact discs. But DeLillo's point may be less about the technology itself than about easy access to the creation of images that are forever fixed and about the impact of such images on the audience. The story points out that the creation of videotapes no longer belongs exclusively to trained cameramen supervised by directors. This gives the videotaped point of view vivid authenticity. Having said this, however, we should note that computer technology in which images may be altered, morphed into forms that never existed in the real world, may lead to a questioning of the image. Seeing is no longer believing when editing takes over.

Readers might judge the narrator to be unusually morbid and nothing like themselves. The need to look tragedy in the face may be human nature, however. He philosophizes about the nature of videotape, speaking almost as a literary critic. He says that it makes children "see things twice," that it defines, that it can have a "jostled sort of noneventness." He views the victim as an actor, mentioning his "underplayed reaction" as he waves nonchalantly to the child. He discusses suspense and the event's lack of accompaniment. The death has become a drama by virtue of the medium of its telling.

The narrator assumes that the audience shares common assumptions and reactions with him, and repeats the direct address "You know" to establish common ground. Having a child as the creator of the videotape gives the event an added horror, since we imagine the effect on the young witness who, as the narrator has pointed out, sees this horrible thing twice. Imagining her emotions makes it more real to the narrator.

He wants his wife to witness it with him and speculates about his reasons for doing this. He is absorbed by the tape's authenticity. Like Walker Percy in *The Moviegoer*, Don DeLillo has his narrator ponder the nature of the reproduced and fixed image: "The tape is supperreal, or maybe underreal. . . . The tape has a searing realness." Videotape is significant for its recurring quality; the viewer can rewind and rerun it again and again. The serial killer is a particularly apt sort of murderer to appear on videotape, since his crime has a similar recurring quality, is like a taped-and-played event. The story itself is much like a videotaped documentary in which the narrator interweaves commentary with the visual images of the tape. However, it more closely resembles a movie review in its synthesis of criticism and textual evidence, although it is a brutally personal one.

The settings of the three stories in this cluster are extremely different. Katherine Mansfield sets her garden party in a realistic setting, suffused with the romantic glow of its young protagonist's point of view as she sorts out issues of social class and the manners surrounding death. Gabriel García Márquez provides a setting appropriate to the magical realism genre in which he writes; the setting is realistic enough, though exotic to most readers, but the events have a fairy-tale quality, as his subtitle allows. Setting in DeLillo's story is confined to the videotape and its double audience, the narrator and the child as he imagines her. Ironically, because it is closer in time and experience to current readers, DeLillo's taped event may seem most real. Although most of us have never seen a murder, we have witnessed thousands in the way that DeLillo's narrator describes this one. Not every story that includes children is a tale *for* children, though we may argue that García Márquez means his title ironically.

All of these stories assume a sophisticated audience able to catch the irony and fill in the gaps of the text. Both DeLillo and García Márquez may in fact be writing about how we interpret texts, bringing our own character and emotions into the reading. Dead bodies are palimpsests, like old parchments that have been written upon, layer after layer. Since they cannot speak for themselves, we fill in the gaps with our projections, our unquestioned warrants and assumptions. The characters of the three stories in this cluster write their own lives onto the silent image of the corpse, revealing themselves by their interpretations. The less we know about the dead person, the more the living characters tell us about themselves.

DISRESPECTING DEATH (p. 1532)

JOHN DONNE
Death Be Not Proud (p. 1532)

As an Anglican priest who was a contemporary of William Shakespeare, John Donne wrote sermons, satires, and a great many highly original poems. His major themes are religion, love, and death. His *Holy Sonnets*, considered his most skilled work, reflect these concerns. Like many of Donne's poems, "Death Be Not Proud," personifies an abstract concept, death, in the kind of extended metaphor called a conceit. The sonnet is constructed as a rhetorical argument, a refutation of the power of death. Addressing death directly, the speaker summons his evidence with an analogy comparing death to rest and sleep, something that human beings welcome. What's more, death is the final agent of the soul's *delivery*, its deliverance to God, or perhaps its final rebirth. He goes on to characterize death as a mere tool of other powers, then ends his argument with the paradox that because the Christian wakes to eternal life, death itself will die.

Death was an ever-present reality for the people of Renaissance England, and John Donne had experienced the deaths of many family members. The wife he passionately loved gave birth to a new child almost every year in a time when women frequently died from the complications of childbirth. She died after sixteen years of marriage in 1617, soon after their twelfth child was delivered stillborn. Six of Donne's children preceded him in death. His letters often speak of his own illnesses, and he once wrote a friend, "I am afraid that Death will play with me so long, as he will forget to kill me; and suffer me to live in a languishing and useless age. A life that is rather a forgetting that I am dead, than of living." Death for Donne in his later years seems like an aging cat, toothless, forgetful, and arbitrary. But the letter is from a later date than the poem, which may have been written as early as 1611, the same year that the King James Version of the Bible was published. The *Holy Sonnets*, subtitled "Divine Meditations," owe much to his own translations of the biblical Psalms, and may be read as religious and philosophical exercises that explore the Christian faith. Perhaps the true intersection of his obsession with death and his personal history would come later.

In many of his poems, Donne has his speaker address someone or something in a dramatic monologue that readers are expected to imagine overhearing. The situation is much like a formal debate in which the opponents each seek to persuade not each other but a listening audience. John Donne, as both a clergyman and a member of Parliament, would have been familiar with both direct and indirect ways of swaying an audience. He uses an Aristotelian argument that seeks to prove the opposition completely in the wrong. Of course, it is impossible to present an argument without revealing something of oneself. The speaker is proud of his defiance of death. His tone is mocking, almost jeering in its sarcasm. Perhaps its strong language is merely bravado, a cover for fear. Or the speaker may seek out death, taunting him into striking.

The poem assumes that the audience will share the speaker's warrants about eternal life after death. But even readers who do not believe this may relate to the concept of death as a rest from life. The intellectuality of the speaker and his skill with language are not consistent with naiveté, and we trust such an ethos. But considering his argument in terms of logos, we might charge him with begging the question. Before we can believe that death should not be proud, we must believe the doctrine that Christ has conquered death and the grave. Donne preaches to the choir, to people who are already supposed to believe that death is powerless.

The poem flows so well as an argument that we may not notice its Shakespearean sonnet structure or its traditional rhyme scheme. For modern readers, the final couplet does not rhyme, though it would have rhymed in many Elizabethan dialects. The final line may be read with the rhythms of iambic pentameter, since it is perfectly regular in its meter. Imagining Donne in the pulpit or in Parliament, however, we might hear a strong voice emphasizing each syllable of the final phrase for a strong, sermonic ending.

As a starting point for death's answering sonnet, we might share with students Donne's fears of old age as expressed in the letter above. Recalling how deeply the poet loved his wife, death might taunt him with their separation. Perhaps death's sonnet will show us a picture of what it would be like to live forever in a decaying and tiresome world. Considered in this light, especially in view of T. S. Eliot's admiration of John Donne's poetry, perhaps "The Wasteland" and other pessimistic texts of the Modernist movement of the twentieth century provide a reply from death much like that proposed by our question.

DYLAN THOMAS

Do Not Go Gentle into That Good Night (p. 1533)

Like Theodore Roethke's "The Waking," which may have been influenced by this poem, Dylan Thomas's "Do Not Go Gentle into That Good Night" is written in the highly structured form called a villanelle. The villanelle began as a French verse form that originally addressed trivial and lighthearted themes. Thomas uses it for the serious purpose of responding to his father's death, thus transforming the form and making it his own. Always experimental in some way, Thomas's dramatic readings of his poetry in the 1950s made him an important voice in twentieth-century poetry. He plays not only with the conventions of form but with language as well. Although "Do Not Go Gentle into That Good Night" does not fracture syntax or use words in the unusual ways that characterize many of his more ambiguous poems, he uses rich imagery and highly metaphoric language to express his deep emotion as he exhorts his dying father to resist death.

Repetition is extremely important to the effect of the poem. It is like an incantation, or perhaps like one of the Welsh sermons the poet heard in childhood. In a villanelle, specific lines must be repeated according to a set pattern. But Thomas employs parallelism in numerous other ways. He repeats the word *rage* at the beginning of the repeating imperative sentence. It is difficult to read the line aloud without clenching one's fists and speaking from the gut. He parallels different sorts of men in a sermonic fashion: "wise men," "good men," "wild men," "grave men," and finally the particularized "you, my father." The sermon builds rhetorically to its strongest point. Implied comparisons and puns give the poem complex layers of meaning. The word *grave* speaks of both seriousness and mortality, and the sight of dying men is "blinding," implying both enhanced light and the loss of it at the same time. Students might enjoy tracing the contrasting images of light and dark in the poem.

The meanings of various images may become less clear the more closely they are examined. Some metaphors have an odd negativity. For example, "wise men" resist the dark because of the absence of "lightning" in their words, and "good men" resist for the equally empty reason that their "frail deeds might have danced." For the speaker of Thomas's poem, blessing and cursing are ironically linked as expressions of his father's life force; either or both are desired as representations of the rage that resists death. Each line of the poem is suffused with paradox.

People who are freezing to death tell of a seductive impulse to curl up and go to sleep. Others tell of near-death experiences in which they have a great desire to remain in the peaceful passivity of the moment rather than return to the voice of the people calling them back to consciousness. In Sophocles' tragedy *Antigone* (p. 1306), the heroine reaches out to her dead family in the underworld, finally free from the suffering and shame brought about by curses on her father Oedipus. Although it is doubtful that Dylan Thomas envisions a loving reunion between his father and his father's loved ones, he concedes the desire that human beings feel for death, even as we dread or fight it, by calling it "good." The frightening opposition to the "dying of the light" mentioned in the most significant refrain would be an awakening into darkness. Light symbolizes a power in the human being, and Thomas refers to other images of light or something like it in all but the last stanza. But it has been pointed out that these references have a strange negativity. Thomas says in the first stanza that "Old age should burn," but the word *should* leaves open the possibility that his father's old age will not catch fire. In the second stanza, the "wise men" apparently could have "forked lightning," but didn't. The "good men" of the third stanza might have seen "bright" deeds dance, but they do not. The "wild men" of the next stanza did something with the sun, but it seems to have been the wrong thing. The "grave men" of the penultimate stanza "see with blinding sight" a potential conflagration that is compared to "meteors," but this has not yet happened. Consequently, all of them resist death.

Thomas goes through the list of different types of men and their failings before revealing that the poem is a dramatic monologue to the speaker's father. Most of us cannot remember the first time we heard or read this poem, and its familiarity makes it difficult to imagine the effect of leaving this information to the end. It will be interesting to look at student responses to the question if there are some reading it for the first time. We might intuit that the impact is greater because of this technique of seeming to address the audience in the abstract at first and then particularizing the message. Both the tantalizing ambiguity of the poem and the technical difficulty of writing a villanelle make this an impressive text. Attempting to write in structured forms may be a good exercise, but a better strategy for writers may be to keep forms like the villanelle and the sonnet in mind for use when content seems suited for them. For most of us, putting the form first limits creativity.

John Donne's poem assumes a Christian faith that sees death as conquered, even though human beings die physically. Therefore, death is not to be feared, and it probably is not to be fought as strongly as Thomas suggests. Donne might not advise the dying father to resist death so strenuously. Thomas, on the other hand, sees death as a "dying of the light," an end of human understanding. He might not see the hope of life after death as a consolation, certainly not as a victory. Donne sees it as a paradox that when death seems at its most triumphant, the human being saved by God's grace enters into eternal life. Thus, when death wins it loses. Thomas's poem, as we have seen, is filled with paradox when examined closely, each stanza containing opposites. Which use of paradox readers see as more effective will depend upon their religious faith, perhaps, and their tolerance for ambiguity. The diction of the two poems also influences the reader's understanding. The conventions of the 1600s called for pronouns like *thee* and *thou* when addressing God, and archaic forms like *think'st*. The vernacular of Thomas's poem, on the other hand, uses words we hear every day. Their syntax also gives a hint about time period. Both poems use imperative sentences, but Donne's word order — "Death be not proud" where we would say, "Death don't be proud" — separates current readers from the speaker. Although Thomas's sentences are difficult, they are fairly straightforward in their word order. Finally, the worldviews of the speakers help us to date them. Attitudes toward death have changed in literary circles, and the foregrounding of religion would be less likely in a twentieth-century poem than in one written three hundred years earlier.

WISLAWA SZYMBORSKA

On Death, without Exaggeration (p. 1535)

In 1996 at the age of seventy-three a Polish woman named Wislawa Szymborska won the Nobel Prize for her poetry. She has been called a poet of the ordinary, and has said that she aims for a style that is without artifice. Deceptively simple, her poetry often deals with war, especially World War II. The Warsaw Ghetto and Auschwitz are part of her personal experience, and her confrontations with mortality begin there. She brings war down to earth with her irony. Postwar Europe is seen through the eyes of a worker: "After every war / someone has to tidy up. / Things won't pick themselves up, after all" she says in one poem. In "On Death, without Exaggeration" she catalogs the things that death cannot do, giving the homely art of "baking cakes" and the human quality of a sense of humor equal importance with astronomy and engineering. And again, she tells us that it can't "clean up after itself." Like John Donne in "Death Be Not Proud," Szymborska jeers at the incompetence of a personified death.

By referring to death throughout the poem by the neutral pronoun *it*, the poet simultaneously dehumanizes death even as she personifies it. Death is like a programmed robot, lacking all creativity and spontaneity. Furthermore, she spends most of the poem telling us what death can*not* do, her negative definition elaborating the vitality that surrounds the hollow impotence of death. Her technique models her title, using understatement rather than hyperbole to make death look foolish. When we stop to think about the reality of death, especially the sort of death Szymborska knew during the war, it seems ironic to think it possible to exaggerate death. How could we make death seem more dreaded and fearful than it really is? Some readers might charge Szymborska and Donne with denial. When Szymborska uses the word *exaggeration*, perhaps she means the sort of attitude we see in Emily Dickinson's "I like a look of Agony," in which death seems to have the upper hand.

To Szymborska, life lived in the present moment overcomes death, who always arrives too late to steal the time we've already lived. Death is never retroactive. The speaker criticizes humanity for "lending a hand" to death, but even this does not overcome the constant regeneration of life. Like a good argument, Szymborska's poem gives specific examples, saving her most vivid ones for last. She grants death's strengths but goes on to continue her recital of its failures. Like Donne in "Death Be Not Proud," she ends with paradox. Just at the point of what seems its greatest victory, death is defeated by its very nature.

All three of the poems in this cluster speak of death without exaggeration. The strong emotion of Dylan Thomas's "Do Not Go Gentle into That Good Night" might seem exaggerated at first reading. Yet death is seen as something that can be resisted, raged against. In Donne and Szymborska, death is ridiculed as awkward and clownish. In all three poems, death is an absence of power: Donne denies death any pride, Szymborska subverts the concept of death as omnipotent, and Thomas makes it analogous to the absence of light. Szymborska's poem seems more lighthearted than the other two. She sets the stage for this by saying that death "can't take a joke," implicitly inviting us to laugh at death with her. Donne takes a similar tack, but a full acceptance of his argument requires a leap of faith. Szymborska, on the other hand, privileges earthly existence. Rather than defeating death by awaking to eternal life, everyday people defeat death just by living. Because she foregrounds everyday life and overcomes death by persistence rather than struggle, we might recognize Szymborska as a woman without reading the prefatory notes. The description of growing embryos seems especially female in its concerns. But, as we have seen with many texts, writers often use personas quite different from themselves. It would be interesting to spring the poem and the author's name, impossible for English speakers to identify as male or female, on students at the beginning of the unit, asking them to guess the age and gender of the poet.

REFLECTING ON KILLING ANIMALS (p. 1538)

GEORGE ORWELL
Shooting an Elephant (p. 1538)

George Orwell's "Shooting an Elephant" recounts an arguably true story of an event that took place during the writer's tenure as a colonial policeman during the 1920s in British-controlled Burma, now the country called Myanmar. Interestingly, Orwell's essay was published in 1936, the year Rudyard Kipling died. Kipling had written many stories and poems set in colonial territories, usually from the point of view of the ordinary British soldier. Students undoubtedly know *The Jungle Book* and other Kipling stories still read by children, and they may have encountered Orwell's *Animal Farm*, a vastly different animal tale that satirizes totalitarian government. Because Kipling's texts do not overtly question the assumptions of empire, interested readers might wish to compare them with Orwell's critique of British domination in Burma in the essay we include here. Enterprising instructors might begin the discussion of "Shooting an Elephant" by playing a tape of a musical rendition of "On the Road to Mandalay" or reading the Kipling poem that has a retired soldier in London longing to return to the "Burma girl" he imagines still waits for him where "the dawn comes up like thunder outer China 'crost the bay." This context can be used to encourage students to question the warrants of imperialism, and some may

384

draw parallels with the American economic or military presence in various parts of the world.

Most current readers will have no trouble finding animal rights issues in Orwell's essay, though they may not immediately recognize the elephant as a metaphor for an unwieldy British Empire. Recently reopening the country to Western tourism, the oppressive dictatorship of Myanmar capitalizes upon images of working Asian elephants, now considered to be an endangered species because of human exploitation, to emphasize the relatively untouched simplicity of a romantic, exotic Burma that can still be sold to visitors. Eric Blair, who later renamed himself George Orwell, joined the Indian Imperial Police at the age of nineteen in 1922. Burma had been annexed into the British Empire as a province of India in 1886. At first, relations were friendly, but British injustices quickly led to resistance by the Burmese, with Buddhist monks leading strikes and protests. Exclusive clubs, like the Gymkhana, were strictly off limits to people of color, no matter what their social station.

While Orwell recognizes the abuses of imperialism and hates them, he does not romanticize the Burmese either. He feels trapped between his guilt for being part of the colonial system and his shame and anger in the face of the contempt and manipulation of the oppressed people. In the fictionalized *Burmese Days*, he relates the autobiographical story of an inspection of a suspect to determine whether the man is a repeat offender. As the policemen check the buttocks of the prisoner for bamboo scars from earlier beatings, a missionary chances by and says, "I wouldn't care to have your job." It was brought home to the writer that, in spite of his seemingly superior position, the colonial effort was at base an unmanly enterprise. "Shooting an Elephant" captures a similarly degrading situation in which the policeman, as an agent of empire, is forced to behave shamefully in order to maintain a facade of superiority.

The writer begins the essay by discussing his frustration with the double bind he finds himself in. He tells the reader that his guilt about "doing the dirty work of Empire at close quarters" oppressed him, even while he fumes against "the evil-spirited little beasts who tried to make my job impossible." It is a truism of oppression that the oppressors become as trapped in their roles and as shaped by the system as the people who are oppressed. The essay illustrates this helplessness to escape the predetermined role. It also reveals the strong motivating force the fear of shame has in the human psyche.

For young men, especially, the fear of being laughed at for a lack of masculinity, for a failure of power, may also be significant. Perhaps it is no coincidence that the concept of honor and the march of conquering armies tend to go hand in hand. Orwell's introspective description of his internal conflicts shoots down pretensions about the glories of empire and masculinity more surely than his bullets fell the elephant. The younger Orwell, Eric Blair, can see the Burmese as beastly, can fantasize about stabbing a Buddhist priest in the gut, but the older Orwell has the 1930s perspective of one who has studied poverty and oppression on a larger scale. For this reason, he is able to describe the young policeman's struggle to recognize the evils of imperialism with some distance.

The shooting of the elephant could have been avoided at several points. His primary motive for responding to the problem in the first place is curiosity. Later, he comes close to abandoning the search for the elephant when rumors become confusing and he thinks the story may be a hoax. Events take on their own momentum when he accepts a rifle. He could have justified not shooting the animal because of the elephant's value or because it has calmed down, but by this time the crowd expects him to do it. In paragraph 7, Orwell explains eloquently why the young man feels he must do this, tying his individual dilemma to the hollow hypocrisy of empire. He compares the imperialist to "an absurd puppet . . . a sort of hollow, posing dummy," and says that the oppressor "wears a mask, and his face grows to fit it." (A quick survey of the art of South Asia will provide interesting visual parallels for these images.)

Like the British Empire in Burma, the elephant dies slowly, painfully, and awkwardly. The narrator emphasizes the "senility" that overcomes the enormous beast. Orwell's language does not spare us the ugliness or the brutality of the elephant's agonizing death, and he makes it clear that the whole effort is characterized by incompetence. Throughout the description the reader realizes, because the narrator makes it painfully clear, that arrogance and lack of knowledge have caused this specific death just as similar attitudes have caused the ugliness and brutality of empire and the clumsy dismantling of empire. Colonialism is a huge, unwieldy monster gone mad, and its end is not graceful. George Orwell is a master of language and has written about the subject in both fiction and nonfiction. Perhaps it is this mastery that makes "Shooting an Elephant" a popular essay for anthologies. The essay provides good examples of narrative technique. It has vivid descriptions and comparisons, a clear sense of cause and effect, suspense, and specific narrative action paced to carry readers along quickly at times and to slow us down at others. The essay may also be popular because students weary of ambiguity appreciate Orwell's clear explanation of the issues he is addressing.

ANNIE DILLARD

The Deer at Providencia (p. 1544)

Because excerpts from Annie Dillard's nonfiction frequently appear in anthologies, students may have encountered her piercing honesty about nature and life. For readers brought up on the cute bunnies of Walt Disney cartoons, Dillard's attitude may come as a shock. Although she often finds mystical significance in nature, she seldom romanticizes it. In an earlier chapter of *Teaching a Stone to Talk* titled "Living like Weasels," Dillard gropes toward her philosophy for living. She would like to live as she imagines the weasel does, she says, "open to time and death painlessly, noticing everything, remembering nothing, choosing the given with a fierce and pointed will." She does not flinch as she observes the world, and she accepts the paradox of "choosing the given." There is a steeliness to this refusal to sugarcoat life. Life is not sweet, as she sees it, and she has no patience with attempts to pretend that it is.

In her autobiography *An American Childhood* (1987), Dillard compares life to standing under a roaring waterfall:

> It is time pounding at you, time. Knowing you are alive is watching on every side your generation's short time falling away as fast as rivers drop through air, and feeling it hit. . . . Knowing you are alive is feeling the planet buck under you, rear, kick, and try to throw you; you hang on to the ring. It is riding the planet like a log downstream, whooping. Or conversely, you step aside from the dreaming fast loud routine and feel time as a stillness about you and hear the silent air asking in so thin a voice, Have you noticed yet that you will die? (125–26)

Perhaps "The Deer at Providencia" comes at a time of stillness, but its stillness does not bring peace but a tense, bitter irony. In *Pilgrim at Tinker Creek*, the book that won her a 1975 Pulitzer Prize, Annie Dillard ponders whether the earth has been created "in jest or in earnest." "Cruelty is a mystery," she says, "and a waste of pain." But she goes on to say that human beings almost universally recognize "beauty, a grace wholly gratuitous." It is a mystery that the world contains both in outrageous plentitude. Annie Dillard's original and creative style and her keen skill with metaphor and description attract experienced readers, but many students find her tedious, morbid, and incomprehensible. They may find "The Deer at Providencia" especially uncomfortable to read. We might prepare them by having them create their own metaphors for life, and then write responses to Dillard's observations about the prevalence of both cruelty and beauty in the universe.

In "The Deer at Providencia" the North American men on the trip to the South American jungle expect a North American woman to have a tearful, sentimental reaction to the cruelty they see. Most readers, both male and female, would feel impelled to free the animal and may be angered by Dillard's enjoyment of the deer meat. She describes eating a fish with relish, but the images remind us that she is eating something that was recently alive, and with the pain and fear of the little deer in our minds we are reminded that the eating of meat always involves an act that is essentially heartless. Not only does she resist the cuddly animal images of Disney, but she rubs them in, comparing the entangled deer to the less cute but familiar childhood tale of Brer Rabbit and the Tar Baby. Most readers do not find this image humorous, and wonder why she has been willing to watch for fifteen minutes as the animal struggles. We may ask why she chooses to tell this story.

The experience of Alan McDonald, a man who has been burned twice, is obviously connected in Annie Dillard's mind, and both stories are examples of the same mystery, the mystery of cruelty, the "waste of pain" she had addressed a few years earlier in *Pilgrim at Tinker Creek*. After she relates McDonald's story and her fascination with it, she states her lesson in an enigmatic sentence: "This is the Big Time here, every minute of it." Annie Dillard looks at the cruelty of life and forces us to look with her, not because she does not care, but because she cares fiercely and refuses to flinch. *This* is life, she insists, just as surely as beauty: this mysterious excess of pain. In describing these stories as mysteries rather than issues, Dillard takes them out of the arena in which reasonable people may disagree. She implies that the unfairness of pain exists as a fact and can be wondered at but not argued. Such arbitrary cruelty cannot be justified by any proofs. After we have felt the impact of this truth, she allows us to see her pity for the deer at the end of the story. But she refuses to admit even this moment of pathos, hinting that such feelings are absurd in a world in which such things routinely happen. The Spanish word *Providencia* calls us back to her questioning of God, the Divine Providence that created such a world. The word implies that God may be a blind and unfeeling force of nature, a sort of fate, rather than a kind and loving father.

Annie Dillard, like George Orwell, finds herself in a culture that is vastly different from her own. She seems less narrow-minded than Orwell. Rather than seeking to impose her values, she observes and accepts the givens of her hosts. She is not an imperialist. Still, she is keenly aware that others are observing her behavior. She is pleased to shock the men with her difference from most North American women. Left on her own, we might expect her to free the deer, though she would coolly watch it being eaten by a jaguar or struggling in quicksand. And even then, we could expect her to imagine the reader observing her, even in solitary moments. After all, she even allows us to watch her at her mirror. Perhaps she is not as different from Orwell as we might think at first. Both narrators seek to prove to an audience how tough they are. Seen from this perspective, both writers are willing to reveal qualities their readers may hold in contempt. Both allow us to watch them as they grapple with hard realities. Whereas Orwell tells a traditional narrative as an illustration of his disillusionment with empire, Dillard takes a more cinematic approach, cutting from one scene to another, with brief commentary to hint at connections between her stories of arbitrary cruelty. Each is dramatic and intense in its own way.

Gender is important to both essays. Dillard proves that she does not share the weakness, or perhaps the compassion, of most women of her culture. Orwell suggests that imperialism forces men to behave in ways that maintain a facade of power, but that the results are recognized as impotent and thus laughable. Not only is the colonial policeman trapped into proving he is a man, but he is trapped into acting as a *white* man is scripted to act. Both writers must contend with both gender and culture as they decide how to behave.

ESCAPING LIFE: CRITICAL COMMENTARIES ON MARSHA NORMAN'S *'NIGHT, MOTHER* (p. 1549)

MARSHA NORMAN
'night, Mother (p. 1550)

To illustrate inductive organization, in which evidence mounts in increasing importance and the claim is asserted as a concluding statement, we might use a cumulative folktale with the double title "No News Is Good News; or, What

Killed the Dog." A traveler returns home and asks his servant if there has been any news. The servant begins with the bad news that the master's dog has died. Then in the process of telling what killed the dog he reveals that the dog has died from eating burnt horse flesh, that the horses have been killed when the house burned down because of candles around his mother-in-law's coffin, and that the mother-in-law has died of shock because the traveler's wife ran away with his best friend. "But other than that," the storyteller drawls in an Appalachian accent, "there ain't been no news."

From Kentucky, a traditional hotbed of the storytelling art, Marsha Norman uses inductive organization in a similarly ironic way as she cumulatively reveals more and more about the oppressive relationship between Jessie Cates and her mother Thelma in the course of the play *'night, Mother.* In the midst of household details that are trivial in the extreme, Jessie reveals in a matter-of-fact way that she is going to kill herself after handling the chores on her list and giving her mother a manicure. This sets up a situation that builds suspense as the audience wonders if Jessie will really go through with the suicide or if her mother will be able to talk her out of it. As the play proceeds, Thelma comes up with reasons for Jessie to live, but her argument is refuted at every point by Jessie, who takes each piece of evidence as another reason to go ahead with her suicide plans. Ironically, the audience comes to believe that Jessie may be correct in her decision as her mother gradually reveals the extent to which she has controlled her daughter's life in a misguided attempt to protect the family from the shame of what she sees as Jessie's disability, having "fits." We learn that Thelma has even manipulated Jessie's marriage and that other family members have suffered from the repercussions of Thelma's surreptitious control. For the first time, Jessie is actually *taking* her own life, a life that has been dominated by Thelma. When Thelma points out that Jessie does not have to commit suicide, Jessie declares that this is exactly why she likes it. She claims her autonomy in this way, finally having her say.

Although a synopsis of the story might give the impression that Thelma is the villain of the drama, she seems to be misguided rather than evil. After hearing the gunshot from behind the closed door of Jessie's bedroom, she cries for her daughter and asks her forgiveness. "I thought you were mine," she explains. And this truth about motherhood, the destructive power of the assumption that children belong to their parents, is the point of the story. Ironically, Jessie says early in the play that she wants the gun for protection, but she has been unable to protect herself from her mother's protection, the mother's failure of trust that has prevented the child from becoming her own person. Yet, in spite of its serious themes of codependency and suicide, there is a grim humor to Norman's dialogue. At one time, Thelma offers to sing all night to keep Jessie alive. Later, when she finally accepts her daughter's decision, she decides that she will not go to her son's house after the deed is done, since "All they've got is Sanka." Most of the humor comes from the ironic juxtaposition of everyday triviality with the desperation of the suicide situation and of the lives that have led to it. Ordinary actions and comments take on a wryly humorous quality in the light of Jessie's impending suicide.

Although her mother assumes that Jessie wants to commit suicide because of her epilepsy, both Jessie and the audience realize that it is Thelma who is troubled by her daughter's condition, not Jessie herself. Thelma has kept this a dark secret, even from Jessie, as she has her husband's similar condition. She has managed her guilt and shame about the "fits" her daughter and husband have by working to hide the epilepsy from everyone. It is this motherly appropriation of their lives, hiding the information they need to be fully functional human beings, that steals Jessie's life from her as it may have stolen her father's life earlier. Jessie knows that suicide is her only way to be independent, but it ironically becomes the avenue through which the two women are able to truly communicate for the first time.

The dialogue makes it clear that Jessie's suicide is a positive move on her part and that the control of her epilepsy has given her the clarity of mind to make this independent decision. She kills herself because she is well, not because she is troubled about being sick. Thelma at first argues that the gun won't work and the bullets are too old, but Jessie shows that she knows what she is doing, has acquired new bullets, and has an alternative plan if this gun doesn't suffice. When Thelma threatens to call Jessie's brother, Jessie answers that she will go ahead and kill herself now, then moves to hang up the phone, explaining that this is "private." Mama implies that Jessie will not succeed, that she will have one of her fits and miss, shooting her ear off or winding up a vegetable. Jessie assures her that she can do the job. Thelma brings up the conventional objections that everyone is afraid of death, that we don't know what death is like, that suicide is a sin. These objections support Jessie's assertion that suicide is right for her. She is always cold anyway, Jessie insists, and she likes quiet; death is profound privacy, and — surprising herself — she realizes that Jesus could be considered a suicide, so sin is not an issue. Thelma counters that Jessie can't use the towels, the gun, or the house to kill herself, since these belong to Thelma. Jessie offers to make coffee. Mama's suggestion that she wait to see what she gets for her birthday opens up the important revelation that Jessie can predict exactly what each relative will give her, each present patently lacking any sense of Jessie as an individual. (Later, Jessie will leave gifts for these relatives that reflect her keen sense of who they are and what she wants them to learn.)

Thelma spends much of the play making wrong guesses about Jessie's unhappiness and offering solutions based upon them. She continues to try to fix things for Jessie, and eventually assumes that she is the cause. Jessie will not allow her mother to appropriate the suicide as something that is about Thelma rather than Jessie. When Thelma insists finally that she cannot let Jessie go because she is her child, Jessie refutes this: "I am what became of your child," she counters. Although some readers will insist that now that the issues are out in the open Jessie could go on to live differently, most will see Jessie as winning the argument. She can only be her own person, really be heard, if she goes through with the suicide.

Unlike many plays, *'night, Mother* takes place in real time, with clocks ticking away the time onstage. This foregrounding of time keeps the audience aware of the limited amount of time the characters have to complete their dialogue and hints at the ending when Jessie decides that her time is up. Once, Thelma even postulates that death, rather than being quiet, may be like a ringing alarm clock that you can't shut off, and at another point she picks up one of the clocks and winds it. The prominent place of time adds to the sense of panic as Thelma looks for ways to persuade her daughter to continue living. As the emptiness of Jessie's life becomes apparent, however, the audience comes to expect that she will carry out her plan. If the play ended differently, most readers would feel a sense of despair and defeat for Jessie. Thelma, on the other hand, has expressed her desire to go on, rather than to think about things. It is clear that she is capable of surviving, and though stunned, she ends by taking care of the business of telephoning her son. The ending is not tragic; rather it is honest, perhaps even triumphant. Jessie wins the argument, asserts her autonomy, and will finally express herself by this final, decisive action.

The presence of only two characters on the stage focuses our attention on their claustrophobic relationship. Jessie insists that her privacy be maintained for once, and this allows the full story of her mother's domination of her life to surface. But offstage characters are important. We first hear of Jessie's father as she searches for his gun, and we're told that the gun may be in the shoebox that held the shoes he died in. She would prefer to kill herself with his gun. We hear that he once dropped the gun in the mud, a fact that takes on new importance when we learn that he, like Jessie, had seizures that were covered up by the protective Thelma. Daddy is Jessie's soul mate, a quiet man who has an artist's soul, to his wife's great frustration. He is laughable to others because he only pretends to fish and instead makes figures from pipe cleaners. Because they are so closely linked, understanding something of Daddy's place in the family helps us to understand both Jessie and Thelma. Also absent, but important to the relationship between Thelma and Jessie, the ex-husband Cecil seems from one angle to be a pawn of the mother and from another to be a factor in the daughter's decline. Although Mama has caught Cecil in adultery, she has kept this from Jessie. For all her neediness, however, Jessie claims to have chosen smoking over Cecil when forced into a choice. She values smoking for its quietness, the quality she loved in her father.

Other characters, though kept offstage, help to develop the main characters. Dawson and Loretta seem to be lacking in imagination, though not in pretension, and Jessie resents their intrusion into her privacy. A hint of sibling rivalry may be indicated, though as the man of the family, Dawson has a great deal of influence in this household. Jessie faults her brother both for not really knowing her and for knowing too much about her. This is especially telling when Thelma reveals that Dawson is routinely called to carry Jessie to her bed after she has had a seizure. Thelma's friend Agnes, like Loretta, can be brought up as a subject of humor, but she also helps us to see how outsiders may see Jessie. Agnes is afraid to come to the house because of Jessie, perhaps for the same reasons she loses her job at the hospital. Jessie's strangeness goes beyond anything that could be attributed to the epilepsy Thelma finds so shameful. Jessie's son Ricky, like her father, helps us to understand Jessie, because she sees him as similar to herself.

Some readers may criticize Marsha Norman for painting a positive picture of suicide, but she provides her own answer to this when Thelma says that Jessie's son Ricky will think that killing is not wrong. "[It's] only a matter of time, anyway,"

Jessie answers, perhaps glancing at a clock. If she thought she could influence her son, she would not kill herself. Jessie draws an analogy between death and getting off the bus at a bus stop. Jessie wants to choose her own stop. Because many people fantasize about making a statement by means of suicide, it might be useful to discuss whether outsiders read suicide in the way that the suicide victim would hope. Jessie does not care, but perhaps most readers do.

CRITICAL COMMENTARIES:

LISA J. MCDONNELL, From "Diverse Similitude: Beth Henley and Marsha Norman" (p. 1584)

SALLY BROWDER, From "'I Thought You Were Mine': Marsha Norman's *'night, Mother*" (p. 1584)

JENNY S. SPENCER, From "Norman's *'night, Mother*: Psycho-drama of Female Identity" (p. 1586)

Within the literary text, readers can explore with safety many contradictory experiences we would never emulate in our own lives. We can follow Emily Dickinson's narrator into eternity, follow Tim O'Brien's soldiers into the killing fields, or watch the slow dying of George Orwell's elephant from the perspective of postcolonial theory. From the same sort of perspective, we can understand Jessie's suicide in Marsha Norman's *'night, Mother* as a declaration of independence, a gaining of self, even while we admit the paradox that such an act in real life would be a loss. We may agree with Lisa McDonnell that death is Jessie's only avenue to "peace and dignity as an individual." In the midst of what McDonnell characterizes as an "adversarial" relationship, Jessie seems to seek silence most of all. It has been silence that Thelma resents in her husband and in her daughter, and both have illnesses that thrust them into silence; both finally retreat from Thelma into the silence of death. Yet it is Thelma's silence that has caused much of the damage to her daughter's psyche.

Many of our college students are beginning to experience the almost surreal transition that occurs as parents begin to accept them as adults. In the happiest of circumstances, they come back to school after Thanksgiving or Easter break and relate the strange sensations of being treated as familiar, but honored, guests at the family dinner table, lingering for after-dinner coffee with their parents to toss around ideas they've encountered at school. Some instructors have experienced this change as parents, realizing with inexpressible satisfaction that our former adversaries have become interesting young adults we would gladly choose as friends. As Sally Browder points out, Jessie has failed to find herself as a person who is independent of her mother, has never developed "a sense of self . . . power . . . meaning in life." Unlike the lucky ones among our students and children who have parents who facilitate their equality, Jessie has been unable to free herself from what Browder calls "the security of an unequal relationship."

Thelma's silence, her inability to be honest with her daughter from an early age, makes suicide seem the only alternative. Browder does not cast blame but insists that it is the belief that the mother is solely responsible for her daughter's happiness that leads to the dependency that Jessie feels only suicide will cure. The converse would be just as destructive, when children are made to feel responsible for their parents' self-esteem. Readers who have not considered such issues may be influenced by the psychoanalytic view to read the play in terms of autonomy rather than suicide. Classes might brainstorm ways that daughters — or sons — can find independent identities and develop honest relationships with parents before suicide seems the only option.

Certainly, most women do identify with the mother/daughter struggle in *'night, Mother*, and the play is, to a great extent, gender specific. As Jenny Spencer points out, men may react to the play differently because they are accustomed to seeing women as objects of sexual desire rather than as complex human beings. Before reading this commentary, we might want to survey male and female students for their gut reactions to the play. It is likely that generational differences may appear as well, since many women of college age have little patience with other women who remain dependent.

RETURNING TO LIFE (p. 1588)

ELIZABETH BOWEN
The Demon Lover (p.1589)

The demon-lover motif that Elizabeth Bowen calls upon in her title is an ancient one, perhaps going as far back symbolically as the temptation of Eve in the Garden of Eden. More explicit connections can be made with the Scottish border ballad called "The Demon Lover" that first appeared in the broadsides of the seventeenth century, one of the first popular uses of the medium of print. Many British and Appalachian folk singers have recorded the song, based on texts collected in Francis James Child's *The English and Scottish Popular Ballads* of the nineteenth century, other collections, or versions in oral tradition. An audiotape shouldn't be difficult to find if instructors want to add it to the class context for reading Bowen's short story. Readers interested in British literary history will enjoy the discovery that both Samuel Pepys and Sir Walter Scott wrote down versions of the ballad being sung in their times.

In its many versions, the story is basically the same: A vulnerable and naive young woman exchanges vows with a dangerously attractive and mysterious man that she barely knows; events occur that cause the lovers to be separated; the woman goes on with her life, marrying and perhaps having children; the lover returns after many years and carries the woman off, often to an evil fate, in punishment for her broken vows. Sometimes the lover is a man, but more often he is supernatural, an evil revenant returned from the dead or the Devil himself.

Current readers will not have to leave the twentieth century to find parallels. Students will be able to think of many examples from popular literature, film, and television. For example, soap-opera viewers will testify that characters who die cannot be expected to stay buried for long, but to return after recovering from miraculous plastic surgery to complicate the lives of heroines who have established new love interests. Fans of slasher movies know that the killer will return like any good zombie in time for the next sequel. The vampires of Anne Rice, the diverse ghouls of Stephen King, and the eerie psychopaths of Dean Koontz may occur to other readers. Audiences of every generation have enjoyed being frightened by the idea that those presumed dead may return to exact vengeance, that the forbidden lover will show up when least expected, to ensure that the faithless one's sins will find her out.

The beginnings of the novel in English have been analyzed as belonging to this genre. The seducer of Samuel Richardson's *Clarissa* or Thomas Hardy's *Tess of the d'Urbervilles*, Bram Stoker's Count Dracula, the darkly brooding men of the novels of the Brontë sisters, and their many descendents in the gothic romance genre all represent the demon-lover type, the dangerous and romantic man a woman is powerless to resist. Repressed women need an excuse to indulge in sexual passion, and the demon lover provides a devil-made-me-do-it out. But the culture demands that the woman pay for her sins — perhaps the breaking of vows, but more likely the unwise making of vows in the first place. Therefore, the satisfying ending demands that her leaving of home and family, whether willingly or through deception or force, leads to her ultimate destruction. Sex and horror go hand in hand because undomesticated love is forbidden but oh so tempting.

Elizabeth Bowen structures her version of the demon-lover tale in a way designed to build suspense. The title signals us to look for sinister clues from the beginning, and the diction further builds the atmosphere of danger. Even before the lady of the house enters her closed London home she notices the "unfamiliar queerness" of the street. We are told that "no human eye watched," inviting the question of whether supernatural eyes might watch instead. A cat, often a symbol of the occult, walks the rooftops, and the word *dead* is used to describe the air. The description of the house is oddly violent: The wallpaper has a "bruise," and the floor has "claw-marks." As the language paints its eerie atmosphere, the narrative action is paced so that suspense slowly builds. Just before she spots the letter, for example, she stops "dead" — that word again — and a dash further slows the pace.

Suspense is further heightened by the gaps in the text. We do not hear her promise to her lover, and the flashback provides few clues to its exact nature. The scant details about her demon lover only increase the sense of danger. We are told that this flashback takes place twenty-five years earlier, during World War I. During wartime, girls frequently promise to wait for their soldiers, just as the soldiers promise to return. These promises tend to be broken more often than they are kept. But the details hint that this is not a sweet wartime romance. He is cold, "without feeling," and even causes her physical pain. She seems to be in a trance during this time, and her mother interprets his interest as obsession rather than love. He has a stalkerlike quality, and hints that he will be near her even when he seems far away. At one point, she pictures his eyes as "spectral glitters," making us wonder if he is human.

Our students may want to discuss the issue of distinguishing between obsessive relationships that make us uncomfortable and healthy love relationships that bring out our strengths. Mrs. Drover may be having this experience now because World War II evokes the same feelings. Her life seems to have been quite boring and safe. She is called a "prosaic woman," a description we might want to explore in class discussion. She seems to have married because this is what one does, and because there had been some concern for a time that she would not attract a suitable husband. She wears a string of pearls, a seemingly timeless indicator of conventional good taste. But overall she does not seem to be a very pleasant person. She is the sort of woman who comes to the house without announcing the visit because she hopes to catch the caretaker in suspected neglect of duty. We are told that her "most normal expression was one of controlled worry, but of assent." We are told her exact age — forty-four — which is about as middle-aged as one can be. Student readers, perhaps to the consternation of some instructors, will see this age as particularly sexless and boring. Though we may identify with her growing perplexity and sense of dread, most readers will not see her as sympathetic. She may look in the mirror to check on the reality of the situation but also may be concerned about how she looks.

Throughout, she seems conscious of being watched, and there are hints that this may be a recurring experience since her separation from the demon lover years earlier. Alert readers will note that the letter's presence in the house suggests the supernatural character of this experience, since she has had to force the door open. The enjoyment of reading "The Demon Lover" comes with our questioning of whether this really happens or if she simply imagines it in response to the crisis of the London Blitz. One arguable theory may be that the sinister taxi driver is actually Death, as he may have been all along. This reading might compare Mrs. Drover's taxi ride with Emily Dickinson's carriage ride in "Because I could not stop for Death —" (p. 1508). Mrs. Drover has been unable to recall her lover's face, but sees with terror exactly who is driving the cab at the story's end. It is a good narrative strategy to leave the face a mystery, since description would have robbed the story of its ambiguity.

ROBERT OLEN BUTLER

Jealous Husband Returns in Form of Parrot (p. 1594)

Like Elizabeth Bowen's "The Demon Lover" earlier in this cluster, Robert Olen Butler's "Jealous Husband Returns in Form of Parrot" can be paralleled to items of popular culture. In fact, this narrative and the other stories of Butler's *Tabloid Dreams* have their genesis in the popular culture of pulp newspaper headlines. Students can find current examples in the checkout line of the grocery store or look for collections — sometimes authentic, sometimes apocryphal — on the Internet. A few favorites: *Missing Baby Found Inside Watermelon: He's Alive!*; *Gust of Wind Blows Midget Balloon Peddler 20 Miles!*; *Statue of Elvis Found on*

Mars! Tabloid newspapers provide good examples of materials we would *not* use in an academic research paper but might be interesting sources to read for examples of logical fallacies and for evidence that fails close examination for appropriateness, believability, consistency, and completeness.

Like their cousins the urban legends, tabloid stories sometimes reveal the warrants and underlying prejudices of their audiences and creators. The UFO stories about Roswell, New Mexico, for example, feed into convictions that the government is hiding important information from the public. They also may reflect a need to believe in superior beings who will relieve us of responsibility for the earth and its inhabitants. The Internet, often a valuable source of information, has its share of legends as well, and requires truly critical reading to sort out which is which. Robert Olen Butler transforms the legends, however, into creative writing.

Often linked with Tim O'Brien as an interpreter of the Vietnam War, Butler's tone differs greatly from O'Brien's and he especially seems to have fun with his quirky stories that begin as tabloid headlines. His dark, grotesque humor may remind readers of Eudora Welty or Flannery O'Connor. Butler's "Woman Uses Glass Eye to Spy on Philandering Husband" could be a companion piece to the story we include here. It gives us a (unique) point of view of adultery from a woman who discovers her glass eye can see on its own. The title character of "Woman Struck by Car Turns into Nymphomaniac" begins her story with a critique of the tabloid genre, a neat bit of verisimilitude and double irony.

"Jealous Husband Returns in Form of Parrot" as a tabloid headline might reveal warrants that hold reincarnation — or more precisely metempsychosis, in which the dying spirit enters an animal — as a possibility after death, especially as a way of reaping one's karma for mistakes in past lives. It also reflects the human fascination with talking animals that feeds interest in apes who learn sign language, dolphins who communicate with complex squeaks and whistles, and parrots who identify shapes, colors, and simple objects in controlled experiments. Because language structures our world and sets us apart from other species, we equate it with intelligence in animals, perhaps rightly so. Some studies indicate that parrots do not simply echo what they hear, but are capable of simple concept formation. Interestingly, parrots can go insane when abused or neglected, plucking out their own feathers and screaming in agony. It is not impossible that a parrot could commit suicide.

As a parrot, the narrator struggles to articulate the words he knows, as he tells us in the first line. Although we intuitively feel that this may be the experience a real parrot would have as it attempted the physical task of reproducing sounds, we realize that even as a man he has been unable to express his feelings. In fact, he tells us that he had deliberately silenced himself as a husband because his anger and jealousy alienated his wife. Now he finds the words he can speak inadequate to explain his situation. When he relates his emotions about his wife to us, his language comes to us through a filter of bird thought. He notices the beauty of her nose for the first time because it has a slight hook, describes her eyes as "nut-brown," and evokes their lovemaking in metaphors that would be meaningful to a bird. He had been "an egg hatched beneath her crouching body . . . entered as a chick into her wet sky of a body." Later, he is sorry for her when he sees her naked, because he sees her as "plucked." Like a writer struggling to articulate thought and experience, the narrator consciously laments the inadequacy of his language and unconsciously reveals his own nature as he tries to explain. We recognize his warrants as those of a bird.

Butler's story is ironic and grotesque. Readers may find it both hilarious and sad. We may feel that the jealous husband gets what's coming to him and find it humorous when he falls off the tree limb, especially when as his bird-self he responds to the memory with flapping wings attempting flight. It may be less funny when as a bird he forgets about glass and smashes against the window, but some of us will smile at the ironic aptness of the event. After reading the story, we may find fresh significance in the parrot behavior Butler describes with such precision. His comments to the wife's lover make us laugh to find that from such a limited vocabulary he is able to summon up fitting insults.

Appropriately, the story does not reveal whether the husband's jealousy was justified. We are never told, for example, if the woman he tries to spy from the tree limb is indeed his wife. Even the narrator must concede that though she is sexually active now, she has a right to be so since her husband is to all intents and purposes dead. The intertextual connection may be accidental, but when the narrator says in the sixth paragraph, "It's all the same for her," some readers may be reminded of Robert Browning's Duke of Ferrara in "My Last Duchess" (p. 1376 in the "Making Judgments" chapter). Both men are disturbed because their wives, perhaps innocently, look at other men and enjoy the pleasures of life. The parrot continues to be jealous, but he is helpless to take action because the gap is too wide for him to communicate what he feels. Butler keeps both the parrot and the reader out of the bedroom, perhaps for the same reason he does not reveal whether her adultery is actual or imagined. His helplessness and jealousy are more intense because so much is imagined rather than known.

The scene in which he sees the human beings naked comes at the end of the narrative and emphasizes how changed the parrot is from the man he was. Like the strongest piece of evidence in an argument, this revelation of difference belongs near the end where its impact is most convincing. When his most eloquent outpouring of language proves sadly ineffective, he ends his life as a parrot. Whether we interpret his flight into the window as suicidal or as a longing for freedom, he no longer holds on to his obsession for his wife. Like so many literary texts that end in suicide, the act is ambiguous, and we may question whether he seeks death or his authentic self.

At times, both Mrs. Drover of Elizabeth Bowen's "The Demon Lover" and the parrot of Robert Olen Butler's story may strike the reader as unsympathetic characters. By the story's end, we may feel empathy for the parrot, since most of us have struggled to articulate our feelings, and we can imagine what it must feel like to be trapped into observing one's most obsessive fears played out while we are helpless to escape. In Bowen's story we observe Mrs. Drover from the outside, third-person perspective; and although we may relate to her horrified attempts to claw her way through the glass of the taxicab windows, most readers feel satisfaction at the ironic and deliciously twisted ending more strongly than empathy for the character. Butler's story is also laced with irony, but the first-person account allows us to know the parrot intimately and to feel compassion for him. Both are imprisoned behind glass, a particularly cruel situation. They can see the place of escape, but the way to it is blocked. They have other similarities as well, since earlier actions have led to their entrapments. "The Demon Lover" is clearly a horror story. Although it presents supernatural or psychologically thrilling events, it does so in a realistic manner that makes the unlikely seem possible. "Jealous Husband Returns in Form of Parrot" is less obviously a horror story, since its basic premise invites laughter and skepticism. Still, by the story's end, many readers may be willing to classify it as a horror story, though a highly ironic one.

Many students may be more familiar with the horror genre than their instructors and will be able to generate criteria for a good horror tale. Any definition should allow for believability, however. We must be pulled into the story's reality far enough to experience its pathos, especially the fear that makes us look over a shoulder for the demon or check for feathers now and then. Like the difference between first-person and third-person perspectives in the two stories in this cluster, the difference between present tense and past tense is most felt in terms of the distance we maintain as readers from the characters of the stories. Although his story is less believable, most readers will find it easier to identify with the parrot of Butler's story than with the woman of Bowen's because of the immediacy of Butler's first-person, present-tense narration.

WHEN DISASTER STRIKES: CULTURAL CONTEXTS FOR BHARATI MUKHERJEE'S "THE MANAGEMENT OF GRIEF" (p. 1600)

BHARATI MUKHERJEE
The Management of Grief (p.1601)

The cliché contends that tragedy brings people together. Although this may be true, tragedy also divides, bringing individuals and groups of people into conflict as they deal with grief and anger in different ways. Issues arise about how problems should be addressed or where blame should be assigned. As this book is being written in 1999, television news programs are filled with discussions of a school shooting near Denver, Colorado. As a result, gun-control advocates protest a National Rifle Association convention and ask for tougher laws. Others look for the genesis of violence in video games, music, and the Internet. Some survivors celebrate forgiveness whereas others choke on frustration. One father takes down crosses erected for the young killers and calls for the teaching of absolute right and wrong in the public schools. Speakers at televised funerals call for Christian conversion. A generation that grew up demanding its own autonomy during the 1960s and 1970s seriously intones the wisdom that parents should search the rooms of their adolescent children and read their diaries. Parents, school administrators, police, magistrates, and "the media" are castigated for various sins of omission. A famous, controversial lawyer has contacted the only African American family among the victims, but in his first interviews about the issue he obviously gropes for guilty parties to sue, moving away from specifics into pathos about the tragedy. Each individual or group finds evidence in the tragedy to support widely divergent assertions. Like any disaster involving violent death on a large scale, the Air India bombing and the later TWA 800 crash raised issues of their own.

For Bharati Mukherjee, brought up in India, and now a U.S. citizen, but for many years a Canadian, multiculturalism is a primary issue. Like many vocal members of "visible minorities" in Canada, Mukherjee sees that nation's official government policy as destructive and insensitive, in spite of its intent to be respectful of ethnic diversity. To a certain extent, her position is based on personal experience. Mukherjee values the autonomy of the individual, an attitude in many ways antithetical to the culture of her native India, where everyone knows his or her place and is expected to live accordingly. Even her name, Mukherjee points out, sends an immediate message that she is of a specific caste and culture — in her case a Bengali Brahmin of the highest caste. But even these fortunate circumstances are limiting and isolating, in Mukherjee's opinion. Her father's game plan had her earning her M.F.A. in Iowa and then returning to India to marry a man of her father's choosing. Instead, Mukherjee married a Canadian classmate, Clark Blaise, thus choosing individuality over culture.

Speaking of her years as a professor in Canada, Mukherjee describes the underlying racism of the dominant culture: "I was frequently taken for a prostitute or a shoplifter, frequently assumed to be a domestic, praised by astonished auditors that I didn't have a 'singsong' accent. The society itself . . . routinely made crippling assumptions about me, and about my kind." She believes that the "multicultural mosaic" of which Canada is so proud encourages such stereotypes, along with a separatism that amounts to de facto segregation. In both Canada and the United States, she maintains, official multiculturalism does not allow for the inevitable changes that take place when cultures come into contact. Instead, it "implies the existence of a central culture, ringed by peripheral cultures. . . . the establishment of one culture as the norm and the rest as aberrations." Because she feels that individual differences become absorbed into the stereotypes of the group, Mukherjee rejects "hyphenation" as an "Asian-American," resisting such categorization. This stance sometimes brings her into conflict with others of Indian descent, who see her as having abandoned her heritage, and with some members of the academic establishment, who see her views as reactionary. Mukherjee's protagonist in "The Management of Grief" begins as a somewhat more conventional woman of the ethnic subculture of Indian immigrants in Canada, but by the end of the story she has worked her way through grief into the beginnings of autonomy.

In many ways, "The Management of Grief" is a story about culture. In the *American Heritage English Dictionary*, the primary definition of culture is "the totality of socially transmitted behavior patterns, arts, beliefs, institutions, and all other products of human work and thought." Other definitions emphasize that culture consists of shared patterns that identify the members of a culture while excluding nonmembers. The loss of close relatives or friends to death is an experience that is common to all human beings. But responses to this loss are not universally the same. The management of grief is to a great extent culture specific. Still, as Mukherjee would remind us, responses of all individuals within an ethnic group are not necessarily the same. One widow finds comfort in her swami, whereas the protagonist chooses Valium. The Indian culture dictates that "it is a parent's duty to hope" and reminds the men that they have a duty to remarry. But the disaster changes cultural configurations. As the narrator describes it, they have "been melted down and recast as a new tribe." Because of a family history that has caused her parents to reject traditional culture, the protagonist is between two worlds even before the tragedy occurs.

Judith Templeton, the naive social worker assigned by the Canadian government to lead the survivors through the stages of grief and bureaucratic paperwork, has trouble fitting her charges into the little boxes of managed grief. She has her chart detailing the stages of grief — rejection, depression, acceptance, and reconstruction — and she busily goes about her job of checking off each stage for the victims. But she cannot see that the Indian survivors handle grief differently, that if the stages are the same, their manifestations may not appear in ways she will recognize.

Shaila seems to be handling her grief well because on the surface her behavior seems closer to that of the mainstream culture. At first, she is numb, surprised to be so calm and controlled. This "normal" first stage, she tells us, is not what the Indian culture would consider normal. In Ireland, she thinks her sons may still be alive. Western psychologists would call this denial, but the Indian community understands it as the duty to hope. Shaila goes through depression, evidenced by not eating or brushing her teeth. But her friend's swami says that depression is selfish. She explodes in anger, must deal with her feelings about the Sikhs, feelings that Western culture would find understandable as part of the grief process. Perhaps she comes to acceptance in a vision of her husband, something if related to the social worker might cause alarm. His instructions to carry on bring about action on her part, but her final release and reconstruction begin at the story's end. Instead of finishing what she has begun with her husband and sons, the voices tell her *"Your time has come."* She is now through the stages of grief, and she is on her own. She is particularly culture-free at this point, able to act without preconceived notions, Canadian or Indian, of how she must proceed.

The title is ironic. Grief should not be managed, Mukherjee implies. Those most connected with cultures, official or traditional, seem most concerned with getting the grief of others safely under control. Ms. Templeton has her list, the traditional families in India find wives for the men, and the Hindu religion offers escape for Kusum. Judith Templeton tries her best, but is unable to see past her own culture of social work. Mukherjee may use her as a metaphor for Canada's official policies of multiculturalism that manage the complexities of constantly transforming human groupings and regroupings into a reductive mosaic, each tile hardened in place. The intentions are good, but the results, according to Mukherjee, are deadly to the individual.

From the opening lines, gender is important in the story. It begins with the strangeness of having other women in the kitchen and ends with a woman striding through the park alone. For a mature woman, there is no pressure to remarry, as there might have been for a man. It is less likely, too, that a man would need permission to move into acceptance and to "*Go*" and "*be brave.*"

CULTURAL CONTEXTS:

CLARK BLAISE AND BHARATI MUKHERJEE, From *The Sorrow and the Terror: The Haunting Legacy of the Air India Tragedy* (p. 1614)

A comparison of the nonfiction account cowritten by the same author with the short story "The Management of Grief" can demonstrate how a difference in purpose and genre may change the emphasis a writer uses to interpret the same events. Although there is considerable overlap, and we can see how Mukherjee has woven many real-life details into her fictional story, the fictional and nonfictional narratives differ in focus. The story has the protagonist's time in Ireland begin at the shore of the bay where the plane went down, where she and her friend are able to imagine their husbands and children to have escaped somehow, even as they discuss fate and contemplate suicide. We see a male engineer, a representative of rationality, as he floats his borrowed roses in the bay and encourages the women to hope. The "lucky ones" are referred to with irony, since they are the survivors who are able to identify their loved ones, but the protagonist has dry clothes packed for her sons and is secretly "ecstatic" that she cannot find their bodies.

Verisimilitude is achieved as Mukherjee creates composites and compresses and shifts details of the actual tragedy for use in her fiction. Unlike the short story, which explores the impact of the tragedy on one woman and on others as seen through her eyes, the chapter from the nonfiction book emphasizes the process of identifying bodies on a variety of representative survivors. This account begins by describing in an objective voice the horrifying business of accurately matching recovered corpses with the identities of people known to be on the Air India flight. Although the fact is not brought out in the Blaise and Mukherjee text, it is now known that one of the many careless errors made by the regional Canadian airline that checked the luggage containing the bombs through was the failure to match luggage with passengers. The terrorists had never even boarded the planes on which they indirectly planted the bombs, insisting that their bags be directed to Air India flights. With this in mind, it is supremely ironic that the bureaucracy works so tediously to correctly account for each dead body. In the short story, Shaila is never able to find the bodies that match her family, but in the actual incident every body is identified.

Like the social worker in the short story, the Canadian bureaucracy is characterized as more interested in efficiency than in compassion. Whereas criticism of this seemingly cold approach is implied in the short story, it is explicit in the nonfiction narrative. Irish acts of compassion are held up in contrast to Canadian paper shuffling. It is telling that officials are unwilling to provide temporary visas for Indian citizens, seeming to suspect an immigration scam. It has been pointed out elsewhere that when the Air India flight went down, then Canadian Prime Minister Mulrooney sent a letter of condolence to his counterpart in India, even though most of the people lost were *Canadian* citizens. The underlying assumption seems to be that members of ethnic minorities still belong to the home country, are somehow not *real* Canadians. Grief must be managed so that emotional remarks do not set off riots or emphasize problems with airport security.

The authors make the tragedy specific and concrete by using examples of survivor experiences and reactions, often quoting them at length, and using their pathos to critique the official handling of the disaster. Both the story and the book chapter have as one underlying purpose Mukherjee's position that Canadian multiculturalism policies hide unquestioned warrants that are fundamentally racist and arrogant. Students who wish to explore the validity of this position will find articulate arguments on both sides. Some authors provide convincing evidence that readings of the failure of Canadian multiculturalism like Mukherjee's are based strictly on anecdotal impressions. They maintain that such judgments can be disproved by statistics showing increased applications for Canadian citizenship among ethnic minorities, their active participation in established political parties with increased representation in Parliament, the lack of evidence that people vote as members of ethnic blocs, overwhelming interest in English and French second-language programs among immigrants, and increased acceptance of mixed marriages like that of Blaise and Mukherjee themselves.

Nevertheless, Blaise and Mukherjee are convincing in their descriptions of actions that fail to consider cultural differences in attitudes toward death and mourning. They characterize the survivors as "private and noble, in their terrible grief," reminding readers that we have been allowed to listen in on Shaila's thoughts, realizing that she is often feeling something quite different from what she appears to be feeling on the surface. We might also remember the older couple who have lost their adult children but refuse to fill out the forms that will put the estate in order. They continue in their "duty to hope" and will not allow the government to manage their grief. The attitude of the writers is implied throughout by the details that they choose to include. For example, the repetition of the symbolic "Pink and Yellow forms" speaks volumes about what the writers see as the actual focus of those who set themselves up to help the survivors. Although they let examples of Irish kindness and family grief speak for themselves, with little commentary, they select from the many possible anecdotes the ones that effectively carry out their purposes.

NEW YORK TIMES, "India Arrests Sikh in '85 Bombing of Jetliner" (p. 1623)

After reading two narratives about the aftermath of the 1985 Air India explosion, readers will find the terse *New York Times* report of the arrest of Manjit Singh sketchy, at best. The tone is almost telegraphic, and there is no sense of human tragedy. In fact, the focus of the article is on the Sikh terrorist and the

Indian context of the crime. The first paragraph outlines the basic fact that 329 people died in the bombing, but no mention is made of their nationalities. The assumption seems to be that this is primarily an issue of interest to people who want to know something about the politics of India. It is not presented as the solving of a mass murder that killed a great number of North American residents, many of them children and young people born and raised as Canadian citizens.

The second paragraph gives brief details about the criminal and his arrest. Some readers will recognize that the name Singh immediately identifies the man as Sikh; perhaps the alias is more significant in Indian culture, but it may strike some readers as the ironic equivalent of changing one's name from John Smith to Bill Smith. Bharati Mukherjee has pointed out, however, that one's last name carries a great deal more cultural weight in India than it does in a less class-bound Western context. The police commissioner, on the other hand, has a Hindu name. We are told in the third paragraph that Singh attempted suicide upon his arrest. This, too, may be ironic for readers who realize that he has managed to circumvent airport security in a way that allows him to commit murder without being forced to accompany the bomb on the flight.

The fourth paragraph establishes the political context and demonstrates Singh's documented history as a Khalistan insurgent. Audiences who know that Pakistan was created as a Muslim homeland by partition in 1947 when the Indian subcontinent was released from British control may find significance in the facts presented here, but for most readers the locations will be simply names. Perhaps the Bombay byline explains the focus. Later paragraphs continue to emphasize India and the background of this particular terrorist. We may be startled to learn in paragraph 10 that 15,000 people, a staggering number, have been killed in the Sikh campaign in the years since the bombing of the Air India flight in 1985. But the article is written in a way that gives this number and the 329 victims of the bombing no more emphasis than the two baggage handlers killed in Japan in the same terrorist effort. This coldly factual account may reveal cultural bias or simply a failure to notice the enormity of the information being conveyed. We can assume, however, that readers who no longer remember the bombing and are not particularly interested in Indian politics will fail to understand the issues Blaise and Mukherjee raise in their texts. Readers will have to be quite imaginative to detect any pathos in the disaster for which Singh has been arrested.

We might compare this account with those that are still familiar in 1999, many years after a similar event in Lockerbie, Scotland. What possible reason can exist for the difference in attention these two crashes have received other than cultural bias? A more complete comparison we might make in our classes would be with a *Wall Street Journal* article written in 1989 by William M. Carley in response to the Lockerbie case. The full title of the article as found in full text on the UMI Proquest Electronic Index backfile is worth consideration: "Fearful Skies: Airline Security Offers Only Weak Protection Against Bombs on Jets — Air India Disaster Shows How Systems Can Be Defeated by Sophisticated Terrorist — The Bored X-Ray Operators." Beginning with brief context about the Lockerbie crash, which interestingly killed fifty-nine fewer people than the Air India explosion, Carley makes the point that terrorists can easily get around airport security procedures, partly because the safeguards in place are often inadequate and poorly carried out. Our students will appreciate this full account of how Canadian Pacific Airline's procedures were circumvented, even though watchers of Indian politics had warned officials of the likelihood of a terrorist attack on the anniversary of the storming of the Sikh Golden Temple in India by Indian troops a year earlier. Extra security was provided, but dogs that could have detected the bombs were refused. Employees noticed that the men requested standby and were willing to pay any price for tickets, insisting that their baggage be checked through all the way to Delhi and Bangkok, even though Air India flights had not been confirmed, but acceded to their demands rather than slow down the boarding procedures. Other airport employees provided only cursory examinations of luggage.

Unlike the *New York Times* story, the *Wall Street Journal* piece, published two years earlier, makes the Canadian context of the events clear. The international nature of the story and the issue of airport security that is of interest to most North American readers are ignored by the *New York Times* article.

Shaila from Mukherjee's short story "The Management of Grief" would undoubtedly be angry about the relegation of this story to that of local concerns in India. Certainly, Mukherjee herself would take it as further evidence of unexamined assumptions that are prejudicial in nature. Because they are brown-skinned ethnic Indians, she would believe, these people are not even acknowledged to be Canadian citizens, and there seems to be none of the sense of outrage at their deaths that accompanied the later Lockerbie and TWA 800 disasters. The possibility that the *New York Times* article, originating in Bombay, may be written by an Indian reporter is no excuse, since Mukherjee, and presumably Shaila by 1992, have no more patience with Indian parochialism than they do with thinly disguised Canadian bias.

SAM HUSSEINI, "Profile in Unfairness" (p. 1625)

Whereas some critics of the airport incompetence that led to the Air India bombing in 1985 might insist that any Sikh traveling on June 22 should have been detained and searched, others, including Bharati Mukherjee, remind us that the bomb was not planted by the terrorists because their religion or ethnicity made them evil, but because this was part of their agenda as Khalistan activists. It is even possible to support the formation of a Sikh homeland without believing that this must be achieved by violent action. Mukherjee has her protagonist in "The Management of Grief" recognize that her anger toward Sikhs unrelated to the bombing is unjustified, though understandable. Her point, in fact, is that stereotypes are destructive. For the same reason, the profiling of people who typically commit certain crimes depends upon stereotype.

An American of Jewish descent who looks vaguely Middle Eastern tells of uncomfortable experiences in airports. A single woman and a university professor who looks younger than her age, she often travels alone and travels light, sometimes with just a backpack. One experience, at Heathrow Airport in London while making connections on a flight from New York to Israel, she describes as quite frightening, her detention and questioning apparently based on nothing other than appearance and destination. Currently in the news are assertions that police should be stopped from profiling drivers as possible criminals based on profiles that often foreground race, and conflicting contentions that schoolchildren should be profiled to predict their potential for violent actions as adolescents.

At the end of his article Sam Husseini describes profiling as "brazenness." He might have easily said *racial and religious prejudice.* Although the crash of TWA 800 turned out to have been caused by mechanical failure rather than terrorism, Husseini claims that fear and prejudice generated by theories for its cause have led to measures that discriminate against certain groups. He begins by relating three anecdotes, tied to current events and presumably representative examples, and follows this with his own personal experience. He points out the equivocation of defenders of profiling, who euphemistically label it "passenger analysis" instead, and he questions the warrants underlying criteria for added questions and searches. He refutes the notion that profiling is an important tool of security, maintaining that it does not do the job. As evidence for this he mentions one case in which a "white seminarian" — doubly eliminated from racial and religious profiling — was discovered to have grenades. The example seems particularly unrepresentative of those who have been convicted of terrorist attacks in recent years and fails to consider that Timothy McVeigh or Unabomber survivalist types might also fit current profiles. He further uses air accidents to refute the idea that profiling will prevent air disasters. He appeals to the authority of Supreme Court Justice Thurgood Marshall and relates as his last piece of evidence a news reporter's approval of El Al's policy, which includes "young, dark-skinned men" as needing a second look.

Still, when contrasted with the anecdotes that Blaise and Mukherjee relate about the effects of terrorism, the indignities of those subjected to airport searches for whatever reason may seem like an acceptable trade-off to readers who travel often. When we realize that alert employees could have spotted the Sikh nationalists who sabotaged the Air India flights — did, in fact, remember them in retrospect as suspicious because of their behavior and demeanor — we may find Husseini's arguments weak and self-serving. Unlike William Carley in the *Wall Street Journal* article mentioned in connection with the previous text in this cluster, Husseini does not suggest alternatives, but perhaps this is not his point. Although it would increase time in airports greatly, perhaps everyone should be checked as thoroughly as those who fit a profile, thus eliminating the prejudice factor. When an Arab criticizes El Al, we might be tempted to ignore his argument as based on traditional enmities and religious bias. Readers may also note that he is paid to have just this opinion, though this does not mean he does not hold it personally.

We may walk a fine line between maintaining civil rights and ensuring safety. Certainly, all people of good will would want to eliminate prejudice, but a good case may be made for being realistic about the dangers of a world filled with people willing to die or kill over political, social, religious, or simply personal issues. Students might want to develop an anonymous survey or questionnaire that seeks out the warrants people might use for determining if a person poses a threat, asking respondents to describe the sort of behavior, demeanor, or appearance that would put them on guard. Would their criteria be the same in an airport as on a deserted street or in their dormitories?

LEARNING FROM PERSONAL ENCOUNTERS WITH MORTALITY (p. 1628)

AUDRE LORDE

The Transformation of Silence into Language and Action (p. 1629)

Known as an outspoken woman who proudly proclaimed her identity as a Black militant lesbian poet, Audre Lorde seems an odd person to address the topic of silence, as she does in this essay. In the late 1970s, being black and militant meant taking a vocal, confrontational stance within the African American community. Such a position could arouse the animosity of people, both black and white, who felt that progress could best be achieved by passive resistance or working quietly within the system. To speak as a black militant aroused hate among conservatives and bigots, and was risky but reluctantly tolerated in the mainstream, perhaps being a bit exotic and trendy among academics and liberal thinkers, who were the first audience for this text. But to speak out loud in the 1970s as a gay man or a lesbian was startling, even embarrassing to many audiences. Audre Lorde's feminism was strongly rooted in the realities of both her race and her sexuality. She boldly uses women's eroticism for political purposes in both poetry and prose.

Looking back at her biography, it is interesting to find that the child who would become the poet and vocal activist did not speak until she was four years old. Her parents were immigrants to New York from Granada, and perhaps the lilt of West Indian speech is responsible for the legend, perhaps true, that when she began speaking, she spoke in poetry. She hints in "Black Mother Woman" that her internal battle to pull language and action out of an innate urge toward silence may come from childhood "myths of little worth" and the "nightmare of weakness" that lay underneath her mother's anger and "heavy love." It was long a fact of life in most cultures around the world, including our own, that women were not heard in any direct way.

In 1978, the year after Lorde delivered this speech at a Modern Language Association convention, Tillie Olsen's *Silences* discussed the many ways that most women, and both men and women of the poor and working class, were long denied voices in literature and intellectual thought. Tracing the use of the word *silence* in feminist rhetoric would make an interesting study of how an issue of definition intersects with social and political issues. Many women writing around the time of Lorde's speech were addressing the question of how to emerge from silence so that their voices would really find an audience and effect the changes that were needed. African Americans, too, were working to be heard.

In this text, Lorde explains that her confrontation with mortality reinforces her need and obligation to use the power of language to promote survival. Although this time the growth was benign, Lorde would later have breast cancer and would die of liver cancer in 1992. After her mastectomy, Lorde refused to have reconstructive surgery or to wear a prosthetic bra, choosing instead to stand straight and tall and allow the absence of her breast to be seen. This was consistent with her authenticity, her determination to boldly be herself. The largest health center established to serve the gay and lesbian community now bears her name. Such institutions are needed, advocates say, because lesbian women often neglect their health. The questions most doctors ask women assume that patients are heterosexual, and lesbians often find that honest responses invite disapproval while silence may skew diagnoses. "Your silence will not protect you," Lorde insists.

Speaking mostly to women, specifically to women who teach English or other languages at the university level in her first context for this essay, Lorde assumes that they will know that women have been underrepresented in the literary canon. She also assumes that they are sometimes afraid to speak out. In paragraph 6, she challenges her audience to examine their own silences and fears. She challenges her readers to define themselves, as she has done. Because her audience is vitally interested in language, in paragraph 10 she calls upon each individual to find her role within a community working to transform language. Writers, she maintains, have the responsibility to make sure that they speak the truth, but also to make sure that the language they use is true. We might ask our students to think about what she means by this. How do style and content interact? Can one be true if the other is dishonest or too self-protective?

For Lorde, silence itself is self-destructive, can make you sick, can even make you die. She has made this choice, and it works for her. But we might point out that in many times and places her speaking out would lead so directly to her death that she would not be heard. Anyone who has ever watched a few minutes of the lowest variety of television talk show may be convinced that not all speech is positive, that some secrets should be worked out in private. Although it may be healthier for gays and lesbians to be open, for example, we might argue that "outing" people against their will before they feel ready is not helpful. Nor do we want to allow hate speech, even if it is sincerely felt. Airing prejudice in a safe environment, on the other hand, can lead to self-examination and change.

Often, in class discussions, individuals are surprised to realize that their warrants reveal previously unrecognized prejudices. Most will deny that they are racially prejudiced, and the most sexist of young men often think they love and respect women. Homophobia is prevalent, though usually kept safely under the cover of political correctness. So most will deny that Lorde's statement of who she is really relates to their own fears. Whether we force them to confront their unconscious biases in class or not will depend upon our teaching methods. We can take opportunities to reveal our own confrontations with biases as they crop up and make it clear that we all have stereotypes that have developed over the years as we construct reality from the cultural materials at hand. Our students need to know that the proper response to these moments of self-knowledge is neither denial nor guilt, but honest analysis, accompanied perhaps by a nonjudgmental sense of proportion.

Many people, not all of them white, find loud black women scary. Admiration and guilt may both play a part in this reaction. When Lorde says that black women especially "were never meant to survive," she asserts the importance of slavery and patriarchal institutions in American history. Readers often go on the defensive against such accusations, denying that the actions of our ancestors have anything to do with current circumstances. Like personal biases, however, cultural assumptions affect us in hidden ways, much as cancers do. Denying them is as antithetical to survival as avoiding the doctor as a cure for cancer.

Although Lorde eventually died of cancer, she survived with it for fifteen years, using the time to speak out as she does here. And while, as she points out, "Death . . . is the final silence," her use of language and action as a counter to silence means that she still speaks today. The fact that we are reading this over twenty years after its first publication means that death has not silenced Audre Lorde. This earlier confrontation with mortality undoubtedly armed her for the battle with cancer that was to come, serving to bring her life into focus. Just as she uses intimations of cancer as a means of finding power for speech, we should biopsy the unexamined prejudices that are uncovered in the course of our intellectual lives and use them to move toward the "harsh and urgent clarity" of authenticity.

JUNE JORDAN
Many Rivers to Cross (p. 1633)

Although the essay we include here is about the suicide of her mother rather than about breast cancer, June Jordan is a survivor of the disease that Audre Lorde uses to confront mortality in the preceding text in this cluster. Referring to her own use of personal experiences as a means of gaining the power to speak out, June Jordan began her address at a San Francisco benefit for Breast Cancer Action in the late 1990s by saying, "Activism is not issue-specific. It's a moral posture that, steady state, propels you forward from one hard hour to the next." In much the same way Audre Lorde spoke of overcoming silence in the 1970s, Jordan urges her audience not to give in to an ingrained sense of powerlessness.

She says that her first reactions to her diagnosis of cancer cast herself as the enemy, since evil — no longer an abstract or external concept — had taken over her body. But she soon learned that she was not alone but part of a community, that action can be taken to combat the 178,000 new cases of invasive breast cancer that are diagnosed in the United States every year. "I see this as an intolerable status quo!" Jordan shouts. "These facts justify hysteria and disruptive running through the streets." But Jordan also finds strength within herself. She can be an activist about breast cancer, as she has been about the injustices she experiences as a black woman, because she has what she calls *privilege*. Her advantages include "a childhood that forced me to fight back or die.... a West Indian temper.... an elite education that enables me to sort, and assess, and synthesize all kinds of information." In addition, as a poet, she has "the task of making rather than breaking connections," and as a survivor she has obligations to others.

As we see her doing in this essay from the 1980s, June Jordan continues to use personal tragedy to examine the nature of power and survival for women. She is concerned with issues of both gender and race, especially how the politics of race affect women and children. Her place as an African American thinker defies easy categorization. As a young woman, she was involved with the Congress of Racial Equality (CORE), going on a freedom ride, reporting on the Harlem riot of 1964, and bouncing around ideas with Malcolm X. Though she owes much to the Black Power and Black Arts movements and to earlier civil rights efforts, Jordan has been bitterly critical of the sexist assumptions of some black leaders, believing that they seek to silence women and diminish their importance. At the same time, she critiques feminist leaders for their failure to consider the importance of mothering and teaching children. She has written everything from children's books to brutally explicit poetry to treatises on international issues. In "Many Rivers to Cross" she speaks of her mother's many deaths, the injustice of a life powerless before racism and sexism, and she vows to live in such a way that others will know when she is dead. And, as we see her doing in her later speech about breast cancer, she confronts mortality with the determination to lift up other women along with herself.

Although she mentions her mother's suicide in the first sentence of "Many Rivers to Cross," Jordan begins talking about herself even before the first sentence is over. If this were an essay memorializing her mother, we might have cause for complaint. Like the mother in Marsha Norman's play *'night, Mother*, this daughter quickly makes the suicide of a family member about herself rather than the person who has died. Some readers may be alienated by this attitude. One complaint may be that it is unclear at first that she is speaking about the repercussions of her divorce when she describes her need for a job and new home, not that she has been dependent upon her mother for these things all along. Those of us who have dealt with death, however, find that all the circumstances of our lives at the time become indelibly connected to the event. We can never recall one without the other. This may explain why Jordan juxtaposes these events, but she has a rhetorical purpose as well. By the time we return to her mother, we realize that the narrator is in the midst of experiences specific to her position as a woman. Therefore, we are prepared for her focus on her mother as a woman who is in a difficult and oppressive marriage while also being powerless because she is poor and black.

When students are asked to write autobiographical essays, they often feel the need to tell everything exactly as it happened and think that they cannot use dialogue unless they remember the speaker's exact words. But professional writers like Jordan often use fictional techniques when writing autobiography. The dialogue captures the flavor of the event and does not have to be exact. Jordan uses dialogue to carry the action along, to reveal the characters of the real people she describes, and to focus the reader's attention on the details she wants to emphasize. Jordan uses this extended personal anecdote to say something about women and work. She discusses this explicitly at the end of her essay, making the connection for the reader. She forecasts her topic by referring to her need for a job at the story's beginning. By framing her essay in this way, she achieves a unity that the reader may sense more than notice consciously.

Jordan is angry at her father. Some of her immediate anger may be influenced by her feelings about the husband who has recently betrayed her. To a certain extent, Jordan is angry at all men, but more precisely, she is angry at the patriarchal system that causes such pain to women like herself and her mother. Another family member, interpreting the marriage of Jordan's parents through their own warrants, might describe the older man in different terms. Jordan sees her father's failure to realize that his wife is dead as a metaphor for the silence and powerlessness of her mother's life and the insensitivity of her father to the needs of the women in his family. Some readers will see the writer as harsh in her judgments. Others may assert the truth of what she says.

Audre Lorde and June Jordan have strikingly similar visions of work and of many other things. Both feel strongly that black women have a unique obligation to speak out and to work as part of a community for the good of many. Both understand the problematic nature of their positions as feminists and black activists, since the work of these two movements sometimes come into conflict as problems are addressed. Both freely use the materials of their most deeply personal experiences to move others into action and new perspectives. Both have cultural roots in the Caribbean, where language is a critical issue in the battle for political and cultural autonomy.

Experience tells us that many students will come to college with contempt for personal narrative in essays. They have been taught, or have misread their teachers, that their own experiences are invalid, that only hard evidence and the voices of received authority should be included in an essay. Many will be uncomfortable with Jordan's narrative and will judge it as poor writing. But although Audre Lorde speaks more directly to the audience at hand and does not tell a story as Jordan does, she urges that writers to do exactly as Jordan has done. In this cluster, we may see Audre Lorde providing the theory that June Jordan puts into practice. Each writer is capable of both.